The War for the Union

"Contrabands" Building Stockade at Alexandria, 1861

The War for the Union

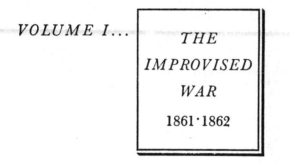

VOLUME I...

THE
IMPROVISED
WAR

1861·1862

by ALLAN NEVINS

KONECKY&KONECKY

ACKNOWLEDGMENT

The author wishes to express his appreciation for material aid given in the preparation of these last volumes of *The War for the Union* to the Guggenheim Foundation, the National Foundation on the Arts and Humanities, and Columbia University. He is deeply indebted to the staffs of the Library of Congress and of the Henry E. Huntington Library at San Marino, California. Without the active support of his colleagues Ray Billington, E. B. Long and John Niven, these volumes would never have been completed. The greatest debt is to Lillian K. Bean whose untiring effort can never be repaid. He also acknowledges gratefully the assistance of his daughters Anne Loftis and Meredith Mayer and his wife Mary Nevins. Finally, he would like to express his gratitude to Joseph G. E. Hopkins of Charles Scribner's Sons for his unflagging patience and devotion to the task of editing these volumes.

Allan Nevins

Konecky & Konecky
150 Fifth Avenue
New York, NY 10011

ISBN: 1-56852-296-7

Printed and bound in the USA

PREFACE

THE CIVIL WAR, fought by every element in the Northern and Southern population, was a people's war, a *Volkskrieg*, in a fuller sense than any earlier conflict of modern time. On both sides the resourcefulness, stubborn courage, and devotion to high aims, the disorderliness, theatricality, and impatience, were alike popular traits. Behind the uprising after Sumter lay the demagogy, selfishness, and blindness of the period since Winfield Scott had occupied Mexico City; years of yeasty growth, leavened by little political honesty or wisdom, which the author has described in four previous volumes, *Ordeal of the Union* and *The Emergence of Lincoln*. They reflected little credit on the people. Now suddenly the storm changed the atmosphere. The people, both Confederates and Unionists, rose to the most desperate effort of their history. The tenacity with which the North fought on to total victory and the South to almost total ruin vindicated their claim to heroic strength of character, and left the country memories which partially redeem the record of a needless war.

This volume and those which follow, treating the plain people as the real heroes and heroines of the war, have as a primary theme the impact of the war on national character. Their thesis, insofar as a single idea can be applied to a struggle so manysided, is that the war measurably transformed an inchoate nation, individualistic in temper and wedded to improvisation, into a shaped and disciplined nation, increasingly aware of the importance of plan and control. The improvised war of 1861–62 became the organized war of 1863–64. The invertebrate country of Bull Run days, goaded by necessity, gathered its energies together, submitted to system, and became the partially-structured country which heard the news of Five Forks. Northern manufacturing enterprises that had been unicellular became complex and organic; primitive transportation lines became parts of a fast-growing network; mercantile undertakings, professional groups, and cultural enterprises, gelatinous in 1861, became muscular enough to bear their share of the burden. To organize armies, to organize the production of arms, munitions, clothing, and food, to organize medical services and finance, to organize public sentiment—all this required unprecedented attention to plan, and an unprecedented amount of cooperative effort. The resultant alteration in the national character was one of the central results of the gigantic struggle.

No writer treating the Civil War as a detached unit could fail to give equal emphasis to the Southern and the Northern story. This history, however, has been planned to cover a much longer period, and its emphasis therefore falls on what is permanent in the life of the nation. From this standpoint much of the Confederate effort appears too transitory to require detailed treatment. The interesting Confederate Constitution, for example, never came into full operation, died in 1865, and had practically no influence on national polity. My regret over the abbreviation of the Confederate story is diminished by the fact that Southern historians have provided several admirable records. In the same way, my regret that tactical military operations are crowded out of a work devoted primarily to political, administrative, economic, and social history, is diminished by the fact that the long list of books of military history is daily swelled by useful additions.

While the people are Hero in the Civil War, they could have accomplished nothing without leadership. A full treatment of Lincoln and his Cabinet, as of the civil leaders of the South, as they responded to growing war demands, is reserved to the next volume. But by the close of 1861 it was becoming clear that Lincoln also was hero of the conflict in a very special sense. For historical reasons the country depended on its professional politicians for guidance. In the first year only a few important figures were drawn from business and industry to hold important executive posts in Washington: notably Anson Stager and Thomas A. Scott in the War Department, and Gustavus V. Fox in the Navy Department. The politicians controlled. And with some merits, what faults the politicians disclosed! Seward performed great services; but his proposal that the North provoke a war with Spain and France to extricate itself from its difficulties, as criminal as it was stupid, must make Americans blush that they had a foreign minister capable of such an act. Chase also did important service; but his uncontrollable vanity and ambition tempted him to mean courses. The ablest man would have failed in Cameron's place, but Cameron was both erratic and incompetent. Montgomery Blair was the most contriving member of an incredibly contriving, self-interested family. Well it was for the republic that out of such a political milieu rose a Chief Executive who combined the noblest qualities of the heart with a singularly lucid intellect and a piercing vision.

The author gratefully acknowledges the help of the Carnegie Corporation and its head, Mr. John Gardner; of Mrs. David Levy; of Mr. Lessing Rosenwald; of Mrs. Jean Conti; of Dr. Abraham Flexner; of Mr. Frank E. Hill; of Professors David Donald and Louis Starr; of Mr. Bruce Catton and Mr. E. B. Long; of Miss Marian McKenna and Mrs. Mira Wilkins; of Dr. Wayne Andrews; of Dr. John Pomfret and the staff of the Huntington Library; of Drs. Carl White, Richard Logsdon, and Roland Baughman of the Columbia University Library; of Dr. Joseph Rappaport, Dr. Saul Benison, and of a host of others generous in aid as in sympathy.

Allan Nevins
The Huntington Library,
May 1, 1959

CONTENTS

Winds of Doctrine

IT IS LATE afternoon of the first day of March, 1861; early spring in the South, but still winter in the North. The sun, sloping westward, shines brightly on the whole eastern half of the United States, filling the Atlantic bays with light, gilding the Appalachian crests, and giving the Mississippi valley a promise of vernal warmth. It finds the people busy with their wonted occupations. Ships crowded with immigrants are gliding into Boston and New York. Factory smoke curls over all southern New England, the Philadelphia area, and the Pittsburgh gateway. Railroad lines, glistening toward the West, hum with traffic; the rivers are dotted with steamboats from St. Paul to New Orleans. While the Gulf plains are already green, in the Carolinas and Tennessee farmers begin to follow the receding frost with black furrows.

To the spiritual ear, a medley of voices rises to the skies. From a minister: "Peace! Let us have peace." A brisk merchant: "Our city board of trade calculated ten years ago that we might have thirty million people by this census. I scoffed at them. But now the government figures our population at 31,375,000. What a market!" A promoter breaks in: "And see where the growth lies! Pennsylvania's up 600,000, New York's up 800,000, but Illinois is up by nigh on to a million. The Northwest—that's the coming country." A blander voice succeeds: "But don't forget Georgia. Ten years ago she was lagging. Now she has more than a million people. And don't forget that cotton calls the tune, either." Peace, industry, growth, hope, seem for a moment universal.

Then harsher voices break in. From several quarters: "War!—we must prepare for war." Discussion grows heated. A Yankee speaks: "Nobody blames the South for having slavery; the whole world is to blame. But I do blame them for wanting to spread it over the whole West." A Virginian replies: "All over the West nothing! Hasn't Kansas just come in as a free State? Aren't Minnesota, Oregon, California all in the Union as free States? When do *we* gain anything?" "Gentlemen, gentlemen!" interposes a New Yorker. "Haven't you read Seward's latest speech? He says we have more than a

I

million square miles of territory left, enough for twenty-four new States. And though much of this area lies far south and has been under a slave code for years, how many slaves live in it? Seward says just twenty-four; one for each new State. Climate and soil govern the issue. We are quarreling about nothing."

At this a Kansan sharply interrupts. "*Who* makes the quarrel? You Southerners do. James Harlan of Iowa told Congress: 'You offensively thrust slavery on us as a great good to be desired and extended and perpetuated by all the powers of the national government.'" An Illinoisan applauds: "And we stand with Lyman Trumbull, who says, 'A Union which can be destroyed at the will of any one State is hardly worth preserving.'" But a Southerner responds with deep feeling: "No, it is *you* who make the quarrel. Jefferson Davis spoke the exact truth when he said, 'The temper of the Black Republicans is not to give us our rights *in* the Union, or to allow us to go peaceably *out* of it.'"

Three cities on which that March sun shines warmest are centers of special tension: Montgomery, Charleston, Washington. The outer streets of Montgomery, with fine houses, churches, lawns, and trees, are lovely, but the center of town is untidy. The neo-classical State capitol is not yet worthy of its noble site above the Alabama. A brick building close by, topped by a Confederate flag, houses the new government. Its broad whitewashed hall is full of chatting politicians. Their voices compete with the noises drifting in from outside: a company at drill, a band, hucksters, and, at the fountain near the principal hotel, an auctioneer selling a few slaves.

A Mississippian: "Ten days yesterday since we swore in Davis as provisional President. We're making progress. You Georgians should be satisfied. You have Alec Stephens as Vice-President and Robert Toombs as Secretary of State."

A Georgian: "Poor consolation for losing the Presidency. Except for his one weakness"—he crooks his elbow significantly—"Bob Toombs would have made a better chief than Davis. But I grant you Porcher Miles may be right when he says, 'Mr. Davis was the choice of the whole people of the South.'"

An Alabamian, soothingly: "Nobody should complain. Each of the seven States has a member of government. Alabama has Leroy P. Walker as Secretary of War. Louisiana has Judah P. Benjamin as Attorney-General. South Carolina has Christopher G. Memminger in the Treasury. Texas has John H. Reagan as Postmaster-General—a smart man even if he did begin life as a plantation overseer. And Florida has Stephen R. Mallory, raised down Key West way, to head our navy if we ever get one."

A South Carolinian: "We're making a nation, and at record speed too.

They tell me the permanent Constitution will be ready in another week. We'll adopt it unanimously, just as we've taken all important steps unanimously. If we only had more States!"

The Georgian again: "Don't worry; the seven today may be twice that many soon. Here is a letter Herschel V. Johnson has just written: 'I look with intense anxiety to the action of the border States. If they join us, we will constitute a respectable power among nations and shall be able to maintain an advancing career. If they adhere to the old Union, I shall regard it as a precursor of their emancipating at an early day. That will be a calamity on us. Without expansion, slavery must be limited in duration. But with a Southern Confederacy of fourteen States, we can maintain the Monroe Doctrine and acquire, when necessary, other lands suited to slave labor.' "

The South Carolinian: "If fighting begins, Tennessee and North Carolina and Virginia will come soon enough; maybe Maryland, maybe Kentucky and Missouri. Commissioners have gone to Washington to demand Sumter again. That's where the first blow may come."

Sumter! On this first day of March, the name is on everybody's lips. In Charleston the atmosphere is feverish. Every square contains soldiers camping or drilling; many of them in gray trousers and jackets, with yellow facings and palmetto buttons. Some ships in the harbor carry palmetto flags; so do the massive storehouses fronting the wharves. Three miles out the famous fort frowns over the harbor entrance. To South Carolinians it looks formidable, though actually it is small by European standards, is mainly of brick, not stone, and shows errors of construction—the inflammable barracks are within the walls. All the promenaders on the Battery are talking of it:

Cautious Speaker: "Heaven knows what answer the commissioners will get. This is what the Buchanan Administration wrote Governor Pickens when we demanded Sumter just after we fired on the *Star of the West* last January. 'If, with all the multiplied proofs which exist of the President's anxiety for peace . . . . the authorities of South Carolina shall assault Fort Sumter and peril the handful of brave and loyal men shut up within its walls, and thus plunge the country into the horrors of civil war, then upon them and those they represent must rest the responsibility.' If weak Buchanan won't give Sumter up, how can Lincoln do it? We are on the brink of what Buchanan calls a horrid civil war."

Fiery Speaker: "Maybe—maybe not. Buchanan didn't resent the firing on the *Star of the West*, though New York and Pennsylvania voted him men to fight with. When Lincoln sees that he must give Sumter up to avoid fighting, he'll do it meekly enough. Why, the South has already seized a long list of national forts and arsenals."

Conservative Speaker: "Lincoln won't give Sumter up for two reasons. First, the eyes of the country are on Sumter as a test case; the eyes of every Republican governor, every Republican Senator. Second, he has no power to give it up. Joseph Holt put that in a nutshell for Buchanan. The President can no more cede Sumter back to South Carolina constitutionally than he can cede the District of Columbia back to Maryland."

Fiery Speaker: "I differ. R. M. T. Hunter of Virginia was correct when he told the Senate that Washington has no right to hold the Southern forts. The legislatures ceded these places to the government, not for pecuniary considerations, but for the defense of the States. Now they cannot possibly be used for defense, and *may* be used for offense."

Conservative Speaker: "I repeat, we were within an inch of war last January. The Sumter garrison was on the very point of firing on Fort Moultrie when the *Star of the West* retreated. Major Anderson then threatened to use his guns to close the harbor. Fort Sumter is a bomb—with a time fuse attached. When her provisions run low six weeks hence, we shall see what stuff Lincoln is made of."

Washington, three days before the inauguration, is agitated by precisely that question: What stuff is Lincoln made of? General Winfield Scott has brought a thousand regular troops into the city, who are supported by volunteer companies. Batteries are being strategically placed. Leading Republicans are besieging the President-elect in Parlor No. 6 of Willard's Hotel. The streets are thronged with a heterogeneous mass: office-seekers, newspapermen, Baltimore plug-uglies, mere tourists, jubilant free-soilers.

Office-seeker: "Did you see what the Washington correspondent of the New York *Herald* said about Lincoln ten days ago? He wrote: 'He is unequal to the crisis, and will feel it so sensibly when he arrives here that it is inferred he will rush for safety into the arms of some man of strong will, who will keep his conscience and manage the government.' The *Herald* says this will be either Seward, with Wall Street, the Cotton Whigs, and the conservative Republicans behind him, or Salmon P. Chase, supported by Horace Greeley, William Cullen Bryant, Ben Wade, Lyman Trumbull, and other hotheads."

Newspaperman: "The New York *Tribune* takes a more judicious view. It thinks pretty well of Mr. Lincoln. Its correspondent, James S. Pike, says that as soon as Lincoln takes office, he will be under such pressure as no man in the country ever suffered before. Will he make heavy concessions to the South? Pike doesn't know, but he says Seward will advise him to do so. And he concludes that the Lincoln Administration will try to preserve peace. 'My conjecture,' he writes, 'is that its stature will about come up to the old compromise standard.'"

Republican: "I have just seen a letter by George W. Julian of Indiana after he talked with the next President. Julian assured a friend: 'Lincoln is *right*. His backbone is pronounced good by the best judges.' "

Second Republican: "And I have just talked with Senator Charles Sumner, who manages to keep in touch with everything. He quoted to me a telling remark by Old Abe. Lincoln said that the Administration and the party must not become 'a mere sucked egg, all shell and no meat—the principle all sucked out.' " [1]

Thus began the uneasiest and most momentous March in American history; the last peaceful March for four agonizing years. The sun went down on a Confederate President who in his recent inaugural, after praying for peace, had said: "if . . . the integrity of our territory and jurisdiction be assailed, it will but remain for us with firm resolve to appeal to arms and invoke the blessing of Providence on a just cause. . . ." It went down on a President-elect in Washington whose inaugural address, after pleading for peace, contained an unequivocal pledge: "The power confided to me will be used to hold, occupy, and possess the property and places belonging to the government, and to collect the duties and imposts." If the words of the two leaders stated anything, they stated a frontal collision.

1 Julian's letter about Lincoln's backbone, undated but by internal evidence written about March 1, is in Julian Papers, Indiana State Library.

1

The Crisis

IT WAS in a somber mood that Americans read Lincoln's inaugural plea to the seceded states, March 4, 1861. Men still living could recall the nation as it took shape in Washington's Presidency—and already it was rent into discordant halves! Harrowing as the hour was to those who thought only of the domestic future of America, it was yet more distressing to those who recalled what the Founders had often said about her world mission. Not many years earlier Tocqueville had written: "From the eighteenth century and the [French] Revolution, as if from a common source, two streams flowed forth; the first led mankind toward free institutions, the other led mankind toward absolute power." The young nation which, as Lincoln had said in Independence Hall on his way to Washington, once offered the world such hope of liberty and equality, might now become an object of derision and reproach. As Columbia faltered, the European champions of absolutism gained in arrogance.

For while America stood convulsed and divided, never had her living example of freedom, democracy, and humanitarianism been more needed by other peoples. Of Tocqueville's two streams, the grimmer seemed triumphing. In France, the glowing dreams of 1789 forgotten, a pinchbeck Napoleon exercised swaggering powers. He commanded the army and navy; he decided on alliances and wars; he dominated the discordant European concert. He appointed the ministers, the council of state, the senate, and the high court; he laid before the legislative assembly its principal bills; and he convened and adjourned that body at will. Subject only to mass opinion, he strove to cow even that monster into subjection. He chained the press, exiled enemies, prohibited political meetings, and turned universal suffrage into a farce. Nor was the situation better in most other lands of the Continent.

Across the Rhine in Prussia, government lay in the hands of a reactionary king and a hidebound group of Junkers intent on perpetuating the principles of feudalism. Since 1848 constant efforts had been made to turn back the hands of the clock. The people had been abused by an unscrupulous police, a postal espionage that spied upon the letters of men high and low, von Roon's strict enforcement of three-year conscription, and a ministry which interpreted the constitution by nullifying its more liberal provisions. In the background, like a shark circling a shattered boat, waited Bismarck, a fierce believer in the Prussian crown, Prussian absolutism, and Prussian power; eager to bring parliamentary institutions to the kill.

Elsewhere men could speak of Tocqueville's free impulses in the language of the Psalmist: "Oh how suddenly do they consume away, perish, and come to a fearful end!" The circling sun looked down on camps and cannon, gendarmes and prisons, provocateurs and plotters. From the convict settlements of Siberia to the garrisons of Polish towns, Russia was a terrorized land. In the Orient, despotism ruled unchecked from the Levant to Mongolia. Throughout the Austrian domains, Hapsburg absolutism had restored all the tyrannies existing before the tempest of 1848: among the Italians of Venetia and Lombardy, the Hungarians, the Bohemians, and the volatile Austrians themselves. The old stagnant order had momentarily quivered when in 1859 Vienna had been compelled to cede Lombardy to Piedmont, and would quiver again when a new imperial constitution was written this very year; but the constitution would remain mere paper. Spain lay in her accustomed torpor. The whims of Isabella II, swayed by religious fanaticism and ideas of divine right, the intrigues of a court camarilla, the feeble conservatism of weak, short-lived ministries, the obscurantism of a church which hated literacy and freedom of thought—all these forces kept the Spanish people enchained.

The Old World power where freedom broadened slowly down was Britain; the Britain of that middle-class devotion to social progress typified by John Bright and Richard Cobden, of the strong moral impulses represented by Gladstone, and of the increasing domination of thought by Manchester Liberalism and its ideas of peace, free trade, industrial energy, and governmental *laissez faire*. But, always a land of compromise, Britain at the moment was ruled by the aristocratic Whigs under the jovial, clearheaded, imperious Palmerston—"old Pam," a great believer in freedom abroad, and a strong brake on its progress at home—and the cautious Lord John Russell, once active in reform but now warily immobile. Under their government the ruling principle of Lord Melbourne, "Why can't they leave it alone?" had full sway. If the abuses which the Chartist movement had tried to extirpate no longer flourished unchecked, change came in but slowly. The cardinal points of the People's Charter, universal male suffrage, the secret ballot, abolition of property qualifications for the House, and salaries for members, were still to be gained. The poor were voteless, gross inequalities among constituencies persisted, and education lay beyond the reach of half the children of the land.

The social structure of Britain was still stratified by harsh class lines and honeycombed by ancient abuses. Westminster still held Ireland under an oppressive yoke. Power and privilege rested with the nobility, gentry, and upper-middle classes, and so long as Palmerston and Russell kept office, change would be gradual.

Had the prospects of freedom abroad been hopeless, the paralysis of America might have seemed less deplorable. It would not have mattered that the spirits of Washington, Adams, and Jefferson could no longer be invoked to fight alongside those of Burke, Fox, and Condorcet. But under the superficial ice of reaction the liberal currents ran with tremendous force. In England the orderly popular agitation of the masses was too stubborn to be stayed. The voices of reform—Dickens, Kingsley, Harriet Martineau, John Stuart Mill, and even Tennyson with his denunciation of "Timour-Mammon grinning on a pile of children's bones"—were loud and eloquent; a bolder Whiggism was coming gradually to birth. Bright and Cobden, the *Daily News* and the *Spectator*, the great social ameliorists like Shaftesbury, and such battlers against orthodoxy as Buckle, Lyell, and Darwin, were stirring the pool of opinion. In France, despite the bitter humiliations of 1848–49, the battlers for freedom—Victor Hugo, Gambetta, Chevalier—never lost heart. The victories of Garibaldi, Victor Emmanuel, and Cavour in Italy heartened the friends of liberty all over Europe. Clough and the Brownings sang of the Italian cause. Exiles like the German Forty-eighters rejoiced when Italy in 1859 emerged as a European power, and in Hungary and Poland patriots plucked up heart.

Never might the example and encouragement of a free, united, progressive America have been more effective. For three generations, in a world of fitful political progress and frequent relapse, the Western republic had represented to uncounted millions a sober, steady hope. It was the brightest governmental and social experiment ever made. The young nation had no monarch, no aristocratic institutions, and almost no vestiges of feudalism. It was without fixed class lines, without official prejudice as to religion, and without bars to the refugees from European lands. "Power, at thy bounds," Bryant wrote, "calls back his baffled hounds." That suffrage should be the right of every adult male, that the highest authority should repeatedly be given to men of the poorest origins, that public moneys should be spent on schools and not armies, that social equality should be enforced by opinion as vigorously as it was protected by law, all seemed to European liberals a kind of miracle. The experiment was new and its scale was unprecedented. Would the republic endure? Or would its failure, like that of some democracies of the past, prove that only a centralized autocracy could govern wide areas and large populations with efficiency?

The situation in which the United States stood on March 4, 1861, was thus of decisive import to half the world. The disruption of the republic would feed the confidence of every despot from the Hermitage on the Neva to Francia's palace in Paraguay, and strike dismay to the Sheffield foundry-man, the Lyons silk weaver, and the Bavarian peasant. The circumstances in which disruption was threatened, moreover, were peculiarly painful.

The nation had endured part slave, part free, for seventy years under the Constitution. During that period the opinion of the civilized world respecting slavery had radically altered. The institution was arraigned by the conscience of enlightened men in older lands, condemned by most people of the Northern States, and deplored by a considerable body of Southerners. It stood indicted not only as profoundly immoral, but as a grievous economic, social, and political handicap to the nation. All progress at the South was clogged by the necessity of restraining and disciplining a helot population, of keeping it in ignorance, and of fettering agriculture and industry by its low capacities. The governing whites could not escape from the unhappy influence, intellectual and moral, of the retarded blacks. In the long run the situation was intolerable. The honor, moral integrity, and international influence of the nation all demanded that it be brought to an end. Yet during these seventy years America had done singularly little for the slaves. It had not attached them to the soil, protected their family life, or provided for their schooling. Many vocal Southerners had departed so far from the Jeffersonian abhorrence of slavery that they now declared it a permanent institution. Since its vitality depended on expansion, most Southerners demanded the right to enlarge its bounds.

A powerful party had arisen in the North, determined to end the expansion. Lincoln as its leader had also proclaimed a much larger and more radical idea: the idea that the nation must accept the principle that slavery was a temporary institution, and at once take thought on the grim questions of when, and how, and under what safeguards it would be abolished.

It had always been clear that acceptance of this principle by a majority of Americans would precipitate a sectional crisis. Since slavery interpenetrated and conditioned all Southern life, the main body of Southerners, proud, sensitive, apprehensive of racial amalgamation even while permitting a great deal of miscegenation, regarded the principle with doubt or horror. To talk about ending slavery in a distant, indefinite age was hard enough; to think about ending it in 1870 or 1890 was terrifying. The Republican party wished the

South to face realities. Lincoln said bluntly that the crisis must be reached and passed; that is, the South must honestly face the great principle, and agree to its soundness. Then, patiently, cooperatively, South and North could agree on ways, means, and times for extinguishing the anachronistic system. Lincoln knew that, as Jefferson had said, the South had the wolf by the ears. He knew that both sections shared responsibility for the origins and growth of the institution, and both should bear the burden of getting rid of it. But on this one point he was firm: it must be put in the path of ultimate extinction.

The election of 1860 had proved two facts. It showed that a majority of Americans were now in favor of halting the expansion of slavery, and so setting a period to its existence; for most Douglas Democrats wished to put bounds to it by popular sovereignty just as the Lincoln Republicans wished to fence it in by Federal restriction. It also showed that the South could not be brought to meet and *pass* the crisis; that it balked at accepting the principle of the transiency of slavery. A dominant body of Southerners stubbornly insisted on dealing with slavery and race relations only in their own way and at their own leisure. Thus alone, said some, can we keep it as a positive good. Thus alone, said others, can we feel safe from the agonies of a precipitate social and economic revolution. Robert Toombs gave the Senate the conditions on which the South would remain in the Union. They were that its people should have equal rights to migrate to the Territories with *all* their property; that property in slaves should be protected like any other, leaving control over slavery to the States; that persons committing crimes against slave property should not be permitted to take refuge in other States; that fugitive slaves should be surrendered; and that Congress should pass laws to punish all who, like John Brown, aided invasion or insurrection in any State.

A group of leaders, in a carefully planned conspiracy, took steps which first split the Democratic party and so ensured Lincoln's election, and which then used his election to inspire Southern secession. As they did so, Southerners emphasized their own interpretation of the Constitution. The nation, they said, was a confederation of sovereign independent States. Already the South had suffered heavily from the North in taxation, tariffs, and an unequal distribution of national benefits; and they would not tolerate the erection of a consolidated democracy, for this, as Calhoun had predicted, would end in control, proscription, and political disfranchisement.

The whole future of the American nation, as the chief exponent and shield of liberal democracy, was thus placed in doubt by a struggle concerning an institution which the moral impulses of the age pronounced a blot on the national shield, and concerning the constitutional ideas involved in this contest. Sensitive leaders felt keenly the tragic bearing of the convulsion on world affairs. Many Southerners winced at the renunciation of Jeffersonian principles by their hotheads.[1] Many Union men saw that the meaning of the American dream to mankind was being put to the test. "I felt great repugnance in drawing the sword against my own kindred," wrote a Kentuckian, "but now when I see that a dissolution would be regarded all over Europe as a condemnation of republicanism, I feel there are no ties sacred enough to withhold me from the battlefield."[2] Charles Sumner had returned from Europe in 1860 after an observation of affairs in France, Italy, and Britain which convinced him that liberalism was slowly moving forward, always alert to the American scene. "I need not say to you," he wrote a British friend, "that I find much to disappoint me in the tone of persons and things. I long to see my country beautiful, great, and good, and am unhappy."[3]

Would the country recapture the international ideal held aloft by Washington in his Farewell Address? "It will be worthy of a free, enlightened, and at no distant period a great nation to give to mankind the magnanimous and too novel example of a people always guided by an exalted justice and benevolence." Now the vision of the founder, like a torch dashed to earth, seemed quenched by darkness.

1 T. S. Gourdin of Florida, editor of the *Southern Confederacy*, wrote that with the formation of the Confederacy, "we must abandon the old idea of our forefathers that 'all men were born free and equal,' and teach the doctrine of the diversity of the races, and of the supremacy of the Anglo-Saxon race over all others. We must take the ground never dreamed of by the men of '76, that African Slavery is right in itself, and therefore should be preserved." Quoted in N. Y. *Tribune*, March 12, 1861.

2 Cassius M. Clay, St. Petersburg Legation, June 30, 1861, to Francis Lieber; Lieber Papers, H.L.

3 Sumner to the Duchess of Argyll, Washington, May 22, 1860; H.L.

Peace or War?

"GOD GRANT that the Constitution and the Union shall be perpetual," exclaimed Buchanan to the crowd when he reached his Lancaster home just after Lincoln's inauguration. Most Americans still believed a sectional adjustment possible without bloodshed. They were naturally optimists; they had discounted radical threats for so many years that they could not now take them at face value, and the idea of a brothers' war was too monstrous to seem credible. A reporter of the New York *Tribune* speculated on the use to be made of the extra troops in Washington when the capital "resumes its wonted quiet." Rebellion had asserted itself, but civil war had not begun.

As yet, only seven States had left the Union. In at least three, Georgia, Alabama, and Louisiana, strong evidence existed that a really fair plebiscite might have shown a majority for the national tie, while in the four others, Mississippi, Texas, South Carolina, and Florida, vigorous minorities had opposed secession. Southerners could not point to a single right except that of the prompt return of fugitive slaves which was being abridged or directly threatened, and some of the Northern States with personal liberty laws were repealing or amending them. While half a dozen Republican governors, led by E. D. Morgan of New York, Richard Yates of Illinois, and N. P. Banks of Massachusetts, recommended that such laws be wiped from the books, Rhode Island, Massachusetts, and Vermont took appropriate action.[1] If the South had no concrete grievances of importance, many asked, why should it revolt? Had not Congress just submitted, by two-thirds vote in each chamber, a constitutional amendment forbidding any change in the organic law which

---

[1] On this subject see Appleton's *Annual Cyclopaedia*, 1861, pp. 436, 452, 556, 576 ff., 634; McPherson, *Pol. Hist. of the Rebellion*, 44; Rhodes, *Hist. U. S. from the Compromise of 1850*, III, 253; Randall, *Civil War and Reconstruction*, 229. Ohio had no law, but Governor Dennison urged conditional repeal in other States. The governors of Maine and Michigan opposed repeal. The total number of cases arising under personal liberty laws was probably small; see W. B. Hesseltine, *Lincoln and the War Governors*, 103 ff., 124 ff. Lincoln said that if the laws were as bad as Southerners asserted (he had never read one), they should be repealed.

would enable the government to interfere with slavery inside a State? [2] Was it not certain that this amendment, if needed to save the Union, would be quickly ratified?

In the wide border area, when Lincoln entered the White House, the situation appeared hopeful. The Delaware legislature, after hearing a secessionist agent from Mississippi, had voted down his proposals—the house unanimously. Governor Thomas H. Hicks of Maryland, though asserting that the State sympathized with the South and hoped to see it given new guarantees, had stubbornly refused to call an extra legislative session as a first step toward rebellion, and had been overwhelmingly supported by the people. In Kentucky the senate, appealing to the South to recede, voted more than two to one against a State convention. Arkansas chose a convention with a decidedly conservative majority, and Missouri elected one which did not include a single advocate of immediate secession. In Virginia, the house in January had voted down a secessionist resolution. The Unionists had carried the elections for a convention, and from the moment that this body met in mid-February, it had been under the sway of astute conservatives. North Carolina, in a popular election, defeated the call for a convention, and at the same time chose eighty-two conservatives as against thirty-eight secessionists to sit in that body if it ever met. The people of Tennessee likewise voted decisively against a convention, and still more decisively for a Unionist majority of delegates.

"Here are eight of the fifteen States," rejoiced the New York *Tribune*, "declaring that they wish and mean to stay in the Union, and not follow the defeated and bankrupt officeholders into the abyss of secession, treason, and civil war." The borderland, lamented the Charleston *Mercury*, was ready to accept much less than the proposed Crittenden compromise, which would have restored the Missouri Compromise line across the Federal Territories and protected slavery south of it.[3] Many Union men, believing that the cotton States had been thrown into revolt by a temporary emotional reaction following Lincoln's election, thought that a counter-reaction might soon hurl the fire-eaters into oblivion.

Lincoln shared this hope. Three days after the inauguration, Representative T. A. R. Nelson of Tennessee, a strong unionist of the American Party, obtained an interview at the White House. Lincoln said that he was anxious to maintain peace, and believed that the Federal revenues should not be col-

---

[2] This passed the House Feb. 28 by 133 to 65; the Senate March 2 by 24 to 12; *Cong. Globe*, 36th Cong., 2d Sess., 1285, 1403.

[3] N. Y. *Tribune* March 7, 1861; Charleston *Mercury* Feb. 14, 1861. For action of the border States see *Ann. Cyc.* 1861, pp. 256, 257; 395; 442–444; 677–679; 729–731.

lected in the seceded States until men had time for reflection. As he still regarded Southerners as members of the national family, he was not inclined to deny them mail facilities. Congress was equally hopeful and still more anxious for peace. Up to the end of its session on March 3, it had been careful not to give the South needless offense. No Republican Senator made any effort to press the bill outlawing slavery in the old Territories which the House had passed in the first session of the 36th Congress. It was not necessary (New Mexico after ten years of slavery protection had only twenty-two slaves, ten of them transients), and not politic.[4]

Nor did the Republican majority, passing bills to organize the new Territories of Dakota, Colorado, and Nevada, include any formal prohibition of slavery. It was a basic Republican doctrine that the natural state of any Territory was one of freedom, and that action was hence unnecessary; but the party leaders also wished to avoid any provocative act. Nor did Congress pass any measure giving the President military weapons to meet the crisis. Two bills for this purpose—"force bills," in Southern parlance—were introduced in the House, but not carried.

All but a few extremists hoped for peace, but on what terms? The answer was clear. To men of the North and the borderland, with a restoration of the Union; to men of the cotton kingdom, with a peaceable separation. All efforts at an arrangement had thus far proved abortive. The Crittenden compromise, which Lincoln opposed, had been defeated by a substitute resolution affirming that no need existed for amendment of the Constitution. Though this resolution passed, 25 to 23, only when six senators from the lower South refused to vote, the Republicans were mainly responsible for it. They had three main reasons for defeating Crittenden's plan. The first was that, protecting slavery south of 36° 30', it might stimulate Southern annexationist schemes in Mexico, Central America, and Cuba. The second was that it nominally handed over to slavery a region nearly as large as the original thirteen States, which had come to the United States as free soil, without a single slave when annexed; and it did this at a time when the party, declaring its solemn conviction that the government had no power to plant slavery on soil previously free, had just elected Lincoln on a platform forbidding slavery extension. The third reason, comprehending the other two, lay in Lincoln's moral imperative: the South must agree that slavery was temporary.

Meanwhile, the Peace Convention, with its eminent delegates from twenty-one States, had foundered in floods of oratory. The shrewd Adams-Seward

---

4 Representative Nelson describes his interesting interview with Lincoln in the Knoxville *Whig*, March 19, 1861. For slavery in New Mexico see the speech by C. F. Adams in *Cong. Globe*, 36th Cong., 2d Sess., Appendix, 124-127.

plan for putting an end to quarrels over slavery in the Territories by immediately admitting the whole Southwest (the present area of New Mexico, Arizona, Nevada, and Utah) as one State had been rejected by Southerners, for that State would obviously come in free.[5]

Yet most men still believed that peace would be preserved. They calculated, on the basis of the vote for Lincoln, Douglas, and the Bell-Everett ticket, that a decisive majority of Americans wished for peace, moderation, and compromise. Those who, like Zachariah Chandler of Michigan and Barnwell Rhett of South Carolina, wanted "a little bloodletting," were a small minority.[6]

[I]

Southern expectation of peace was based on the idea that the North would yield. Secessionist leaders hoped that the Lincoln Administration would let the new cotton republic go its way without hindrance. Many in the deep South cherished an illusion that Yankees were interested only in money-grubbing. Utterly materialistic, secessionists told themselves, Northerners lacked the fine sense of honor and fighting spirit which characterized the best "Southrons." Moreover, according to the Dixie view, these New Englanders or Ohioans, aware that they would soon be worsted, shrank from conflict. Had not all the great American generals, Washington, Andrew Jackson, Winfield Scott, Zachary Taylor, been Southerners? Had not the Mexican War been won mainly by Southern troops? Did not military schools, military parades, and military adventures appeal to the South, while Northerners kept their noses in ledgers? This confidence was buttressed by Northern talk of peace, the anti-war fulminations of Northern Democrats, a faith in border State protection, and a feeling that the South was irresistible.

Secessionist leaders had taken note of Franklin Pierce's irresponsible assertion that before any Northern army reached the South it would have to fight organized forces in its own section. Unfortunately, they heard many similar Northern voices.

Douglas, telling the Senate on January 3 that peace was the only sane course, declared that if war began, reunion would be impossible. The alternatives were subjugation and extermination on one hand, and separation on the other; and since extermination was unthinkable, he felt convinced that war would mean "final, irrevocable, eternal separation." His follower Senator

5 Nevins, *Emergence of Lincoln*, II, 397 ff., details measures and efforts in Congress and elsewhere for peace; see also Randall, *Civil War and Reconstruction*, 200 ff. The Adams-Seward plan is best followed in the manuscript diary of C. F. Adams.
6 The phrase is Zack Chandler's; Nevins, *Emergence of Lincoln*, II, 411, 412.

George Pugh of Ohio found the idea of coercing the South "utterly revolting." John A. Logan of Illinois echoed them, saying that war would not only fill the land with widows and orphans, but result in "disunion forever." Henry M. Rice of Minnesota assured the Senate that it must never expect the Northwestern States to vote a man or a dollar for war. Numerous journals spoke in like terms. The Detroit *Free Press* had the effrontery to predict that if a conflict came, "*that war will be fought at the North*," and to threaten that in Michigan 65,000 men would interpose between any Union army and the Southern people. The Cincinnati *Enquirer* warned coercionists that if Ohio troops were called out, they might march against the government, not for it.[7]

Southerners could not believe that the North was capable of war when they read that citizens in southern Ohio, Indiana, and Illinois, assuming that disunion would be permanent, proposed taking the lower part of these States into the Confederacy. This was a very real movement. "I believe, upon my soul," the editor of the Chicago *Tribune* had written Senator Lyman Trumbull in January, "that if the Union is divided on the line of the Ohio, we shall be compelled to struggle to maintain the territorial integrity of this State." Samuel Medary, former territorial governor of Kansas and Minnesota, had just established a journal in Columbus, Ohio, which pledged obstruction to the use of force. Similar fulminations came from the Chicago *Times and Herald*, controlled by Cyrus H. McCormick, the New York *Day Book*, and the Boston *Courier*. No paper was blunter than the New York *Express*:

If the people of one section madly proposes to itself the task of trying to whip the other, the hope of reconciliation is extinguished forever. . . . There is a chance that fraternal relations, though temporarily ruptured, may one day be restored, if peace is preserved.

When the municipal elections this spring, from Cleveland to Chicago, revealed a shift in favor of the Democrats, hope that this party might prevent coercive action increased in the South. Buchanan later denounced the politicians and editors who assured the Confederacy it would have powerful allies. "This, with the persistent inaction of Congress and General Scott's 'views,' induced the leaders of the Cotton States to believe there was but little danger of Civil War."[8]

---

7 Pierce fruitlessly wrote the other ex-Presidents (Tyler, Fillmore, Van Buren, Buchanan, a singularly uninspiring lot) proposing a meeting to suggest remedial measures. Douglas' speech is in *Cong. Globe*, 36th Cong., 2d Sess., Appendix, 35–42; Pugh's *Ib.* 29–35; Logan's *Ib.* 178–181. Pugh spoke Dec. 20, 1860; Logan, Feb. 5, 1861. Vallandigham called coercion "atrocious and fruitless"; O. C. Hooper, *The Crisis and the Man*, 7. Rice's speech is in *Cong. Globe*, 36th Cong., 2d Sess., 1373. Cf. Wood Gray, *The Hidden Civil War*, 45 ff.

8 C. H. Ray quoted in Wood Gray, *op. cit.*, 45; O. C. Hooper, *op. cit.*, 1–35; A. C. Cole, *Era of the Civil War*, 253–257; N. Y. *Express* (controlled by Benjamin and Fernando Wood), Jan. 16, 1861; Buchanan, July 1, 1863, to Royal Phelps, in Miscellaneous Presidents'

Still greater was the Southern faith in a protective borderland shield. If this area was against secession, it was equally adamant against coercion.

Hicks of Maryland declared that his State would make common cause with its sisters in resistance to tyranny if need arose. Even Unionists in Kentucky asserted that they would desert the government if it used force. The Virginia house with but five dissenting votes denounced any thought of coercive action. In Nashville the legislature served notice that if any Union force were sent south, Tennesseeans would join as one man in repelling the invaders. These declarations had fervent conviction behind them. The great majority in the border region, Southern in origin, tastes, and sympathies, would feel a blow against Southern culture as one which smote themselves. Devoted as they were to the Union, they shrank from the idea of saving it by blood. And behind their antagonism to force lay a hope that if time were allowed for reflection, the two sections would find reason overcoming passion, and agree on a reasonable compromise.

The feeling of the cotton States that war was impossible because they were unconquerable was partly braggadocio, for the region was rich in Captain Bobadils. It sprang more rationally, however, from the military preparations they were making, and the deep hold taken by the doctrine that King Cotton ruled Britain and France.

The new republic, against countless handicaps, was trying to establish forces able to face the Northern regulars and militia. Its Congress had passed legislation creating a provisional regular army of 10,500 officers and men, including 4 brigadier generals and 9 colonels. P. G. T. Beauregard, resigning from the Union army, had been appointed brigadier and hurried to the command at Charleston. An act of February 28 authorized the President to receive State forces if tendered, or volunteers with State consent. Southerners hoped that their troops, under the new flag of 3 stripes, red, white, and blue, with a union of 7 stars, would soon number 50,000. Meanwhile, the States were filling their ranks. Mississippi in January had authorized the formation of a division of infantry and was sending a force to Pensacola. Its volunteers came in more rapidly than they could be equipped, officered, and drilled. In Louisiana the secession convention established 2 standing regiments, 1 infantry and 1 artillery, while by mid-February the State had issued arms to 28 volunteer companies with a strength of 1765. A similar story could be told of the other cotton States. On March 9, under a law passed

---

File, NYPL. Buchanan laid the blame for "go in peace" utterances on certain Republicans, but Democratic leaders were of course much the more numerous and flagrant offenders. "My voice was unheeded," he wrote, "though I often warned them [the secessionists] that the first gun fired at Charleston would unite all parties."

three days earlier authorizing the President to ask for any number of volunteers up to 100,000, Secretary of War L. P. Walker called on all the seceded States to furnish quotas, chiefly for garrisoning forts; and he stood ready to issue a further call at any time.[9]

Meanwhile, the Montgomery government was blithely taking over a great part of the arms and munitions lodged in old Federal repositories. It deeply galled the North to read of large stores thus "stolen" from the United States. New Orleans on March 6 gave an imposing ovation to General David E. Twiggs, fresh from his surrender (still in national uniform, and before passage of the State ordinance of secession) of nineteen army posts in Texas. Bands pounded along Canal Street, which was dressed in pelican bunting and palmetto flags; oratory resounded, cheers echoed; and Twiggs, his large bald head uncovered, bowed right and left from his barouche with General Braxton Bragg, heading files of troops. Early in the year Southern forces had taken over Fort Pulaski at Savannah, Fort Morgan at Mobile, and Fort Barrancas at Pensacola, with their contents. The head of the navy department, S. R. Mallory, was busy recruiting sailors.[10]

Even if peace reigned, it seemed probable that the Confederacy might be more of a military nation than the United States. At first it would use its armed power to deter the North from attack. Then its ardors might turn elsewhere. Vice-President Alexander H. Stephens, after predicting to an Atlanta audience that Sumter would be surrendered, the North would accept the situation, and the border States would eventually join their sisters, spoke in Columbus, Georgia, of martial conquests. The Confederacy, acting on the principle that slavery must be extended and perpetuated, might in time acquire Cuba and parts of Mexico and Central America.[11]

Altogether, the cotton kingdom flexed its muscles with a sense of exuberant strength. Its leaders had cherished the forecast of Langdon Cheves at the Nashville Convention: "Unite and you shall form one of the most splendid empires on which the sun ever shone." And never for a moment did the Deep South forget what Senator James H. Hammond and others said of its power to rally European support. A threat to the cotton kingdom would be a stroke at the jugular vein of the greatest naval powers of the globe.

"The first demonstration of blockade of the southern ports," prophesied Major W. H. Chase of Florida in the January issue of *De Bow's Review*,

9 J. D. Bragg, *Louisiana in the Confederacy*, 53–55; *Statutes at Large. Provisional Govt. CSA*, 43–52; O. R. I, iv, pt. 1, 135; N. Y. *Tribune*, March 19, 1861.
10 Moore, *Rebellion Record*, I, 7 ff.; Twiggs, a Georgian by birth, was soon made a major general in the Confederate army, but was too old for active service.
11 Columbus *Sun*, quoted in N. Y. *Tribune*, March 19, 1861; Johnston and Browne, *Alexander H. Stephens*, 356, 363, 396. Slavery was the cornerstone, said Stephens.

"would be swept away by English fleets of observation hovering on the Southern coasts, to protect English commerce and especially the free flow of cotton to English and French factories. The flow of cotton must not cease for a day, because the enormous sum of £150,000,000 is annually devoted to the elaboration of raw cotton; and because five millions of people annually derive their daily and immediate support therefrom in England alone, and every interest in the kingdom is connected therewith. Nor must the cotton states be invaded by land, for it would interrupt the cultivation of the great staple." Even the Northwest, he continued, would act to protect the free ports and markets of the South.[12]

Cotton would maintain peace, for cotton ruled the world.

[II]

Most Northerners expected peace to prevail for a quite different set of reasons. They thought that the seven cotton States had no vital grievances and would soon come to their senses, that the new republic was too weak to be viable, and that the border area would offer persuasive arguments for a return. They had seen so many other crises—1820, 1833, 1850—disappear that they gave rein to cheering hopes. "I guess we'll keep house," said Lincoln. They had heard so much gasconade that they lumped most secessionists with the fire-eaters. "I incline to believe," wrote Charles Eliot Norton on March 5, "that they will not try violence, and that their course as an independent Confederacy is nearly at an end." In a let-them-cool-down mood the *Atlantic* published a resigned quatrain:

> Go then, our rash sister! afar and aloof—
> Run wild in the sunshine away from our roof;
> But when your heart aches and your feet have grown sore,
> Remember the pathway that leads to our door!

On the absence of substantial Southern hurts, Douglas was emphatic. He argued that the South had gained more than if the line of 36° 30′ had been revived by the Crittenden amendment. "There stands your slave code in New Mexico protecting slavery up to the thirty-seventh degree as effectually as laws can be made to protect it. . . . The South has all below the thirty-seventh parallel, while Congress has not prohibited slavery even north of it." It was true that slavery had a legal right to spread farther than for climatic and economic reasons it might actually go. What a Southern historian was later to call the natural limits of slavery had perhaps been reached. Charles Francis

---

12 *De Bow's Review*, vol. 30, January, 1861; Chase, an ardent secessionist, argued that the potency of cotton made Southern armies and fleets superfluous.

Adams was equally derisive as to Southern grievances. To complain of personal liberty laws which had never freed a single slave, of exclusion from territory which slavery could never hope to occupy, and of fear of Federal interference with slavery in the States, against which the North was now willing to erect a solemn bar—this was puerile. Adams called upon the Southerners to recover from what he called "panic, pure panic." [13]

Adams, like Seward and many others, was certain the Confederacy must soon collapse from inner weakness. It could never be more than a secondary power, he declared; never a maritime state. It labored under the necessity of keeping eight millions of its population to watch four millions. If independent, it would have to guard several thousand miles of frontier against the flight of slaves to territory where they could never be reclaimed. "The experiment will ignominiously fail." So thought John W. Forney, writing his Philadelphia *Press* from Washington that anybody who talked with secessionists could see that they lacked heart in their enterprise, and looked forward to the speedy collapse of their whole conspiracy. Douglas, who never faltered in his hope that inner weakness would undo the new nation, announced late in March: "Division and discontent are beginning to appear in the revolting Southern Confederacy." [14]

Always bold and imaginative, Douglas was revolving a plan of which he spoke to William H. Russell of the London *Times* and others; a plan for a North American customs union embracing Canada, Mexico, and the United States, which he hoped would pave the way to reunion. Like others, he believed in the healing power of delay. He wished to fix a conciliatory character upon Administration policy, and, as he told friends, to "tomahawk" the Administration if it took a belligerent line. On March 6 he therefore gave the Senate an elaborate misinterpretation of Lincoln's inaugural as a pacific manifesto. He was delighted, he said, to find Lincoln so conservative in temper, for the Union could never be cemented by blood. The President had promised to abstain from any offensive acts, had let clear Federal rights lie dormant, had suggested that the Constitution be amended, and had promised to allow the people to devise such changes as they desired. Furthermore, he had declared that in every exigency he would lean to friendly solutions. [15] Douglas went on, in a pernicious warping of Lincoln's words:

13 Sandburg, *Lincoln: The War Years*, I, 120 ff.; C. E. Norton, *Letters*, I, 219; Adams in *Cong. Globe*, 36th Cong., 2d Sess., *Appendix*, 127 (Jan. 31, 1861); Douglas, *Cong. Globe*, 36th Cong., 2d Sess. (March 25, 1861), p. 1504; *Atlantic*, May, 1861.

14 Adams, *ut sup.;* Forney is quoted in Springfield *Republican*, March 19, 1861, Douglas in Chicago *Morning Post*, March 27, 1861.

15 Russell, *My Diary North and South*, April 4, 1861, for Douglas' plan; *Cong. Globe*, 36th Cong., 2d Sess. (March 6, 1861), pp. 1436–1439. But Douglas frankly told Welles that he had no influence. The Democratic party had broken up; the Republican party had no use for him; nobody would follow him. *Diary*, I, 34, 35.

In other words, if the collection of the revenue leads to a peaceful solution, it is to be collected; if the recapture of Fort Moultrie would tend to a peaceful solution, he stands pledged to recapture it; if the recapture would tend to violence and war, he is pledged not to recapture it; if the enforcement of the laws in the seceding States would tend to facilitate a peaceful solution, he is pledged to their enforcement; if the omission to enforce these laws would best facilitate peace, he is pledged to omit to enforce them; if maintaining possession of Fort Sumter would facilitate peace, he stands pledged to retain its possession; if, on the contrary, the abandonment of Fort Sumter and the withdrawal of the troops would facilitate a peaceful solution, he is pledged to abandon the fort and withdraw the troops.

Of far greater importance, in this crisis, was Seward's belief in peace. The veteran New York politician, who for a dozen stormy years in the Senate had closely observed Southern friends and enemies, and who as a man of tortuous expedients believed that expediency ruled human conduct, was certain that war could be avoided. As Gideon Welles put it later, Seward had no doubt that he could set to work immediately the new Administration came in, reconcile the main differences, and within ninety days restore harmony to the nation. *He* was head of the Republican party, and *he* would be the real power behind the weak railsplitter. During the brief month of William Henry Harrison's Administration he had dominated that President; during Zachary Taylor's sixteen months he had again swayed the scepter; now he would be Grand Vizier once more. Thrusting Lincoln aside, he would rely on time, forbearance, and patience to bring the cotton States back.

"I learned early from Jefferson," Seward had told the Senate, "that in political affairs we cannot always do what seems to us absolutely best." He would like to see all the Territories organized at once into two States, one Southwestern, one Northwestern, reserving the right later to subdivide them into several convenient new States; but such a reservation was constitutionally impossible, and he believed that the embarrassments resulting from the hasty incorporation of two areas of such vast extent and various characteristics and interests would outweigh the immediate advantages of halting the slavery quarrel. To admit one great Southwestern State was as far as he would go. Meanwhile, he would trust to cool second thoughts:

When the eccentric movements of secession and disunion shall have ended, in whatever form that end may come, and the angry excitements of the hour shall have subsided, then, and not until then,—one, two, or three years hence— I should cheerfully advise a convention of the people, to be assembled in pursuance of the Constitution, to consider and decide whether any and what amendments of the organizational law ought to be made.[16]

16 Welles, Nov. 27, 1872, to I. N. Arnold, Arnold Papers, Chicago Hist. Soc.; *Cong. Globe,* 36th Cong., 2d Sess., Jan. 12, 1861.

Seward, thin and worn, said just before Lincoln came in: "The majority of those around me are determined to pull the house down, and I am determined not to let them." [17] He had written Lincoln on February 24 that he knew the real peril much better than his Republican colleagues in Washington, and that only the soothing words which he had spoken "have saved us and carried us along thus far." A man of ripe political experience, he could show impressive astuteness, and had a fine capacity for persuasive public speech. Yet he revealed at times superficial thinking, erratic judgment, and a devious, impetuous temper, which were the more dangerous because he was cockily self-confident. He had immense vanity; in fact, remarked the British minister, so much more vanity, personal and national, than tact, that he seldom made a favorable impression at first.[18] Now he was sure that he could restore the Union with one great if—if Lincoln would let him take the helm.

Justice John A. Campbell of the Supreme Court, a mild, sagacious Alabama unionist, attended a dinner party which Douglas gave shortly before the inauguration and which Seward dominated as the great power-to-be. When asked for a toast, Seward proposed: "Away with all parties, all platforms, all persons committed to whatever else will stand in the way of the American Union." After dinner, Campbell told the company that slavery was a transitory institution, which though yet strong in the deep South was steadily dying in the border area. Once the Constitution was amended to protect slavery in the States from any national interference, the only question would be that of New Mexico, which was unsuited to slavery anyhow. "How, Mr. Seward," he asked, "can you fail to effect an adjustment?" The Senator replied: "I have a telegram from Springfield today in which I am told that Senator Cameron will not be Secretary of the Treasury, and that Salmon P. Chase will be; that it is not certain that Cameron will have a place in the Cabinet; and that my own position is not fully assured. What can I do?" He had hoped that Simon Cameron might abet his conservative labors for peace.

What he did was to make a last-minute movement to keep Chase, whom he feared as a radical, out of the Cabinet. When this failed, he nevertheless took the State Department, confident that he could manipulate Lincoln and so save national peace.[19]

Horace Greeley likewise believed a rapid readjustment possible. His suggestion that the erring sisters go in peace was qualified by his insistence that they should first prove that a majority of their people wished to go, for he was

17 C. F. Adams to R. H. Dana, Jr., Feb. 28, 1861; Dana Papers, MHS.
18 Newton, *Lord Lyons*, I, 117; Nicolay and Hay, *Abraham Lincoln: A History*, III, 319, 320.
19 Campbell, undated memorandum "Relative to the Secession Movement," Confederate Museum; Nevins, *Emergence of Lincoln*, II, 452–455; N. Y. *Weekly Tribune*, April 30, 1861.

confident that in Florida, Alabama, and Louisiana no such majority existed. Even late in the spring he told a Cooper Union audience that the Southern people were at heart for the old ties. "I believe that the tide makes for the Union, and not against it; that secession is exhausting itself as a fever; and if it can be judiciously handled for a few months, it will burn out." S. F. B. Morse proposed an amicable temporary separation pending negotiations for a new and better Union. The two peoples should conclude an immediate alliance, divide the national property, and sever the flag (the blue union diagonally, the stripes horizontally) until such date as their junction should again make the banner one.[20]

This faith that if Lincoln's Administration accepted the status quo, vigorously waving a palm branch, the cotton domain would come back, was shared by that old Jacksonian Democrat George Bancroft. He assured an English historian that Southern leaders had seceded only with a view to reconstructing the Union on their own terms, possibly with New England (as Bennett's *Herald* suggested) left outside. John Bell of Tennessee, lingering in Washington after March 4 and repeatedly seeing Lincoln, entreated the President not to molest the Confederacy, for any attempt to reinforce the forts or collect the revenues would result in bloodshed and Border State secession. He advised an indefinite truce. The more the cotton States armed and the heavier the taxation they imposed, the sooner would a wave of popular discontent rise, resulting at last in a friendly reconstruction. Bell might have quoted such voices of discontent as the New Orleans *True Delta:*

The odds and ends of every faction which have combined themselves together to precipitate the cotton states into revolution have shown an audacity which Marat, Danton, or Robespierre might have envied. Special privilege, a rag money aristocracy, and favored classes, will now be fastened upon unfortunate Louisiana; and in return the people will have the consolation derivable from the reflection that one of her greatest domestic interests is destroyed and her importance as a state of the Union dwarfed into a pigmy association with decaying, retrograding, and penniless confederates. The depth of our own degradation for the time distracts the attention of the people from the progress of oligarchical usurpation and tyranny in our sister States, which are made participators with us in a humiliating calamity.[21]

If worst came to worst, in the opinion of some Northern observers, unity could be restored on the basis of Manifest Destiny; that is, on the common ambition of powerful groups North and South to take possession of the whole continent and its islands.

20 Morse manifesto, undated, S. F. B. Morse Papers, LC.
21 M. A. DeWolfe Howe, *Bancroft,* II, 135–136; *True Delta,* April 10, 1861. Bell's views are summarized by M. J. Crawford, writing March 3, 1861, to Toombs; Toombs Letterbooks, South Caroliniana Library.

[III]

The realities of the crisis were grimly different from these dreams. Peace, as time proved, was impossible. It was impossible because neither North nor South could now yield. Both were prisoners of the situation created by long years of paltering and evasion.

The Confederacy must stand fast because its goal was not readjustment, but independence. The successful secessionist conspiracy had been a drive, we repeat, to give the people of the Deep South full power to settle their own problems in their own way. Retreat would mean a sacrifice of their constitutional principles, a humiliating blow to their pride, and a definite subordination to the North and Northwest. The heads of the Confederacy were not bluffing, but in deadly earnest. They were determined to maintain their new nation at all hazards and whatever cost.

Certainly every public and private utterance emphasized the permanency of their government. Mrs. Jefferson Davis, who like her husband would have preferred to see the Union kept intact on Southern terms, wrote Buchanan on March 18 that she had found the opposition in Montgomery to reconstruction quite violent. "I fear me greatly, my dear old friend, that you are really the last of an illustrious line." This was the conviction of John Slidell of Louisiana. He wrote S. L. M. Barlow, one of the first great corporation attorneys of New York and an ardent Democrat of conservative views, that reconstruction was a hopeless idea at any time or under any conditions. "At this point there is unanimity of feeling of which you can form no idea without passing some time amongst and mixing freely with our people." We could quote other men at tiresome length. Louis T. Wigfall of Texas in the Senate on March 7 repeated Robert Toombs' statement that the seceded States would never come back under any circumstances. Treat them as independent and the nation could have peace, he vociferated; treat them as part of the Union and it would have war. Wlliam M. Browne, former editor of the Washington *Constitution*, now in the Confederate State Department, was amazed by Northern talk of reconciliation. "Knowing, as we do here," he wrote from Montgomery March 6, "the temper of the people, not the politicians—their hopes, aspirations, resolution, and resources—we look upon union as impossible as the annexation of the Confederate States to Great Britain in their old colonial condition."

The roots of this Southern determination ran deep indeed. Secession, as old Barnwell Rhett said, was not the work of a day, but had been preparing for twenty years.[22]

22 Slidell to Barlow, New Orleans, March 24, 1861, Barlow Papers; Browne to Barlow, March 6, 18, 1861, *Ibid*. Still only in his middle thirties, handsome, wealthy, and cultivated.

Sectional pride, and sensitiveness to sectional honor, had played a large part in crystallizing Confederate resolution. The South was denied equality in the Union, men argued, when it was debarred from taking its slave property into the common Territories. This feeling of sectional jealousy and patriotism more than any other explains the surge of rejoicing that swept across the cotton kingdom as the secession ordinances were adopted. How humiliating now to fall back! But material motives played their part. Convinced that the South was systematically exploited by Northern merchants, brokers, shippers, and bankers, estimating that Yankee harpies bled it of a hundred and fifty millions a year, and resentful of Northern tariffs, coastal trade monopoly, and fishing subsidies, Southern leaders believed they had issued a declaration of economic freedom. They would build a richer agriculture; they would have their own flourishing ports and fleets; they would make New Orleans, Mobile, Charleston, and Savannah opulent seats of finance and industry.

But above all, Southern determination rested on a sense of fear which had grown more acute ever since John Brown's raid; a foreboding that they could never entrust the intertwined problems of slavery and race adjustment (they feared that emancipation would mean eventual amalgamation, a negroid South) to a Northern majority. "A crisis must be met and passed"; but they refused to *pass* it—to take the decision to put slavery on the road to ultimate extinction. They feared Northern clumsiness, precipitancy, and ruthlessness. Henry W. Hilliard of Alabama stated this frankly in a letter to a New England friend. "It is supposed," he wrote, "very generally, that we apprehend some immediate mischief from Mr. Lincoln's administration; some direct and plain interference with our rights; and we are appealed to by our northern friends to await some hostile demonstration on his part; we are reminded that his character is conservative. . . . Now all this may be conceded, and yet if the whole southern mind could be brought to yield implicit faith in these assurances, still the attitude of the southern states would remain unchanged. It is not any apprehension of aggressive action on the part of the incoming administration which rouses the incoming administration to resistance, but it is the demonstration which Mr. Lincoln's election by such overwhelming majorities affords, of the supremacy of a sentiment hostile to slavery in the nonslaveholding states of the union." [23]

The South contained many who felt a repugnance to slavery. Hilliard

---

Barlow belonged to the Buchanan wing of the party. Keitt of South Carolina said, "I have been engaged in this movement ever since I entered political life"; Springfield *Republican*, Jan. 19, 1861. A Northerner interviewed Davis, Toombs, and R. M. T. Hunter in Washington in December and January of the secession winter, and presented his report, "Conversational Opinions of the Leaders of Secession," in the *Atlantic*, Nov., 1862, pp. 613–623. All three regarded secession as final; Toombs and Davis spoke of using force to sustain it.

23 Quoted in Springfield *Republican*, Jan. 1, 1861.

knew that world sentiment was hostile to it. What he meant was that the Lower South could not commit its fate, in its position of delicacy and peril, to a sectional majority which might prove heedless and dogmatic. This was the Hobbesian ultimate of fear, the chief cause of war; the fear of a people that its way of life would be overthrown by a rival power and creed. The South could not turn back.

[IV]

Still less could the North yield on the mighty issue of disunion. How long had its leaders been explicit on that point! "Liberty and Union, now and forever, one and inseparable"—every schoolboy knew the reply to Hayne. "Our Federal Union: it must be preserved!"—every Northern youth thrilled to Jackson's sentiment. Webster had said in his Seventh of March speech that the idea of peaceable secession was an absurdity. Henry Clay that same year had declared that if any State put itself in military array against the Union, he was for trying the strength of the nation. "I am for ascertaining whether we have a Government or not—practical, efficient, capable of maintaining its author-ity. . . . Nor, sir, am I to be alarmed or dissuaded from any such course by intimations of the spilling of blood. If blood is to be spilt, by whose fault is it?" Thomas Hart Benton had fiercely asserted that the Union must be upheld, if need be, by arms, and President Taylor had promised cold shot and hempen rope to traitors. Lincoln but echoed these leaders when he placed in his inaugural his single veiled threat to Southerners: "In your hands, my dissatis-fied fellow-countrymen, and not in mine, is the momentous issue of civil war."

Beyond a sentimental attachment to the idea of Union, beyond old fealties, loomed irreducible material considerations. Divorce usually means a partition of property. Men might pause but briefly over the question whether they could divide the Fourth of July, Yorktown, Lundy's Lane, and Buena Vista; but the government held title to vast physical possessions. Said the Chicago *Tribune:* "No party in the North will ever consent to a division of the national territory, the national armaments, the national archives, or the national treasury." A President consenting to it would have courted instant impeachment. What of the Southwest? If peaceable secession were permitted, the Confederacy would lay claim to part of New Mexico and Arizona, with hope of a frontage on the Pacific. Confederate sympathizers in Texas, Arkansas, and Missouri would almost certainly attempt to seize the Indian Territory, a key to the Southwestern domain. Where would the international border be drawn, and how would it be policed? Once demarcated, that boundary would certainly be crossed by numberless runaway slaves—and streams of free Negroes; it would be invaded by Northern agitators; and new John Browns would raid more Harpers Ferries.[24]

How, asked John Minor Botts of Virginia in a letter to disunionists, are you going to dispose of the Mississippi River? That question stung Northwestern emotion like a poisoned barb. Let the South try to sever the stream, said Douglas, and the men of Illinois would follow its waters inch by inch with the bayonet to the Gulf. The lower part of the great river had been paid for out of the common purse for the common national good. When Northerners read that Mississippi had placed a battery at the Vicksburg bluffs which was halting steamboats bound downstream, their blood boiled. Congressmen and editors spoke in no modulated tones. "We would like to see them help themselves," retorted the Memphis *Evening Argus*. Later the Confederate Congress conceded the full and free navigation of the river, but it made no provision for the landing or transshipment of cargoes. As river boats could not go to Europe nor ocean ships ascend to St. Louis, import and export shipments were thrown under Confederate power. Amos Kendall, the veteran Jacksonian, told an Illinois friend that if he were an editor he would make the nation ring with his protests. He would declare that the West should never submit to such a situation; that its industrial and commercial interests were hanging over an abyss; and that when Southern complaints touching slavery had been removed, the seceding States must reënter the Union—under compulsion if necessary.[25] He knew that compulsion was war.

It was obvious, moreover, that the precedent of Southern secession might be fatal to the entire national future. Winfield Scott in the "Views" he had sent Buchanan had babbled of a land of four capitals, at Albany, Washington, Columbia, S. C., and Alton or Quincy, Illinois. Each of these four new countries would have ports on navigable waters. But what if some interior States were shut out of the new confederations and left landlocked? What if Michigan could at any time join Canada, closing the Soo? For that matter, what if the Confederacy found Texas becoming opposed to slavery, withdrawing from the new bond, and making herself independent again? American stability, credit, prestige, and power would be dealt shattering blows by a principle of withdrawal which held the potentialities of unlimited dissolution—of national suicide. A once great nation might be Balkanized. The idea, abhorrent to all thoughtful Northerners and many Southerners, was abhorrent most of all to those who saw the nation as a beacon-light of stability, moderation, and freedom in a disorderly world.

24 Clay's speech (a reply to Dawson of Georgia) is in *Cong. Globe*. For Benton see *Thirty Years*, II, 200; for Douglas' views, Milton, *Eve of Conflict*, 396; the editorial in the Chicago *Tribune*, Dec. 12, 1860, was repeated more emphatically Dec. 22.
25 Kendall to J. D. Caton, March 14, 1861; Caton Papers, LC.

Farewell, if secession prevailed, to all ideas of American greatness, and of American leadership of the liberal forces of the globe! Instead, the emergence of two jagged, unhappy, mutually resentful fragments, one a slave-mongering nation of oppressor and oppressed, the other a nation compelled to militarize itself and debase its temper and institutions because of an antagonistic neighbor. Farewell to the old fraternalism, optimism, and idealism, now to be replaced by a Peloponnesian atmosphere, a hostility like that of Athens and Sparta, Rome and Carthage!

Northern unwillingness to yield was heightened by the growing conviction that however fervent was the emotion of the cotton States, it had been brought to its climax by a conspiracy as deliberate and selfish as Catiline's. A deep anger burned in many Northerners as they read of this conspiracy. The Nashville *Patriot* during the recent Presidential campaign had arraigned W. L. Yancey, Barnwell Rhett, and Porcher Miles as its leaders. It had related how the conspiracy began with the Southern Convention in Montgomery in May, 1858; how the Southern League, to promote a great Southern party, had been systematically organized; how Yancey had persuaded the Alabama legislature to assert that it would never submit to the domination of a sectional Northern party; and how he had induced the Democratic State convention in Alabama on April 23, 1859, to declare that unless the Federal Government gave slavery positive protection on the high seas and in the Territories, it would use its best endeavors to withdraw from that government. The *Patriot* described how Yancey appeared in Charleston as leader of the disunionists and helped engineer the disruption of the Democratic Party, simply to make sure of Republican victory and subsequent secession.[26] "Then we can excite the South to rise," Yancey had said.

The *National Intelligencer* in Washington took up the conspiracy thread and pursued it further. In that careful, moderate paper a noted Southerner, a former member of Congress, published on January 9, 1861, his *j'accuse*. "I charge," he wrote, "that on last Saturday night a caucus was held in this city by the Southern secession Senators from Florida, Georgia, Alabama, Mississippi, Louisiana, Arkansas, and Texas." They resolved, he went on, to seize all political and military power in the South. They telegraphed orders for the drafting of final plans to seize all forts, arsenals, and custom houses; they sent advice that the secession conventions then or soon to be in session should pass ordinances for immediate withdrawal; and they directed the assembling of a secession convention at Montgomery on February 13. In order to thwart any attempted interference by Washington, they determined that the seceding States

26 Widely republished, South as well as North; for example, in Selma, Ala., *Reporter*, July 26, 1860.

should temporarily keep their members sitting in Congress. "They have possessed themselves of all the avenues of information in the South,—the telegraph, the press, and the general control of the postmasters." [27]

"Have we not known men," Andrew Johnson presently asked the Senate, "to sit at their desks in this chamber, using the government's stationary to write treasonable letters; and while receiving their pay and sworn to support the Constitution and sustain the law, engaging in midnight conclaves to devise ways and means by which the government should be overthrown?" [28] Stephen A. Douglas went further. He believed, with Charles Francis Adams, that the conspiracy embraced a plan to seize the Capitol before Lincoln could be inaugurated there, and to paralyze the government; a plan which only the unexpected strength of the Virginia Unionists in the election of 1860 frustrated.

Because of the tremendous sentimental and moral values attached to the Union, because of the impossibility of dividing its assets and dissevering a land where the greatest river systems and mountain valleys ran athwart sections, because secession meant a chain process of suicide, because the integrity of the republic was the life of world liberalism, and because to most observers it seemed that a squalid conspiracy had turned natural Southern aspirations and apprehensions to unnatural ends, the North could never give way. Certainly Lincoln would not give way; his inaugural address had clearly stated his determination to maintain the Union and hold its property. But in believing that he could do this and still avoid war, he made three errors. First, he temporarily underrated the gravity of the crisis. Second, he overrated the strength of Union sentiment in the South, as he showed in a futile effort to persuade Sam Houston of Texas to rally the nationalist groups. And lastly, as David M. Potter says, he misconceived the conditional character of much Southern Unionism. These were errors of the head, not of the heart, and because of the confused and murky situation were natural enough.[29]

27 This letter was vouched for by the eminent editor W. W. Seaton. Arkansas, not yet seceded when Lincoln took office, stood on the brink.

28 *Cong. Globe*, 37th Cong., 1st Sess. (July 27, 1861), 297.

29 Jefferson Davis wrote later that he knew war was inevitable. He had served long in Washington beside Northern leaders. "With such opportunities of ascertaining the power and sentiments of the Northern people, it would have shown an inexcusable want of perception if I had shared the hopes of men less favored with opportunities for forming correct judgments, in believing with them that secession could be or would be peacefully accomplished." "Lord Wolseley's Mistakes," *North American Review*, vol. 149, Oct., 1889, 475. In his Senate speech Jan. 10, 1861, he had predicted long years of war, terrible devastation, and a final peace between two republics. He wrote to Governor Pickens, Jan. 13: "We are probably soon to be involved in that fiercest of human strife, a civil war." Lincoln would never have written that! Davis knew that *no* Federal Government worthy of the nation could avoid meeting with arms the policy he was helping carry through. Even Buchanan, since the revolution in his Cabinet, was not that feeble! "When Lincoln comes in," wrote Davis to Franklin Pierece, Jan. 20, "he will have but to continue in the path of

[V]

The Confederacy in March faced a vital issue: Should it wait or strike? If it waited, it might gain by finding time to install its government, organize its resources, and import foreign materials. It might also lose by giving Union sentiment in large areas, such as northern Alabama, time to reassert itself once the first fine rapture of independence began to decline. But above all, its attention was centered on border States. If it waited, would they gravitate to the Confederacy, or fix their allegiance yet more firmly in the Union? If it struck, would the shock make them embrace secession or recoil from it?

The best opportunity for a stroke presented itself at Fort Pickens on Pensacola Bay and Fort Sumter in Charleston Harbor, two thorns in Confederate flesh. Pensacola was much the less sensitive spot. Florida was not South Carolina. Here a Yankee lieutenant occupied Pickens, which could be easily reinforced from the sea, with a tiny body of troops under a workable arrangement that he should hold his island fort unharmed while Florida forces occupied the neighboring mainland positions without disturbance.[30] Danger of an explosion was slight, and he had provisions for five months.

Sumter held a different status. Recent events had made it to Northerners a symbol of the maintenance of the Union, and to Confederates a symbol of foreign intrusion. Radical Northerners believed that it must be held, radical Southerners that it must be taken. Under Robert Anderson, a veteran of the Mexican War, it symbolized the choice between acquiescence in secession, or stern resistance to it.

Confederate leaders had forcibly indicated their determination to attack Sumter if it were not quickly evacuated. Judah P. Benjamin wrote S. L. M. Barlow in New York as early as January 17, 1861, that an act of war impended at Sumter or Pickens. "At neither can it be long delayed." When Jefferson Davis was elected President, William Porcher Miles of South Carolina was at hand in Montgomery. He favored an early assault, but urged his State government not to permit it until the Confederate authorities gave the word. Our attack, he wrote, would necessarily plunge the new nation into war with the United States, and that before the six other States were prepared. Davis on March 1 appointed Beauregard to command at Charleston. As he did so he informed the Governor, Francis W. Pickens of South Carolina, that he was anxious to vindicate Southern rights territorial and jurisdictional, and that he

---

his predecessor to inaugurate a civil war." Dunbar Rowland, ed., *Jefferson Davis, Letters, Papers, and Speeches*, V, 36–38. Potter's statement is in *Lincoln and his Party in the Secession Crisis*, 375.

30 On Lieutenant Slemmer and his opponents see O. R., I, i, 333–342.

had discussed with Beauregard the works needful to reduce Sumter most speedily. Confederate authorities hurried a colonel to New Orleans to buy fifteen tons of cannon powder for immediate shipment to Charleston. The moment the governor of Florida read a synopsis of Lincoln's message he telegraphed Pickens in South Carolina: "Will you open at once upon Fort Sumter?" [31]

Yet before Lincoln took office, the Buchanan Administration, fortified by the addition of Edwin M. Stanton, Joseph Holt, and John A. Dix to the Cabinet, repeatedly warned the Confederate leaders that an attack on the fort would mean war. Buchanan not only refused to withdraw the troops from Sumter, but declined to promise not to reinforce them. Indeed, as he wrote later, he uniformly declared he would send reinforcements whenever Major Anderson requested them or the safety of the post demanded them. Joseph Holt, as Secretary of War, met South Carolina's demands for evacuation with the stiffest denials. The United States held absolute sovereignty over the fort, he declared; the government possessed no more authority to surrender it than to cede the District of Columbia to Maryland; the small garrison was not a menace, but was maintained to protect South Carolina from foreign foes. If rash leaders assaulted Sumter "and thus plunge our country into civil war, then upon them and those they represent must rest the responsibility." [32]

Charleston throughout March resounded with martial activities, for Beauregard put new energy into preparations for war. He found the harbor already bristling with guns, every point of access from the sea fortified, the channel obstructed, and watch maintained to make sure that not even a small boat reached Fort Sumter. Charlestonians, their State troops drilling day and night, thought they had done everything possible. But Beauregard mobilized a large body of Negro laborers to strengthen the harbor defenses, improved the position of the guns, enlisted more artillerists, and hastened the arming of small vessels to operate in coastal waters. Secretary of War Walker urged him on: "Give but little credit to rumors of an amicable adjustment," he wrote March 15. During battery practice a heavy ball struck the Sumter walls; and though an officer was sent at once to explain that it was a chance shot, Charlestonians guessed that their gunners were fixing the range of the fort. A floating battery was heavily armed to be anchored near Sumter. [33]

31 Barlow Papers; Miles Porcher to F. W. Porcher Feb. 9, 1861, Amer. Art. Assn. Catalogue Feb. 5, 1929, p. 39; Davis to Governor Pickens, A. S. W. Rosenbach Collection; Memminger, Feb. 16, 1861, to Col. M. A. Moore, Memminger Papers South Caroliniana Lib. Gov. W. O. Perry to Gov. Pickens, March 5, 1861, Pickens-Bonham Papers LC.
32 Curtis, *Buchanan*, II, 541 ff.; Holt, Feb. 6, 1861, to Attorney-General J. W. Hayne of S. C., N. Y. *Tribune*, Feb. 9, 1861.
33 O. R. I, i, 275, 276; Charleston correspondence, March 9, 10, in N. Y. *Tribune*, March 13, 16, 1861.

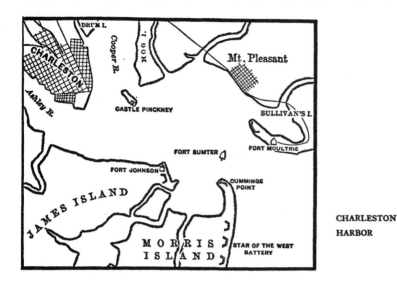

CHARLESTON
HARBOR

Many officers were spoiling for a fight. Beauregard, reporting March 22 that all his batteries would be in full trim in a few days, was able to add that Sumter was nearly out of fuel and provisions. Five days later he expressed hope that the fort would soon surrender, for the uncertainty ought not to last beyond the period when he had completed all his preparations to compel Anderson to surrender.[34]

[VI]

Meanwhile, in Washington, Abraham Lincoln, new to high office, totally untrained in administrative duties, inexperienced in the leadership of Congress and public sentiment, and quite unacquainted with his Cabinet, had to face a multiplicity of problems with scanty assistance and amid constant distractions. For secretarial aid he had only two men, John Hay and John G. Nicolay, both able, but very young, very green, and very provincially Western. The country would have gained had Lincoln brought some capable Republican of more experience, like Horace White of the Chicago *Tribune* staff, who had reported the Lincoln-Douglas debates, to reinforce them. The first week Lincoln had to receive callers in droves, meet the diplomatic corps as it paid its respects, address delegations from six States, handle a swollen mail, and hold his first formal Cabinet meeting (March 9). That week Seward, on whose friendly if contriving advice he could best lean, was ill with lumbago.

In his first days Lincoln had to fill the principal existing vacancies before the Senate adjourned its short special session; to consult with General Scott on the bad position of the army, whose two principal administrative officers, Samuel Cooper as adjutant-general and Joseph E. Johnston as quartermaster-

34 O. R., I, i, 280, 283; Beauregard to Walker, March 22, 27.

general, leaned to the South; and to study the possibility of keeping Maryland, Virginia, Kentucky, and Missouri in the Union. Washington was speculating on antagonisms within the Cabinet, with Seward, Cameron, and Bates understood to be moderate, while Chase, Montgomery Blair, and Welles supposedly held more extreme views.[35] Martin J. Crawford, one of three Confederate commissioners whom Jefferson Davis had just sent to Washington to explore the chances of a treaty of amity, was busily inquiring as to the intentions of the new regime, and reporting to Montgomery on March 6 that Seward and Cameron could be relied on to maintain a peace policy. Another commissioner, John Forsyth, arrived on his heels, and both men began using ex-Senator Gwin of California and Senator R. M. T. Hunter of Virginia in an effort to establish unofficial relations with Seward.

When did Lincoln have time to ponder the one question that mattered: the question what course could best serve the cause of peace and reunion? Not during his first levee, which so jammed the White House that for an hour those who wished to leave had to get out through the windows. And not while he was incessantly besieged by office-hunters and Congressional patronage-dispensers. At first he refused to limit his hours for seeing people. But when he found that he had no time to take a drink of water, he fixed them at ten o'clock till three, and later at ten till one.[36]

Lincoln thought it appalling that while the national house was on fire at one end, he had to be letting out rooms at the other. Sane observers were equally aghast. We have no national policy, no administration plan, one of Greeley's friends lamented near the end of March; while the government crumbles underfoot, the only problem considered is whether some supplicant should be a tide-waiter, a village postmaster, or an Indian agent. But the system existed; the President had no escape.

He was in fact the focal point of pressures which reached out to every town and county with a sizable Republican vote. After filling his Cabinet, he had but one important personal appointment to make—that of Hiram Barney, a capable attorney, to be collector of the port of New York. Barney, a friend of William Cullen Bryant, had extended Lincoln some valued courtesies at the time of the Cooper Union address, and had supported him in the Chicago convention. The President took a certain interest also in sending Charles Francis Adams to London, W. L. Dayton to Paris, Norman Judd to Berlin, and that eccentric egotist Cassius M. Clay to St. Petersburg. In the main, however, his appointments had to be parceled out to clamorously selfish men and groups.[37]

---

35 Blaine, *Twenty Years*, I, 285, 286.
36 N. Y. *Herald*, March 9, 1861; Helen Nicolay, *Lincoln's Secretary*, 82, 83.
37 The Barney appointment is discussed in Alexander, *Political Hist. N. Y.*, II, 390–396; cf. Wm. Allen Butler (a law partner), *A Retrospect of Forty Years*, 349, 350.

Every Republican in Congress wished to strengthen his political organization; every editor coveted a post-office connection to swell his subscription list; every jobless politician wanted a salary. The Illinois members, for example, met in conclave to draw up a slate of appointments to be requested of Lincoln. After dividing marshalships, district attorneyships, and territorial posts, they demanded a slice of foreign-service pie. Senator Lyman Trumbull wanted two consulships, Representative Elihu Washburne one, and Representative W. P. Kellogg one. Joseph Medill of the Chicago *Tribune*, meanwhile, wished one of his staff made the new Chicago postmaster. "If Mr. Scripps has it," he explained, "the country postmasters of the Northwest would work to extend our circulation." And Illinois was but one State! Three-quarters of the March correspondence of the typical Senator, Representative, or Cabinet member in this hour of crisis pertained to jobs. A clamor of greed and grumbling filled the capital.[38]

In this matter Lincoln was the victim not merely of the national system, but of the special necessities of the Republicans. They did not as yet have a coherent, well-organized party. It had been born some half dozen years earlier as a patchwork of local organizations; it had fought the campaign of 1856 under a hastily-chosen nominee as a coalition of new, uncertain State organizations, and had lost; in the three years after 1856 it had largely disappeared from view as a national entity. Its enthusiastic rally in 1860, a marvel of improvisation, might have failed again but for the Democratic schism. Its members included former Whigs, former Know-Nothings, former Freesoil Democrats, and young men who were simon-pure Republicans. Now it needed the cement of national office to make it a unified, well-knit party on a truly national basis. Its chieftains— governors, Senators, Representatives, editors, State and local committeemen— were resolved that it should obtain this cement, and anxious to determine its quality. Lincoln was well aware that parties are essential to democratic government, and that his Administration could not possibly succeed without strong party support. In the hours he gave to applicants he was not merely dividing spoils; he was building a foundation.

Throughout March the hotels were jammed. In one, three hundred unbathed men slept in the dining room. Anybody could get into the White House, and nearly everybody did. The physical and psychological pressure on

38 Medill's letter, March 4, 1861, is in the Lyman Trumbull Papers, LC; see also the Washburne Papers. Among the dissatisfied elements the Constitutional Unionists were prominent. Edward Everett resentfully noted that in Maryland, Kentucky, and Missouri, where the Republican vote had been trifling and the Constitutional Union vote tremendous, Lincoln had bestowed the three great plums on Republicans—Montgomery Blair, Cassius M. Clay, and Edward Bates. Everett, March 31, 1861, to Sir Henry Holland; Everett Papers, MHS.

Lincoln was crushing. On March 14 one correspondent shouldered his way through the fragrant throng. "I saw the President this morning, and his whole air was that of not only a worried but an ill man. He would require a fortnight's rest, it seemed to me, to enable him to let off a joke or a jolly backwoods reminiscence." Not until hundreds of appointees had been confirmed, and the special Senate session had ended on March 28, could the Administration give wholehearted attention to the grave national issues.

To add to Lincoln's difficulties, Douglas as the chief Democratic leader spent March indicating that he would harass the Administration mercilessly unless it sacrificed almost everything for peace. He seemed a very different Douglas from the man who had recently talked of hanging traitors. For one reason, he was trying to pull the defeated Democratic party together, and to rally Union forces in the South. For another, he was drinking heavily again, a fact which explained some excesses of language and one bout of fisticuffs on the Senate floor. But when all allowances are made, his attacks were outrageously sharp. He introduced a resolution calling on the Administration to tell the Senate how many forts, arsenals, and navy yards it held inside the seceded States, with what forces, and with what intentions. His object, he stated, was to press the government into a definite avowal of policy. In his opinion, it had but three courses open: It could amend the Constitution to preserve the Union, it could assent to a peaceable division, or it could make war to subjugate the lost States. "The first proposition is the best and the last is the worst," he declared.

If Douglas wished assurances that Lincoln would not wantonly provoke war, he got them. Senator Fessenden, assuring him that the President would use no questionable powers and violate no law in an effort to collect the revenues, obviously spoke for Lincoln. It was not clear that the government had any right to collect customs dues aboard a warship, and it would certainly not do so without explicit mandate from Congress. Yet day by day Douglas kept up his scoriac outbursts, often using bitter personalities. His manner was satanically provoking. Sometimes he exhibited a heavy-handed malignity, sometimes he was patronizingly sarcastic. You state that you mean peace, he said tauntingly, and yet pass laws that cannot be enforced without war. You talk of maintaining the Federal authority, yet you have not a Federal officer, acting by your authority, in the whole secession area. However affronted, his opponents thought it best to bite their lips in silence.[39]

One eloquent foreign voice, in these dark days, was raised to hearten Amer-

---

39 *Cong. Globe*, 36th Cong., 2d Sess., 1436 ff. "I expect to oppose his [Lincoln's] administration with all my energy on those great principles which have separated parties in former times," Douglas said March 6; but on a Constitutional amendment to settle the slavery issue, he would support Lincoln.

ican friends of freedom. Elizabeth Barrett Browning wrote an American acquaintance that some evils were worse than civil conflict. "My serious fear," she declared, "has been, and is, not for the dissolution of the body but the death of the soul—not of a rupture of states and civil war, but of reconciliation and peace at the expense of a deadly compromise of principle. Nothing will destroy the republic but what corrupts its conscience and disturbs its frame—for the stain upon the honor must come off upon the flag. If, on the other hand, the North stands fast on the moral ground no glory will be like your glory." [40] These were the sentiments of millions of lovers of the Union.

Most men on both sides in the sectional struggle felt that they stood upon sound moral ground. It was all-important that the leaders on each side, and especially on the Union side, should act on high principle and not expediency. Would Lincoln, so untried in great responsibilities, yield to the heavy pressures for peace at any price—for delay beyond the point of no return? Or would he stand by his declaration that evasion must stop? Before the answer was given, a quietly desperate struggle between him and Seward had to be decided.

40   N. Y. *Independent*, March 10, 1861.

$$\boxed{3}$$

Contest for Power: Seward and Lincoln

LINCOLN headed what was essentially a coalition government. His Cabinet represented groups of diverse origins and principles—conservative Whigs, freesoil Whigs, Union Democrats of Jacksonian cast, and radical adherents of new Republican ideas. Of its members a majority—Secretary of State Seward, Secretary of the Treasury Chase, Secretary of War Cameron, and Attorney-General Bates—had aspired to the Presidency, and Chase and perhaps Seward hoped for that prize in the future. The Cabinet had not even the semblance of unity, and its level of responsibility was low. As the diaries of Chase, Bates, and Secretary of the Navy Gideon Welles show, they had no trust in each other. Several were at critical moments to prove disloyal to the President; and at least two were so undependable that part of their duties had to be taken over by others, Cameron ceding certain military responsibilities to Chase, and Bates certain responsibilities over civil justice to Seward. Lincoln, like other leaders of coalitions which included headstrong men (Lloyd George in the First World War, for example), had to fight for his tenure of power. His first battle was to be for the control of his Administration, his second for the control of military strategy—and others were to follow.

From the moment South Carolina seceded, Seward had been actuated by the idea of compromise; from the moment he took the State Department, he had cherished a belief that he could dominate Lincoln. Having led rough Zack Taylor when he was only Senator, now as the ablest Cabinet member he would lead the rustic neophyte from the Sangamon. Recent events strengthened his confidence. He had revised the inaugural address, put his friend Cameron into the Cabinet even if he had failed to keep Chase out, and easily established himself as Lincoln's chief adviser.[1]

To comprehend Seward's attitude, we should glance at a few comparative

---

[1] The exact extent of Seward's influence over Lincoln is hard to gauge. But we may agree with Douglas that it was much greater than it should have been. Lincoln often sat listening to his breezy, genial, cynical talk and drew profit from his experience. It was temporarily an Eisenhower-Taft situation, rather than a Wilson-Underwood situation. Welles, I, *Diary*, 34, 35.

facts. He was almost eight years older than the President. When little Abe Lincoln was a ragged backwoods lad trudging to log schools in Indiana for brief intervals of ciphering, Seward was studying at Union College. While Lincoln was keeping store, splitting rails, and surveying at New Salem, Seward was leader of the New York Senate. The year 1842 found Lincoln a struggling Springfield lawyer; it found Seward completing four busy years as governor of the Empire State. When Lincoln left the House in defeat after one term, Seward sat in the Senate as almost the peer of Clay or Webster. Throughout the 1850's Seward seemed the chief embodiment of the freesoil cause; no other Republican leader gained so much experience or renown; and wearing the laurels of twelve years of versatile Senate service, he entered the party convention of 1860 the leading candidate and to most citizens unquestionably the strongest man—to be beaten by a raw Western attorney.

Just before the inauguration he inspired a friend to publish in the New York *Evening Post* a letter presenting him as a paladin of peace, who would effect an early restoration of the Union if only New York enemies, fanatic abolitionists, and (it was hinted) an inexperienced President did not prevent him. The letter writer lamented that never before had so many members of Congress been open applicants for Presidential favors. "This, and the impression which exists that Mr. Lincoln is opposed to any form of compromise, makes members firm who ne'er were firm before, and creates obstacles to the settlement of our difficulties which ten words from the lips of Mr. Lincoln would dispel in a moment." [2] Let Seward be the *deus ex machina!* A Southern commissioner reported what was doubtless an accurate transcript of Seward's loose, fluent talk just after the inauguration. "I have built up the Republican party, I have brought it to triumph, but its advent to power is accompanied by great difficulties and perils. I must save the party, and save the government in its hands. To do this, war must be averted, the negro question must be dropped, the irrepressible conflict ignored, and a Union Party to embrace the border slave States inaugurated. . . . [Then] the people of the cotton States, unwillingly led into secession, will rebel." [3]

It is certain that the three main ideas in this passage were really held by Seward. First, he believed that *he* must take the leadership; he had so written

2 This letter in the *Evening Post* was acridly dissected by the N. Y. *Tribune* of Feb. 27. We are credibly informed, said the *Tribune*, "that the very language of this letter is the same as has been repeatedly used by Mr. Seward in private conversation." Greeley very wrathfully accused Seward of trying to take charge of the Administration and reduce Lincoln to a cipher.

3 Forsyth, March 8, 1861, to Robert Toombs; Toombs Letterbook, South Caroliniana Library, Univ. of S. C.

his wife. Second, he believed that the Republican Party must be broadened into a Union Party, powerful in the border States, and quiet on the slavery issue. Third, he assumed that if the seven cotton States were isolated, their people would soon beg for readmittance. Winfield Scott wrote Seward on March 3 outlining various alternatives before the government, and ending with alternative number four—let the seceded States depart in peace. This implied that the head of the army regarded Seward, not Lincoln, as general manager of the new regime, and Seward showed the letter widely around Washington to confirm that belief and strengthen the peace party.

Back of Seward's policy lay a profound moral defect. He could not take the great issue of Southern intransigence, so all-important to the future of the nation, with due seriousness. He thought that any storm, even this, could be controlled by cunning management, party bargains, and dexterous maneuvering; he did not realize that he was facing men in deadly earnest, whose determination was fixed, and was dealing with a movement far too powerful for mere shrewd manipulation. Douglas, among others, saw through his shallow conceit. Douglas knew that he had been hand-in-glove with various Southern Senators all winter, playing a dangerous game with them. The time for games had now passed.

[I]

On inauguration day Sam Ward, son of a rich New York banker, skilled lobbyist, and friend of many leaders in both parties, launched an effort to encourage Seward's peacemaking. He wrote the Secretary that he had talked with several Confederate leaders; that he had learned that Robert Toombs was the master spirit of the new government (an illusion Toombs liked to create); and that the Southern Congress was adamant for independence. He warned Seward that if the Southern commissioners who had come to open negotiations in Washington were sent back unrecognized, President Davis could not restrain the incensed South Carolinians from attacking Sumter. His informants, ex-Senator W. M. Gwin of California and Senator R. M. T. Hunter of Virginia, thought that the question of treating with the commissioners ought to be submitted to the Senate, where twenty-two favorable Democratic votes could be counted on.

It is clear that Ward, Gwin, and Hunter assumed that Lincoln was a nullity, and hoped that Seward would so manage affairs as to preserve peace.[4]

4 Ward's letters are in Bancroft, *Seward*, II, 542–545; see also Crawford, *Genesis*, 322; Rhodes, *History*, III, 328: Bancroft, *Seward*, II, 111.

In Montgomery, meanwhile, Judah P. Benjamin was voicing the indignation of the Confederate Government over the way in which Washington let matters drift, and its determination shortly to seize the forts.

Seward was perfectly willing to hold indirect parleys with the Confederate commissioners. He allowed Gwin, a warm sympathizer with the South, to run back and forth between him and the three agents, Martin J. Crawford, A. B. Roman, and John Forsyth, who regarded themselves as envoys of a foreign power. While the trio threatened immediate blows against Forts Sumter and Pickens, Seward pleaded for delay and peace. Finally, the commissioners sent the Secretary a memorandum agreement (March 8) offering a wait of twenty days in return for a promise that the existing military position would be preserved in every respect. Seward meanwhile assured Sam Ward that the Administration would take no warlike steps; and Ward delightedly urged his New York friends to buy stocks and keep on buying.[5] Momentarily, the commissioners hoped they had entrapped Seward. If he signed their memorandum, he in effect recognized the Confederacy![6] When the paper arrived, however, the wily Secretary was abed with lumbago and declared that his physician had forbidden him to transact any business whatever. Gwin at this point dropped his dubious and doubtless distasteful activities as a go-between.[7]

Seward was certainly too shrewd a fox to be ensnared. However anxious he was to take a conciliatory line, evacuate Fort Sumter, and charm the Confederate States back into the Union, he could not possibly recognize the commissioners as agents of an independent government. Undiscouraged, the three emissaries persuaded Senator Hunter to accept the role of intermediary. When on March 11 the convalescent Seward returned to the State Department, he found that conservative slaveholder on his doorstep. The Secretary was embarrassed and uneasy, and when Hunter pressed him, merely said that he would ask the President about the propriety of an informal interview. Next day he wrote Hunter that he could not see the commissioners. Nevertheless, Crawford and Forsyth remained of good heart, informing Toombs cheerfully on March 12:

> While . . . a refusal to treat with us . . . in the absence of the evacuation of the Charleston and Pensacola forts is, from our point of view, certain war, the Administration still talks of peace. A gentleman from Tennessee had a half hour's private conversation with Mr. Lincoln this morning, and he assured him there would be no war and he was determined to keep the peace. . . . Mr. Crittenden of Kentucky told Mr. Crawford this morning that General Scott was also for peace, and would sustain Mr. Seward's policy, and if

5 Ward, March 9, 1861, Barlow Papers.
6 The commissioners to Toombs, March 8, 1861, Toombs Letterbook, South Caroliniana.
7 W. M. Gwin, MS Memoirs, Bancroft Library, Univ. of California, 190–200.

Sumter should be evacuated we think it will be the influence of General Scott upon the President which will produce that result. . . .

We are still of the opinion that Fort Sumter will be evacuated.[8]

Lincoln at this point, in fact, almost made up his mind that the evacuation of Sumter was a military necessity. Major Robert Anderson, commanding there, had suddenly reported on February 28 that he did not think an attempt to reinforce the post could succeed without 20,000 disciplined men. This had astonished the outgoing Secretary of War, Joseph Holt. Anderson had been told to report frequently on the condition of his garrison and on any warlike preparations around him; he had not suggested that the preparations were threatening or that reinforcements were needed; nevertheless, since an exigency might arise at any moment, Holt had quietly prepared a small expedition which was ready to sail from New York on a few hours' notice with troops and provisions. Now Anderson estimated that a relief attempt would be hopeless without forces far beyond the nation's immediate means—large naval units to break past the defenses into Charleston Harbor, and a powerful army to overwhelm the hostile fortifications from the rear. Where were the warships and the troops? Only eight companies were stationed in Washington, and only seven at Fort Monroe—all required where they were.[9]

It was all too true that Anderson's position was increasingly precarious. The South Carolina authorities permitted him to buy meat and vegetables in Charleston only from one market day to another, and forbade him to lay in a stock of nonperishables like flour.[10] In Washington, A. D. Bache of the Coast Survey and Col. J. G. Totten, chief engineer of the army, agreed that the strengthening of Fort Moultrie, the erection of land batteries, and the obstruction of channels had put Sumter in grave danger. Army officers talked of Charleston as "a new Sebastopol." Nearly the entire available force of South Carolina was in the field, and squads of recruits were arriving in an unsteady stream from other Southern States—even Maryland. Special trains were leaving Richmond with mortars, shot, shells, and ammunition. Even as Lincoln took his oath Governor Pickens telegraphed the Tredegar Iron Works: "Please send 400 shells for Dahlgren guns in addition to those already ordered."[11] The floating battery was anchored within range of Sumter, and Beauregard expressed confidence that he could blow Anderson out of the place at a moment's notice.

But various Union leaders refused to believe that a huge fleet and army

8 Toombs Letterbook, South Caroliniana Library.
9 Secretary Holt to Lincoln, March 3, 1861; Robert Todd Lincoln Papers, LC. It would take weeks to bring back the small forces garrisoning the Southwest.
10 N. Y. *Tribune*, March 11, 1861.
11 See telegrams of L. P. Walker, Pickens, and others in Pickens-Bonham Papers, LC.

would be needed to save Sumter, and declared it outrageous to talk of giving up the fort. Gideon Welles shook his beard with the exclamation, "Astounding!" Attorney-General Bates was resentfully perplexed. Above all, Postmaster-General Montgomery Blair, determined that the Union must be maintained at any cost, was profoundly stirred.[12] His brother-in-law Gustavus V. Fox, a man of determined chin and bald, domelike brow, systematic and energetic, and an Annapolis graduate who had overseen the transport of troops to Vera Cruz during the Mexican War, felt the same way. Blair had just brought him to Washington from his business in Massachusetts to advise General Winfield Scott, head of the Army, and he was ready to play his part. When Lincoln on Saturday, March 9, held his first Cabinet meeting, everyone agreed that more information was needed.

That same day Lincoln asked Scott to answer three questions in writing: How long could Sumter hold out? Could it be reinforced or supplied during that period with existing means? If not, what additional forces would be needed? On the following Monday, March 11, Scott laid his depressing answers before Lincoln. Sumter had hard bread, flour, and rice for only 26 days, with salt meat for 48; and to relieve the fort with existing resources was impossible, for he would need a strong fleet, 5000 additional regulars, and 20,000 volunteers.

These responses shocked Lincoln. He held Scott in high respect, for the old general had always been deeply attached to the Union, and there was of course no question of his impressive military achievements. Lincoln had supported him when he was the Whig Presidential candidate in 1852. He trusted Scott sufficiently to be appalled by his report. What he did not realize was that Scott in this matter was largely an echo of Seward, who adroitly manipulated him, and that the commander at times showed evidences of senility, although, as we shall see, he could if aroused plan ably and boldly. When the President on March 5 had requested Scott to be vigilant in maintaining all Federal forts and posts, the General had done almost nothing.[13] But this Lincoln did not yet know.

It is not strange that on these three days, March 9–11, Lincoln almost

12 O. R., I, i, 196–198; Bates, *Diary*, 177, 178; Welles, *Diary* (retrospective), I, 4.
13 Lincoln, worried over Fort Pickens at Pensacola, on March 11 repeated in writing his order to Scott to maintain Federal positions. Next day Scott started orders to the commander of some troops on the warship *Brooklyn* off Pensacola to land his company to reinforce Pickens. But this order was not obeyed! The naval commander refused to let the men land. He wrote Secretary Welles April 1 that such a movement "would most certainly be viewed as a hostile act, and would be resisted to the utmost." He would not begin the war under Scott as head of the Army, though he would willingly obey any order from Welles as head of the Navy. "Omitted Letters" in G. V. Fox Correspondence, N. Y. Hist. Soc.

gave way. In Washington the *National Intelligencer*, long the nation's principal Whig newspaper, appeared with an earnest editorial plea for withdrawal. The *National Republican*, a newspaper close to some Administration leaders, the same day explicitly announced that the Cabinet had decided to evacuate both Sumter and Pickens. It is possible that Seward nudged the elbows of both editors. Certainly he helped spread word of an imminent evacuation, and told J. C. Welling of the *National Intelligencer* to convey the news to a Union leader in the convention which Virginia was then holding. On the 12th the Charleston *Courier* and *Mercury* announced that Sumter would soon be in Confederate hands without a fight.

This news, in fact, rapidly spread through the country. The New York *Herald* carried a dispatch on the 12th denouncing the reports as a stockjobbing scheme, and a cloak for secret Administration efforts to strengthen the fort. But next day it ate its words. "I am able to state positively," wrote the Washington correspondent, "that the abandonment of Fort Sumter has been determined upon by the President and his Cabinet."

Fierce and swift was the wrath of all radical Republicans. The lobbies of hotels rang with denunciation. Ben Wade's profanity was fearful to hear. Greeley's *Tribune* uttered an angry wail. To give up the fort in the first fortnight of power! To abandon what Buchanan in spite of all his imbecility and cowardice had held! This would be an acknowledgment that the Union was dissolved forever unless it was saved later by the most abject concessions. Perhaps, wrote Greeley, the North really was too demoralized to act with vigor, or perhaps circumstances necessitated the step; but he could not help thinking that if the Administration were to accept disunion, it might begin with a step less humiliating. John A. Dix commented that the grief and anger of the North would almost ruin the Administration. Western Congressmen were particularly indignant.[14]

[II]

Yet Lincoln had not fully made up his mind, and Lincoln still gripped the reins.

The anxious Cabinet held two sessions on March 14, the first from ten to one, the second from four till seven. The members now divided sharply on Scott's report that evacuation was practically unavoidable. Montgomery Blair, a tall, ministerial-looking attorney who as a boy had often listened to the talk of his father and Andrew Jackson, and who believed that his West

14 N. Y. *Times*, *Tribune*, *Herald*, March 12-15, 1861; note especially J. S. Pike's Washington correspondence in the *Tribune*.

Point training enabled him to speak on military topics, led the opposition to surrender. Since nullification days his family had made the word "Union" a shibboleth. He had represented Dred Scott before the Supreme Court. Now he felt certain that Winfield Scott was growing imbecile, and that neither Seward nor Cameron understood the kind of action that the crisis demanded. Violence was not to be met by temporizing. "It is my deliberate opinion," he had recently written, "that if such a policy is acted on we shall have a long and bloody war and permanent disunion"; on the other hand, if a strong Northern blow were struck, the Southern masses would rise against the Confederate Government.[15] One root of the difficulty, in Blair's opinion, was the widespread Southern conviction that all Yankees lacked courage. Appeasement by the surrender of Sumter would convince them of this, and simply make a collision more probable. The Southern Gascons needed a lesson, nor should it be costly. And Montgomery Blair was only one of many who believed that a firm attitude would mean a shorter war.

Blair came to the Cabinet armed with a plan for the naval relief of Sumter prepared by his brother-in-law. Gustavus V. Fox proposed sending to Charleston, under convoy of the seven-gun vessel *Pawnee* and the revenue cutter *Harriet Lane*, a steamship laden with stores and two tugboats. If on reaching Charleston they found Confederate gunboats opposing their entry, the two warships must destroy or drive ashore the Southern craft, Major Anderson assisting with his guns. Then, at nightfall, the tugboats would run past the shore batteries and relieve the fort. Even if one tug was lost, the other could deliver the stores and a limited number of troops, after which the tugs would be abandoned while their crews joined the garrison. The scheme was endorsed by experienced sailors. At Kinnburn on the Black Sea eight British gunboats one night had safely passed Russian forts mounting eighty guns. What Fox was now proposing was something like the running of Vicksburg and Mobile during subsequent naval operations. However, two naval men who at first leaned to the plan, Commodore S. H. Stringham and Commander J. H. Ward, shortly became convinced that it was impracticable.[16]

Seward protested violently. He was adamant in his opposition to any attempt at relief. It was the duty of the Administration, he argued, to defer to the opinion of General Scott, Major Anderson, and other high military officers that any such effort would be abortive and costly. A relief expedition would precipitate hostilities, and if war was to begin, the North should not strike the first blow. Alongside Seward stood his old friend Cameron, the conservative Indiana wirepuller Caleb B. Smith whom Lincoln had reluctantly

15 Blair, Jan. 23, 1861, to John A. Andrew; Andrew Papers, MHS.
16 Fox's plan is in *Confidential Correspondence of G. V. Fox*, I, 8 ff.

appointed to the Interior Department, and, with some reservations, Attorney-General Bates.[17]

The two Cabinet meetings reached no conclusion. Thereupon Lincoln, desiring a more considered statement of views, on the 15th sent every Cabinet member a letter asking whether, as a political measure, it was wise to try to provision Sumter. To this query Blair alone gave an unqualified yes. He declared once more that firm action would do more than weak appeasement to avoid prolonged bloodshed and end the rebellion. Chase took a stand which, had it been widely known, would have astonished the nation. He had gone into the Cabinet with the reputation of an unflinching radical, the doughtiest champion of those whom C. F. Adams called the ramwells—that is, the diehards. But at the moment it was actually true that, as Greeley's Washington correspondent wrote, he was no extremist, but "moderate, conciliatory, deliberate, and conservative." [18] One important factor in his hesitation was his fear that a war would be very difficult, and perhaps impossible, to finance. He was under pressure from Eastern bankers who had warned him that they would not take his pending eight-million-dollar loan unless the government pursued a peace policy. Now he wrote Lincoln that if relieving the fort meant enlisting huge armies and spending millions, he would not advise it. It was only because he believed that the South might be cajoled by full explanations and other conciliatory gestures into accepting the relief effort without war that he supported it. That is, he was for relief only with careful explanations.

The other replies said no. Wordy letters of Caleb B. Smith and Gideon Welles boiled down to a simple statement that relief would be politically unwise. Cameron stressed the weight of adverse military opinion. Bates, like Seward, emphasized the argument that the North ought not to provoke hostilities. Our right is unquestionable, he wrote, and we have the means to act. But "I am willing to evacuate Fort Sumter, rather than be an active party in the beginning of civil war." Seward's position hardly needed restatement. While he declared that the nation must be kept intact even if this ultimately meant war, he argued that Sumter was useless, and conciliation would give the Unionists of the South an opportunity to rally and undo the work of the fire-eaters. He would try to collect the national revenues, but only at sea. "I would defer military action on land until a case should arise when we would hold the defense. In that case, we should have the spirit of the country and the approval of mankind on our side." Essentially true is the statement which Montgomery Blair later made: "Alone in the Cabinet, I resisted the surrender

17 Welles, *Diary*, I, 8 ff.
18 N. Y. *Tribune*, March 6, 1861.

of Forts Sumter and Pickens and the dissolution of the Union which that surrender signified, and put my resignation on the issue." [19]

Lincoln yet hesitated. That he inclined toward an early evacuation is indicated by three pieces of evidence. The first is that on March 18 he placed a
memorandum in his office papers summarizing the arguments for and against
it, with the weight heavily against any effort at relief. The second is that on
the same day he sent inquiries to Welles (about naval force), Bates (about legal
right), and Chase (about general practicability) respecting the offshore collection of tariff duties, an indication that he leaned toward the plan suggested by Seward. The Secretary of State, according to Welles, was spending much of each day at the White House, vigilantly informing himself of
every act, word, and idea of Lincoln and the other Cabinet members. The
third bit of evidence is that Montgomery Blair in desperation wrote out his
resignation, determined to quit if no effort were made to relieve Major
Anderson.

The President was keeping an uneasy eye on Virginia, where on February
4 a convention had been elected to deal with the problems of the hour. The
Union men had won a decisive victory, which Seward had hailed as a gleam
of sunshine in a storm. Only 30 unconditional secessionists had been elected
among 152 members, and by a vote of more than two to one the people required that any findings of the convention must be submitted to a plebiscite.
Disunion had met "a Waterloo defeat," declared the Richmond *Whig*. But the
Unionists represented various shades of opinion, and if the North attempted
coercion, a majority would at once become disunionists. Through confidential
channels, both Lincoln and Seward tried to keep in touch with the convention.

In fact, Lincoln immediately after his arrival in Washington had talked
one evening for several hours with a border group which included the venerable William C. Rives of Virginia, Judge George W. Summers of that State,
and James B. Guthrie of Kentucky, head of the Treasury under Franklin
Pierce. All had gathered in a semicircle about the President-elect, who sat
awkwardly in a chair, his feet on the rungs, his elbows on his angular knees,
and his large hands cupped under his cheeks. After telling a story drawn

19 To Cassius M. Clay, Dec. 31, 1881; Henry B. Joy Collection. Chase was actually
willing to let the cotton States go. He later wrote Alphonso Taft that he had taken the view
that the government had two feasible alternatives: to enforce the laws of the Union everywhere, or to recognize the Confederacy of seven States as an accomplished fact, let it try
its experiment of separate nationality, and forbid any further dismemberment of the nation,
enforcing its authority vigorously. April 28, 1861; Chase Collection, Univ. of Pa. It is an
equally striking fact that Charles Sumner also had been conditionally ready to let the cotton States depart in peace. He had written the Duchess of Argyll, Dec. 14, 1860, that he
approached the question with the greatest caution, and that if secession could be restricted to
the seven States, "I shall be willing to let them go." Sumner Papers, HL.

from his frontier law experiences, and one from Aesop, both of which made good points, Lincoln laid down the principles on which he said he would stand firmly: slavery must not be extended into any Territory, and the laws must be faithfully executed. Various men spoke. At last Rives, a dignified and impressive figure, made with trembling voice an eloquent plea. He referred to the potential horrors concealed in the lowering clouds, and to his own profound love of the Union. But if Lincoln resorted to force, he said, Virginia would secede, and old as he was he would fight for Virginia.

At this Lincoln uncoiled his huge frame from the chair, advanced a step, and according to one account said: "Mr. Rives, Mr. Rives! If Virginia will stay in I will withdraw the troops from Fort Sumter." The story has a plausible ring. It is certain that Lincoln was intensely concerned lest Virginia go out, and hopeful that the convention would adjourn without action. He later told John Hay about the call of these border leaders. "He promised," Hay records in his diary for October 22, 1861, "to evacuate Sumter if they would break up their convention, without any row or nonsense. They demurred. Subsequently he renewed [the] proposition to Summers, but without any result. The President was most anxious to avoid bloodshed." Lincoln remarked that it would be sound policy to trade a fort for a State. But the Virginia convention kept on sitting, obviously in order to vote secession if the government took any step that could be construed as coercion.[20]

[III]

In this duel of Montgomery Blair with Seward, it momentarily seemed that Seward was winning. But the situation was suddenly changed by a dramatic intervention.

Blair apprised his father, the venerable Francis P. Blair, living at Silver Springs near Washington, of his probable resignation. The stalwart Jacksonian, one of the elder statesmen of the nation, a founder of the Republican Party, and a great power throughout the border area, was fiercely aroused. At the next session of the Cabinet (apparently Monday, March 18) he followed

20 Charles S. Morehead of Kentucky, who was a member of the Peace Convention in Washington, later described this meeting in a speech reported in the Liverpool, O., *Mercury*, Oct. 13, 1862. He had served a term with Lincoln in Congress, and Lincoln sent word through a friend asking him to call. It was Morehead who then arranged to bring in Rives, Guthrie, General Donovan of Missouri, and Judge George W. Summers of Virginia. The conversation began at nine in the evening in Lincoln's quarters in his hotel. Morehead told also of meeting with Seward, who pledged his honor that no collision would take place between North and South. " 'Nay,' said he, 'Governor Morehead,' laying his hand on my shoulder to make it more emphatic, 'let me once hold the reins of power firmly in my hands, and if I don't settle this matter to the entire satisfaction of the South in sixty days, I will give you my head for a football!' " For editorial comment see N. Y. *Tribune*, Nov. 6, 1862.

Montgomery to the White House, ensconcing himself in Nicolay's office. As soon as the meeting broke up, he sought Lincoln. He found the President in the Cabinet room reading the written statements of the members. "Will you give up the fort?" Blair demanded. Lincoln did not say. He merely replied that nearly all the Cabinet favored it.

"It would be treason to surrender Sumter, sir," trumpeted the old man. He told Lincoln that the step would "irrevocably lose the Administration the public confidence." Acquiescence in secession would be a recognition of its constitutionality. Scott was timid and senile; as for Seward, the man had never known what principle and firmness meant. "If you abandon Sumter," Blair declared, in effect, "you will be impeached!" And returning to Silver Springs, he wrote the President that while he did not question Scott's patriotism, he regarded Seward as a thoroughly dangerous counselor.

Lincoln's secretaries tell us that he was at heart for holding Sumter, and that only the bulk of adverse opinion had shaken his resolve. The aged Blair produced a telling effect. "His earnestness and indignation aroused and electrified the President," recalls Gideon Welles; "and when, in his zeal, Blair warned the President that the abandonment of Sumter would justly be considered by the people, by the world, by history, as treason to the country, he touched a chord that responded to his invocation. The President decided from that moment that an attempt should be made to convey supplies to Major Anderson, and that he would reinforce Sumter." This is a gross overstatement. Lincoln did not yet fully make up his mind. When he did decide, it was on the basis of complex factors, not Blair's plea alone, and this final resolve was to provision Sumter, not reinforce it. But the plea was nevertheless potent.[21]

Lincoln, still hesitant, determined to send personal agents to Charleston as investigators. Montgomery Blair proposed that Gustavus V. Fox make a quick visit to look into the position of Sumter, and Lincoln consented subject to the approval of Cameron and Scott. Immediately afterwards the President arranged an inquiry into the political situation. Stephen A. Hurlbut of Illinois, an old associate, a Charlestonian by birth and a whilom law student under the famous South Carolina jurist James Louis Petigru, was in Washington. He would command the confidence of prominent Charlestonians. On March 21 Lincoln asked him to hurry down and test Seward's supposition that South Carolina harbored many crypto-Unionists. Hurlbut, telegraphing his sister that he was making her a visit, at once departed. Lincoln's friend Ward Hill

---

21 Rhodes make no mention of Blair's call on Lincoln; neither do Nicolay and Hay. It was briefly noted in Crawford's *Genesis*, p. 368. Welles, *Diary*, I, 13, 14, gives a fuller account, and Smith, *Blair*, II, 9–13, fuller still.

Lamon, who had come from Springfield to seek the Federal marshalship in Washington—a big, loquacious bumbler of more self-assurance than discretion—also went down. In fact, he and Hurlbut traveled together, each supposing that *he* was the principal emissary.

Fox should be back on March 25th, Hurlbut and Lamon on the 27th. A final decision would have to be made immediately afterward. The Virginia convention still marked time. Public opinion North and South still waited in rising anxiety.

[IV]

The intentions of Confederate leaders, meanwhile, were in no doubt whatever. They meant to establish their independent republic forever. William M. Browne spoke for nearly everyone at Montgomery when on March 22 he warned a New York friend that they would attack Sumter if Federal troops were not soon removed. "I am still very confident we shall have a collision," Judah P. Benjamin informed S. L. M. Barlow on April 3. "We have almost certain intelligence of an intention to reinforce Pickens, and that is of course war, and must be so treated by us at all hazards." [22]

The Confederate commissioners were later to accuse Seward of flagrant deception in leading them to believe throughout March that the evacuation of Sumter was imminent. But that the commissioners themselves attempted to delude and deceive Seward by tacitly encouraging his belief in eventual Southern return there is no doubt! Crawford admitted as much when early in March he notified Toombs that he had acquiesced in Seward's plea for delay, on condition that the existing status be rigidly preserved. "His reasons, and my own, it is proper to say, are as wide apart as the poles; he is fully persuaded that peace will bring about a reconstruction of the Union, whilst I feel confident that it will build up and cement our Confederacy, and put us beyond the reach either of his arms or diplomacy." He did not tell Seward that! [23]

The same point was made with yet greater vigor by Crawford and A. B. Roman in a letter of March 26. Poor Seward still thought that peace would lead to a reunion. Very well, they would fool him to the top of his bent. "We believe the peace party is strengthening every day in the North, and we further believe that every day's peace lessens the chance of war. . . . We know that we are independent of this government, living under our own Constitution, and enforcing our own laws, levying tribute upon the North,

22 Barlow Papers.
23 March 6, 1861; Toombs Letterbook.

and doing all things which a free people may of right do. These things aid us at home in solidifying our Government and preparing our people for any emergency; abroad it gives us power, character, and influence. We should do nothing therefore lightly to disturb our rapid growth, and show us less prepared for war than this Government supposes us to be." [24]

As intermediary the commissioners were now employing John A. Campbell of the Supreme Court, a lover of the Union, and a man of fine integrity, cultivation, and tact. He and Seward were old friends who could talk frankly. To some interviews Campbell took Supreme Court Justice Samuel Nelson, a New York Democrat of nearly seventy. Just what promises did Seward give? Just what deceptions did he practice? [25]

Campbell on March 15, after seeing Seward, told Crawford he felt confident that the Administration contemplated no change prejudicial to the Confederacy, and that Sumter would be evacuated in five days. This of course reflected his conversation with Seward. The five days having expired, the commissioners asked Campbell to inquire into the delay. Three times on March 21–22 the judge again saw Seward. Once more Campbell on returning from these talks expressed unabated confidence that Sumter would shortly be evacuated, and that no change would be made in the status of Pickens.

At one point Seward most improperly let his expectations of imminent evacuation carry him away. Judge Campbell remarked that he was going to write a letter to Jefferson Davis. "What shall I say to him on the subject of Fort Sumter?" he inquired. "You may say to him," replied Seward, "that before that letter reaches him—how far is it to Montgomery?" "Three days," rejoined Campbell. And Seward completed his sentence: "You may say to him that before that letter reaches him, the telegraph will have informed him that Sumter will have been evacuated."

Nevertheless, the commissioners well understood that all this represented no pledge by Seward, but simply expressed his confidence that he could manipulate Lincoln and control events. They well knew that inside the Cabinet and party a terrific struggle was taking place. They realized that, as Crawford and Roman ungenerously put it on March 26, "The *courage* and *pertinacity* of Mr. Chase [they should have written Blair] may prevail over the craftiness and timidity of Mr. Seward." "We believe," they reported, "that he [Seward] will impress the President so strongly with his wisdom that he will ultimately control him, but this may be a mistake, and he [Lincoln] may at last fall upon

---

24 March 26; *Ibid.*

25 Campbell was hotly denounced in Alabama for his unwavering adherence to the Union He and Judge Nelson shared a conviction that they could combine loyalty to the Union with opposition to coercion. It was Judge Nelson who, after talking with Seward, arranged for Campbell to serve as intermediary.

the other side." Clearly, they were under no deception. They possessed a correct view of realities.

Playing for high stakes, the commissioners used every possible tool, every expedient, every device. Not satisfied with two Supreme Court justices as go-betweens, they soon utilized the Russian minister, Stoeckl. Roman conversed with Stoeckl in fluent Louisiana French, and made a tentative plan for a meeting, seemingly accidental, between himself and Seward at Stoeckl's residence. This fell through. Meanwhile, the commissioners still used threats. Crawford, for example, had Campbell tell Seward on March 14 that Sumter was a point of the greatest possible danger, as hostilities might commence at any moment. At all times the commissioners, speaking scornfully of Seward behind his back, hoped to use him as a cat's-paw. "It is well that he should indulge in dreams that we know are not to be realized," they had exultantly commented to Toombs.[26]

The Confederate Government was coolly determined to parley so long as negotiations seemed profitable, and to begin shooting when violence became expedient. Toombs on April 2 wrote the commissioners in derision of Seward's hopes: "It is a matter of no importance to us what motives may induce the adoption of Mr. Seward's policy by his government. We are satisfied that it will redound to our advantage, and therefore, care little for Mr. Seward's calculations as to its future effects upon the Confederate States." [27] Dr. Gwin returned in April from a trip to Mississippi, full of confidence in the future of the Confederacy.[28] We know that Northern acts of apparent acquiescence in separation were not strengthening the Unionists in the South, but weakening them.[29] That combative young Virginia orator Roger A. Pryor, who had just resigned from Congress, was traveling through the Carolinas assuring hearers that one resolute Confederate blow would bring the upper South into the new republic.

26 Letters of Crawford and later Crawford, Forsyth, and Roman in Toombs Letterbook, March 8, 22, 25, 1861. It is fair to say that Seward at first seemed as willing as Roman for the meeting at Baron Stoeckl's, and withdrew from the arrangement only because he feared unfavorable publicity.
27 Bancroft, Seward, II, 119. James G. Randall in Lincoln the President, I, 324, speaks of Seward's "definite pledge of evacuation," as do other writers. This is a misuse of words. No pledge was given because (1) Seward obviously had no power to give one, and (2) Campbell's reports clearly state a prediction—a belief in strong probability—but not a categorical promise. It is plain from the commissioners' reports that they at first accepted Seward's belief, but that by March 22 they were doubtful, and that on March 26 they knew that he would probably lose his game. If the Commissioners did not know that Seward was characteristically loose of speech, anybody in Washington could have told them.
28 Curtis, Buchanan, II, 539.
29 William Watson, a young Scottish engineer of Baton Rouge, and F. A. P. Barnard of the Univ. of Mississippi, are among a number who so declare; Watson, Life in the Confederate Army; John Fulton, Memoirs of F. A. P. Barnard, 276, 277.

Seward had gradually evolved a definite program. He hoped that the Virginia convention, after rejecting secession, would call a meeting of delegates from the border States, as some leaders talked of doing; that this body would formulate a plan of reunion; and that a national convention would follow. Actually, he was playing with a dangerous idea.[30] The proposed border gathering might easily result in a new wave of secession and a Border Confederacy, which would first try to dictate to both North and South a set of terms for reunion; then if the North balked, as well it might, the border area would have grounds for joining the cotton States. By April, however, sentiment in Virginia was plainly shifting toward abandonment of the Union, and secessionist managers in the convention were inclined to drop the idea of a Border Confederacy.[31]

Suppose that Seward's idea of a national convention to hammer out terms of reunion had ultimately prevailed. Would the seven Confederate States have responded? On the contrary, the probability was that the gap would have steadily widened. Each side would accommodate its institutions, usages, and requirements to the new order. Under shelter of the Confederacy a large body of special interests would spring up—mercantile groups fostered by its low tariffs; shipping groups nourished by the direct trade between New Orleans, Mobile, and Charleston on one hand, and Liverpool, London, and Havre on the other; planting groups able to buy more cheaply in Europe than in the North; thousands of officeholders and contractors paid in Confederate money; publishers, writers, editors, lecturers, and politicians capitalizing on Confederate nationalism; and manufacturers exploiting the cry, "Buy Confederate wares." Erstwhile doubters would find that the cotton kingdom could really do without the North and West. Meanwhile, many Northerners would lose their sense of shock over the rending of the national fabric. Peace feeling in many Northern communities would grow. Tokens of this trend were already appearing. Wendell Phillips was silenced by a mob when he tried to speak in Cincinnati late in March. Elections early in April resulted in the defeat of two Republican Congressmen in Connecticut and two more in Rhode Island, and in Democratic victories in St. Louis and other important cities; a reaction attributed to confusion and discouragement among Union men.[32]

---

30 George W. Summers of the Virginia Convention indirectly let Montgomery Blair know that he and his associates hoped to call a border convention in Nashville or Frankfort, submit a plan of compromise to both sides, and adjourn until fall. Meanwhile they would begin the spring canvass to defeat secessionism in Virginia. Summers to J. C. Welling, March 19, 1861, Blair Papers, LC.
31 Wash. correspondence dated April 1, 1861, in N. Y. *Tribune*.
32 For election results see N. Y. *Herald*, April 6, 7, 10.

Sam Ward, who not only talked with Southern leaders in Washington but traveled in the South, formed a more astute judgment of the situation than Seward. Later, in the spring of 1862, he heard Seward say that if the South had been allowed to go in peace, within two years it would have come back. "I differ from you," he declared. "I found among the leaders a malignant bitterness and contemptuous hatred of the North which rendered this lesson necessary. Within two years they would have formed entangling free trade and free navigation treaties with Europe, and have become a military power hostile to us." [33]

[V]

What of the investigators sent to Charleston? Gustavus V. Fox posted back with encouraging word that a relief expedition was quite practicable. The vital requirement, in his opinion, was a naval force strong enough to drive off the petty warships in the harbor if they offered resistance. "All else is easy." He told the President that Scott's adverse judgment was worthless, for the question of sending a squadron past the forts at night was naval, not military. He compiled for Lincoln a list of various operations in which ships had passed land batteries with impunity. At Blair's instance he appeared at several Cabinet meetings to advise the President, and in one had the satisfaction of hearing the eminent engineer Colonel G. M. Totten declare his plan feasible.

On Fox's heels returned Stephen A. Hurlbut, who had seen a number of prominent Charlestonians. "From these sources," he wrote, "I have no hesitation in reporting as unquestionable—that separate nationality is a fixed fact—that there is an unanimity of sentiment which is to my mind astonishing —that there is no attachment to the Union." It would be useless, he reported, to appeal to the laboring masses. Power in South Carolina and the Confederacy was swayed by men who, while they desired to avoid war, intended and expected a peaceable separation, after which they believed that the two sections would be friendlier than before. "But it is equally true that there exists a large minority indefatigably active and reckless who desire to precipitate collision, inaugurate war, and unite the Southern Confederacy by that means."

The Confederacy would never turn back, warned Hurlbut; unless the United States resisted, at least five States (he had no information on Louisiana and Texas) were irrevocably gone. As yet, he believed that the garrison at Sumter could be withdrawn without insult, but in another week even that

33 March 27, 1862; Barlow Papers.

would probably be impossible. "I have no doubt that a ship known to contain only provisions for Sumter would be stopped and refused admittance." He closed with a note of warning. This was a time to expect the worst, and to be prepared for it; to yield only from strength, not from weakness; and if not to yield, to be yet more amply prepared.

The bumbling Lamon likewise returned with an oral report that no real Union party existed in South Carolina, that the people of the cotton States were infuriated, and that the masses were being hurried into open rebellion. He had talked with Governor Pickens, former Representative Lawrence Keitt, Postmaster Huger, and the Unionist James Louis Petigru; and Petigru himself had declared that the only alternatives now were peaceable secession or war. Lamon was in close touch with Seward. It was under Seward's influence that he actually told Governor Pickens that he had come to arrange for the withdrawal of the garrison, and that after his return he wrote the governor that he would be back in a few days to assist in the evacuation! He also gave Major Anderson the impression that no relief would be attempted. All this was outrageous, and when Lincoln heard of Lamon's letter to Pickens, he indignantly denied that the man possessed any authority to make such a statement.[34]

The critical hour had now struck. Congress, the people of the country, the merchants and manufacturers suffering from a grave interruption of business, the Virginia convention, all were in anxious suspense. The uncertainty as to Administration policy must be ended. On March 28 a series of events brought matters to a head.

First, the press that morning published dispatches revealing that General Scott a fortnight earlier had ordered the *Brooklyn*, lying off Pensacola, to reinforce Fort Pickens. Actually, as we have seen, it had *not* been reinforced because its commander would not obey Scott's orders, but the press did not know this. Much more importantly, Lyman Trumbull that day introduced an ominous resolution. Expressing the impatience of the unyielding Republicans, it breathed a hint of impeachment. "Resolved," it ran, "That in the opinion of the Senate, the true way to preserve the Union is to enforce the laws of the Union; that resistance to their enforcement, whether under the name of anti-coercion or any other name, is encouragement to disunion; and that it is the duty of the President of the United States to use all the means in his

34 G. V. Fox, Confidential Correspondence, I, 12. Hurlbut's long and well written report is in the R. T. Lincoln Papers; see also Nicolay and Hay, III, 391, 392. For Lamon's report see his *Recollections of Abraham Lincoln, 1847-65*, 70-79; Lamon's communications with Pickens and Anderson are in O. R., I, i, 221, 222, 281, 282. See also Crawford, *Genesis*, 337. Lamon's papers in the Huntington Library throw no light on the subject except to confirm his general ineptness.

power to hold and protect the public property of the United States, and enforce the laws thereof. . . ." This was a shot aimed straight at Seward.[35]

And in the third place, Lincoln's first state dinner, held that evening, was followed by a dramatic scene. Just as the party at the White House broke up, he called his Cabinet into a separate room, shut the door, and with evident emotion told them that Scott that day had advised evacuating Fort Pickens at Pensacola as well as Sumter. Montgomery Blair tells us that a silence of amazement followed. Everyone knew that Seward had prompted Scott. The hush was broken by Blair's impassioned denunciation of the old general—in effect a denunciation of Seward. As it was common knowledge that Pickens could be held indefinitely, Scott's advice was obviously given on political, not military, grounds.[36]

Blair knew that Seward had overshot his mark. Lincoln's emotion proved it. To give up Sumter under military necessity would be bad enough, but to give up Pickens as well would be ignominious surrender. The Cabinet without dissent (Cameron was absent in Harrisburg) condemned Scott's recommendation. Its members knew that Trumbull's resolution was supported by a large majority of Senate Republicans, and a vociferous body of Northern opinion. In a recent caucus of Republican Senators, only three had dared to advocate the abandonment of Sumter, while the others had angrily denounced any such act as national dishonor.[37]

Lincoln unquestionably felt a sense of betrayal when he told his Cabinet of Scott's stand. That night, knowing that he must meet the crisis, he did not sleep. He rose greatly depressed. To a friend he remarked that he was "in the dumps"—for he knew that he must try to relieve Sumter, and relief meant war.

When the Cabinet met again at noon on March 29, a desultory discussion showed that Seward was now on the defensive. He hardly dared lift his voice. Nobody but the feeble Caleb B. Smith concurred in the proposal to give up both forts, and he only if military necessity should dictate it. Bates finally cut through the talk with a suggestion that Lincoln should state his questions, and all should give their written replies on the spot. These replies, some of them headed "In Cabinet," revealed a marked crystallization of opinion.

35 Wash. *National Intelligencer*, N. Y. *Herald*, *Times*, Phila. *Press*, etc.; *Cong. Globe*, 36th Cong., 2d Sess., p. 1519.
36 Nicolay and Hay, III, 394; Welles, *Lincoln and Seward*, 64-69, with Montgomery Blair's letter to Welles, May 17, 1873. Scott had earlier, March 17, sent Secretary Cameron a memorandum which is given in O. R., I, i, 200, 201. The state dinner is graphically described by W. H. Russell, *My Diary North and South*.
37 The Confederate commissioners, writing Toombs on March 22, reported that the Senate caucus was "violently and bitterly opposed" to evacuation, and that "their influence and power has been brought to bear on the Govt. to prevent it." Toombs Letterbook.

Chase had now firmly made up his mind. "I am clearly in favor of maintaining Fort Pickens and just as clearly in favor of provisioning Fort Sumter," he wrote. "If the attempt be resisted by military force Fort Sumter should, in my judgment, be reinforced." Welles was equally emphatic. "I concur," he stated, "in the proposition to send an armed force off Charleston with supplies of provisions and reinforcement for the garrison at Fort Sumter, and of communicating, at the proper time, the intentions of the government to provision the fort, peaceably if unmolested." He thought resistance highly probable, and held that this would justify the government in using all the force at its command. He concluded: "The time has arrived, when it is the duty of the government to assert and maintain its authority." Bates declared that Pickens should be supplied and reinforced at all hazards, and a naval force should be kept on the Southern coast sufficient to blockade any port. As for Sumter, the time had come either to evacuate or relieve it.[38]

Caleb Smith in his written opinion proposed evacuating Sumter as a necessity, but defending Pickens, blockading the Southern ports, and enforcing the collection of revenues. Seward was of course for abandoning Sumter immediately. But even he declared that he would at once, and at every cost, prepare for war at Fort Pickens and in Texas, to be waged, however, only to maintain the possessions and authority of the United States. It is certain that at heart he really wished to give up Pickens. It is also certain that he yielded ground only because he saw that the opposition to his ideas was so overwhelming that he would lose all chance of maintaining his leadership unless he shifted his stand.[39]

Blair, anxious for the immediate relief of Sumter, stood triumphant. A fortnight earlier a majority of the Cabinet had been against that step; now three out of six were for making the attempt, and the other three were for militant action at other points—action that would mean war. Seward remarked to Montgomery C. Meigs that all men of sense saw that war must come.[40] This, however, may have been either adroit dissimulation or a passing mood of discouragement, for he still clung to the hope that, by hook or crook, he could maintain peace.

Opinion among the sterner Republican leaders was hardening, for they perceived that if mere drift prevailed much longer, pacifism in the North would infect many people. Henry J. Raymond's *Times* had declared ten days earlier that it saw "a growing sentiment throughout the North in favor of

38 Bates, *Diary*, 180. It was Sam Ward who reported Lincoln's depression; letter to Barlow, March 31, 1861, Barlow Papers. Text of Bates's paper in Robert Todd Lincoln Papers; essential excerpts in Nicolay and Hay, III, 429–432.
39 Seward's biographer Bancroft believes that his statement that he now wished to hold Pickens was just a pretense; C. W. Elliott in his *Winfield Scott*, 703 ff., takes the same view.
40 Meigs, MS Diary.

letting the Gulf States go." Thurlow Weed's Albany *Evening Journal* agreed with the *Times* that Lincoln should never adopt a coercive policy without the sanction of a special session of Congress. Even that influential New England organ, the Springfield *Republican*, was reluctant to hold the cotton States by force.[41] Impressed by both the rising intransigence of the Lower South and the vigor of the Northern peace party, and feeling that national salvation or ruin must be put to the test at once, most Republican chieftains were becoming insistent that Lincoln take a resolute stand.

Ben Wade shared the views expressed in Lyman Trumbull's militant resolution. In seven States, he told the Senate, the people were dominated by usurpers. "A military despotism tramples their rights under foot," and they should be rescued at once. Zack Chandler of Michigan spoke with characteristic vehemence. If the Administration did not act to maintain the Union, he would quit the disgraced soil of the United States and join the Comanche Indians. Wigfall of Texas retorted that the Comanches had already suffered too much from contact with the whites, but Chandler was in deadly earnest.[42] Owen Lovejoy was too warmly devoted to Lincoln to use harsh language, but he wrote the President in blunt terms that he must relieve the fort, or—an unconstitutional act—recognize the Confederacy. Greeley was declaring that if Sumter had of necessity to be given up, the nation would be heartsick; but that if the Administration surrendered Pickens as well, it would sink lower than Buchanan's, and America would become a second-rate power. Carl Schurz was writing Lincoln to predict general disheartenment and loss of the fall elections if he did not send reinforcements forward. Bryant of the New York *Evening Post*, Forney of the Philadelphia *Press*, and Medill of the Chicago *Tribune* were demanding a firm stand.[43]

From some quarter a call went out to the stanchest Republican governors to assemble in Washington if they could, and Curtin of Pennsylvania and several others prepared to hurry to the capital.

[VI]

Thus it was that the last act of the drama began; an act which reached its climax in Seward's final desperate effort to seize the rod of authority from Lincoln.

Lincoln was now ready to use Gustavus V. Fox's plan for sending pro-

41 N. Y. *Times*, March 31, April 3; Albany *Evening Journal*, March 23; Springfield *Republican*, March 20–26, 1861.
42 *Congressional Globe*, 36th Cong., 2d Sess., p. 1514 (March 27, 1861); Halsey Wigfall, Washington, March 30, to Louise T. Wigfall, Wigfall Family Papers, Univ. of Texas.
43 N. Y. *Tribune*, March 27, and see the editorial "Come to the Point," April 4, 1861; Springfield *Republican*, April 11, 1861. Lovejoy's and Schurz's letters in the Robert T. Lincoln Papers are typical of a number there.

vision ships to Sumter, with warships behind them in readiness for use. He asked Fox to write a memorandum on the requirements of the expedition. In a dozen lines, Fox suggested that the *Pawnee*, *Pocahontas*, and *Harriet Lane* be prepared for sea, that a large steamer and three tugs be hired, that three hundred sailors and two hundred soldiers be ordered ready for service, and that provisions be collected sufficient for a hundred men during one year.[44] Approving this scheme, Lincoln on March 29 directed the War and Navy Departments to get the expedition ready to sail by April 6; and although he later explained to Congress that it was to be withheld or sent forward as circumstances dictated, only some strong evidence that retention would save Virginia and pave the way to reunion could now alter his decision. That decision made war almost inevitable. Lincoln gave his order in the deepest agony of spirit. On March 30 he had a bad sick-headache, and "keeled over," as Mrs. Lincoln put it, for the first time in years.[45]

Seward also was in profound agony of spirit. Would he have to confess that Montgomery Blair and the Congressional iron men had worsted him, that Lincoln had rejected his guidance, and that his dream of replacing the Republican Party by a Union Party, saving the country, and emerging as the greatest statesman of the century, had dissolved? He still had faith in appeasement. Was that faith to be quenched in torrents of blood?

The policy Lincoln had thus far pursued needs little explanation. His inaugural address had been one long plea for patience, forbearance, and the avoidance of rash action. He had called for "patient confidence in the ultimate justice of the people," had asked the nation to "remain patient," and had reminded everyone that "nothing valuable can be lost by taking time." He had given Southerners a solemn pledge: "The government will not assail you, unless you first assail it." He had announced that he would avoid provocative acts to allow the people "that sense of perfect security which is most favorable to calm thought and reflection." After this, he had to strain patience even to the point of seeming infirm. But he had made two facts entirely clear. He would not tolerate secession, "the essence of anarchy," and he would use the power confided to him to hold the property and places belonging to the government, and to collect its revenues. He could not fail to provision Sumter once that was shown possible, or to hold Pickens.

A different judgment must be delivered on Seward's policy. It had one fine aspect in its humanitarian and idealistic quality. Growing up with the republic, he had talked with Jefferson, had sat at the feet of John Quincy Adams, and had labored side by side with Webster, Benton, and Clay. He

44 Nicolay and Hay, III, 433; O. R., I, iv, 227.
45 Message of July 4, 1861; Nicolay and Hay, III, 434. Sam Ward, writing S. L. M. Barlow March 31, quoted Mrs. Lincoln on the President's prostration; Barlow Papers. All witnesses testify that the double strain of the crisis and the office-seekers had worn him to exhaustion.

cherished the lofty vision of a Union of fraternal concord, and had written that image into the single eloquent passage of Lincoln's inaugural. But his course had a base aspect in its devious duplicity. Ever since March 4 he had been partially deceiving Lincoln on one side, and the Southern commissioners (themselves brazen deceivers) on the other. He had been using the aged Scott as a tool; Scott's memoranda on the heavy forces needed to coerce the South, on the impossibility of reinforcing Sumter, and on the desperate plight of Pickens, precisely fitted Seward's policy. He continued to stand in a most equivocal position in relation to the Southern commissioners, and as late as April 7 sent Judge Campbell a message: "Faith as to Sumter fully kept. Wait and see."[46]

Once Lincoln determined to send a relief expedition to Sumter, Seward saw that he must change his strategy. To maintain an ascendancy over the President, he would have to move boldly and fast. On April 1, Greeley's *Tribune* blazed with headlines: "Fort Sumter to be Reinforced. Views in Favor of It. A Peaceful Movement. The Attack Left to the South." The dispatch below, dated from Washington March 31, stated that heavy pressure had been brought to bear for holding Sumter at all hazards; that Northwestern members of Congress (this meant Trumbull, Lovejoy, Elihu Washburne, Zack Chandler, Ben Wade, and others) were specially urgent; that feeling in the Cabinet had changed; and that several naval officers were now confident that steamships could run the Charleston batteries. This was so correct that the correspondent obviously had some inside informant. Next day the Confederate commissioners telegraphed Toombs in Montgomery: "The war wing presses on the President; he vibrates to that side." Secretary of War Walker at once telegraphed Beauregard in Charleston to treat the Sumter garrison as a force with which he might at any moment be in conflict.[47] In Virginia secession feeling had hardened; the cord with the Union was ready to snap at any moment.[48]

46 See Bancroft, *Seward*, II, 123 ff.; Gideon Welles, *Lincoln and Seward*, 59, 60; Elliott, *Scott*, 70 ff. Seward on April 1 talked with Campbell, and wrote out for him an explicit assurance: "I am satisfied that the Government will not undertake to supply Fort Sumter without giving notice to Governor Pickens." This of course alarmed Campbell, who asked if Lincoln had undertaken to supply Sumter—as he had. "No, I think not," replied Seward. "It is a very irksome thing for him to surrender it. His ears are open to everyone, and they fill his head with schemes for supply. I do not think he will adopt any of them. There is no design to reinforce it." So Campbell some years after the event remembered Seward's words. If his report is accurate, Seward was counting on Lincoln's retreat, or was self-deceived, or to cloak his own defeat was deceiving Campbell. See Campbell's MS "Facts of History," Crawford Papers, LC. Blair believed that Seward was capable of any trickery. "Nobody," he wrote, "has ever long associated with him who had not heard him recount by the hour his successful political strategy." Welles, *Lincoln and Seward*, 68.
47 O. R., I, i, 284-286.
48 On April 6 the Richmond correspondent of the N. Y. *Herald* wrote: "The revolution is daily gathering strength." He added that Unionists in the State convention were anxious to adjourn before the tide swept it into disunion.

Sumter, according to Fox, could hold out only till mid-April. Seward had but a few days in which to retrieve the situation. His acts bore the stamp of almost insane desperation.

First, he attempted to substitute for the relief of Sumter, which meant war, a diversionary expedition to Fort Pickens. On the afternoon of March 29 he took to the White House his friend Montgomery C. Meigs, widely known as the West Point engineer who had built the Rock Creek aqueduct and was in charge of the Capitol wings and dome. On the way he explained that he wished to hold Pickens and the Texas ports, letting the conflict begin there if the Confederates chose. Lincoln asked if the Pensacola fort could be held. "Certainly," replied Meigs, "if the navy does its duty." The upshot, after Meigs had prepared and submitted a detailed plan, was that Lincoln told him to take it to Scott at once: "Tell him that I wish this thing done, and not to let it fail unless he can show that I have refused him something he asked for as necessary." And Scott, stiffening his tall frame, quoted Frederick the Great: " 'When the king commands, all things are possible.' " [49]

Thus was authorized a movement that Seward hoped might become a substitute for the Sumter effort, and so gain delay. He and Meigs drove rapidly ahead with their plan. They fitted out vessels laden with troops and stores. They put Lieutenant David D. Porter and Colonel Harvey Brown in naval and military command respectively. Needing a warship powerful enough to beat off possible assailants, they fastened upon the one strong ship readily available, the *Powhatan;* and they prepared for Lincoln's signature orders commandeering that vessel, which in the pressure of business he signed without proper inspection.

Seward saw to it that the closest secrecy surrounded the expedition. To nobody on the ships but the commanders, and to nobody in Washington but the President and Seward's close group, was the destination known until the squadron was within sight of the sand dunes of Pensacola. Secretary Welles of the navy was not consulted, and the *Powhatan* was taken from him without his knowledge just as he and Fox were planning to send it to accompany the Sumter relief expedition!

In the second place, Seward made a direct plunge for the powers of the Presidency. That Lincoln was suffering terribly from his multitudinous anxieties, from the unending harassment of patronage hunters, from the conflict between his hatred of bloodshed and his determination to do his duty, was

49 Meigs, MS Diary, LC; Nicolay and Hay, III, 436, 437; Meigs in the *National Intelligencer,* Sept. 16, 1865, replying to G. V. Fox. Scott in January had renewed earlier pleas to Buchanan to be allowed to reinforce Pickens, but nothing effective was done; *Memoirs,* II, 622–624. Lincoln assented because he thought all along that whatever happened at Sumter, reinforcement of Pickens would help assure the country of Administration staunchness. *Collected Works,* IV, 424.

plain to everyone. His prostration by migraine was immediately followed by a most unusual flare of temper. On March 31 a California delegation called to protest against the influence of Senator Edward D. Baker over appointments, and presented a paper severely reflecting on Baker's motives. For a quarter century Lincoln had counted Baker one of his dearest friends; he had named a son for him; he respected his oaken character. Tearing the paper into shreds and flinging it into the fireplace, he dismissed the group with stinging words.[50] The next day Seward chose to hand the overburdened executive what he hoped would be a decisive document, his paper entitled "Some Thoughts for the President's Consideration." He proposed that he should take the helm; what was more, that he should provoke a war with Spain and France.

This memorandum has usually been treated as an inexplicable piece of folly. Seward remonstrated with Lincoln for his supposed lack of policy, domestic or foreign; declared that the central question must be changed from slavery to union versus disunion; stated that he would let Sumter go because it was generally associated with the slavery question; and asserted that he would simultaneously reinforce all the Gulf forts, and put the scattered navy in readiness to blockade the South, for this would bring the issue of union to the front. This part of the memorandum was erratic enough. But the really startling section was Seward's plan for healing national division by precipitating a great foreign conflict:

I would demand explanations from *Spain* and *France*, categorically, at once.

I would seek explanations from Great Britain and Russia, and send agents into *Canada, Mexico,* and *Central America,* to rouse a vigorous continental *spirit of independence* on this continent against European intervention.

And if satisfactory explanations are not received from Spain and France, Would convene Congress and declare war against them.

But whatever policy we adopt, there must be an energetic prosecution of it.[51]

Seward calmly offered to assume all responsibility, and pursue and direct the new policy incessantly.

The fact was that the Administration possessed a domestic policy, which Lincoln had outlined in his inaugural. It had also a foreign policy, embodied in Seward's own instructions, approved by Lincoln, to our envoys. Moderate but firm, these instructions directed our ministers to assert that the government would never consent to a dissolution of the Union; that the United States was determined and able to maintain its integrity; that it wanted no help, and would brook no interference. Our envoys were told never to discuss

50 This scene is described by the Washington correspondent of the N. Y. *Tribune,* April 1, 1861.
51 Text in Nicolay and Hay, IV, Ch. I.

the merits of the quarrel between North and South as if they admitted of argument. They were to emphasize the commercial advantages of a preservation of the Union. They were also to use language of generous forbearance in speaking of the South; and they were to declare that if war came, it would be by the act not of Washington, but of its armed, open, and irreconcilable enemies.[52]

Seward's plan was foolish indeed, but it was not such incomprehensible folly as has always been supposed. The usual explanation is that he thought merely of the unifying effect of a foreign war. He did, of course, think partly of this. He knew that chauvinism is always latent in every nation, that American editors and politicians always got a ready response to anti-Spanish, anti-French, and anti-British utterances, and that Douglas, Cass, and others had often given reckless vent to xenophobia. In a speech at the New England Society dinner in New York the previous December, Seward himself had been cheered for boasting that if a foreign foe attacked the metropolis, "all the hills of South Carolina would pour forth their populations to the rescue." [53] But Seward's plan was more subtle in nature than a mere effort to merge the sectional conflict in intercontinental conflict.[54]

The key to his scheme is found in reports by the British minister, Lord Lyons, of various conversations with the Secretary; and its essence lay not in the idea that South Carolinians would leap to defend New York, but in the idea that they would strongly object to seeing New York conquer Cuba without their help. It was war with Spain that Seward had primarily in mind, and this because he knew that powerful Southern forces had long desired just such a war. He never thought of embroiling America with Great Britain. That would be far too doubtful a contest. But he did believe that the United States could easily defeat Spain, which had just invaded Santo Domingo, and that in defeating her could swiftly overrun Cuba and Puerto Rico.

The moment Washington opened war on Spain, Seward believed, the cotton States would tremble lest Cuba become free soil—either as an independent republic, or a State of the Union. That, indeed, had long been a bugbear of the Lower South. To avert such a calamity, he hoped that Southerners would join the attack. If the Confederacy did not forego its independence to share in the new conquest, then the United States would at least gain a great island base for operating against the Confederates, and for closing the Gulf. It would also

52 See instructions to C. F. Adams, *Diplomatic Correspondence, 1861*, p. 59.
53 Seward, *Works*, IV, 649.
54 This is the view of Seward's motivation stated, for example, by Nicolay and Hay, by Rhodes, and by Bancroft in his *Seward*, II, 134–137. But these writers had not studied Lyons' dispatches in the British Foreign Office. Seward was far too much of a Talleyrand to be actuated by simple motives.

gain other advantages: The ending of the slave trade to Cuba, a closer relation-ship with Great Britain, which had long tried to destroy that monstrous traffic, and the enhanced respect of other nations. If France entered the war, the United States would also seize the French islands.

Seward disclosed these views in a number of confidential talks with Lord Lyons this spring. In one conversation he suggested that America and Britain should sign a convention for suppressing the Cuban slave trade and guarantee-ing the independence of Santo Domingo. He expatiated at the same time upon the readiness of the United States to defy Spain, and upon the fruits she might win from a Spanish war. "For his own part," he said, "he should have no ob-jection to make an anti-African-Slave Trade demonstration against Spain; if she were rash enough to provoke it. Such a demonstration might have a good effect upon the Southern States. These States had always held that the mainte-nance of slavery in Cuba was essential to their own safety. It might not be a bad lesson to them to see how much they had put at hazard by attempting to withdraw from the protection of the United States." [55]

That Lincoln was thunderstruck by Seward's cool proposal that he should divest himself of his constitutional functions, delegate the Presidential authority to another, bury in oblivion the great freesoil victory, and arbitrarily thrust the nation into war with a European power—perhaps two powers—need not be said. His management of the situation offered a signal proof of his statesman-ship. That same day he wrote a short reply characterized by tact, common sense, and firmness, which annihilated Seward's proposals, but left Seward un-harmed. He knew, of course, that not a word of the matter must reach the public. This reply remained in Lincoln's papers. Perhaps it was shown to Seward; perhaps Lincoln, with characteristic magnanimity, decided that it would be kindlier to transmit its substance orally. Not until a quarter century had elapsed did Lincoln's secretaries give the world its first knowledge of the incident.[56]

The President pointed out that in his inaugural address he had defined his domestic policy—he would "hold, occupy, and possess the property and places belonging to the government" and would collect the duties and imposts—and that he still maintained that policy. Seward had approved it, but Seward now proposed to abandon Sumter. As for external affairs, he and Seward had been preparing circulars and instructions to ministers in perfect harmony "without even a suggestion that we had no foreign policy." Upon Seward's closing proposition that whatever policy was adopted must be energetically prosecuted,

---

55 British Foreign Office Papers (hereafter cited F. O.), 4/1137, Lyons, May 11, 1861, to Lord John Russell.
56 See Roy P. Basler, ed., *Collected Works of Abraham Lincoln*, IV, 316-318.

and either the President must do this himself or devolve the responsibility on some member of his Cabinet, Lincoln commented: "I remark that if this must be done, *I* must do it. When a general line of policy is adopted, I apprehend there is no danger of its being changed without good reason, or continuing to be a subject of unnecessary debate; still, upon points arising in its progress, I wish, and suppose I am entitled to have the advice of all the cabinet."

From that hour the question who should lead the nation was decisively answered.

Seward, still hoping that the Sumter expedition might be held back while the Pickens relief squadron went forward, had a third card to play—a weak and dubious card. On April 2 or 3 he asked Allan B. Magruder, a Virginia Whig practicing law in Washington, to accompany him to the White House, where Lincoln was expecting their call. The President requested Magruder to hurry to Richmond, and bring G. W. Summers, a Union leader in the Virginia Convention, to Washington. It was common knowledge that Virginia now teetered on the edge of secession, and some believed that public sentiment might force the convention to declare for it at any moment. As Virginia acted, so would North Carolina, Tennessee, and perhaps Kentucky. If they all seceded, the Confederacy would become highly formidable. Seward hoped that using an influential intermediary, the Administration might arrange a last-minute bargain, agreeing to let Sumter go if Virginia would stay in the Union. On the way back from the White House, the Secretary still expressed confidence that the troubles would blow over without war, and the Union be saved! Magruder hurried off, and on April 4 he returned, not with Summers, but with another Virginia Unionist, Colonel John B. Baldwin.

Of the ensuing conference between Lincoln and Baldwin we have no first-hand account. We possess only Magruder's confused statement of what Baldwin told him, published fourteen years later. From this narrative it appears that Lincoln was in great agony of spirit, but that at no point did he offer to evacuate Sumter, and that he regarded the die as cast in favor of its relief. His first words were, "Mr. Baldwin, I am afraid you have come too late." And when Baldwin begged him to issue a proclamation waiving the right to hold Sumter and Pickens, and calling a national convention, Lincoln looked at him with manifest disapproval. "Sir," he said, "that is impossible." [57]

57 No episode of the time is murkier than this interview arranged by Seward. Magruder's "A Piece of Secret History," *Atlantic*, vol. 35 (April, 1875), 438–445, is hazy and obviously inaccurate. The subject is again hazily treated in several letters by George Plummer Smith to John Hay, Jan. 7, 9, 20, 1863, in the Robert Todd Lincoln Papers. John Minor Botts in *The Great Rebellion* briefly mentions it. Baldwin made no proposal to the convention. In 1866 he published a pamphlet on the interview (Staunton, Va.) which categorically asserts that Lincoln made no offer, and said repeatedly, "I am afraid you have come too late." Cf. W. L. Hall, "Lincoln's Interview with John B. Baldwin," *South Atlantic Quarterly* (1914), XIII, 260–269.

[VII]

It was indeed too late. Both sections by this date believed that war was at hand. On April 4 Lincoln received a letter written by Major Anderson on the first saying that by sharp economy he could make his rations last about a week longer. Startled, the President bade Secretary Cameron order Anderson to hold out until the 11th or 12th, and tell him that the relief expedition would go forward. On the 6th the *Powhatan* sailed from New York for Fort Pickens, precipitating an acrid quarrel between Seward and Welles. The Secretary of the Navy, justly incensed that Seward should have taken his most effective warship and crippled the Sumter expedition without even notifying him, never ceased to believe that his colleague was a double-dealer—particularly as Seward so bungled Lincoln's order transferring the *Powhatan* to the Sumter force that it went to Pensacola after all! [58] On the 6th, Lincoln started a State Department clerk to Charleston to notify the governor of South Carolina, in very placatory terms, that the government would attempt to supply Fort Sumter with provisions only. He also sent an army lieutenant with word that if South Carolina did not resist the provisioning, the United States would not attempt to throw in unannounced arms or ammunition.

And at last the Sumter expedition got off. The little *Harriet Lane* sailed April 8; the transport *Baltic*, with Captain Gustavus V. Fox, troops, and stores, went off with two tugs on the 9th; and the *Pocahontas* on the 10th. This limping, scattered exit was appropriate to an expedition which had been tardily planned, weakly organized, poorly equipped, and belatedly dispatched. But at any rate, it was on its way.[59]

The country waited tensely. A number of Northern governors who had

58 He signed the order "Seward" instead of "Lincoln," and Captain Mercer could not obey it. Welles tells the story in his *Lincoln and Seward*, 54 ff., with graphic detail and strong feeling. He also penned a sixteen-page narrative, undated, which is partially quoted in *The Collector* (Walter R. Benjamin), LXIX, No. 4 (April, 1956). Orders and letters concerning the Sumter and Pickens expeditions will be found in O. R., I, i, where Meigs's statements are particularly useful.

An interesting adventure story is connected with the Pickens expedition. When Welles on April 6 received word that Captain Adams had not obeyed orders to reinforce Pickens, a piece of news which took him and Lincoln aback, he summoned Lieutenant John L. Worden. It was just before midnight. Welles gave the young man secret dispatches to be carried to Adams. Donning civilian garb, Worden set off at once. On the way to Atlanta he found his car filled with Southern troops, and fearing he might be searched, memorized the dispatch and destroyed it. It was nearly midnight on April 10 when he reached Pensacola. He had to obtain a pass to reach Captain Adams from General Braxton Bragg. Later Bragg said he got the pass only by asserting that he had an oral message of a peaceful nature; Worden denied making any such statement. At noon on the 12th the young man reached Adams. That night Pickens was reinforced by 470 soldiers, marines, and a few days later, a further reinforcement of about 600 men was added. With a garrison of 1100 and provisions for six months, Pickens was safe. See the Worden Papers, Lincoln Memorial University, Harrogate, Tenn.

59 O. R., I, i, 230–236, 245, 291.

met in Washington to reinforce the Senators and Representatives demanding action, and to counteract Seward, waited. The stock market waited. Thurlow Weed and Samuel Blatchford, on what they thought inside information, sold out their shares and waited. A fog of secrecy closed in upon government offices. All the departments, by strict Presidential order, debarred reporters. Seward directed that any clerk who admitted a stranger to his room without express permission should be dismissed. New York correspondents told Sam Ward that the Cabinet was as impenetrable as the Venetian Council of Ten: "The oldest rats and foxes can glean nothing." [60]

By the 12th the little fleet should be off the Charleston bar. Lincoln knew that any moment thereafter the telegraph might bring news of war.

60 S. W. Crawford, *Genesis*, 416, 417; Sam Ward to S. L. M. Barlow, April 6, 10, Barlow Papers.

The North Lurches to Arms

NEWS THAT an expedition had started for Sumter fell upon Charleston like a tensely awaited tocsin. The first word came by irregular channels. Seward, who had kept the expedition to Pickens secret even from Welles and Cameron, the two Secretaries most concerned, divulged the Sumter plans to a newspaper correspondent and friend, James E. Harvey, whom he had just nominated as Minister to Portugal. Harvey, a native of South Carolina, at once telegraphed Charleston: "Positively determined not to withdraw Anderson. Supplies go immediately, supported by naval force if their landing be resisted. A Friend." [1] Then on Monday night, April 8, Lincoln's two messengers reached the city with their official notification. One of them, learning that the Confederacy would allow no provisioning of Sumter, at eleven in the evening started back for Washington. An hour later, amid a heavy rainstorm, seven guns from Citadel Square gave the signal for an immediate muster of all reserves. Hundreds of men sprang to arms; the home guard clattered through the wet streets arousing laggards; and all night the long roll kept citizens awake. By dawn 3,000 men had been called to the colors, and telegrams were summoning 4,000 more from the interior.

It was now necessary for Montgomery to make *its* momentous decision. What Davis would do could hardly be doubted. To be sure, no military reason whatever existed for an attack on Sumter. The victualing of the fort might reasonably be regarded as a mere maintenance of the status quo. But as dominant Northern sentiment made it necessary for Lincoln to try to maintain the post, so dominant Confederate sentiment necessitated its reduction. Any retreat might dangerously encourage Southern Unionism.

---

1 Seward's act was susceptible of being read either as impulsive folly or double-dealing. Why tell a South Carolinian? Montgomery Blair always believed this was another move to wreck the Sumter expedition. The dispatch, he pointed out, was sent the very day that Lincoln ordered the expedition; it was sent by Seward's intimate friend; and when Senators tried to have Harvey removed from his diplomatic post, Seward prevented them. Letter to S. L. M. Barlow, 1865, no day, Barlow Papers. See O. R., I, i, 187, for the telegrams; Nicolay and Hay, IV, 32, for Seward's lame explanation.

When Beauregard telegraphed the message from Lincoln, Secretary of War Walker at once notified President Davis. The Cabinet, hastily summoned the morning of the 9th, realized the gravity of the issue. They deliberated long and earnestly. Walker, the Secretary of War, an Alabamian who was well aware of his section's unreadiness for conflict, was reluctant to move.[2] Toombs was still more averse, for he predicted that an attack would open a bloody civil war, and he could not take the responsibility of advising it. As they talked he grew more decided. "Mr. President," he pleaded, "at this time it is suicide, murder, and will lose us every friend at the North. You will wantonly strike a hornet's nest which extends from mountain to ocean, and legions now quiet will swarm out and sting us to death. It is unnecessary; it puts us in the wrong; it is fatal." [3] But others took a different view. Judah P. Benjamin had committed himself to an assault. So had C. G. Memminger, the head of the Treasury. Senator Jere Clemens of Alabama said later that he heard J. G. Gilchrist, an Alabama leader, address Walker in impassioned terms: "Sir, unless you sprinkle blood in the face of the people of Alabama, they will be back in the old Union in less than ten days!" [4]

The strong current of radical Southern feeling carried Davis along with it. A host of men in the cotton States were impatient for a blow. From Austin to Beaufort, they were angered by the failure of the Confederate commissioners to obtain any Northern concessions. "These men," stormed the Savannah *Republican*, "should require to know within five days whether the forts on our soil, and justly belonging to us, are to be given up, or whether we shall be compelled to take them by force of arms." Already Georgia troops had left for Pensacola in readiness to attack Fort Pickens. South Carolina could hardly be restrained any longer. Davis feared that the peppery little State would act for itself, with resultant confusion, and he knew that most people of the Lower South would regard further delay as cowardice. Representative David Clopton of Alabama had expressed their view weeks before: "The argument is exhausted, further remonstrance is dishonorable, hesitation is dangerous, delay is submission, 'to your tents, O Israel!' and let the God of battles decide the issue." [5]

The Cabinet decided to strike for a multiplicity of reasons: A desire to bring the hesitant borderland, Virginia at its head, into the Confederacy without more ado; a hope that the North would offer more bluster than fight;

2 So L. P. Walker wrote S. W. Crawford, *Genesis*, 421.
3 Stovall, *Toombs*, 226; U. B. Phillips in his life of Toombs accepts this statement.
4 Jeremiah Clemens in a speech at Huntsville, Alabama, March 13, 1864, reported in N. Y. *Tribune*, March 24.
5 Savannah *Republican* quoted in Charleston correspondence, April 2, N. Y. *Tribune*, April 5, 1861; Clopton to C. C. Clay, Jr., Dec. 13, 1860, Clay Papers, Duke Univ.

a conviction that Britain and France must soon recognize the nation on which they depended for cotton. But above all, Southern nationalism impelled the government. The idea that a Federal fort should be maintained in one of the principal ports of the Confederacy seemed intolerable, while the desire to display Southern prowess in arms had grown irrepressible. On the 10th, Secretary Walker notified Beauregard that he should at once demand the evacuation of Sumter, and if it were refused, proceed to compel its surrender.

A bare chance of prolonging peace yet remained. The following afternoon, Beauregard sent three aides to demand Anderson's surrender. The major, in handing them a written refusal, remarked: "Gentlemen, if you do not batter the fort to pieces about us, we shall be starved out in a few days." [6] Actually, with stern belt-tightening, he could have subsisted on his dry stores longer.

This statement Beauregard naturally deemed so important that he telegraphed it to Montgomery. President Davis and Secretary Walker conferred. Walker then replied that the government did not wish to bombard Sumter needlessly. If Anderson would state a time for his evacuation, and would promise meanwhile to fire no gun without provocation, "you are authorized thus to avoid the effusion of blood. If this or its equivalent be refused, reduce the fort as your judgment decides to be most practicable."

Four men—James Chesnut, a former South Carolina Senator and wealthy plantation owner who had said that commerce, culture, and Christianity derived their "chief earthly impulse" from slavery, Roger A. Pryor, the fiery Virginia lawyer, duelist, and secessionist, and two aides—took the proposal to Anderson just after midnight on the night of April 11-12. After a long conference with his officers, he offered to evacuate Sumter by noon of the 15th, engaging meanwhile not to open fire unless he received orders from his government or additional supplies.[7] He thus went as far as he could to meet Walker's demands. Actually, Anderson, a Kentuckian, believed that Sumter ought to be given up for both political and military reasons. He did not wish to be relieved or reinforced, and he disapproved of the relief expedition.[8]

But Chesnut, Pryor, and the two aides, reading his answer on the spot, decided that his proviso, which left him free to use his guns to cooperate with a relief force trying to enter the harbor, was unacceptable. Rejecting the terms, they informed Anderson that their batteries would open in an hour. In this

6 O. R. I, i, 301.
7 O. R. I, i, 14; Crawford *Genesis*, 422–426.
8 See his letter of April 8, 1861, O. R. I, i, 284. Anderson was married to a Georgian, and though by conviction he was a Unionist, he had a natural sympathy with the South. His disapproval was partly founded on his belief that the expedition must fail disastrously. Then, too, he felt very bitter about being left sitting on so exposed a limb. Among his many letters, published and unpublished, that of April 8, 1861, to Lorenzo Thomas, O. R. I, i, is specially interesting

they took upon themselves a tremendous responsibility. They might have telegraphed Walker again, and could have had Davis' reply in a few hours. A wait would have cost nothing. The victualing expedition would in any event have been a failure, for without the *Powhatan* it lacked sufficient strength to provision the fort against Confederate opposition.[9] But the four had color of authority to act, and were impatient. Pryor two days earlier had told a crowd that he knew the way to put Virginia into the Confederacy in less than an hour by Shrewsbury clock: "Strike a blow!"

On the day just ended, April 11, both North and South seemed to know that war was but a few hours away. In Montgomery the War Department was swamped with applications from regiments, battalions, and companies for active service. In Washington the swearing in of volunteer militiamen, begun the previous day, was continued, and sentries were stationed on all roads leading into the city. By nightfall the capital was garrisoned by about 500 regulars and 700 militia. The Confederate commissioners departed, first sending Seward a letter in which they charged that the Administration had grossly deceived them.[10]

Charleston that day had been full of rumors—a false report that the Federal fleet was just off the bar; a true report that the *Harriet Lane* had been sighted; reports that Anderson would and would not surrender. With business suspended, thousands flocked to the waterfront. Occasional armed patrols swirled up and down the streets. At nightfall a bombardment was reported imminent. Some people congregated before the two newspaper offices, while others climbed to the housetops. Trains poured new spectators into the city, who hurried to the Battery. Signal lights burned and flashed in the harbor, where the sea was calm under bright stars. Soon after midnight a speck-like boat moved toward Sumter; men waited while St. Michael's intoned two, then three; four came, and the speck moved away from the fort.

Then, at four-thirty, as the east began to pale, the dull boom of a mortar came from Fort Johnson, and a moment later a shell burst just over Sumter. It was a signal shot. A brief pause ensued. Then other guns announced that war had begun; among them, the columbiad of the iron battery on Morris Island was fired by that exultant secessionist, Edmund Ruffin of Virginia.

9 Admiral Porter later asserted that as the Charleston bar had only thirteen feet of water and the *Powhatan* drew twenty-one, she could not have crossed it, or have gotten within five miles of the Confederate guns. "Statement" in Crawford Papers, LC.

10 One of the gloomiest Washington observers was E. M. Stanton, lately of Buchanan's Cabinet. On April 10 he commented caustically that the Administration was "panic-stricken." On the 11th he reported a general distrust of the sincerity of Lincoln and the Cabinet, and a sharp diminution of loyalty within the city. But Stanton was always morose and censorious, Curtis, *Buchanan*, II, 538–542.

[I]

Looking backward, we can now see that a conflict between North and South had been certain when Lincoln was inaugurated. Nothing the government might legitimately have done could have averted it. The seven States of the cotton kingdom were determined to erect a separate republic; the United States was determined to maintain the Union. At some point and some moment battle was certain. It would have taken place at Pickens if not at Sumter, in Texas if not at Pickens, or on the banks of the Mississippi if not in Texas. The powerful groups which had carried secession through would never turn back; no government in Washington worthy of the name could assent to the disruption of the nation.

The point at which the Civil War could possibly have been averted lay much further back. If the plan of Yancey, Rhett, and others to divide the Democratic Party at Charleston had been defeated, as with more Southern wisdom it could have been, Union men might well have controlled the situation in that party and the South. If the timid, irresolute Buchanan had acted at once after South Carolina's secession to call a national convention, a remedy for Southern disaffection might have been devised. But by March 4 war could no more be prevented than the Niagara River could be halted on the brink.[11]

Nevertheless, the conduct of affairs both North and South between March 4 and April 14 furnished a spectacle as painful as it was confusing.

In Washington, what situation could have been more anomalous than that of a President moving in one direction, and his chief Cabinet officer moving in another, while Congress and subordinate leaders groped in the dark? It is impossible to acquit Lincoln of great clumsiness. His central policy was sound: he would hold all the national forts and places he *could* hold, and let the South make war if it attacked them. But he groped his way, failing to act incisively. He should have ascertained more rapidly the exact length of time Sumter could hold out, the precise temper of Montgomery, and the true possibilities of

---

11 A careful sociologist studying the origins of war in general states that the pattern rarely shows a spiral movement of public opinion that gets out of control and ends in a stampede. Instead, it shows that groups representing some special or political interest lay their plans for war well in advance. These men coolly weigh their chances—their ability to arouse sectional or national sentiment in favor of some "cause," their economic potential, their relative military strength. The decision to make war is in most instances reached months or even years before the first shots. Thus the Samuel Adams-James Otis group long planned the Revolution; the European coalition began in 1792; the Austrian ultimatum to Serbia was planned in March, 1909; Mussolini set the dateline for the Ethiopian war a good two years in advance; Hitler long planned the attack on Poland. The Civil War conforms to this pattern. Yancey and others planned to sunder the Democracy, "fire the Southern heart," and precipitate secession. *Cf.* Theodore Abel, "The Element of Decision in the Pattern of War," *American Sociological Review*, Vol. 6 (December, 1941), 853-9.

victualing Sumter. Instead, showing too little personal initiative, he left it to Seward and Scott to tell him how long Sumter could stand without reinforcement. He left it to Montgomery Blair and Gustavus V. Fox to find out that a possibility of reinforcing it did exist. He left the real intentions of the Southern leaders and people to guesswork.

Moreover, Lincoln as yet gave his associates no sense of authentic and alert leadership. Most Cabinet members thought that he was concerting measures with Seward. Yet on April 1, Seward was convinced that no policy existed and that Lincoln was incapable of formulating one. Montgomery Blair in the opposite faction decided that Lincoln had no backbone, no principle, no policy but a mistaken readiness to yield, and he called in his father to turn the balance. Winfield Scott thought Lincoln weak, or he would never have proposed to abandon Pickens. Judge Campbell believed leadership totally wanting. "The tone of the [inaugural] message will be followed," he wrote, "and its recommendations will be allowed to slide, as are the expressions common to that class of thieves known as politicians." [12] Charles Francis Adams, visiting Washington March 28, got from Seward an alarming picture of the President: "No system, no relative ideas, no conception of his situation—much absorption in the details of office dispensation, but little application to great ideas. The Cabinet without unity, and without confidence in the head or each other." Adams' call on Lincoln confirmed this image: ". . . the course of the President is drifting the country into war, by its want of decision. . . . The man is not equal to the hour." [13]

As for Seward, his conduct was highly exasperating. He could not shake off the delusion that he was to be prime minister and show the rough railsplitter how to act. Worse still, he totally miscalculated the national situation. He thought that if peace were kept at any price, the South would drift back. Instead, every day these seven States, with a domain stretching from Charleston to Corpus Christi and from New Orleans to Atlanta, with important economic groups anxious for all the low-tariff gains they could seize, with politicians hungry for Confederate office, with poets, editors, lawyers, ministers, physicians, and others ardently nursing the idea of Southern independence, with a rising generation proud of Dixie virtues and scornful of Yankee vices, would drift further away. Once fully established, such political separations—like those of Southern Ireland from Britain, Norway from Sweden, Pakistan from

12 Campbell's first notes on Lincoln are severe. The inaugural he called a mere stump speech. "It is wanting in statesmanship—of which he has none—and dignity and decorum. I should call it an incendiary message, one calculated to set the country in a blaze. He is a conceited man—evidently he has been a great man in Springfield, Illinois." To his mother, March 6, 1861, Campbell Papers, Alabama State Archives.
13 Adams, MS Diary, March 28, March 31, 1861.

India—have a way of making themselves permanent. Too much pride, too many selfish interests, too fervent a loyalty, crystallize within the new boundaries.[14] Montgomery Blair was more straightforward than Seward, but he equally miscalculated the situation. He thought that a few hard blows at the the Confederate oligarchs would move the Southern people to overthrow their government and come back into the fold. He totally misconceived the inevitable Southern response to blows.

The Confederacy showed an equal lack of wisdom. Still more unfortunately, its leaders showed little indeed of the tormented shrinking from war that was to be found in Washington.

The firing on Sumter was an act of rash emotionalism. What would it really matter if it remained for months in Northern hands? It offered neither impediment nor threat to the Confederacy. Let it alone, and although at some point the North could certainly have fought to maintain the Union, a period of Northern inaction was not only possible but probable. Given Seward's belief in waiting, and Lincoln's vast patience and forbearance, a protracted pause might have ensued, during which the Confederacy could have exported cotton, imported arms and munitions, stocked defense plants with machinery, and drilled troops. The astute Alexander H. Stephens, counseling delay, showed more statesmanship than Jefferson Davis. Indeed, Davis might well have recalled that in January he had written Governor Pickens to leave Sumter alone: "The little garrison in its present position presses on nothing but a point of pride."

But the callousness evinced in Montgomery's rush into battle is especially discreditable. In Washington the debating, the hesitations, and the agony of the leaders, at least point to an underlying sense of the awful responsibilities of the hour. In the end the government gave Charleston courteous notice that it was sending supplies to a famished garrison, protested its pacific temper, and declared that it would not fire until fired on. In Montgomery, however, the debate was brief and hasty; neither Davis, great gentleman though he was, nor any associate showed real agony of spirit; and the final decision put it in the power of Beauregard, living in "an ecstasy of glory and rhetoric," [15] and two impetuous aides to start the bloodiest war of the century.

The one bright element in the history of these six dark weeks is the complete integrity of purpose exhibited by Lincoln. Adhering to his oath, he never wavered in his determination to hold Pickens. He wavered on Sumter only

14 Even restricted to seven States, the Confederacy would have had an area of 560,000 square miles, a population of 5,000,000, and resources far excelling those of most nations of the globe. Arkansas seemed likely to join in any event, adding some 53,000 square miles and 435,000 people.

15 T. Harry Williams, *Beauregard*, 50.

when the highest military authority told him it could not be held, and reverted to his determination when other authorities reassured him. He did not for a moment share Seward's delusion that appeasement would solve the problem, or Montgomery Blair's delusion that the Southern people were not really behind their leaders; he saw the realities. That he lacked vigor, foresight, and organizing capacity is all too clear. He did not clearly understand the currents of opinion in the South. But his honesty of intention was plain. A humane, kindly man, he felt the greatest distress over the impending bloodshed. A patriot who had devoted his best thought to the Constitution, laws, writings, and traditions handed down by the architects of the republic, he grieved over the demolition of the harmonious structure they had built. He wrestled with himself in the sleepless hours recorded by his secretaries. But his purposes were always elevated, and when war came he could feel that he had but performed his sworn duty.

In your hands, not mine, he had told Southerners, lies the issue of peace or war. The shells that burst over a Federal fort, awaiting a victualing expedition which had orders not to fire unless it was fired upon, gave the answer to that statement.[16]

[II]

The thunderclap of Sumter produced a startling crystallization of Northern sentiment. Apathy had seemed in the air. The timidities of Buchanan, the futilities of the Peace Convention, the later alternations of hope and fear, had given rise to a sense of helplessness. But Sumter disclosed the irrevocable determination of the Lower South to divide the nation; Anderson's hoisting of the white flag on the 13th, followed by his evacuation of the fort next day, was a stain upon Northern honor. Anger swept the land. From every side came news of mass meetings, speeches, resolutions, tenders of business support, the

16 The efforts of some Southern historians (C. W. Ramsdell, "Lincoln and Fort Sumter," *Journal of Southern History*, III, 259 ff.; Clement Eaton, *A History of the Southern Confederacy*, Ch. 21) to suggest that Lincoln needlessly brought on the war by trying to provision Sumter may be left to fulfill their presumed purpose of comforting sensitive Southerners. Ramsdell did not explore the question whether Davis needed to attack the Federal fort! Lincoln was required by the Constitution to protect the properties of the United States; he could have been impeached had he failed to do so; he had explicitly pledged himself in his inaugural to do so; and dominant Northern sentiment demanded that he do so. He warned the South in direct terms that he would do so. The proposition that he should have let Sumter go in the hope of ultimate reunion is really a proposition that he should have broken his oath and defied the public will just to take a fearful risk—the risk of division into two and perhaps several jangling, inferior republics. Confederate leaders meanwhile yielded nothing, and promised nothing but defiance. See James G. Randall's decisive refutation of the Ramsdell thesis in *Lincoln the Liberal Statesman*, and in *Lincoln the President*, II, 342–350.

muster of companies and regiments, the determined action of governors and legislatures.

In this eruption of emotion most Northerners took unthinking pride. It seemed a purifying hurricane which swept away all sordid aims. Idealists had been disheartened by the trickeries, bargains, and compromises of the past ten years; by the Ostend Manifesto, the Nebraska Act, the Lecompton swindle, the filibustering, the corruption, and the absorption in moneymaking. Now, they said, the flame of devotion to the principles of Washington, Hamilton, and Marshall was burning brightly again. Even the most timid took courage, even the most partisan became firm nationalists. As mass meetings cheered the Union and Constitution, as churches followed Trinity by flinging the Stars and Stripes from their steeples, and as armories resounded with the tramp and clash of drilling troops, many felt that they had emerged into an effulgent new era. They forgot that excitement was not patriotism. They forgot that an ounce of planning, forethought, and coordination was worth many pounds of passionate demonstration.

The very basis of organization was endangered by the delusion that victory would be quick and cheap. The New York *Commercial Advertiser* spoke of the rebels as a "small minority." Greeley's *Tribune* exulted in the notion that the first week would see 10,000 men in Washington, the second 20,000, the third 40,000. Raymond's *Times* believed the "local commotion" could be quelled "effectually in thirty days." The Philadelphia *Press* also deemed a month sufficient, while the *Public Ledger* seemed to think that a mere proclamation would suffice.[17] In Chicago the *Tribune* declared that the west alone could end the conflict in two or three months. Soldiers, politicians, and ministers all had the optimism that Lowell's Hosea Biglow later ruefully recalled:

> I hoped, las' Spring, jest arter Sumter's shame
> When every flagstaff flapped its tethered flame,
> An' all the people, startled from their doubt,
> Come musterin' to the flag with sech a shout,—
> I hoped to see things settled 'fore this fall,
> The Rebbles licked, Jeff Davis hanged, an' all . . .

One of the few immediate attempts to analyze the uprising was made by the historian Bancroft. While the politicians had been wavering, he believed,

17 *Commercial Advertiser*, April 15; N. Y. *Tribune*, April 17; *Public Ledger*, April 15, etc. *Harper's Weekly* observed (May 4) that men might as well fight as try to do business. "The war has begun and the trade of the year is as thoroughly ruined as it can be. We shall do no mischief by prosecuting the war vigorously. By prosecuting it vigorously we shall secure peace and fair trade next year." An astounding somersault was performed by the *Independent*, which had shared W. L. Garrison's pacifism. Now it praised war as a vital defense of the Constitution, a restorer of national life, and a divine retribution for slavery; but it too expected a short war. May 4, 11, etc.

the people had pondered the situation and had reached four basic conclusions. One was that the populous Northwest could never let the lower course of its great central waterway pass into foreign hands. The second was that dwellers on the upper Chesapeake, its headwaters flowing from New York and Pennsylvania and its principal railroad clasping the West, felt the same jealous anxiety over their communications. As a third consideration, people feared the expansive temper of the Confederacy. It claimed Maryland, Virginia, Washington and the States below, it claimed Missouri, it claimed the best avenues to California, and it claimed the boundary with Mexico—which it would soon invade. So, wrote Bancroft, "I witnessed the sublimest spectacle I ever knew," an irresistible rush to the defense of law, order, and liberty.[18] It is strange that Bancroft said nothing about the passionate attachment of millions to the idea of Union, inculcated by every national leader from Franklin to Webster, and nothing about the fact that the success of the great American experiment in democratic self-government, as an example to the world, depended on maintenance of the Union.

Major Anderson, his officers and men, reached New York April 18 to meet a wild demonstration. Joseph Holt soon reported a talk with him. "He was satisfied," wrote Holt, "that the course pursued had been the means of fixing the eyes of the nation on Sumter, and of awakening to the last degree its anxieties for its fate; so that . . . its fall proved the instrument of arousing the national enthusiasm and loyalty. . . ."[19] This was just what Lincoln meant when he shortly told Orville H. Browning of Illinois that the plan of supplying Sumter had in a sense succeeded: "They attacked Sumter—it fell, and thus, did more service than it otherwise could."[20]

18 M. A. DeWolfe Howe, *Bancroft*, II, 137–138.
19 Anderson came in on the steamer *Baltic;* Holt to Buchanan, May 24, 1861, Curtis, *Buchanan*, II, 550, 551.
20 Browning's report of Lincoln's words, not written down on the spot but recorded later, cannot be regarded as literally accurate. Lincoln said something like this statement; it was a gloss on his careful explanation of his course in his first message to Congress in July; and he meant that although the North failed to hold Sumter, the sudden and unnecessary Southern seizure of it aroused Northern determination. Browning, *Diary*, July 3, 1861. He meant just this when he wrote Gustavus V. Fox on May 1 in similar terms. A really trustworthy report of Lincoln, closer to the event than Browning's, can be found in the letter of Senator Garrett Davis of Kentucky, April 28, 1861, detailing an interview in the White House "early last week." Lincoln was "frank and calm, but decided and firm." He said that he had decided not to try to reinforce the Sumter garrison, "but merely, and only, to supply its handful of famishing men with food," a purpose he had distinctly communicated to the Southern authorities. "The President further said, that events had now reached a point where it must be decided whether our system of federal government was only a league of sovereign and independent States, from which any State could withdraw at pleasure, or whether the Constitution formed a government with strength and powers sufficient to uphold its own authority, and to enforce the execution of the laws of Congress." Frankfort, Ky., *Commonwealth*, May 3, 1861.

[III]

Clear-sighted Americans saw that the whole issue of the war, and with it the position of the United States in the world, depended on the border States. If all of them went out, the Union could not be saved. If even Kentucky and Missouri went out, along with Virginia and Tennessee, Northern victory would be almost impossible. The next few weeks, deciding this question, would decide almost the whole game. Could they be held?

The next six weeks, April 14–June 1, were a period of touch and go. It was touch and go whether Maryland and Baltimore would not fall under the control of secessionists; whether Washington would not be captured and Lincoln and his Cabinet put to flight; whether the Virginia forces which seized Harpers Ferry and Norfolk would not close in on some other important point; whether Kentucky and Missouri would not slip away; whether so many army officers would not resign as to cripple the nation. In facing these contingencies, the Administration paid in dire anxiety for its failure to take some elementary precautions for war. While the South armed itself, Washington had done nothing. True, Seward and Lincoln wished to avoid provocative steps. But would it have been provocative to get a few more regulars into Washington from the West, or to suggest to Governor Curtin that two strong militia regiments be ready at Harrisburg? Fortunate it was that Curtin *had* taken a few simple steps, and that the recently elected governor of Massachusetts, John A. Andrew, had done more. Fortunate it also was that Virginia did not possess a governor as impetuously earnest as Curtin, and as farsightedly efficient as Andrew.

For although Virginia moved, she moved slowly. Her convention on April 17 passed an ordinance of secession subject to popular ratification in May. Word of this "resumption of sovereignty," telegraphed over the North, ended the fatuous predictions that Arkansas alone of the hesitant States would secede. However, declared Greeley's *Tribune*, the rebels might gain little, for Richmond would have to give close attention to the angry Unionists of western Virginia and the restive slaves. Some support was lent this view by the heavy vote against the secession ordinance, 55 to 88, by Governor Letcher's previous unwillingness to leave the Union, and by the convention's tardiness in placing the State in full cooperation with the Confederacy—no alliance being effected until April 25. Vice-President A. H. Stephens, hurrying to Richmond, complained that Virginians were far behind the times and preferred talk to war.[21]

Nevertheless, the position of Washington was serious. Lincoln's proclamation of April 15 asking for 75,000 militia was indignantly rejected by the

21 *Tribune*, April 19, 1861; Johnston and Browne, *Stephens*, 399 (April 25).

governors of Virginia, North Carolina, Kentucky, Tennessee, and Missouri, and given only a conditional response by Maryland and Delaware.[22] It was of course heartily accepted by all the others, and the War Department fixed the State quotas, asking New York for 17 regiments, Pennsylvania 16, Ohio 13, Illinois 6, Massachusetts 2, and so on—each regiment to consist, as nearly as possible, of 780 officers and men. But the militia system at once showed its characteristic state of decay. In some cities it consisted only of amateurish bandbox forces, which had served to hold balls, grace public parades with showy uniforms, and attend inaugurations; in smaller places it mustered an array of rural bumpkins. One of the familiar gems of Congressional humor was a speech by Tom Corwin ridiculing the Kentucky militia "generals" who restored their men after their drill by a treat of watermelons and whiskey at a country store. Now it was necessary to call out volunteers to create new militia regiments. The want of depots of proper arms, clothing, and other equipment was distressing. And how get them to Washington? Could that city be properly garrisoned in time?

While the Charleston batteries still pounded Sumter, the Confederate Secretary of War boasted in a Montgomery speech: "The flag which now flaunts the breeze here will float over the dome of the old Capitol at Washington before the first of May." [23] Various Southern journals predicted that a column from the Lower South, reinforced in North Carolina and Virginia, would seize the Federal District before the North could defend it. Which nation would first mass its troops on the Potomac? Tidewater Virginia seemed to spring to arms overnight. The day of Sumter a New Orleans businessman sent a Yankee friend a threat: Davis had 60,000 troops ready to march, "and all say here that Baltimore, Philadelphia, and New York will be taken within thirty days. . . ." [24] While W. H. Russell reported to the London *Times* from Montgomery that the Confederacy intended to attack and hold Washington, the British minister, Lord Lyons, wrote that the principal fear of the Lincoln Administration was for the city.[25]

When Virginia seceded, the tiny detachments scattered through Washington were strengthened, more troops and cannon were placed at the Long

22 O. R. Series III, i, 67 ff. deals with this militia call. The governors sent their first contingents to the field, under Lincoln's call, organized as brigades and divisions. They therefore took the generals of militia, like Ben Butler, who had more idea of military organization than anyone else at hand.

23 N. Y. *Evening Post*, April 23, 1861.

24 For the brag by Secretary Walker, a fire-eating protege of Yancey, see N. Y. *Evening Post*, April 23, 1861. This paper erroneously reported that Jefferson Davis had reached Richmond to lead an immediate attack on Washington. For the New Orleans letter dated April 11, see N. Y. *Tribune*, April 24.

25 Frederick W. Seward, *Seward 1846–1861*, p. 545; Russell, *My Diary* (London ed., 1863), I, 259, 260.

Bridge, and batteries were posted on strategic hills. New volunteer companies were set to drilling. Two irrepressible gentlemen dangerous chiefly to their own side, Senator James H. Lane of Kansas and Cassius M. Clay of Kentucky, organized companies of their own, Lane bivouacking his men in the East Room of the White House. Veterans of 1812 shakily stumped into line. A home guard of elderly men, fitly called the Silver Grays, was whipped together. All told, the national capital in the first anxious days after Sumter had for its protection one dilapidated fort twelve miles down the Potomac, six companies of regulars, about two hundred marines at the navy yard, two companies of dismounted cavalry, and the flatfooted, flatchested, untrustworthy militia or uniformed volunteers of the District, numbering fifteen companies on April 13 and about twice as many a week later.[26]

Winfield Scott's plan, if the city were attacked by overwhelming force, was to make a citadel of the Treasury Building, with the President and Cabinet in the basement, and all the troops concentrated about Lafayette Square.

The general hoped for the best; when the news of Sumter came, he expected the early arrival of a war steamer to cruise the Potomac, and some artillery from the regular forces in the Northwest. Lincoln imperturbably continued his accustomed round of conferences and other duties, only now and then revealing his deep anxiety—as in an impulsive walk to the arsenal, whose doors stood open unguarded. The general alarm nevertheless continued great. When on April 18 the first little force arrived from the North, five tough-looking companies of Pennsylvania militia whom Curtin, with the aid of a regular officer, Fitz-John Porter, had hurried off, only slight relief was felt. Unfortunately, these men had only thirty-four muskets and no ammunition! But they could be equipped, and they were marched to the Capitol. Word also came that a stronger body of Pennsylvania volunteers was on the Susquehanna opposite Havre de Grace.[27]

[IV]

This was improvisation, but one governor, Andrew of Massachusetts, had really planned. Early in January he had begun to equip all the volunteer com-

26 Scott's daily reports to Lincoln, R. T. Lincoln Papers; Margaret Leech, *Reveille*, Ch. 4. John G. Nicolay, sitting in the White House, thought that the District Militia were politically unreliable, and might turn against the government, so that they would all find themselves looking down the muzzles of their own guns. "We were not only surrounded by the enemy, but in the midst of traitors." To his wife, April 26, Nicolay Papers, LC. Winfield Scott had told a Cabinet meeting that he thought Fort Washington could be taken by a bottle of whiskey.
27 Leech, *Reveille*, 65; Nicolay and Hay, IV, 70, 71; W. B. Wilson, *Acts and Actors in the Civil War*, 24 ff.

panies and set them drilling nightly. Before darkness fell on the day of Lincoln's call for troops, colonels of regiments at New Bedford, Quincy, Lowell, and Lynn had orders to muster on Boston Common. April 16th found them parading under the elms, drums beating, flags flying. Next day the governor commissioned Ben Butler as commander of the brigade, and before night all four regiments had departed for the front.[28] The Sixth Massachusetts, 800 strong, went first by rail. Breakfasting next morning at New York hotels, they marched down Broadway, beflagged, crowded, and throbbing, to the Hudson ferry. The band played but a single bar of "Yankee Doodle" before it was drowned out. The roar of cheers, the thrashing handerchiefs and banners, the hot emotion of the densely jammed spectators, made the scene the most impressive that men could remember. But at that moment secessionists in Baltimore were busy arousing mob passion.

Baltimore, the third city of the nation, had half the population of Maryland. More than a third of her great trade was with the South and Southwest. For weeks the Baltimore *Sun* and *Examiner* had been stirring the bitter waters of anti-Northern feeling. "If we are to grow, thrive, and prosper as a manufacturing city," the *Sun* had declared, "our sources of prosperity must be in the South." Ross Winans, who had introduced the eight-wheeled railroad-car system and established in Baltimore the largest railroad machine shops in the country, a man sometimes rated hardly second in wealth to William B. Astor, was helping to finance the secessionist cause. Such merchants as Johns Hopkins and William T. Walters did a huge Southern business. Slave property in the State was valued at sixty to seventy million dollars. The tidewater arm had immemorial ties of blood and sentiment with Virginia. Louis M. McLane, just back from diplomatic service in Mexico, had told a secessionist meeting that he favored confronting any Northern force on the Susquehanna with arms. Most officers of the city government, the mayor excepted, were on the secessionist side, and so were a majority of the legislature, which the loyal but wabbling Governor Thomas H. Hicks refused to call into session. The city was a powder tub ready for a match.[29]

28 Lossing, *Civil War*, I, 401, 402; Schouler, *Massachusetts in the Civil War*, I, 49 ff.
29 Senator Anthony Kennedy told the chamber in 1863 that "in 1860 the trade of the city of Baltimore, according to the report of her chartered Board of Trade, amounted to $168,000,000; $26,000,000 over her great railroad lines to the West, and $100,000,000 directly to the South and Southwest." *Cong. Globe*, 37th Cong., 3d Sess., pp. 1374, 1375. This was an exaggeration. According to the Baltimore correspondent of the N. Y. *Tribune*, March 12, 1861, Pennsylvania, Ohio, and Indiana bought almost two-thirds of the general merchandise sold in Baltimore, the Upper South the other third, and the Lower South but a small amount. But Baltimore, struggling amain with New York and Philadelphia, greatly valued her Southern connections. The influential Severn Teackle Wallis, who had studied law with William Wirt, leaned to the secessionist side and wrote many editorials for the *Examiner*. By the census of 1860 New York and Brooklyn had 1,072,300 people, Philadelphia had 562,-500, and Baltimore 212,400.

As the cars of the Sixth Massachusetts rumbled across upper Maryland, Southern sympathizers poured into Monument Square; not a ragged, disorderly rabble, but a well-dressed crowd numbering merchants and lawyers of note. Shortly before noon on the 19th the troop train drew into the President Street station. The men had to be moved across town to the Camden Street station— and the mob was gathering fast. By quick, determined action, the troops might have kept control of the situation, but a series of disastrous errors was made.

One error was that of the mayor, who had sent police to the Camden Street station, a mile from the true danger point. Another was that of the colonel, who should have unloaded his men, formed them in solid column with bayonets fixed, and marched them across town at the double-quick, but who instead kept them in the cars, to be drawn slowly by horses along tracks in Pratt Street. When the mob obstructed the cars, attacked them with paving stones, and tore up the tracks, most of the regiment had to climb down amid a rain of missiles. Somebody fired, and before the melee ended, four infantrymen and a larger number of the mob had been killed and many injured. The city police finally did most to restore order. Although the Sixth reached Washington at five in the afternoon, seven companies of unarmed Pennsylvania volunteers remained at the President Street station until they were sent back to the Susquehanna.[30]

Anti-Northern feeling rose higher than ever in Baltimore. "The excitement and rage of everyone, of all classes, of all shades of opinion," reported the British consul, "was intense. Strong Union men harangued the crowd, declaring they were no longer such, and demanding immediate action."

That day brought news that the little Union garrison at Harpers Ferry had destroyed arms, armory, and arsenal, and retreated across the Potomac to Hagerstown, Maryland. At Norfolk the commandant of the Navy Yard was about to scuttle all but one of the warships there afloat. Baltimore, raging like a hornet's nest, would ambuscade any fresh Federal troops who attempted a passage. Thus hostile forces ringed Washington. When a body of Ohio militia reached Pittsburgh on April 19 on their way to the capital they were suddenly halted by orders from Governor Dennison, who had heard that Cincinnati was about to be attacked. The burning question was whether Maryland and Virginia secessionists, while the entire border rose, would cut off all access to Washington.

During four days, April 19-22, bellicose Marylanders swept both city and State government before them like straw upon a flood. Cowed by the violent

30 For the riot, see G. W. Brown, *Baltimore and the Nineteenth of April, 1861;* Marshal George Kane's report to the police board, *Cong. Globe,* 37th Cong., 1st Sess., 200, 201; Mayor Brown's report, O. R. I, ii, 15-20; N. Y. *Tribune,* May 9, 1861.

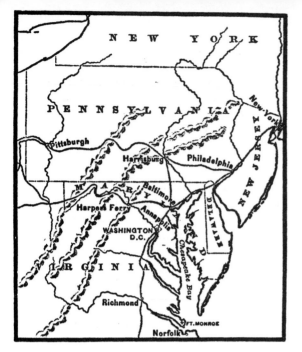

ROUTES OF APPROACH
TO WASHINGTON

Southern demonstrations of the 18th and 19th, Governor Hicks gave way. He had thus far stood by the Union, refusing a special session of the legislature, and pledging Lincoln four regiments if they were used only in Maryland and the District of Columbia. But now he told a seething crowd in Monument Square that he would suffer his right arm to be torn from his body before he would raise it to strike a sister State; he telegraphed Lincoln, "Send no more troops here"; and he announced that his main object was to save the State from civil war. Mayor George W. Brown made a concurring declaration that no Maryland boys would fight the sons of other States. The two wrote President John W. Garrett of the Baltimore & Ohio advising him to take all Northern soldiers back into Pennsylvania. Worse still, Hicks, Brown, and Police Marshal George P. Kane agreed in midnight conclave that the best way to avoid a renewal of the fighting between rioters and Union troops would be to destroy the railroad bridges connecting Baltimore with the North. Kane, thinking he had an authorization to do this, sent out gangs which demolished the short Canton bridge just outside the city, the long bridges over Gunpowder and Bush Creeks (arms of the Chesapeake), and two wooden bridges at Cockeysville fifteen miles north of Baltimore.

No step could have done more to isolate Washington. The seat of government was cut off from the loyal States by rail through Baltimore from the night of April 19. Meanwhile, the mob remained dominant in Baltimore throughout April 20-21. It shut the President Street station, forced Unionists to haul down their flags, and patrolled the streets trying to seize Union soldiers.

Kane, espousing the secessionist side, was ready to go to any length. He telegraphed a Maryland Congressman to send out messengers to arouse Virginia and Maryland riflemen and hurry them to Baltimore: "Fresh hordes will be down upon us tomorrow. We will fight them and whip them, or die." On the 21st the wires were cut, and Washington thereafter could send telegrams north only by the precarious Harpers Ferry route.[31]

The reign of terror continued until April 24th. Hundreds of Unionists were driven from Baltimore, and thousands more fled. When Ben Butler arrived in Philadelphia on the 20th with 800 Massachusetts militia, he found the direct route to Washington closed. With instant resourcefulness he took his troops by rail to Chesapeake Bay, put them on a boat, and steamed down to Annapolis. Governor Hicks having the effrontery to protest against this landing on sacred Maryland soil, Butler delivered a spirited rebuke. If necessary, he said, he was ready to treat Maryland as enemy territory; and taking possession of the frigate *Constitution*, so dear to Yankee hearts, he announced that this partially consoled Massachusetts for the loss of her sons.

Meanwhile, Governor Hicks surrendered to the demand for a special session of the secessionist-controlled legislature; [32] and hard on Ben Butler's heels the New York Seventh, a crack parade regiment, also had to take the bay route to Annapolis. One of its officers was the gifted Major Theodore Winthrop, who wrote a graphic account of its southward journey. Some 1700 Pennsylvania militia, partly unarmed, had revolted against their detention on the Maryland boundary, and were marching down the empty railroad line toward Cockeysville north of Baltimore. In Washington, Lincoln himself uttered the anguished cry: "Why don't they come? Why don't they come?" Speaking to the Massachusetts soldiers, he said that he didn't believe there was any North; the Seventh Regiment was a myth—"You are the only realities."

In his alarm and indignation, the President immediately after the Baltimore riot summoned Mayor Brown and Governor Hicks. On Sunday morning, April 21st, Brown and three prominent Baltimoreans (Hicks was ill) were ushered into the President's office, where General Scott and the Cabinet joined them. Though Lincoln was anxious to avoid fresh collisions, he made clear the absolute necessity of safe transit for Federal troops. No forces would be used against Maryland, he said, and none for aggression upon the South. But Wash-

31 Kane's story as given in the *Congressional Globe, ut sup.*, is scathingly interpreted there by Representative Francis Thomas, who had no doubt of his disloyalty. He was arrested and long held in confinement. Governor Hicks and Mayor Brown both denied later that they had really intended the destruction of the bridges, and it seems they had given only a limited and partial assent. G. L. P. Radcliffe, *Governor T. H. Hicks and the Civil War,* 54 ff.

32 For Hicks' explanation see the speech he later made as Maryland Senator, *Cong. Globe,* 37th Cong., 3d Sess., 1376, 1377; an enlightening statement on the whole situation.

ington *must* be protected, and since troops could no longer be safely brought up the Potomac, they *must* cross Maryland. General Scott underlined this warning. It was not a question of using Baltimore streets, he said. Regiments might by-pass the city by taking the water route to Annapolis or wagon roads to the Relay House just southwest of Baltimore.[33]

Mayor Brown assured Lincoln that the city authorities would do their utmost to prevent mob interference with the roundabout routes. Lincoln then directed that the Pennsylvania militia at Cockeysville either march around Baltimore to the Relay House, or go back to York and Harrisburg.

It was an extraordinary spectacle, this of the President of the United States and the general of its armies parleying with a mayor and suspending the right of national troops to march through his city to save Washington. When later it became known, it aroused intense indignation in the North.[34] But it reflected the disorganization of the hour: the lack of efficient action to forward troops from New York and Philadelphia; the poor information facilities of the government, which remained ignorant of the fervid Northern rising; above all, the want of antecedent military preparation in Washington. Under the circumstances, Lincoln acted sagaciously. He did not have sufficient military power to risk enforcing a right of transit, and provocative orders might have stirred tens of thousands of wavering Marylanders to join Virginia in attacking the capital.

[V]

Then by April 25 the skies cleared. In Maryland the Unionists rallied. It is true that in Baltimore the secessionists and neutralists remained dominant; the city council appropriated half a million for defending the place, Mayor Brown asked citizens to lend their arms and ammunition, and Southern sympathizers organized companies to repel the Northern "myrmidons."[35] But many eastern Marylanders realized that if Baltimore continued obstructive it would be stormed and perhaps laid in ashes, while western Marylanders were mainly loyal. News arrived that troops were concentrating in Pittsburgh,

---

33 Actually the Overland line from the Northern Central R. R. to the Relay House, the point eight miles southwest of Baltimore where one branch of the Baltimore & Ohio led to Washington, was more difficult than Scott believed. No good common road of less than thirty miles connected the two railroads. President J. Edgar Thomson of the Pennsylvania Central wrote from Philadelphia April 23 that more vigor should be shown in organizing troop movements, that Baltimore should be put under martial law, and that Maryland should be made to feel the weight of national power. O. R., I, ii, 587, 596–597.
34 See N. Y. *Tribune* editorial, May 3, 1861.
35 Radcliffe, *Hicks and the Civil War*, 67.

York, Philadelphia, and other cities.[36] Federal units took possession of the railroad from Philadelphia to Perryville on Chesapeake Bay, strengthened the track, brought down new locomotives, arranged for three trains a day, and got three steamboats plying to Annapolis.

"If the route from Annapolis to Washington City is open," J. Edgar Thomson wrote Secretary Cameron April 23, "we have transportation facilities on the Chesapeake equal to the movement of fifteen thousand troops a day to your city, together with any amount of provisions, etc." And the Annapolis–Washington railway *was* open. Ben Butler had found in an Annapolis railroad shed a rusty half-dismantled locomotive, and had asked his men if anybody could repair it. A private stepped forward to reply: "That engine was made in our shop; I guess I can fit her up and run her." Cameron had Vice-President Thomas A. Scott of the Pennsylvania Central take a body of picked railroadmen, including young Andrew Carnegie, to Annapolis to help put the line in order. Annapolis was suddenly full of troops, waiting for the first train.[37]

When Thursday the 25th dawned in Washington the spirits of loyal men had sunk to a low ebb. The city still seemed hemmed in by rebel elements, and Southern sympathizers were exultantly circulating rumors of a Virginia drive. General Scott was getting ready to issue General Orders No. 4, which went out next day: "From the known assemblage near this city of numerous hostile bodies of troops it is evident that an attack upon it may be expected at any moment." The North was trembling for the capital. In Albany, Governor Morgan heard the "most painful reports" of its peril. In Philadelphia all city regiments were detained by a woeful deficiency of guns and ammunition.[38]

Then, at noon, a mighty shout came from the Sixth Massachusetts encamped on Capitol Hill. They had seen a troop train drawing into the station. Citizens began running pell-mell to the scene. As the train stopped a wild burst of cheering was heard even at the Treasury. Under a bright sun, the trim ranks of the Seventh were soon marching up Pennsylvania Avenue, whose sidewalks filled magically. The men kept soldierly step under their unstained banners, and when their band struck up onlookers danced with delight. On they came, past Willard's, past the Treasury, through the White House grounds, and under the very eaves of the mansion. Lincoln emerged to wave

36 When Ben Butler in Philadelphia heard of the attack on the Sixth Massachusetts, he not only hurried Col. Munroe's regiment to Annapolis, but telegraphed to Governor Andrew for artillery; and Andrew leaped to throw new bodies of troops aboard trains. They reached New York the night of Sunday the 21st, clattered aboard two waiting transports on Monday, and sailed with all possible speed to join Munroe at Annapolis.

37 O. R. I, ii, 596; *Butler's Book*, 202.

38 O. R. I, ii, 600–602.

them a greeting, the happiest-looking man in town. As an Illinois man remarked, "He smiled all over." [39] Then the footsore, sunburnt privates, turning back to the marble-paved courtyard of Willard's, half-stripped to splash
in the fountain. That evening they too went into bivouac on Capitol Hill,
enlivening the soft spring night by selections from their band.

Troops now poured steadily into Washington. Colonel Elmer Ellsworth's
Zouaves, recruited largely from the New York Fire Department, left for the
capital. The Seventy-first New York arrived and found quarters in the temporary hall erected for the inauguration ball. The first Rhode Island came
in, commanded by a West Pointer recently with the Illinois Central, the burly,
bewhiskered Ambrose E. Burnside, and accompanied by the slender "boy governor," William Sprague of the rich cotton-textile family. The Twelfth and
Sixty-ninth New York, the First and Second Connecticut, the New Jersey
Brigade, and other units were soon being disposed about town. A scurrying,
squealing covey of transports, ferries, and small boats kept Annapolis harbor
busy. Even Westerners arrived; Secretary Chase on the 24th had besought
the Ohio authorities to add 50 per cent to their contingents, and hurry them
forward by the Pennsylvania Central—"Delays and mistakes are dangerous."

The soldiers represented American life in all its colorful contrasts. Some
of the First Zouaves were dangerous criminals, some of the Seventh the fashionable elite of Gramercy Square, many of the Yankee boys mill-hands,
many of the Westerners fresh from the plow. Ben Butler made merry over one
fearful hardship suffered by the Seventh New York. They left behind at
Annapolis a thousand velvet-carpet campstools which never caught up!

For the moment the fast-arriving soldiers found their experience entrancing.
It was nearly all gaiety, movement, color, and adventure.[40]

Three units were soon quartered in the Capitol, the Sixth Massachusetts in
the Senate, the Eighth Massachusetts under the dome, the Seventh New
York in the House. Odors of lilac and horse-chestnut blooms drifted in at the
windows. At daybreak reveille blared through the dim interior. Chaffing,
shouting, and singing, the soldiers marched for their meals to the hotels, where
they scuffled with squads of waiters for food. The regiments competed hotly
with each other in drills. The Rhode Islanders attracted particular attention
by their natty uniforms, shining arms, and long baggage trains, with vivandières
(a short-lived feature) adding a romantic touch. Dress parades, band concerts,
and "universal promenading" made Washington livelier than ever before.
With trees leafing out, shoals of ambitious men arriving to seek military com-

39 N. Y. Tribune, April 26, 1861, Wash. correspondence.
40 See Theodore Winthrop's delightful essay, "Washington as a Camp," Atlantic, vol. 8
(July, 1861), 105–118.

missions, and shops busy, the city was too prosperous to listen to secessionist sympathizers. As the May sunshine grew hotter and the streets livelier with uniforms, most units moved under canvas. They specially liked the large Sibley tent; a wrinkle, wrote Theodore Winthrop, taken from savage life, for it was the Sioux tepee made more compact, handsome, and, if the flaps were kept open, healthy.

The rapid increase of Federal strength completely changed the situation in Maryland. Some men had been for rough action; Governor Morgan of New York had telegraphed Cameron to open a way through Baltimore "cost what it may," and the First Zouaves had boasted that they could go through the city "like a dose of salts." [41] But a refluent wave of Union sentiment soon surged across the State. General Scott late in April created the Department of Annapolis, a belt twenty miles wide on each side of the Annapolis–Washington railway, with the iron-fisted Ben Butler in command, and placed all eastern Maryland, outside this belt, in the Department of Pennsylvania under Major General Robert Patterson. Baltimore began a grand-jury investigation of the riot. [42] When Hicks met the legislature in Frederick its members were overawed by the massing of Union forces and the strength of loyal sentiment in the central and western counties.

Baltimore was soon in an especially chastened mood, for the mob outbreak and flight of citizens caused a collapse of rents, realty prices, tax receipts, and trade. When businessmen asked the government to restore railway service, telegraphs, and mails, Secretary Cameron refused until Federal forces controlled the city and his own agents the railroad offices. Before the end of April, Fort McHenry had been heavily reinforced, Fort Morris garrisoned, and gangs of men put to work restoring the railway bridges. On May 5, Ben Butler's troops occupied the Relay House. Next day the Northern Central Railroad was in full running order, and a Union recruiting office was opened on Baltimore Street. Finally, on the night of May 12, Butler used a thousand men and a battery to occupy Federal Hill commanding the city, and seize some arms about to be shipped south. The movement was dramatically executed in thick darkness, amid a violent thunderstorm, the lightning gleaming on the fixed bayonets. [43]

Increasing numbers of troops poured into Washington. Throughout large parts of the North men had volunteered in throngs, anxious to serve before

41 Morgan's letter, April 25, 1861, is in O. R. I, ii, 600.
42 O. R. I, ii, 607, 611.
43 N. Y. *Tribune*, May 16, 1861, on Baltimore business troubles; *Butler's Book*, 227–230. The British consul, reporting to his government April 27 that many of the laboring classes were in a state of starvation, feared rioting and revolt, and sent his family to Philadelphia for safety; FO 5/778.

the short war ended. In Indiana, Governor Morton announced the day of Lincoln's call that he could forward 30,000 men instead of the six regiments requested. When a Massachusetts volunteer was asked in New York how many were coming, he replied: "How *many?* We're *all* a-coming." New York authorized the enlistment of 30,000 two-year men. Money, too, was poured out generously. Congress, in its anxiety to avoid provocative action, had made no special appropriation available before it adjourned. All loyal States, all large cities, and many towns, however, were ready to appropriate funds. What occurred in the Empire State was typical. While the common council of New York City on April 22 voted a million to equip regiments and half a million for the families of soldiers, a tumultuous city mass meeting appointed a Union Defense Committee which immediately raised large sums. The Brooklyn common council set aside $100,000 for the Thirteenth Regiment and its dependents. Rochester made available $130,500; Buffalo $50,000; Troy $10,000. All this was in addition to a State appropriation of three millions signed by Governor Morgan a few days after Sumter.[44]

Men (untrained) and money were momentarily plentiful. But where were the arms, uniforms, tents, blankets, and camp kitchens? Where was the barest organization for feeding troops, drilling them, and nursing them when ill? What, above all, was to be the method of coordinating national, state, and local efforts, a vast jumble?

Coordination moved like a rusty oxcart. The fate of Major-General John E. Wool, commander of the Department of the East, offers an example. He arrived in New York on April 22, and from quarters in the St. Nicholas Hotel threw himself into the work of providing arms and forwarding troops.[45] He ordered the Federal quartermaster and commissary offices in New York to give transportation and thirty days' rations to each soldier bound for Washington; he conferred with the Union Defense Committee on plans for relieving the capital; he chartered transports and armed steamers for troops; he sent ammunition, gun carriages, and provisions to Fortress Monroe; he directed Governor Richard Yates in Illinois to send a force to seize possession of the arsenal in St. Louis (for his jurisdiction extended to the Mississippi); he telegraphed Frank P. Blair to aid the movement; he ordered heavy cannon and other war materials to Cairo; and when Ellsworth's Zouaves were held up by stupid State orders he sent them forward. He had efficient co-workers in

44 O. R. I, iii, *passim*, for a wealth of material; N. Y. *Tribune*, April 23, 1861, for interviews with volunteers; J. A. Stevens, ed., *Minutes, Correspondence, and Reports of the Union Defense Committee* (1885). Connecticut showed an equally militant temper. While the legislature voted two millions and guaranteed every soldier ten dollars a month in addition to Federal pay, Hartford raised $64,000, New Haven $30,000, and other places similar sums.
45 Wool Papers, N. Y. State Library.

Chester A. Arthur, the State's assistant quartermaster-general, who from a downtown office arranged for feeding, clothing, and to some extent arming the soldiers, and John A. Dix, chairman of the Union Defense Committee. The Committee on April 31 adopted resolutions praising Wool's energy and ability, and the value of his long experience and military skill.

But at that very moment Wool was ordered back to Troy; and when he asked why, Cameron replied that his emergency activities, while Washington was cut off and could not be consulted, had seriously embarrassed the War Department! [46]

Shortages, confusion, and delays reigned paramount. Of small arms an apparently adequate supply existed on paper in public repositories, but for three reasons troops often went without them. Many were too poor to use, facilities existing for their distribution were weak, and Scott wished most of the best pieces kept for long-term troops, not issued to three months' militia to be abused and lost. The government had no cannon foundry. Uniforms, blankets, tents, and medical equipment were all in very short supply. Food was abundant, but its preparation and distribution were so poor that units detained in populous cities—for example, Pennsylvania troops in Harrisburg and Philadephia—were literally half-starved. The press soon reported that some companies in the capital itself had but two meals a day, and those of bread, fat salt pork, and water. Governors and adjutant-generals found it easy to write orders and sign contracts, but the arms and goods were slow to arrive.

Even barracks and proper camps were wanting. Early in May the diarist George Templeton Strong found several hundred men stuffed into a building at Broadway and Fourth Street, the air mephitic and ammoniacal—"I never knew before what rankness of stench could be emitted by unwashed humanity." [47] The installation of Washington troops in public buildings was eloquent of the slapdash improvisation of the time. Amid the general indiscipline, it was no wonder that a private whose regiment was visited at the Capitol by Lincoln remarked saucily to the President: "Now, sir, stand by us, for we mean to stand by you."

All over the country, the ninety-day regiments departed with the most rudimentary equipment. New York had better resources than some other States. Yet a large part of the Eighth New York went southward in citizens' dress and without arms. When the Thirteenth New York, the pride of Brooklyn, marched to its transport, about 200 of its 650 men were left be-

46 Dix, *Dix*, II, 1–16; George F. Howe, *Arthur*, 24; Stevens, *Union Defense Committee*, *passim*; O. R. I, ii, 160.
47 Strong, *Diary*, III, 148. For difficulties of Mobilization see K. P. Williams, *Lincoln Finds a General*, II, 796–800.

hind because they had no muskets. The others had received them, with knapsacks and blankets, at the last hour. As for the Sixty-ninth New York, it embarked only after scenes of indescribable confusion. Men accepted and men still clamoring for acceptance had crowded early that morning into Prince Street. Here, in front of Colonel Corcoran's house, a large truck was stationed. "The rush at this point," wrote a reporter, "was perfectly tremendous, so eager were the men to obtain their equipment. The captain of each company was stationed on the vehicle, and here the acceptance or rejection of the recruits occurred." As each man was enrolled a blanket was thrown over him. He was passed to another man, who snatched off his hat and put a regimental cap on his head. Still another man thrust a musket into his hands, while others gave him a tin plate, knife, fork, and tin cup.[48]

The War Department was a scene of hurry, endless intensive work, uncertainty, and chaos. Cameron hired all the clerks and copyists his rooms could hold. He, the commissary-general, and the quartermaster-general kept their forces busy without reference to clocks. Some men stayed in the building twenty-four hours a day, gobbled food brought from a restaurant, and caught a few hours' sleep on a settee. Yet from troops everywhere still came reports of hunger, discomfort, and general mismanagement.

Most serious of all was a conflict of views in high circles. General Scott thought that troops should be brought to Washington even if ill equipped; Secretary Cameron maintained that no large number should come until they had a full outfit for camp and field. Lincoln, deferential to Scott's military experience, inclined to take his side.[49]

[VI]

It is in the light of these difficulties that we must weigh the question whether Lincoln erred in not calling at once for more than 75,000 ninety-day men. Douglas said that *he* would have called for 200,000. Greeley clamored for a large force. "Assuming that the crushing out of the rebellion is a question of time and cost only," the *Tribune* commented, "we hold it cheaper to employ 400,000 men in six months than 200,000 to close it up in a year." Lincoln might have been wiser to call for 100,000 or 150,000 men, and assuredly should have made the term longer. But if a larger number had been demanded, the confusion, the hardships of ill-fed, ill-clothed, ill-housed troops, and the public irritation over duplication, waste, and shortages, would have been multiplied. Moreover, the problem of costs was serious. As matters

48 N. Y. *Tribune*, May 9, 1861; G. T. Strong, *Diary*, III, 132; N. Y. *Tribune*, April 24.
49 Meneely, *War Department in 1861*, 159 ff.

stood, Chase was despondent and harassed, uncertain whether money could be raised for exigent needs. The President underrated the formidability of the Confederacy, the determination and talent of its leaders; he hoped, with Seward, that the flame of revolt would still die down, and he feared that too threatening a military effort might affect border State sentiment adversely.[50]

In one decision, that not to call Congress into special session, Lincoln made no error. For several reasons it was wise to defer the session for ten weeks, and public opinion approved his course.

It was necessary, first of all, to make sure that Washington was a safe place in which to sit. In the second place, he could do everything essential without Congressional action; in fact, during the emergency Congress would be rather an encumbrance than help. As a third consideration, key men of Congress would be summoned as wanted. Thus before the end of May, Senator William Pitt Fessenden of Maine got a letter from Chase saying that Lincoln wished him and other important members of the Senate Finance Committee to come to Washington at once to help prepare financial measures. Finally, so long as Lincoln and Seward cherished even faint hopes of a peaceable conclusion and a restoration of the Union, they feared the loud hostility of radical-minded members of Congress to compromise measures.

But action in Washington depended in great measure on action by the States in revolt. What, in these weeks, was the Confederacy doing?

50 For discussion of this subject see Ropes, *Story of the Civil War*, I, 111, 112; Comte de Paris, *Civil War*, I, Book II, Ch. IV; and such later writers as Fred A. Shannon, *Organization and Administration of the Union Army*, I, 31 ff. Ropes points out that Lincoln's call for 75,000 was followed on May 3 by a call for 42,034 three-year volunteers, 22,714 men for the regular army, and 18,000 men for the navy. Altogether, this raised the available army to 156,861 men, and the navy to 25,600 men, "certainly a very respectable force." Kenneth P. Williams has a judicious treatment of call for troops in *Lincoln Finds a General*, II, 796–800.

5

The Confederacy at War

THE ARDOR of the South after Sumter was as impressive as that of the North—and the lack of hardheaded planning just as remarkable. Feeling was even more vehement, indeed, than above the Potomac. Since the South had no great cities, scenes of mass enthusiasm were impossible. But its young men had been even quicker to enlist, and its women more eager to applaud them. Its clergy were as ready to consecrate stands of colors, its propertied men as generous in subscribing to loans, as in New England. In all the towns bands played, military companies paraded, bonfires blazed, and orators harangued the crowds.[1] Rural districts were equally exuberant. John B. Gordon, leading some North Georgia volunteers in coonskin caps from Atlanta to Montgomery, found the line of travel in unbroken uproar. Troops gathered at the stations under banners of strange device; fires lighted the hilltops; fife-and-drum corps shrilled and thumped; cannon exploded their salutes; and girls rushed aboard the cars to pin blue cockades on the men.[2] A war of resistance to tyranny, a struggle for freedom like that of 1776—so everybody believed. Sang ardent Henry Timrod: "Hath not the morning dawned with added light?"

For the moment an astonishing unanimity seemed to possess most of the South. A Northern journalist traveling through the Gulf States found the Unionists "completely crushed out for the time."[3] In countless breasts, of course, affection for the old nation contended with loyalty to the new. In South Carolina the aged Alfred Huger melted into tears when he thought of the past; in Virginia the youthful John S. Wise watched the Stars and Stripes hauled down with indescribable emotions. Many dissenters were prudently silent.[4] But so convinced were most Southerners of the right of secession and so sternly did they condemn coercion that Lincoln's call for troops brought

---

1 A. H. Bill, *The Beleaguered City*, 38, 39, pictures the excitement in Richmond.
2 Gordon, *Reminiscences*, 10.
3 Albert D. Richardson, letter in N. Y. *Tribune*, May 18 (dated May 10), 1861.
4 Russell, *My Diary*, Chs. 13–17 deal with feeling in S. C.; Wise, *The End of an Era*, 160. The real extent of the Union feeling in the South will be considered later.

a wave of anger that overthrew all differences. In an instant, the editor of the *Southern Literary Messenger* told the novelist John P. Kennedy, the proclamation transformed 75,000 Virginia Unionists into bitter enemies of the United States. Conservative leaders of the Virginia convention turned about face.[5]

Instantly the center of Southern interest moved from Charleston to the Potomac. Jefferson Davis on hearing of Sumter telegraphed his congratulations: "All honor to the gallant sons of Carolina, and thanks to God for their preservation." But at once he sent further messages: the governor of Virginia was asking for troops, and the regiment at Columbia and a regiment from Charleston were needed on the James, for the defense of the northern boundary of the Confederacy had suddenly become a matter of extreme urgency.

It was certain that Virginia would leave the Union, the only question being whether she would go at once or wait for the border States. Her convention went into secret session. Not only most delegates from the western counties, but some others, contended for delay. While they debated, mob excitement in Richmond rose until Union members feared violence; but the pause was brief. On April 17 the convention by the before-noted vote of 88 to 55, with 10 members absent, passed an ordinance of secession, to be submitted to the people May 23. Meanwhile the convention assumed supreme authority, and Governor Letcher ordered all military units to hold themselves alert. A fresh wave of enthusiasm rolled over Richmond. John Tyler joined in addressing a "spontaneous people's convention" sitting in town; Letcher had the Confederate flag, with an eighth star for Virginia, hoisted over the capitol; and a nocturnal procession flowed through the streets, cheering an orator who predicted the capture of Washington within sixty days.[6]

The alliance of Virginia and the Confederacy was quickly cemented by formal compact. When State leaders appealed to Montgomery for succor, Davis and the Cabinet prevailed on Vice-President Alexander H. Stephens to leave Georgia for Richmond on April 19. On his way north he spoke at station after station, insisting that Washington be taken as soon as possible. Though the South mingled aggressiveness with apprehension, the cry "On to Washington!" was fervently raised. Reaching Richmond on April 22, Stephens conferred with John Tyler and six other commissioners on a treaty of alliance with the Confederacy, and addressed the convention, outlining Southern policy. Already Richmond was so full of soldiers, with more pouring in by every train, that Governor Letcher soon had to stop the flow.

On April 24 the alliance of Virginia and the Confederacy was signed. Next day the convention ratified it. This step, momentous in itself, was potent in its influence on North Carolina and Tennessee, still delaying action.[7] The old Dominion lent the cause a dignity it had not before possessed, and promised to bring new and valuable leaders to the government and army.

That the South had spiritual qualities of its own which in several respects were superior to those of the North few impartial observers denied; and these qualities Virginia had once shown at their best. When Southerners asserted that they were maintaining a special way of life which independence alone could safeguard, they meant not only the social system based on slavery, but a dignity, repose, jealousy of personal honor, and courtesy that the hurried Yankee world could not match. They might be leisurely to the point of indolence, but their best circles stood closer to the Renaissance ideal of humanism; they might possess less social conscience than the Puritanic reformers of the North, but they had a mellower urbanity, and a keener sense of the romantic. Versatile Virginians like William Byrd and Thomas Jefferson had established the humanistic tradition of the South, and the Virginian John Esten Cooke had come nearest the spirit of Walter Scott. The slave-selling State of 1861 had slipped downward, but it was still a proud State.

[I]

Like the North, the Confederacy underestimated the magnitude of the struggle before it. Until autumn, most people anticipated a short contest. When the Confederate Congress met on April 29 in Montgomery to deal with what Davis called a declaration of war by Lincoln, it showed a confident optimism. Davis in his message dwelt with pride on the response of the South to the crisis. Transportation companies had freely offered the use of their lines; a convention of Southern railway presidents in Montgomery had not only reduced the rates for men and munitions, but had offered to accept compensation in Confederate bonds; farmers, mechanics, and professional men had all been eager to make sacrifices. Age and youth alike had rushed to the colors, and men of high civil rank had been willing to enlist as privates. We shall never be subjugated by arms, proclaimed Davis. He told Congress that he had 19,000 men under arms in various places, that 16,000 more were being assembled in Virginia, and that under existing legislation he planned to organize forces of 100,000, to be ready for instant action. He

7 Davis, *Rise and Fall*, I, 328 ff.

asked for a new grade of command, that of general, to outrank the major-generals of various States.[8]

"You count without your host," a brother-in-law of Jefferson Davis had told Charles Sumner the previous winter; "when the fighting begins it will all be north of the Susquehanna." [9] This idea that the resistance of Northern Democrats to all Yankee war measures would defeat coercion quickly died. But the Southern muster of force was so prompt and exuberant that multitudes believed in a quick victory. Many Southerners were persuaded that inasmuch as the North had grown rich at their expense, collecting fat brokerages and shipping charges, making fortunes by buying raw cotton cheap and selling cotton textiles high, and levying tariffs on Southern consumption, the Yankee economy would collapse after secession. "Look at the four hundred millions in Northern losses," exclaimed Alexander H. Stephens in May; "the leeches are now realizing whose wealth sustained them!" As news of the Northern business depression floated down, Southern editors gloated over the prospect of grassy New York streets. The South was one of the richest lands in the world, exulted the Richmond *Examiner,* and the North one of the poorest—sixty-eight Boston bankruptcies in a week proved it. Many who did not go so far as this nevertheless held that much of the Northern strength was artificial, and that of the slave States basic and impregnable. While the Yankee world depended on manufactures for which the demand might wither overnight, the South relied upon farm commodities for which the market exceeded the supply. The Northern economy was topheavy, the Southern stable.

We have already noted the allied concept, related to Napoleon's sneer at the nation of shopkeepers, that the commercial-minded Yankee lacked fighting spirit. To some the war lay between gentlemen and yeomen on one side, and "vulgar, fanatical, cheating counter-jumpers" on the other. Beauregard was convinced that the average Southerner was physically stronger than the average Northerner. "Yankee trash" was a familiar phrase, varied by suggestions that most New York soldiers were thugs and jailbirds.[10] Southern newspapers and letters of the spring of 1861 are full of vaunts that one Confederate equaled five of Lincoln's "myrmidons," that a Southron (another favorite term) could whip a Yankee with one hand tied behind his back, and that Northerners could be defeated with children's popguns. Unfortunately, John B. Gordon later ruefully remarked, they wouldn't fight that way! Such gasconade is common in all wars, but in this one many Southerners believed it.

8 *Messages and Papers of the Confederacy,* I.
9 Sumner to Duchess of Argyll, Boston, June 4, 1861, HL.
10 W. H. Russell quotes both the counter-jumper phrase and Beauregard; *My Diary,* Chs. 18, 19. He notes also the thug-and-jailbird characterization, Ch. 30.

"Just throw three or four shells among those blue-bellied Yankees," a Northern newspaper correspondent heard a young man tell a crowded car in North Carolina, "and they'll scatter like sheep." This correspondent was so pained by the oft-repeated declaration that Yankees were cowards that he almost rejoiced in the brilliant prospect the South enjoyed for learning the truth.[11]

Even if the North fought well, averred many Southerners, it could never subjugate a freedom-loving people who battled on the defensive for their homes and institutions. As Great Britain had failed in the Revolution, so Federal power must fail now. What did it cost the government to get fifteen hundred Seminole warriors out of the Everglades? demanded a Tennessee Congressman. Thirty millions! "When you talk of conquering States, the whole arithmetic fails of figures to count the cost." [12] Distance was a defense. Above all, a population of eight millions determined to die rather than yield could no more be beaten down than the Swiss had been by the Austrians, the English by the Armada, or the Dutch by Philip II. This belief had a poignant intensity. When John Tyler traced the Anglo-Saxon struggle for liberty and self-determination from Magna Charta down through Naseby and Saratoga to Sumter, he touched a vibrant chord. But all the defenses named might prove treacherous.[13] River and railroad could conquer distances; the "inside lines" of the South lost meaning when a Union army moved up the Tennessee into the heart of the Confederacy; and the North too could state principles which steeled the arm and exalted the spirit.

When rugged John H. Reagan of Texas declared that if war came the South would show how brave men could die, Emory B. Pottle of New York uttered a rejoinder of ringing truth. "I do not doubt it," he told the House, "and I tell the gentleman that he knows little of the North if he thinks the example will be thrown away upon us. Sirs, you do injustice to our common ancestry if you doubt that we can meet the shock of battle upon equal terms with you. Who doubts the courage of either section?" While the Southerners had a greater taste for military pursuits, no statement was more fallacious than the frequent remark that they displayed a superior fighting ability.[14]

11   Gordon, *Reminiscences*, 7; Albert D. Richardson in N. Y. *Weekly Tribune*, May 18, 1861.
12   James H. Thomas in *Cong. Globe*, 36th Cong., 2d Sess., p. 437.
13   Richmond *Examiner*, April 20, 21.
14   *Cong. Globe*, 36th Cong., 2d Sess. (Jan. 25, 1861), 570. Perhaps the Southerners did have a greater aptitude for war, for it is true they rode and shot better—at first. But Northerners and Southerners were the same people, with essentially the same characteristics. If the Southerners possibly had a little more ardor, the Northerners possibly had a little more endurance; but both statements are dubious. The best brief statement of the differences between Northern and Southern troops is in Comte de Paris, I. He thinks the Northerner somewhat superior, as being better educated, and therefore more resourceful and quicker-minded, but he was a prejudiced witness.

The Southerners' faith in a short war derived much, finally, from their before-mentioned confidence in the power of cotton. From Jefferson Davis to the humblest farmer, countless men accepted the doctrine so often preached by James H. Hammond and others that cotton was king. A child can break a thread of cotton, wrote Benjamin H. Hill of Georgia, but on that thread hangs the world.[15] W. H. Russell, dining in Charleston, heard a Carolinian tell the British consul that England was a helpless subject of this potentate. "Why, sir, we have only to shut off your supply of cotton for a few weeks, and we can create a revolution in Great Britain." Even a steward on a Mississippi River steamboat assured Russell that all the world could not beat the South, for King Cotton was autocrat of Europe.[16] If the Upper South doubted his potency, in the Lower South few questioned the weight of his scepter. It was a dangerous theory, for it encouraged a policy which played into the hands of the Northern blockade.

The wilder Southern utterances on this subject had long amazed Britons. "There is something truly astonishing," the London *Economist* had said in 1851, "in the infatuations which seem to possess the Southern States of America." If civil war took place, "no bribes, however enormous, would induce the English people—or any class among them, however interested in the result—to lend its aid to a revolt which they believe to be utterly unprovoked, the result of the worst political passions, and likely to end in the degradation of the Southern States."

The London *Spectator* had spoken in similar terms. Lord Derby, head of the Conservative Party, quoting the Charleston *Mercury* on the power of cotton to make Britain recognize and even ally herself with a Southern republic, termed such statements the fruit of a distempered fancy. He warned Southerners that Britain would not intervene, that any reduction of the Southern cotton supply would merely stimulate its cultivation from Brazil to India, and that they would find themselves hoist by their own petard. In the five years 1845–49, the South had supplied Britain with 84 per cent of her cotton requirements, and the rest of the globe had given her 16 per cent. In the five years 1855–59, the South had furnished but 76 per cent, and other countries 24.[17]

The cotton kingdom cherished its dream because it knew so little of European realities. Few Southerners were students of the economy of other nations; fewer still traveled attentively abroad or talked with foreign businessmen. The fact that the South was provincial enabled the ignorant Governor R. K. Call of Florida to gain wide credence for his statement that Britain

15 Quoted by Coulter, *The Confederate States*, 184, 185.
16 Russell, *My Diary*, Chs. 14, 51.
17 Full material on this subject may be found in a pamphlet, "Disunion and Its Results to the South," dated Washington, Feb. 18, 1861, of anonymous authorship; HL. It warned the South that King Wheat, King Corn, and other kings were more powerful than cotton.

completely depended on the South. "A failure of our cotton crop for three years would be a far greater calamity to England than three years' war with the greatest power on earth." [18]

[II]

The second session of the Provisional Confederate Congress, a unicameral body whose members were appointed by the State secession conventions, sat in hot, humid, mosquito-ridden Montgomery from April 29, and dealt with problems of the utmost magnitude. It was a mediocre body, indebted to the secrecy of its sessions for its short-lived reputation for sense and courage. As one member remarked, it had few if any superior minds, and seldom held a debate marked by noteworthy wisdom. Its informality was reminiscent of Washington: the same want of dignity and earnestness, the same spectacle of feet on desks, dark-circled spittoons, buzzing gossipers, and lobby vultures sharpening their beaks. Most of the ability of the South was drained into the Army, Cabinet, and diplomatic service. In Howell Cobb as president it had an urbane leader until he left to pursue martial glory. Thomas S. Bocock of Virginia, who had once barely missed election to the national speakership, entered early in May. Others of repute included William Porcher Miles of South Carolina, Benjamin H. Hill of Georgia, and Louis T. Wigfall of Texas; in general, however, observers wondered why so many hacks had been chosen.[19]

Congress not only gave Davis the large force for which he asked, but permitted him to accept volunteers without State consent. It authorized an issue of $50,000,000 of 20-year 8 per cent bonds, or, alternatively, an issue of $30,000,000 in such bonds and $20,000,000 in treasury notes, not bearing interest. It debated an embargo on the export of cotton by sea, and prohibited the payment of debts beyond the confines of the border States. Obviously, these enactments all possessed cardinal importance.[20]

The first gave the Confederacy the partial—but only partial—basis of an army bound to serve for three years unless it won an earlier peace. This was something the Union did not have for long months to come. Down to Sumter

18 Letter of Governor R. K. Call of Florida to John S. Littell, pamphlet dated Feb. 12, 1861; HL.
19 See the sketch in T. C. DeLeon, *Four Years in Rebel Capitals*, 31, 32, and the full account in E. M. Coulter, *The Confederate States of America*, Ch. VII. The United States later published the *Journals* of the Confederate Congress in seven volumes, and the Southern Historical Society has published press reports of proceedings.
20 Coulter, the *Confederate States*, 134 ff.; Eaton, *History of the Southern Confederacy*, 54 ff.; Johnston and Browne, *Stephens*, 401–404. The Provisional Congress lasted from Feb. 4, 1861, to Feb. 17, 1862, holding five sessions. The first Congress, which was the first body elected by the people, met Feb. 18, 1862. W. C. Rives, a member, wrote scathingly of the Provisional Congress to A. L. Rives, Aug. 14, 1861; Rives Papers, Univ. of Virginia Library.

the Confederacy had been receiving militia and volunteers for six months or a year, and only by consent of their States. Now that the situation had radically changed, the President was authorized (May 8, 13) to receive up to 400,000 men, without delaying for State permission, who would serve for three years or the duration. Recruits wishing to enlist for only six or twelve months might still come in as members of a State unit. An array of short-term, intermediate-term, and long-term troops therefore soon appeared at the front, some of them State volunteers, some militiamen, and some national volunteers. The resulting confusion and jealousy were serious.

It would have been far better for the Southern cause could a uniform enlistment of three years have been prescribed. But Secretary Walker, whom Alexander H. Stephens called "rash in counsel, irresolute in action," and who haggled over prices when the Confederacy needed every gun it could obtain, furnished poor leadership; while Congress and the people could not believe in three years of battle and bloodshed. President Davis almost alone had publicly and constantly predicted a long and costly war.[21] For these prophecies, ardent advocates of secession had berated him as slow and conservative; now hotheaded patriots abused him as pessimistic and feeble-hearted. Vice-President Stephens, at this stage in sympathetic rapport with Davis, also told everybody that the conflict would be prolonged and sanguinary, would require the severest sacrifices, and would fail if the people did not show endurance. He was similarly attacked. As the troops gathered, all exuberance and thirst for the clash of arms, many feared only that victory would be won before they could share it. Their elders anticipated a few fierce combats, and then a negotiated peace of independence.

In passing its first financial measures, Congress again took shortsighted views. The new head of the Treasury, Christopher G. Memminger, a Charleston attorney who had long been chairman of the finance committee of the South Carolina House, had methodical industry, but no particular expertness, vision, or force of personality, and he also thought in terms of a short war. He had begun work in a bare room in Montgomery, unswept, uncarpeted, unfurnished, and without a cent of public money, so that even his desk and chair were paid for from his own pocket. His whole official term was to be a career of expedients, and the first emergency measures were typical of those to come. He made it plain that he expected no great immediate revenue from import or export duties, and not more than $15,000,000 the first year from direct taxes, which most of the States assumed anyway and paid

21 Davis insists on this in his *Rise and Fall of the Confederate Government*, with ample evidence; and his final speeches in the United States Senate show that he had a clear expectation of a long, savage conflict. For Walker see C. A. Evans, *Confederate Military History*, I. This fastidious Alabamian, disliking contractors, groaned: "No *gentleman* can be fit for office."

in their own notes. The seeds of a lusty inflation were sown in the market-ing of $50,000,000 of treasury notes.

Happily for his power to meet the most immediate needs, he obtained some $560,000 in Federal cash and bullion from the mint and custom house in New Orleans, while various States, towns, and individuals—Alabama in the van with $5,000,000—made loans or gifts. But it was clear even in the spring of 1861 that the Confederacy would float to victory or defeat on a sea of paper.[22] Not until the spring of 1863 did Congress pass a comprehensive tax law—too little and too late.

The bill for an embargo on cotton was of course simply an application of the Confederate doctrine that King Cotton, by judicious squeezes on the British windpipe, could compel foreign assistance. We hold the aces, rejoiced the Charleston *Mercury*, and we shall bankrupt every cotton factory in Britain and France if those nations do not acknowledge our independence. Other newspapers advised the planters to keep the cotton on their plantations; thus it could neither fall into Union hands nor relieve that desperate European stringency which would soon force foreign intervention. The cotton mer-chants, the warehouse owners, the insurance writers, and the factors doing a brokerage business all united in urging retention of the great staple. Before long the principal British consuls in the South reported to the foreign office that planters and government were alike determined to carry through a plan of economic coercion: no cotton except in return for recognition and the breaking of the Northern blockade! The first bill for an embargo, with such popular feeling behind it, seemed certain to pass; so did later bills.

But not quite. When embargo came to the point of enactment, an unseen but easily identifiable influence halted it. Jefferson Davis saw clearly that while the threat of such a law might effectively influence foreign opinion, actual passage would carry pressure too far. So unfriendly a measure would anger the British and French governments. The proper pose of the Con-federacy was that of an anxious friend of free commercial intercourse, only too ready to ship its staple abroad once the North permitted. The President therefore let Congress pass bills cutting off trade with the United States, and forbidding exports of Southern crops to Europe except through Southern ports, but he went no further.[23]

22 J. C. Schwab, *The Confederate States*, 10 ff. Some Federal money and bullion were obtained at the Dahlonega (Ga.) mint, and the Charlotte (N. C.) assay office. The Con-federacy provided for a million dollars in interest-bearing notes in March, 1861. The total of specie on which it was able to lay hands during its whole existence amounted only to $27,000,000. Schwab, 43.

23 See Frank L. Owsley, *King Cotton Diplomacy*, Ch. I. Congress did levy a duty of one-eighth of one per cent a pound on cotton exports, to pay the interest on early loans (Feb. 28). Davis, *Rise and Fall*, I, 486; Schwab, 239, 240.

The first civil policies of the government had thus been fairly well fixed when a convention in Raleigh unanimously passed a secession ordinance for North Carolina on May 20, and Virginia by overwhelming popular vote on May 23 decided in favor of leaving the Union. The way was now open for a transfer of the capital of the Confederacy to Richmond. When Vice-President Stephens visited Virginia, he had all but promised that this step would be taken. The Virginia convention issued a formal invitation which filled most members of Congress with enthusiasm. They were heartily tired of Montgomery, with its wilting temperatures, pestiferous insects, and still hungrier lobbyists and office-seekers. The city's hotels were overcrowded, dirty, and ill served; the flies were fearful; the streets lifeless and uninteresting. Richmond by comparison was a metropolis. President Davis vetoed the bill for the transfer, but Congress at once repassed it.[24]

Some Southerners believed that strategic considerations pointed to the choice of a railway center less exposed to Federal attack: Lynchburg, Chattanooga, or Nashville. The arguments for Richmond, however, were overwhelming. The importance of the city as a rail and iron-manufacturing center, its Tredegar Works holding a national reputation, and the value of northern Virginia and the Shenandoah Valley as storehouses of grain, meat, and other supplies, made their defense absolutely vital. As it was certain that the most formidable army of the Confederacy would soon hold positions between the James and the Potomac, command could best be exercised from Richmond.

Sentimental factors were also potent. Here on the historic James stood a handsome capitol building; here was Crawford's statue of Washington, with its attendant cluster of Virginia celebrities; here were spots hallowed by Jefferson, Patrick Henry, George Mason, Madison, and John Marshall. And finally, certain political arguments had great weight. Since part of the border area was still hesitant, since the Lower South had launched secession and many feared that the cotton kingdom would dominate the Confederacy, and since the primacy of Virginia in the Southern sisterhood could not be denied, Richmond was to be preferred above all other cities of the new nation.[25]

Howell Cobb predicted that Virginia soil would soon become a vast battleground, dyed with the blood of the bravest Southern heroes. Even those who derided his suggestion that at critical moments members of Congress might doff their togas and buckle on their armor, felt that the government could well gain from proximity to its forces.[26] Communications both north and south would be easier, and to plant the capital so far toward the front

24 Bill, *Beleaguered City*, gives an interesting sketch of the transfer.
25 Coulter, *Confederate States*, 100, 101.
26 Speech at Atlanta May 22, 1861, *Ann. Cyc.*, 140.

would show a sense of strength. At this date Stephens and others expected
President Davis to take command of the Army of Virginia in person, and
some believed that the brief, sharp conflict would be mainly confined to the
Old Dominion.[27] It took time to reveal the disadvantages of an exposed position not quite 110 miles from Washington and close to tidewater. It also
took time to show that the choice of Richmond had some unfortunate effects
on the broad lines of Confederate strategy, for it reduced the scale of army
movements, and it strengthened the natural tendency to favor Eastern as
against Western demands.

With a distinguished entourage, Davis left Montgomery on Sunday
evening, May 26, for Virginia. All along the way, at Atlanta, Augusta,
Wilmington, Goldsboro, and other towns, crowds assembled which, despite
announcements that the President was ill and wished privacy, demanded
speeches. Shouts of "The old hero!" and "We want Jeff Davis!" brought
him out for a few fervent sentences. Having reached Richmond, he drove
behind four white horses, between cheering banks of people, to the Spots-
wood Hotel. The sound of saw and hammer vibrated from Capitol Hill, where
buildings were being altered for the new government. Davis, with Toombs
and the State Department and Memminger and the Treasury, took up offices
in the former custom house. The War Department under Walker, with other
departments and bureaus, found rooms in the ugly brick Mechanics' Institute, where the headquarters for Virginia troops occupied the top floor.

[III]

Alexander H. Stephens, fierily addressing a crowd at Atlanta, told it that
however long the struggle, triumph was certain. "We have now Maryland
and Virginia and all the Border States with us. We have ten millions of
people with us, heart and hand, to defend us to the death. We can call out
a million people, if need be; and when they are cut down we can call out
another, and still another . . . a triumphant victory and independence, with
an unparalleled career of glory, prosperity, and independence, await us." [28]
But did the Confederacy really have the Border States?

Once Lincoln called for troops, the secession of Virginia, North Carolina,
Tennessee, and Arkansas was so certain that the Confederacy immediately
treated all four as quasi-members. Although all had been fundamentally
Unionist in sentiment, the hostility of all to coercion was overwhelming.
What the ablest Southern religious editor, George McNeil of the *North*

27 Johnston and Browne, *Stephens*, 403.
28 N. Y. *Tribune*, May 9, 1861.

Carolina Presbyterian, had said of his State was essentially true of the others. After taking pains to ascertain popular feeling, McNeil had written an article addressed to the nation declaring that although three-fourths of the North Carolinians were anxious to preserve the Federal tie, while only one-fourth stood for secession, practically all of them would resist coercive action. "We have yet to see an individual who would tolerate an invasion of the South." In other States the secessionists had been a distinct minority. Tennessee had voted decisively against a convention to debate separation, and East Tennessee had voted four to one. In Arkansas the *State Gazette* had declared March 30 that all informed men put the Union majority at fully 20,000.[29] History, wrote an agonized Virginian, would record that a majority in the Old Dominion carried their struggle for national unity to the point of pusillanimity and dishonor.[30] But a great majority were against coercion.

Why? If they believed in the Union and the Union was attacked, why join the assailants and not the defenders? Theoretically, because they did not believe in the indissoluble Union of which Washington repeatedly spoke, but in the dissoluble Union of John Taylor of Caroline. They held the compact theory of the Federal tie. Emotionally, because they felt themselves identified with the Lower South. Pragmatically, because they saw that slavery and other special economic interests which they shared with the cotton kingdom would be endangered by its defeat. But if they ever thought of themselves as true Unionists they had a twisted logic and a confused set of loyalties; they should have called themselves tepid, conditional, and halfway Unionists. Andrew Jackson would have applied more scorching adjectives. They had none of Jefferson's conviction, as expressed in a letter to Washington in 1792, that the rending of the Union into two or more parts would be an evil of incalculable proportions.

In Virginia the result of the referendum at once became foregone. The most prominent "Union" men in Richmond, including several who had been emphatic in their assertions of attachment to the nation in recent public meetings, took their stand with Governor Letcher. John Baldwin of Augusta County, who had spoken powerfully for the Union in the convention, wrote the Staunton *Spectator* that their only hope now was in "making ready for the biggest fight that is in us." Only one Unionist leader of high rank remained unyielding: John Carlile, after resisting secession on the convention floor until adjournment, returned to western Virginia to lead the struggle against it there. Throughout the tidewater area a spirit of intimidation reigned:

29 *North Carolina Presbyterian,* Nov. 24, 1860; *Ann. Cyc.* 1861, p. 678, for Tennessee; *Arkansas State Gazette,* March 30, 1861.
30 Wm. Frazier, Rockbridge, Va., May 20, 1861, to Horatio King; H. King Papers, LC.

No Union man dared vote his convictions, and opposition to secession was measured only by absenteeism from the polls. Vigorous use was made of Senator James Mason's letter stigmatizing antagonists as traitors, and of a judicial charge to a grand jury declaring that any citizen who adhered to the Federal government might be indicted for treason.[31]

Under these circumstances, the referendum was a farce; the State had really been out of the Union since April 17 and the plebiscite simply ratified a *fait accompli*. The soldiers voting in their camps, where any opposition voice would have been drastically silenced, were practically unanimous. The piedmont counties were almost as solidly for the ordinance as the tidewater area. Most localities in western Virginia were against it, but they stood alone. Had a fair, calm election been possible, Norfolk County, which sold much produce to Northern cities, and the counties around Washington, connected with the free States by commercial and social ties, would have polled a large Union vote, but prudence dictated abstention. "At Alexandria," wrote a Falls Church man who successfully stood for Congress this spring, "where there were really some four hundred Union men, only some forty votes were given for the nation"; the others were sullenly silent.[32] Many who voted for secession did so with long, sad thoughts.

North Carolina seceded with a greater outward show of unanimity, but a deeper inner division. Even among the Democrats, few had tolerated a spirit of fire-eating radicalism. Non-slaveholding groups had long and energetically opposed the efforts of slaveholders to pass tax measures favorable to their own interests. W. W. Holden, the erstwhile secessionist editor of the *North Carolina Standard*, so changeable that he was called the Talleyrand of the State, had come over to the Union position. The proportion of slaveowners in the commonwealth was smaller than in its neighbors, and most of them held comparatively few hands. Among the Quakers and the small upcountry farmers abolitionist sentiment possessed great vigor. No State had more genuine reluctance before Lincoln's call for troops, just as none after joining the Confederacy contributed more valorously to the cause.[33]

When Lincoln issued his call, Governor John W. Ellis not only denounced him for warring upon popular liberties, but seized the arsenal at Fayetteville, with 37,000 small arms and 3,000 kegs of powder, the mint at Charlotte, and three forts on the coast; asked for the enrollment of 30,000 men; and promised

31 Beverley B. Munford, *Virginia's Attitude Toward Slavery and Secession;* C. H. Ambler, *History of West Virginia.* Files of the *National Intelligencer* throw special light on the Virginia struggle.
32 Letter of Charles H. Upton in N. Y. *Tribune*, May 28, 1861.
33 C. C. Norton, *The Democratic Party in Ante-Bellum N. C.* (1931), *passim;* Elizabeth Y. Webb, "Cotton Manufacturing in North Carolina 1861–65," *N. C. Hist. Rev.*, (April, 1932), 117–137.

the Confederacy a regiment. Holden swung back to secession in an editorial, "We Must Fight." A special legislative session arranged the election of a convention on May 13, which eight days later unanimously passed a secession ordinance. For the moment most opposition was overborne, although some old Whigs, like George Badger, grumbled over the methods used, and would have preferred a declaration of independence to one of secession. Here, as in Virginia, true Unionists held their tongues. Jonathan Worth, a leader of special elevation who had lately written that nineteen-twentieths of the people he saw were for the old national tie, now sadly recorded: "The voice of reason is silenced. Furious passion and thirst for blood consume the air." He still believed that no separate government could ever be as good as the united nation men were pulling down.[34]

Tennessee in the last Presidential election had given John Bell, champion of the Constitution and the Union, a decisive majority over Breckinridge. At a Nashville meeting shortly before Lincoln's inauguration, Bell had expressed the hope that all would yet be well with the nation. Large parts of the State were as much opposed to a rupture of the national bond as Ohio or Pennsylvania. The Nashville *Democrat*, defending the Union to the last, declared that leaders of the Deep South had plotted to betray the border. "We must expect that the cottonocracy will attempt to precipitate a war with the General Government, with the express purpose of dragging Tennessee into their meshes." [35] The popular vote taken to elect a convention had indicated that approximately 92,000 of those who voted were in favor of the Union, and only 25,000 for abandoning it.

It therefore required determined effort by the secessionist governor, Isham G. Harris, a radical proslavery attorney of force and ability, and by the secessionist majority in the legislature, to carry Tennessee rapidly into the Confederacy. When Harris informed Lincoln that the State would raise 50,000 men, if necessary, to defend Southern rights, influential citizens published an address urging a neutral stand. Harris convoked the legislature only to confront a hostile minority. An ordinance for submitting independence to popular vote passed the Senate 20 to 4, but the House only 46 to 21, and another ordinance for an alliance with the Confederacy met similar dissent. Actually Harris was staging a *coup d'état*, for the legislature had no authority to vote an alliance. This measure (May 1) committed Tennessee to the Confederate cause, just as a law to raise an immediate force of 25,000, with a reserve of 30,000, and to issue bonds for $5,000,000, committed it to military

---

34 J. G. de Roulhac Hamilton, *Correspondence of Jonathan Worth*, I, 99, 149. Holden in the *Standard* on Feb. 15, 1861, predicted that secession and war would end in abolition of slavery, repudiation of debts, general beggary, and military government.
35 Quoted in Havana, Ill., *Squatter Sovereign*, Feb. 28, 1861.

action. When the referendum was taken on June 8, the people went to the polls without real power to decide the result. As in Virginia, they could only ratify a *fait accompli*. Nevertheless, 47,238 voted no, as against 104,913 voting yes, and in East Tennessee the result was 32,923 for the Union, 14,780 against it.[36]

Like Virginia and North Carolina, Tennessee had such strong bonds of blood, social similarity, and economic interest with the Lower South that she was certain to join it. But East Tennessee, had Northern forces been within reach, might well have done what West Virginia did to remain in the Union.

The situation in Arkansas presented some unusual features. There, as in other border States, many slaveholders had been conservative Unionists. It was the slaveholding districts that had voted most strongly for Bell or Douglas, while northern and northwestern Arkansas, an area of small farmers with few slaves, had given Breckinridge his small majority. Among the well-to-do the old Whig tradition remained strong, while many believed that secession would jeopardize slavery. After Lincoln's election, however, the slaveholding counties caught fire from the revolt of the cotton kingdom, while the hillier sections showed a strong attachment to the nation. Doubtless the small farmers had voted for Breckinridge as an expression of Southern sentiment, but now realized that they would fare much worse in a divided than a united country; doubtless also the slaveholders, while actuated largely by sectional emotion, were now inclined to believe that their human property would be safer in the Confederacy than in Lincoln's Union. At any rate, the voting on the Presidency and then on secession showed that in the two distinct geographical areas of Arkansas an abrupt change of alignment took place in the winter and spring of 1860–61. The planters who had so largely stood for Bell or Douglas now ardently espoused the Confederate cause, while the farmers of northwestern Arkansas in particular turned to a staunch Federal allegiance.

The governor of Arkansas bade Lincoln expect no troops, and prepared to lead the people in resisting Northern "usurpations." The State convention which had recently adjourned was hastily reassembled (May 6). As it passed an ordinance of secession with a shout, one former Union delegate after another rose to declare his entire loyalty to the South. The convention authorized the governor to call out 60,000 men (an inflated figure, for the white population was under 325,000!), and to issue $2,000,000 in bonds. State troops seized Fort Smith. No referendum now being deemed necessary, on May 18 Arkansas formally joined the Confederacy. But as in Tennessee, a stubborn opposition simmered under the surface—an opposition that was to make the

36   J. W. Fertig, *The Secession and Reconstruction of Tennessee*; J. W. Patton, *Unionism and Reconstruction in Tennessee*; *Ann. Cyc.*, 1861, pp. 679–683.

area adjoining Kansas a Union stronghold, and that was eventually to rally behind the one brave delegate who risked his life by voting no on secession, Isaac Murphy, and lift him to the governorship of the reconstructed State.[37]

Altogether, the secession of the Upper South, adding four new stars to the Confederate flag, was a very different process from that of the cotton king-dom. Instead of a reckless surge of emotion we meet anxious deliberation, anguish of heart, a bitter clash of opinion, and dark forebodings of the future. We meet men who flung sternly reproachful cries at the North: "We struggled so long, we sacrificed so much!—and now your measures leave us no choice." We meet other men who addressed the Confederate leaders with yet more passionate rebukes: "We fought so hard for your rights, we gained so much and held such firm expectations of gaining more!—and now you drag us into a needless war, where we must stand the brunt of invasion, and our sons must die for your desperate policies." We meet States almost or quite torn physically asunder by the uncontrollable forces of the time. We meet the finest spirits and ablest generals of the South, thrust, they believed, into decisions which were at once disastrous and unavoidable. Here in the wide borderland lay the most poignant tragedy of a tragic period.

[IV]

One of the finest spirits who felt constrained to an unhappy choice, Robert E. Lee, sent on May 5 a letter to a Northern girl who had requested his photograph. "It is painful," he wrote, "to think how many friends will be separated and estranged by our unhappy disunion. May God reunite our severed bonds of friendship, and turn our hearts to peace! I can say in sincerity that I bear animosity against no one. Wherever the blame may be, the fact is that we are in the midst of a fratricidal war. I must side either with or against my section or country. I cannot raise my hand against my birthplace, my home, my children. I should like, above all things, that our difficulties might be peaceably arranged, and still trust that a merciful God, who I know will not unnecessarily afflict us, may yet allay the fury for war. Whatever may be the result of the contest, I foresee that the country will have to pass through a terrible ordeal, a necessary expiation perhaps for our national sins. May God direct all for our good, and shield and preserve you and yours!" [38]

The tide of secession, running with such fresh force after Sumter, gave

---

37 L. L. Harvin, "Arkansas and the Crisis of 1860–61" (MS Master's Essay, Univ. of Texas) covers the subject in detail. See also David Y. Thomas, *Arkansas in War and Recon-struction*. The secessionists in Arkansas had been watching events, ready to seize any op-portunity.

38 Private source; not "my section *of* country," as Freeman, *Lee*, I, 475, has it.

the South many of the ablest officers of the army and navy. In all, nearly a third of the nation's commissioned military men, 313 in number, resigned. The War Department offices were also partly stripped. Of ninety regular employees there in 1860, thirty-four were gone by midsummer of 1861. Three had died, and some had perhaps been displaced for age, ill health, or political reasons, but most of them had left to join the South.[39]

Among the resignations those of Robert E. Lee, Joseph E. Johnston, E. Kirby-Smith, Franklin Buchanan, and Matthew Fontaine Maury were longest remembered. Those of lesser stature included Colonel Samuel E. Cooper, the adjutant-general, and Major John Withers, assistant adjutant-general. Cooper's course awakened the keenest censure in the North, for he had been born in New Jersey; his mother was a New Yorker, his father a Massachusetts man; he had entered West Point from New York, had played an efficient part in the Seminole and Mexican wars, and had spent nearly ten years in his important post. But the influence of his Virginia wife, sprung from the George Mason family, his Virginia home, and his close friendship with Jefferson Davis, proved paramount. He became adjutant- and inspector-general of the Confederacy, to serve throughout the war. Colonel Lorenzo Thomas, who took his place, was nearly sixty, more experienced, and more energetic, but vain, unstable, and of poor judgment.

Highly creditable to Joseph E. Johnston was the mental anguish he suffered in deciding to resign. This gallant soldier, shrewd, cautious, systematic, was a Virginian through and through, his father a soldier under "Light-Horse Harry" Lee, his mother a niece of Patrick Henry. But since graduation from West Point his whole life had been given to the Union. He had been wounded five times in the Mexican War; he had been first to plant a regimental flag on the walls of Chapultepec; he had been a staff officer with the Utah expedition, and in 1860 had become quartermaster-general of the army. Officers who consulted him in the spring of 1861 found him pacing up and down his Washington office in deep thought, his fine head bent forward, his absorption so complete that he had to be addressed several times before he awoke. One visitor heard him muttering to himself in painful perplexity. Overwrought, he exploded at the slightest interruption. Finally, on April 22, when Virginia's departure was certain, he closeted himself with Secretary Cameron.

"I must go with the South," he said, in effect, "though the action is in the last degree ungrateful. I owe all that I am to the government of the United States. It has educated me and clothed me with honor. To leave the service is a hard necessity, but I must go. Though I am resigning my position, I

39 A. Howard Meneely, *The War Department, 1861*, 106–109. The Cameron Papers and Gideon Welles Papers, LC and NYPL, contain much on the resignations.

trust I may never draw my sword against the old flag." He wept, and tears stained his cheeks as he hurriedly left the room.

Major E. Kirby-Smith, a son of Florida whose army experience and connections were chiefly in the South and Southwest, had resigned early, but with only less travail. He wrote his mother that he had broken all the ties that bound him to the army "not suddenly, impulsively, but conscientiously and after due deliberation." He was the youngest man in the force to be senior major of his regiment, twenty years in advance of his contemporaries. "I sacrifice more to my principles than any other officer in the Army can do." But he would rather carry a musket in the cause of the South than be commander-in-chief under Mr. Lincoln. He departed with a State that the Union had bought with national funds.[40]

Robert E. Lee reached his critical decision much more easily, for as his principal biographer writes, it was the product of instinct, not deep reflection. He was too clearsighted not to recognize the true character of the movement in the cotton kingdom. Writing his wife in January, 1861, he had said that if the upper tier of States trusted the Gulf secessionists, they would be "dragged into the gulf of revolution." The word "dragged" was deliberately chosen. The same month he wrote his son Fitzhugh that secession was naught but revolution. "The framers of our Constitution never exhausted so much labor, wisdom, and forbearance in its formation and surrounded it with so many guards and securities, if it was intended to be broken up by every member of the Confederacy at will. It is intended for 'perpetual union,' so expressed in the preamble, and for the establishment of a government, not a compact, which can only be dissolved by revolution or the consent of all the people in convention assembled. It is idle to talk of secession." He had recently been made colonel of the First Cavalry, and brought to Washington to be near headquarters. To friends he said that he had a profound contempt for the business of secession.[41]

40 On Johnston see Cobb's MS Reminiscences of Washington in 1861, Cameron Papers, LC. Johnston wrote in resigning that he hoped some thirty years' service, "with as much labor, hardship, danger, and loss of blood as the duties of the military service in this country often imposed, may be thought to entitle me to early consideration of this communication." Letter of April 22, 1861; extra-illustrated set of *Battles and Leaders*, HL. Johnston was the only general officer who went to the South from Federal services; Lee was a colonel. But Johnston was a staff, not a field officer, a fact which entered into the subsequent disputation about rank. Gov. Letcher made him a major-general of Virginia troops two days after Lee got a similar appointment. Kirby-Smith's letters to his mother, written from Texas March 3, March 25, 1861, in the Kirby-Smith Papers, Univ. of N. C., are illuminating. While the family name appears to have been Smith, I follow the DAB form of Kirby-Smith.

41 On the events leading up to Lee's resignation the letters in Fitzhugh Lee's life are illuminating, but Fitzhugh's comment is misleading, and Long's life is a better guide. Douglas Freeman states that Lee decided by instinct, without thought; see both his life and his DAB article. Lee's own story is given in his letter to Reverdy Johnson, Feb. 25, 1868, in

After this, why did he act (as he measurably did) against his own convictions? Unquestionably, because of State and local loyalties, family affections and interests, and personal ties too strong to be sundered. Winfield Scott, who not only thought Lee the ablest officer in the army, but had a warm personal fondness for him, openly avowed his desire to have him made the principal Union field commander. Lincoln and Cameron were ready to accept this judgment, but so uncertain of Lee's fidelity to the Union that they asked old Francis P. Blair to talk with him. The two met at Blair's house on April 18. Lee's answer was unhesitating. He declined Lincoln's quasi-offer, stating frankly that although opposed to secession and deprecating war, he could take no part in an invasion of the South. He did consent to discuss the subject with Scott, and went directly to his headquarters, but again said no firmly.[42]

Meanwhile, Virginia had left the Union, and the president of the Virginia convention informed Lee that, at the instance of Governor Letcher, it wished to make him commander-in-chief of the Commonwealth forces. On April 20 he presented his resignation, writing that it would have been offered earlier but for the struggle it had cost him to separate himself from—what? Not from the Union, of which Virginia had been the strongest pillar in Washington's day, but "from a service to which I have devoted the best years of my life and all the ability I possessed." Hurrying to Richmond, he received an ovation in which all the State leaders joined, and took up his command April 23.

How tremendous a loss the North incurred in Lee's departure it took time to reveal, although many men partly divined it at once. His decision naturally aroused intense Northern bitterness. Erstwhile friends renounced him, the press compared him with Benedict Arnold, and admirers of his father-in-law, the late George Washington Parke Custis, speculated on the grief that his choice would have given to that adopted son of Washington. We can easily understand and sympathize with his course. But it was no allegiance to the Confederacy that he felt, no sympathy with basic Confederate principles; it was

J. W. Jones, *Life and Letters of Robert E. Lee*, 131, 132. John Hay heard a friend of Lee's say in 1863 that he had expressed utter contempt for secession right up to his departure; *Diaries and Letters*, 70. Other sources of prime value are Nicolay and Hay, IV, 97 ff.; Smith, *The Blair Family*, II; Simon Cameron in *Cong. Globe*, Feb. 19, 1868; and Montgomery Blair's letter to William Cullen Bryant, *National Intelligencer*, Aug. 9, 1866. Most lives of Lee are less than candid on his deep aversion to secession and to the intrigues of the cotton kingdom leaders.

42 Lee inherited his State loyalty. His father, "Light-Horse Harry," had exclaimed: "Virginia is my country. Her I will obey." S. F. Horn, *The Robert E. Lee Reader*, 15. But that George Washington would have been horrified by his exaltation of State above nation we may feel morally certain. It was perfectly true also that, as Edward Everett wrote, officers of the army and navy were servants of the government in a peculiar sense. Unlike civil officers, they were engaged and maintained for life, and a State government had no more right than the British government to discharge them from the service. Everett to Charlotte Wise, April 26, 1861; Everett Papers, MHS.

simply loyalty to the proud Old Dominion with which the Lees had for nearly two and a half centuries been associated. Nobody today dreams of questioning Lee's sincerity, devotion to duty, or nobility of mind. Winfield Scott had said, "He is true as steel, sir! true as steel!" But we may well question whether the man who thus preferred State to nation did not lack a certain largeness of view, did not respond to a parochial type of patriotism, and did not reveal an inadequate comprehension of the American destiny.[43]

Maury was actuated by the same motives that swayed Lee. Loving the Union, detesting secession, and hoping to the last for compromise, he believed that his primary allegiance lay with his birth State Virginia and his home State Tennessee. The line of duty, he had written on March 4, was clear: "Each one to follow his own State, if his State goes to war; if not, he may remain to help on the work of reunion." [44] Three days after Virginia seceded he left for Richmond to be commissioned, at fifty-five, commander in the Confederate navy.

Franklin Buchanan showed decidedly less principle. He too loved the Union, rejected the doctrine of secession, and condemned the course of the cotton kingdom. But he loved his native Maryland, where he had relatives and property, felt a horror of abolitionists, freesoilers, and coercionists, and as Gideon Welles observes, was much courted and caressed by Southern sympathizers. As head of the Washington navy yard he had moved in a society predominantly slaveholding. The day after the Baltimore riot he handed Welles his resignation, saying that he could never stand idly by while Maryland blood flowed in the streets of his native city; and he offered his services to Governor Hicks. When it became clear that Maryland was not going out, after all, he tried to withdraw his resignation, but Welles curtly informed him that it was too late. September found him a captain in the Confederate navy.[45]

These accessions greatly strengthened the Confederacy. Lee was worth an army in himself. Not all the officers from the Upper South, however, valued State above nation. In the most anxious April days a Virginia committee headed by the venerable Judge John Robertson called on Winfield Scott at his headquarters. The two men had been fellow students at William and Mary in 1806! But Scott instantly stopped his old college mate: "Friend Robertson, go no further! It is best that we part here, before you compel me to resent a mortal insult." [46] David Glasgow Farragut, a Tennessean by birth and for forty years

43 See Lossing's caustic personal comment in his *Civil War*, I, 421, 422; Washington correspondence in N. Y. *Tribune*, May 9, 1861.
44 D. F. M. Corbin, *Matthew Fontaine Maury*, 186.
45 Charles Lee Lewis, *Admiral Franklin Buchanan*, Ch. 12 ff.
46 Townsend, *Anecdotes of the Civil War*, 4, 5.

a Virginian by residence, kept his uniform, broke with his friends, and sent his family North.

So too, at Carlisle Barracks another Virginian, George H. Thomas, colonel of the Second Cavalry, maintained his allegiance. His sisters never forgave him. Philip St. George Cooke, colonel of the Second Dragoons, stayed in the Union Army with a vitriolic denunciation of the Catilines of the Deep South. The oligarchs of South Carolina, he wrote, had made themselves leaders in revolution and ruin; aided by demagogues and rebellious spirits, they had dragged or dragooned the reluctant voiceless people of six other States into line; and now they were lighting the torch of war for the whole South. "I owe Virginia little; my country much." [47] John Newton and John W. Davidson, both Virginians and both destined to be major-generals, stood fast by the Union.

For its navy the Confederacy gained less than for its army. Southern youth, prizing an army career, had displayed much less taste for the sea. Of all grades and branches, 322 naval officers resigned, some of them men of high ability. At the Annapolis Academy an assistant professor wrote Welles that he was sure of the loyalty of but five men out of forty officers and other gentlemen employed there. A great majority stuck with the flag, however, while the merchant marine offered a reservoir of experienced captains and mates on which the North, but not the South, could draw. [48]

[V]

Virginia had hardly seceded when military action began on its borders. Washington by late April was too strongly held to be attacked. But State troops, under Letcher's orders, at once moved against the valuable Harpers Ferry armory and arsenal, and the Gosport Navy Yard near Norfolk, with its dock, storehouses, and nine warships. As we have noted, the tiny force guarding Harpers Ferry fired the buildings and made a hurried retreat. At Gosport the *Cumberland*, the only ship in commission, was hastily towed to safety. All other property—the vessels *New York*, *Pennsylvania*, *Merrimac*, and others, with provisions, cordage, and machinery—was consigned to flames on the 20th in a spectacular conflagration. The most valuable vessel, the *Merrimac*, would have been extricated, for she had steam up ready to move, but that the cowardly commandant of the navy yard suddenly revoked his permission. While the North felt deep humiliation over these losses, Virginia disunionists thrilled with exultation.

The eight weeks following Sumter witnessed a defiant convergence of

47 See the long letter by Philip St. George Cooke dated June 6, 1861, in the *National Intelligencer*, June 22, 1861.
48 J. R. Soley, *The Blockade and the Cruisers*, 8.

Southern troops upon Virginia. When Jefferson Davis installed himself in Richmond, armies were assembling at Harpers Ferry, covering the Shenandoah Valley, under Joseph E. Johnston; at Manassas, covering the direct approach from Washington, under P. G. T. Beauregard; and at Norfolk, covering the peninsula between the James and York Rivers, under Benjamin Huger and John Magruder. The whole South hummed like a hive of angry bees. Government officers traveling to the new capital wrote that the country seemed one vast camp. The main distributing points were Richmond and Lynchburg, where troops arrived at the rate of 4000 a week. Every train came laden with soldiers and supplies. What was most needed was one directing mind, for until June the Virginia army and the Confederate forces had separate heads.[49]

Like the first Northern recruits, the Confederate levies were a motley host. Most of them were young, and many mere boys; all but a sprinkling of veterans of the Mexican and Indian wars were completely raw; and they were generally ill clad, ill armed, and ill disciplined. The gentlemanlike militia companies of Charleston, Richmond, and other cities presented the best appearance, and volunteers from the backwoods and poor-white areas made the worst. "To see from a distance a mass of these dirty, tobacco-chewing, drinking, swearing, smoking, fetid troops," wrote one observer, "almost leads one to think that the swamps of the Carolinas have become locomotive swamps, as it were, made flesh." The rush to arms had carried into the ranks a good many professional and businessmen who would tarry there but a short time. One company at Harpers Ferry had for captain a Mexican War officer, for first lieutenant a former member of Congress, for sergeant a judge, and for corporal a former United States consul, while the rank and file included lawyers, physicians, and planters.

Camp Lee on the outskirts of Richmond gathered regiments of weird variety, all in exuberant spirits and athirst for battle. The First Texas, flying the Lone Star flag, a unit later to grow into Hood's renowned Texas Brigade; the New Orleans Tigers under the pelican banner; a Zouave unit from Louisiana in scarlet trousers, blue shirts, and richly embroidered jackets; the Third Alabama, smartly uniformed, with a hundred body servants and a mountain of baggage; Georgia troops in green-trimmed butternut, and Mississippians under the magnolia ensign—all fraternized with Virginia lads. One regiment aroused special enthusiasm: the Maryland Guard, its members straggling in by various routes, but all in blue-and-orange Zouave uniforms. Richmond was soon alive with lank North Carolinians, longhaired Arkansans, Tennessee mountain-

49 Files of the Richmond *Whig* and the Baltimore *South;* Kirby-Smith Papers, Univ. of N. C. (he was stationed first at Lynchburg and then at Harpers Ferry); Richmond correspondence, N. Y. *Daily Tribune,* May 27.

eers with fringed leggings, and citified young men from St. Louis and Nashville. Many carried bowie knives or pistols, nearly all drank, and they made fatal duels and affrays commonplace.

While most officers were of superior character, the coarseness, ignorance. and rowdiness of many privates disheartened onlookers. Richmond citizens soon grew disillusioned. Ruffians as well as gallants had leaped to the flag. The New Orleans Tigers included brass-knuckled, dagger-carrying desperadoes, the scourings of the New Orleans levee; the Maryland Guard had some Baltimore plug-uglies; tough frontiersmen and drunken young planters swelled the host. As in Washington, so in Richmond saloons, brothels, and gambling dens began to flourish as never before. Robberies and assaults swamped the police. It was necessary to confine the Tigers to a separate camp. Richmond began to realize that if she was the heroine of a rich historical pageant, her house was no longer her own, and for better or worse all Virginia was tied to the Lower South.[50]

Officers in the Mississippi Valley, refusing to concede that Virginia would be the main seat of war, prepared to fight on a broad front. New Orleans built a breastwork of cotton bales along the levee, armed and manned 12 river steamboats, and by May 15 enlisted 2,000 men. The personnel of a Baton Rouge company indicated the popular character of the first response: 25 mechanics, 24 merchants and clerks, 11 farmers, 9 planters, 4 engineers, 1 lawyer, and 11 miscellaneous. More than a third of this company had been born abroad, and more than a seventh in the North. Gideon J. Pillow, hero of the Mexican War, was expected soon to lead an irresistible army of Valley boys to the rescue of Kentucky and the conquest of southern Illinois. By mid-May the Confederate forces, moving northward from Memphis to New Madrid and Belmont on the Missouri side of the Mississippi, were confronting some 5,000 Union troops at Cairo.

But the South, even more than the North, was fearfully lacking in equipment. Men cried "To arms!"—but there were no arms, no cannon, no uniforms, no medical supplies, beyond those hastily and scantily scraped together. Josiah Gorgas, a man of quiet resourcefulness amounting to genius, reported on May 7 that not quite 160,000 small arms of all kinds were available in the various public repositories within the seceded or seceding States. This included about 15,000 rifles and 120,000 muskets stored in various arsenals east of the Mississippi, a few thousand more in arsenals west of the Mississippi, and a small body of arms belonging to States and military organizations.[51] But many of

50 Bill, *Beleaguered City*, 149-152; Richmond correspondence in N. Y. *Tribune*, May 27, 1861; Bell I. Wiley, *Johnny Reb.*

51 William Watson, *Life in the Confederate Army*; Report to Chairman F. S. Bartow of the Cong. Committee on Military Affairs; Jefferson Davis, *North American Review*, vol. 149 (Oct., 1889), p. 476.

the arms were defective, many so antiquated that they were more dangerous to the holder than the foe, and 'many out of reach. At Harpers Ferry the Virginia troops seized some 5,000 muskets, and what was far more valuable, part of the machinery for making more. At the Norfolk navy yard about 500 cannon, good, poor, or totally unusable, were captured. Of ammunition the South was desperately short.

From every post rose the same complaints. "Words cannot express to you our deplorable condition here," wrote Kirby-Smith from Harpers Ferry May 29, "unprovided, unequipped, unsupplied with ammunition and provisions. . . . The utter confusion and ignorance presiding in the councils of the authorities that were is without a parallel." At Pensacola, W. H. Russell found ammunition on hand for only one day's firing, and poor stuff at that. From Corinth, Mississippi, Julian Alcorn addressed his wife in pathetic terms. "My position is most difficult and perplexing, chief in command of five thousand men, fresh volunteers, poorly clad, rather poorly fed; without a sufficient supply of anything." [52] Governor Letcher later extenuated his blunders in trying to supply the Virginia troops by pointing out that until the arrival of Lee in Richmond he had nobody of military capacity to advise him.

Soldiers from Norfolk to Galveston drilled with every variety of musket, shotgun, rifle, carbine, or fowling piece. They drilled in frock coats, swallowtails, jackets, and shirtsleeves. They guarded their powder, for it was too scarce for target practice. They sweetened their fare of corncake, fat bacon, and peas with molasses fetched in a jug from home. They lightened their evening hours with fiddle and accordion.[53] As the first fever for combat subsided, the impression grew that the great battle to which all looked, and which many believed would be final, was several months distant, for it would take that long to organize the armies South and North. Throughout June the general expectation was still for a short war. Even the perspicacious Judah P. Benjamin, changing his mind, now thought it would last only three or four months.[54] Of the coming horrors of battlefield mutilation, hospital agonies, and home-front exhaustion, few had the slightest premonition.

The wonder was that under these circumstances, amid hurry, guesswork, and reckless expedients, in an atmosphere of shortsighted optimism, so much

52 Kirby-Smith Papers, Univ. of N. C.; Julian Alcorn, June 6, 1861; Alcorn Papers, Univ. of N. C.

53 See, for example, F. G. DeFontaine's "Personal Reminiscences" in the magazine *Blue and Gray*, June, 1893. The drunkenness and rowdyism of many men and some officers mortified their fellows. "I cannot and will not stand such association," wrote W. C. Carrington, July 4, 1861, from Centreville; Brock Collection, HL.

54 An account of Benjamin's change of opinion is given by John Slidell in a letter of July 20, 1861, to S. L. M. Barlow; Barlow Papers. But Slidell, originally confident of a brief conflict, now anticipated a stubborn contest. The fact probably is that many men felt alternations of hope and despondency regarding the duration of the conflict.

was accomplished. Many local leaders showed appalling incapacity. "The imbecility and inaction of some of our State governments," Kirby-Smith wrote, "is and will be almost as disastrous as treachery." [55] Others, however, revealed astonishing resourcefulness.

Virginia was foremost in effective preparation. For this the energy of Letcher and quick organizing capacity of Lee were chiefly responsible. An estimate of the number of troops required for defense of the important points, 51,000 men, had been swiftly made. Quotas had been assigned various parts of the commonwealth, points of rendezvous established, and mustering officers appointed. By mid-June about 40,000 Virginians were in the field. Arms had been distributed: about 2,000 rifles and carbines and 41,650 muskets from eastern and central Virginia, with 13,000 pieces from Lexington, making 56,650 in all. Staff officers, including heads of the commissary, quartermaster, medical, and engineering departments, were acting with fair efficiency. Lee, pleased by the alacrity of the volunteering (except in western counties) was equally gratified by the promptness with which arrangements were made for instructing, equipping, and provisioning the forces. The State arsenal at Richmond had been rapidly expanded and the work of preparing munitions expedited. It had been found necessary to make carriages, caissons, battery wagons, and other items for the artillery, but Lee was able to report on June 15 that 115 guns for field service had already been provided, from which 20 light batteries of 4 guns each, with the requisite horses and harness, had been organized.

In addition, a Navy Department, theretofore unknown in Virginia, had been created. Defensive works had been built on the Elizabeth, James, York, and Rappahannock Rivers, naval batteries numbering some 320 pieces of heavy ordnance had been planted, and ammunition prepared—while some 120 pieces of heavy ordnance had been sent to other parts of the Confederacy. Between April 31 and June 14, Virginia expended for war $1,839,000, a sum which outstanding bills would bring to nearly $2,000,000. The stores and other property purchased, Letcher boasted, had been paid for as bought, and the credit of the State thus fully maintained.[56]

But other States, with weaker executives than Letcher, less gifted military leaders than Lee, and populations less ready for mobilization, lagged in the rear. Organization for war was much more difficult in Alabama, Mississippi, and Arkansas, while the threat of battle seemed less exigent. Nor was Virginia

55 J. H. Parks, *Kirby-Smith*, 127.
56 These facts are drawn from Letcher's message of June 17, 1861; Lee's long report to Letcher June 15; the letter of Captain S. Barron, of the Office of Naval Detail, June 10, 1861, to Letcher; the report of a committee of the Virginia Council June 3, 1861, on a conference with President Davis, and other documents in the Letcher Papers, Va. State Library.

herself without vital deficiencies. J. B. Jones in the War Department wrote June 18: "We have not enough ammunition to fight a battle. There are not percussion caps enough in our army for a serious skirmish." [57]

[VI]

Somewhat belatedly and reluctantly, Virginia transferred her forces to the Confederacy on June 8, 1861. Lee, who would have liked to retire to private life but who never failed to heed the voice of duty, became in some degree an acting assistant Secretary of War, and in part a deputy chief of what would later have been termed a general staff.[58] Beauregard, at Manassas, had an army of perhaps 20,000, which was steadily being reinforced. Joseph E. Johnston, under War Department orders, had taken command at Harpers Ferry, whence he was presently to fall back near Winchester to cover the Shenandoah Valley. "The want of ammunition," he explained in retreating, "has rendered me very timid." [59] Of the 8,000 rough-looking men he found at Harpers Ferry, 1,000 had not been armed, and he lacked artillery horses. Far across the commonwealth, where the hard-cropped tidewater plantations fronted the Atlantic, two experienced soldiers, Huger and Magruder, occupied positions on both sides of Hampton Roads. Huger had been brevetted thrice in the Mexican War for gallantry; in the same conflict T. J. Jackson, the future "Stonewall," had sought command under Magruder because he knew that if hard fighting was to be done, Magruder would be there. Other forces stood at Aquia Creek.

Most of Virginia, save for the western counties beyond the Allegheny wall, was ready to resist a Union onslaught. Along the Mississippi, at Memphis, at Island No. 10, at points just below the Kentucky-Tennessee line, at New Madrid and other Missouri points, forces of the Confederacy were gathering in formidable numbers. Hope rose high in Southern breasts that Missouri and Kentucky might soon be detached to strengthen them. Thus June of 1861 might be called the honeymoon month of the Confederacy. Eleven States seemed solidly inside it. It now held an imperial domain stretching from the Chesapeake to the Rio Grande, from the Georgia sea islands to the Indian Territory and even the far Southwest, from the frontier settlements of Arkansas to the oldest of American buildings in St. Augustine. Everywhere parade grounds echoed to the grounding of muskets and the bark of drill sergeants.

57 *Diary of a Rebel War Clerk*, I.
58 Freeman, *Lee*, I, 515 ff.
59 O. R. I, ii, 934. Johnston reached Harpers Ferry as a brigadier-general in the Confederate service, a post he accepted in preference to that of major-general in the army of Virginia. He found T. J. Jackson there, and Jackson, after insisting on seeing documentary proof of Johnston's seniority in rank, gave him cordial support. Freeman, *Lee*, I, 515, 516.

Troop trains still moved forward past cheering towns, where women thrust knapsacks, flowers, and dainties upon the soldiers. As bands blared, ardent youths remembered that theirs was the race of Agincourt, Yorktown, and Waterloo, and pulses leaped at the thought of new victories. Swords were bright, uniforms were fresh, limbs were unwearied. Despite all the confusion, the inadequacies, the clash of rival ambitions, the future looked roseate; beyond immediate sacrifice lay independence, and beyond that a resplendent national future.

Yet amid the bugles and roses, the pomp and parade, thousands watched what was happening with perturbation and anguish. For every Southerner who cheered, another was torn by regret and anxiety.

The provost-marshal at Cairo arrested a youth of seventeen, obviously guileless and of gentle breeding, as a spy. It turned out that the lad was from Pittsburgh, had served three months with the Twelfth Pennsylvania Volunteers, and had been honorably discharged. On the entreaty of his heartbroken mother he was trying to slip south, braving death to find a brother just wounded in Jeff Thompson's Confederate band.[60] A brothers' war indeed!—as a thousand instances proved; a war sometimes of father against son. It is no wonder that a citizen of Memphis wrote across the hostile lines to Horatio King in Washington to express his grief at what was going on. "It is a magnificent day, the sky is without a cloud, the air perfectly charming it is so bland, and indeed the city is as quiet as a sabbath in the country; but my God, what a contrast does the physical aspect of things present to the state of the country. I never have seen any excitement that approached the present in intensity. Men's passions seem to be surging and rolling like the billows of a storm-lashed ocean. It is terrible, terrible! Where is it to end?" [61] And a million women felt, at least intermittently, like John Esten Cooke's niece Nancie, who poured out her heart to that cultivated Virginia author:

"When will this frightful time be over? Sometimes I think I have gotten used to it, and then again when I am by myself, the thought that all I love best are in such constant danger almost drives me wild." [62]

60 This episode is related in a communication of the provost-marshal at Cairo to Lincoln's friend Gen. John A. McClernand, Oct. 26, 1861; McClernand Papers, Ill. State Hist. Lib. The boy's name was Charles Shaler.
61 J. W. Merriam of Memphis, April 21, 1861, to King; King Papers, LC.
62 Nancie Cooke, June 8, 1861, Cooke Papers, Duke Univ.

6

Struggle for the Western Border

IT WOULD BE erroneous to suppose that in the tense days after mid-April all eyes were bent on Washington, Montgomery, and Richmond. Events in the Mississippi Valley crowded as thickly on each other, and were of equal import to the nation. The Northwest had a body of determined governors—among others Richard Yates of Illinois, who promptly called out 6000 volunteers, took military possession of Cairo, and inspired the legislature to appropriate $3,500,000 for war; Oliver P. Morton of Indiana, who believed that the conflict should be made "instant and terrible"; and Samuel J. Kirkwood of Iowa, who borrowed from his friends to help equip the first levies. They looked southward to a closely balanced border.

Nobody had ever accused the Kentuckians and Missourians of a want of fighting temper. The men who had built palisades against the Shawnees with Harrod, hewed farms from the forest with Boone, and marched to Chihuahua with Doniphan, had bequeathed their children a readiness to face any foe. In the convulsion of 1861, however, the overwhelming desire of the borderland was to remain neutral. Their attitude suggested the nervousness of the bystander who sees that he may suffer more from a quarrel than either participant; but the paramount fact was that they preferred moderation, for in the main they detested as equally repugnant the idea of secession and the idea of abolition. The Bell-Everett platform of the Union, Constitution, and compromise had precisely expressed majority sentiment. Here, as in Maryland, the spring wrote a record of their all but frantic effort to stay out of a conflict which they thought insane.

It is also the record of strenuous rival efforts by the Union and the Confederacy to win them to active collaboration. Their assistance might turn the scale. In this contest, which side would blunder least? If Lincoln emphasized freesoil too much and Union too little, he would certainly fail. If Jefferson Davis pressed too hard and stressed ties of blood and institutions too arrogantly, *he* would fail. The struggle for the border, with its general solidarity of outlook, its mingled devotion to State Rights and to the nation, and its mixed

economic interests, demanded patience, diplomacy, and psychological understanding as much as the exertion of force.

[I]

Of cardinal importance to the salvation of the Union was Missouri, by far
the richest and strongest trans-Mississippi State. Its population was that of
Massachusetts—each had about 1,200,000. It held one of the principal cities of
the nation, St. Louis, with perhaps 175,000 people, and with factories, warehouses, mercantile establishments, influential newspapers, river shipping, and
a well-stocked arsenal. If the secessionists could carry Missouri into the Confederacy, they might cut off Kansas, fan smoldering disloyalty in southern
Illinois, and double the danger of the North's losing precariously-poised
Kentucky.

When Sumter fell, the position of Missouri was doubtful. In the recent
Presidential election Douglas and Bell had run neck and neck, Douglas leading
by fewer than 500 votes. Both had far outstripped Breckinridge. If most of
the aggregate Douglas, Bell, and Lincoln vote were considered a vote for the
Union, the people stood about four to one against secession. Everyone knew
the ardent attachment of the large German population in and near St. Louis
to the Union; everyone knew, too, how much the prestige of the Blair family
and the memory of the firm nationalism of Thomas Hart Benton counted.

But Union men who hoped that no attempt would be made to lead the State
astray soon learned their error. The Missouri *Republican*, the oldest and long
the ablest journal in the area, closely connected with the strongest men and
richest interests of St. Louis, throughout the campaign had exerted its influence in favor of the Union. Nobody had supposed it would waver in its
adherence to the principles of Webster and Clay. Suddenly, however, on
December 31, 1860, it had carried an editorial addressed to the legislature
then just assembling which fell upon Union men like a thunderclap. Northern
wrongs to the South, it declared, demanded redress. The legislature should
call a convention of all the slave States in Baltimore, and meanwhile assemble
a State convention to consider such constitutional amendments as Congress
might submit. If no remedy for the Southern grievances was attained before
March 4, Missouri should then secede.

Union men had rubbed their eyes as they read. Their standard bearer had
deserted to the enemy. "From that hour," writes one of the leaders, Charles D.
Drake, "the secession conflict raged in Missouri as I believe it never would
have raged if that paper had kept on the track it trod before." This is an overstatement, for the conflict was irrepressible. Nevertheless, the stand taken by

the journal did encourage the proslavery and pro-Southern elements, while it discouraged the Yankee freesoilers, liberty-loving Germans, and other groups who had organized as Wide-Awakes for Lincoln. Claiborne Jackson, the proslavery politician who had helped overthrow Benton and who had been elected governor as a Douglas Democrat, now rallied his followers as he hoisted a secessionist standard.

"Probably not one member of either house had, before the people, been an avowed disunionist," adds Drake; "but when that body assembled, it soon appeared that a majority of men in each house was made up of men of that stripe, who were ready to follow Claiborne Jackson's traitorous course." The waters had begun to boil like the Mississippi in flood.[1]

The legislature had given disunionists their cry, "No coercion!" by passing on February 21 a reply to the coercionist resolutions of Ohio and New York: "It is the opinion of the General Assembly that the people of Missouri will instantly rally on the side of their Southern brethren, to resist the invaders at all hazards and to the last extremity." Throughout February a growing bitterness of feeling was manifest on both sides, which Lincoln's inauguration intensified. Claiborne Jackson, more and more ardent in the secessionist cause, had established a confidential correspondence with Confederate leaders. He and his friends had been hopeful that the State convention which, by legislative decree, was elected on February 18 to consider Federal relations, would have a secessionist character. But by a majority of about 80,000 the State pronounced against disunion, choosing not a single secessionist delegate to the convention. After a committee had made a moderate, well reasoned report, the convention voted 89 to 1 that Missouri had no adequate cause for dissolving her connection with the Union. Before March closed, both the legislature and convention adjourned, leaving the State apparently committed to the Union and to peace. Only the extremists who rallied about Claiborne Jackson at one pole and Nathaniel Lyon and Frank Blair at the other demanded belligerent policies.

Impromptu military units long before the inauguration had been drilling on both sides. Along the Missouri River secessionists organized companies; in St. Louis, Unionists formed a strong home guard from the Wide-Awakes. In this situation, the Federal arsenal was the natural object of plots and counterplots. The secessionists hoped that when Washington took decisive action and war began, they could seize the arms and equip their forces to carry Missouri into the Confederacy. Had not the convention voted 89 to 6 in favor of evacuating national troops from Southern forts? The arsenal held enough war materials to

1 Drake's MS autobiography, Mo. State Hist. Soc., is an enlightening document. See also Eugene M. Violette, *A History of Missouri*; Lucy L. Tasher. "The Mo. Democrat and the Civil War," *Mo. Hist. Review*, XXXI, 1937, pp. 402-419

turn the balance in Missouri and perhaps to help the secessionists in Kentucky.

Late in Buchanan's term the national government had taken some steps to protect the arsenal, increasing the garrison to more than 400, with the able, moderate, and unquestionably loyal Major Peter V. Hagner in command. Most Federal officers thought the position safe. Not so Captain Nathaniel S. Lyon, a West Pointer of Connecticut origin and Mexican War experience who was assigned to the arsenal early in February. This thin, sandy-haired, red-bearded little man, his blue eyes full of fire, had learned on the Kansas border to hate proslavery men, and was determined to take every precaution against loss of the post. He had wanted the command himself. Impetuous and explosive, he possessed highly fanatical traits.[2] He assailed the appointment of Hagner as sordid favoritism on the part of General W. S. Harney, head of the Department, declared that Hagner's deliberation in strengthening the arsenal showed "imbecility or damned villainy," and indicted Lincoln himself as lacking resolution to deal with treason. Backed by Frank P. Blair, Jr., he obtained command of the arsenal troops in the middle of March, while Hagner kept control of the ordnance stores; and he gave notice that if Hagner in an emergency opposed the marshaling of home-guard troops to defend the place, he would pitch him into the river.

The taking of Sumter gave the expected impulse to the secessionist movement. Governor Jackson met the President's call for troops with an insulting rebuff. Missourians in general, declared the St. Louis *Republican*, "denounce and defy the action of Mr. Lincoln." The recent election of D. G. Taylor, a wobbly anti-coercionist, as mayor, seemed to enhance the opportunities of the pro-Southern elements for seizing the city and State.

Hungry for the 60,000 muskets, the 90,000 pounds of powder, the 1,500,000 ball cartridges, and the field guns lying in the arsenal, the secessionist legislators bethought themselves of a plan for paralyzing their opponents and making the most of their own strength. They passed a law placing the entire St. Louis police force, the local militia, and the sheriff under four commissioners, to be named by the governor and to sit with the mayor. This meant that Claiborne Jackson could manipulate the police, control the disloyal companies, and perhaps paralyze the loyal home guard. As police commissioners, Jackson promptly appointed three virulent secessionists and one anti-coercionist, who countenanced the dressing of the city with Confederate flags. What Southern sympathizers might do in St. Louis had just been illustrated at Liberty, near Kansas City, where a small arsenal had been seized and the arms distributed in seditious Clay County.

---

2 The eulogistic tone of Ashbel Woodward, *Gen. Nathaniel Lyon*, is countered by the estimate in L. U. Reavis, *Gen. William Selby Harney*.

To Union men—to the incandescent Lyon, to the tall, lithe, hard-hitting, hard-drinking Frank Blair, at forty-one the youngest of the Blair clan and the idol of Missouri Republicans, to James O. Broadhead, a prominent lawyer, it seemed time to strike. To lose the arsenal, standing on low ground near the river and open to attack by water and land, would be to lose everything. Lyon by secret messengers induced Governor Yates of Illinois to put militia, under Presidential orders, on the steamboat *City of Alton.* On the night of April 25 the boat swiftly crossed the river, the militia swarmed ashore, and the arsenal gates were thrown open. Lyon had everything in readiness; 21,000 muskets, 500 rifle carbines, artillery, and large quantities of cartridges were hurried on board. Taken by the steamboat to Alton, where citizens joyously unloaded them, they at once went by rail to Springfield. "The secessionists are euchred," proclaimed the Union men.[3]

[II]

Even yet the situation seemed precarious. Lyon, fortifying the arsenal grounds, urged the enlistment of loyal men and formation of more home guards. Blair was elected colonel of a regiment which occupied Jefferson Barracks, about ten miles from the city. But most of the aristocratic older families of St. Louis sympathized with the South, a turbulent riverfront element might at any moment get out of hand, and much of the interior passionately hoped for Confederate success. In Lexington on the Missouri River, secessionists broke up a Union meeting. Business in Kansas City and St. Louis was half prostrate, thousands were out of work, and many prudent citizens were moving away. Claiborne Jackson actually had little power, but that little he used to make trouble. He called a special session of the legislature for May 3 to consider measures for enabling Missouri to defend herself, and he opened it with a message in which he threw himself squarely behind the Confederacy. He also gave orders, as was his legal right, for the regular annual brief militia encampments. "Our interests and sympathies are identical with those of the slaveholding States," he proclaimed, "and necessarily unite our destinies with theirs." [4] Such sentiments angered the loyal half of the State, which feared that the legislature might really take some provocative step.

3 Carr, *Missouri,* 293 ff., Galusha Anderson, *Border City,* 68 ff., Drake, MS Autobiography, and R. J. Rombauer, *The Union Cause in St. Louis,* 1861, cover the subject in detail. St. Louis contained a subtreasury with Federal money. Blair had led in converting the Wide-Awakes into a home guard military organization under a Committee of Safety; James Peckham, *Lyon and Missouri in 1861.*

4 John McElroy, *The Struggle for Missouri;* Galusha Anderson, *Border City;* T. L. Sneed, *The Fight for Missouri;* W. B. Stevens, *Centennial History of Missouri,* I; Drake, MS Autobiography.

And fanaticism evoked counter-fanaticism. General D. M. Frost, commander of the State militia, at the beginning of May formed a camp of about 700 men in Lindell's Grove on the western margin of St. Louis. He and many of his soldiers stood for armed neutrality. They were too weak, too divided in sentiment, too open in their movements, to menace the city or the now depleted arsenal. Frost, a West Point graduate and responsible man, had in fact offered to assist the Federal commanders in making certain of full national control of government property; an offer perhaps insincere, but worth receiving tolerantly. The governor, who nevertheless hoped that Camp Jackson, as it was called, might eventually be used to take the arsenal, saw to it that the men got arms and ammunition, partly smuggled from Federal sources. On May 8 a steamer from New Orleans brought in cannon and munitions, seized at the Baton Rouge arsenal, labeled "marble" and "ale." The governor had just written Confederate friends that he was confident the State would secede along with Kentucky and Tennessee. "They are all bound to go out and should go out together if possible," he declared, stating that this might be within a month. "Missouri can put in the field today 20,000 men, better armed than our fathers were, who won our independence." [5]

Camp Jackson certainly needed watching, and could not safely be allowed to grow. But its situation, commanded by surrounding hills, was weak; its force was puny compared with the 10,000 well-armed Union troops and loyal volunteers hard by; and all its drills were open to the public. General Harney, a loyal veteran of the Seminole and Mexican Wars, and a man who knew Missouri well, believed that peace could safely be preserved. Yet Lyon, who was new to the State, for he had arrived in February, let his hatred of slavery and puritanical zealotry overmaster him; he rushed into inflammatory action just when calmness was needed.

In his eyes, according to his biographer, Camp Jackson was a fearful menace. Announcements that it would break up on or about May 10 might be only a dark stratagem; and if it did break up, the men might go home to enlist in secessionist units. Moreover, reading of the Baltimore riot, Ben Butler's seizure of the Annapolis railroad, and the Northern mobilization, Lyon decided that it was time to strike a hard blow at secession in Missouri and thus teach traitors their place. The applause which the Northwest had given his raid on the arsenal encouraged him. According to a dramatic but dubious story, he had toured the camp disguised as the venerable mother-in-law of Frank Blair, peering at the militiamen and their piled arms through a black veil as his wheelchair was pushed down the alleyways, and noting indignantly that one

5 Full text of letter in *Loyal Legion Papers, Missouri Commandery*, I, 23–25. Cf. Smith, *Borderland*, 230 ff.

company street was called "Davis," and another "Beauregard." Enlisting the support of Blair and three other members of the committee of safety—though two members objected that a Federal marshal might easily replevin the Baton Rouge arms—Lyon prepared to attack the camp. He would demolish this nest of rebels—he would show hesitant neutrals which side to choose! On the 10th he moved several thousand troops about the camp, summoned its officers to surrender, and made the militia prisoners.[6]

This was reckless enough. Still more injudicious was Lyon's decision not to parole the disarmed militia, but to march them into St. Louis as a spectacle. Southern sympathizers had poured into the streets, excited and resentful. As they saw the dejected prisoners file past under guard of Yankee and German volunteers, passions broke loose; they hurled first gibes, then stones; and at a point where a unit called Die Schwarze Guard by friends and Dutch Black-guards by enemies had halted, a collision occurred. Lyon's forces began firing indiscriminately, twenty-eight persons were killed or mortally wounded, scores were injured, and the city was thrown into an uproar.

This was the blackest day in all St. Louis' history. Fear and anger rose on both sides to the fever point. Next day a new affray cost six lives. The secessionists raged against Lyon, German newspapers, and the home guard; loyal citizens kept a sullen silence. Inevitably, some Union men in Missouri and many readers of brief and distorted accounts of the affair in the Northern press hailed Lyon as a hero whose resolute action had saved the State. That legend, popularized in history and fiction, has survived.[7] But the truth is that Lyon and Frank Blair, Jr., both rash, headstrong, and excitable, had dealt an unnecessary stroke, aroused emotions better left quiescent, and in one day done far more harm to the Union cause and the best interests of Missouri than Frost and Claiborne Jackson, left alone, could have accomplished in a month. Their action, under the excitement of the time, is understandable, but it was unwise.

From this moment Missouri was given over to four years of violence and a cruel intestine war. As rumors spread that German volunteers were threatening to burn the city, a thousand people fled town in a single afternoon. Some streets were left entirely deserted. Not until General Harney, returning to headquarters, published a reassuring proclamation, was calm partly restored. While disloyal elements were only partly cowed in the city, the Missouri River

6 General Harney, who as departmental commander would certainly have restrained Lyon, was temporarily absent from the area; in fact, Lyon deliberately took advantage of his absence. Frost, apprised of the coming attack, wrote Lyon declaring he had no disloyal designs, and again offering to help preserve peace and order in the area. O. R. I, iii, 7–8.

7 See the accounts in the *Annual Cyclopaedia*, 1861, pp. 660, 661; in John Fiske, *The Mississippi Valley in the Civil War* (highly misleading); in Winston Churchill, *The Crisis;* and in Nicolay and Hay, IV, 198 ff.

belt was vibrant with Southern feeling. Reports reached many towns that German troops and antislavery fanatics were butchering men, women, and children. Some communities rose en masse, determined to arm themselves with pitchforks and scythes, if nothing better, march on St. Louis, and stamp out the violence. Only later reports and the news of Harney's judicious measures partially allayed the anger. That sagacious commander ordered all the German volunteers out of the city, replacing them by United States regulars; kept riotous groups off the streets; closed political meetings; punished crime; and searched the town for arms, confiscating more than a thousand rifled muskets and two small cannon. Most of the citizens who had fled soon returned.[8]

However, Harney could not undo the harm wrought by Lyon and Blair; for the moment the news of the St. Louis bloodshed reached Jefferson City, full civil war in the State lay just ahead. A scene of angry pandemonium in the legislature gave way to determined action. The governor's bill to arm the State on the Confederate side had till then slept; now it was revived, passed with instant speed, and sent to Claiborne Jackson to be signed. Cooperation with the Indians was authorized. The members had hardly gone to their lodgings to sleep when a telegram that Lyon and 2,000 men were marching to seize the governor and legislature roused the town. Bells were rung, the legislature was convened in midnight session, and new measures were passed to arm the State.[9] In the next five days the legislature paid every cent in the treasury into the military fund, authorized Jackson to borrow another million to equip troops, and empowered him to organize the military forces, seize the railroads and telegraphs, lease a foundry at Boonville to manufacture arms, and do anything else needful.

The governor acted with energy to throw Missouri on the Confederate side. Secessionists poured into Jefferson City and other mustering points. As major-general in command Jackson appointed Sterling Price, a highminded man of Virginia birth who had been colonel in the Mexican War, Congressman, a courageous Democratic governor, and president of the recent convention. He was a conditional Unionist until the aggressive acts of Lyon and Blair converted him to secession. Another former governor, J. S. Marmaduke, who had also been a conditional Unionist, went into the State forces. Secessionist forces seemed about to dominate most of the State outside St. Louis. Some of them, collecting in irregular bands which drove Union men from their homes, inaugurated the guerrilla activities which in time seemed likely to make half of

8 St. Louis correspondence dated May 13 in N. Y. *Tribune*, May 14, 1861. The Columbia (Mo.) *Statesman*, April–June 1861, throws valuable light on events from the Union standpoint. On March 28, 1862, the *Statesman* published revealing letters by Claiborne Jackson written during the crisis.

9 Peckham, *op. cit.*; W. F. Switzler, *Illustrated History of Missouri*, 315.

Missouri a desert.[10] On the Confederate side all was unity and determination.

One result of the reckless Blair-Lyon policy, on the other hand, was to divide the Union supporters. General Harney did his utmost to restore confidence in moderate policies. He of course never wavered in his allegiance to the Union cause. Missouri must remain loyal, he declared; he would maintain the national authority wherever his arm could reach; and he would never tolerate the recent legislative enactments, the fruit of needless excitement. Though he endorsed Lyon's coup (a necessary act, despite his private doubts), he spoke in what he called "tranquillizing" terms, and asked authority to enlist an Irish regiment to mollify the general feeling against Federal forces which were composed almost entirely of Germans. Had it been possible, he would have dismissed the home guards. Blair and Lyon watched this policy with hostility.[11]

What was more serious, Blair and Harney soon clashed on the question of a truce. In his sagacious way, the veteran general began negotiations with Price, asking him to suspend the recent military act. A meeting followed, at which the two agreed on a pacific manifesto (May 21). Both, they said, were intent on "restoring peace and good order," and relied on the Federal and State governments to effect this. Price would use all his State forces to maintain order; Harney would make no military movements likely to create excitement or jealousy. Thus was proclaimed an armed truce like that which Lincoln was countenancing in Kentucky, a sensible procedure. On May 29, Harney reported that the State was gradually being pacified, and this was true.[12]

Lyon and Blair, however, outraged by Harney's course, did their utmost to bring it into discredit. During May, Blair began pulling wires in Washington for Harney's removal and the appointment of Lyon in his stead. The peppery soldier from Connecticut reported to Washington on June 3 his belief that a Confederate movement into northwestern Arkansas was being coordinated with mysterious and industrious shifts of Price's forces toward southwestern Missouri. The two collected and made the most of stories of secessionist outrages on Unionist farmers and villagers, some true, some untrue.

Inevitably, conservative Union men aligned themselves behind Harney, while radicals took the side of Blair. Among the moderates was Ethan Allen Hitchcock, another veteran soldier of honorable record, who later declared that he had drafted the Price-Harney agreement. Among the radicals was the editor of the Missouri *Democrat*, the most influential Republican journal in the

10 Smith, *Borderland*, 241, states: "Much of the later bitterness with which guerrilla warfare was carried on in Missouri was probably due to the feelings engendered by the occurrences at Camp Jackson."
11 Harney's course may be followed in his letters to the War Department, O. R. I, iii, 373 ff.
12 O. R. I, iii, 375–382.

State. As Blair made it clear that he must have Harney's head on a platter, the schism extended to the Cabinet in Washington. Montgomery Blair exerted himself fiercely on the side of the brother he hoped one day to see in the White House. Attorney-General Bates took Harney's side, but without energy. It became plain, though Lincoln hesitated, that the general's tenure was coming to a close.[13]

The Blairs had a motto of rule or ruin—of fighting to a finish. With clan spirit, they fought always for each other. It is evident that Frank Blair intended to be the Missouri Warwick, dominating the State politically and militarily. Lincoln was unwilling to give Lyon the command, declaring that he seemed too rash. Finally, however, he yielded to the pressure and sent Frank Blair an order for Harney's removal, to be used only if an emergency arose which justified such extreme action. The day after sending it, overcome by doubts of its propriety, he followed it with another letter, in which he impressed upon Blair that it was to be delivered only if Blair thought this "indispensable." Of course Blair did think so. In characteristically ruthless fashion, on May 31 he gave the humiliated Harney the order for dismissal.

Now the path was open for disrupting the truce. On June 11, at a long-famous conference in the Planters' House in St. Louis, Blair and Lyon faced Price across a table. The Covenanter and the Ironside met the Cavalier. They grimly laid down demands that Price, who had long detested Blair, could not meet. In fact, they declared they would yield not one inch for the sake of State concord. Price strode out to rally his forces, and to begin open war.

In thus carrying Missouri into full civil war before mid-June, Blair and Lyon acted according to their honest conviction and best lights, but with rash arrogance. In great part, the horrors and losses from which this unhappiest of States was to suffer were traceable to their precipitate, intolerant course. Born fighters both, they preferred mortal conflict to a patient reliance on compromise and delay. Although the situation was full of danger, the preponderant evidence indicates that Harney was right in believing that the loyal Missourians needed only time and tranquillity to consolidate their position in the Union. As he said, Union men outnumbered secession men in the interior of the State two to one; in St. Louis, which had nearly one-sixth the population of the State, Union sentiment was not only ascendant, but was bulwarked by strong Federal forces; and Missouri was half surrounded by Kansas, Iowa, and Illinois, all belligerently devoted to the Union. The truce which Harney had made with Price offered more advantages to the North than the

13 Smith, *Blair Family in Politics*, II, Ch. 29; Snead, *Fight for Missouri*, 100 ff.; E. A. Hitchcock, *Fifty Years in Camp and Field*, 431. Nicolay and Hay, IV, 217 ff., take the side of the Blairs, for Lincoln accepted that side; but Lincoln did not yet know how selfishly contriving the Blairs often were.

South, for every day of peace fortified loyal sentiment. It is clear that Price, an honorable conditional-Union man anxious to see difficulties composed, was doing all that he could to restore order. He had kept his promise of dismissing his force.

Blair, however, insisted on having his way. He had exceeded the authority which Lincoln entrusted to him in giving Harney his dismissal, for that act was by no means indispensable to meet an emergency, as Lincoln had stipulated. Lyon was still more insistent on taking his own course. This Yankee captain was as intemperate in speech as in action. "Rather than concede to the State of Missouri for one single instant the right to dictate to my Government in any matter however unimportant," he had told Price, "I would see you . . . and every man, woman, and child in the State dead and buried. This means war." [14]

Four days after the conference in the Planters' Hotel, fighting commenced at Lexington. It was certain that the Union forces could in time conquer the State. But it was also certain that their conquest would leave it seething with hatreds, divided county by county, even farm by farm, by the bitterest antagonisms, and racked with internecine war. Of all border States, we repeat, Missouri was destined to suffer most, and her suffering was to a great extent the work of three men: the fire-eating Claiborne Jackson, the fanatical Lyon, and the ambitious Frank Blair. Her strength was to fall mainly on the Union side, but it was nothing like the strength she might have exerted.

[III]

In Kentucky, Union feeling up to the time of Lincoln's inauguration had been strong. The lifelong teachings of Henry Clay still swayed many hearts. Kentucky had been the first-born child of the Union, her sons had been nationalists since the War of 1812, and most of her river counties looked to Cincinnati and Pittsburgh as their natural gateways. Just before the Presidential election the Kentucky and Ohio legislators had held a fraternal gathering at Columbus, Ohio. John Bell's Constitutional Union Party had carried the State. Many slaveholders believed that the only safety for the peculiar institution, which must wither if exposed to the chill blasts of world opinion, lay in the Union. Even Paducah, closely connected by trade with the Gulf States and the center of a populous slaveholding district, kept a Unionist majority.

To be sure, Kentuckians were so intimately bound by blood, culture, and institutions with Virginia and North Carolina, which had mainly peopled the State, that the thought of war with the South was abhorrent. If majority

14 Quoted by Snead, 199, 200; he was present. See also Smith, *Borderland*, 253. Lyon's aide quotes him in only a slightly less bloody-tongued utterance; Peckham, 248.

sentiment was firmly against secession, it was just as strongly against coercion of the secessionists.[15] But in the recent election the vote for Bell, Douglas, and Lincoln had totaled 93,073 as against 53,143 for Breckinridge. Kentuckians had enthusiastically supported Crittenden's proposals for compromise, as an alternative; many looked favorably on Governor Beriah Magoffin's plan for guaranteeing slavery within the States, enforcing the return of fugitives, and drawing a new territorial line along the 37th parallel.

The State had its share of able men. Leslie Combs, a veteran of the War of 1812, a Whig leader who had once been Clay's ablest lieutenant at the State capital, and an inspiring speaker, was as stanch in his devotion to the nation as the conscientious, universally respected John J. Crittenden. James Guthrie, first citizen of Louisville and the ablest banker and railroad executive of the region, was destined to bring both his influence and his invaluable Louisville & Nashville Railroad to the Union cause. Kentucky, in contrast with her slave neighbor up the river, was happy in having such a trio to battle the Southern sympathizers Breckinridge and Magoffin.

It was an agonizing hour for the fair land of bluegrass and rhododendron. Foreseeing that war might soon roll along the Ohio and Cumberland, that family might fight against family, that armies from the northern and eastern counties might battle against armies from the southern and western, the best leaders had looked to compromise, and, if that failed, to neutrality.[16] Combs had denounced the "Destructionists"—the men North and South who used every device to create bitterness. By shrewd action, the moderates had managed to keep control of the situation. Early in January the Bell-Everett chieftains, meeting in Louisville, had established a Union State Central Committee to organize their followers behind a moderate Unionist program, and thus had done much to keep in hand the special legislative session which met January 17.[17] Possibly Breckinridge hoped that this body would "precipitate"

15 The Frankfort *Commonwealth* and Lexington *Observer and Reporter*, both Union Journals, steadily inveighed in March and April, 1861, against secession. The former attacked (April 12) the "trickery and cunning of the conspirators" of the Deep South ever since they had disrupted the Democratic convention in Charleston.

16 Many Kentuckians were worried about navigation rights on the Mississippi. C. F. Burnham, a member of the legislature, wrote James S. Rollins of Missouri March 15, 1861: "We will denounce the piratical laws of the Southern Congress on the obstruction of the navigation of the Mississippi and the imposing of tariff duties on shipping on that stream. We will take nothing from them as a concession, we *demand* its free navigation as a *right* which must never be interfered with." Rollins Papers, Mo. Hist. Soc.

17 An unsigned memorandum to Lincoln, dated April 1, 1861, written probably by Green Adams, is in the R. T. L. Papers. "In Kentucky the Union party has a majority of about 40,000," it states. "They are faithful and loyal to the general government and the Constitution, anxious for its supremacy being maintained and above all are anxious for Peace. But the minority, and it is a dangerous minority, are open or disguised disunionists according to locality."

the State into secession. If so, he was foiled. "Thank God," Combs wrote later, "there were found loyal and patriotic Democrats who preferred principle to party—their country to a selfish and arrogant faction—and they united with us to save the Union." [18]

The moderates had no difficulty in defeating Governor Magoffin's scheme for a convention to consider the secession issue. Instead, the legislators demanded that the South halt its secession movement, and that the North give up all idea of coercion. They also invited the other States to join in a national convention. To Breckinridge, who delivered a speech declaring that the Union could not be restored, and that Kentucky should mediate for continued peace between the two independent confederacies, they listened coldly.

When Sumter fell, the passionate anxiety of the people to keep their State from becoming a battleground for contending armies found immediate expression. Governor Magoffin telegraphed Lincoln that Kentucky would furnish no troops "for the wicked purpose of subduing her sister Southern States," but a week later refused a similar call for men from Jefferson Davis. The State Union Committee declared that Kentucky could tie herself neither to the chariot wheels of the Lincoln Administration nor the Gulf State wagon, and should repel any invasion of her sacred soil. Guthrie told a Louisville meeting that it would be equally wrong to supply militia for the national government or to raise volunteers for the Confederacy. To be sure, plenty of excited and bellicose partisans could be found, those for the Union chiefly in the cities and eastern Kentucky, those for the cotton kingdom in the wealthier agricultural districts. The great majority, however, with a fervor which in retrospect appears pathetically sincere, hoped to avoid setting brother against brother. They had a premonition of the terrible moment when at Missionary Ridge the Fourth Kentucky, U.S.A., lined up in full view of the Fourth Kentucky, C.S.A., and kinsmen stared down each others' muzzles.

Let the war, wrote one editor, the brilliant George D. Prentice of the Louisville *Journal*, find the Transylvania land calm in armed neutrality, an asylum for victims of the carnage, "a sublime example to her erring sisters." Let her, wrote a poet, rise serene above strife:

Orbed in order, crowned with olives, there invoking peace, she stands. . . .

Magoffin by proclamation warned both the Federal and Confederate governments not to encroach on Kentucky soil, and forbade citizens to make any hostile demonstrations against either side. While he leaned strongly to the secessionist position and continued to urge a State convention, Union strength

18 Combs in N. Y. *Tribune*, May 9, 1861; letter dated Lexington, Ky., April 29. For an excellent general account of events see E. M. Coulter, *The Civil War and Readjustment in Kentucky*.

easily sufficed to hold him in check. The governor momentarily believed that he might persuade Ohio, Tennessee, Indiana, and Missouri to join Kentucky in a movement for mediation. Leaders of Tennessee and Missouri, when he opened negotiations, seemed responsive, but Governors Morton and Dennison north of the Ohio returned emphatic negatives.[19]

Inevitably, Magoffin seemed to the leaders both in Washington and Richmond to be playing a double part. For a time after Sumter, he secretly let Confederate recruiting agents operate in Kentucky; then, conscious of the danger of provoking stern Federal action, he drew back. By April 24, General Gideon J. Pillow was warning the Confederate War Office that the governor, surrounded by Black Republicans, was undependable. "I condemn and utterly abhor his neutral policy, or rather his alliance with Lincoln; but yet I am satisfied that he will ultimately break the shackles with which he is now manacled." [20] Lincoln's informants were equally certain that Magoffin was allied with black secessionists and Jefferson Davis. In reality, he was honestly torn between his Southern sympathies and his love of the Union. He was author of the plan by which six arbiters, chosen by party caucuses, drew up a neutrality agreement that had been given approval in advance by the legislature. Despite his temporary sanction of some secret Confederate recruiting, he was substantially loyal to this agreement.

And secession received a crushing moral blow in Kentucky when on May 4 voters went to the polls to elect a Border State convention which the legislature had called to meet later that month in Frankfort. At the last moment the Southern Rights party, foreseeing defeat, withdrew its ticket, so that a full Union slate was chosen. But it was the size of the vote which counted. Two-thirds as many ballots were cast as in the recent Presidential election, and the Union vote in Louisville was substantially larger than the Presidential vote.[21] Clearly, Kentucky would stand firm—unless rash Federal leaders, by gratuitous violence, thrust the southern and eastern sections into the arms of the Confederacy. The legislature which Magoffin called into a new session May 6 found the election results a clear verdict for the Union; and this verdict

19 *National Intelligencer*, April 18, 1861. Former Senator Archibald Dixon also stood for neutrality; see Coulter, 41 ff. Senator Garrett Davis was wholeheartedly for neutrality. "Let Kentucky look for herself. . . . Let her stand immovable as a rock peering above the tempest-tossed ocean." Frankfort *Commonwealth*, May 3, 1861. But the lion-hearted Joseph Holt had no use for neutralists. This Kentuckian, now living in Washington, wrote a long letter May 31 to J. F. Speed, published in the Louisville *Journal*, saying the ship *Union* must be saved: "The man who, in such an hour, will not work at the pumps, is either a maniac or a monster."
20 O. R. I, xlii, pt. 2, 68–70.
21 Louisville *Journal*, May 6, 1861; *Ann. Cyc.*, 1861, pp. 396, 397. The border convention proved abortive, only Missouri and Kentucky sending delegates.

was presently underwritten by a special election to fill Congressional seats, nine of the ten districts selecting stanch Union men.[22]

In this critical hour Lincoln displayed masterly comprehension and alertness. He believed, as he wrote later, that to lose Kentucky with her 1,200,000 people and her strategic position on the Ohio and Mississippi would almost be losing "the whole game." Avoiding threats, showing a warm feeling for his and his wife's birth State, offering promises of kindly treatment, he kept the velvet glove over the iron gauntlet. To Garrett Davis he gave the friendliest assurances, saying:

That he intended to make no attack, direct or indirect, upon the institutions or property of any State; but on the contrary, would defend them. . . . And that he did not intend to invade with an armed force, or to make any military or naval movements against any State, unless she or her people should make it necessary by a formidable resistance of the authority and laws of the United States. . . . That he contemplated no military operations that would make it necessary to move any troops over her territory—though he had an unquestioned right at all times. . . . That if Kentucky made no demonstration of force against the United States he would not molest her. That he regretted the necessity of marching troops across Maryland, but forces to protect the seat of the United States Government could not be concentrated there without doing so; and he intended to keep open a line of communication through that State to Washington City, at any risk, but in a manner less calculated to irritate and inflame her people.[23]

At once, in mid-May, Kentucky assumed a formal status of neutrality. The House voted 69 to 26 that the Commonwealth should take no part in the war except as mediators and friends to the belligerents. Governor Magoffin announced a strict neutrality in terms that might have been used by Brazil or Norway. Good Kentuckians, he declared, should refrain from words or deeds likely to "engender hot blood."

Many Kentucky merchants, busy with invoices and ledgers, continued to trade profitably with both North and South. Louisville remained such a great collecting center for goods shipped into the Confederacy that she aroused the jealous wrath of Cincinnati. Although early in May Union troops blockaded the Mississippi at Cairo, trains continued to puff southward on the Louisville & Nashville, bulging with provisions, clothing, shoes, and hardware. Even munitions leaked through. Groaning wagons swelled the flow, for corn that sold

[22] The Congressional elections were held June 30; the vote was Union, 92,460; State Rights, 37,700.
[23] Garrett Davis' letter describing his interview with Lincoln, written to George D. Prentice from Baltimore April 28, was published in the Frankfort *Commonwealth*, May 3, 1861, and reprinted in *Cong. Globe*, 37th Cong., 2d Sess., Pt. 4, pp. 82, 83.

at twenty cents a bushel north of the Ohio fetched fifty cents farther south. This trade had the tacit consent of Lincoln, anxious to keep Kentucky's good will, and bitterly did Northwestern governors and editors upbraid him. Not until August 16, nearly a month after Bull Run, did he bow to recent Congressional legislation by proclaiming a stoppage of commercial intercourse with the South. And even after that, under a liberal permit system instituted by Chase in the Treasury, trade with the South continued in Kentucky on a reduced scale.

[IV]

It was certain that Kentucky, barring some revulsion of sentiment, was safe for the Union. It was also certain that neutrality could not permanently endure. A sense of tension and imminent conflict pervaded the State. "We will remain in the Union," wrote Garrett Davis, "by voting if we can, by fighting if we must, and if we cannot hold our own, we will call on the General Government to aid us." [24]

The State, everyone agreed, had to be armed. But who would control its forces? Magoffin asked the legislature to appropriate $3,000,000 to be used by himself and Adjutant-General Simon Buckner in augmenting and arming the State Guard, already a strong body. Buckner was in secret correspondence with the Confederate leaders. When the governor proclaimed himself commander-in-chief of all State forces, the legislators took alarm. They placed the military under a board of four trusty Union men, created a home guard to counteract the State Guard, and required privates and officers of both organizations to swear allegiance to the Union. The military board were directed to take charge of the State arsenal at Frankfort, and of every gun, bullet, and pound of powder in State possession anywhere. Thus was Samson shorn of his locks. Many communities had been mustering local units. Those which stood for the Union now found themselves strongly supported by the board, the legislature, and Union leaders who had direct communication with Lincoln and Stanton. [25]

By the end of May the Unionists had thus gained decided advantages. Lincoln's friend Joshua F. Speed, a wealthy businessman in Louisville, and his older brother James Speed, an influential jurist there, threw their energies into support of the national government. The President quietly sent out Major Robert Anderson and Naval Lieutenant William Nelson, both Kentuckians.

24 May 16, 1861, to McClellan; O. R., III, i, 236.
25 See the letter of "Union" in Frankfort *Commonwealth*, May 29, 1861, describing how the legislature "in the name of an outraged people have taken from the hands of the Governor all his military power."

Anderson was directed to establish an office in Cincinnati to recruit Kentucky and West Virginia volunteers, while Nelson was to distribute 5000 government muskets and bayonets among loyal men. Senator Garrett Davis and various associates visited Cincinnati for arms and distributed them to companies far and wide. Anderson decided, on the advice of Guthrie, the Speeds, and others, that it would be impolitic to try to raise any Kentucky regiments for the Union army, for this would break the nominal "neutrality." Organization and arming of home-guard units, however, proceeded rapidly.[26] Meanwhile, the loyalty oath compelled Simon Buckner to carry a large body of the State Guard into Confederate service farther south—the Louisville *Journal* shrieking after him: "You are the Benedict Arnold of the day! You are the Catiline of Kentucky! Go, thou miscreant!" [27]

As these advantages were gained, however, a sharp difference of opinion developed in the North. Lincoln, certain that Kentucky was the very pivot of the war, remained willing for the time being to accept her "conditional Unionism." That neutral status, he believed, would save the State intact while sentiment for full participation developed. The government posted large Union forces at Cairo, but did not attempt to enter Kentucky. Early in May, Colonel B. M. Prentiss at Cairo felt some fear that Confederate troops might suddenly be concentrated at Columbus, the Kentucky terminus of the railroad from New Orleans, and attack him. An officer of Kentucky militia therefore called to say that he would equally resist a Northern invasion from Illinois, and a Southern invasion from Tennessee. Although Lincoln accepted this attitude, much Northern sentiment found it intolerable. Who is not for us, many said, is against us!

Lincoln's tolerance of wavering elements, his insistence on a cautious, placatory policy, struck aggressive Northerners as both impolitic and irresolute. To them no Halfway House was permissible; better an open traitor than a hypocrite. Governors Morton, Yates, and Dennison asserted that they were ready to move forward sufficient troops to support a vigorous Union regime in Kentucky. Northern editors began contrasting the decided action by which Blair and Lyon had discomfited Claiborne Jackson in Missouri with Lincoln's kid-glove handling of Magoffin. A little boldness, they said, will bring numerous Kentucky regiments to our colors and shorten the war. When Major Anderson, under Administration orders, rejected a regiment raised among Kentucky Unionists, and its heads appealed to leading members of Congress, their response was emphatic: If Kentucky chooses to leave the

26 Nicolay and Hay, IV, 234 ff.; Coulter, *passim*. The Frankfort *Commonwealth*, June 7, 1861, carries Garrett Davis' long statement to a legislative committee on the work he had done to aid Anderson and Nelson in distributing arms from Cincinnati and Louisville.
27 September 27, 1861.

Union because the nation accepts the voluntary service of her sons, let her try! Old Tom Ewing, born the year the Constitution went into effect, who had read Virgil in the Ohio wilderness, opposed Jackson's financial measures, and served in Zachary Taylor's Cabinet, wrote Crittenden: "There can be no truce or compromise until the opposites have met in force and measured strength—and the sooner the better." [28]

Unquestionably, however, Lincoln showed the greater wisdom. While the slowly gathering Northern armies were still largely unequipped, Virginia had joined the Confederacy, formidable forces had gathered at Richmond, Manassas, and Harpers Ferry, and fighting had begun in western Virginia and central Missouri. Lincoln did not want the flames to spread—as yet—to Kentucky. He knew how easily a few echoing shots could loose an avalanche of passion. One Kentucky Unionist, reporting late in April that every town and precinct was organizing military companies, added: "If the war is general between the two sections I presume more havoc will be made in this State than anywhere else." [29] Men might sneer at what James Russell Lowell termed Lincoln's "Little Bo-Peep policy," but he intended to stay that havoc. He wanted to see the State kept an integer until its position in the Union column was fairly secure.

The President did allow himself one jest on the subject. A Kentucky State senator wrote him a bombastic protest against the stationing of troops in Cairo. Lincoln replied, in a letter unfortunately lost, that if he had only known that Cairo, Illinois, was in this Kentuckian's senatorial district, he would not have sent any soldiers within a hundred miles of the point. [30] But his conviction was clear and firm.

Time proved his sagacity. To the last year of the war Missouri, where Blair's rough policy had prevailed, was a source of deep anxiety and a potential liability; but Kentucky, though much more exposed, soon became one of the bastions of the North. She gave in all perhaps 75,000 men to the Union armies as against a third that number to the Confederacy, and under the shock of invasion, as we shall see, stood firm. [31]

28 *Cf.* Lossing, *Civil War*, I, 460 ff.; Anderson to J. J. Crittenden, June 25, Thomas Ewing July 8, 1861, Crittenden Papers, Duke Univ.
29 C. F. Burnham of Richmond, Ky., April 22, 1861, to James S. Rollins; Rollins Papers, Mo. State Hist. Soc.
30 Frankfort *Commonwealth*, May 29, 1861.
31 J. S. Johnston gives this estimate in *Confederate Military History*, IX, 201.

7

Struggle for the Eastern Border

THROUGHOUT the early weeks of the war the Stars and Stripes over the national capitol were challenged by a Confederate banner in plain view on the Virginia hills, a symbol of the proximity of danger not lost upon the troops who were fast turning the sleepy town into a busy garrison city. The unfinished white obelisk of Washington Monument, a litter of stone blocks, sheds, and derricks about its base, and the skeleton Capitol dome, its iron ribs stark against the sky, were symbolic too; they seemed eloquent of the incomplete national edifice. Washington was full of new sights and sounds; the tramp and clatter of regiments drilling; parades with drum and fife; whitish-brown camps springing up all along the slopes of the northern outskirts; guns practicing at the navy yard. As May and June brought hot, dry days, mule-drawn trains of army wagons churned dust into the air—"Real estate is high," jested the citizens—and stenches increased.

The first strategic necessity, from the Union point of view, was to make Maryland secure, seize western Virginia, and fortify the south bank of the Potomac. Only when Washington felt that it was safe, could it turn to larger tasks. For a time the area within a half-arc drawn fifty miles north and a hundred and fifty west of the city was of burning concern.

Maryland, whose half-million white people could not long ignore the facts of geography, was undergoing a rapid change of sentiment. It was more fortunate than Kentucky in that a great river was its southern, not northern, boundary. Temporarily the confused Governor Hicks talked of neutrality. He not only told the legislature when it met April 26th that the State's only safety lay in a neutral position, but actually proposed to Lincoln that Lord Lyons, the British minister, be asked to mediate between the "contending factions"! This chimera of neutrality beguiled the legislators into a denunciation of both Southern secession and Northern coercion. The House sent deputies to Lincoln to protest against seizure of the Maryland railroads and treatment of the State as a conquered province. James M. Mason, recently senator from Virginia, had hurried to Baltimore to talk with the speaker, other officers, and many members, whom he reported so "earnest and zealous in the cause of the South" that he felt sure they would take steps "to place the authority of the State in hands ready and competent to act with Virginia." But beyond a few protests, and an academic declaration in favor of Southern independence, the Southern sympathizers in the legislature dared not go.

Dominant sentiment was swinging to the Union side. "A large majority of the inhabitants," reported the British consul, "including the wealthy and intelligent portion, are only waiting for sufficient encouragement and protection to avow their loyalty"; and a little later Reverdy Johnson, head of the Maryland bar, who was denouncing secession as treason and bringing his influence as former senator and attorney-general to the support of the Union, noted that national sentiment was fast increasing. Confederate destruction of property of the Chesapeake & Ohio Canal and Baltimore & Ohio Railroad assisted in the revulsion. When Maryland elected members of Congress early in June the Union won the entire slate.[1]

From their fortified position on Federal Hill overlooking Baltimore, the Union forces brooked neither open opposition nor covert treachery. Ben Butler, arresting the gray-haired ironmaster Ross Winans on the charge that he had made 5000 pikes for rebels and committed other offenses, declared that hanging a man worth fifteen millions would teach traitors a lesson. Winans was released in chastened mood. Governor Hicks also rapidly saw a new light. On May 15, to meet the President's request of a month earlier, he called out four regiments; and although they were not accepted, the time for ninety-day troops having passed, recruiting stations steadily sent forward Union volunteers. Indeed, throughout the war Maryland nearly filled its quotas. Before long the governor was collecting arms to keep them out of the hands of Southern sympathizers and taking other steps in aid of the Union. The adherence of West Virginia to the North naturally strengthened the national cause in the State. Replying to secessionist demands that Maryland follow her sister Virginia, the novelist John P. Kennedy demanded, "Which Virginia?" [2]

Like other border areas, eastern Maryland remained hotly divided in sentiment. Many women flaunted secessionist rosettes; haughty citizens ostentatiously brushed their coats as they passed Union soldiers; heads of the City Club shut its doors against Northern officers; newsboys sold Confederate songs and caricatures; shop windows carried pictures of Davis and Lee; crowded theaters applauded Southern sentiments. On the other side, women

1 House Document A, 1861; E. M. Archibald (British consul), April 27, 1861, FO/5 778; G. L. P. Radcliffe, *Hicks and the Civil War*, 78 ff.; James M. Mason, April 25, 1861, to the governor of Virginia, Mason Papers, Va. State Library.
2 Radcliffe, 97–104; *Butler's Book*, Ch. V; O. R. II, i, 563 ff.

who sympathized with the North presented flags to Union regiments; men cheered the national banner; appreciative crowds watched Yankee parades. Some families saw brother aligned against brother. But the division and peril never approached that in Missouri; like little Delaware with *her* obstreperous slaveholders, Maryland was entirely safe.[3]

[I]

On the morning of May 7, 1861, a group representing a recent convention of governors in Cleveland called at the White House. Morton of Indiana, Yates of Illinois, Dennison of Ohio, Curtin of Pennsylvania, and others had met to concert their plans. The deputation told Lincoln that they would furnish any number of men required to smash the rebellion if he would only press a determined and spirited policy. While they did not defend the impatience expressed in some quarters, they declared that their states required some assurance that the government was in earnest and would go forward energetically, without compromises. These governors feared Seward's influence over Lincoln.

"A question had arisen," wrote young Nicolay in his diary, "as to how these States should protect their borders. If for instance Kentucky should secede, as was feared, Cincinnati would be insecure without the possession of Covington Heights across the river. Yet if they took them, the whole State would be in arms at the pretended invasion. The General Government had not indicated what it would do in this case. Ohio desired to know. . . ."[4]

Ohio would have to wait before invading Kentucky, but along another broad front Ohio could act at once. Obviously, western Virginia, like Maryland, could never be surrendered to the Confederacy. Its strategic value was altogether too vital to the nation. This mountainous district offered a buffer zone protecting eastern Ohio, western Pennsylvania (including Pittsburgh), and the flank of any Federal army which marched into the Shenandoah Valley. It covered a long stretch of the Ohio River. It fairly secured the Baltimore & Ohio Railroad, the one line which with its direct links joined Washington with Louisville, Indianapolis, and St. Louis; a line enabling the United States to transfer troops between the eastern and western theaters much more readily than the South could move them. The protection which West Virginia gave eastern Kentucky would presently make the invasion of eastern Tennessee, toward Knoxville, much easier; while it was not actually valuable as a base for striking into the Confederacy, it did help protect some of the points

3 For Delaware see Harold Hancock, "Civil War Comes to Delaware," *Civil War History*, II (Dec., 1956), No. 4.
4 Nicolay Papers, LC. Nicolay does not give us Lincoln's reply.

of debouchment for energetic invasion of the South. Finally, retention of these western counties, with more than 350,000 population, kept fully 30,000 men out of the Confederate army, and at times tied up sizable Confederate forces.

The action taken by western Virginia after Sumter showed how irresistibly, in a crisis, popular feeling can burst through all artificial barriers. The people beyond the Alleghenies, bound by natural economic ties more closely to their northern neighbors than to eastern Virginia, had cared little about the so-called wrongs of the South, but very keenly about the maltreatment they suffered from the Tidewater and Piedmont. They complained that they were grossly underrepresented in the legislature, that the three-fifths rule in counting slaves deprived them of their share of seats in Congress, that they were outrageously overtaxed, and that while very poor in communications they got nothing like their share of public improvements. By no means least, they felt aggrieved by the disdainful attitude of proud eastern planters and merchants toward the "mountaineers." [5]

For each of their complaints they could offer substantial evidence. Trans-Allegheny Virginia in 1860 had 135,000 more white people than eastern Virginia, yet under the constitution the eastern counties held control of the Senate. Despite its larger white population, the west had only five Congressional seats, the east eight. Inasmuch as slaves under twelve years of age were exempt from taxation and older slaves were assessed much below their true value, the east, according to Francis H. Pierpont, the principal western leader, each year escaped paying $900,000 in taxes justly its due; and inasmuch as the State had built no railways nor canals west of the Alleghenies, practically all of the $30,000,000 by which the State debt had been augmented since 1851 had gone for internal improvements in the east. [6]

Small wonder that the Morgantown *Star* declared that the grievances of the western folk against Richmond were tenfold greater than those of the slaveholders against the Yankees! If Virginia were now to float the cotton kingdom kite aloft, the westerners did not mean to be hitched to the extreme tail. They knew how vulnerable they were to attack. Cannon on the Ohio shore could demolish Wheeling, converging forces could crush the panhandle in an iron vise, and troops could sweep up the Monongahela for a hundred miles. It is evidence of the astonishing blindness of the leading Virginia secessionists that they paid no heed to monitions that the westerners would no longer be mere hewers of wood and drawers of water.

5 James C. McGregor, *Disruption of Virginia*, 73–75; and see his maps.
6 McGregor, 76; E. C. Smith, *Borderland*, 105. It was one of the weaknesses of slavery that it helped breed sectionalism in some States, and encouraged the older and richer sections, in general, to discriminate against the newer and poorer.

When the Virginia convention voted its ordinance, the trans-Allegheny unionists had already determined to form an independent State. Some of their delegates in Richmond, evading arrest, hurried home by way of Washington. Others held a hasty consultation in the Powhatan Hotel, decided that as soon as they were safe beyond the mountains they would call a convention and carve out their new commonwealth, obtained passes from Governor Letcher, and took the most direct road back, braving threats of violence. A few days later they were inciting their fellow citizens to resolute action. In eloquent speeches they explained how the barons of the lowland had swept the State into war, expatiated on the insults they had received, and assured the people that their only safety lay in separation. In Wheeling, a delegate fresh from Richmond exhorted men to enlist so effectively that a week later a regiment was ready. The Wheeling *Intelligencer* argued uncompromisingly for the Union and a new mountain star in the flag. In Wellsburg, the citizens, after hearing another fiery speaker, hurried a committee to Washington, obtained 2000 small arms from the War Department, returned to the panhandle, and distributed them to eager recruits.[7]

The movement, spontaneous, full of extralegal irregularities, and varying from place to place in public support, spread like the wind. Community after community held mass meetings. One gathering of special note at Clarksburg, the birthplace of Stonewall Jackson, called a convention in Wheeling for May 13, each county to elect at least five delegates.[8] But this somewhat premature summons, carried to every hamlet, met an uneven response, for it stated no clear object, and did not intimate that the convention would have any special authority. When on the appointed day more than four hundred men met in Wheeling, they represented only twenty-five counties, and included few persons of note. John S. Carlile, a self-educated, forceful man whose oratorical gifts had carried him into Congress, and whose aggressive championship of the Union had made some Richmond secessionists thirst for his blood, emerged as the leader, but he was overruled when he suggested immediate steps to create a new State.

Northern observers who believed that western Virginia was aflame for the nation were only partly right. It was not only love for the Union but resentment over their special grievances which actuated the majority. Like most border people from the Patapsco to the Missouri, West Virginians were ready to cry: "A pox upon your warring houses!" This May convention in Wheeling

7 W. P. Willey, *An Inside View of the Formation of the State of West Virginia*, 51–53; Smith, *Borderland*, 189.

8 Virgil A. Lewis, *How West Virginia Was Made, passim.* All the 150 counties of Virginia were free to send delegates; the only question was how many counties would respond. West Virginia later incorporated a half hundred.

voted almost unanimously that secession was intolerable; but, pausing, it then took a moderate and prudent course. To plunge forward immediately and create a new State, as Carlile suggested, would estrange many conditional Union men and drive some into the arms of the rebellion. Western Virginia as a whole was unready for so bold a step. Under the shrewd guidance of Francis H. Pierpont, an attorney and coal dealer of Wheeling, the delegates agreed that if the secession ordinance was approved in the pending referendum, a special election should be held for a second convention in Wheeling.[9]

This course was sagacious, for probably a majority of the people were then equally against a disruption of the Union and a disruption of Virginia. A delayed State of fifty counties was certainly better than an immediate State of twenty-five. Western leaders did their best to roll up a heavy negative vote in the referendum on secession. They succeeded, for although the returns have disappeared, it is known that in twelve typical counties of the northwest, the vote was nearly ten to one for the Union.[10] They had candidates for Congress named in three districts. They appealed to Lincoln and the governors of Ohio and Pennsylvania for assistance, and Dennison of Ohio ordered George B. McClellan, just appointed the State commander, to concentrate his troops on the Ohio ready to cross as soon as Virginia's secession was officially declared. Some Northerners were disappointed by the delay; the Philadelphia *Press*, New York *Tribune*, Cincinnati *Gazette*, and other journals which had been eagerly hailing a new mountain commonwealth dedicated to liberty and nationality wrung their hands. But caution afforded time for sentiment to harden.

Hardly was news of Virginia's final decision received before the western hills and valleys began to witness stirring scenes. McClellan's glittering columns swung across the Ohio and pushed on, without him, in a converging movement from Marietta and Wheeling. On June 3, in the first real field action of the war, a little Confederate command which had been putting the torch to railroad bridges was surprised and routed at Philippi. Virginia troops had begun moving up from the southern borders of the region. Officers on both sides, however, reported that the people were overwhelmingly for the North, and as McClellan soon drove the Confederates back, Pierpont and his associates could proceed unchecked with the work of political reorganization. They had a new plan—a better plan.[11]

9   Lewis, *op. cit.*, 34 ff.; Smith, *Borderland*, 194 ff.
10   J. M. Callahan, *History of West Virginia*, I, 352.
11   Pierpont in an autobiographical sketch in the Brock Papers, HL, gives himself entire credit for the plan to be adopted. He first explained it to the Committee of Safety which had been organized, he states, saying: "When our State is organized and recognized at Washington, then we can divide." The Committee and leading men of Wheeling endorsed

Our business, they announced when the second Wheeling convention opened—a gathering in which thirty-four counties and four-fifths of the trans-Allegheny population were represented—is not to create a State, but to preserve one. "Let us save Virginia, and then save the Union." In other words, establishment of a new State was postponed in favor of the creation of a government which purported to speak for all Virginia, and expected to receive recognition as such from Lincoln. Under this plan, Union men were to be elected to all State offices, and Washington was to treat their regime as constitutionally sovereign all the way from Norfolk to Wheeling. A precedent for Lincoln's action had been found in President Tyler's decision in 1844, later upheld by the Supreme Court, recognizing one of two rival State governments in Rhode Island as valid.[12]

Thus "the Restored Government of Virginia," using the regular seal of the Commonwealth with the words "Liberty and Union" added, rose in June in opposition to the Virginia of the Confederate sisterhood. The convention unanimously elected Pierpont, apparently principal author of the plan, as governor. Showing exuberant energy, he helped organize a loyal legislature, collected $40,000 from the national government as Virginia's share of public land sales since 1841, and within fifty days raised ten regiments of troops, nine of them composed of Virginians. The legislature elected two Senators, who were at once admitted to Congress along with three Representatives—against the strenuous protests of James A. Bayard of Delaware.[13] Lincoln, in his message opening the new Congress in July, emphatically declared the legitimacy of the Wheeling regime: "These loyal citizens this government is bound to recognize and protect as being Virginia." It is clear that the President, as Attorney-General Bates suggests, had helped devise the scheme.[14] Bates wrote in his diary:

I have good relations with all the leading men of that region who come here. At first, we had some difficulty in weaning them from their long-conceived thought of a new State, stretching from the Blue Ridge to the Ohio. That done, they assumed to be Virginia, and are now represented in both Houses and fully recognized. This is "at once an example and fit instrument"

---

the plan. When the second Wheeling convention met, the delegates were told of the plan, and they "went to work with a will." See also W. P. Willey, *Inside View*. But he seems to have had powerful collaborators in Washington.

12 Lewis, *How West Virginia Was Made*, 369-372; O. R. III, i, 378. This second Wheeling convention began June 11, 1861.

13 John S. Carlile and Waitman T. Willey were elected Senators. Bayard was a crypto-traitor in thought if not act. He wrote S. L. M. Barlow as late as June 27 arguing for an agreed division of the nation on the line of the Potomac and Ohio Rivers, predicting a despotic military regime in the North, and declaring that the country was much too large anyway for a representative government; Barlow Papers.

14 Bates, July 14, 1861, to J. O. Broadhead; Broadhead Papers, Mo. Hist. Soc.

for bringing back all the States, and restoring the integrity of the Union. It needs but a slight change of circumstances to induce East Tennessee, West North Carolina, North Alabama and perhaps North Georgia, to follow the example. There is another inducement to this course, of a coarser nature, which will have a greater effect in fact than will be openly avowed. By treating the proceedings of the Rebel Governments within the States as unauthorized and simply void, they will get rid of enormous debt liabilities without incurring the odium of downright repudiation.

This example of Virginia, and its recognition by the General Government, has already struck terror into half the insurgent States. Its moral influence in settling the contest will be equal to at least 50,000 of our best troops.

The new plan, which turned out to possess no such political potency as Bates hoped, was destined shortly to dissolve into the simple original project for a separate State. Creation of the "restored" government thus became a roundabout, awkward, perplexing mode of effecting the inevitable partition. What was important was the fact that as early as June, 1861, this important area was detached from Virginia; detached to make an effective shield for southeastern Ohio, southwestern Pennsylvania, the Baltimore & Ohio, and the armies west of Washington; and detached to be also an effective corridor for threatening the Confederacy.

[II]

Suddenly the military border moved south; the secession of Virginia met a sharp counter-stroke. On May 24, ten thousand Union troops breakfasted on the soil of the Old Dominion. Richmond's adherence to the Confederacy having become effective the day before, it was now constitutional for Lincoln to use force to repossess the national property in the State.

The troops found this march a poetic experience. Before officers of the New York Seventh dismissed parade on May 23, the privates saw their colonel parleying with others. Something was in the wind! Soon irrepressible cheers from the company streets greeted orders that the men be ready to march at a moment's notice. "Alexandria!" "Harpers Ferry!" "Richmond!" they exulted. It was a clear night of full moon, refulgent, mild, and dewy. At an hour past midnight the drums beat; the men fell into column, tramped through the shadowy trees to the highroad, and soon swung through outer Washington. A pause ensued while a Jersey brigade, 3000 strong, passed them, the troops chaffing each other gaily. Then they resumed the march, till they saw a broad pathway of reflected moonlight shining on the Potomac, and opening their files, rumbled out on the Long Bridge. As they reached the Virginia shore, dawn was breaking. Directly in front of them stood the sinking moon, bright and handsome as a new twenty-dollar gold piece, a splendid oriflamme. On they went past a racecourse to a ridge, where the Jersey boys, their picks and spades ringing amid abundant profanity, were constructing a tête-du-pont to protect the bridgehead. As the sun rose some New Yorkers took a hand. Others curiously inspected Lee's Arlington House, its paint fading, its yard weedy, its propylaeum of stuccoed columns crumbling a little, and its interior presenting to Theodore Winthrop "a certain careless, romantic, decayed-gentleman effect, wholly Virginian." [15]

General Scott had planned to have the 75,000 three-months men, once Washington was safe, entrench themselves on Arlington Heights, and then move against Harpers Ferry, while nine or ten regiments meanwhile made a thrust against Fort Monroe. He acted none too soon. Confederate pickets had been seen on the Heights, and engineers were surveying positions for batteries. At Alexandria, Lieutenant-Colonel A. S. Taylor of the Virginia forces had orders to defend the town unless overwhelmingly outnumbered.[16] Cannon planted at Alexandria could close the river and batter the public buildings of Washington. But now, as strong forces of Union infantry, artillery, and cavalry crossed the Long Bridge and the Aqueduct Bridge at Georgetown, only a few shots were fired. Staking out lines, throwing up earthworks, posting cannon, the Union troops immediately built Fort Corcoran on the Arlington estate and Fort Runyon not far away, the first strong points in a system of Virginia fortifications which ultimately became ten miles long. The North was elated. It applauded Irvin McDowell, whom Secretary Cameron—much to the irritation of Winfield Scott, who had other plans —had ordered to head the movement.[17]

Yet the blundering confusion inseparable from hasty Federal improvisation was at once evident. Five days later McDowell reported that Alexandria remained almost totally unfortified because the men had no transportation to the hills, no tools, and worst of all, no plans; that horses were starving; and that many of the scattered troop units were getting insufficient food because they lacked wagons, established lines of communication, and officers with enough experience to look after them.

One incident of the occupation had a poignant meaning to both North and South. Of the young Northern officers none was better known than

15 Theodore Winthrop, "Washington As a Camp," *Atlantic Monthly*, Vol. 8 (July, 1861), 105–118.
16 O. R. III, i, 233; O. R. I, ii, 24.
17 Scott had opposed the rapid promotion of McDowell because he thought it injured General J. K. F. Mansfield, who, distinguished as chief engineer under Zachary Taylor in the Mexican War, had been appointed to command the Department of Washington, and had been foremost in urging the seizure and fortification of Arlington. See *Committee on the Conduct of the War*, II, 37.

Colonel Elmer Ellsworth of Illinois, head of a Zouave regiment which he had drilled into remarkable efficiency. Lincoln and others knew that his life had been a heavy struggle against poverty, a model of stainless virtue, and an example of burning ambition channeled into public service. He had long since dedicated himself to an important cause, the complete reorganization of the militia system of the United States. He had studied every branch of military science; and to illustrate his principles, he had organized in May, 1859, a company which he drilled to such discipline, endurance, skill, and energy that when taken on an eastern tour, it aroused the admiration of all beholders. Nominally a law student in the Lincoln-Herndon office, he had traveled to Washington with the President-elect's party. Then, working night and day, he had gone to New York to enlist his model regiment.

Springing up the stairs of the Marshall House in Alexandria to haul down the Confederate flag, he was shot on his descent by the proprietor. This Virginian, James W. Jackson, knew that his action meant instant death, but—as devoted as the youthful Illinoisan—he never hesitated. Flags South and North went to half-mast. Jackson's body was carried to an obscure grave, while Elsworth's was taken to lie in state in the East Room of the White House and to become the center of a memorable funeral demonstration in New York.[18]

Scott's blow heartened the North, which a month earlier had seen Washington threatened and now could claim a small corner of Confederate soil. Nevertheless, to carry Southern outposts on the fringe of the capital was no great feat. The really important point before Washington was Manassas Junction, twenty-five miles southwest of Alexandria, which Ben Butler had already urged Scott to take by storm.[19] Here, where the railroad running south from Alexandria to Richmond joined a line from the Blue Ridge, Confederate forces had collected in such strength that a heavy price would have to be paid for gains.

[III]

On the whole, the North had achieved a great deal in holding most of the debatable borderland. To protect Washington, it had to use military force to keep the whole upper Chesapeake region safe; to protect Ohio, it had to gain the strategic prize of West Virginia. Although the Western borderland was too new to have reared many true statesmen, Kentucky had produced

18 Ellsworth's death probably inspired John Hay's poem written long after, "Thanatos Athanatos" (Deathless Death) on "Soldier boys who snatched death's starry prize":
"Their memories hold in death's unyielding fee
The youth that thrilled them to the fingertips."

19 Parton, *Butler in New Orleans*, 105.

in Henry Clay an illustrious apostle of nationalism and moderation, and had raised up lesser men who shared his pride in the republic and faith in compromise. These successors, whose spirit harmonized with Lincoln's, now kept the commonwealth in the Union, and prevented angry factions from flying at each other's throats. Missouri alone represented a partial failure. Its one eminent leader, Benton, had left no inheritors; rather, the angry partisans, the David Atchisons, Trusten Polks, and Henry T. Blows, had found equally intemperate successors. The State had been saved to the Union, which had every geographical advantage in taking it, but saved only in a feverishly diseased condition which was certain to grow worse. A Southern historian remarks that the Confederacy lost Kentucky because it was too impatient to be tolerant, and too impetuous to be tactful. The North had lost the best possibilities in the Missouri situation by the same errors.

Strategically, the North held the entrances to the Shenandoah Valley, the Cumberland and Tennessee Rivers, and the Lower Mississippi. In population it had much the greater part of some thirty-four million people; in resources, it had grain, meat, minerals, factories, and shipping in abundance. Many vital parts of the Confederacy lay in a comparatively narrow strip along the Atlantic and Gulf, from Norfolk at one extremity to the Rio Grande at the other—exposed everywhere to attack by sea. Of the remainder, the interior States of Tennessee and Arkansas were vulnerable by river invasions. Far different would have been the situation had the Confederacy rounded out its domains by seizing Kentucky, Missouri, and western Virginia. The balance then would have swayed against the Union.

8

Grandiose Plans and Blundering Leaders

WHEN SENATOR HENRY WILSON and Judge Rockwood Hoar spent May 1 paying calls on Lincoln and every Cabinet member to urge aggressive fighting, they spoke for millions of fellow citizens. In a war of the people, the masses always chafe for headlong action. Like a sluggish river which a thunderstorm has made swift and angry with rising water, the feeling of the North since Sumter had become fierce and impatient. Wait until Jefferson Davis' legions rolled over the Potomac to tweak the noses of the Northern garrison? Never! In the East the cry was for an early seizure of Richmond, in the Northwest for a rapid march down the Mississippi Valley, and everywhere for the resolute suppression of rebellion and punishment of traitors. It would cost something, but even editors who dilated on practical difficulties believed with Greeley that when Lincoln had 30,000 brave men in Washington, 45,000 more ready for the field, and 500,000 at home biting their nails for service, Virginia might as well surrender.[1]

In this hour of indignant emotion the voice of dissent was largely drowned. Fervent supporters of the Union were cheered by the emergence of a strong party of war Democrats under Stephen A Douglas. The moment he heard of Sumter, the Illinois Senator abandoned his attacks on the Administration and began urging it to grimmer effort. "What would I do with the traitors left in Washington?" he said to an inquirer. "If I were President, I'd convert or hang them all within forty-eight hours."

He was quick to call at the White House. Lincoln later said that he was the first to warn him of impending trouble in Maryland, to point out the advantages of the Chesapeake–Annapolis route, and to emphasize the importance of holding Fort Monroe. The Associated Press at once announced that he had pledged the fullest support to the Union. Hastening west, he

1 N. Y. *Tribune*, May 2, 1861.

spoke in Cleveland, Columbus, Indianapolis, Chicago, and above all, in the Springfield so familiar with his voice.

An audience tense with anticipation jammed the State capitol as the Speaker, young Shelby M. Cullom, introduced Douglas. He rose magnificently to the occasion, presenting himself as no mere baiter of the South, but an earnest patriot determined to fortify his people. That experienced political reporter, Horace White, wrote later that he could not imagine any orator, ancient or modern, exhibiting greater power.[2] The idol of Midwestern Democrats clearly thought the nation in terrible peril. He addressed a vast unseen audience as he appealed for unity, disclaimed any personal ends—"There is no path of ambition open to me in a divided country"—and urged a mighty effort. "The shortest way to peace," he said, "is the most stupendous and unanimous preparation for war. The greater the unanimity the less blood will be shed. The more prompt and energetic the movement, and the more important it is in numbers, the shorter will be the struggle."

Though the Illinois legislature had already proved its determination, Douglas' influence was much needed to win over one section of the Democratic press and politicians. Newspapers like the Cincinnati *Enquirer*, Indianapolis *State Sentinel*, and Chicago *Times and Herald*, along with some hesitant members of Congress, awoke to a new sense of duty under his prodding. The *National Intelligencer* shortly published a letter by Douglas, dated May 10, recalling the wholehearted backing that Clay and Webster had given Jackson in the nullification crisis.

When Douglas penned this letter he was prostrated in his Chicago home by inflammatory rheumatism and other ailments. He had long overworked, drunk too much, and generally neglected his health. His death on June 3 was mourned as nothing short of a national calamity even by journals that had opposed him for years. Had he lived he would doubtless have resumed his partisanship on many questions of policy, but his scorn for copperheadism would have been bitingly expressed. He would have been a constant advocate of energetic war measures, would have cooperated warmly with such old-time Democrats as Gideon Welles, whose appointment to the Cabinet he had applauded, and would have lifted his voice across the battle lines to assure former followers in the South that peace might be had on the basis of a restored Union, but with nothing less. He had already told Lincoln that Seward was too moderate, and was exerting too much influence on the Administration.

---

2 White, *Lyman Trumbull*, 153. Cullom wrote later that he had never been so impressed by oratorical genius; March 19, 1883, to I. N. Arnold, Arnold Papers, Chicago Hist. Soc. See also the *Atlantic*, "Reminiscences of Stephen A. Douglas," vol 8 (August, 1861), 205–213.

"Who can take his place?" lamented Representative S. S. Cox of Ohio. Had he continued to lead the War Democrats, then men like Fernando Wood, Vallandigham, and Bayard would have played a lesser role, and the party would have exercised a healthier influence in national affairs. One lack which Lincoln felt sorely was a cooperative yet critical Democracy.[3]

[I]

The question of the grand strategy to be pursued by the growing Federal armies had to be determined at least roughly before Henry Wilson's aggressive war could be begun. The atmosphere of haste, ignorance, and makeshift fostered a variety of conflicting plans. Not only did the country have nothing remotely resembling a general staff, but its military leaders had never given the slightest attention to problems of an intersectional war. Cameron, however expert in political intrigue, had neither the technical knowledge nor imagination to devise broad war plans. From the outset, divisions on strategy were evident in the Cabinet, the army, and the public. Three main proposals soon emerged: Blair's, Scott's, and McClellan's.

Montgomery Blair's proposal was for quick hard blows in Virginia, based on the theory that the Southern masses were not behind the Confederate government and would soon forsake it. Thus the conflict, waged also with psychological weapons, might be short. He wrote Governor Andrew of Massachusetts on May 11:

I have great difficulty in impressing my policy upon the Administration in the condition of things here. The great obstruction in the way in the past and in the present is Gen. Scott. He does not appreciate as I do the condition of things at the South. He regards the whole Southern people as consolidated in hostility to the North and thinks of making war upon them as if making war upon a foreign government whereas the truth is that the conspirators who have got arms in their hands under color of state authority are scarcely more obnoxious to the North than they are to the great masses of people at the South, but they have armed themselves under color of one pretext or another, so that even the armed men who would desert from their policy have no longer any election, and the unarmed masses—the Union men of the South— are overawed by the armed marauders that Jeff Davis has sent throughout the country.

3 The fullest inheritor of Douglas' mantle was James W. Sheahan, editor of the Chicago *Morning Post*, an able, intelligent, and patriotic Democratic organ. It is a misfortune that Douglas' letters to Sheahan, a hundred or more, seem to have perished. In his obituary editorial in the *Post*, Sheahan wrote, "He poured forth his opinions respecting men and measures with the utmost freedom." I. W. Morris, of the Democratic House delegation, declared that Douglas had no confidence in Vallandigham, "as I know from frequent conversations with him," either as a man or a politician. Chicago *Morning Post*, July 12, 1862. The *Post* of July 22, 1862, has the best text of the Chicago and Springfield speeches.

It would require but a very inconsiderable part of the forces at our command to put down this band of plunderers, if used vigorously, and as soon as they are put down, the deliverers will be welcomed in Virginia, as they now are in Maryland. . . .

It would be hard to say which was the more fatuous, Blair's belief that the South would at once turn against Davis' government, or his illusion that Union forces could strike a powerful blow before May 22. He went on:

My suggestion has been that we should at once organize a Southern Army. To do this we should select a leader for the Southern Army, give him his staff, select the best, the most accomplished of our officers to surround him, detail troops, procure transports, and organize a great army that should rendezvous at Hampton Roads and menace Norfolk and Richmond. The band of marauders that now pervade the State of Virginia would then rush to meet the threatened invasion, the people of Virginia would speak their real sentiments at the approaching election, and their votes if not our ballots would drive the marauders out of the State on the 22d instant.[4]

More realism underlay Scott's famous anaconda plan for crushing Southern resistance by combining a naval blockade with concentric military pressures.[5] In outlining this scheme for enveloping the Confederacy by tight cordons on its northern frontier, the Mississippi, and the Gulf and Atlantic coasts, Scott emphasized his conviction that it would bring the secessionists to terms with minimal losses. He even thought that an invading army of 60,000 volunteers and 25,000 new regulars could take possession of the Mississippi. He proposed, while sealing up the Atlantic and Gulf ports, and using one large force to hold the rebels in Virginia, to organize this striking army of perhaps 85,000 on the Ohio River, give them four or five months' hard drill, and then, when frost had killed "the virus of malignant fevers below Memphis," to move them and a flotilla of gunboats rapidly down the Mississippi to New Orleans, garrisoning towns and posts at proper points.

Scott assumed that the great majority of Southerners supported the Confederate government, and would fight hard. He believed that they could muster a main army of 100,000 to 150,000 men to defend Richmond. Rather than attack this array, he thought it good policy by cordon and blockade to starve the South into submission. He told August Belmont that he was confident of achieving a peace by the spring of 1862.[6]

Scott's plan was radically defective in concentrating attention on the ter-

4 Andrew Papers, MHS. Blair's knowledge of Southern sentiment was pure divination or guesswork; he thought the Blair family necessarily understood Southerners.
5 For Scott's plan see O. R. I, li, pt. 1, pp. 338, 339, 369, 370, 387.
6 Scott's correspondence with McClellan's O. R. I, li, pt. 1, 338, 339, 369, 370, 387, is supplemented by material in Elliott, *Scott*, 720 ff., and Swinton, *Army of the Potomac*, 41, 42. For the statement to Belmont see Belmont's letter of June 7, 1861, to the Rothchilds in *A Few Letters and Speeches*, 47.

ritory of the Confederacy and the weakening of its people, when the Confederate armies were the true objects of attack. An amateur could point out objections. How could Scott keep the large Confederate army in Virginia immobile? What if Southerners took the offensive in the Ohio and Mississippi valleys before Union forces moved? What if 80,000 men were totally inadequate, if the fortresses on the Mississippi held out, and if the blockade proved leaky? These objections all stemmed from Scott's inattention to Southern armies as the true centers of operations. An antogonist is not knocked out by blows on his extremities.

Nevertheless, Scott's plan had great merits. He precisely identified a number of cardinal factors in the war: the importance of blockade, the need for careful labor in drilling and equipping armies, the value of cool weather for Southern operations, and the priority to be given recovery of the Mississippi. In the end, the South was actually to be largely paralyzed by a combination of pressures. He showed insight, too, in warning everybody against the impatience of Northern politicians and public, when hasty action might mean disaster. When on May 3 he formed the Department of the Ohio and appointed McClellan its commander and the leader of the projected invading force, he urged the young general to emphasize preparation: "Lose no time, while necessary preparations for the great expedition is in progress, in organizing, drilling, and disciplining your three months' men, many of whom, it is hoped, will ultimately be found enrolled under the call for three years' volunteers. Should an urgent and immediate occasion arise meantime for their services, they will be the more effective." The slow, inexorable strangulation of the Confederacy by the coils of an anaconda represented by the blockade, the capture of coastal strips and ports, the conquest of the Mississippi, and the advance of encircling armies, was indeed—when joined with field victories— to be the main road to victory.

Scott's plan also evinced a grasp of the strategic fact that large armies invading the South would have to get their supplies by river or rail, and be tied to these facilities. Until Sherman marched to the sea through one of the few areas which produced a rich food surplus, the river and railway map was to be pretty much the map of war.[7] It is curious to note, however, that Scott's proposals for seizing the Mississippi rested entirely on a campaign downriver; the naval conquest of New Orleans from the Gulf was not proposed until much later.

McClellan himself, only a fortnight after the war began, had prepared an all too impetuous plan. When promoted from his State position in Ohio to be department head and major-general in the regular army, he learned con-

7 On this fact see Spenser Wilkinson, *War and Policy*, 37.

fidentially of Scott's plan for marching "an iron band" of 60,000–85,000 troops along the Mississippi River, supplied by boats. He did not like it; indeed, when he wrote his memoirs long after, he remained convinced that occupation of the Appalachian chain early in the war would have yielded more rapid and decisive results than any thrust down the Mississippi. He at once laid before Scott two other proposals for using an army of 80,000 Northwestern troops as soon as it could be mustered and disciplined. One plan was for throwing it across the Ohio River at Gallipolis, marching it up the Great Kanawha Valley, and deploying it to capture Richmond. Promptly executed, wrote McClellan, this movement would not fail to relieve Washington, and if aided by a decided advance in the east, "secure the destruction of the southern army." A cooperating column could occupy Louisville and prevent any interference by Southern troops operating from Kentucky. McClellan's alternative proposal was to move the 80,000 men across the Ohio at Cincinnati or Louisville, march straight to Nashville, "and thence act according to circumstances." [8]

Scott demurred, and found no difficulty in explaining to Lincoln the weakness of the two schemes. What about enlisting and equipping the men McClellan wanted in such a hurry? What about the difficulty of overland transport across such great distances and rough terrain? What about angering western Virginia and Kentucky by thus invading them? Scott contrasted McClellan's strategy of dagger blows with his own over-all strategy of encircling pressures. "For the cordon a number of men equal to one of the general's columns would probably suffice, and the transportation of men and all supplies by water is about a fifth of the land cost, besides an immense saving in time." [9]

That Lincoln at first leaned toward Scott's faith in deliberate anaconda pressures is evident from a number of facts: His continued deference to Scott's military experience and wisdom, his restriction of the May call for troops to some 42,000 volunteers and some 22,700 regulars, his statement to Congress when it met in July that he hoped for a speedy termination of the war, and his letter to Simon Buckner declaring that he wished to suppress the insurrection with the least possible annoyance to well-disposed people

8 O. R. III, li, pt. 1, pp. 338, 339. A Swiss observer later propounded the curious theory that it was an error to make Washington, which could be amply covered by gunboats on the Potomac and by forts, the main Eastern base. Instead, a great fortified camp should have been created at Harpers Ferry, giving Washington flank protection, and offering opportunity to advance on Richmond, the Shenandoah, and western Virginia. Lieut.-Col. Ferdinand Lecomte, *The War in the U. S., A Report to The Swiss Military Dept., Aug., 1862* (N. Y., 1863).

9 May 2, 1861; O. R. III, li, pt. 1, p. 339 (Scott's endorsement on McClellan's letter of April 27, 1861).

everywhere. Seward of course continued to shrink from bloody battle and hold to his faith in reconciliation. Even Chase, dismayed by his financial problems, was in no mood to press for large-scale aggressive war. Attorney-General Bates assured a Missouri friend that he would rather save the nation by overawing all opposition than by fighting, and would as far as possible avoid bloodshed. The Administration, he explained, was convinced that the Chesapeake and the central Mississippi were the two controlling areas that must be held with massive grip. The first would dominate the Maryland–Virginia region, and the second with the ocean blockade would shut the South in an iron prison.

Thus the whole Cabinet, except Montgomery Blair, down to midsummer of 1861 accepted Scott's belief that a systematic tightening pressure all round the South would swiftly bring its people to terms. A happy dream! [10]

Indeed, the central defect of all Northern thought in these months was a gross underestimation of difficulties and dangers. Scott underestimated the power of the South to strike while his "cordon" was being knotted. McClellan —who actually asserted that his columns, after taking Richmond and Nashville, could rapidly converge on Pensacola, Mobile, and New Orleans—underestimated the Confederate ability to halt his march. Blair underestimated Southern devotion and tenacity. Impatient editors and politicians forgot Daniel Webster's dictum that, in war, if there are blows to be given there are also blows to be taken. The few who foresaw a protracted conflict founded their ideas on wrong premises, though Scott showed more wisdom than most men in saying the struggle might take two or three years because its weapons would be as much economic as military. [11]

[II]

Scott, as the architect of grand strategy, maintained a firm grip on the military helm. He labored under various maladies of age. After dinner he would call his body servant to wheel his roomy armchair around and put his feet up for a nap; sometimes he fell asleep in the midst of a conference. He was

10 Scott wished to divide his 85,000 troops into two bodies. The smaller would board river transports, headed and flanked by powerful gunboats; the larger would march by land as nearly abreast as practicable, supplied by heavy freighters. They would begin somewhere on the Ohio and proceed "on the first autumnal swell in the rivers." O. R. III, i, 177 ff.; Elliott, *Scott*, 722. General John A. Dix had a somewhat similar plan. He would make no offensive move until November; use the summer to train troops in camps of instruction; garrison Washington with 50,000 men; and in autumn launch two invading columns of 100,000 men each, one in Virginia, the other in the West. Morgan Dix, *Memoir of John A. Dix*, II, 28, 29.
11 Scott predicted to Seward, Chase, and Cameron a three-year war: "For a long time thereafter it will require the exercise of the full powers of the Federal Government to restrain the fury of the non-combatants!" Marcus J. Wright, *General Scott*, 330.

nevertheless capable, if some crisis arose, of twelve or fourten hours' work a day. His headquarters in a shabby brick building on Seventeenth Street were crowded with officers, politicians, contractors, newpapermen, and railway officials. An unending stream of mail and telegrams poured in on him.[12] Experienced, systematic, and conscientious, he had a much better grasp of business than Secretary Cameron. An Ohioan who brought McClellan's special scheme for ending the war to Scott learned that many radical politicians were impatient of the general's anaconda plan. But he found Scott's headquarters a busy place where decisions were quick and clear, and the atmosphere electric; when he called on Cameron he found an aimless, cluttered, evasive office.[13]

Scott had to sustain the first Southern strokes, the loss of Norfolk and Harpers Ferry—blows that more vigilance on the part of the Administration might have blocked.

The navy yard opposite Norfolk, three-quarters of a mile long and a quarter-mile wide, contained riches at which we have already glanced: Machine shops, foundries, an ordnance building, a sawmill, sail lofts, and at least 2000 cannon, 300 of them new Dahlgren guns. Among the warships were the huge three-decker *Pennsylvania* of 120 guns, and the steam-frigate *Merrimac*, its engines in need of repairs. Nothing had ever been done to fortify the navy yard, and the nearest troops were at Fort Monroe, separated by many miles and much water. The failure of the Lincoln Administration to garrison the place of course arose from its unwillingness to give offense to Virginia or provoke the Confederacy. Not until more than a month after the inauguration was the commodore in charge of the yard ordered to get the ships and other movables ready to be taken beyond danger, and even then he was warned to take no steps that would give needless alarm.[14]

A single regiment at Norfolk, supported by the warships anchored at the yard, could have held both places until reinforcements arrived; and with Fort Monroe at their backs, the Union forces could have dominated that whole corner of Virginia. But as matters stood, when a Virginia officer arrived on the scene April 18, he was able to take rapid action for the seizure of invaluable materials. Bringing up the Richmond Grays and six hundred men

12 E. D. Keyes, *Fifty Years' Observation;* Elliott, *Scott,* 724. The general fell asleep while talking to an Iowa delegation under Senator Grimes.

13 A. F. Perry, *A Chapter in Interstate Diplomacy, Papers,* Ohio Commandery Loyal Legion, III, 333–363.

14 Gideon Welles treats the question of the capture of Norfolk at length in his *Diary,* I, 41–54. He admits that the local commander showed feebleness and incapacity, while some associates were treacherous. But Welles says in his own defense: "In repeated verbal applications to General Scott in the months of March and April, as a precautionary measure, I met a refusal, on the ground of military necessity and inability to comply. He had not, he said, troops to defend Harper's Ferry. . . ."

from Petersburg, he called out the military companies of Portsmouth and Norfolk. The Northern commodore had delayed until too late in getting the *Merrimac* into the safety of Hampton Roads. An engineer from Washington had repaired the machinery and gotten up steam, and explicit orders had come to put all the more valuable ships in safety. But the fatuous commodore listened to junior officers who told him that no danger existed. "How could I expect treachery on their part?" he asked later. "The mere fact of their being Southern men was not surely a sufficient reason for suspecting their fidelity!" [15]

Too late Washington awoke to the situation, and replaced the commodore by the vigorous Captain Hiram Paulding, who made a frenzied attempt on the night of April 20–21 to destroy everything at the yards. Much of the property, however, survived his torch and dynamite. Taking possession of the smoking premises at dawn on the 21st, the Confederates were able to salvage the dry-dock, foundry, ordnance building, and other structures, much of the machinery, and hundreds of good cannon. [16] They soon began shipping ordnance to other places. Before long, heavy guns with fixed ammunition had been placed at almost every exposed point on the entire Southern coast, and at numerous entrenched camps inland. The Confederates simultaneously seized Fort Norfolk near the city, with about 150 tons of powder and many loaded shells. Of the warships, the *Merrimac* and the *Plymouth* were raised, and the former was converted into an ironclad of formidable strength. Besides gaining all this, the Southerners were able to intrench themselves in a position that would cripple any future Union movements in the region of the lower York and James. Warships issuing from Norfolk could attack along a wide coastline. [17]

Harpers Ferry lay within a short march of Washington and southern Pennsylvania, and by prompt action it also might have been held. The capture of the armory and arsenal was later described by one of the principal Confederate officers engaged as a purely impromptu affair. From the begin-

15 This officer, Charles S. McCauley, had received his orders April 10. See also Lossing, *Civil War*, I, 393, for details.
16 See report of a Virginia officer sent to inventory the place; Richmond *Enquirer*, Feb. 4, 1862, quoted in Lossing, I, 397, 398.
17 John A. Dahlgren, an inventive officer who had given the country an efficient ordnance workshop, and who took command of the Washington navy yard when Franklin Buchanan joined the Confederacy, wrote in his diary, Feb. 3, 1862: "It is now evident that the pivot of affairs lay in the period beginning at the time when the attack on Sumter was decided, and the abandonment of Norfolk. The loss of Norfolk was almost fatal; could that have been held, the fate of Virginia might have been otherwise. The Department had one month to send there a suitable Commandant and officers, which was not done. So the latter deserted and the former was helpless. How much it has cost, only to ward off the consequences of this mistake. . . ." M. V. Dahlgren, *Memoirs of John A. Dahlgren*, 355.

ning of the year the superintendent had warned the Ordnance Bureau that an attack might be imminent. Yet only a tiny force was sent to guard the machinery, the ammunition, and the 20,000 rifles, and by April 18 it was reduced to forty-five men. Though at that moment 20,000 rifles were absolutely priceless to the Union, the War Department had half a company to watch them! This rash exposure invited attack. Ex-Governor Henry A. Wise laid the plans; volunteer officers at a night meeting April 16 at the Exchange Hotel in Richmond worked out the details; the railroads of northern Virginia promised transport; and volunteer companies were alerted for orders from Governor Letcher. Troop units from Staunton, Charlottesville, Culpeper, and other points gathered in Winchester, and on the night of the 17th marched to the Ferry. Expecting a sharp battle, they were astonished when they found the arsenal blazing but deserted, for the little Union guard, warned that the enemy were at hand, had destroyed the munitions and stolen away. The novelist Hawthorne later described the ruins as dismal piles of broken bricks and smashed pillars, amid which lay gunbarrels in heaps of hundreds, twisted by the flames and rusted by weather.[18]

Had only a fighting regiment been there! During the first week the Confederates kept but 1300 raw recruits at the place. This force stopped a train which was carrying General William S. Harney, just humiliated by Frank Blair, from St. Louis to Washington. As sympathetic Confederate officers escorted the captured officers to a Richmond train, Harney gazed at the few hundred soldiers in sight, and with a twinkle inquired of the commander: "Where is your army encamped, general?" [19] Three batteries that the Southerners brought up had no caissons and no horses.

Within the next month, however, the Confederates raised their detachments at or near Harpers Ferry, commanding the confluence of the Shenandoah and Potomac, to the 8,000 men already noted. Still more important, they sent a Mexican War veteran to take command—the first appearance of Thomas J. Jackson on the stage where he was to become immortal. In the worn, dingy blue uniform of a professor at the Virginia Military Institute, Jackson instituted a rigid discipline and brought system into all the camp arrangements. With his six feet of height, powerful limbs, and strongly marked features set off by a heavy beard, he was an impressive figure. The troops quickly learned that he was gentle with the ignorant but unsparing with shirkers. Alert, energetic, a master of quick military movement, he merited his future sobriquet only in that his large frame and determined air gave him a rocklike firmness. "The

18 Statement by Col. Roger Jones, *Battles and Leaders*, I, 125; Hawthorne, "Chiefly About War Matters," *Atlantic*, vol. 10 (July, 1862), 43–61.
19 *Battles and Leaders*, I, 119, 120.

presence of a master mind," writes a subordinate, "was visible in the changed condition of the camp"; and this influence persisted after the command was transferred on May 23 to Joseph E. Johnston.

And who faced Johnston? A soldier near seventy, who after fighting in the War of 1812 and Mexican War, and spending decades in business, had been mustered into service as a ninety-day major-general of volunteers—Robert Patterson of Pennsylvania. On June 3 he took command at Chambersburg, Pennsylvania, of a little army consisting chiefly of Keystone militia. He at once proposed an advance against the Confederates on Maryland Heights, a sound strategic move. Scott approved the undertaking and sent him reinforcements, merely enjoining him to attempt nothing without a clear prospect of success, for the enemy would profit from even a drawn battle. When Patterson advanced with about 15,000 men, Johnston not only abandoned the Heights, destroyed the railroad bridge, and retreated south of the Potomac, but fell back to a point near Charlestown, Virginia. On June 16, Patterson repossessed Harpers Ferry—after the Confederates had carried off all the valuable arsenal machinery.[20]

But what then? He telegraphed Scott, saying that he wished to make the Ferry his base and march on Winchester. Scott quite properly asked the reason, writing him: "The enemy is concentrating upon Arlington and Alexandria, and this is the line first to be looked to." He was right, for the Confederates were gathering their forces at Manassas, hoping to advance on Alexandria; and Jefferson Davis had written Beauregard on June 13 that he planned soon to unite Johnston's troops with Beauregard's to give the advance impressive strength. Patterson remained where he was.

Although Scott had lost important pawns in the Norfolk naval base and Harpers Ferry arsenal, he had high hopes of the larger game.

[III]

On May 28, four days after troops moved across the Potomac to seize Alexandria, Brigadier-General Irvin McDowell was appointed head of the Department of Northeastern Virginia. This alert, capable officer, tall, deep-chested, and strong-limbed, had a reputation for efficiency, but in singularly limited fields. An Ohioan of Scotch-Irish family, a West Pointer in the class of 1838, a man of cultivation and foreign travel, he had served almost exclusively in staff positions. Duty at the Military Academy, in Mexico as adjutant-general

---

20 See Robert Patterson, *A Narrative of the Campaign in the Valley of the Shenandoah.* Scott's letter of instruction to Patterson was dated June 8, 1861; O. R. I, ii, 694. John Sherman served briefly on Patterson's staff.

to Wool, on various departmental staffs and at army headquarters—such was his record. He was liked by Scott, who had known him since he entered the army, and by Secretary Chase, influenced by the fact that McDowell came from his own town of Columbus. But McDowell was a man of distinct faults. He talked unguardedly, and was given to sharp sayings which helped make him one of the most unpopular officers of the army. He was a gargantuan feeder, who would soon show a portly figure and puffy face. And even Chase, while lauding him as brave, truthful, able, and intensely earnest, criticized his brusque aloofness. "He is too indifferent in manner," commented Chase. "His officers are sometimes alienated by it. He is too purely military in his intercourse with his soldiers." [21]

McDowell, as he later testified, never believed in Scott's march down the Mississippi. But he did agree with Scott that they must drill a large army, work which would take four or five months at least, and he contemplated no early battle.

Unit after unit was sent across the Potomac, until on June 24 McDowell was able to report that he had twenty infantry regiments, "good, bad, and indifferent," of nearly 14,000 men, with 250 cavalry and one serviceable field battery of 6 rifled guns. As more troops were steadily arriving, he hoped soon to have a field army of 25,000 men, leaving 10,000 in the Washington fortifications. McDowell held the sound conviction that long wagon trains groaning with impedimenta were unsoldierly.

It is difficult to describe the levies assembled under McDowell except in terms of a rabble. The peasants who milled about Wat Tyler with clubs and pitchforks were little inferior in equipment and training. To be sure, a few regulars theoretically seasoned the mass with some discipline and experience— one infantry battalion, a few cavalry and the single battery [22]—but actually they had no effect upon it; for the army was really made up of ninety-day militia, eager for discharge in July, and the first of the green three-year men who had responded to Lincoln's call in early May. Many Johnny Raws did not know how to fold their blankets properly, handle firearms safely (Senator Wilson, appalled by the accidents, urged that they be deprived of revolvers),

---

21 James Harrison Wilson, dining with McDowell, was impressed by his vigor. But noting that he gobbled up every dish within reach, finishing with an entire watermelon, he agreed with Gen. J. B. McPherson that he was too greedy a gourmand to be a good general. *Under the Old Flag*, I, 66. Carl Schurz writes that his censorious temper made him by the fall of 1862 the most hated officer in the entire army. But Chase, while granting his faults, attributed his unpopularity partly to the fact that he turned a harsh face toward all marauding and looting, and that he worked his troops down to Spartan fighting trim. Schurz, *Reminiscences*, II, 382, 383; Chase, Sept. 4, 1862, in Chase Papers, Pa. Hist. Soc.

22 This on June 24; three additional companies of regular artillery were in the Washington intrenchments. O. R. I, ii, 718 ff.

dig intrenchments, or otherwise take cover under fire.[23] The two inveterate camp enemies mentioned by Defoe in *Memoirs of a Cavalier*, idling and sotting, stalked through the Union lines. Later one commander explained a disaster by saying that although the men had not marched enough to tire them, "They had been loafing around a great deal; had been out a great deal of nights, and had been broken of their rest, and had not had full rations."

Reluctance to drill, an insubordinate temper, and a tendency to shirk hardship were general. W. H. Russell saw camps which stank abominably because the men had dug no latrines. He saw a soldier, diving into an earth-pit, halted by a sergeant's yell: "Dempsey, is that you going into the magazine wid yer pipe lighted?" On the march the recruits stopped to pick blackberries, refill their canteens, and lounge. Many officers, petty politicians or local dignitaries, were so incompetent that the story of captains ordering their companies to "Swing around like a barn door" were not wholly apocryphal.[24] The Massachusetts businessman, J. M. Forbes, transacting military business in Washington early in June for Governor Andrew, was alarmed by what he saw. One stupid officer infuriated him: "Of *such materials* is the U. S. Quartermaster's Department now composed!" He wrote prophetically: "I shall be surprised if they don't get a *big scare* at Washington one of these days, and should be glad to see our [Massachusetts] preparations of all *essentials* so complete that we could on a pinch hurry off our six Regiments at short notice. Tents and wagons in such a case might follow later." [25]

Nor was this amateur army given proper headquarters organization. McDowell, who had been partly educated in France and had spent 1859 traveling and studying there, knew the paper requirements of an army. His motley force was grouped in five divisions of 2,000 to 3,600 men each, but the five brigadiers, Samuel P. Heintzelman, Theodore Runyon, D. S. Miles, Daniel Tyler, and David Hunter, were poorly acquainted with their duties, with their subordinates, and with their own capacities. Nobody, not even McDowell, had ever handled a division before; Hunter and Heintzelman, both West Pointers, had been majors before the war, but Hunter only as paymaster in Mexico. For staff work McDowell assembled the proper number of quartermasters, commissary officers, and medical officers, and assigned men to ordnance, signal service, inspection, and engineering, but regulars were so few that he had to employ many novices.

McDowell's own headquarters was lamentably under-officered. He had no chief of staff to help him take comprehensive views and to catch up his work if

23 Henry Wilson, June 27, 1861, to Governor Andrew; Andrew Papers, MHS.
24 George W. Bicknell, *Hist. 5th Maine;* Samuel Merrill, *The 70th Indiana*, etc.; *Committee on the Conduct of the War*, II, 182.
25 Forbes to Andrew, June 9, 1861; Andrew Papers, MHS.

he were disabled; nor did he have any group to help him make plans, move forces, and see that his orders were executed. W. H. Russell, breakfasting with him on July 6, found him unaccompanied by any aide. When they walked later through the Washington streets, not one of the many soldiers they passed saluted. No military police or provost guard was available to keep order among the troops, who bought liquor at will and at night became drunkenly riotous. Some days later, Russell on reaching Washington from Annapolis found McDowell alone on the station platform, peering anxiously into the cars for two batteries that had gone astray. Russell expressed astonishment to find an army commander running such errands. "I am obliged to look after them myself," sheepishly explained McDowell, "as I have so small a staff, and they are all engaged out at my headquarters." But he had no real staff at all, observed Russell; just some plodding pedants to write memoranda and ignorant young fellows to strut about.[26]

His intelligence service was practically nonexistent. Telling Russell that a decent map of Virginia was unprocurable, he admitted that he knew little or nothing of the country in front, and had no cavalry officer capable of making a reconnaissance.

For these defects McDowell was far from being solely responsible. Winfield Scott, irritated when Cameron ordered McDowell across the river, had vainly urged the general to protest. In his displeasure he treated McDowell coldly, impeded the flow of troops to his camps, and denied him expert assistance. Clinging to his Mississippi plan, Scott wanted nothing but a holding operation in Virginia. "No additions were made to the force at all," testified McDowell later. "With difficulty could I get any officers." In vain did McDowell tell Secretaries Cameron and Chase that his burden was too great for one man, and that he could not organize, discipline, and lead his army without trained aides.

Scott's irritation increased when McDowell felt it necessary to argue before a Cabinet meeting against the Mississippi expedition on the ground that it would encounter excessive obstacles and perils. To capture New Orleans, said the general, the North should take Pakenham's short route. The head of the new Department of Washington, General J. K. F. Mansfield, also showed jealous chilliness toward McDowell.[27]

It could not justly be said that McDowell and his five division commanders

---

26 Russell, *My Diary*, July 16. Gurowski, *Diary 1861–62*, p. 61, says he saw McDowell do detail work which even in a half-organized army belonged to the chief of staff. Russell's opinions, corroborated by testimony before the Committee on the Conduct of the War, are expert, for he had seen much of armies and campaigns, and edited in London the best military periodical in the world.

27 *Committee on the Conduct of the War*, II, 37 ff.

gave their troops insufficient drill; the difficulty rather was in the wrong kind of drill. Numerous parades in June found the troops marching with increased precision. When on the 17th Cameron and McDowell reviewed eight infantry regiments, with some cavalry and artillery, in the most imposing military display yet made, spectators voiced a lively admiration. But of long route marches, charges, scaling exercises, and target practice there was almost none. Had the war been a contest in drill-ground evolutions, the army would have done well. As it was, McDowell shortly had to explain that his men were so unused even to light marching-order loads that a force which should have covered a six-mile road in four hours without strain actually took eleven hours and arrived in exhaustion. Though by June 20 his lines extended twenty miles along the Potomac and at some points reached ten miles into Virginia, offering room for businesslike maneuvers, his idea was to break in his troops gradually.

By that date three armies had taken shape in Virginia: Patterson's at ruined Harpers Ferry, Ben Butler's at Fort Monroe, and McDowell's. McClellan had largely completed his successful West Virginia campaign.[28] Lyon commanded a small force in Missouri with which he hoped to purge the State. But what armies! The authors of over-all strategic plans talked of sweeping marches to New Orleans, to Nashville, to Richmond, to Mobile and Pensacola; and here were crude, poorly armed cohorts that for the most part could not be trusted to march twenty miles in hostile territory. Any dream can be indulged by men who plan in the supramundane spirit of Simon the Magician. It is now time to turn to an examination of realities, and measure the discipline, equipment, morale, and cohesion of the legions that had been assembled to vindicate the unity of the republic.

28 One of McClellan's subordinates on June 3, with a small Indiana brigade, routed a Confederate force with such hot pursuit that the event was termed "the Philippi races." Then on July 11, W. S. Rosecrans, second in command, defeated the Confederate forces on Rich Mountain led by John Pegram and W. S. Garnett. Credit for the West Virginia campaign lay as much with the subordinate officers, including the able Jacob D. Cox, as with McClellan.

9

The Greenhorn Armies

THE TRADITIONAL DISTRUST of Anglo-Americans for military establishments had long been reflected in their treatment of regular troops. In
America as in Britain the army had been starved. Captain Jenks of the Horse
Marines had been as much a figure of fun as Tommy Atkins. The American
regular force, absurdly small for its severe duties on the Indian frontier, and
totally inadequate as a nucleus in the event of foreign collision, nevertheless
satisfied the nation. After the Mexican War its strength had been fixed at
10,120. Later its numbers were enlarged, especially when in 1855 four regiments were added; but just before the Civil War it barely exceeded 16,000.
This, as one administrator after another pointed out, was insufficient to keep
the western tribes in order.

The flames of Indian hostilities had flickered up at many points in the West
during the 'fifties, falling and rising again, but never quite being extinguished.
One reason for adding the four new regiments in the middle of the decade
was that a detachment of troops had just been murdered by the Sioux. In Texas
and New Mexico punitive expeditions were needed to suppress Indians guilty
of outrages on the settlers and the emigrant trains. A considerable force under
Harney had to invade the Sioux country, partly to protect western Kansas
and Nebraska, and partly to keep the Oregon Trail clear. In the Territories of
Washington and Oregon sharp fighting took place. The line of the Indian
frontier in the Far West grew more perilous as emigration and settlement
thickened. In 1857 the Secretary of War, reckoning that an aggregate of 6700
miles of emigrant roads had to be watched, declared that his forces found adequate protection impossible. The country had sixty-eight forts of a large and
permanent character and seventy less substantial posts where garrisons were
needed. They were scattered over three million square miles, so that a visit even
to a dozen of the most important required a long, arduous journey. Down to
1861 the War Department constantly besought Congress for more men, and
a better system of strongholds.

[I]

The organization of the army was manifestly defective. Its basis was in part the British army system as it had existed in the colonies, and it retained many defects which the British army had pruned away. The several grades of generals were appointed by the President, but below this rank, promotion by seniority was the inflexible rule, so that no matter how incompetent the officer, he was steadily pushed up the ladder. As Secretary of War Floyd remarked, "The *worst* officer of any army *must*, if he lives, come to be one of the most important and responsible officers under the government," a regimental head. An almost insurmountable wall separated line officers from the staff (that is, medical, quartermaster, commissariat officers), who constituted an independent corps. Seldom serving in the field, the staff could not gain an adequate fund of observation and experience, while their independent status deprived them of proper opportunities as aides to the commanders. The system also begot an unhappy accumulation of red tape and prerogative—of general stuffiness.[1]

When we add that the pennypinching national economy kept the army ill paid, so that a major-general received only $3480 a year, a brigadier $2112, and colonels from $1332 in the infantry to $1512 in the cavalry, we can understand why so many able men left the service. (The Chief Justice was paid $8500; Cabinet members and Associate Justices got $8000, Senators and Representatives $5000.) Lower officers were worse off still. After long, arduous waiting, a captain of infantry had to rear his family on $768 a year, and a major on $888, with small contingent allowances. Although no prudent British father would allow his son to enter the army without private means, in general the British pay was fully double the American scale.[2]

One branch, the engineers' corps, an exception to the general rule, did offer scope to energetic and ambitious young men. For one reason, its activities lay mainly outside the tribal country. "Service in the Indian campaigns," Secretary Jefferson Davis remarked, "though little calculated to excite the military ardor of the soldier, is attended by equal hazard and even by greater privation than belongs to warfare with a civilized foe." It was dirty, exhausting, risky work; icy blizzards, burning heat, raging streams, blinding dust storms, were commonplace incidents of duty; long periods of loneliness and monotony, demoralizing in the extreme, were followed by fierce spasms of hardship and peril.

1 See the annual Reports of the Secretaries of War, 1850–60, particularly those of Jefferson Davis and John B. Floyd.
2 *Harper's Magazine*, Vol. 11 (Sept., 1855), 552–555. It was generally agreed that a captain ought for the good of the service to get at least $1800, a colonel $3000. The pay schedule adopted early in the century had been continued without regard to rising costs. The base pay of $7 a month for privates explained in part the general American contempt for "sogers."

In the engineering service, however, officers might distinguish themselves by road building, dam construction, harbor work, exploration, or erection of public buildings, becoming as famous as Lee or Montgomery C. Meigs.

Throughout the 1850's the army engineers were busy making military roads in the West. They surveyed the Great Lakes, gathering materials for accurate charts and marking reefs and shoals with buoys. Military parties were sent to survey unknown areas and explore the most practicable railroad routes between the Mississippi and Pacific. This was suitable work, for the defense of the Pacific Coast in war would require a railroad, and it was also work which army engineers could best perform. Robert E. Lee found no satisfaction in routine garrison duty, but when assigned to the problem of removing some bars in the Mississippi opposite St. Louis which threatened to destroy the usefulness of the port, he delighted in a task worthy of his best efforts. From beginning to end, Lee's labors had carried him over much of the nation. He improved the channel of the upper Mississippi at Keokuk rapids. He performed engineering work at Cockspur Island near Savannah. In New York Harbor he saw to the making of elaborate changes in Fort Lafayette and Fort Hamilton. Other engineers dealt with assignments just as complex; for example, Captain Randolph B. Marcy, who by 1861 was a veteran of western exploration, skilled in road-marking, fort-placing, and guidebook-writing.

That the regular army was on the whole well officered its severest critics seldom denied. Its leaders had received their training in three schools: West Point, the Mexican War, and various branches of civil life. Many of the best officers of the conflict now beginning had enjoyed a combination of all three.

West Point, as founded in the Jefferson Administration, was originally a school for training military engineers, with a plan based largely upon that of the Royal Military Academy of Woolwich. But under the farsighted, meticulously careful, and progressive administration of Sylvanus Thayer, who in 1817 began re-creating the institution, its course was broadened while its discipline became more severe. "Sylvanus Thayer is a tyrant," Andrew Jackson ejaculated in 1832. "The autocrat of all the Russias couldn't exercise more power!" But he was a wise, benevolent autocrat, and when he left in 1833 the academy had a growing reputation.

Some capable teachers came; Dennis Hart Mahan, for example, whose book on strategy and military history, *Outpost* (1847), proved that he was the best military scientist of his time in America.[3] In 1854 Colonel William J. Hardee, asked by the government to prepare a system of drill which would permit of quicker evolutions, compiled a handbook of tactics based primarily on

3 R. E. Dupuy, *Where They Have Trod*, and Schaff, *The Spirit of Old West Point*, *passim*.

French practice.[4] Immediately introduced at West Point, his tactics became standard in the army. Under Lee, who was superintendent 1853–55, the course was lengthened to five years to make room for English, military law, and more of practical training.

The active service of the Mexican War gave many young officers useful lessons not only in handling troops, but in resourcefulness and persistence. Robert E. Lee was only a captain when, during the march on Mexico City, he made a perilous night journey to headquarters with news of an enemy concentration which Scott called "the greatest feat of moral and physical courage performed by any individual during the campaign." Grant was but a lieutenant when at Cerro Gordo he helped lead the advance over chasms so steep that his men could barely climb the precipices. Robert Anderson was a captain of artillery when, accompanying Scott, he penned the letters to his wife which furnish the most charming and graphic account of the campaign. At Buena Vista, Captain Braxton Bragg fought gallantly to convert defeat into victory, and at the most desperate moment Jefferson Davis did turn the balance with his regiment of Mississippi Rifles. The 900-mile march of John E. Wool from San Antonio to Saltillo, the yet longer march of A. W. Doniphan to Chihuahua, the surprise attack of Persifor F. Smith which destroyed a Mexican army at Contreras, the assault of Joseph E. Johnston on Chapultepec, and the varied service seen by T. J. Jackson and McClellan, all counted as tuition for an infinitely more grueling contest.

Both before and after the Mexican War, West Point men who would later play large parts in the conflict of North and South steadily left the regular army for civil employ. In a country so rich in opportunity, the wonder is that so many—Thomas, Ewell, Lee, Pope, Sheridan, Buell—stayed. Meade, who graduated from West Point in 1835, resigned the next year, but came back to the army in 1842. Hooker, who graduated in 1837, left in 1853 to seek his fortune in California. Sherman, of the class of 1840, forsook the army in 1853 to give restless trials to banking, law, and the management of a military· college. Grant, taking his West Point degree in 1843, was out of the army eleven years later, drifting from occupation to occupation. William S. Rosecrans, of the class of 1842, stayed in military life but a dozen years before engineering, coal mining, and oil refining engaged his talents. McClellan thirteen years after he quit West Point was chief engineer of the Illinois Central. All these men learned much from their wide experience of both civil and military affairs.[5]

4　The Washington *National Intelligencer*, Nov. 2, 1854, states that Hardee's text was taken from the system of the Chasseurs de Vincennes in France.

5　Nearly 300 West Point graduates became Northern generals in the war, and about 150 became Southern generals; E. C. Boynton, *History of West Point*. Sixty-five Southern cadets resigned from West Point to take Confederate commissions.

But the fact remains that the regular army was a poor nucleus for a rapidly expanding force in a great conflict. The limited scale upon which its various branches operated made for inertia, narrowness, and slackness. The medical department, for example, had been organized by Secretary John C. Calhoun in 1818 under an excellent plan. The first surgeon-general, a capable, energetic man, had required every post surgeon to keep full and accurate records upon everything pertaining to climate, disease, and "medical topography" and to forward them to the Medical Bureau in Washington. The next incumbent utilized these records to publish two useful volumes in 1856, one on medical statistics, the other an army meteorological register. But beyond collecting some illuminating if limited information, the Medical Bureau thereafter achieved almost nothing.

Its officers were mere post doctors, who, with one brilliant exception later to be noted, lacked not only experience in the problems of a large medical establishment, but capacity to organize a service to meet these problems. Nobody had really studied camp sanitation; nobody, despite the ghastly lessons taught the British and French in the Crimea, really understood hospital requirements. The same stagnation, hidebound worship of routine, and pettiness of outlook obtained among the rank and file of the quartermaster and commissary departments.

All the principal army services, in short, would have to be rebuilt on a new basis. The regulars were only a trickling little stream which would soon be merged with the plunging waters of a river of volunteers.

[II]

What were the principles and methods by which the construction of a great volunteer army in the North began? We have seen how Eastern governors hurriedly sent the first militia regiments to Washington. But the 75,000 ninety-day men constituted the merest stopgap.[6]

In the initial emergency Lincoln, incessantly busy with other matters, had to depend on the Cabinet. So far as Cameron went, this meant depending on a reed, for that fumbling Secretary let delays, confusion, and blundering over-master him. Salmon P. Chase provided the first clear guidance.

On May 3, as we have noted, Lincoln issued a proclamation calling for 42,034 volunteers to serve three years or the duration, and next day Cameron in General Order No. 15 specified that they should be organized in forty regiments. Lincoln simultaneously directed a small augmentation of the regular

---

6 The three-month men on July 1 actually numbered 77,875; *Ann. Cyc.* The 16,000 regulars were partly needed in the West to hold the Indians in check.

army. It was Chase who inspired these steps. That energetic, ambitious leader while governor of Ohio had carried through a reorganization of the military establishment of the State, lifting it to a new plane of efficiency; he had many military friends; and once war began, he was anxious to see it waged with implacable resolution. If he had had his way, the government would have called for 65,000 more men instead of 42,000. And it was Chase who, by Lincoln's express direction and with Cameron's consent, took up the problem of organizing the new levies.

Just how this astonishing delegation of powers of the War Department to the head of the Treasury took place we do not know. Perhaps at some Cabinet meeting Chase pointed to his experience with military administration in Ohio. Everyone knew that Scott specially respected him, and that McDowell was a protégé; the overworked Cameron was ready to agree; and Lincoln, who had a low opinion of Cameron and was impressed by Chase's masterful, dynamic ways, gladly assented. The moment Chase entered a room energy, system, rapidity (and grasping ambition) entered with him. He asked McDowell, who in the beginning was assistant adjutant-general, and W. B. Franklin, a West Point graduate who was superintending architect of the Treasury, to draw up a basic plan which he revised.[7]

The first question before these men was vital. Should they make a bold new plan for a consolidated national army, or should they accept the traditional reliance on State regiments, State officered and largely State-equipped, to be slowly and imperfectly welded into a national force? In short, should purely military considerations rule, or political and popular pressures be dominant? From the standpoint of professional military men, a dazzling opportunity presented itself. The Administration might use the crisis to demand a unitary national army, its officers to be appointed by Washington; its men to be recruited not by States but by regions or departments; and each regiment to be divided into three battalions, one regularly posted to a home base to enlist and drill recruits so that the command would always be kept full.[8] If Chase and his advisers had asked for this and for a general conscription act, they would have offered the country a military plan which French or Prussian officers could applaud—a plan not unlike that which later enabled the country to fight two world wars with signal efficiency.

But even McDowell and Franklin dared not go so far. They recommended that the three-year regiments be made part of the regular army, with national

7 Schuckers, *Chase*, 183–186; Meneely, *War Department, 1861*, 137 ff.; Upton, *Military Policy of the U. S.*, 234. Franklin had graduated at the head of his class (1843) and fought at Buena Vista; the fact that his father was long clerk of the House of Representatives helped him take national views.

8 Upton, 234.

numerals, and with officers commissioned by the President on nomination by the governors. They suggested that the regiments be apportioned among the States according to their representation in Congress, that the three-battalion system be adopted, and that each Congressional district be required to keep its regiment full. This was a hybrid national-State system. And Chase rejected even this mild advance. He knew that to put boys from Connecticut, New York, or Wisconsin into units designated simply by regular-army numbers, not by State names, would kindle a mighty popular revolt. For himself, he said, he would "rather have no regiments raised in Ohio than that they should not be known as Ohio regiments." He was against the three-battalion plan for volunteers (though not for the regulars), arguing that it would be unwise to abandon a regimental organization with which all State militia were familiar; and he thought that to avoid too great a centralization of authority in the Federal Government, the States should appoint the regimental officers.

In thus sticking to the old-fashioned system, Chase gauged public sentiment well. However great a price that system had cost the nation in the Revolution and the War of 1812, the people would not abandon it. Congress had to ratify his plan, which we shall consider in detail later, and Congress would have balked at a consolidated army. All Illinoisans wanted to speak of "The Fifty-fifth Illinois"; all New Yorkers of "The Eighty-eighth New York."

The next two problems were interrelated: How should the forty volunteer regiments be apportioned among the States, and how rapidly should they be sent to the front? These questions were bound to bring the State and Federal authorities into collision. Aflame with patriotic zeal, a number of governors had encouraged the enlistment of troops beyond reasonable limits, and were under pressure to put them on a firing line. Legislatures had created camps of instruction; State executives had hurried troops to these camps and were feeding and drilling them at great expense; the men were eager to fight, and other groups at home were eager to take their places.

In his general order for the forty regiments, Cameron did not specify State quotas, so that a vast deal of confusion and uncertainty ensued all over the North. The companies drilling in a thousand communities and coalescing into regiments hoped for prompt acceptance by Washington. Their officers besieged the governors, who in turn bombarded Washington for instructions and concessions. Representatives and Senators hurled themselves upon the War Department. As day after day no orders came, the companies continued to drill, parade, and swear, and to write angry letters to political friends.

When the Union Defense Committee of New York found that conflicting laws and orders interfered with the prompt use of fourteen regiments it was equipping, a committee hurried to the capital and held an impatient interview of several hours with Lincoln on May 15. The President agreed that the four-teen regiments might forthwith be moved to Washington.[9] At once jealous Pennsylvanians expressed great indignation. Chiefly from units already drilling, Governor Curtin formed a reserve of fifteen regiments under a new military bill which he pushed through the legislature. These reserve regiments, destined to honorable fame in a dire national crisis, demanded that they get just as fair treatment as the New Yorkers.

Belatedly, Cameron on May 15 did write a letter, not received by some governors for a week, announcing to each State its quota. The one sent to John A. Andrew in Boston was typical of all. Cameron informed the impatient Andrew, who knew that more than ten thousand men were drilling and fuming in the Bay State, that he could send forward only six new regiments. "It is im-portant," wrote the Secretary, "to reduce rather than to enlarge this number, and in no event to exceed it. Let me earnestly recommend to you, therefore, to call for no more than eight regiments, of which six only are to serve for three years, or during the war, and, if more are already called for, to reduce the number by discharge." [10] In State after State, Cameron's strict limitations, and his admonitions to keep recruiting and mobilization down, fell on the public zeal like a chilling fogbank.

Nearly all the principal governors continued to strain at the leash, eager to move further and faster than the War Department thought feasible. Bucking-ham of Connecticut, for example, had made an agreement in Washington with General Scott (sanctioned, he thought, by Cameron) for acceptance of some extra regiments which were imploring active duty. Returning to Connecticut, he was outraged to find this agreement canceled by Cameron's new action on State quotas. Curtin was similarly incensed when Cameron notified him that the government would accept only ten three-year regiments from Pennsyl-vania, for this meant sending large bodies of enthusiastic Keystone volunteers home. Curtin exploded in an angry letter to Cameron: "It would be well for me to understand how authority is divided, so we can move with certainty, and the ardor of the people of this State should not be again cooled by changes." Yates thought that Lincoln's own State was very shabbily treated.[11]

Austin Blair of Michigan, too, a man of radical temper who favored prompt, sweeping, and aggressive policies, condemned the Administration policy of limiting the troops to be accepted. He predicted that the nation would soon rue it. After putting the First Michigan early on the scene in Washington, he

9 N. Y. *Tribune*, May 16, 1861.
10 Schouler, *Mass. in the Civil War*, I, 167.
11 Meneely, 146, 147. Governor Buckingham's troops were to include a regiment armed free of charge by Colonel Colt with Colt's revolving breech-loading rifles (an arm by no means perfected); Buckingham, *Buckingham*, 163, 164.

had pressed forward the preparation of three additional regiments. When the War Department sent him word that it would be better to reduce than increase that number, numerous additional companies drilling throughout Michigan either broke up or found service under the banners of other States. Governor Blair indignantly kept on with his program of training, and had the satisfaction of seeing the Fifth Michigan leave Detroit for Virginia late in the summer. He wished to see overwhelming Union forces hurled upon the enemy like Caesar's legions—"pay them out of his property, feed them from his granaries, mount them upon his horses, and . . . let him feel the full force of the storm of war." [12]

[III]

The fact was that the War Department wished to avoid explaining publicly the chief reason for limiting the armies. This was that to hurry masses of men to Washington before uniforms, arms, camps, and hospitals were ready would be a calamity. Arsenals and armories were half-empty; few depots of military stores existed; tents and uniforms could not be made overnight, or good drill-masters supplied. Of the 30,000 volunteers in Washington, wrote a well-informed journalist on May 15, not more than 2000 would be called soldiers by a British or French general.

When the emergency first developed, Scott thought that troops need be given only a gun and ammunition before going to Washington for full equipment; Chase and Cameron wished to see the States furnish them a full outfit for field and camp before they came. Lincoln at first tended to take Scott's side, but as the dispute persisted saw that his Cabinet officers had the greater reason. The shortage of equipment could be far better understood in Washington than in Indianapolis or Boston, where many imagined that the government had vast storehouses full of everything. Actually, the supply of arms alone was partially adequate, and difficulties of distribution hindered their use. The government had no foundry for cannon. Uniforms, blankets, tents, medicines, all were grossly deficient. Hence it was that Cameron wrote Lincoln as late as July 1 that one of the main difficulties was to keep down the size of the army; hence Lincoln finally informed Congress on July 4: "One of the greatest perplexities of the government is to avoid receiving troops faster than it can provide for them." [13]

The commissary officers in Washington, purchasing large quantities of food

12 Message to the legislature, Jan. 2, 1862.
13 O. R. III, i, 303. Chase was of course partly actuated by his dread of unnecessary expense while the Treasury was still ill served. On this see W. P. Fessenden, Aug. 27, 1861; Fessenden MSS, Columbia Univ.

for the incoming troops, found themselves without organization to distribute it properly. They had insufficient horses and wagons; they had no cooking facilities in many of the buildings where thousands of men were housed. Not only stoves and utensils, but blankets, cots, mattresses, and tents were urgently needed. Forehanded commanders tried to provide for their troops before arrival at the capital. For example, Colonel H. W. Slocum, the popular head of the New York Twenty-seventh, had sent his lieutenant-colonel in advance to see that victuals were ready; but the officer could do nothing, and the men found only two barrels of salt pork. They went to bed supperless and angry. The First Massachusetts, miraculously reaching Washington some two hours ahead of schedule, also found no provisions ready. Those who had no money went hungry the first night. Next morning they rustled up some boxes of salt red herring, soda crackers, and a quantity of wormy, sour ship-bread, and with coffee made in two rusty caldrons found in a hardware store, got the semblance of a meal.[14] In a day when most families breakfasted on stewed fruit, oatmeal, meat or eggs, potatoes, and bread and butter, this was sorry fare.

Such shortages were virtually nation-wide. The governors, so creditably anxious to raise heavy armies and deal stout blows, learned this as soon as they went into the national market for necessaries.

Buckingham of Connecticut, for example, at once found a shortage of arms. His State had a thousand muskets of Mexican War age, and two thousand smoothbore percussion muskets that were practically useless. It owned thirty pieces of artillery, but no caissons or harness. He had money aplenty, but to find good arms to buy was another matter. The difficulties of transport were highly irritating. The First Connecticut left New Haven by sea May 9, a thousand men jammed on a little steamer that could scarcely accommodate two hundred in comfort; no food, little water, and practically no plumbing. He met another shortage in uniforms. The quartermaster-general, paying $7.50 each for a supply, had to take many made of blue satinet, this being a euphonious term for shoddy, a cotton warp filled with reclaimed wool. A New Haven Congressman later charged that many of the uniforms were not worth eighty cents, but shortages had driven the price high. No attention was paid to the size and measurements of the volunteers; and men in uniforms too short or too long, falling into shreds before a month expired, were as ludicrously pathetic as circus clowns.[15]

Yet the governors still insisted on drilling troops, doing their best to equip them, and if possible getting them sent off to some front. Well it was that they

14 Leech, *Reveille in Washington*, Ch. V; C. B. Fairchild, *Hist. of the 27th Regt. N. Y. Volunteers*; W. H. Cudworth, *Hist. of the First Regt. Mass. Infantry*.
15 See Buckingham's Annual Message to the Leg. (May Session), 1861; New Haven *Register*, *Journal*, and *Courier*, June 13–15, 1861; Hartford *Courant*, June 17, 1861.

did so! Anxious to fight a hard war, they were wiser than those who like Montgomery Blair expected a short, easy conflict; wiser by far than Seward, who on April 28 told a New Yorker that the Administration wished to preserve the Union by winning the disloyal to loyalty, not by waging aggressive warfare. Curtin's fourteen reserve regiments were to do some of the best fighting of the war. Buckingham's extra regiments battled on bloody fields, and Connecticut flags were the first planted on the soil of South Carolina and Mississippi.[16]

Even more impatient and aggressive than these men was the redoubtable John A. Andrew of Massachusetts, a host in himself when the war began. "We wish to go *onward*, not to *stand still*," he exhorted a Cabinet member, adding that in defense of the Union, "We relent at no sacrifice." When Cameron on May 15, informing him of the Massachusetts quota of three-year volunteers, earnestly recommended that he furnish no more than eight regiments in all, of whom only six would be three-year men, Andrew was bitterly disappointed. Six regiments! Three had already gone to the camps, leaving only three more to be supplied. Yet at that time more than ten thousand men in Massachusetts were organized into companies, hot for service.[17] How could he select fifty companies from two hundred demanding action? He would not! The legislature had created camps for five volunteer regiments, and, defying Cameron's instructions, Andrew filled them, making these five commands a reserve. However, about three thousand ardent Massachusetts men at once enlisted elsewhere —six companies in New York alone—and others went back to their homes. The general feeling was of chagrin and bitterness, and Andrew shared it.

He continued to press on the Administration the importance of using more men and making war more aggressively, thus shortening the conflict. Visiting Washington, the short, stout, bustling governor, his curling hair disordered, his eyes gleaming behind his spectacles, began to snap at Cameron like a pertinacious airedale. "I shall give you ten regiments fully equipped within forty days!" he exclaimed. Horace Greeley helped to publicize his demands in the press. General Hiram Walbridge of New York, busy to the same end, spoke to Lincoln in Andrew's behalf. At last, in mid-June, Cameron consented to receive ten additional regiments from Massachusetts. By the middle of July the six regiments originally bargained for had all marched off to the front; Fletcher Webster's regiment, which in honor of an illustrious name had been given independent acceptance by the Department, followed on June 24; and before

16 George L. Clark, *Hist. of Conn.*, 391. On Friday, May 10, Governors Dennison (Ohio), Curtin, Blair, and Randall (Wisconsin) spoke from a hotel balcony in Cleveland. Austin Blair said they were daily telegraphing the President, "Call on us for more troops." Cleveland *Leader*, N. Y. *Tribune*, May 9.

17 Pearson, *Andrew*, I, 233; Schouler, *Mass. in the Civil War*, I, 165.

the close of the first week in August three more regiments had gone. This left seven still recruiting.

Thus the little Bay State, with a population of a million and a quarter, was assigned seventeen regiments in all, far more than her due proportion. Despite the governor's forty-day pledge, September arrived before the last regiment was moved forward. But Andrew's radical aggressiveness was unabated. Speaking to this last regiment at a dinner given it on its passage through New York, he demanded relentless military action and hailed the coming day when Southerners would find slavery falling beneath their own parricidal stroke.[18]

The geographical situation of Ohio gave special importance to the zeal of Governor William Dennison, a former Cincinnati attorney who displayed unexpected grasp and energy. It was he who, hearing from friends of the high capacity of McClellan, sent for him, talked with him, and had him made major-general commanding all the State militia. He also sent James A. Garfield to Illinois for 5000 arms, and hurried another agent to New York who got about an equal quantity there and ordered more from England. Dennison took practical control of the railways, telegraphs, and express lines for war purposes; he besought the governors of Indiana and Illinois to join him in invading Kentucky, a proposal vetoed by Lincoln; he argued the thesis that the proper line of defense was not the Ohio River but the mountains below it; and he persuaded the War Department to extend the boundaries of the department assigned to McClellan so that they covered that area. It was Dennison who on May 11 telegraphed Secretary Chase asking him to see that McClellan got a three-year commission, so that he would outrank all others in that theater. "Ohio must lead throughout the war." And it was mainly because of Dennison's preparations that before June two Northern columns were marching into Virginia beyond Parkersburg. Ohio had gone far toward justifying Dennison's insistence on a preëminent role in the war, and her military sons—Hayes, Garfield, McKinley—were to make her a new Mother of Presidents.[19]

New York, too, refused to accept the limits that Cameron tried to place on her efforts. Here the problem of troop supply gave rise to a three-cornered quarrel, sustained with acrid intensity and *opéra bouffe* drama by Governor E. D. Morgan, the Union Defense Committee of the metropolis, and Secretary Cameron. We need sketch only its outlines.

The legislature, thinking Lincoln's call for seventy-five thousand militia inadequate, not only hastened their dispatch, but under a hurried law of April

18 Pearson, *Andrew*, I, 250.
19 Whitelaw Reid, *Ohio in the War*, I, 53–57. By the end of 1861 the attorney-general of Ohio was able to report that the State had furnished, beyond its 22,380 three-month men, no fewer than 77,844 men enlisted for three years. If Dennison had been given his way, he would have raised more, and have sent them more rapidly to the front.

18 authorized the raising of thirty-eight volunteer regiments for two years' service. One two-year regiment had left for the front, and companies of the other thirty-seven were moving to the rendezvous points when Lincoln issued his call on May 3 for three-year troops! Cameron then fixed the New York quota at only ten regiments. He and Morgan forthwith began exchanging angry epistles over the questions whether ten or more should be accepted, and whether for two or three years. The dispute was complicated by a confusing series of War Department dispatches May 13–15 to Morgan, speaking of ten, eleven, and fourteen regiments, and of terms of two years, three years, and "two or three years." Cameron and his chief clerk were themselves confused.

Meanwhile, Cameron wrote the Union Defense Committee that, needing nine regiments "to serve during the war," he hoped the Committee would supply them if Morgan refused to do so. This accentuated a conflict which had rapidly developed between Morgan, who insisted that he and his State military board should keep firm control of military affairs, and the Committee, which after busily organizing regiments wished to get them off its hands and off the expense accounts of the metropolis.[20]

Lincoln himself had to intervene to help arrange a workable compromise. In mid-May, after talking with anxious members of the Defense Committee, he gave them a decision supported by General Scott: he would take fourteen regiments from them if the men would serve three years. In this decision Lincoln was moved by the praiseworthy energy the Committee had displayed when Washington stood in peril, by its subsequent enterprise, and by his realization that its influential members would be most useful to the government in the flotation of loans.[21] Both he and Seward, however, were anxious not to offend Morgan, or to create a situation in which the governor and committee would give more time to fighting each other than to defeating the Confederacy. They hastily assured Morgan that the fourteen city regiments were not to be deducted from the thirty-eight State regiments that Albany was offering, but were to be added.

Seward wrote Thurlow Weed in Albany to this effect. "Tell the Governor in God's name to send on the whole quota," he enjoined Weed. "I will take care of it." Lincoln had General Scott convey the same message to Morgan. Simultaneously, the President warned the Defense Committee that he felt real concern "lest a seesawing commence, by which neither your troops nor the governor's will get along in any reasonable time." [22]

Unfortunately, friction between Governor Morgan, an earnest, businesslike

20 Meneely, 157–160; E. D. Morgan to Cameron, May 10, 1861, Morgan Papers, N. Y. State Library. See James Rawley, *Edwin D. Morgan, 1811–1883: Merchant in Politics.*
21 Chase to Dennison, May 16, 1861, cited in Meneely, 160.
22 Weed, *Life of Thurlow Weed*, II, 333; *Hist. Union Defense Committee*, 185, 186.

man with a rigid sense of the dignities of his office, and the Defense Committee, which was determined to extend its proud record, persisted and grew. While the President and Seward wished fourteen Committee regiments added to the thirty-eight State regiments, Chase and Cameron wished them subtracted. "It is the P——, General S——, and I against the two C's," Seward had written Weed. When the Committee pressed for assurances that it might act independently of Morgan, Cameron on May 18 telegraphed a pointed refusal. He and the President were at partial cross-purposes in the matter. It appears that they were not even well informed of each other's views and actions. While Lincoln on May 22 asked Morgan to come to Washington for a face-to-face discussion, with Committee members present, Cameron the same day dispatched an aide northward to talk with the governor and Committee, and give them a fresh summary of the War Department's position. It turned out that Morgan could not take time to visit Washington.

It also turned out that the Defense Committee, so clamorous for furnishing fourteen regiments, actually had fit recruits for only eight! [23] And Cameron's assistant found that it was by no means certain Morgan could furnish his thirty-eight. It is no wonder that this assistant reported that he had become suspicious of all promises and believed that a high Federal officer should take charge of the whole New York situation.[24]

Ultimately, all the New York agencies that were pressing regiments upon the reluctant War Department won at least a partial victory. That of Morgan might be termed complete. Cameron, after fresh protestations that he would take none but three-year men, finally capitulated and accepted the full thirty-eight regiments of two-year men. The last regiment left the State July 12. But still, in this era of improvisation, confusion waved its scepter. Several of the thirty-eight, unfortunately, had been recruited for three months of Federal service, and two years of State service, so that the men naturally supposed that at the end of ninety days they would be returned to their New York homes. When the War Department ruled that they must complete two full years and held them for the national army, mutinies developed in four regiments, and were not suppressed without great vexation.[25] These thirty-eight volunteer regiments aggregated some 37,000 men. The Defense Committee stuck to its insistence on fourteen regiments. And the noisy, unprincipled Daniel Sickles, who had received special Administration permission to raise a brigade, filled up three regiments by mid-July and soon afterward partially recruited two more.

23 O. R. III, i, 226; four regiments had already gone forward and 4500 men were ready to make up four more.
24 Meneely, 163, 164.
25 Special Orders 322, Aug. 2, 1861; *Report*, Bureau of Military Record 1865, pp. 54 ff.

Altogether, New York during 1861 led the nation by raising more than 120,000 men, distributed among 125 regiments, battalions, and batteries. Of these, not far from half were ready before Bull Run produced a new situation and an urgent new call for troops.[26]

[IV]

Altogether, it was a remarkable chapter of headlong action which the Northern governors wrote in the three months following Sumter. As yet, the republic had more vigor in its State governments than in its still unorganized national departments, headed by inexperienced, overworked, and sometimes weak men. The determined war spirit of the North was far better exemplified by the ablest State executives—Morton, Dennison, and Austin Blair in the Middle West, Buckingham, Andrew, Morgan, and Curtin in the East—than by the uncertain Cameron, the cautious Bates, the conservative Caleb B. Smith, or even Montgomery Blair with his bemused trust in Southern Unionism. To be sure, the governors often moved all too heedlessly and hastily, but they moved with unflinching resolution.

The story in other States was in general outline much like that in Ohio, Massachusetts, and New York. Nearly everywhere, enthusiastic agencies or ambitious men were pressing military units on the governors, sometimes real companies and battalions, sometimes mere paper plans for companies. Nearly all the governors, beset by a thousand local pressures, urged on by newspapers and politicians vocal for aggressive war, and coping with legislatures which were much more ready to provide camps of instruction than to appropriate money for keeping bodies of troops in them for any period, pressed the nation to take troops off their hands—more troops—yet more troops. They were impatient of delays. As Andrew wrote of his own action, they moved "as if there was not an inch of red tape in the world." The governors believed that the Administration was underestimating the task ahead, and the people would have pressed them on from behind even if they had not so believed.

Inevitably, the Administration, with Cameron wringing his hands over chronic deficiencies in supplies, and Chase tormented by financial exigencies, tried first to stem the torrent of proffered troops, then in May and early June partially yielded, and soon thereafter tried again to build cofferdams. As the special Congressional session called for July 4 drew near, Cameron's reluctance to accept troops increased. He already had in national camps a far larger aggregate of ninety-day militia and long-term volunteers than he had ever expected. He, Chase, and several Congressional leaders had been toiling long

26 *Report,* Bur. Mil. Record, 39 ff.; O. R. III, i, 344, 345, 483, 494.

hours on a comprehensive plan to meet the situation. He wanted to accept no more responsibility until Congress had given its approval.

With all real fighting still ahead, the soldiers could take their shortages and privations with summer insouciance. The war was yet in its gala period of cheers, music, exciting new scenes, and exalted patriotism, and a happy release from humdrum toil.

We may take the First New Hampshire as an example. When it struck its tents near Concord at the end of May it rolled southward through green fields, burgeoning woods, and a continuous ovation. Crowds assembled at every station to cheer the special train. At Norwich, Connecticut, the columns, smart in dark gray with red-cord facings, marched aboard two Sound steamers. At dawn next morning they found waiting on the Hudson River pier a Granite State committee with a presentation flag, a bevy of ladies, and a speech. Headed by their band, they marched across Manhattan, impressing spectators with their four women nurses for each company, shining arms, and seventeen four-horse wagons carrying camp equipment, provisions, and ammunition. They dined at the large New York hotels, and as the sun sloped westward marched through more cheering crowds to take their twenty-car train to Washington.[27] Many a farm lad and mechanic in that regiment had never before been twenty miles from home, never ridden on train or steamboat, never seen a city or glittering hotel. The war was romance, the muskets and bayonets were for parade, and the nurses were proof of home solicitude, not a portent of wounds and disease.

In short, confusion, improvisation, and deficiencies that under a grimmer war test would have been intolerable could be grimacingly endured, while excitement and exaltation fixed the mood of the day. On May 26 a frothy wave of emotion surged through Washington. Three guns suddenly boomed from the War Department, the signal that fighting had begun across the Potomac and that all troops must move across the bridge to participate. Dragoons clattered past the Treasury; batteries tore down the Avenue; the Fifth Massachusetts double-quicked toward the Potomac, followed by a Connecticut regiment and District volunteers. Soldiers yelled, civilians cheered, women screamed, and a general uproar followed the yellow coil of dust that marked the onrush. For half an hour Washington was bedlam. Congressmen, buckling pistols to their waists, shook hands and offered jubilant bets on victory. Then, as troops reached the Long Bridge, came word that it was a false alarm growing out of some target practice.

Still the Administration clung to the theory that the Confederacy could best be crushed by anaconda pressures from every side. Lincoln during April

27 N. Y. *Tribune*, May 27, 1861.

had proclaimed the blockade of all Confederate ports, and Scott had written that the government relied greatly on its "sure operation." [28] As rapidly as possible, vessels had been posted outside the chief southern ports. The wife of Senator James Chesnut, living in Richmond and seeing Jefferson Davis frequently, noted on his authority July 16: "We begin to cry out for more ammunition and already the blockade is beginning to shut it all out."

But as news came of the fortification of the Mississippi, and the mustering of formidable Confederate forces in Tennessee and southeastern Missouri, it became plain that Scott's dream of a great amphibian expedition proceeding relentlessly down the Father of Waters would have to be qualified. Seizure of the Mississippi was sound, but it would take time. It also became evident that the large Confederate army gathering under Beauregard at Manassas might have to be attacked shortly lest it attack Washington; that, in short, Confederate movements would do much to determine the grand strategy of the war. On July 1, 1861, the total strength of the Union forces was placed at 186,000. Of these, McDowell had about 30,000 facing Beauregard.

The nation waited. North and South, a sense that the ominous pause of late June and early July preluded fateful scenes of action grew deeper. The armies, excited by small clashes in West Virginia and Missouri, waited. Business, depressed from Maine to Texas by the innumerable derangements of the crisis, waited. Anxious wives and mothers, torn between pride and grief, waited. Throughout the wide South four million Negroes, feeling emotions of wonderment and hope they had never before known, waited. Not since Naseby and Sedgmoor, Camden and King's Mountain, had an English-speaking people, a people above all others used to compromise and hostile to fanaticism, been called upon to understand the tragedy of a civil conflict.

The leaders of the now divided peoples waited too, each resigned, but each apprehensive and sorrowful. When Mrs. James Chesnut talked to Davis, she was impressed by his melancholy outlook, and recorded that throughout all he said ran "a sad refrain." A sculptor friend of Lincoln has written that about two weeks before he left Springfield for Washington "a deepseated melancholy seemed to take possession of his soul." Lincoln had felt a pang of personal grief in the death of Elmer Ellsworth, to whose parents he had written a sorrow-sharing letter. His secretaries were growing used to his smile, "in which there was so much of sadness." [29] Nevertheless, each leader in his own way faced the terrible situation with fortitude.

10

The Union Leaders

BECAUSE THE national organization for waging a great war was wretchedly rudimentary, Congress, though half deluded by the idea of a short conflict, now had to follow Lincoln's first steps by beginning to construct a system to meet the task which lay before the North. The brunt of the labor fell on Republican veterans whom seniority gave important committee positions.

At high noon on July 4, 1861, portly Hannibal Hamlin let his gavel fall in the Senate, while the brisk, wiry John W. Forney as clerk rapped for order in the House. Both men gazed on sadly depleted chambers. In the Senate, even after Orville H. Browning had taken the vacant seat of Douglas, and two members had been sworn in from newly admitted Kansas, the roster reached only forty-four. For all eleven States of the Confederacy a solitary man, Andrew Johnson of Tennessee, answered the roll. In the House, after the chaplain had instructed God on the realities of the crisis, 159 responded, but two from western Virginia were at once challenged. Everybody anticipated a brief session, and many predicted that it would last only a fortnight, for little beyond initial measures to carry on the war would be discussed.

The organization of the House at this opening of the Thirty-seventh Congress was quickly completed. After one ballot Galusha A. Grow was chosen Speaker over Frank Blair, his nearest competitor, while Emerson Etheridge was elected clerk. Grow, a tall Pennsylvanian of dynamic aspect, with a dome-like forehead and intense steely eyes, was not yet thirty-eight. His rapid rise was attributable partly to talent, partly to the assistance of his law partner David Wilmot, and partly to his zealous championship of homestead legislation. A man of homespun simplicity, a working and not a talking leader, and a former Democrat who had been quick to join the new Republican Party, he was popular both at home and in the House. This former bark spudder of the Tunkhannock frontier, in fact, represented the best type of self-made American. Etheridge, an uncompromising Unionist, had been one of the nine slave-State members of Congress who had fought the Kansas-Nebraska Act. Himself from western Tennessee, he had come to Washington a few weeks earlier to plead for aid to the terrorized Unionists of East Tennessee. His election was a tribute to a courageous man who, his friends said, would be murdered if he returned home.

Frank Blair's appointment as chairman of the House Military Affairs Committee, a post in which he would collaborate with Henry Wilson of the Senate Committee, gave promise of energetic action. Thaddeus Stevens of Pennsylvania, beginning his fourth term, took the powerful and thankless chairmanship of Ways and Means. His senatorial counterpart was William Pitt Fessenden of Maine, equally shrewd but far milder in temper. The wise, equable old John J. Crittenden of the House Committee on Foreign Affairs had the task of working with the strong-willed Charles Sumner of the similar Senate body. These chairmanships would carry throughout the war, except that Blair, entering the army, would give way to William A. Richardson of Illinois, and Crittenden, dying in 1863, to Daniel W. Gooch of Massachusetts. It will be noted that Crittenden, the Nestor of Congress, whose national service had begun as Jefferson left the White House, had gladly taken a House seat at the end of his Senatorial term.[1]

In the Senate, New England was now clearly dominant. The departure of Seward and Chase for Cabinet posts had given Sumner, Fessenden, Henry Wilson, and John P. Hale of New Hampshire greater prestige than ever. Hale was head of the naval affairs committee. Westerners grumbled over the fact that Yankees also held the chairmanships of the committees on postoffice, claims, patents, printing, and public buildings.[2] Sumner, by virtue of his real if stilted oratorical power, literary talent, pedantic learning, friendships among the principal intellectual luminaries of England and America, and record as an implacable warrior against slavery, loomed highest among the members. Even on the Republican side many distrusted his fanaticism, egotism, and harshness of language, and all were irritated by his pomposity, which led Lincoln to remark that although he had seen little of bishops, "Sumner, you know, is my idea of a bishop." To border members his puritanical intolerance often seemed edged with malice, as if in assailing Southern institutions he was as much interested in injuring white men as in helping blacks. But nobody of sense ever questioned his ability, integrity, or elevation of purpose. His critical attitude toward Seward, though their disagreements impeded the conduct of foreign affairs, was well warranted.[3]

---

1 Crittenden had accepted a Federal post in Illinois as early as 1809.

2 The only New England Senator who did not have a chairmanship was the newcomer Lot M. Morrill of Maine. One House observer later wrote that New England's quasi-monopoly of posts "created no small degree of jealousy and ill-feeling in other sections"; Blaine, *Twenty Years,* I, 323.

3 C. F. Adams, *R. H. Dana,* II, 253, 258. Dana believed that Sumner in his large and influential correspondence with Britons denounced Seward freely, but this was untrue.

Most of the prominent Midwesterners in the Senate were of New England derivation. Lyman Trumbull of Illinois, Lincoln's friend, came of the famous Connecticut family. Ben Wade of Ohio had been reared in western Massachusetts on a poverty-stricken hill farm, never outgrowing its rough vocabulary. Zack Chandler of Michigan, a man of unbounded self-confidence, aggressiveness, and radicalism, sprang from a rural New Hampshire township; and so did James W. Grimes of Iowa, a leader of iron independence and shrewd judgment. Timothy O. Howe of Wisconsin, who had courageously insisted that the Fugitive Slave Act ought to be obeyed, could speak of his Maine origins. On sectional questions all these descendants of New England tended toward a certain uniformity of view. Trumbull, for example, for all his general moderation, often voted with his radical colleagues.

The House, far more than the Senate, had an acknowledged chieftain. When James G. Blaine in 1881 undertook to name three parliamentary leaders in America who had taken positions comparable with that of Chatham in the British legislature, he listed Clay, Douglas, and Thaddeus Stevens of Pennsylvania. Here again was a son of New England, for Stevens came from Vermont, and had graduated from Dartmouth. Close thought, wide reading, and grim conviction, with long practice at the bar, gave him an unrivaled power in debate. His broad shoulders, pushed up in a perpetual shrug, bore a tremendous head of peculiar shape—broad at the back and high in front, with a heavy ridge above the deep-set, lustrous eyes. His strongly-marked features were formidable, for the stubborn chin and projecting lower lip, beetling eyebrows, and ready frown gave him a pugnacious appearance. His large frame was ungainly, and his walk, since he had a clubfoot, lumbering. When he spoke, his high-keyed voice flung out his crisp, sententious, neatly turned sentences with belligerent decision. Humor, picturesqueness of language, and literary eloquence he seldom employed, but he possessed a dry wit of Damascene sharpness with which, his face solemnly impassive, he would sometimes take off an opponent's head so dexterously that he convulsed the House.

Above all, however, his lucidity, force, and grasp of fact and principle made him feared. He remembered dates, figures, and precedents with invariable exactness. Those who were stung by his brusque manner and savage sallies to grapple with him were usually swiftly downed by his battering-ram mind and devastating use of his tenacious memory. In conducting House business, he detested technicalities, tricks, and trifles; by a few whip-crack sentences he would bring members back to the main point. He had an overmastering sense of the magnitude of the issues confronting the republic, which made him scornful of defenders of slavery or palterers with treason. He demanded that the war be fought with unrelenting vigor, he insisted on extirpating the taproot of secession, and just now he meant to keep the House hard at work until an effective Administration program had been enacted. In this determination he had efficient aides. One was Elihu B. Washburne of Illinois, the most vigilant and conscientious of the western members, whose eight years' experience made him an expert in the rules of the House; another was Owen Lovejoy of the same State, fierily eloquent for the emancipation cause for which his brother had died; and a third was the hardworking Justin S. Morrill of Vermont.[4]

Both House and Senate leaders were anxious to work with Lincoln in prosecuting the war effort, but both were already determined to move further and faster than he thought wise. Between Sumner and Lincoln useful friendship was destined in time to develop, founded on a mutual esteem which overrode their immense incompatibility of temperament. Sumner, who had enough of an uncertain, flickering greatness of his own to divine the far deeper, more stable greatness of Lincoln, had quickly made himself a familiar of the White House. He was learning to admire Lincoln's patient sagacity, his passion for justice, and the Euclidean precision of his intellectual processes, even though the President's magnanimity seemed weakness to him, and the President's humor (a quality of which Sumner had none) quite incomprehensible.

Thaddeus Stevens kept away from the White House and the departmental offices. Stubbornly, even belligerently, independent, he would have regarded friendly calls on the President as a fawning on power. He wished to be free to attack Cabinet officers with incisive criticism.[5] He had bitterly resented the appointment of Cameron to the War Department, regarding himself as better Cabinet material and coveting the Treasury. He thought Lincoln too tardy, too ready to temporize and compromise, too anxious to consult public sentiment. As yet, however, he was willing to restrain his impatience and cooperate energetically with Administration leaders.[6]

For the time being the Republicans, so new to power, had real unity. For

---

4 Here are more Yankees of rural origin; Washburne, like the Lovejoys (both Owen and the martyred Elijah) came from Maine.

5 Because Stevens made many enemies, cared little for appearances or public opinion, and drew a saturnine mask over his private life, dubious gossip and legend clustered about him. But beyond a propensity to gambling, no important dereliction was ever proved by real evidence. He had many kindly traits, including a warm liking for young men, a passionate sympathy for the handicapped and abused (to whom he gave freely), and great devotion to his mother. He visited her annually, and said that it was the greatest joy of his life that he was able to present her "a well-stocked farm and an occasional bright gold-piece which she loved to deposit in the contribution of the Baptist church which she attended." Josiah Bushnell Grinnell, who knew him well, credited him with a character of great sensibility. "On a reverse in business partial friends proposed a gift of one hundred thousand dollars—a gift delicately declined in further proof of a sensitive rather than of a sordid nature." *Men and Events of Forty Years*, 189.

6 A. K. McClure, *Lincoln and Men of War-Times*, includes a discerning chapter, pp. 277-295, on Lincoln and Stevens.

that matter, there was temporarily much truth in what one member said, that Congress had only two parties, Union and anti-Union. Most of the true War Democrats aligned themselves with War Republicans. Lincoln was urging formation of a Union Party, which duly appeared this summer in New York and other States. No trouble would be encountered in carrying the needed measures.

Among Lincoln's many worries, however, one was the question of the real extent of Democratic support. He eagerly questioned members and scanned the early debates. In the Senate the worst Border dissenters, notably James A. Bayard of Delaware, James A. Pearce of Maryland, Trusten Polk of Missouri, and most hostile of all, John C. Breckinridge, he thrust outside serious consideration. Representing the hard-shell slaveholders, they held ideas that had been antiquated in Monroe's day. Polk, Breckinridge, and Jesse D. Bright of Indiana were later to be expelled for disloyalty, and Breckinridge was to command Confederate troops.

It was the Douglas Democrats who counted, and happily for the Administration, they showed the right mettle. Had their leader been present he would have differed from the Republicans on important issues, but he would have been a very Hampden in national patriotism. The brilliant E. D. Baker of Oregon, Lincoln's beloved friend, evinced the same militant spirit that had made him colonel of a regiment in the Mexican War. James A. McDougall of California, another old friend, John R. Thompson of New Jersey, and that stanch Jacksonian Unionist, Andrew Johnson, who had risked his life in opposing the Tennessee secessionists, were all dependable. Determined to crush the Confederacy, these Valiants-for-Truth despised any Faint-Heart. They would fight to the last against what McDougall called "the mad assault of misguided men on the integrity of the Union."

In the House some Douglasites threatened to show a more lukewarm spirit. The rhetorical S. S. Cox of Ohio, from the Cincinnati district, who touched a hornet's nest by accusing the Western Reserve of being slow to answer the war trumpet, declared that he would fight to restore the Union, but for nothing beyond that goal. "I will vote for what is required to enable the Executive to sustain the Government—not to subjugate the South, but to vindicate the honor, peace, and power of the Government." His whole attitude was wittily equivocal; but then Cox, a graduate of Brown and a former editor of the *Ohio Statesman*, might be trusted not to go too far in defending the South. His worst offense was a resolution suggesting that Lincoln should appoint seven conservative Northerners, including Van Buren, Filmore, and Pierce, to confer with seven Southern commissioners on peace and Union; an effort to muddy the waters, but not so bad as Clement L. Vallandigham's resolution forbidding the President to call out more troops until he named peace commissioners to accompany them to the South.[7] Cox was more than offset by a bold Douglas man from the Springfield district in Illinois, another of Lincoln's friends, John A. McClernand, who made speeches with a Jacksonian ring. Still another Democrat, H. B. Wright of Wilkes-Barre, replied to Vallandigham as to a Catiline:

> I want to see no peace that is established upon the overthrow and disintegration of the republic. . . . When they come to us and ask terms for these unholy and unrighteous acts, I am willing to say to them that we will take your terms into consideration when you lay down your arms and abandon the project of a southern confederacy. . . . The offenses have been too severe and too great to go unpunished. . . . The kind of subjugation about which I speak is the subjugation of traitors, in order that patriots may live, and in order that the benefits of our laws and institutions shall prevail. If the gentleman from Ohio calls that subjugation, I tell him I am in favor of such subjugation.[8]

The shades of Jackson, Polk, and Douglas, which throughout the session seemed to cheer on the Unionist Democrats, were certainly present when one of the memorable scenes of senatorial history took place on August 1. From the first day the former Vice-President, Breckinridge, had flown one poisoned shaft after another into Northern ranks. He had charged the Republicans with guilt for the war, had accused Lincoln of hasty, arbitrary passion in calling forth the largest army ever seen in the hemisphere, and had predicted that a year of fighting would bury all constitutional liberty. The feeling that this Kentuckian, with all his dignity, grace, and felicitous diction, was as deadly an enemy of the Union as Jefferson Davis, had grown until an explosion came. The topic under debate was a bill to use martial law to suppress insurrection and sedition.[9]

Breckinridge, his face flushed with emotion, gained the floor. "The drama, sir, is beginning to open before us," he declaimed, "and we begin to catch some idea of its magnitude." Under this demand for the regulation of military affairs, he went on, lurked a sinister plot for the confiscation of Southern property and emancipation of Southern slaves. Every day, the Constitution was being trodden more brutally under foot. Public and personal liberties

---

7 *Cong. Globe*, 37th Congress, 1st Session, 28 (McDougall); 96 (Cox).
8 *Idem*, p. 98.
9 Breckinridge, just forty, had studied at Center College, the College of New Jersey, and Transylvania, and had gained renown at the Lexington bar. He had held that after Sumter the Union no longer existed, and favored the secession of Kentucky, but temporarily accepted the neutral status of his State. Southerners now expected him to act as defender of the Confederacy, and he did so. A speech he made July 16 assailing Republicans for not accepting the Crittenden Compromise was called "treasonable sophistry" by the N. Y. *Tribune*.

were dying. Ruin, utter ruin, awaited the South, North, and West alike; heavy contending armies might desolate the whole continent, and what would be the result?—two enfeebled and implacably hostile nations. He quoted Calhoun's assertion: "War is disunion, eternal and final disunion."

During this tirade Baker, who had raised a regiment of volunteers now in camp near Washington, entered the chamber in his colonel's uniform, carrying his fatigue cap and riding whip. He gained the floor. As a boy he had seen the brilliant London pageant with which Nelson was carried to his grave, and he was the more fervently American because he was an adopted citizen. He began calmly, putting Breckinridge some searching questions. But his feelings quickly carried him away. The nation was waging war, he said; its armies must advance beyond the jurisdiction of civil courts; the commanders must therefore exercise authority over life, liberty, and property. Breckinridge wished to halt the armies and yield to rebellion. What, then, were the pleas he was making? Were they not intended to blunt the Northern weapons and animate Southern fighters? "Sir, are they not words of brilliant, polished treason, even in the very Capitol?" The galleries broke into applause, but he continued:

What would have been thought if, in another Capitol, in another Republic, in a yet more martial age, a senator as grave, not more eloquent or dignified than the Senator from Kentucky, yet with the Roman purple flowing over his shoulders, had risen in his place, surrounded with all the illustrations of Roman glory, and declared that advancing Hannibal was just, and that Carthage ought to be dealt with in terms of peace? What would have been thought if, after the battle of Cannae, a senator there had risen in his place, and denounced every levy of the Roman people, every expenditure of its treasure, and every appeal to its old recollections? . . . It is a grand commentary upon the American Constitution that we permit these words to be uttered.

Fessenden replied in a stage whisper to the question about the Roman traitor: "He would have been hurled from the Tarpeian Rock." The speech, made so impressive by Baker's sudden striking appearance on the scene in military uniform, so filled with fire and logic, reverberated throughout the country. What does it matter, asked Baker, if we expend materials and money without measure? "In a year's peace, in ten years at most of peaceful progress, we can restore them all"—and as guerdon of their toils, they would have the reunited nation, the Union, the Constitution, and a free government, unvexed by the treason which Breckinridge was preaching.[10]

10 This scene, rendered more memorable by the fact that Baker soon sealed his fealty to the flag with his death, was later described by many who saw it. See the accounts in Blaine, *Twenty Years*, I, 344, 345; Forney, *Anecdotes of Public Men*, I, 42 ff.; Henry L.

[I]

The atmosphere of Washington as Congress sat was hardly conducive to thoughtful debate. Regiments steadily streamed into the capital. Through the open windows members heard the blare of bands and stentorian commands of officers, and caught the gleam of gun barrels and gay colors, as troops marched from the trains. With a hundred thousand soldiers in the Washington area, the city seemed an ever vaster camp. Pennsylvania Avenue had been so cut up by Army wagons that riding over it was like traversing a corduroy road. The streets were thronged every afternoon and night by tipsy, quarrelsome troops, who crowded the saloons, brawled on corners, or stood lonesomely in doorways. Bloody altercations were frequent, for drunken men flourished bayonets and revolvers without rebuke. The Washington police consisted of a day force of only sixteen men and an auxiliary night guard of fifty paid by the national government. Though the mayor had fixed 9:30 P.M. as closing hour for saloons, the rule was widely disregarded. On July 4 most proprietors shut their drinking places because they feared the soldiers would get out of hand, as many did. Among the troops swarmed undesirables of many kinds. The city, wrote one private, "is lousy with secessionists, and is the den, the very lair, of swindlers."

Washington shops were filled with martial trappings—swords, epaulets, dirks, pistols, and spurs. Bookstores displayed volumes on infantry tactics, artillery drill, and camp management, along with titles like Count Gasparin's *Uprising of a Great People*, and patriotic sheet music. One officer bought for twenty-seven dollars books whose titles he loosely recorded:

Callan's *Military Laws*	Mahan's *Out Posts*
Halleck's *Military Art*	*Standing Orders Seventh Regiment*
Nolan's *Cavalry Horse*	*School of the Guides*
Maxims, etc., on the Art of War	Benet's *Court Martial*
The Art of War	*Ordnance Manual*
Casey's *Tactics*	Field Manual Battalion Drill

Field Manual on the Evolutions of the Line [11]

All the hotels and boardinghouses were now jammed, with rooms renting at premium prices. "Soldiers are cheated here most unmercifully," wrote one. Lobbies were crowded with generals (Lincoln told of a boy who threw a stick

---

Dawes, "Two Vice-Presidents, John C. Breckinridge and Hannibal Hamlin," *Century Magazine*, July, 1895. Breckinridge, thinking that Sumner had uttered the remark on the Tarpeian Rock, at once scathingly denounced him; *Cong. Globe*, 37th Cong., 1st Sess., 376 ff.

11 See the statement by the Commissioner of Public Building in the Report of the Secretary of the Interior, Nov. 30, 1861; Washington newspapers; and the MS Diary of Colonel J. A. Mulligan in the Chicago Hist. Soc. Mulligan bought the books listed.

at a dog and hit five brigadiers), colonels, and majors in every variety of uniform; with Zouaves in red, blue, and gray; with men of crack militia regiments, sailors in bell-bottom trousers, and cavalrymen in boots. Among the epaulets moved women flaunting their finery. "Hoops and buttons have the highways and byways, ogling each other," wrote a disgusted Western officer. "Beauty and sin done up in silk, with the accompaniment of lustrous eyes and luxurious hair, on every thoroughfare offer themselves for Treasury notes."

Of all the hotels, Willard's stood preëminent. It was more clearly the center of the Union, observed Hawthorne a little later, than the Capitol or White House. "You are mixed up with office-seekers, wire-pullers, inventors, artists, poets, prosers (including editors, army correspondents, attachés of foreign journals, and long-winded talkers), clerks, diplomatists, mail contractors, railway directors, until your own identity is lost among them." Political mendicants were irrepressible once more, for the business depression had augmented their numbers. They swarmed into departmental offices, pursued Congressmen to their rooms, and thrust letters of application into reluctant hands on the streets. The hot, dingy city gave the general impression of a vast miscellaneous disorder. It was little wonder that visitors took refuge from its stench and struggle in juleps, gin slings, whiskey-skins, and brandy smashes.[12]

As the place grew more crowded, its sanitary condition became worse. The medical authorities had good reason to fear an outbreak of typhoid among civilians and troops. Even yet the Washington aqueduct to bring water from Great Falls was unfinished, for much grading and facing with masonry remained to be done on the tunnels, while work on the distributing basin had been interrupted when laborers were hurried off to erect intrenchments on the Virginia shore. The Washington canal in the heart of town, constructed at great cost and regarded at first as a valuable improvement, had become an intolerable nuisance. It was a grand open receptacle for nearly all the filth of the city. The sewage from public buildings, hotels, and many private residences drained into it, and had filled it in many places with accumulations of offensive soil and rank vegetation above the water level. This sewer stretched within almost a stone's throw of the Capitol, Treasury, and White House. As an official report declared:

The accumulated filth and excrement of the city is constantly held in a state of semi-solution in this hotbed of putrefaction, by means of the ebb and flow of the tides, over a surface of more than a million square feet. And whatever portion of it ultimately finds its way into the Potomac River is spread

12 Mulligan, MS Diary; Hawthorne, "Chiefly About War Matters," vol. 10, Atlantic (July 1862), 43–61.

out in thinner proportions over several hundred acres of flats immediately in front of the city, the surface of which is exposed to the action of the sun at intervals during the day, and the miasma from which contaminates every breath of air which passes, from that direction, through or over the city.[13]

The unfinished state of the Capitol pained many of its occupants. Though government provision for work on the dome had stopped a fortnight after Sumter, the contractors had decided to go ahead at their own risk. The porticoes and steps of the Capitol wings had still to be completed; part of the interior of the wings was unfinished; and the bronze statute of Freedom to rise over the whole was still in progress. It was painful, also, to have the entire basement of the Capitol devoted to a huge army bakery. Fat bakers in white aprons and paper caps busied themselves in rooms once sacred to clerks and committees. The crypt under the rotunda was used for storing flour. Army wagons clattered over the lawns and walks, and smoke from the ovens drifted into the rooms where Congress sat. When flues were installed, they discharged the smoke into the hot air pipes for warming the Congressional Library, so that it was impossible to make winter use of the books until the bakery was removed.

Happily, however, most Capitol rooms had been so thoroughly renovated that few traces remained of its brief use as a barracks. Buchanan's portrait had been removed from the rotunda, and the names of secessionist Senators erased from their desks. The shrubbery had been renewed, the walls repainted or whitewashed, the floors polished, and the chambers carpeted with a cool matting. The White House, too, had been refurnished—though Lincoln rather liked the battered furniture which remained in various rooms. To a fashionable New Yorker who condoled with him for dwelling in so dilapidated a mansion, he dryly replied: "All I know is that it is much the nicest house I have ever lived in." [14]

It was well for everyone in the government to realize that the nation's business was now war. The day Congress met, a parade of New York troops swept along Pennsylvania Avenue. Lincoln, the Cabinet, and other dignitaries watched it from a pavilion near the White House, and later he, Scott, and others spoke briefly to the throng.

13 Commissioner of Public Buildings in Interior Dept. Report, Nov. 30, 1861; Report of R. Seymour, Senate Misc. Doc. 83, Thirty-eighth Cong., 1st Sess., 20.
14 See Senate Exec. Docs. Nos. 1 and 2, 37th Cong., 2d Sess., on the state of the public buildings, and the Washington aqueduct. The Treasury had also been entirely renovated after troop occupancy, the soldiers at one time having used every room from basement to attic.

[II]

If Republican feeling was adamant for the Union, it had not yet hardened into a demand for action against slavery. The venerable Crittenden offered on July 19 a long-famous resolution on the objects of the war. It declared:

... that this war is not waged, upon our part, in any spirit of oppression, nor for any purpose of conquest or subjugation, nor purpose of overthrowing or interfering with the rights or established institutions of these States, but to defend and maintain the supremacy of the Constitution and to preserve the Union, with all the dignity, equality, and rights of the several States unimpaired; that as soon as these objects are accomplished, the war ought to cease.

This Crittenden resolution carried in the House 117 to 2, the dissenters being Charles J. Biddle of Philadelphia, Democrat, and A. G. Riddle of Ohio, Republican. In the Senate the resolution passed 30 to 5. Southern leaders, who had frequently accused the Republican Party of intending to destroy their institutions, might have found in it a proof of forbearance, and it unquestionably helped placate border sentiment.[15]

Lincoln's message to Congress was calm and mild, addressed to reason and not passion. Its most caustic passages related to Virginia, whose leaders, he believed, had tricked him by pretending adherence to the Union at the very time that they were concerting aid to the Confederacy. Now war would sweep over them: "The people of Virginia have thus allowed this giant insurrection to make its nest within her borders, and this government has no choice left but to deal with it where it finds it." Much of the message was devoted to a justification of his course in the Sumter crisis. If he had yielded, he wrote, the Union would have gone to pieces, and republican government would have tottered. He could not betray so vast and sacred a trust. He and those supporting him had chosen their course "without guile, and with pure purpose," and they must press forward with manly hearts to victory. But he uttered not a single harsh word upon the Southern people.

The President's request that Congress give the government at least 400,000 men and $400,000,000 precipitated a debate as hot as the July sun that swung over Washington. Not that anybody doubted that the great new volunteer army must and would be created without delay. The three-month men would be returning home immediately; the forces under McDowell, McClellan, and Lyon were obviously insufficient to sweep through the South; and the country was eager for decisive action. Congress was actually determined to give Lincoln not less that 500,000 men. But the mode of organizing this force, the system of choosing, measuring, and replacing its officers, the standards of pay and

15 Cong. Globe, 37th Cong., 1st Sess., 222, 223. Passage took place in the House July 22, in the Senate July 25. It was by no means a firm commitment.

subsistence, and several lesser questions, excited grave differences. The War Department, too, would have to be strengthened, and members differed about the means.

Every effort was made by Administration leaders to expedite action. The very first bill introduced in the Senate was Henry Wilson's measure for the new volunteer army. Reported out of committee within a week, on July 10, it was passed after rapid discussion before the day closed, 34 to 4. It provided the 500,000 troops that Senate leaders thought necessary. Unfortunately, the Senate's action had been *too* hasty; a day later Wilson called the measure back from the House for changes, some of them important. On the 12th he presented it again, and it at once passed in amended form, 35 to 4. The House that same day took up a measure of its own, whipped into shape by Frank Blair and his committee, which it passed without delay. A conference committee ironed out the differences, and on July 18, only a fortnight after Congress met, an act was ready for Lincoln's signature. He signed it July 22.[16]

Quick work!—but in this brief period some interesting questions had been discussed. One was the length of service. An Ohio Democrat in the House, objecting to the three-year term fixed by Republican leaders, which he said proved that the government had no faith in its ability to quell the rebellion promptly, argued for one year on the ground that volunteers would be much more easily found for a short term. The majority insisted on three years or the duration of the war. A minority also opposed the figure of 500,000 fixed by the two military committees. Surely, declared McClernand of Illinois, Lincoln and Scott had known the number actually needed when they proposed 400,000. Various border members, notably Senator Saulsbury of Delaware and Representative Burnett of Kentucky, went further. Half a million men smelled to them of a war of subjugation, and Saulsbury proposed 200,000, which he thought enough to defend Washington and the North while a peaceful solution was being arranged. The angry majority voted him and four other border Senators down.[17]

[III]

Sitting until August 6—and its pace was soon accelerated by Bull Run—Congress in twenty-nine working days passed seventy-six public acts, ranging from the volunteer army bill to the creation of a better police force for Wash-

16 *Cong. Globe*, 37th Cong., 1st Sess., 50–54, 64, 147, 194, 205. The nation now stood at much the point in this war which it had reached in the Revolution when Congress, under date of September, 1776, provided for the enlistment of 88 battalions of 750 men each to serve for the duration.

17 The men who voted with Saulsbury were Trusten Polk (Mo.), W. P. Johnson (Mo.), Anthony Kennedy (Md.), and Lazarus Powell (Ky.).

ington. A great increase in the navy was authorized, and eleven regiments were added to the regular army.

The augmentation of the regular army provoked much opposition, for as we have said, most Americans regarded the regular establishment with contempt. Many of the soldiers were misfits, who had enlisted more often from love of adventure, idleness, drunken impulse, or fear of civil punishment than from patriotism. A majority of them lived the sullen, stupid lives of men without wives or family, and without ambition. They usually served in lonely, uncomfortable frontier posts, spending most days in monotonous drill and evenings in dull vacuity. Bad officers tyrannized over them, and good officers gave them no comradeship. Naturally, they turned to drink, gambling, and horseplay, their privations proving less hurtful than their degradations. Although the army held a better position than in Europe, parallels for Thackeray's picture in *Barry Lyndon* were easily found, and many American captains would have echoed Lord Melbourne's statement that the worst men make the best soldiers. The Anglo-Saxon distrust of standing armies in time of peace was reinforced by the special American feeling that in a land so full of opportunity, something was wrong with a man who found refuge in the military.

The Administration proposal to add 24,000 men to the regulars therefore elicited a variety of adverse arguments. Some in both houses, including Lovejoy, Trumbull, and E. D. Baker, thought that in view of the great new volunteer army, more regulars were unnecessary, and that once added, it would be hard to reduce their numbers. Senator Grimes believed that good men had too great a prejudice against the regulars to enlist, that a large standing army was unrepublican, and that after the war it would be an intolerable expense. In the House, Blair's Military Affairs Committee took the position that the volunteer army would be adequate to win the war, and that if the regulars were to be strengthened, it should be at the end of the conflict. Bluff Henry Wilson supported the expansion that Scott and the War Department asked.[18] However, he blurted out that if he had his own way, he would disband the regulars entirely and distribute their officers among the incoming volunteers:

The truth is, that this army of ours is paralyzed toward the head. Your ablest officers are young captains and lieutenants; and if I wished today to organize a heavy military force, such as we are calling into the field . . . I would abolish the [regular] army as the first act, and I would then take officers

18 *Cong. Globe*, 37th Cong., 1st Sess., 40–49, 124, 125, 148–154. Much of the account of the British regular army in Dr. John Brown's paper on Dr. Henry Marshall in *Horae Subsecivae* might be applied to its American counterpart. For a later phase of the bad situation see R. de Trobriand's *Army Life in Dakota*, Lakeside Press ed., xxii, xxiii.

from the Army, and place them where their talents fit them to go, without reference to the ranks they occupied in the old regiments.

The augmentation passed only with a proviso that when the war ended the regular army should be reduced to 25,000 men. Another amendment, potentially important, authorized the high command to assign regular officers to the volunteers to heighten their efficiency, guaranteeing them their old army positions when peace came. Thus a halting step was taken toward merging some of the experienced officers into the raw army.

Despite this new legislation, the standing army really gained little in strength. By the end of the year, when hundreds of thousands had entered the volunteer forces, only about 7,000 had joined the regulars. They preferred the citizen army partly for its more genial, tolerant discipline, and partly for its better name, but most of all because of State loyalty. Lincoln, signing the bill July 29, thought it in the main good; but actually it had both good and bad sides. The new regiments of regulars proved, on the whole, better officered and disciplined than the volunteers, and when scattered among the Eastern and Western armies, set an example of cleanliness in camp and steadiness in battle. But they absorbed a body of regular captains and lieutenants who, distributed through the volunteers, might have done much to improve their fighting quality.[19]

Already a new star, dimming the luster of Scott's name, was rising fast and influencing Congress. McClellan, against the opposition of the old general, swiftly wrote into law his demand for adequate staffs. On July 30 he penned the measure; next day Henry Wilson introduced it; and McClellan took pains to lobby for it—showered, as he moved through the Capitol halls, with congratulations on his West Virginia feats. Scott's opposition to large staffs was grounded largely on the fact that he had managed affairs in Mexico with only two aides! The new law, signed by Lincoln on August 5, authorized the President to appoint such a number of aides as might be requested by all major-generals and commanders of higher rank (Scott being a brevet lieutenant-general). The immediate object was to give McClellan, previously restricted to three aides, as large a staff as he wanted, but other general officers also profited. Later on Cameron, troubled by a thousand politicians, journalists, and excitement hunters who wanted to get on somebody's staff, thought

19 The regulars by the end of 1861 had a strength of only 22,425; *Report of the Provost-Marshal General*, I, 102; cf. Upton. McClellan thought that either the regular army should have been broken up temporarily, and its members sprinkled among the regiments and staffs of the volunteer army to instruct and discipline that body, or it should have been built up to real strength, and used as a select reserve for critical junctures. *Own Story*, 97. Part of the regulars had to be kept in the West. Thus the Ninth Infantry remained in California to control Indians during the war, and the Fifth Infantry was busy with Indians in New Mexico.

that the law should be amended to fix some limitation. By and large, however, the Act was a necessity.[20]

One additional measure, the enlargement of the War Department, had the greatest urgency. The personnel with which Cameron was trying to manage the greatest war effort of the century was hardly strong enough to deal with a sizable Indian outbreak.

The department occupied a drab little two-story brick structure adjoining the White House grounds, its gaunt homeliness slightly relieved by a colonnade of white Corinthian pillars occupying about one-third of the elevation. Here in a narrow office the intellectual-looking Cameron, his forehead wide and high, his eyes gleaming under his frosted brow, moved nervously about, seeing the endless stream of army men, commission hunters, and contractors, jotting down memoranda which he instantly lost, and jerking out directions to assistants. Crowded into the same building were the adjutant-general, quartermaster-general, commissary-general, chief engineer, and chief of ordnance. The offices of the surgeon-general and paymaster-general had been placed in another small building at E and Fifteenth. The whole War Department personnel had numbered but ninety when Lincoln was elected, and so many experienced men were lost during the secession upheaval that only fifty-six were still serving in the late summer of 1861, the harassed bureaus being compelled to take on assistants without legal authority. In passing judgment on Cameron, we must bear in mind that for nearly four months after Sumter he had to struggle along with a creaky, antiquated administrative mechanism, operated by a mere handful of men.

Under the new legislation a War Department of decent strength became possible. Cameron had been helped from the start by his tireless friend Thomas A. Scott of the Pennsylvania Railroad; and Scott was now made Assistant Secretary in charge of all government transportation lines. The adjutant-general, Lorenzo Thomas, promoted to be brigadier-general, was given an assistant adjutant-general with a colonel's rank, and eighteen other assistants with ratings from captain to lieutenant-colonel. The office of commissary-general had been in particularly bad shape, for its two aged heads had been quite unequal to their mounting duties, and it was of the first importance to strengthen them with capable helpers. The overburdened quartermaster-general, Montgomery C. Meigs, who would eventually prove one of the principal architects of Northern victory, received twenty-seven new staff officers, all soon as busy as beavers. And so it went down the line. The surgeon-general's office, headed by the feeble, stubborn Clement A. Finley, an ill-educated army

---

20 McClellan, *Own Story*, 82, 114, 136; *Cong. Globe*, 37th Cong., 1st Sess., 361, 385, 441; O. R. III, i, 705.

surgeon who had risen to his place by seniority, was beyond rescue by any effort that Congress could yet make, but it was somewhat improved by the provision of new medical personnel.

One striking provision of the new legislation permitted the use of women nurses in the general permanent army hospitals. Another gave each regiment a chaplain, who must be an ordained clergyman of some regular Christian denomination—for an effort by Vallandigham of Ohio to obtain recognition for the Jews unhappily failed.

[IV]

To wage the war, greater financial resources were an urgent necessity. Chase had estimated that not less than $320,000,000 would be needed in the next year; but because he thought the conflict would be short, and wished to find out how much the tariff law of March would yield, he proposed raising only $80,000,000 by taxation. Congress therefore passed an act authorizing him to borrow a quarter of a billion dollars during the year by the sale of treasury notes, in denominations of not less than $50, bearing interest at the rate of 7.3 per cent, a $5,000-dollar note thus returning its holder a dollar a day; or by the sale of coupon bonds at 7 per cent, not redeemable for 20 years. A direct tax of $20,000,000 a year was levied in fixed proportions on the States and territories, ranging from $2,604,000 for New York to $3,240 for Dakota Territory. Congress also imposed a few new tariff duties for revenue, notably on sugar, tea, and coffee; and voted an income tax which was not to be effective for ten months. On its final day it enacted a confiscation law, declaring that all property used in supporting the Confederate cause was a lawful subject of prize and capture.

In debating the direct tax, sectional feeling naturally flared high. Middle Western members vigorously denounced the basis of assessment, which was real estate alone, asserting that while their farms would be heavily burdened, the mortgages, bank and corporation stock, and manufacturing property of the East would be taxed lightly if at all. Representative Isaac N. Arnold of Illinois computed that his State would pay practically 7 mills on its property, while Massachusetts would escape with 2.6 mills. To these complaints Thaddeus Stevens answered that while the direct tax would indeed fall most heavily on the New States, any internal revenue taxes on horses, carriages, watches, liquors, and so on, would be paid chiefly by the large cities and older States. The new income tax, which on British experience Stevens thought might be the most equitable of all, would also eventually rest hard on the East. The bill passed the House 77 to 60, with prominent Westerners of both parties—Arnold, Frank Blair, William S. Holman, S. S. Cox, George Pendleton—opposing it. The vote in the Senate was 34 to 8, and of the 8 no fewer than 6 were openly or covertly hostile to the whole war effort.[21]

The creation of a large public debt at the high interest rate of 7 per cent or more a year provoked astonishingly little debate for so portentous a measure. The sum authorized exceeded any previous total of national indebtedness. But Congress agreed with Chase that for a short war borrowing was a sound principle; and it accepted the view of financial leaders that the loan could not be floated with a lower interest return. Banks of New York, Boston, and Philadelphia, rallying at once to the task of distributing treasury notes to the public, found it far from easy.

Debate raged fiercely, however, around the confiscation bill. John J. Crittenden threw his great prestige against it. Since Congress had no power to touch slavery within the States, he argued, when it undertook to confiscate slave property used in aid of the rebellion it performed an unconstitutional act. Thaddeus Stevens retorted that this constitutional argument would come ill from rebels who were seeking to overthrow the Constitution. A better rejoinder was made by William Kellogg of Illinois. True, we have no power to legislate on slavery, he declared. But we do have power to punish treason by confiscation, taking a man's house, land, and furniture; and we can similarly take his right to service in another, for the penalty operates on the individual, not the institution.

In the course of debate Lyman Trumbull added an amendment under which any slave who was permitted by his owner to work on any Confederate fort, navy yard, dock, ship, or intrenchment, or to give any military or naval service whatever to the rebellion, was set free. Breckinridge raged against this amendment.[22] Although the bill was fought to the end by most Democrats and Border members, it passed the House 60 to 48, and the Senate 24 to 11.

The slavery question in one form or another, in fact, kept cropping up throughout the session. The general feeling of Republicans was expressed by Senator Henry S. Lane of Indiana, who stood by the Crittenden resolution. "But let me tell you gentlemen, that although the abolition of slavery is not an object of the war, they may, in their madness and folly and treason, make the abolition of slavery one of the *results* of this war."

Another dramatic scene took place in the Senate when Andrew Johnson rose to plead for the rescue of his people of eastern Tennessee. This stout

21 John A. Bingham of Ohio clashed with Roscoe Conkling of New York, and Schuyler Colfax of Indiana with Justin S. Morrill of Vermont, on this sectional issue. *Cong. Globe*, 37th Cong., 1st Sess., 325 ff.

22 "I tell you, sir," declared Breckinridge, "that amendment is a general act of emancipation." *Cong. Globe*, 37th Cong., 1st Sess., 262.

champion of the common man, self-taught or rather wife-taught but a powerful debater, had escaped the Confederacy through the Cumberland Gap, leaving his people enduring an Iliad of wrongs: houses broken open, property
pillaged, leaders arrested, and unoffending citizens murdered. He did not beg
help as a suppliant, he said; "I demand it as a constitutional right." Had his rugged
mountain folk been given 10,000 stand of arms when the contest began, they
would have asked no further assistance.

Drama also attended the vehement clash between John C. Ten Eyck of
New Jersey, demanding that Congress appropriate a million and a half for
one or more armored ships or floating batteries, and various opponents
who talked of naval "jobs." The debate showed that French and British experiments with armored ships had attracted wide attention, and that the French
ironclad *La Gloire* and British ironclad *Warrior* were regarded as potential
threats to American ports. Out of this debate was to come the means of building—in the very nick of time—the armored *Monitor*.[23]

Inevitably, and healthfully, the short session mustered a thin battle line
of defenders of civil liberty. Congress just before adjourning passed an act
punishing with fine and imprisonment those who conspired to overthrow the
government or resist its authority. This was mild enough, and far more alarm
justly sprang from Lincoln's suspension of the writ of habeas corpus within
definite geographical limits. He had begun with a proclamation covering the
Washington-Philadelphia lines of communication (April 27). Senator James
A. Pearce of Maryland condemned not the suspension, but the unguarded
nature of the step and the arbitrary acts committed under its shelter.

In Great Britain, as he and others pointed out, martial law had been very
sparingly used—not in the Gordon riots, nor in the Chartist disturbances, nor
in grave Irish troubles. When used, it had carried a careful limitation of the
period during which persons arrested might be held without bail or main-
prize. But in Maryland, a State predominantly loyal and now perfectly quiet,
troops had marched into various towns to search for arms, had forcibly entered houses, had seized men without any decent ground for suspicion, and
had imprisoned them without orders from superior authority. The police commissioners of Baltimore, said Pearce, had been jailed without any grand-jury
indictment or specification of illegal conduct by any other agency, simply

23 Ten Eyck was specially interested in the ironclad vessel called the *Stevens Battery*
lying incomplete at Hoboken, with $812,000 necessary to finish it. The eminent Robert L.
Stevens had modeled and constructed it without a dollar of compensation, and his brother
Edwin Augustus Stevens, his executor and heir, had now offered to give his skill and services
free to make the ship available. Most naval experts, while uncertain of the value of such craft
as cruisers, agreed on their importance for harbor defense. *Cong. Globe*, 37th Cong., 1st
Sess., 345-347. The Senate passed the measure Ten Eyck desired by the close vote of 18
to 16.

because General N. P. Banks had accused them of "some purpose not known to the Government"—and they were still imprisoned!

When the Senate Judiciary Committee under Lyman Trumbull brought in a bill to authorize, define, and regulate the use of martial law, a chorus of dissent broke forth. It would be tiresome to trace the debate, and it suffices to say that both advocates and antagonists realized that the subject was extremely delicate. Everyone agreed that in suppressing rebellion the military authorities needed large powers and would certainly take them; but nearly everyone agreed that to define these powers was a dangerous matter—too much might be granted, or too much withheld. Loyal and disloyal men were intermingled in many communities; suspicion often fell on the wrong person; oaths meant little to scoundrels; and in some areas patriots had less trust in the regular courts than in military tribunals. "There is difficulty environing us everywhere," said Senator Edgar Cowan of Pennsylvania. Trumbull regarded his bill as the most important of the session. "I think that the idea that the rights of the citizen are to be trampled upon and that he is to be arrested by military authority, without any regulation by law whatever, is monstrous in a free government." Yet he admitted that the measure might not accomplish its object.[24]

Thus it was that the bill, opposed by some because it limited existing powers too much, and by others because it extended them too far, was postponed from day to day until it failed. On the final Senate vote for postponement, radical Republicans like Fessenden, Collamer, and Wade stood alongside balky conservatives like Bayard and Saulsbury. The sphere of military control remained undefined.[25]

[V]

Congress adjourned on August 6 in a very different mood from that in which it had first met, for military disasters soon to be described had chastened it. It had accomplished the legislation generally expected of it; now the executive branch had to make the most of the new laws. The President and Cabinet probably drew a breath of relief when it rose, for they felt freer. Power was steadily passing from the legislative to the executive, and the country looked to Lincoln for action.

Though generally cooperative, Congress had shown a natural jealousy of its functions. One of the first measures wanted by the Administration was

24 This subject is fully covered in *Cong. Globe*, 37th Cong., 1st Sess., 332–343. McDougall of California, for the Douglasite wing of the Democracy, advocated throwing out almost the whole bill.

25 *Cong. Globe*, 37th Cong., 1st Sess., 374 ff.

a resolution validating all Lincoln's acts, orders, and proclamations, including his suspension of the writ of habeas corpus. Because Congress believed that it alone had power to suspend the writ, this ran into heavy opposition. All efforts to carry it failed until the end of the session, when the validation, shorn of any mention of habeas corpus, was tacked to a bill increasing the pay of army privates, and thus smuggled through.[26]

For three reasons the President had not attempted to exert much direct influence on the activities of Congress. The first was that he had full confidence in such leaders as Henry Wilson and Frank Blair in military affairs, and Thaddeus Stevens in finance; the second that he was preoccupied with the army movements in front of Washington; and the third that he was also engrossed in the politico-military affairs of Kentucky and Missouri. So long as this short session gave him the men and money he needed, and did not move too harshly in confiscating Southern property, he was content to let it alone. He disliked even the mild confiscation act passed, and doubtless grimaced over Thaddeus Stevens' vituperation in the debate: "If their whole country must be laid waste and made a desert, in order to save this Union from destruction, so let it be." [27] But he signed the act without protest. Lincoln was never a leader of Congress in the sense in which Woodrow Wilson, Theodore Roosevelt, and Franklin D. Roosevelt later often led it, and now, as a novice in the Presidential chair, he was specially hesitant. Later on, the bungling military and financial legislation might have been improved had he played a prime minister's part; but that time had not yet come, and nobody was disturbed because his message contained not a single proposal for legislation beyond the curt request for troops and money.

Lincoln did not yet loom up the colossal central figure in Washington which he was subsequently to become. Intimates saw him in various lights, but not yet as a great man. All Presidents grow in office, but he was to grow far more than most of them.

The glimpses that soldiers and public got of him were of a pleasant, honest-minded, awkward man. Troops saw him at parades, looking kindly and a bit absent; once holding his two little boys by the hand; taking off his hat clumsily at the salute to the flag and putting it on again country-fashion, gripped by the rear rim; stooping as a boy came by with a pail of water to take a great swig. When Francis Lieber, the German-American expert on international law, was taken by Seward to call, he decided that Lincoln was better than people thought him, "but oh, so funny!" Seward in departing said, "I shall immediately return with Lord Lyons; you had better put on your black

26 N. Y. *Tribune*, Aug. 7-10, 1861.
27 *Cong. Globe*, 37th Cong., 1st Sess., 415.

coat—you ought to have put it on for Dr. Lieber." To this jocular remark Lincoln replied: "I intended to do so, but the doctor will excuse me; I was not aware it was so late." It was easy for prejudiced men to make cutting remarks. "That sand-hill crane in the Presidential chair," wrote one correspondent; "the joking machine men call Abraham Lincoln." [28] Himself unassuming, he was no respecter of persons. One reason why Charles Francis Adams, Sr., carried from the White House so unfavorable an impression was perhaps that Lincoln showed no awe of Adamses, and half-ignored the Quincy man to talk about political appointments with Seward. Robert Gould Shaw, calling in all the hurly-burly a fortnight after Sumter, formed a truer impression:

> We were shown into a room where Mr. Lincoln was sitting at a desk, perfectly covered with papers of every description. He got up and shook hands with us in the most cordial way, asked us to be seated, and seemed quite glad to have us come. It is really too bad to call him one of the ugliest men in the country, for I have seldom seen a pleasanter or more kind-hearted looking one, and he has certainly a very striking face. His voice is very pleasant; and though, to be sure, we were there only a few minutes, I didn't hear anything like Western slang or twang in him. He gives you the impression, too, of being a gentleman.[29]

His sense of the tremendous responsibility on his shoulders deepened his natural melancholy. Above all, it deepened his thoughtfulness. What casual callers could not see beyond the kindness, honesty, and sadness that shone from his angular, furrowed countenance was this ingrained thoughtfulness. They would depart impressed by the wonderful mobility of his face, which could be grimly uncompromising, touchingly careworn, or infectiously mirthful. They could not see, when the door shut, the quick change to intense earnestness as he studied papers, or to concentration as, in the words of Nicolay, "he would sometimes sit for an hour in complete silence, his eyes almost shut, the inner man apparently as far from him as if the form in his chair were a petrified image." [30] Habituated to meditation from his lonely frontier boyhood, trained to precise logical processes by the law, he brought to the Presidency a capacity for intense lucid thinking matched by no other executive. His mind was slow and cautious, but in clarity it excelled Hamilton's, in penetration Madison's, and in weight Webster's. One of his greatest

28 The N. Y. *Tribune* correspondent Samuel Wilkinson so called Lincoln in letters to S. H. Gay; Gay Papers, Columbia University.
29 C. F. Adams, Sir., MS Diary, MHS; MS Diary of Robert Gould Shaw, May 2, 1861.
30 Helen Nicolay, "Characteristic Anecdotes of Lincoln," *Century Magazine*, vol. 84 (August, 1912), 699.

gifts as President, to be revealed in due time, was his ability to think problems through to irresistible conclusions.

His other great qualification was his intuitive understanding of the popular mind, and of political necessities and possibilities. He knew that to be a great statesman he had to be a great politician, like Jefferson and Jackson before him. More than these men, he believed in the goodness and wisdom of the whole people; they could not be fooled long, and he was the last man to wish to fool them. The aggressive Thaddeus Stevens thought that he ought to have led opinion more trenchantly, even recklessly; but Stevens closed his career saying, "My life has been a failure." [31] The patient, watchful Lincoln knew that it was better to be accused of tardiness than to be rash in policy or impracticable in method. He, not Stevens, was the true Commoner. He had no excessive regard for Congressmen, among whom he had once sat, and not only usually resisted any Congressional encroachment on his sphere of action, but was ready at need to invade what Congress deemed its sphere. But his regard for the people never failed.

The Whig tradition, which so many Republicans inherited, regarded Congress as the prime seat of national power, and Clay, Webster, and Seward had labored to make it just that. Lincoln, however, shared the Democratic view—the Jackson-Polk view—that the President as the direct representative of the people should be the vital source of governmental energy. Serving in Congress and later watching affairs closely, he had seen how efficiently Polk acted as commander-in-chief, and how he managed the Mexican War in all its details, administrative, fiscal, and military. He saw Polk, even more effectively than Jackson, tell Congress what to do; he was unquestionably aware that Polk drove his Cabinet with tighter rein than any former President, and the lesson was not lost on him—only he substituted tact for dictation.

He was always ready to manage Congress by giving its members jobs, letting them romp a little with contracts and appropriations, and lending them a hand at logrolling. He specially valued his Congressional spokesmen, like faithful William Kellogg of Illinois and headlong Frank Blair. Nobody showed more consummate skill in dealing with politicians of varied types, often crass, selfish, vain, or corrupt. In time he was to exercise this skill masterfully in handling the ambitious Chase, the unscrupulous Ben Butler, the self-centered Sumner, and the dictatorial, tempestuous Stanton. His magnanimity never failed—he gave even his sleepless rival and frequent detractor, Chase, the

---

31 Quoted by A. K. McClure, *Lincoln and Men of War-Times*, 286. McClure writes that Lincoln "never cherished resentment even when Stevens indulged in his bitterest sallies of wit or sarcasm at Lincoln's expense."

Chief Justiceship—but neither did his skill. When he turned from the politicians to the people, however, his attitude was one of deference to a higher power. While he knew that he must take the responsibility for decisive enunciations of policy, and did so, he also knew that he did not manage the people: in the last analysis, they managed him.

During this spring and summer of 1861, people poured through the White House in a steady stream. They numbered old Illinois intimates laden with advice, politicians bearing opinions and demands, contractors, youths seeking commissions, inventors, adventurers anxious to raise irregular commands, officers after promotion, governors, Congressmen. "It would be hard to imagine a state of things less conducive to serious and effective work," writes John Hay, "yet in one way or another the work was done. In the midst of a crowd of visitors who began to arrive early in the morning and who were put out, grumbling, by the servants who closed the doors at midnight, the President pursued those labors which will carry his name to distant ages. There was little order or system about it; those around him strove from beginning to end to erect barriers to defend him against constant interruption, but the President himself was always the first to break them down. He disliked anything that kept people from him who wanted to see him, and . . . he would never take the necessary measures to defend himself." And his time was not all wasted. He gained much information, some ideas, a good deal of cheer, and above all steady inspiration, from the thronging callers.[32]

Ideally, the Northern war effort should have been run with consistent system, energy, and flair for organization; but this was quite outside Lincoln's nature. Nor was the country ready for this. It needed a half-century of national growth to enable Wilson to organize his Cabinet, the War Industries Board, the War Labor Board, the General Staff, and other agencies for efficient centralized control of a great war.

Lincoln's principal failure in the first half of 1861 was his neglect to create some group or agency to collect facts and analyze opinions bearing upon national war resources, on men, munitions, and manufacturing capacity, on enemy strength, and on the best fields of military action. With a fumbling, nerveless Secretary of War, no General Staff, no office in Washington acquainted with industry, commerce, and labor, and no intelligence bureau, such an advisory agency would quickly have become invaluable. Sir William Robertson, when made Chief of the Imperial General Staff in 1915, outlined

32　See James G. Randall, *Lincoln the President*, Vols. I and II, *passim;* John Hay, "Life in the White House in the Time of Lincoln," *ut supra;* Charles A. Dana's dictated notes on Lincoln in Ida M. Tarbell Papers, Allegheny College; William O. Stoddard, *Inside the White House in War Times;* Tyler Dennett, *Lincoln and the Civil War in the Diary and Letters of John Hay;* David Donald, *The Enduring Lincoln.*

to the War Office under Kitchener what he thought was the nation's cardinal need. It was "a supreme directing authority whose function is to formulate policy, to decide on the theatres in which military operations are to be conducted, and to determine the relative importance of these theatres." This authority, civilian in personnel, was to gather information through many channels, chiefly military. It was to suggest the men to carry out policy, and under the Prime Minister "exercises a general supervision over the conduct of the war." [33] The United States needed something of the kind in 1861.

[VI]

Nobody could expect Lincoln's relationship with his constitutional advisers, the Cabinet, to be systematic, nor to find him making the Cabinet an effective, coherent body. He expected each Cabinet member to "run his own machine," as he put it. But in the summer of 1861 it was already clear that his relations with the Cabinet would never be satisfactory. The executive group showed nothing of the unselfish cooperation, the earnest association and consultation for the public good, the cordial unity in dealing with Congress, that have marked many Cabinets; and the nation thereby lost heavily.

In part the difficulty lay with the peculiar constitution of the Cabinet. Made up largely of men who had been eager rivals for the Presidency, and who headed special factions in the Republican Party, it lacked basic harmony. Deep personal antagonisms marred relations between Montgomery Blair and Chase, between Welles and Seward.[34] But beyond this, the President was too careless, independent, and busy, after the first weeks, to attempt to create executive unity. "Why do you talk about a Cabinet?" presently burst out Chase to a friend. "There is no Cabinet to be member of." This was precisely the complaint of Greeley's *Tribune*. Lincoln had so withdrawn himself from those to whom he should be closest, grumbled Greeley, and had formed such a set habit of acting or not acting just as his own judgment dictated, that "the impression has become almost universal in the popular mind . . . *that he has no Cabinet, in the true sense of that term.*" Attorney-General Bates felt himself an outsider; I am merely a Law Officer, he declared. Secretary Welles, too, was outspoken in censuring the lack of any system:

I have administered the Navy Department almost entirely independent of Cabinet consultations, and I may say almost without direction of the President, who not only gives me his confidence but intrusts all naval matters to

33 Sir Frederick Maurice, *Atlantic Monthly*, vol. 137 (June, 1936), 772 ff.
34 Welles writes: "Between Seward and Chase there was perpetual rivalry and mutual but courtly distrust. Each was ambitious. Both had capacity. Seward was supple and dexterous; Chase was clumsy and strong." *Diary,* I, 139.

me. This has not been my wish. Though glad to have his confidence, I should prefer that every important naval movement should pass a Cabinet review. . . . So in regard to each and all the Departments; if I have known of their regulations and instructions, much of it has not been in Cabinet consultations.[35]

Welles' statement was quite valid for the first part of the war. Governor Dennison of Ohio returned from a trip to Washington reporting that the departments were little governments in themselves. Lincoln had said to him: "Now, Dennison, if Jeff Davis was to get me and I told him all I know, I couldn't give him much information that would be useful to him." [36]

In the absence of general Cabinet consultation, Welles specially resented the opportunity thus given the wily, experienced Seward to push himself forward as chief adviser to the President. Lincoln, he thought early in the war, lacked self-reliance. Perplexed by events, the President relied too much on the far wider knowledge of Seward, whose self-confidence, talkativeness, and easygoing geniality had a ready appeal. No one else, Welles jealously noted, attempted to obtrude himself, or even to suggest that other Cabinet members should be consulted on some of the important measures of the government. Chase alone, greatly irritated by Seward's presumptions, made an occasional effort to talk intimately with Lincoln, learn what was going on in other departments, and offer counsel. Later in the war Welles and Chase were to transfer their antagonism for a time from Seward to Edwin M. Stanton, for the Secretary of War then seemed nearest the seat of power. Wrote Chase:

The President decides all questions concerning the war either by himself or with the advice of the Secretary of War and Commander in Chief [Stanton and Halleck]. The Heads of other Departments, unless perhaps that of the State, are so rarely consulted that they might as well not be consulted at all. Of course being intensely interested in what goes on I can't help saying what I think occasionally; but I do not see good enough come of it to make me vain of my influence.[37]

As this statement suggests, Lincoln was determined to manage the war effort himself, and the determination grew as he increased in wisdom and power. He was not going to let the Cabinet direct any considerable part of it. He had emphatically put Seward in his place on April 1, although retaining him as a close friend and adviser. He overruled Cameron in the matter of the Massachusetts and Pennsylvania regiments. He got General Scott to support him in overruling Cameron again in the critical step of making the able

35 Chase to E. D. Mansfield, Oct. 27, 1863, Chase Papers, Pa. Hist. Soc.; N. Y. *Tribune*, Jan. 27, 1865 (editorial); Bates, Aug. 13, 1864, to J. O. Broadhead; Broadhead Papers, Mo. State Hist. Soc.
36 MS Diary of Wm. T. Coggeshall, Military Secretary to Dennison, Foreman Lebold Coll.
37 Welles, *Diary*, I, 131–139 (Sept. 16, 1862); Chase to Hiram Barney, July 21, 1863, Chase Papers, Hist. Soc. of Pa.

Montgomery C. Meigs quartermaster-general.[38] Generals were soon to be as great a problem to him as politicians. At first he deferred too much to Scott, as he did to Seward, but he was sufficiently vigilant to refuse to let the hot-headed Nathaniel Lyon take command in Missouri. The self-distrust of which Welles speaks was partly a mask. He had a way of drawing out interlocutors with questions, as if still undecided, when his mind was quite made up.

"Mr. Lincoln was always the master," said Charles A. Dana later, "and he did not put on the appearance of it at all. He never gave a hair's breadth, never gave way—he always had his own way. The relations between him and all the Secretaries were perfectly cordial always and unaffected, and without any appearance of his thinking himself the boss, but it was always his will, his order, that determined a decision." This is an overstatement, especially for Lincoln's first year, but it has essential truth. Edward Everett Hale shortly described Lincoln's combination of firmness and tact in different terms. "Nothing shows the power of the President more at the present moment," he wrote after visiting the White House early in 1862, "than the way in which every person you meet thinks and gives you to think that he and the President are hand in glove, and indeed, quite agree." [39]

The inadequacies of the White House secretarial staff were numerous. One observer remarked caustically of John Hay: "As he looks like seventeen, he is under the necessity of acting like seventy." Its main defect, however, was that it was too small. Time quickly developed one specially grievous need: A fact-finding agency responsive to the President's special demands. A single efficient man with reference books and filing cabinets might have done much. Lincoln could not depend on his Cabinet members for many facts about their spheres of concern; on Stanton for exact figures of army strength, for example. He could not depend on anybody for good material on geography and topography; when the main Eastern army went to Harrison's Landing, nobody could tell him what the Landing was like. He could never depend on generals for reliable data on enemy strength. Most of all, he needed more information on the men he appointed to military and civil office. Often he groped in the dark. Somebody to sift official reports, run through newspapers, and approach politicians for critical and confidential judgments would have been invaluable. Of course Lincoln would still have made mistakes. But he would not so readily have appointed John Pope to a command in which he almost ruined the Union cause, or have sent the feeble Dayton as minister to France.

In the summer of 1861, however, both President and Cabinet were yet un-

---

38 Lincoln, *Collected Works*, IV, 394, 395.
39 Dana's Memoranda, Ida M. Tarbell Papers, Allegheny College; Hale's Memorandum April 26, 1862, in E. E. Hale, *Memories of a Hundred Years*, II, 189, 190.

tried. The quality of the statesmanship possessed by Lincoln, Chase, Seward, and their associates remained to be tested. The sculptor L. W. Volk had made a life mask of Lincoln in Chicago in the spring of 1860; the sculptor Clark Milles was to make another in the spring of 1865. The contrast between the two faces would measure the ordeal through which the President was to pass, and the growth he would attain, in four of the most harrowing years of our history.

11

The First Test of Strength

BY THE TIME Davis reached Richmond and Beauregard partly organized his command at Manassas, the grand strategy of the Confederacy had taken shape. On land, a generally defensive policy was to be pursued while the new nation awaited aid from cotton-starved Europe. The Confederate Congress declared a defensive attitude by resolution just after Sumter, Jefferson Davis proclaimed it in his message to Congress, and Robert E. Lee as head of the Virginia forces asserted it in special orders: "The policy of the State, at present, is strictly defensive." Since the Confederacy as yet lacked strength to invade the North, the defensive policy, despite Beauregard's protests, was inescapable. It imposed on the South a manifest disadvantage in the loss of the initiative. While the North could choose its point of attack, the Confederacy was like a wary duelist, waiting to parry a lunge or a slash. One countervailing advantage was the ability to use distance for defense, transferring troops by inside lines, so far as transport facilities permitted—for inside lines are useless without traffic arteries—while the Union was making long outside marches. Another advantage was the power of awaiting attack behind entrenchments.

The defensive military policy of the South would have had far greater effectiveness if the section had been buttressed by natural physical barriers. Unhappily for its generals, the Confederacy had no Pyrenees, no Vosges, no Carpathians, while the South found it utterly impossible to gain and hold the Ohio, which might have been a real rampart. West and northwest the section was pierced by great rivers: the Mississippi, the Red, the Tennessee, the Cumberland. From Ohio, the Monongahela led southward; from Pennsylvania the Shenandoah Valley opened a corridor. Eastern Virginia was singularly exposed. The Potomac tributaries and the York, Rappahannock, and James, all admitted hostile armies well within the Old Dominion. From the sea, Wilmington, Charleston, Mobile, and above all New Orleans seemed readily assailable. The Confederates lay in a besieged fortress with many entry-ports open. Nevertheless, the principal Southern leaders believed they could withstand all

Union attacks until the Yankees grew tired of the butchery, or Europe intervened.[1]

The energy that the South might have put into a rapid exchange of cotton for arms while the seas remained fairly open went instead into a brisk but essentially futile campaign of privateering.[2] Davis' proclamation (April 17) that all who wished to use privately armed ships to resist Northern aggression might apply for letters of marque sent a spasm of activity through Southern ports. Two days later Lincoln proclaimed that any Southerner molesting American commerce under such authority would be subject to the penalties for piracy; but of course the North could not hang captured privateersmen, for instant retaliation would have followed. Southern leaders being eager to get the "militia of the sea" into action, the rebel Congress passed comprehensive legislation, signed by Davis early in May, which secured to holders of letters of marque and reprisal practically the whole proceeds of their captures. The same law gave Northern merchantmen in Southern ports thirty days to get home, a privilege which the North did not extend to Southern ships. Bounties were offered for the destruction of enemy warships of superior force, and for every naval rating taken prisoner.[3]

The enthusiasm in Southern seaports for the combined opportunity of striking the Yankees and pocketing a neat profit was feverish. Wharves, counting-rooms, and hotel lobbies responded with talk of Drakes to sweep the ocean. The New Orleans *Daily Crescent* dreamed that within 4 months at least 750 swift vessels averaging 4 mighty guns apiece would be crippling the Northern strength. Unhappily for the Confederacy, some of the best Southern ships were seized in Northern harbors. Three fine vessels of the Charleston line, the *South Carolina, Massachusetts*, and *James Adger*, with the *Bienville* of the New Orleans line, were soon Northern cruisers. What they might have done for the South is suggested by the feats of the *Nashville*, also of the Charleston line, which served the Confederacy as transport, privateer, and warship. However, despite the Southern lack of good shipyards and mechanics, some busy hornets were soon sent out.

1 On Confederate strategic policy see Davis, *Rise and Fall*, I, Ch. VI; Clifford Dowdey, *The Land They Fought For*, 126; Eaton, *Southern Confederacy*, 124, 125. John M. Daniel in the Richmond *Examiner* inveighed against the "policy of retreat"; see editorials June 12, June 15, July 2, etc., and F. S. Daniel, *The Richmond Examiner During the War*.

2 The exchange of cotton for arms at this date could not have been large, nearly all the 1860 crop having been exported or sent to New England, but it might have been useful. See Owsley, *King Cotton Diplomacy*, 25 ff.; Coulter, *Confederate States*, Ch. X; J. H. Reagan, *Memoirs*, 113; Schwab, *Confederate States*, 13–16, 233, 234.

3 Statutes, Provisional Govt. CSA, 2d Sess., Ch. III; Richardson, *Messages and Papers of the Confederacy*, I, 60–62; Robinson, *The Confederate Privateers*, 17–20, 30 ff.; and on Washington's belated offer to adhere unconditionally to the Declaration of Paris outlawing privateers, 64th Cong., 1st Sess., Senate Doc. 332. For fundamental material on the Confederate privateers see *O. R. Union and Conf. Navies*, Series II, i, 247–249.

New Orleans on May 16 dispatched the little steamer *Calhoun*, which that same evening captured a Maine bark with 3,000 barrels of lime. She was immediately joined by two other New Orleans privateers which began cruising the Gulf. Beauregard had urged Louisiana to fortify the Mississippi below the city, arming Forts Jackson and St. Philip with the heaviest guns to be found, and constructing heavy booms, one of timber and one of barges, across the river. This was delayed, but the privateers delighted Creole hearts. Charleston, meanwhile, had her first privateer active June 2, when the schooner *Savannah*, armed with one 1812-style eighteen-pounder, put to sea on a brief and unfortunate cruise. After capturing a Maine brig laden with Cuban sugar, she was seized by a Union warship. Landed in New York, the small crew were ironed, confined in the Tombs, and tried for piracy, with the death penalty staring them in the face until the jury happily disagreed.[4] Another Charleston privateer named for Jefferson Davis, a brig armed with five English guns of 1801 vintage, went to sea in June, and soon captured a Philadelphia freighter and a Massachusetts schooner. A third, the *Dixie*, sailed in July and within four days placed a prize crew aboard a Yankee bark full of coal.

By this time merchants and shipowners in all North Atlantic ports were clamorous for an immediate intensification of the blockade. Even if the Confederacy could place only a few dozen privateers on the ocean, unless its ports were quickly sealed it would deal Northern commerce a staggering blow. Steamship companies, shippers, and insurance interests demanded that the government put guns and gunners on important steamers like those which brought forty millions in gold from San Francisco to New York every year, furnish convoys on dangerous routes, and station warships in such busy sea lanes as Vineyard Sound.[5]

Even during May, blockading vessels trailed their smoke across the skies outside Charleston, Savannah, Mobile, and New Orleans. But no Yankee ever uttered a frostier understatement than Secretary Welles's remark that the navy was "not as powerful or in numbers as extensive as I wished." When Sumter fell, only forty-two ships, including tenders and storeships, were in commission. Six were in Northern ports, four at Pensacola, one on the Great Lakes, and the others dotted over the globe from the Mediterranean to the East Indies. With authority from Lincoln, Welles instantly ordered the buying or leasing of twenty vessels.[6] He assigned an Atlantic force the task of closing

---

4 Four of the twelve jurors stood for acquittal; see Robinson, *Privateers*, 135-147, for details.

5 Nineteen New York insurance companies demanded that the navy give immediate protection to commerce; O. R. I, i, 9.

6 Welles established in New York an advisory board of five, including Governor E. D. Morgan, William M. Evarts, and Moses Grinnell, to assist in forwarding men and supplies. His MS diary contains some matter not in the published version.

Confederate ports from the Chesapeake to Key West, and shortly divided it into North Atlantic and South Atlantic squadrons under Louis M. Goldsborough and Samuel F. Du Pont respectively. A Gulf squadron was instructed to shut every port in that area. Blockade runners were soon being captured. The seizure of three British ships off Charleston on May 22 posed a difficult diplomatic question, which was settled when the government, after Seward appealed to Welles, released them.[7]

It was soon evident that no exterior patrol would suffice to shut the Southern ports. Along such an extended coast, with so many inlets, harbors, and bays, it was easy for blockade runners and privateers to slip in and out. Only when some of the major ports had been captured could the movement of ships be brought under control. By July conversations were under way between the army and navy upon an amphibious expedition against Wilmington. Meanwhile, the navy had let contracts for the hurried construction of warships. The sloop *Tuscarora* was launched at Philadelphia on August 22. "Her keel was growing in the forest three months ago," boasted Welles. Vessels of every size and shape were also bought for refitting and arming. "Alas! It is like altering a vest into a shirt to convert a trading steamer into a man of war," lamented Du Pont, but the work went on. Although summer found the blockade still highly ineffective, naval officers could reflect that the war was young.

The South, indeed, by midsummer had a premonition of the days when imports would cease, and shortages become crippling. Northern commercial interests equally felt a foreboding of grave damage to the American merchant marine. Long so proud, it might be swept from the seas or compelled to take refuge under foreign flags.

[I]

On land, meanwhile, the time had come for harder blows. North and South, the clamor for fighting grew ever more strident. In Richmond the rebel war clerk Jones wrote in his diary for June 12: "The vast majority of our people are for 'carrying the war into Africa' without a moment's delay." [8] From Washington a gallant New York soldier, Francis Barlow, destined to become known as the boy general and to have his monument reared at Gettysburg, wrote that the demand for crushing the enemy made a campaign so imperative that if Lincoln objected, he might be replaced by a military dictatorship.[9] "Already the murmurs of discontent are ocean-loud against the slow and cau-

7 West, *Welles*, 117; J. R. Soley, *The Blockade and the Cruisers*, 8, 9.
8 Jones, *Rebel War Clerk's Diary*, I, 51.
9 Francis Barlow had enlisted as a private April 19, married the next day, and left his bride at the church to go to the front. His letter of May 27, 1861, is in the S. L. M. Barlow Papers.

tious courses of the war. I see this in the files of responsible and pervading correspondence which crowd the Secretaries' mails, and I know it from the President himself."

The sight of troops pouring to the front gave people on each side a false impression of strength. When Beauregard left Montgomery for the Virginia front on May 29 his train, according to a Boston-born physician aboard, counted 148 cars, all filled with troops bound for Augusta and points north, and drawn by two locomotives.[10] This may be an exaggeration, but it is true that Southerners who cheered massive troop trains expected a prompt advance. Jefferson Davis explained to Joseph E. Johnston on July 13 that a North Carolinian who accused the government of wantonly holding back 17,000 eager men from his State was writing nonsense. Volunteers swarmed everywhere, but Davis had to tell these eager units: "I have not arms to supply you."[11] In Washington, it was assuredly a mistake to show members of Congress on July 4 an imposing military pageant, some 25,000 troops filling Pennsylvania Avenue like a blue river, while their tread sounded like dull thunder, for the spectacle made many members recklessly impatient. "This was war," wrote one. "We should bring on the battle."[12]

Each side underrated the need for preparation, and undervalued the fighting quality of its opponents. "It was a favorite notion," wrote General Barnard later, "with a large class of Northern politicians (and the people too) that nothing but an imposing display of force was necessary to crush the rebellion."[13] Surely, since pioneers had fought under Andrew Jackson at the wave of a hat, a regiment hardly needed three months' drill! Why wait, when only a thirty-mile march was needed to overwhelm the enemy?

Both the Confederate camp at Manassas and the Union camps before Washington were slovenly. Neither army had properly assembled and organized its baggage trains, tents, food arrangements, or medical supplies. Beauregard could have said precisely what McDowell did say later: "I had no opportunity to test my machinery, to move it around and see whether it would work smoothly or not." Yet each section waved aside reasons for delay. "True enough, you are green," men admitted. "But the enemy is green too—you are all green alike."[14]

The North had a taste of the bloody realities of war on June 10. Ben Butler —urged on by Montgomery Blair, who denounced the "miserable do-nothings" in Washington and expressed confidence that a march to Richmond would be easy—moved that day to capture two Confederate posts, Big and Little Bethel,

10 Dr. Martin McQueen in Syracuse *Journal*, May 27, 1861.
11 O. R. I, ii, 976–977.
12 A. G. Riddle, *Recs. of War Times*, 29.
13 Barnard, *The C. S. A. and the Battle of Bull Run*, 42.
14 Hurlburt, *McClellan and the Conduct of the War*, 103.

a few miles from Fort Monroe. The command was given to an incompetent. He used faulty old maps, sent out two columns on a night march which, instead of joining hands and cooperating, actually fired into each other, and by this tragic mishap gave the alarm to the Confederates at Little Bethel, who fell back on Big Bethel. He then completely botched an attempt to flank this well-chosen position, where the enemy was protected by a swampy creek and a battery of guns. As Butler later wrote, "Everything was mismanaged." The Union forces withdrew just as the Confederate leader, fearing reinforcements from Fort Monroe, himself retreated! The reason which the Northern commander later offered for retiring was that his troops were hungry from long marching. Actually they had covered about eleven miles, and if they had halted to eat lunch from their haversacks, they could have kept the position the enemy was abandoning! [15]

It was evident, meanwhile, that the Northern forces were loose, clumsy, and inharmonious. The aged Scott reigned without actually ruling. He had three armies, Patterson's in the Harpers Ferry area, McDowell's at Alexandria, and Ben Butler's at Fort Monroe, which he failed to coordinate, and whose commanders all distrusted him.[16]

Patterson, who on June 28 had 14,350 men facing Joe Johnston's 10,700, made a series of erratic movements. Elated by his success in driving Johnston from Harpers Ferry, he thought that with Scott's support he could win a brilliant victory; but Scott, with superior insight, disapproved of his plans, and withdrew some of his troops. The result was that the Pennsylvania general believed that he had been checked just as he was on the point of seizing a bright advantage. Had he held Charlestown just south of the Potomac, he would have been in a position to strike at Winchester, intercept Johnston if that general suddenly moved to join Beauregard at Manassas, or himself march rapidly to reinforce McDowell. Instead, he put himself in a remoter position at Martinsburg.[17] Relations between Scott and McDowell continued bad, with Scott petulant and McDowell resentful. By July 16–17, returns for the McDowell-Mansfield command in the Washington-Alexandria area showed

15 On the two Bethels, see *Butler's Book*, 266–270; Swinton, *Army of the Potomac*, 31. The saddest loss at Big Bethel was that of Theodore Winthrop, a more than promising American man of letters.

16 Lossing, *Civil War*, I, 525, 526; Swinton, 33, 34; O. R. I, ii.

17 For Patterson's Shenandoah operations see O. R. I, ii, 156–187, 607, 694; his own *Narrative* is best read in the light of T. L. Livermore's careful paper on the campaign in Military Hist. Soc. of Mass., I, *Campaigns in Virginia 1861–62*. Alonzo H. Quint's *The Second Mass. Infantry* gives an interesting view. Patterson when forced to retreat had to endure silently a great deal of public criticism. "Great injustice is done you and your command here," John Sherman, who had been on his staff, wrote from Washington June 30, "and by persons in the highest military position." When Patterson placed his forces at Martinsburg they were behind Johnston, who was thus free to move to Manassas at any time with Patterson trailing in his rear.

37,321 officers and men present for duty, but McDowell felt that Scott had denied him the staff, equipment, and latitude in training which he needed.

If Patterson and McDowell distrusted the head of the armies, Butler's opinion was scorching. The day he was appointed major-general, May 16, he called on Scott to exchange angry accusations. Scott accused him of running terrible risks in Baltimore, thwarting the government's pacific plans, and showing general highhandedness. Butler retorted that Scott knew nothing of the situation, had made dangerous concessions to the disloyal mayor, and should have helped him suppress the murderous plug-uglies. Though Cameron and Chase urged the indigant Butler to stay in the service, and Montgomery Blair assured him he was entirely right, his irritation grew when he found Fort Monroe shockingly ill equipped. It had no horses, no proper water supply, no provisions but hardtack and meat; the seven or eight thousand men he commanded were insufficient to do more than keep Magruder at bay. The sympathetic Blair, who had hoped to see Butler march direct on Richmond, wrote Cameron on June 22 in high dudgeon. Instead of 20,000 men with proper artillery, cavalry, and wagon trains, Butler had less than half that force, no transport, no cavalry, and few guns. Blair added:

My want of confidence in the enterprise of the General-in-Chief grows. Besides, he does not approve our policy and is not heartily with us. He means to play Pacificator. I counsel you to take these matters into your own charge, seeing that you have the responsibility.[18]

The West Virginia campaign furnished new evidence of want of plan and liaison in Washington. McClellan exaggerates the facts when he declares that from first to last he had no "advice, orders, or instructions from Washington or elsewhere," and acted on his own initiative; for actually he got some helpful information from Scott. But he was left altogether too much to his own resources. He issued a proclamation to the people of West Virginia of strong political tinge, and an equally political address to his soldiers. When he sent Lincoln copies, with a letter explaining his reasons for the invasion, he got no comment from President, Secretary of War, or General Scott. It was unfortunate that Cameron and Scott did not fully and promptly inform McClellan of their plan of action in front of Washington. Had they done so, the troops flushed with victory at Rich Mountain might have marched, as McClellan suggested, toward the Shenandoah to help Patterson pin down Joseph E. Johnston.[19]

18 See *Butler's Book*. Blair in the rough draft of his letter to Cameron included a sentence later deleted: "As our friend Chase even has fallen out with the Genl I hope we will pluck up courage to take our affairs into our own hands." Blair Papers, LC.

19 See McClellan's published *Report*, 15–17, 51, 52; for Scott's advice see O. R. I, ii, 648, 743, etc.

[II]

Like two wrestlers glowering at each other across the ring, McDowell and Beauregard early in July faced each other across twenty miles of broken Virginia countryside. The Union commander, after detaching about 6,000 men to protect his communications, had 30,000 troops with 49 guns; the Confederate general had some 22,000 men with 29 guns. Both might be rapidly reinforced—the Southern army by Johnston's Shenandoah force, which at the beginning of July comprised about 11,000 men with 20 guns, and the army of McDowell by Patterson's larger force.[20] In this matter of reinforcing Beauregard and McDowell the Confederacy held the advantage, partly because Johnston could use the railroad from Winchester to Manassas, while Patterson had no ready means of reaching the area.

The Administration had good reasons for wishing to see McDowell offer battle. One was that the ninety-day men were soon to quit, they hoped to see action before they left, and obviously they ought to be used. Another was that European governments might be impressed by Northern vigor. The most important, however, was that Northern morale must be sustained.

Impatient Congressmen varied their debates by grumbling loudly about procrastination. Wagons and horses were needed? Well, buy them! Regiments had to be organized into brigades and divisions? Well, shove them in! Zack Chandler, who came to the Senate full of plans for seizing rebel property, thought that Scott could avoid hard fighting just by showing a little energy: he could simply surround the scoundrels, make their case hopeless, and compel them to retreat to Richmond. Chandler and others were talking about hanging the worst traitors as soon as they were caught.[21] Half of the press was ringing with demands for hard blows. As an echo of Horace Greeley's suggestions, Fitz-Henry Warren, a Washington correspondent of the *Tribune*, wrote his famous "Forward to Richmond" article; Greeley allowed Charles A. Dana to repeat and reinforce it in subsequent issues; and other newspapers caught it up. "Forward to Richmond! Forward to Richmond! The Rebel Congress must not be allowed to meet there on the 20th of July!"—so from June 26 onward ran the *Tribune's* daily iteration of "The Nation's Battle-Cry." [22]

20 On numbers see Ropes, I, 127, 128; *Battles and Leaders*, I, 175; O. R. I, ii, 309, 487. A few ninety-day men did quit just before the battle, and the position of the whole body affected Union morale.

21 Chandler to his wife, Washington, June 27, 1861, Chandler Papers, LC; F. W. Banks, Washington, July 9, 1861, to S. L. M. Barlow, Barlow Papers; Washington correspondence dated July 11, 12, in N. Y. *Tribune*, July 13, 1861.

22 Cf. Charles A. Dana, "Greeley as a Journalist," N. Y. *Sun*, Dec. 5, 1872; and Dana's dictated statement to Ida M. Tarbell in Tarbell Papers, Allegheny College. Dana had been with the *Tribune* since 1847 and in some of Greeley's absences had taken full charge.

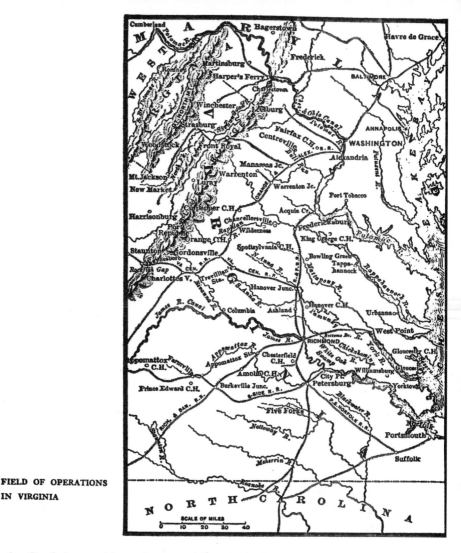

FIELD OF OPERATIONS
IN VIRGINIA

SCALE OF MILES

On the Confederate side various prodders, including the Richmond *Examiner*, had made Jefferson Davis nearly as anxious to hazard battle as Beauregard. Davis wrote Johnston July 13 that the one great object was to give the Southern columns capacity to take the offensive and prevent the junction of the enemy's forces.[23]

Nothing could have been more haphazard than the way in which McDowell's forward thrust was determined upon. First, Scott orally asked him to submit a plan of operations against Manassas, with an estimate of the men needed. Second, McDowell sent his plan to Scott, who read and approved it. Third, a council was held June 29 in the East Room of the White House attended by Cabinet members and leading officers. McDowell read his plan,

23 O. R. I, ii, 976, 977.

on which nobody made any comment except Mansfield, commanding in Washington, who said that he had not thought about the matter, knew nothing about it, and was unprepared to speak! The relation of Patterson's army to the movement was discussed, and one participant states that Scott explicitly promised to have it keep the Confederates in the Shenandoah engaged: "I assume the responsibility for having Johnston kept off McDowell's flank." Finally, McDowell submitted his plan to the army engineers, who made no constructive suggestion. In short, no real debate on the wisdom or mode of the attack took place.

Once the plan was accepted, McDowell had great difficulty in implementing it. Some regiments crossed the Potomac late, and a few not till the very day he was to start his army. He set out with no baggage trains, and though he possessed ammunition wagons and ambulances, had no facilities to carry food or tents. The men carried three days' rations in their haversacks. Said the jealous Mansfield, in effect, "I have no transportation to give you." Said Meigs, head of the quartermaster arrangements: "I have transportation, but Mansfield does not want me to supply it until the troops move." Said the overburdened McDowell: "I agree to that, but between you two I get nothing." So he set off, telling Scott he was not really ready to go: "So far as transportation is concerned, I must look to you behind me to send it forward." The egregiously bad marching of his troops McDowell explained by saying that Americans were unused to foot travel. Starting on Tuesday morning, July 16, the army did not reach Centerville until Thursday afternoon, when it camped until the battle advance began Sunday morning the 21st. Why?—partly because its provisions had not come up.[24]

Actually, McDowell's plan was well conceived and well drafted. By defeating Beauregard at Manassas, he would not only dispel the threat to Washington, but seize the important junction between the Orange & Alexandria Railroad and its lateral branch to the Shenandoah. He had the advantage of superior numbers, better ordnance, about 1600 regular soldiers, and the prospect of a timely reinforcement by Patterson. But a sharp check at Blackburn's Ford on the Bull Run July 18 discouraged his men, who wondered whether the Confederate line could really be penetrated. He and the army engineers used the next two days trying to discover the best place for attack. Meanwhile Patterson, whose duty was to hold Joseph E. Johnston, marched in precisely the wrong direction. He had been alarmed by vague reports that he had 30,000 to 40,000 troops before him. In a half-hearted demonstration, he moved toward

24 McDowell dates the East Room conference June 29; Montgomery C. Meigs says the beginning of July. See McDowell's testimony, *Comm. on Conduct of the War*, II, 35 ff.; Meigs Papers, Box IV, LC; and O. R. I, ii, *passim*, full of material on the campaign.

Winchester and Johnston on July 16, but then next day retreated to Charlestown, and a little later pulled still farther back to Harpers Ferry. Johnston no sooner learned that Patterson had fallen back than he exultantly set his troops in motion, hurrying them on as fast as he could to join Beauregard.

The result was that on July 20 the main body of Johnston's force joined Beauregard. His intelligence service, for he had Major J. E. B. Stuart's cavalry to scout for him, was as superb as Patterson's was worthless. While Patterson was asking Scott for aid at Harpers Ferry, Johnston's command was fraternizing with the defenders of Manassas. This, said McDowell later, was "the fatal thing" that decided Bull Run.

Yet it was not the only fatal element. At first the Union advance on the 21st seemed victorious. Pressing against the Confederate left, McDowell's raw volunteers threw the Southerners back in some disorder. The main fighting began about ten; at noon the battle was raging heavily beyond Bull Run, around and on the hill capped by the Henry farmhouse; reports of a disaster swept Richmond. The gallant James S. Wadsworth of New York thought at two o'clock that the Union army had won the field. But command liaison on the Union side was very poor, so that troops moved in piecemeal and raggedly. Then, soon after three, a new part of Johnston's army, fresh from the trains, arrived on the scene—the brigade of E. Kirby-Smith. That force, delivering a severe discharge of musketry, followed it with a hot charge. Some Union elements stampeded, and as Beauregard ordered an attack along the whole line, the Union troops were swept back. By five they were in full retreat.

Beauregard had possessed complete warning of the Federal advance, for at 8:00 P.M. on July 16 a sealed letter, brought him by relays from the Confederate spy Mrs. Greenhow in Washington, had announced in cipher that McDowell had been ordered to move. Early next morning he telegraphed the news to Jefferson Davis. On the 17th the Richmond authorities had been able to order Johnston's Army of the Shenandoah to join Beauregard, and T. J. Jackson's brigade had forthwith led the van in the march to the nearest railroad station. Scott, meanwhile, had failed to give Patterson positive orders.[25]

Not only were the Southern forces better coordinated, but they had better officers and showed superior morale. During the battle the Confederate generals kept close under fire. Johnston and Beauregard were in the front lines at critical moments, Brigadier-General B. E. Bee was mortally wounded, Colonel

25 See Col. Alfred Roman's *Beauregard*, I, 71 ff. (practically an autobiography); Johnston's *Narrative*, 50 ff.; Gen. James Wadsworth's testimony in Committee on the Conduct of the War, II; Swinton, *Army of the Potomac*, 58, 59; Ropes, I, 131 ff. Swinton and Ropes emphasize the defective leadership and uneven fighting on both sides. *Comm. on Conduct of the War*, II, 103. By Patterson's own statement, he could have held Johnston with 8,000 men; *op. cit.*, 107. A mass of military dispatches may be found in O. R. I., li, pt. 2.

J. F. Thomas, chief ordnance officer, fell while leading broken troops back into battle, and Jubal Early was equally intrepid. It was while Bee was appealing to his South Carolinians to sustain the honor of their State that he pointed to a brigade of the Army of the Shenandoah standing on the Henry house hilltop awaiting the Northern onslaught: "Look, there is Jackson with his Virginians standing like a stone wall against the enemy." [26] The men responded by a spirited charge. Young Jeb Stuart, leading two companies of cavalry, made his first appearance on a battlefield by a timely onslaught against the Union right flank, sweeping through the supports of two Federal batteries and leaving the guns an easy prey to an advancing regiment of Virginians. Throughout the hottest part of the battle the Confederate morale rose.

The Union troops had the disadvantage of advancing over unknown terrain against a foe of unknown strength. Raw troops fight more steadily when stationary, as most of the Confederate units were; in attacking they become confused and disorganized. Many Northerners entered the fight hot, tired, and thirsty from previous marching. Sights of wounds and agony frightened the green men. General William B. Franklin went forward with the Fifth and Eleventh Massachusetts to try to extricate an exposed battery. The infantrymen could not be brought up to the mark: they would rush forward, deliver a volley, and then, instead of taking hold of the guns, fall back to a safe place to reload. The Union artillery was badly served, and Griffin's expert West Point Battery showed the usual contempt of regulars for volunteers. Early in the combat it tore through the New York Seventy-first at top speed for a front-line position, cutting the regiment in two. Later, it ran out of ammunition. The caissons tore recklessly back for a fresh supply, scattering the units in their path, and men who saw the horses and gunners madly ripping out for the rear, thought all was lost—and ran too.

The Union retreat, at first orderly, quickly became a disgraceful rout. As Beauregard's lines swept forward, the panic grew, and soon men were in headlong flight, amid heat, dust, anguish, and terrific profanity. W. H. Russell, riding forward on horseback, found himself among the first fugitives. "What does this mean?" he demanded, and an exhausted officer gasped: "Why, it means that we are pretty badly whipped." [27]

The scene between Manassas and Alexandria that evening was never to be forgotten. The fields were dotted with fugitives, mounted officers outstripping

26 *Century*, XLVIII, vol. 48 (May, 1894), 155, 156.
27 Russell's vivid description, *My Diary*, Ch. 50, is corroborated by the photographer Mathew Brady, caught in the flight; Representative A. O. Riddle, quoted in S. S. Cox, *Three Decades*, 158; Horace White, *Lyman Trumbull*, 165–168. Trumbull, who had gone to the battle with Senator Grimes and others, wrote: "Literally, three could have chased ten thousand."

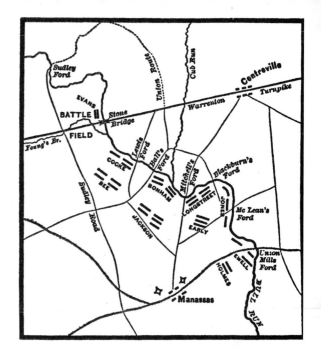

BULL RUN
DISPOSITION OF
CONFEDERATE FORCES

privates afoot. Down the Centreville highway poured a river of wagons, ambulances, soldiers belaboring mules, and dirty, disheveled troops. Every vehicle was jammed with men, who threw out even ammunition to make room. The ground was covered with provisions, overcoats, knapsacks, blankets, muskets, canteens, and cartridge boxes. Drivers whipped their teams; reeling soldiers clung to stirrups and wagon gates; and at every interruption of traffic masses of troops yelled frantically with rage: "The cavalry is on us! Get along, get along!" Over the crossroads rose columns of dust, for here, too, masses of troops were fleeing as from some unknown terror. As the flight roared northward, its noise like that of a great river, more and more men fell out from exhaustion. At Centreville some fresh reserve regiments formed line on a good defensive slope, and the fleeing forces might well have considered themselves safe.[28] But when a neighboring battery opened fire, the thud and flash precipitated a fresh panic.

It was the familiar story whose moral Kipling later compressed into three lines:

Ye pushed them raw to the battle as ye plucked them raw from the street,
And what did ye look they should compass? War-craft learned in a breath
Knowledge unto occasion at the first far view of Death?

In Washington that Sunday intense suspense had gripped everyone. Scott, anxious to allay men's anxiety, talked confidently of success and went to

28 A reserve brigade under Miles and a brigade under Richardson, in and just beyond Centerville, had taken no part in the fighting, maintained good order, and served as a dependable rear guard; Ropes, I, 153.

church at eleven. Early in the afternoon the President began receiving telegrams every quarter hour from Fairfax Court House, three or four miles from
the battlefront. They at first gave the impression that the Union forces were
retiring, and Lincoln, alarmed, went to see Scott, whom he found asleep. The
General explained that the noise of battle was often misleading, for the wind
made the firing seem first near, then far. Lincoln, returning to the White
House, found news that the battle still raged, but that McDowell now seemed
to be winning. Pleased by word that the Confederates had been driven back,
he went for a ride. His secretary Nicolay records:

At six o'clock . . . Mr. Seward came into the President's room with a
terribly excited and frightened look, and said to John [Hay] and I, who were
sitting there, "Where is the President?" "Gone to ride," we replied.
"Have you any late news?" said he.
I began reading Hanscom's dispatch to him.
Said he: "Tell no one. That is not so. The battle is lost. The telegraph says
that McDowell is in full retreat, and calls on General Scott to save the capital,
etc. Find the President and tell him immediately to come to General Scott's." [29]

[III]

The Confederates made no real pursuit. By a determined thrust from either
the east or west, they might have turned the small reserve force at Centreville.
Some regiments on the Confederate left did ford Bull Run and set out to
follow the fleeing troops, but were recalled by a staff command given in error.
That night President Davis and the principal Confederate generals held a
battlefield conference.[30] Davis was at first willing to send the freshest units,
the brigades of Ewell, D. R. Jones, and Longstreet, in pursuit, but because
doubts were thrown upon a major's report that he had seen a wild flight, with
abandoned wagons and choked roads, he finally decided against the step.
Johnston believed that his raw troops, poorly supplied with food and ammunition, could not execute forced marches and attack the fortified lines before
Washington. He thought his troops more disorganized by victory, indeed, than
the Union forces by defeat. Beauregard also opposed an attempt at pursuit.
Previously hot to take the offensive and advance on Washington, he now declared that the prostration of the men, the shortage of supplies—the Manassas
army had never possessed food for more than two days, and sometimes no
rations at all, while it now held only enough ammunition for half a battle—and
the general confusion, forbade a forward thrust.

29 Nicolay to his wife, July 27, 1861; Nicolay Papers, LC.
30 Davis had reached the battlefield just in time to witness the rout of the Union forces,
and at once exultantly telegraphed his War Department that 15,000 Confederates had defeated 35,000 Federal troops. Roman, *Beauregard*, I, 111.

This decision deeply disappointed both Richmond and the many Southern sympathizers in Washington. Mrs. Greenhow, who had repeatedly assured Beauregard that the Union works south of the Potomac had been barely commenced and mounted few guns, and that a Confederate advance was greatly dreaded in the capital, ended more than one dispatch after Manassas: "Come on! Why do you not come?" But Johnston and Beauregard made a correct decision. By an implacable pursuit, flogging on their tired soldiers, the Confederates could have taken more prisoners and stores, making the defeat still more humiliating. But as they approached Washington they would have met the reserves from Centreville, the divisions of Mansfield and Runyon, some 11,000 Pennsylvania troops who arrived on Monday, and perhaps Patterson's force. Beyond the fortifications lay the Potomac. The night after the battle a dull, drenching rain began which continued all next day, turning the roads into mud. The railroad bridge across Bull Run had been destroyed. And the Confederates were hungry. Their commissary service, in the hands of the ill-tempered, inept Colonel Lucius B. Northrop, who had refused to let Beauregard sweep the area south of Washington clean of provisions, was distressingly inefficient.[31]

Even without pursuit, the Confederates claimed fully 1200 prisoners; 28 fieldpieces of good quality, 8 of them rifled, with more than 100 rounds for each gun; some 500 muskets and 500,000 rounds of ammunition; and horses, wagons, caissons, and ambulances. Losses on both sides have been variously computed, but the best source places the Union killed at 481, the Confederate at 387.[32]

The exultation of part of the Southern press and public was not only unrestrained, but tinged with an arrogant tone. "The breakdown of the Yankee race, their unfitness for empire," declared the Richmond *Whig*, "forces dominion on the South. We are compelled to take the sceptre of power. We must adapt ourselves to our new destiny. We must elevate our race, every man of it, breed them up to arms, to command, to empire."[33] The Louisville *Courier-Journal* was equally insolent. The South, remarked the editor, had until a few

31 "The want of food and transportation has made us lose all the fruits or our victory," wrote Beauregard, July 29. "We ought at this moment to be in or about Washington, but we are perfectly anchored here, and God only knows when we will be able to advance; without these means we can neither advance nor retreat." Roman, *op. cit.*, 121, 122. George Cary Eggleston in *A Rebel's Recollections* emphatically states the view of those who thought the army should have pursued. Jubal Early in his reminiscences emphatically agrees that advance was impracticable and impolitic; *Narrative*, 43–46.

32 O. R. I, ii, 327, gives Union killed 481, wounded 1011, and missing 1216; the Confederate killed at 387, wounded at 1582.

33 July 23, 1861. One able Southerner, the engineer R. H. Lucas, said he would not give ten cents on the dollar for New York property; Manigault, MS Recollections, Univ. of N. C., 326, 327.

weeks since governed the North as its Norman ancestors had governed the Saxon churls. The Yankee revolt would not last long, for, "dastards in fight and incapable of self-government, they will inevitably fall under the control of a superior race. A few more Bull Run thrashings will bring most of them once more under the yoke, as docile as the most loyal of our Ethiopian chattels."[34] *DeBow's Review*, picturing the North as divided and half-prostrated, predicted that the battle would confirm the independence of the South.[35]

Needless to say, responsible men like Davis and Lee knew that the test had only begun.

34 Quoted in Rossiter Johnson, *War of Secession*, 70.
35 September, 1861.

12

A Resurgent North

THE EFFECT of Bull Run at the North, as its meaning sank in, was as stimulating as a whiplash. It blew away illusions like rags of fog in a northwest gale. Andrew D. White, a young upstate New Yorker already winning prominence as an educator, heard of the battle as he was entertaining Charles Sumner's younger brother, fresh from Washington. White was angry over a recent statement by Seward that the Administration had determined to end the rebellion even if it took 50,000 men to capture Richmond and dictate terms that summer. In what kind of dreams was Seward indulging? White and George Sumner agreed that defeat was healthy if it stopped such fatuous misconceptions.[1]

The defeat brought Northern dissidents to better support of the war, and stimulated every State to intensified effort. Illinois telegraphed the War Department offering seventeen regiménts. Indiana telegraphed offering ten. As regiments of ninety-day men were mustered out in New York, the rank and file showed a strong desire to reënlist—but with the stipulation that they must have officers of real capacity. The first shock in Washington had been appalling. To see McDowell's rabble, a host of dirty, ragged, hungry men, come pouring in to beg food from door to door and sink to sleep on pavements and doorsteps; to see the hotels crowded with road-stained officers, some brazen, some ashamed—this disheartened loyal citizens. But the *National Intelligencer*, indignant over reports North and South that the city was frightened, published a front-page editorial August 3 to declare that the capital remained undaunted, undiscouraged, and confident of ultimate success.

A second Northern uprising was at once evident. Governor Curtin, now justified in his insistence on a State reserve of fifteen regiments fully armed and ready for an emergency, could claim first place in the movement. The arrival of his troops in Washington just after the battle heartened the North. Volunteers thronged forward. Seward five days after the battle wrote Charles Francis Adams in London that military and civil panic had quickly ceased, and the

1 White, *Autobiography*, I, 87–88.

true result was already seen in a vigorous reconstruction of the war effort on an expanded scale.[2] Within a fortnight a strong new army of more than 75,000 men, enlisted for three years or the duration, was in the training camps.

A complete reorganization of command was clearly necessary. At the very moment that public confidence in McDowell fell to zero, the press was spreading broadcast a Napoleonic proclamation from McClellan:

Soldiers of the Army of the West!
I am more than satisfied with you.
You have annihilated two armies, commanded by educated and experienced soldiers, intrenched in mountain fastnesses fortified at their leisure. You have taken five guns, twelve colors, fifteen hundred stand of arms, one thousand prisoners, including more than forty officers—one of the two commanders of the rebels is a prisoner, the other lost his life on the field of battle. You have killed more than two hundred and fifty of the enemy, who has lost all his baggage and camp equipage. All this has been accomplished with the loss of twenty brave men killed and sixty wounded on your part.[3]

These statements were the more impressive because their author had served with distinction in Mexico, had been an official observer of the Crimean War, and combined a West Point education with managerial experience in business. McClellan was careful to point out that *he* had inspired his men: "I have not hesitated to demand this of you, feeling that I could rely on your endurance, patriotism, and courage." The New York *Herald* led the press in extolling him. "The name of General McClellan is upon every lip," it declared July 15. Cabinet members, military men, and the universal populace joined in his praise; "Hurrah for McClellan!" men even shouted in the streets. His energy, skill, and organizing efficiency delighted everybody.

His one-month campaign to conquer northwestern Virginia indeed appeared to be brilliant. Nobody could deny his high administrative capacity. A critical scrutiny, however, would have demolished some of his eloquent pretensions. He had possessed a heavy preponderance in numbers, and one still heavier in firepower, for the Confederates were poorly equipped. He had marked advantages of transport in the use of the Baltimore & Ohio on the north and the Great Kanawha on the south. He operated in a friendly country. At Parkersburg, for example, his troops had met a general ovation, "gray-headed old men and women, mothers holding up their children to take my hand, girls, boys, all sorts, cheering and crying, 'God bless you!'" The campaign hardships of which he spoke feelingly ("long and arduous marches," "insufficient food," "inclemency of the weather") did not bother a young Ohio officer named

2 *Diplomatic Correspondence*, 1861.
3 This pronunciamento was dated July 16; O. R. I, ii, 205–208. All the younger generals then fancied themselves embryo Napoleons, and cultivated Napoleonic rescripts; except a few who thought themselves Wellingtons.

Rutherford B. Hayes serving with him. On the contrary, Hayes exulted in the fine mountain scenery, clear streams, wooded slopes, and generally warm, clear weather.

McClellan's handsome, soldierly presence, kind, modest manners, and evident care for his troops, made a happy impression. The obverse of the medal was his readiness to lay claim to credit belonging to others, to depreciate and rebuke subordinates publicly, and to exaggerate the enemy strength. A colonel had won Philippi while McClellan sat at his office desk in Cincinnati. At Corrick's Ford, General T. D. Morris, with 1800 men, had routed the enemy and killed Robert S. Garnett, the Southern leader (July 13). Two days earlier Union forces had been aided in the most important battle, Rich Mountain, by a lucky accident. General W. S. Rosecrans was to attempt to turn the Confederate flank and attack the heights from the rear while McClellan assaulted in front. As Rosecrans advanced, his pickets seized a farm youth who led them by a secret way directly behind Colonel John Pegram's entrenchments on the mountain, where they won an overwhelming success. McClellan, by contrast, did badly; he failed to attack at the proper time, scaled the mountain late, and lost the chance of completely crushing the enemy.

While understating the forces opposed to subordinate officers like Jacob D. Cox and Rosecrans, McClellan constantly overstated those facing himself. Cox complained later that the general had systematically depreciated him. He had similarly written General Morris a series of insulting reprimands, culminating in the statement that if Morris asked for any more reinforcements, "I shall take it as a request to be relieved from your command and return to Indiana." When McClellan publicly castigated Rosecrans, that general sent him a reasoned justification closing with a spirited rebuke: "Review, if you please, that letter which you have put on record, and say whether, after you receive this, both private feelings and public interest are likely to be the better for it." [4]

McClellan's official Rich Mountain report seemed to give all the credit to himself. Yet J. D. Cox could truthfully assert that Rich Mountain disclosed some characteristics of McClellan that were destined later to come out more fully. "There was the same overestimate of the enemy, the same tendency to interpret unfavorably the sights and sounds in front, the same hesitancy to throw in his whole force when he knew that his subordinate was engaged." [5]

On the very Sunday night of Bull Run Lincoln began to draft new plans.

4 For this West Virginia campaign see O. R. I, ii, 194 ff.; McClellan's *Report*, and his *Own Story*; Ambler, *History of West Virginia*, 335 ff.; J. M. Callahan, *Semi-Centennial History of West Virginia*, 154 ff.; Festus P. Summers, *The Baltimore & Ohio in the Civil War*, 69–89; J. W. Thomas, "Campaigns of McClellan and Rosecrans in West Virginia, 1861–62," *West Virginia History*, vol. 5 (July, 1944), 245–308; and Jacob D. Cox, *Reminiscences*, I, 64 ff. Cox was one of the first (but far from the last) of talented officers from civil life to feel the enmity of West Point leaders.

5 Cox, *Reminiscences*, I, 58.

When two days later he finished this private memorandum of nine points of military policy, he said nothing about a changed military leadership; this was not necessary. His program embraced the strengthening of the blockade, of Butler's force, and of the Shenandoah army; it called for reorganizing Mc-Dowell's army, and pushing operations in the West; and it demanded the rapid dispatch of the new volunteer recruits to the Washington camps. A few days later Lincoln added that Manassas Junction and Strasburg should be seized and permanently held, with an open line from Washington to Manassas.[6] He was planning a fresh advance on that route. Nobody now talked of an easy march down the Mississippi, or from Cincinnati across country to Mobile, or even, as Montgomery Blair had done, from Fort Monroe to Richmond. The main object was to strike the formidable Southern armies, and in Washington, one voice chose the leader: McClellan.

Hot July days; hot contentions wherever Congressmen gathered; hot letters passing back and forth, like E. M. Stanton's denunciation of Administration "imbecility" to Buchanan; mint juleps and gin slings pouring down hot throats. On July 26, McClellan reached the city. Ambition burned in his brain as, calling on Scott, he heard that he was now where Napoleon had stood after Arcola: "Soldiers, like a torrent you have rushed down from the heights of the Apennines!" Next morning brought a call on Lincoln—their first meeting. He met the President coolly and confidently, and was invited to attend the Cabinet meeting at one. Scott was jealous of that invitation, declaring, "You shall not go when *I* am not asked," and he detained McClellan. The general had to explain this later to Lincoln, who was wryly amused.[7]

Within ten days after Bull Run, nearly the whole high command under Scott was changed. Patterson, his term of service expiring, gave way to N. P. Banks on July 27. In West Virginia, Rosecrans took McClellan's place. Frémont was just settling himself in Missouri. McClellan at once set about reorganizing his forces. He found on arrival at his Washington headquarters that he had about 50,000 infantry, less than 1000 cavalry, 650 artillerymen, and 30 cannon. He also found that the streets, hotels, and barrooms were full of drunken officers and men absent without leave from their units, "a perfect pandemonium"; that not a single regiment was properly encamped; that no preparations had been made for defense, not even to the placing of troops in military positions; and that the forts on the Virginia side lay detached, with no real defensive line.[8] McClellan further discovered that Scott was not the

6 Lincoln, *Collected Works*, IV, 457, 458; Nicolay and Hay, IV, 368.
7 McClellan, *Own Story*, 66, 67.
8 McClellan's dark picture in his *Own Story*, 66, 67, which enhances the magnitude of his achievement in reorganization, is to be taken with some reserve. Progress *had* been made in manning the fortifications; O. R. I, ii, 755, 756.

only officer with an excessive jealousy of his own position; neither McDowell nor Mansfield was cordial to the young officer now placed over them.

At any rate, the holiday was over. Grim war had begun.

[I]

The North was now busy raising its great new volunteer army of 500,000. The spirit needed was that of Tom Paine in an earlier crisis: "I call not upon a few, but upon all; not on this State or that State, but on every State; up and help us; lay your shoulder to the wheel; better have too much force than too little, when so great an object is at stake. Say not that thousands are gone, turn out your tens of thousands." But more than a determined spirit was required.

This really tremendous Union task of the summer and fall, the raising, equipping, and organizing of some 500 regiments, the greatest citizen army in history, demanded a careful Federal plan. This plan should have comprehended five desiderata which were not met: a close Federal control of the work, with due regard for State pride; an accurate determination of the State quotas; full use of regular army officers and men, widely distributed, to help train and command the new army; careful selection among both civilians and regulars for officers; and an end to the use of independent private recruiters in raising companies and regiments.

Congress was partly at fault for the lack of realistic plan, but the larger blame falls on Secretary Cameron, of whom a wrong view has been taken. He was not dishonest, for no proof exists that as Secretary he took a penny not his own. This veteran spoilsman was not a whit more inclined to play politics with his high office than Chase or Blair. But he was an incompetent administrator; flustered, inexact, forgetful, he had no ability to organize an efficient War Office as Chase and George Harrington organized an efficient Treasury, and Welles and Gustavus V. Fox organized an efficient Navy Department. He lacked vigilance in guarding against contract abuses; and worst of all, he was totally unable to plan.

The Military Act which became law on the morrow of Bull Run was a curious mixture of merits and defects. It did provide for a three-year army, the President to call forth the men as needed and apportion them among the States on the basis of population. It did provide that the President might appoint major-generals and brigadier-generals from the regular army. It did take a few precautions to ensure greater efficiency among subordinate officers than they had shown at Big Bethel and Bull Run. From colonels down, they were to be chosen as before under State laws, the higher officers in the main to be appointed by the governors, and the lower elected by the men; but every general commanding a separate department or army was authorized to create a board to examine the qualifications and conduct of any officer. If the board's report was unfavorable, the officer's commission would be canceled. The mere existence of this provision did something to improve the character of the army.

The faults of the Act, however, were glaring. It would have been wise to scatter officers and carefully picked men of the regular army widely among the incoming volunteers to leaven the whole lump with their sound ideas of discipline. General Scott, however, insisted on maintaining the regular army practically intact, and Cameron supported him. Nor was Congress inclined to differ from them. Most members at this stage of the war distrusted West Point as a school of Southern, aristocratic, snobbish flavor, and believed that gifted amateurs could quickly become efficient generals; that men like Ormsby Mitchel, Lew Wallace, Frémont, Jacob D. Cox, and Carl Schurz were quite as good as the McDowells, Mansfields, Lyons, and McClellans. Senators John Sherman and Ben Wade merely expressed a general prejudice this summer in assailing West Point. "I know," said Fessenden in replying to Sherman, "that the Senator from Ohio has peculiar views about this institution. He thinks commanders are born, not made. I do not. I think they are made. I think education is necessary." [9] Greater seminal use of the best regulars, say one to every twenty-five volunteers, would not only have promoted efficiency, but would have had a nationalizing tendency; yet it was never tried.

Under the new law, as under the old, recruiting was by States and localities, with provision for reimbursing them for the costs of raising, arming, paying, and transporting troops to the point where they entered Federal service. This was an irresponsible, extravagant, and confused method.[10] Regimental officers were commissioned by the governors, not the President. Naturally privates thought of themselves as Vermont men, Wisconsin men, and Pennsylvania men, not as national troops; and colonels and majors looked to Yates, Morgan, and Andrew for control and support, not to Washington. The provision that regimental vacancies should be filled by letting the men elect lieutenants and captains while officers chose majors and colonels added to the decentralizing tendencies of the system. Congress, in this plan, seized on what Emory B. Upton later termed the worst vice in State practice; fortunately, it was short-lived.

A few farsighted men perceived that ideally the North needed a national army. Early in the summer of 1861, ex-Governor Rodman Price of New Jersey, James L. Curtis of New York, and John C. Frémont held a conference at the Astor House in New York, where they drew up a plan for the free interchange of Eastern and Western troops. Curtis went to Washington, and

9 *Cong. Globe*, 37th Cong., 1st Sess.
10 Emory B. Upton, *Military Policy of the U. S.*, 260.

persuaded Frank Blair to lay the proposal before Cameron. The Secretary approved of it, as Curtis wrote Frémont, "and advised my proceeding forthwith to raise regiments and send them forward to St. Louis. Mr. Blair, Sr., suggested that he (Frank) should see President Lincoln and ask his approval. The President said, after reading the paper, that it was a grave and important suggestion, that he would submit it to the Cabinet." Though Attorney-General Bates termed it the best idea of the day, the Cabinet failed to approve it. Curtis remained hopeful, believing that if Cameron assented, Frémont might take ten thousand Pennsylvania troops west.[11] However, the plan came to nothing, for it conflicted with State pride and the regional prejudices of many people. To the end of the war the Western forces remained largely of Western origin, the Eastern forces of Eastern antecedents. John Pope actually wanted a complete Illinois army, kept intact, moved as a body, and officered by Illinoisans from corporals to major-general.[12] And as a second consideration, the War Department was totally unequipped to raise a national army. State adjutant-generals and other officers had to shoulder the task of preparing forces.

When the Comte de Paris after service on McClellan's staff came to explain the organization of the huge volunteer army to Frenchmen, he found much to censure. To him the fundamental weakness of the system so hurriedly devised this summer was the want of any means by which the national government could enforce discipline. Having no power to appoint or demote officers below the rank of brigadier-general, the Federal authorities possessed but a nerveless grasp of the army. From colonels down, the great host of officers looked to the State capitals; all arrangements were temporary, and nearly all were tinged with politics; the troops never felt the insistence on efficiency which a firmly constituted hierarchy of command, exempt from party pull and push, could offer. Many politically favored officers shot rapidly to a colonelcy, brigadiership, or, like Ben Butler, still higher, simply for lending their influence and bringing forward a body of troops. More than one subaltern of the regular army, made a colonel, grew disgusted with volunteers and politics, and returned to minor rank in his old regiment. When regiments disbanded, officers lost their places. A sense of uncertainty pervaded the whole officer corps.[13]

The Comte also specially censured the failure to provide a vigorous system of recruitment to fill vacancies caused by battle, sickness, and desertion. Once a regiment left its State, no more men applied to its recruiting office—if it had any. The influential leaders who had formed it were far away in camp; the choice places had all been filled; and public sentiment was interested in raising

11 Curtis, N. Y., Aug. 6, 1861, to Frémont; Blair-Lee Papers.
12 Pope to Yates, Yates Papers, Ill. State Lib.
13 Upton, 258; Comte de Paris, *Civil War*, I, 266, 267, 273, 274.

new units, not in strengthening old ones. A sharp battle, or a week in a malarial area, might cut an outfit in half, but the new regiments coming in furnished it no reinforcement. These fresh regiments brought all the inexperience that had cost their predecessors so dear, while the example and tuition of the veterans, which might have been so useful under a process of consolidation, were left unused. Meanwhile, the old skeleton regiments were often too weak to be effective in battle. Some army commanders tried to repair this defect. McClellan, for example, shortly issued General Order No. 105 requiring that volunteer regiments should immediately report deficiencies in strength to the Adjutant-General, and that incoming men should be requisitioned to fill the gaps. In practice, however, these orders were but partially executed.[14]

The volunteer army, as the war proceeded, thus became filled with regiments of three-quarters, half, or quarter strength, sometimes given good replacements, sometimes weak ones, and sometimes none at all. They were officered by men selected sometimes for capacity, but frequently for family influence, militia experience, or personal or political reasons; more often than not, by aggressive men whose organizing enterprise or community popularity brought them to the front. Promotions and replacements of officers were often arbitrary, and sometimes the morale of a regiment was ruined for months by a single wretched choice; the Tenth Massachusetts Volunteers from the Berkshire area, for example, almost went to pieces when it got an incompetent major.[15] The first Massachusetts three-year men marched off under a colonel whom Charles Francis Adams, Jr., termed "a notorious incompetent"; and Adams assured his father that all the Bay State regiments but one were so wretchedly officered this summer that it would be a miracle if they did not disgrace themselves. At Big Bethel, indeed, a brigadier did disgrace Massachusetts.

In the West, Joseph Medill begged Senator Trumbull to see that Brigadier-General S. A. Hurlbut was denied confirmation. He had been drunk in Chicago every day for a week; he led his Zouave regiment off for Missouri still so drunk he could hardly walk; and the city, with 1500 sons under his command, felt outraged by his appointment. Nevertheless, he stayed. Half the good volunteer colonels could have echoed the plaint of the head of the Eighteenth Illinois: "I have some 4 or 5 officers in my regt who are utterly worthless."[16]

14 Cf. Shannon, *Organization*, I, 190. A typical regiment reduced to a shadow of its old strength was the Twentieth Massachusetts Volunteers, whose historian, George A. Bruce, states that after Mine Run late in 1863 it mustered but 150 officers and men present for duty, having suffered to that date 745 war casualties.
15 J. K. Newell, *The Tenth Mass. Volunteers, passim.*
16 W. C. Ford, ed., *Cycle of Adams Letters*, I, 12, 13; Medill, July 13, 1861, Trumbull

Privates could be punished summarily for any misdemeanor. But officers, as the Comte de Paris noted, had to be brought before a court-martial for even small offenses, and could not be given as much as two days' confinement without formal sentence. The trial process, borrowed from the little regular army with its high sense of officers' prerogatives, thus became a shield to protect officers guilty of neglect, misconduct, or even gross insubordination.

Fortunately, the legislation for the new army did contain provisions which made it possible to strengthen the higher command. Representative A. S. Diven of New York wished to write into it a requirement that the President must select the six new major-generals and eighteen new brigadiers from West Point graduates, or officers who had spent at least five years in the regular army, or men whose war service had proved their ability to command.[17] Since this was felt to be too restrictive, it failed. But Senator James W. Nesmith of Oregon, who held enlightened views upon military management, fared better with a permissive amendment, allowing the President to select general officers from the line or staff of the regular army.

Saying that he knew major-generals and brigadiers who could not pass an examination as first lieutenant in any militarily advanced country, Nesmith spoke feelingly of the murderous results of appointing politicians and other upstarts, totally ignorant of the art of war, as ranking commanders. It was not true, he declared, that men would be happier under amateurs of popular repute from their own States; when shells burst and bullets hissed, they preferred an officer who knew his profession. Henry Wilson warmly seconded him, and the amendment passed.[18]

[II]

Just how was the new army of half a million raised? On the morrow of Bull Run no spur was necessary, for the people felt a grim determination to get the war fought and won. The governors, telegraphing offers of fresh troops, asked how many would be accepted. The War Department's invariable answer was, "Send them all"; and thus by noon of July 24, fully 75,000 had been taken, with more coming.[19]

Lincoln thought it unnecessary to issue a new proclamation calling for volunteers, and unwise for the moment to apportion quotas among the States. The policy of the War Department was to accept, under blanket authority of

---

Papers, LC; Col. H. R. Lewis, Mound City, Ill., Sept. 7, 1861, to McClernand, McClernand Papers, Ill. State Hist. Lib.
17 *Cong. Globe*, 37th Cong., 1st Sess., 95–100.
18 *Cong. Globe*, 37th Cong., 1st Sess., 52.
19 O. R. III, i, 140 ff.; N. Y. *Herald*, July 25, 1861.

the half-million bill of July 22, all the troops the governors believed they could raise, just as fast as they could muster them. Throughout the late summer and fall Cameron periodically besought the governors to send on all the regiments they had organized. Sometimes he engaged to supply arms and other equipment, but more frequently he suggested that the States provide their own muskets, uniforms, and the like, sending the bills to the Treasury.

Lincoln made requests on the same basis. He asked Governor Morgan to provide 25,000 three-year men, for example, but in such informal fashion that the request does not appear in the records; and it was not until nearly a year later, when it became necessary to determine what New York's quota *should* have been in order to reach a basis for determining the size of a fresh demand, that the proper share of the Empire State was fixed.[20] Morgan was quick to comply with Lincoln's request and to do more. Four days after Bull Run he issued his own proclamation for the 25,000 men, and almost immediately added an extra four regiments.

Other governors showed equal alacrity in meeting the nation's demands. It soon became clear that the half-million men, and more, would be obtained without difficulty. The real question was whether the troops would be raised efficiently, equitably, and under the best organization permitted by the new law. As we might expect, hurry and improvisation answered this query with an emphatic No.

While the States were raising their fresh regiments, the ninety-day men were returning home. The governors, heartily abetted by the War Department, hoped to induce many to reënlist. In numerous instances, however, these short-term veterans set something like an adverse backfire blazing. They brought home shocking stories of weak officers, bad camps, and uncoordinated army movements. Thousands, too, became rebellious over the delay—and sometimes the total failure—to pay them for their services. Several Pennsylvania regiments which reached camp near Harrisburg and found no provision whatever made for their shelter, subsistence, or compensation, grew mutinous. They filled the city with men searching for quarters and means of cooking rations, threatened to seize the money in the Adams Express office, and frightened citizens with angry talk of breaking open the shops. Governor Curtin had to detail a regiment of three-year troops to protect the capital, while young Don Cameron begged his father to send the troops at once to camps nearer their homes. In the end they were moved to encampments scattered over the State, where paymasters pacified them.

20 Phisterer, *N. Y. in the War of the Rebellion*, I, 22, 23. An Act signed by Lincoln July 31 gave him power to accept volunteers without previous proclamation and in whatever numbers he thought desirable; O. R. III, i, 372.

Similar episodes took place in Ohio, though Governor Dennison had gone to Washington especially to make sure that the troops would be promptly paid and mustered out. In New York, too, Governor Morgan complained to the War Department that failure to recompense the old regiments discouraged new enlistments.[21]

Much worse were the confusions and jealousies created everywhere by the readiness of the War Department to permit and even encourage recruiting by individuals and irregular groups. For this practice, which angered the governors, burdened the army with many deplorable officers, and produced widespread confusion, Lincoln as well as Cameron was to blame.

A chorus of protest came from the State capitals. "I hope," Morton of Indiana telegraphed Cameron July 25, "the War Department will accept of regiments only through me." The same day Governor Kirkwood of Iowa informed the Department that he would countenance no more regiments raised by individuals. A Pennsylvania official who indignantly inquired whether it was not now illegal to accept troops otherwise than through the governors could hardly have been calmed by the assurance that it was entirely legal, and that the Department had accepted twice as many from ambitious colonels as from State executives. Yates of Illinois was particularly exasperated. Telegraphing the Department repeatedly for exclusive authority to handle all State recruits, he got no answer until on August 14 he burst out to Cameron: "I could have had troops today sufficient to have opposed any force but for the interference from Washington in accepting independent regiments without notice to me, breaking up our organization." The Secretary at once gave him the desired authority. But five days later Austin Blair was making the same indignant protest. "I will furnish all the troops you call for," wrote Blair, "much sooner and in better order than these independent regiments can." [22]

The intentions of Lincoln and Cameron were good. They wished to expedite recruiting, fan the war spirit, and strengthen the impression of government eagerness to accept all the men who crowded forward. The Secretary seems to have surmised that all objection would be removed if the regimental officers were required to apply to their governors for commissions, and then ordered to report in Washington as soon as possible.[23]

This, of course, was far from the fact. Industrious village Hampdens, and budding Harrisons and Houstons, donning their sashes, duplicated State re-

21 O. R. III, i, 358–366 for Pennsylvania; *Ibid.*, 357, for Ohio, and Reid, *Ohio in the War*, I, 56; O. R. III, i, 415, for New York. The Paymaster-General himself went to Harrisburg late in July to iron out the difficulties.
22 O. R. III, i, 350, 390, 409 ff., 410, 428.
23 Cameron to O. P. Morton and Edwin Morgan, Aug. 29, 1861, O. R. III, i, 465; Austin Blair to Cameron, August 19, 1861, Austin Blair Papers.

cruiting efforts. They drained more troops from one area than another, with resultant ill feeling. They demanded colonelcies and captaincies. Meanwhile, they created an apparent competition between State and Federal recruiting. In New York, for example, Dan Sickles, the murderer of Philip Barton Key, used his characteristic swagger and impudence to organize his own brigade. He and his officers were contemptous of State authority, holding themselves quite above it. It required a general order from Cameron, placing all independent regiments in New York under Morgan, and emphasizing the governor's authority to reorganize, officer, and equip such regiments in the way he thought best, to bring Sickles down to earth. This order ended a highly embarrassing situation; and as it placed no fewer than sixteen independent regiments under clear State authority, Albany greeted it with profound relief.[24]

Other States, however, continued to suffer. The much-harassed Dennison of Ohio telegraphed Cameron on August 25 asking whether he had empowered a certain man to raise an artillery regiment. "If so, for God's sake withdraw the authority. Such a commission will make a farce of the public service." It was impossible to pursue any system in organizing Ohio troops, he added, so long as these irregular units raised their heads from Ashtabula to Hamilton. Ohio was actually raided from outside, two regiments being offered to Oliver P. Morton in Indiana. When Morton hesitated to accept them, the War Department wired him: "Lay aside etiquette. Organize soldiers as rapidly as you can. Get them, no matter where from, so they are good, loyal men." Not until September 10 did the outraged Dennison obtain authority to reorganize and equip all regiments.[25]

But even he had less to endure than Governor Curtin of Pennsylvania, a party rival of Cameron's. Stung beyond endurance, Curtin finally made a fervent plea to Lincoln. After pointing out that the new military law permitted the President to accept independent units only when the States failed to respond, he went on:

> On the 26th day of July last a requisition was made on the Executive of this State for ten regiments of infantry in addition to the forty-four already furnished. . . . Active measures were immediately taken to comply with the requisition, but unfortunately the Government of the United States went on to authorize individuals to raise regiments of volunteers in this State. Fifty-eight individuals received authority for this purpose in Pennsylvania. The direct authority of the Government of the United States having been thus set in competition with that of the State, acting under its requisition, the

---

24 S. W. Burt, *Memoirs*, 46, 47; O. R. III, i, 483, 484.

25 Frémont had empowered John A. Gurley to send him volunteers from Ohio, and some recruits were actually sent to Missouri from the State; O. R. III, i, 466, 473 (Indiana), 519, 520 (Missouri). The authority on Sept. 10 was Special Order No. 243; O. R. III, i, 495, 496.

consequence has been much embarrassment, delay, and confusion. . . . The result is what might have been expected—that after a lapse of twenty-six days not one entire regiment has been raised in Pennsylvania since the last requisition. There are fragments of some seventy regiments, but not one complete; yet men enough have been raised to form near thirty complete regiments.[26]

Yet a week after Curtin's appeal, the War Department was authorizing James S. Negley of Pittsburgh to finish organizing an independent brigade of three or more regiments, thus piling confusion on confusion. When Cameron finally acted on Curtin's protest, he rebuked the governor for having written directly to the President. He also explained that Lincoln had never received the letter, for it had been filed in the War Department without having been read by anybody—which under Cameron seems to have been standard departmental practice for countless papers; and Cameron himself had not seen it until a messenger from Curtin brought him a copy! Cameron forthwith issued another special order placing all independent units in Pennsylvania under full authority of the governor; and the department took steps to chase out of the State some zealous recruiters from New York, Illinois, and California—complete outsiders and interlopers.[27]

Much more might be said on this strange tolerance of independent recruiting. Ben Butler and John A. Andrew became combatants in the most complex, protracted, and celebrated case of individual interference with State recruiting, which shook all New England, and supplied enough tragi-comic episodes for an *opéra bouffe*.[28] A President more exact, systematic, and vigilant than Lincoln, a Secretary more alert and clearheaded than Cameron, would have prevented these difficulties. It was bad enough, though unavoidable, to put recruiting under twenty-odd States, not the nation; it was far worse to let hundreds of ambitious men, some patriotic, some selfish, and most of them unfit, romp about the field.

However, despite all vexations, the recruits, from farm, forge, factory, store counter, and professional desk, rolled in. The initiative was taken by communities, local leaders, or both interacting. Village or town authorities would hold a mass meeting; politicians would deliver stump speeches, ministers would pray, the local editor would read the peroration of Webster's Reply to Hayne, the crowd would sing "America"—and young men would enroll their names. Or the local militia company would form a nucleus, or some burning patriot would raise an oriflamme.

A typical piece of New England recruiting is described by Thomas W. Hyde, a Maine lad who was soon brevetted a brigadier in his middle twenties.

26 *Ibid.*, 439, 440.
27 O. R. III, i, 491–534.
28 Meneely, 213–221; Schouler, *Mass. in the Rebellion*, I, 275–281; O. R. III, i, 810–866.

He heard the news of Bull Run in the shipbuilding town of Bath. Together with Senator Fessenden's son, he got State authority to raise men, opened an office, and advertised that soldiers would receive $22 bounty, $15 a month with full equipment, and $100 with lifelong glory when mustered out. Before long squads of eager young men were housed in Sibley tents dotting the beautiful green slopes between the State House at Augusta and the Kennebec. The officers of the various companies, summoned to ballot for regimental leaders, chose a regular-army captain for colonel, a three-month sergeant for lieutenant-colonel, and the reluctant Hyde for major. "I did not know then," he writes, "that the principal duties of a major were to ride on the flank of a rear division, say nothing, look as well as possible, and long for promotion." Off they went—the band playing them to the train, handkerchiefs waving from every farmhouse, cheers at every station, and lunch in Faneuil Hall.

Meanwhile, a typical piece of big-city, large-scale recruiting was furnished by the Fifty-fifth Illinois in Chicago. The attorney David Stuart, a friend of Douglas, obtained Cameron's direct authority to raise the 2,000 men of the Douglas brigade, put his own money and best energy into the effort, secured the aid of Democratic politicians and several Methodist ministers, and with the magic name of Douglas to assist him, had the brigade ready for service before October ended.[29]

The now rampant war spirit overcame every impediment: the high cost of getting and initially maintaining the recruits, for the nation reimbursed the States and the individuals concerned for only a part of their expenses; the want of a proper allotment system to provide for soldiers' families; the lack of arms; the irritations of dealing with hidebound, narrow-minded, arrogant fossils in the national quartermaster and commissary establishments, and endless departmental red tape. Senator Grimes wrote Cameron in mid-September that if the government would adopt the allotment-ticket system used in the navy, Iowa would soon send him 4,000 men even better than those already accepted; and before the close of the month, the War Department did belatedly set up home-allotment procedures. State complaints, fervent and long-continued, also got rid of an asinine War Department rule that no fewer than a company minimum, sixty-four men, could be mustered into service at one time. Recruits sometimes had been kept waiting six or eight weeks, without uniforms, blankets, or rations, and with not even a lieutenant sworn in to command them, until they reached the magic total of sixty-four. But after Cameron, responding to the protests of Morgan and Dennison, abolished

29 See Thomas W. Hyde, *Following the Greek Cross; A Committee of the Regiment, The Story of the Fifty-fifth Illinois*. Stuart, who was under a cloud because he had been involved in a notorious divorce case, proved a good officer; Hyde became one of great distinction. Fessenden's son was slain at Second Bull Run.

the rule, volunteers were sent, as fast as their names could be signed on muster rolls, to convenient camps, and set to drilling. A first lieutenant would take charge of half a company, and a captain and second lieutenant were added when full strength was reached. This new plan worked well.[30]

Still the men came in: a rush in late July, a new flood in August, and fresh hosts in early fall. They came in spite of a fundamental change in the economic situation. Business all summer had been depressed, but the harvest season and the letting of innumerable contracts created an autumn boom. Farms, shops, and war industries drained away the surplus labor supply. Skilled hands in particular thought twice before taking army pay, even after it had been lifted to what some foreign observers deemed an exorbitant figure. As the cost of living rose, men with family responsibilities could not be happy about a wage of $11 a month, even with a bounty of $100, as authorized by the military act, superadded.[31] Inevitably, such social and economic pressures made for an army of youths and young men. Veterans later used to say, "The war was fought by boys," and although this was not true, a little more than 13 per cent of the enlistments were 18 and almost 30 per cent were under 21. Officers, too, were generally young; in the volunteer army the mean age at entrance into service was found to be 30.44.

[III]

The gathering of the huge volunteer forces in and about Washington was an inspiring sight, which gave many who witnessed it an exultant confidence. The new volunteers, though even by fall far from being well-taught soldiers, were much superior to the ninety-day men. "Finer material could not be found in physique," wrote W. H. Russell after seeing a review held by McClellan and McDowell, marred by only one tatterdemalion unit sent from New York City. He thought no division of the regular army line in any country of the globe could show a greater number of tall, robust men in fine physical trim. The big, hearty, outdoor recruits who composed so great a part of the popular host—the lumberjacks, fishermen, hardfisted young farmers, stevedores,

30 New York State by November had main recruiting depots in the metropolis, Albany, and Elmira, and not fewer than twenty regimental camps in the interior of the State. These tent camps had been created to make it more convenient for recruits to assemble for drill, and to gain the active aid of prominent citizens. Morgan to Cameron, Nov. 4, 1861; Morgan Papers, N. Y. State Lib.

31 Governor Morgan was so much impressed by these high costs that he tried to give a premium of $2 a recruit to anyone who brought in not less than 32 acceptable men to one of the main depots. This special bounty he thought would not cost more than $25,000 for the State's 25 new regiments, and would do much to stimulate enlistments. But Cameron refused to foot the bill, and the governor revoked his order in mid-October. O. R. III, i, 452, 453, 465; Burt, *Memoirs*, 54.

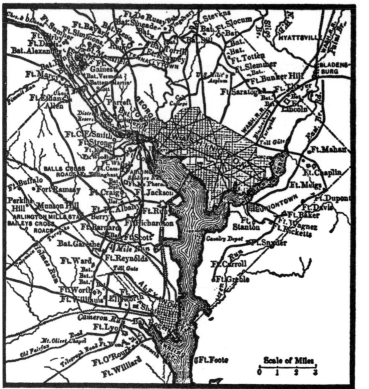

WASHINGTON AND
ITS ULTIMATE
DEFENSES

and draymen—stood hardship well; but it was soon noted that the clerks, bookkeepers, schoolmasters, and mechanics from the towns, even the men most delicately nurtured, stood it rather better. As greater precautions were taken, and as crisp autumn weather came on, the health of the army, in the East more rapidly than in the West, improved.[32]

While Washington had still all the confusion of a great armed camp, the military elements had become more orderly. The surrounding hills were whiter than ever with tents, for the reinforcements had spread over them, but the camps showed system and cleanliness. One observer, standing on an eminence at sunset, saw with his spyglass the evening parades of 34 regiments. On another occasion he counted 150 army wagons in line on Pennsylvania Avenue, and an hour later saw a drove of 700 fine cavalry horses clattering over the Long Bridge. But the barrooms were empty of army blue, roistering soldiers had disappeared from the streets, and officers in hotel lobbies were few. Their places had been taken by hundreds of sad-eyed citizens come to look for

32 Russell, *My Diary*, Aug. 26, 1861; *Following the Greek Cross*, 21, 22; Adams, *Doctors in Blue*, chapters 3, 10. The Sanitary Commission with incomplete data found that in the first year Western troops had a much higher sick rate than Eastern, and enlisted men one much higher than officers. For age of the troops, see the Sanitary Commission pamphlet, "Ages of U. S. Volunteer Soldier" (1866), which abounds in interesting facts. It gives the average age of 1,012,273 volunteers at date of enlistment as 25.8.

relatives lost since the battle or lying in hospitals. The new provost guard was so efficient that it stopped Ben Butler as he was getting into his carriage at the National Hotel, and held him until he was identified.

The numbers, energy, and determined spirit of the host seemed to promise great victorious movements to come, perhaps ending in the lightning flash of a new Solferino. Captain J. R. Hawley of Connecticut, later to become editor, governor, and Senator, reached the capital late in September. He breakfasted at the Soldiers' Retreat, a large rough new building for feeding troops, washed in another big structure hard by fitted with tanks and troughs, and, marching with his regiment two miles up Fourteenth Street, encamped in an open field.

"Oh, but this is grand!" he wrote his wife. "Troops, troops, tents, the frequent thunder of guns practising, lines of heavy baggage wagons, at reveille and tattoo the air filled with the near and distant roll of drums and the notes of innumerable bugles—all the indications of an immense army, and yet no crowding, no rabble. Nobody knows how many there are, but I guess from certain facts that there must be over 200,000 in all—including those across the river and in General Banks's division. Indeed, I have good evidence that there are about 275,000, *not* including Gen. Dix's command at Baltimore." [33] Although this was an overestimate, already many believed that the new army was a formidable human machine that should soon roll inexorably and victoriously southward.

33   Hawley, Sept. 25, 1861; Hawley Papers, LC.

13

Giant in Swaddling Clothes

ANXIOUS though the people were to get on with the war, the late summer lull had at least this important effect: It gave North and South a pause to assess their situation. They began to comprehend that they were locked in a life-and-death grapple. Ex-Senator John Slidell of Louisiana wrote S. L. M. Barlow just before Bull Run that in all the South he did not know a solitary man who would reëstablish the Union on any terms. "You can scarcely hope to subjugate us. We *know* that you cannot, and if your views prevail, there can be no other termination of the war than by the mutual exhaustion of both parties."[1] The idea bit deep that the war must be fought to a devastating conclusion. Assistant-Secretary of War P. H. Watson told McClellan that the rebels would persist to the death gasp.[2] Though great numbers on both sides still looked forward to 1862 as the year of victory, most men of sense knew that the contest might be protracted, that it would test the people to the utmost, and that it would produce a new America.

Lincoln sat daily for long hours in his office on the south side of the White House; the kind of office that a county judge or prosperous doctor might be expected to have. Its furnishings were a large cloth-covered table for Cabinet meetings, a smaller table where the President usually wrote, a high wall desk with pigeonholes for papers, two horsehair sofas, an armchair, and some straight-backed chairs. Over the marble mantel of the brass-fendered fireplace hung a faded steel engraving of Jackson. Elsewhere on the wall were a photograph of John Bright, and a number of framed military maps. His secretaries, Nicolay and Hay, gave him efficient help, and a young Illinois newspaperman, W. O. Stoddard, went through the mail to sort out trivial or offensive letters. Other assistants he had none except an occasional clerk lent from some department. The offices of Cabinet members were equally primitive. They had changed little since 1800. The same wooden tables, desks, pigeonholes, and ledger-size copybooks as in John Adams' day, the same quill pens and scuffed carpets,

1 July 20, 1861, Barlow Papers.
2 Chase, *Diary and Corr.*, 50, 51; this talk was Nov. 11, 1861.

and the same anemic staffs docketing papers, surrounded Chase, Welles, Cameron as they struggled with visitors.[3]

These executives looked out on a nation which seemed as vertebrate as a jellyfish. They could ask for aid from individuals, but not from capable associations or societies, which hardly existed. The war necessarily had to be a vast social and economic as well as military effort. But where were the leaders trained in social and economic organization? The nation had only small managerial groups and little skill in cooperative effort. Of the 8,200,000 people whose occupations were noted by the recent census, 3,300,000 were farmers, planters, and farm laborers, and many more were indirectly connected with agriculture. A shrewd observer, Sir Morton Peto, shortly estimated that seven-eighths of the population was engaged in tillage or the callings materially dependent thereon; an understandable exaggeration.

This agricultural country, just passing through a transportation revolution, was fairly well organized for farming and for all kinds of communication— by railways, canals, telegraphs, and express systems. The manufacture of farm machinery, the handling of farm products, the milling of grain, the packing of meats, the sending of a new host of settlers westward every year, and the supply of this host with consumption goods, were all competently done. As yet, however, they did not carry the country far from the old order of small enterprises, local outlooks, and unrestricted individualism.

A war machine can be built quickly and efficiently only if many components already exist. The Department in 1861 had no difficulty in making decisions. It soon found that the half-million volunteers embodied under the July legislation would wear out shoes in two months and uniforms in four; they therefore needed 3,000,000 pairs of shoes and 1,500,000 uniforms a year. It was easy to decide that they must have mountains of arms, a hundred miles of wagons, great base hospitals, and incredible miscellaneous supplies. The difficulty lay in implementing the decisions.

Problems of selection became acute; which firm could really fill the orders? Problems of scheduling were even more perplexing; how could everybody down the line of supply be told just what was needed, and when, and where? Industrial discipline was as important as military discipline; factories, contractors, and agents had to be held to rigid performance. And nobody knew the indispensable facts! Figures of industrial capacity, lists of companies, data on car supply, information on the ability of heads of firms—all this was beyond the reach of the tiny Washington departments. Such terms as "coordination," "priorities," "allocation of materials," and "flow of supplies" lay far in the future; the idea of "production management" was beyond human

3 Leonard D. White, *The Jacksonians*, 548.

ken. The realities which such words represented could no more exist in
America of 1861 than the roof of an unbuilt house could float in mid-air, for
no supporting structure existed.

The government which was now girding itself for war labored under the
sharpest limitations. It had always been a government of noninterference,
made for the freedom of the individual; of calculated inaction, to give State and
local agencies the fullest scope; of economy, passivity, and short views.

No national banking system existed. Washington paid no real attention to
agriculture; a weakly supported, feebly administered bureau in the new Interior Department represented the only Federal provision for the fundamental industry of the land. So important a subject as public health had never
engaged the attention of any national bureau, or for that matter, of any State.
In Europe the English sanitarian Edwin Chadwick, the French pathologists,
and the new school of medical statisticians had spurred the leading governments into at least elementary attention to public sanitation. But Americans
were stone deaf to their one eminent figure in the field, Lemuel Shattuck,
whose report on conditions in Massachusetts (1850) had met blank indifference.[4] So, too, the transportation revolution which was remolding America
proceeded without any attention in Washington save for land-grant legislation and a few Far Western surveys. Any proposal that government
guidance should accompany government subsidies would have met a hostile
wall.

One significant index of the weakness of the central government was the
deficiency of trustworthy statistical data. The national censuses were ample
in numerical facts, decently accurate, and issued with really useful interpretation. A few cities and one State, Massachusetts, had systems of vital
registration; New York took an efficient census of its own in 1855. As yet,
however, the country was without the great mass of trustworthy data later
to be gathered continuously by numerous Federal agencies.[5]

Statistics are a function of complexity in government as of society, for
whenever new problems demand new solutions it becomes necessary to probe
into exact conditions and measure precise results. For want of an apparatus of
consistent fact-finding, Americans groped in the dark in meeting the crisis
of 1861. When armies had to be raised, for example, it was important to
know the ages of the male population. The census merely furnished facts on
the population, male and female, in each five-year bracket to the age of
twenty, and each ten-year bracket thereafter; all this set down by counties.

4 John Koren, *History of Statistics;* and see the article on statistical needs by ABC in
National Intelligencer, May 29, 1856.
5 Such as the Bureau of Agricultural Economics, Interstate Commerce Commission,
Bureau of Foreign and Domestic Commerce, Bureau of Labor Statistics, and Bureau of Internal Revenue, to name but a few.

Hence in the fifteen–nineteen age bracket, the government did not know how many were boys of fifteen, and how many young men of nineteen. In the succeeding age bracket, it did not know how many were twenty, and how many were twenty-nine. Yet by the date of the Civil War, all important European nations but Switzerland had permanent statistical bureaus under proficient management. The proposals for such a bureau in Washington, made by S. B. Ruggles and others, had met stubborn opposition from state-rights quarters.

In short, Lincoln presided over a weak government which suddenly had to be made strong. And behind the government lay a largely inchoate society; a society which believed in accomplishing the impossible, but whose libertarian bent made accomplishment terribly difficult. A tremendous gulf separated the unformed nation of the Civil War from the nation that in the next great conflict was to mobilize its energies so massively under the Council of National Defense. Where were the technicians in 1861? Where were the efficient business administrators? Where were the thousand organizations, industrial, commercial, financial, professional, to lend them support? Where were the principles and precedents?

If we briefly examine this society, we shall see that Great Britain in the first throes of the Napoleonic struggle had been better adapted to wage war than the shambling, uncertain American giant of 1861. "Organization" is a key word, and from one point of view the transformation of an unorganized land into an organized nation was the key process of the Civil War.

[I]

The country we have called invertebrate, and this invertebracy reflected a deeply ingrained spirit. "In the United States," wrote August Laugel during the conflict, "there is a horror of all trammels, systems, and uniformity." [6] Americans were hostile to discipline and jealous of every encroachment on personal freedom. As autumn leaves fell on drilling soldiers and thickening lines of factory hands, some observers saw that old ways were falling too. "The Great Rebellion a Great Revolution"—so ran the title of a *Herald* editorial on November 24, 1861. Our manufactories have been revolutionized, said the paper, our mode of living has been changed, and "everything the finger of war touches is revolutionized." A few discerning men saw the essence of this revolution. It was the conversion of a loose, inchoate, uncrystallized society into one organized for a mighty and many-sided effort.

6 Laugel, *The United States During the War*. The roots of individualism ran deep into frontier experience, and deep also into the Protestant emphasis on individual interpretation of truth and the individual will; deep too into Nonconformist tradition, Lockean and Jeffersonian ideas of the right of revolution, and egalitarian principles.

Crèvecœur in delineating the American had emphasized his love of independence and impatience of control. Cooper and Melville depicted a population of unfettered, self-assertive character. "Call me Ishmael!"—even that was better than repression. Emerson's chapter on "Solidarity" in *English Traits* contrasted British unity—"marching in phalanx, lock-step, foot after foot, file after file of heroes, ten thousand deep"—with American separatism. Thoreau, living on a patch of ground, experimenting with civil disobedience, and giving up his little pencil factory to preach an ideal society of noble villagers, and Cooper crying, "God protect the country that has nothing but commercial towns for capitals," [7] appealed in different ways to deep American instincts.

Most people instinctively veered away from strong social and economic combinations just as they veered away from strong government. John Taylor of Caroline, sharing Jefferson's idealism, inveighed against "monopoly and incorporation," and argued that capitalist combinations went arm-in-arm with a powerful centralized government, both fostering caste rule, the exploitation of farmers and laborers, and social injustice. Such doctrine, like the appeals of William Leggett and George Henry Evans to radical workmen, harmonized with the natural attitude of millions. Horace Greeley, anxious to better both the farmers and city wage earners, and striving to democratize the land system, was too wise to attack industry. Like a good Whig, he wished to see it grow. But he never lost his suspicion of the larger forms of business organization. In the midst of war the *Tribune* published long indictments of corporations: their profiteering, mismanagement, nepotism, and the tyrannies of their agents and officers. They were "heartless," wrote Greeley.[8]

Reared in an ungirt, unplanned society, Americans since the seventeenth century had been busy improvising. The first demand of the frontier, farm, and small shop was for such improvisations as the log cabin, the long rifle, the hand-hewn chest, the Conestoga wagon, and the overshot water wheel. The term "homemade" had a wider application in America than elsewhere. An ingenious people not only respected the amateur but belittled the expert. Peter Cooper building his engine *Tom Thumb*, Lincoln patenting his device for lifting boats over shoals, Goodyear spilling his rubber on a stove, Ezra Cornell wrecking his pipe-laying machine so that he could string his telegraph on poles, all believed that an amateur could do anything, and many concluded that organization would inhibit the gifted amateur. Generations later, Henry Ford reflected this attitude by shunning organizational charts, destroying business forms, and refusing to assign fixed duties to officers of the huge Rouge plant.

7 Cooper, *Correspondence*, II, 404.
8 See, for example, the long editorial April 3, 1863, entitled "Manufacturing Mismanagement."

Even in old Eastern cities, experts commanded little regard. Young James B. Angell, entering the office of the Chief Engineer of Boston in 1851, found that the staff had worked their way up from rodmen's jobs by rule-of-thumb methods. Work was under way on the Cochituate water system. It turned out that Angell was the only man in the whole office who had studied calculus and could deal with the involved formulae for water problems. This went to prove the force of Francis Wayland's argument that it was high time American colleges dealt less in theology, and more in science and technology.[9]

The nation was full of good craftsmen and husbandmen, able to work alone or in small groups. Company B of the Tenth Massachusetts, a Berkshire regiment, contained a typical array: 23 farmers, 3 merchants, 2 teamsters, 2 shoemakers, 2 hostlers, 2 carpenters, a seaman, laborer, clerk, bookkeeper, painter, peddler, blacksmith, calico printer, cloth manufacturer, and cheese-factory superintendent.[10] Such men, facing ordinary problems, could improvise with happy dexterity. But war presents innumerable large-scale problems, which demand experts supported by large-scale organizations. In time both the experts and the organizations were to appear—and with them would emerge a new nation.

As they appeared, the country lost a certain freshness and bucolic charm, and the strength which it gained was a coarser strength; but the gain was greater than the loss. The dynamism of national life, with population moving westward, new towns shooting up, and immigration combining with a high birth rate to stimulate growth, had kept life plastic and full of picturesque novelty. Successive frontiers had meant successive rerootings, seldom deep or strong. American life was to remain dynamic, but it would soon be dynamic in a different way, with larger elements of a disciplined, hardened kind. Its roots were to go deeper, and the plastic freshness was to be exchanged for well-planted power.

Much of the lack of organization was basically immaturity. The nation had no standard time, so that New York, Philadelphia, Washington, and Pittsburgh kept what time each city or its railroads liked. Only two American cities in 1860 had paid fire departments; all the others—New York until 1865, Philadelphia until 1870—depended on volunteers. All New England in 1860 had only three hospitals; the entire South had one in Charleston, one in Savannah, one in Mobile, "perhaps one" in Richmond, and one in New Orleans renowned for its wretchedness.[11]

Only an immature country would have endured the wretched postal facilities against which New York and Boston committees had protested in 1856. James Harper, Peter Cooper, and others that year pleaded for a uniform

9 Angell, *Reminiscences*, 78; Wayland, *Thoughts on the Present Collegiate System* (1842).
10 J. K. Newell, *The Tenth Mass. Volunteers*.
11 E. W. Martin, *The Standard of Living in 1860*, 233-236.

two-cent rate on letters, for in all large cities private carriers profitably distributed mail at that rate, and in New York about ten million letters were privately carried as against a million sent by post. The committees asked for compulsory prepayment by stamps, and free letter delivery in all large towns. In Europe dead letters were returned to senders; in the United States they were simply burned—four to five millions yearly. Though some reforms were adopted, the situation continued wretched. Although in 1860 the American population materially exceeded the British, the number of letters posted in the United States was only 184,000,000, one-third the 564,000,000 posted in Britain. The post office had three regular rates on letters, five surcharges, and forty-nine rates on papers and periodicals. Drop letters in New York numbered 1,500,000 in 1860; in London, 63,200,000.[12] "We are now enduring a postal system," remarked Putnam's Magazine, "which worries government, vexes and injures the public, demoralizes the officials, and pleases nobody." Bryant's Evening Post asserted that a barrel of flour could be sent by an express company from New York to New Orleans more quickly than the government could transport a letter over the same ground.[13]

The horror of all trammels, system, and uniformity, to use Laugel's phrase, prevented farmers from associating in production or marketing. Rural cooperation had taken firm root on the European continent immediately after the Napoleonic wars, and by 1860 was gaining maturity in Denmark, Germany, Switzerland, and other lands. New Zealand was soon to show how strong it could become in a pioneer community. The large size of American farms, mobility of the population, and individualistic temper of rural areas prevented any similar growth in the United States; nor did the government offer the slightest encouragement. Similarly, national labor unions as yet counted for almost nothing. In 1857 nine or ten such unions had been gaining vigorous stature when the panic felled all but three, the typographers', the hat finishers', and the journeymen stonecutters'. Before Sumter a few others, including the iron-molders' union under the indomitable William H. Sylvis, emerged. None had much vigor, for a half-dozen environing forces were unfavorable: the steady immigration of unskilled labor, lingering public hostility toward "conspiracy" in the labor market, the adolescent character of the factory system, the ruthlessness or paternalism of employers, and again the strong individualism of native Americans.[14]

12 Representative Hutchins of Ohio in 1862 vigorously attacked the postal abuses in Congress; see editorial, N. Y. Tribune, June 25, 1862.
13 Dec. 13, 1855; and still true in 1860. The government had issued its first stamps in 1847.
14 Commons, et al., I, 335–453, gives the history of unions destroyed in the panic of 1857, and of the revival down to the war; see also George R. Taylor, The Transportation Revolution, 252 ff., 283 ff.

Thus neither agriculture nor labor when the war began was able to speak with united voice, furnish the government trained administrative talent, or lend any organized assistance to the war effort. Business and finance of course offered more resources, for they could not exist without some degree of organization. Nevertheless, it was a rudimentary degree, with short-comings more conspicuous than strength; as we shall see if we examine even the best-developed field, that of transportation.

[II]

Transportation could be expected to make comparatively rapid progress in systematization, for it was nurtured by the vast American distances, the irresistible westward movement, and the general American restlessness. The development of the West had seemed the nation's great primary task. The building of turnpikes, canals, and railroads to carry people across mountains, prairies, and plains, the shipment of crops eastward and a thousand varieties of commodities westward, and the necessity for extending the commercial and cultural interchanges of new and old states, had required careful planning and administration of communications.

The east-west railroads, particularly north of the Ohio, were in 1860 the country's most imposing business creations, their securities the very core of the investment market. National expansion had required an increasing con-solidation of railway controls. The Pennsylvania, for example, had attained a more extensive dominion than most people realized. Its main Philadelphia-Pittsburgh line, with branches and leased strips, covered 423 miles, of which 250 were double-tracked. This, however, was but the beginning. In 1856, three lines westward, in Ohio, Indiana, and northern Illinois, had merged as the Pittsburgh, Fort Wayne and Chicago. The Pennsylvania, which had in-vested substantial sums in building the three lines, received nearly $770,000 in stock. Thomas A. Scott, the Pennsylvania's vice-president and general super-intendent, was appointed to the board of the new company; George W. Cass, a director of the Pennsylvania, was made president. For all practical purposes the Pennsylvania thereafter controlled an additional 465 miles of railroad in the Middle West. Before 1860, the Pennsylvania had come to dominate about 165 miles of railroad reaching to the Ohio River and through southern Ohio, and about 200 miles running northwest from Pittsburgh to Cleveland. Thomas A. Scott again appeared on the boards of the tributary roads.[15]

The same process which gave the Pennsylvania an imperial system could

---

15 H. V. Poor, *History of the Railroads and Canals of the U. S.*, I, 470 ff.; H. W. Schotter, *Pennsylvania Railroad Company, 1846–1926.*

be traced in the development of the New York Central. At the outbreak of the war, this line from Albany to Buffalo, and the connecting Lake Shore and Michigan Southern, gave a group headed by Erastus Corning control over 650 miles of continuous rail into Chicago. The Erie, a hill-and-valley line from New York (Piermont) to Dunkirk on the lakes, was as yet still seeking a westward extension. But the Baltimore and Ohio, which ran to Parkersburg, made connections there to Cincinnati, and thence extended to St. Louis by a controlling arrangement with the Ohio and Mississippi, was very powerful indeed, and thirty-eight year-old John W. Garrett, its recently elected head, was a man of wide influence. Paralleling the early boundary between the Union and Confederacy, the B. & O. was to play an important role in the conflict. It was a source of great strength to the North by 1861 that three strong trunk lines, obviously soon to be joined by a fourth, connected the northern seaboard with the midwest.[16]

Other remarkable achievements in organization were the anthracite railroads, with their docks, freight yards, and coal trestles. Of the north-south lines the Illinois Central, as yet terminating at Cairo, and the Louisville & Nashville, a 185-mile road completed on the eve of conflict, had great importance. In the South the Memphis & Charleston, finished in 1857 on a line through Atlanta, cherished dreams of a grandeur it was never to attain.[17] Since every isolated community longed for the scream of a locomotive, ideas of growth animated the whole railroad world. Superintendent J. G. Kennedy of the Census, announcing that the railways of the nation had hauled 26,000,000 tons on their 30,800 miles of track in 1860, declared that three-quarters of this bulk had been created in the previous decade.

Yet from the standpoints of management and equipment, the railroads had a rudimentary aspect. The British expert S. F. Van Oss, writing much later, remarked on their adolescent traits. "Englishmen live in a country which has arrived at maturity; America still is in its teens." [18] Slow wood-burning locomotives ran all too often over rickety tracks on erratic schedules. The existence of at least eight different gauges required frequent loading and unloading. Most railway heads were less interested in methodical organization and progress than in slapdash policies and quick returns. Management tended to be autocratic, one man or a small clique controlling lines large or small. Speculation exulted in almost unchecked license. Few large roads had arrived at a scientific allocation of functions among their officers; the B. & O. was in fact conspicuous

---

16 Festus P. Summers, *The Baltimore and Ohio in the Civil War.*

17 A Confederate quartermaster officer testified that Southern railroad managers showed "the best business talent" in the South; O. R. IV, ii, 882.

18 Van Oss, *American Railroads as Investments*, 10.

for its well-planned departmentalization.[19] Still fewer lines had heads of pre-eminent ability. The two strongest executives were Garrett, trained in his father's commission house, and J. Edgar Thomson of the Pennsylvania, a proficient engineer who had studied railroad practice in Europe. The mere promoter was much more common.

The rule of small business salaries applied to railroads as to other establishments. In 1856 the Illinois Central cast about for a chief engineer. As its officers had seen George Brinton McClellan's report on his survey of a railway route across the Cascade Mountains, they selected him. His captain's pay had totaled $1,326 a year. President W. H. Osborn offered him $3,000 a year for three years. He showed marked administrative enterprise. Before long he was in general charge of railroad operation in Illinois, and by the end of 1857 was vice-president. He helped meet the depression that winter by harvesting Lake Michigan ice to be sold by the carload all the way to Cairo when summer became torrid. Early in 1858 he contracted with a group of steamboat owners to establish an Illinois Central line of packets to New Orleans, thus for the first time linking Chicago and the Gulf by scheduled year-round transportation. Yet his salary remained $3,000,—a proof of the low esteem for managerial talent.[20]

The fact was that the transportation revolution presented some remarkable feats in organization alongside glaring gaps and failures. No pageantry of the time excelled that of the western rivers. The mile-long line of boats smoking and throbbing at the St. Louis levee, surpassed by a still longer line at New Orleans; the floods of pork, tobacco, corn and cotton that the Ohio, the Cumberland, the Arkansas, and the Red poured into the central Mississippi stream; the motley passengers—fur traders, immigrants, Indians, soldiers, cotton planters, land speculators, gamblers, politicians, British tourists; the inter-city rivalries, the desperate races—these made the steamboat world a tremendous spectacle. The 1600 steamboats which plied the Mississippi before the war had cost perhaps $60,000,000; the 900 steamboats, barges, and flatboats which

19 As early as 1848 it had a master of transportation, a master of the road, a master of machinery, and a general superintendent, along with division superintendents; Hungerford, *The Baltimore & Ohio*. Centralized purchasing by large roads, even the B. & O., was unknown; each large department purchased for itself.

20 33rd Cong., 1st Sess., House Exec. Doc. 129; C. J. Corliss, *Main Line of America*, 90, 91. It need not be said that the broad foundation of all transport in the republic was the ox, mule, and horse, the cart and wagon. Between 1850 and 1860 the number of horses rose from 4,337,000 to 6,249,000, giving an average of one horse to each family of five. The number of asses and mules rose from 559,000 to 1,151,000, predominating in the South; a panegyric of the mule may be found in the census volume on Agriculture, p. cxiii. It is significant of the survival of primitive rural conditions that the number of working oxen rose from 1,701,000 to 2,255,000, the South having 858,500 and the Middle West 820,000. *Ibid.*, cviii-cxv.

plied the Ohio carried an annual Cincinnati-Louisville commerce valued at $35,000,000. This traffic on the great water highways, creating cities wealthier than Venice or Shanghai, represented no inconsiderable planning and organizing. Packet owners made various attempts at combination, but they were loose and abortive. During the war, the immense flotillas were to prove invaluable to the Northern armies. But the railroads already threatened them, the conflict strengthened the railroad lines, and before long the gaudy steamboat commerce was to prove as evanescent as the caravel.

In maritime commerce, meanwhile, defects of American planning and enterprise cost shipowners dear. The beautiful clipper ships, the transatlantic packets flying the Black Ball flag, and the coastal vessels had written proud pages in the American record. But on the Atlantic, the British-owned Cunarders showed better organization and safer management than their Yankee rivals operated by Edward Knight Collins, naval architect and shipping merchant. In twenty-six transoceanic passages in 1852 the Collins ships made much the faster time; but a strain of American recklessness appeared in the exclamation of Captain Asa Eldridge of the *Pacific*, "If I don't beat the *Persia*, I will send the *Pacific* to the bottom." Successive misfortunes, including the loss of the *Arctic* in 1854 with more than 300 dead, the foundering of the *Pacific*, and the withdrawal of the government subsidy, were too disastrous to be survived. Meanwhile, American shipbuilders clung tenaciously to wooden vessels propelled by sails or paddle-wheels, though British builders were turning to iron ships and screw propellers. Even the boasted *Vanderbilt* was a wooden ship with two walking-beam engines and two great paddle-wheels forty-two feet in diameter. The emigrant business began passing to British vessels. In the summer of 1857 the *National Intelligencer* carried a significant article, "Losing Our Carrying Trade." It pointed to reports that the better organized British yards were building 300 oceangoing steamboats: [21]

What are to become of sailing vessels when these 300 ocean steamers, or even one-half of them, shall be navigating the Atlantic Ocean? Already sailing vessels have to content themselves with the most bulky and least profitable freight; passengers, specie, light and costly goods, and so on being carried almost exclusively by steamers. The mode of travel and transportation upon the ocean is undergoing the same change that has already taken place on land; the old slow coach or vessel is being cast aside for the rapid rail-car and the storm-defying steamer. England, seeing this inevitable change, has, with the sagacity, prescience, and bold energy which characterize her, thrown her-

21 Louis C. Hunter's admirable *Steamboats on the Western Rivers*, 237–240, 308–357, covers organization and disorganization in the river steamboat business in careful detail. On Atlantic shipping see R. G. Albion, *The Rise of New York Port, 1815–60*; George W. Sheldon, "Old Shipping Merchants of New York," *Harper's Monthly*, vol. 84 (Feb., 1892), 457–471; *National Intelligencer*, July 25, 1857.

self forward in this revolution, and has covered, and is covering, the great highways of commerce with her steamers, and taking from all other nations, and especially from us, the most profitable portion of the carrying trade of the world.

New England might have been expected to organize large-scale transportation with special acumen. Instead, the section conspicuously failed in farsighted organization. The Boston & Worcester was completed in 1835, and the Western, from Worcester to the Hudson opposite Albany, in 1842. But down to the war the two railroads had not been united, though of course through trains were run over them. Moreover, Boston had no connecting railroad across upper New York to the lakes. The Boston-Albany line was fifty miles longer then the rival New York-Albany line, and had to traverse the rough Berkshires, while New York City offered a much better port and a far more magnetic shipping center. Hence, as C. F. Adams, Jr., pointed out, New York railroads, merely by intersecting any line that Boston tried to build across New York State, could draw down its traffic to the metropolis.

Meanwhile, in southern New England unification proved equally unattainable. The Hartford & New Haven was completed during Van Buren's Presidency, and the New York & New Haven was finished in Taylor's, but it was not until a decade after Sumter that they were consolidated. Thus the regime of small affairs continued dominant on the New England railroad scene even while J. M. Forbes was mobilizing Boston capital to help build the Michigan Central, the future Chicago, Burlington & Quincy, and the Hannibal & St. Joseph.[22]

Unevenness—ragged, sporadic action in a desert of individualism—was the keynote of the country's organizational activity. That handmaiden of transport, the telegraph system, was in its way astonishing. From a swarm of small companies a number of large concerns was presently born; and then by a program of consolidation carried out in the fall of 1857, the American Telegraph Company became dominant in the East, while the Western Union held a similar primacy in the West. The American, when Lincoln was elected, had nearly 300 offices and 13,500 miles of wire, controlling the business from Halifax to New Orleans. Over it and all the remaining companies the North American Telegraph Association held a loose control.

The country, which had long suffered from a jumble of little precarious companies, hoped for a reign of order. That might indeed have been the result but for the covert mutual enmity between the American and the Western Union. While the former wished to support Cyrus W. Field's Atlantic cable

22 C. E. Kirkland, *Men, Cities, and Transportation*, I, 127 ff., II, 72 ff.; Van Oss, *American Railroads*.

project, the latter was much more interested in a telegraph line to California. They were rivals in absorbing the surviving independents, and they quarreled violently over relations with the Associated Press, which the Western Union befriended and the American attacked as a dangerous news-gathering monopoly. The telegraph war which loomed up in 1860 showed that organization had gone far, but not far enough.[23]

That other handmaiden of transport, the express system, a uniquely American growth, had been somewhat more completely organized. So efficient were the various express companies that a Boston gentleman who wished to give a dinner party with Western buffalo hump, Ozark wild turkey, New Orleans shrimp, Minnesota wild rice, Georgia scuppernongs, and Shenandoah apples could command them all. The large sums the government used throughout the country were safely handled by express; all the long-distance financial exchanges of the country were conducted in the same way. Consolidation had been nearly as important in this industry as in the telegraph business. A union of two older companies had given birth in 1850 to the American Express, guided by Henry Wells and William G. Fargo, and this in turn soon organized Wells, Fargo to carry on the Western business, and the United States Express Company as an Eastern subsidiary. Various smaller concerns survived. In monetary terms the business was small; but the speed, economy, safety, and responsibility with which the agencies delivered letters, money, and parcels all over the continent made them invaluable to the country, and illustrated organizational enterprise at its best.[24]

The trunk-line railroads, steamboat interests, and telegraph and express companies were well enough organized to serve the Northern war effort effectively. But could as much be said of the equally important manufacturing industries?

[III]

Any reader of the massive report on manufactures in the census of 1860 is struck by the smallness of the units listed. Generally speaking, production rested on a multiplicity of petty establishments. The nation's pig iron came from 286 furnaces, with an average invested capital of about $14,000 each, and an average annual product much below that figure. Pennsylvania, the most

23   Robert L. Thompson, *Wiring a Continent*, 310–342.
24   Alvin S. Harlow, *Old Wayvills, passim*. Henry Wells published in the N. Y. *Tribune*, Feb. 20, 1864, a complete account of his and his companies' achievements. The earliest important line had been W. F. Harnden's Boston-New York package express; Wells had been the first to suggest and execute an express business to Buffalo, then Chicago, and ultimately the Far West. Total operating costs of the three corporations in 1864 were only about ten millions.

important iron State, had an industry of small furnaces widely scattered. In the Lehigh Valley gangs of smoke-grimed, hard-muscled men operated about twenty anthracite furnaces, in the Schuylkill Valley as many more, and in the Susquehanna Valley twenty-five. A westward drift had spawned iron-making centers in the Juniata, Johnstown, and Lewisburg districts, but they too were small; the four furnaces of the noted Cambria works could not average 10,000 tons apiece.

And the manufactories which took the iron? The firearms of the country came in 1860 from 239 establishments, with an average invested capital of less than $11,000. Connecticut, thanks to the Colt, Winchester, and other plants, was the main seat of fabrication, yet the 9 factories at work there employed fewer than 900 people in 1860, and the value of their product fell below $1,200,000. Smallness was equally characteristic of the sewing-machine industry, based upon American ingenuity and readily adapted to war work. Isaac M. Singer had founded his company only in 1851, and was still working hard to effect a pooling of patents and a union of enterprises. The census reported sewing machines made by 74 companies in a dozen States; and the 5 factories of Connecticut, which held the lead, divided an output of some 24,000 machines valued at just over a million.

Some industries of wide fame worked on a surprisingly modest scale. Though John A. Roebling was already well known for his wire-rope and suspension bridges, his Trenton factory had a capital of only $100,000, and its 70 hands made rope worth only $70,000 annually. And though Richard M. Hoe had revolutionized the printing of large newspapers by his rotary presses, the country had 14 press manufacturers, all small, with an aggregate yearly product of less than a million dollars.[25]

Surely, it would be said, the manufacturers who supplied agriculture and transportation had organized large enterprises; and it was true that important foundations had been laid. The largest manufacturer of locomotives, at Paterson, N. J., however, employed only 720 men in 1860 to build 90 engines. The largest car-wheel factory in the country, at Wilmington, Delaware, employed only 200 hands to cast 30,000 car wheels annually. One of the best-known industries in the land was the shovel factory of Oliver Ames & Sons in Massachusetts; running 26 tilt-hammers in 4 plants, it made 250 dozen spades and shovels a day, still rather a small-scale operation. Yet more famous was Cyrus H. McCormick's factory in Chicago, which produced 4,131 reapers and mowers in 1860. To meet varying regional needs, farm-implement manufacturing was widely distributed. In this field several corporations were achieving an impressive capital and a fairly complex organization. Nevertheless, the

25 Census of 1860, *Manufactures;* see the long introduction.

rule of smallness still had general validity. In the single county of which Canton, Ohio, was seat, the aggregate product of fifteen firms or individuals was worth more than twice as much as McCormick's whole output.[26]

New York City and its vicinity had a variety of machine shops which had sprung up principally to furnish iron forgings and castings, together with marine engines, to shipbuilders. They included the Fulton, the Allaire, the Neptune, the Morgan, the Delamater, and the Novelty iron works, with several more in Brooklyn. The works of the Stevens family in Hoboken and the Continental Iron Works at Greenpoint, Long Island, fell into the same category. Nearly all were destined to become important during the war. The Allaire establishment, successor to Robert Fulton's Jersey City shop, dated back to 1816, the Novelty Works to 1830, and the Morgan Works to 1838. At Cold Springs on the Hudson the West Point Foundry also had vigorous engineering facilities, and later planted branch machine shops in New York City. Other sturdy engine-building plants were found on Western waters, at Pittsburgh, Steubenville, Cincinnati, and Louisville. Undertakings of considerable size did not daunt the major shops. The Novelty Works had cast a sixty-ton bedplate for the engine of Collins's ship *Arctic*, the Corliss Engine Works at Providence turned out flywheels 25 feet in diameter, and a Philadelphia machine shop bored castings 18 feet long and 16 feet in diameter.

Yet these machine shops, however ambitious some of their undertakings, were small compared with British works and primitive in organization. They were obviously expansible, but when war demands came nobody knew how fast or effectively they could expand. Although they were becoming more specialized, they offered no products comparable with the finer parts of the reaper or sewing machine.[27]

Of all American manufactures, none had grown so strikingly during the previous half-century as textiles. The first complete textile factory, the Boston Manufacturing Company at Waltham, had been born of war in Madison's day. It had paved the way for the larger factories in the Merrimac Valley, and demand had grown so heavily that the country now had 1,091 cotton factories alone, more than half of them in New England. Massachusetts alone

26 The manufacture of labor-saving farm machinery, naturally one of the greatest branches of American endeavor, had given some men and firms nation-wide renown. S. M. Osborne & Co. in Auburn, N. Y., Adrian Platt & Co. in Poughkeepsie, R. L. Howard in Buffalo, and C. Aultman & Co. in Canton had a general fame. H. & C. Studebaker had begun their wagon business at South Bend in 1852. Already in 1860 a machine bound grain by wire. The census report stated that four-horse harvesters with two men to bind and two to shock could harvest twenty acres of grain a day; "we shall soon have machines that will cut, gather, and bind up the grain in one operation." *Manufactures*, cciv et seq.

27 For the machine shops see N. Y. *Tribune*, Feb. 7, 1863, an informative article; Clark, *History of Manufactures*, 107 ff.; Bishop, *History of American Manufactures*, III, 112.

counted 217 cotton factories; New England employed nearly three-fourths of the capital and made two-thirds of the product in the cotton industry. Some mills, like those of the Sprague family in Rhode Island, were imposing. It was in woolens, however, that the highest degree of concentration had been effected. Worsted manufacture was conducted mainly by three establishments, the Pacific Mills at Lawrence, Massachusetts, the Manchester Print Works at Manchester, New Hampshire, and the Hamilton Woolen Company works at Southbridge, Massachusetts. These three organizations loomed up as giants on the flat American scene with their total of 3,400 hands. The largest, the Manchester mill owned by the Merrimac Mills Corporation, which also made cotton prints in large quantities, was one of the few industrial wonders of the land. At Lawrence a fourth enterprise, the Bay State Mills, had become the world's leading makers of cashmeres, shawls, and other fine woolens. The census commented on the completeness and order of the large New England woolen factories.

A nation needing mountains of uniforms could take encouragement from the vigor of the ready-made clothing industry. It had grown up with democratic mass demand, cheap cloth, and the sewing machine until 3,800 firms with a capital of nearly $25,000,000 were engaged in it. A silent revolution was merging many small shops into large wholesale establishments. The average product was largest in the Middle Atlantic and Yankee shops, approaching $25,000 a year. East of the Alleghenies female hands were giving way to men. The principal cutters and salesmen in the bigger shops were often former merchant tailors, glad to invest their capital and influence in the large units. Thus, "with all the advantages of large capital and machinery," remarked the census, they could "supply every town and village with ready-made clothing at the lowest prices." [28]

Though in a hundred areas industry was forming larger units, even the biggest were still usually ill organized and amateurishly administered. One-man supervision predominated, and managerial problems were solved by trial and error. The McCormick factory was managed by Leander McCormick, Cyrus's brother, and four foremen. The Cooper & Hewitt iron works at Trenton were directed by Abram S. Hewitt, with advice from Peter Cooper and assistance from Edward Cooper. Erastus B. Bigelow, founder of a thriving carpet business, a determined enemy of corporate as distinguished from individual management in manufactures, published in 1858 a testy pamphlet on

---

28 Census, *Manufactures*, xxxii, lx, etc. The making of boots and shoes had grown into a large industry in Massachusetts, which by the State census of 1855 turned out nearly 12,000,000 pairs of boots and some 17,000,000 pairs of shoes. The whole number of shops in the country making boots and shoes in 1860 was 2,439. But as yet the industry was poised between the domestic and factory systems.

the subject.[29] Businesses should not be controlled from commercial and financial centers, he argued, but on the spot; for unity of purpose, one head was worth far more than the divided responsibilities of a large corporate organization. Isaac Singer, Samuel Colt, and Oakes Ames would have agreed. So long as the controlling brain was as keen as McCormick's, Hewitt's, or Bigelow's, it might well be superior to group management. Some industries were specially adapted to one-man control, and some business geniuses had to rule alone.

The most typical American manufactory in 1860 was the property of a man or family who had founded it, ownership passing from father to sons. This was true even of the older houses. The varied enterprises of Phelps, Dodge & Company, for example, were carried on by a close-knit group, members of the Dodge, Phelps, Stokes, and James families. Five men in 1860, of whom "the Christian merchant" William E. Dodge was the best-known, held total ownership and direction. From their Cliff Street offices in New York they managed the largest metals business in the country, a New Jersey bank, railroad interests, wide tracts of timber, iron, and coal lands about Scranton, and other undertakings with quiet efficiency.[30] But incompetents could wreck a business as easily as talented creators could make it. No New England textile mill was more noted than that of the Middlesex Company in Lowell, but its heads lost the entire capital by appalling "mistakes and irregularities."[31] And the trend of the times was toward multiple ownership and management.

As concentration gave birth to larger units, control by individuals and families declined. To reduce costs by standardization of product and improvement of methods; to stimulate or seize upon changes in market demand; to hold orders by prompt delivery of excellent goods—this, no less than growth in size and capital, required a more elaborate managerial organization. Larger buildings, larger stocks of materials, larger working forces, and more complex machinery meant expert planning and supervision. This fact was being illustrated by the shoe industry on the eve of the war. Amid a multitude of domestic producers and tiny cobbler shops, factories of real size had emerged primarily because customers had to be sought, materials purchased cheaply, labor supervised vigilantly, and innovations rapidly adopted. By 1860 steam power was being introduced into the larger manufactories, making the hand power of small shops seem pitifully slow.[32] Lyman Blake's machine for stitching uppers to soles had been invented, and would at once accelerate the tendency toward big and complex shops, with more and more elaborate staffs.

29 Entitled "Depressed Condition of Manufactures in Massachusetts."
30 R. G. Cleland, *Phelps-Dodge 1834–1950*, Ch. III. The Connecticut shops of the Ansonia Brass and Copper Company made a wide variety of products.
31 Crowley, *History of Lowell*.
32 Blanche E. Hazard, *Origin of the Boot and Shoe Industry in Mass.*, 123 ff.

This change in corporate administration, however, was in 1860 still slow and gradual. After all, in most areas the shift from small to large units had to wait on the progress of railroad facilities, and the consequent rise of regional or national markets. State impediments to large-scale organization were formidable. Without notable exception, State laws forbade corporations to hold property in other States, or stock in other companies, except under special charter. It was with great difficulty that legislators grasped the fact that it might serve the general good to encourage companies to undertake broad interstate activities. General incorporation laws were themselves recent, the Connecticut statute of 1837 being the first of broad character. Chief Justice Lemuel Shaw of Massachusetts did an important work 1830–60 in adapting the law of partnerships to corporations, and sheer economic necessity widened the influence of his decisions.

Until after the war, however, joint stock corporations were restricted mainly to railroads, banks, and insurance companies; State and railroad securities remained the staple of the stock exchanges. Manufacturing was not to adopt the corporate form on a broad scale until after Appomattox, and not to own interstate properties until still later. One reason for the formation of the Standard Oil trust as late as 1881 was that State laws blocked such interstate ownership.[33]

[IV]

Of the great range of organized activity among the churches, the educational bodies, the professional groups, the publishers, the writers, the social service societies, and lesser participants in voluntarism, how much was likely to aid a government at war? How much of this activity encouraged the principle of cooperative effort? Very little.

All the powerful church organizations, with two exceptions, had split in two on the sectional issue. The Catholics, an ecumenical body under foreign governance, remained ostensibly united. So, formally, did the Episcopalians, for even after communicants in the Confederacy established a separate church, the General Convention called the roll of the Southern dioceses. The other denominations rallied with fervor to the conflict. Quoting "The Lord thy God is a God of war," Southern Presbyterians, Baptists, and Methodists, as sects, as earnestly aligned themselves with their chosen cause as Northerners of the same churches supported the Union. Probably most Americans gained their

---

33 F. H. Chase, *Lemuel Shaw;* Arthur H. Dean, *William Nelson Cromwell*, 18. New York by an act of 1811 had permitted incorporation by general law rather than by special enactment, but the authority had strict limits.

first lessons in organization and cooperation from their church bodies. These great agencies enrolled millions who knew no society, club, or company, they enlisted men in active continuous work to an extent never equalled even by the political parties, and they touched life at more points than any other body. For women they furnished the one great means of organized expression.

But although the churches were in fact multifariously useful for the war, they were dismayingly limited in their usefulness. North and South, they undertook a great variety of labors. They supplied chaplains for the armies; they distributed Bibles, devotional books, and tracts; they supported revivals in camp; they helped meet problems of poverty and home relief behind the lines. Northern church leaders formed societies to assist the freedmen, inspired the Christian Commission, sent leaders (rather unsuccessfully) to occupy pulpits in conquered areas, and furnished spokesmen to plead the Northern cause abroad. Yet the central purpose of the churches debarred them from intensely practical activity. Their primary concern was with the other world, not with this. After an immemorial concentration upon extramundane activities one day out of seven, they could not give full weekly labor to mundane concerns.

Nor had the concept of social Christianity, as preached in England by Kingsley and Maurice, in France by Lamennais and Buchez, yet reached America. In 1857 the Y. M. C. A. in New York had been torn apart by a secession of nearly 200 members, including prominent clergymen, who asserted that political and social topics, including slavery, were too much discussed, and that the society had wandered from its original objects.[34] This small but significant event emphasized the doctrine that the central business of the church was to save souls and quicken the spiritual life of the people. Any wide departure from that path—beyond, say, raising the $2,500,000 collected by the Christian Commission—would have aroused condemnation.

As for education, it had a far more uneven and precarious organization than religion. When Henry Barnard established his *American Journal of Education* at Hartford in 1855, the principle of a unified system of public schools under State control was fairly well rooted in the North. To implant it had required a long battle against penny-pinching enemies of public expenditures, religious bodies which wished to fractionize the educational system, and fossil obstructionists of "book learning." Associations of teachers and friends of education, fighting this battle, had founded numerous societies all over the East and Middle West.

Yet the results were so uneven and new that no powerful educational bodies useful for war work yet existed. New York and Illinois had not gained separate State superintendents on a permanent basis until 1854, and Pennsyl-

34 *National Intelligencer*, April 30, 1857.

vania until 1857. In 1861 a belt of States reaching from Maine and New Jersey to the far borders of Kansas had permanent State school officers, but only nine, including California and Alabama, possessed regularly organized combinations of State and county administrators.[35] Teachers' organizations had narrow scope and slight vigor. The one important national agency, the American Association for the Advancement of Education, was ten years old; but however commendable, it was unable to rally the nation's teachers in united effort.

Significantly, no educator made an effort to form classes in army camps, convalescent hospitals, or prison camps. The Northern volunteer regiments were full of youths torn from academy or college, of semi-illiterates, and of half-Americanized aliens, apt material for teaching. But no body capable of implementing an educational plan, had one been broached, existed.

The medical profession, like the ministers and teachers, had the aid of schools, journals, and societies in fostering its special aims. But standards of training were so low, quacks and charlatans were so abundant, and public interest in medical advancement was so slight, that the profession lacked organized power.[36] In Great Britain and Europe, S. Weir Mitchell later wrote, medicine by 1861 held places of trust in the government, but in America it was neglected. "Our great struggle found it, as a calling, with little of the national regard. It found it more or less humble, with reason enough to be so." [37] General medical societies had a history running back into colonial days, and before 1861 State-wide societies overspread the whole map east of the Mississippi, save in Louisiana, which left the field to a New Orleans association.

Most early medical societies, however, both State and local, were primarily social organizations of scant authority or prestige. For a time some State governments clothed specified societies with power to license physicians, regulate fees, and punish malpractice. Such authority was in general ill exercised, and the State tended to turn instead to special medical boards. Several close-knit, well-led urban societies gained more repute and influence than the loose State associations. In Philadelphia the College of Physicians, dating from 1789, in Boston the Society for Medical Improvement, from 1838, and in New York the Academy of Medicine, from 1846, all had a distinguished membership, listened to papers of merit, and commanded public respect. Societies in Cincinnati, St. Louis, and one or two Southern cities had dignity. The membership, however, was always smaller than it should have been. Their interest in medical education did not lead in the best direction, and when much later university medical schools of adequate standards came into existence, it

35 Cubberley, *Public Education in the U. S.*, 122 ff., 246 ff.; Cubberley and Elliott, *State and County School Administration Source Book*, 283 ff.
36 H. B. Shafer, *The American Medical Profession, 1783–1850*, pp. 169–173.
37 *In War Time*, Ch. IV.

was from other impulses and indeed against the opposition of some leading medical organizations.[38]

On the initiative of New York physicians, the American Medical Association was founded in 1846. Its committee on education did effective work to improve medical training within the old pattern, urging lengthened terms of study, the use of hospitals for clinical teaching, higher admission requirements, and stricter examinations. It labored also to improve American drugs, inculcate higher ethical principles, and stimulate original research and writing. Holding annual conventions in different cities, it enlisted adherents in each, until by 1856 it had more than 3,000 members.[39]

But on the whole, medical organization when the war broke was in its groping initial stages. Most societies were social or amateurish, and not one had produced a great administrator or initiator. They held banquets, combated quacks, and passed resolutions, but they did much more to promote *esprit de corps* than to increase medical knowledge or influence public opinion. Hampered by financial difficulties, languid interest, factional squabbles, and lack of professional dignity, many of them kept up but an intermittently active existence. The American Medical Association was as yet so narrowly professional, deficient in broad social interests, and fluctuating in strength, that it was of slender general value. Medical education would have to be revitalized before medical associations could grow powerful.[40] No society was able to give the government important aid during the conflict. The chief wartime organizers of medicine, surgery, and nursing were to be a clergyman, a landscape architect, a frontier army doctor, an attorney, and a woman clerk in the Patent Office.[41]

Of all the great professions, that most glaringly deficient in organization was the bar. When the nation sprang to arms, no legal society worth mentioning existed North or South. Although Philadelphia laid claim to a city association founded in 1802, it was nothing more than a lawyers' social club. Even New York City had no bar association until Samuel J. Tilden, under stress of a dire civic emergency in Tweed days, led the way in founding one, and the American Bar Association did not arise till some years later. The earliest State association seems to have been one which led a precarious life in Iowa for some years after 1874. Lawyers with an instinct for leadership or a cause to

38 W. F. Norwood, *Early History of American Medical Societies*, CIBA Symposia, 1947, No. 9.

39 Shafer, 232 ff.; John Shaw Billings, "Literature and Institutions," in E. H. Clarke, *et al.*

40 F. R. Packard, *History of Medicine in the U. S.*; W. D. Postell, *The American Medical Association*, CIBA Symposia, 1947, No. 9; F. C. Stewart, *On the Medical Schools and the Conditions of the Medical Profession in the USA* (1856), 116.

41 Bellows, Olmsted, Hammond, George T. Strong, and Clara Barton; but mention might also be made of three physicians, Drs. Tripler, Van Buren, and Agnew, and a scientist, Wolcott Gibbs.

promote turned naturally to political parties. For improvements in the efficiency and ethics of the bar they looked to legislatures, the State attorneys-general, and the courts.[42] If any officer of the national government wished legal advice—in making appointments to the bench, in drafting legislation, in searching for precedents, in dealing with questions of constitutionality—he could apply to individuals; but help from associations he could not get.

One of the greatest indirect contributions to the war strength of the nation was made by the press, both daily and periodical. It kept the people informed, it more than any other agency molded public sentiment, and despite shrill dissident voices and conflicting policies, it crystallized a spirit of national unity. Daily journalism was competitive in the extreme. In New York City the coarse, fickle *Herald*, the enterprising, solidly informative, and socially radical *Tribune*, the eloquent and cultivated *Evening Post*, and the moderate, judicious *Times* contended for leadership. While their daily circulation was almost wholly metropolitan, by weekly and semi-weekly editions they reached the entire North. Every city had its daily, almost every county seat its weekly.

The country was full of newspapers, read more voraciously, perhaps, than in any other land. New York State had more dailies than all Great Britain. A current story told of a minister who preached hell-fire without effect; but his announcement that the godless went to a land without newspapers made his congregation turn pale and profess conversion.[43]

While outwardly newspapers seemed to illustrate the essence of individualism, actually they possessed a remarkable solidarity. The practice of exchanging subscriptions was universal. A country editor might get twenty or fifty exchanges from all parts of America; he produced a better journal by swift use of the scissors than by laborious employment of the pen, with the result that the content of many newspapers was much the same. The government subsidized this system of exchanges by special postal concessions. A remarkably telling editorial by Greeley, Bryant, or Raymond, by Samuel Bowles or John W. Forney, was certain in the end to appear in many journals. A striking piece of special correspondence in the Chicago *Tribune* or Springfield *Republican* would be widely clipped. The Associated Press, originally a combination of New York dailies to collect news, had by 1860 taken almost complete control of news-gathering in the United States and Canada. Though bitterly assailed as a ruthless monopoly after it defeated the effort of the telegraph companies to establish separate news services, it did its work efficiently and cheaply.[44]

---

42 Charles Warren, *History of the American Bar;* M. Louise Rutherford, *Influence of the American Bar Assn.*
43 D. Macrae, *The Americans at Home,* Ch. 31.
44 Victor Rosewater, *History of Cooperative News-gathering in the U. S.;* Oliver Gramling, *The A. P.*

Indeed, the diffusion of intelligence was one of the best-organized branches of national endeavor. The New York *Tribune* or *Herald* published every night 55,000 copies, with each department—European correspondence, Washington, Albany, and metropolitan news, editorials, Wall Street article, agricultural column, produce and shipping news, letters to the editor—copiously filled; it dealt systematically with advertisements, legal printing, and birth, marriage, and death notices; it provided for paper supply, street sales, local deliveries, and subscriptions—all through carefully coordinated activity. This was possible because each journal had a body of trained employees, an eye to system, and an instinct for the latest inventions. Stereotyping, for example, developed by Charles Craske of New York, came into use just in time for the large war editions. The *Tribune* boasted that in the spring of 1862 its weekly edition circulated more than 150,000 copies, and its semi-weekly 18,000; its consolidated circulation of more than 220,000 copies was, it declared, much the largest in the world.[45] Altogether, it reached fully one-twentieth of the whole newspaper-reading public of the North. Such a feat was impossible without careful organization.[46]

The publication of books and magazines was likewise a vigorous department of American life, for mass education meant mass reading. The Scottish publisher William Chambers, looking primarily at New England, wrote that every American bought and read books—a gross exaggeration; Anthony Trollope declared that Americans were the greatest consumers of literature on earth, taking 10,000 copies of a book where Englishmen took one.[47] Although the invention of electrotyping ten years before the war had reduced costs, during the 1850's the annual dollar value of books trebled. Harper Brothers just before the panic of 1857 turned out 3,000,000 volumes in a single year. To be sure, the purchase of books hardly averaged a dollar a year for adults, but the market well repaid the largest firms. The houses of Appleton, Lippincott, Harper, Ticknor & Fields, Putnam's, and Scribner's flourished while they honorably allied their names with the best literature. *Harper's Monthly Magazine* before the war attained a circulation of more than 100,000; farm journals, religious journals, and women's magazines like *Godey's Lady's Book* were widely read; Robert Bonner's New York *Ledger* was reputed to sell 400,000 copies a week; and the two important illustrated journals, *Harper's Weekly* and *Frank Leslie's*, overcoming their initial crudities, were reaching and instructing great bodies of readers.[48]

45 N. Y. *Tribune*, April 10, 1862.
46 The census reported that in 1860 the nation had 383 daily newspapers, and more than 3250 weekly or semi-weekly newspapers. The totals were steadily growing.
47 Chambers, 219; Trollope, *North America* (1862), I, 271.
48 Martin, *Standard of Living in 1860*, 324, 325.

The largest book-and-magazine houses, like Harper's and Ticknor & Fields, were organized on a sturdy scale. But book-publishing in general was as much decentralized as most manufacturing, for prosperous firms were found all the way from Albany and Richmond to St. Louis and Nashville. Equally noteworthy was the wide diffusion of bookshops; just before the panic at least three thousand shops dealt exclusively in books and periodicals, while nearly seven thousand more sold them in connection with other wares. The book trade was not efficiently managed or systematized, for it perhaps never can be. The American Publishers' Association had recently been founded to bring publishers and booksellers into better relations, and its weekly organ, the *Publishers' Circular*, carried full information on the trade. But as of newspapers, it could be said that the seemingly chaotic book business had more internal solidarity and coordination than men supposed. It was well arranged to stimulate literature, and to keep the nation fairly informed upon events and forces.

While in a narrow view the manysided publishing activities of the North were of limited value to the war effort, in any broad view they were of priceless utility. The press kept the country informed of every phase of government activity, offered a free forum of discussion which was indispensable to the healthy workings of democracy, and through its best journals gave the nation encouragement and inspiration. "We cannot too often repeat that the first duty of the citizen at this juncture is to give the President a generous, confiding, and cordial support," said *Harper's Weekly* just after Bull Run,[49] and most publishers took a similar view in dark hours. One influential pamphlet on the nation's resources, scattered broadcast late in the conflict, was worth a small army.[50] It was unfortunate that in some other areas the national energies were not equally well organized.

[V]

The lack of associative elements, the plastic state of society, and the prevalent individualism, had their compensation. They fostered self-reliance, enterprise, and ingenuity. Blessed with great natural wealth, and aided by capital accumulations, energetic Americans wrought great achievements. "The period following California gold," writes one historian of technology, "developed an apex of individualism perhaps never before and certainly never since attained in the world's history." [51] The ingenuity was as striking as the energy.

49 August 3, 1861 (V, 482).
50 "Our Burden and our Strength," by David A. Wells (1864).
51 Roger Burlingame, *March of the Iron Men*, 312, 313.

Repeatedly a lonely experimenter who knew little of the general state of the arts would devise some memorable improvement. John Deere thus produced his self-scouring plough, Robert L. Stevens his T-rail, Linus Yale, Jr., his famous pin-tumbler cylinder hook, and Crawford W. Long, in an isolated Georgia village, his anaesthetic. Elias Howe thus solved the problem of devising a needle which, working from the top plane only of a piece of cloth, would stitch both its top and bottom.

Herman Haupt, a young Pennsylvania West Pointer, who went into railway construction, was suddenly faced twenty years before the war with the necessity of finding the laws by which the transmission of strains in a trussed bridge was governed. He sat down in a country town in Pennsylvania without books of reference or scientific apparatus, and by experiments on the resistance of timbers, and his own methods of obtaining mathematical formulae, met the exigent requirements of the York & Wrightsville Railroad. He did more; he arrived at some valuable new principles of bridge building. Just before the war, helping direct the boring of the Hoosac Tunnel, and confronted with the task of piercing strange rock strata, he devised drilling machinery comparable with that used in piercing Mont Cenis. In short, without supporting organizations, he repeatedly displayed a triumphant inventiveness. Brought into the army in 1862, Haupt showed his ingenuity in building bridges of novel materials (beanpoles and cornstalks, said Lincoln), making implements for twisting and straightening rails, devising torpedoes, and so on; while his skill in helping several generals move troops and meet fast-changing strategic situations was equally notable.[52]

But were these empiric methods good enough? A significant contrast might be drawn between Charles Goodyear in America and Charles Mackintosh in Scotland. While the Connecticut experimenter, without scientific training or advice, hit on the vulcanization of rubber by stubborn plodding and luck, the systematic Glasgow manufacturer arrived at great results by well-considered steps. He obtained the guidance of the brilliant chemist-surgeon James Syme of Edinburgh, dissolved raw rubber in coal-tar naphtha, and applied the solution as a varnish to cloth. While Goodyear sank into debt, Mackintosh became rich. It was only when well-organized groups placed themselves behind Goodyear's discovery that American rubber products far outstripped the British goods. There could be no question in 1860 that the inexorable process of business consolidation, the steady growth of industrial undertakings in size, and the new scientific knowledge, demanded group activity in place of individual enterprise; but individualism still reigned supreme.

52 See Haupt's pamphlet, "Hints of Bridge Construction," 1841; Frank A. Flower's useful preface to Haupt's *Reminiscences*.

Very different was the situation in England. John Stuart Mill, commenting on the intellectual progress of the working classes, remarked that their advance in the habit of cooperation was equally surprising. "At what period were the operations of productive industry carried on upon anything like their present scale? Were so many hands ever before employed at the same time, upon the same work, as now in all the principal departments of manufactures and commerce? To how enormous an extent is business carried on by joint stock companies. . . . The country is covered by associations." [53]

America was now ready to take wide and rapid strides on the same road. The transportation revolution was creating national markets; they in turn would help create the industrial revolution, with large national agencies of manufacture. Business giants governing huge combinations would soon arise. But as matters stood in 1861, Lincoln never thought of summoning a group of business leaders to assist him in wartime administration; the businessmen had no faculty of cooperation. Except for the Sanitary Commission, the government made practically no use of professional groups in war work; it picked men here and there, but in haphazard fashion. In short, it used little organized machinery, for the machines had never been created. Lincoln might well have found valuable assistance, for example, in a board of transportation. But how was such a board possible in a country where the first through train of freight cars did not pass from the State of New York into the State of Ohio until January 11, 1863? [54]

53 Mill, *Dissertations and Discussions*, I, 196, 197 (Boston, 1864).
54 Edwin A. Pratt, *The Rise of Rail Power in War and Conquest*, 22, 23.

14

McClellan and the Tasks
of Organization

LINCOLN was quick to ask McClellan for a memorandum on his proposed mode of using the new volunteer forces. He replied on August 4 that he would need for his main army of operations about 273,000 men, with 20,000 more for defending Washington and smaller forces to protect Baltimore, Fort Monroe, and the Baltimore & Ohio. His army would require 600 guns, twenty-five regiments of cavalry, proper engineering and pontoon trains, and adequate means of transport, while effective naval cooperation would have to be arranged. Still other troops would be needed to occupy West Virginia, Kentucky, and Missouri, while the size of the army to go down the Mississippi would have to be determined by its commander and the President. Admitting that the total force seemed large and its cost would be heavy, McClellan urged that it would be cheaper to crush the rebellion at one blow, and terminate the war in a single campaign, than to leave the conflict a legacy to the next generation.

Thus something of the optimism of the first months survived even Bull Run. One campaign, one blow!—and McClellan spoke not merely of driving the enemy from Virginia, but of occupying Charleston, Savannah, Montgomery, and New Orleans; in short, moving this great army into the heart of the Confederacy and stamping out resistance at its center. He was soon to tell a group of Philadelphians: "The war cannot be long, though it may be desperate." His memorandum said nothing about the time required for preparing the blow, but it was evident that he wanted plenty of it. He and Scott immediately disagreed as to the first army formations, McClellan insisting that brigades be rapidly united into divisions, while Scott declared this unnecessary, for in Mexico he had used brigades alone. McClellan cut through the dispute by obtaining a War Department order August 20 constituting the Army of the Potomac under his full and direct command.

"I at once designated an efficient staff, afterwards adding to it," McClellan later wrote. His chief of staff, a position new in America, was his father-in-law Colonel Randolph B. Marcy, a West Pointer now nearly fifty who had served on the northern frontier, fought in Mexico, and taken part in the so-called Mormon War; a big, soldierly man of moderate abilities. His adjutant-general was Seth Williams, a brigadier, assisted by Lieutenant Colonel James A. Hardie, both good officers, and the latter especially capable and industrious. As head of engineers McClellan kept the exceptionally clearheaded and experienced Major John G. Barnard, who later completed the Washington defenses and in time wrote a caustic analysis of his chief's generalship. The topographical engineers soon passed under Brigadier-General A. A. Humphreys, remembered as a military historian. As quartermaster-general McClellan appointed Captain (later Brigadier-General) S. Vliet, who loved his wine, but to whose efficiency he paid high tribute.[1]

Army health offered an appalling problem. Typhoid and other fevers raged in the camps. The sick took refuge in improvised general hospitals in and about Washington, some, like the deadly hospital at Cumberland, Maryland, so bad that they became a public scandal. Incoming regiments brought volunteer surgeons ignorant of army methods—and sometimes of everything else. To replace chaos by order McClellan appointed Charles S. Tripler as medical director, an officer who with the general's support did good work, but whose preparations for active campaigning proved inadequate.

As the staff steadily grew to sixty-five in the spring of 1862, it enlisted other notable men. The provost-marshal-general, Andrew Porter, soon halted the straggling, disorder, and criminality which made the Washington camps a byword. Major Albert J. Myer, who had been made head of the signal corps before McClellan assumed control, devised a good system of torch-and-flag signaling, and introduced an insulated telegraph wire which could quickly be strung; indeed, he was the father of the signal service. McClellan's telegrapher, Major Thomas T. Eckert, also organized a service of notable efficiency. This Ohioan, long an expert in telegraphy, was to rise rapidly to the position of general superintendent of military telegraphs in Washington, where he saw

1 O. R. I, v, 5 ff.; *McClellan's Own Story*, 113; McClellan, *Report on the Org. and Campaigns of the Army of the Potomac*, 39 ff., 51 ff.; Swinton, *Army of the Potomac*, 62 ff.; Kenneth Williams, *Lincoln Finds a General*, I, 103 ff. When McClellan took command July 27 the forces around Washington numbered perhaps 53,000. He insisted that his command be termed and organized as an army, while Scott clung to the idea that McClellan ought to head a geographical department. McDowell had already organized brigades south of the Potomac. Under McClellan, a division consisted (ideally) of three infantry brigades of four regiments each, four batteries, and one cavalry brigade. For McClellan to the Philadelphians see Philadelphia *Evening Journal*, Nov. 5, 1861. Gen. Peter S. Michie, an expert, speaks slightingly of Marcy's capacities, but Marcy's books indicate a likely intelligence.

much of Lincoln. The work of his men in the field was as dangerous as it was arduous. The balloonist T. S. Lowe was another young man who had impressed the government before McClellan took charge in Washington. Cameron, after Lowe had made some spectacular ascents, and had sent Lincoln the first telegram ever transmitted from the upper air, made him head of the new aeronautics section of the army. McClellan was glad to encourage him, and although the heavily wooded nature of the country and the difficulty of transporting and flying balloons limited his usefulness, he sometimes obtained information of value.[2]

The general's aides included several striking figures. John Jacob Astor was ultimately to inherit one of the great American fortunes. Richard B. Irwin in time became adjutant-general and historian of the nineteenth army corps. Louis Philippe d'Orleans, the Comte de Paris, saw hard fighting at first hand, which later aided him in the production of a masterly four-volume history of the war. His brother the Duc de Chartres also served on the staff through a long, hard campaign. Altogether, McClellan listed a personal entourage of nineteen, or, if he added the Prince de Joinville, who accompanied his two nephews of the Orleans family to headquarters and stayed for a time, twenty.

The young general stood almost alone in his early recognition of the vital importance of apportioning precise duties among a large body of staff officers, and in this respect showed a more modern understanding of command procedures than Robert E. Lee. His comprehensive grasp of administrative work in general made a startling contrast with the confused, nerveless methods of Cameron's War Department and Scott's headquarters. Although he often played favorites and unjustly criticized subordinates whom he disliked, he cultivated a real esprit de corps in his staff family. His faith in the special equipment and all-sufficing capacity of professional military men to win the war was accompanied by an unhappy contempt for politicians, and, since he was very much a Democrat, a strong dislike of Republican politicians. Indeed, he believed and openly declared that a military elite, to the great benefit of the nation, would thereafter play a larger part in public affairs. He was much more like a French or German general than those of the traditional American variety.[3]

---

2 Myer, who later established the U. S. Weather Bureau, is commemorated by Fort Myer. Eckert wrote a valuable book, *Recollections of the U. S. Military Telegraph Corps During the Civil War.* Mt. Lowe near Pasadena is named for T. S. Lowe, who built an observatory on it.

3 As we shall see, he had a Colonel Blimp attitude toward slavery. Irwin was another staff member later to pen a scathing review of McClellan's command; see his article on the Peninsular Campaign in *Battles and Leaders,* II, 435 ff. Dahlgren reported McClellan's views on the military in the nation's future; *John A. Dahlgren,* by his daughter, 344, 345.

[I]

McClellan struck everyone by his air of energy, confidence, and address. W. H. Russell, hard to please, liked the serenity of his dark blue eye, the firmness of his mouth, and the animation of his features; he liked the general's compact, powerful frame, massive throat, and well-shaped head. Dr. Henry W. Bellows of the Sanitary Commission wrote a more observant description. He too noted the muscular figure, well-knit and perfectly balanced, the handsome regular features, topped by dark, short hair, the calm, direct, and powerful eye. What seemed to him more remarkable was McClellan's leopard suppleness, as graceful as if his movements were controlled by some inner rhythm. "His manner," added Bellows, "is self-possessed, unaffected, though remarkably self-complacent, with natural dignity and frankness. His talk, to the point, earnest, honest, and intelligent. He is not afraid of responsibility; he knows his place, assumes its rights and an interest in meeting its requirements. While I should say that balance, availability of every talent, promptness, superiority to routine, and willingness to stand in the gap were more conspicuous in him than ingenuity, brilliancy, or originality, yet there is an indefinable *air of success* about him and something of the 'man of destiny.' "

It was this aura of destined greatness, this assurance radiated by a man not yet thirty-five, which made Napoleonic comparisons inevitable. "He looked like one who always had succeeded and always will succeed." Already men talked of him as the next President.[4]

A man of resolution, force, and belief in his star, but of more self-esteem than of absolute self-confidence; a soldier of long training, keen observation, and settled convictions, but not of imagination, depth, or subtle analysis—this was McClellan. His early environment had not been altogether fortunate. He had been all too carefully reared in Philadelphia, his father an active, prosperous, disputatious physician; the city was conservative, and the rather aristocratic circles in which he received his education and formed his social tastes were distinctly so. He was contemptuous in early years of "these wretched Dutch and Irish immigrants." The Mexican War and his regular army experience had confirmed his natural distrust of volunteers, an attitude unfortunate in the head of the greatest volunteer army in history. There was something decidedly spoiled in the temper of this proud, ambitious, inwardly haughty leader. As A. K. McClure, who knew him well, remarked, he would have taken the rough buffets of war better had he once been a ragged alley

4 H. W. Bellows to his wife Sept. 12, 1861, Bellows Papers, MHS; when the Prince Napoleon in August, 1861, repeated to McClellan Lord Lyons' remark that he would be the next President, the general "answered with a fine, modest, and silent smile"; "The Tour of the Prince Napoleon," *American Heritage,* August, 1957.

urchin, used to playing and fighting with other boys of tough material. From the time he was admitted to West Point by special permission at the age of fifteen and a half, until he was made vice-president of the Illinois Central at thirty-one, he had too easily won success after success. His lucky appointment in 1855 as an army observer in the Crimean War enabled him not only to study military affairs in Europe, but to talk with dignitaries of the highest rank, including the French and Austrian emperors.[5]

Being spoiled, he could be arrogant when given full rein, and petulant when crossed. Already his treatment of Jacob D. Cox in the West Virginia campaign had been unfair, and that of W. S. Rosecrans, whom he termed a silly, fussy goose, ungenerous. To cooperative subordinates and to admirers he showed a natural affability and kindliness. As Dr. Bellows put it: "His voice is sweet, his address affectionate, his manner winning." Because of this, of his leaderlike qualities, of his real mastery of the minor arts of war, and of his solicitous care of his troops, officers and men came to adore him. "How those brave fellows love me," one officer reports his saying, "and what a power their love places in my hands." A better man would have emphasized obligation rather than power.[6]

Behind the mask of seeming serenity and self-confidence, however, lay a great deal of self-distrust; behind the apparent energy, dynamism, and boldness lay caution and timidity. His services in Mexico had been those of an engineer. At Sevastopol he had stayed only two weeks (October 16–November 2, 1855), all in the British camp, and at the beginning of a siege that was destined to endure almost a year; he spent most of his time inspecting the Russian defensive works and measuring the Allied difficulties, and departed full of admiration for the fortifications erected by Todleben and the valor of the Russian defenders. It was the belief of the best authorities (Marshal Niel, General Wolseley, and Todleben himself) that a fierce, determined attack on Sevastopol late in September, 1855, would have carried that fortress, and that by declining to attempt it and cautiously sitting down to a prolonged siege, the Allies played into the Russian hands; but if McClellan knew this fact, he does not mention it in his reports.[7]

During his European tour he carefully inspected various military works in Austria, Prussia, and other countries; but it seems significant that he lingered over defensive positions, evincing no interest in the study of offensive strategy or tactics. In the West Virginia campaign his dispositions had been excellent,

5 W. S. Myers, *McClellan*, 16; McClure, *Recollections of Half a Century*, 316.
6 Myers, 190–194; Donn Piatt, *Memories of Men Who Saved the Union*, 295.
7 McClellan, *Reports* (35th Cong., Special Session, Senate Exec. Doc. No. 1). The British in the Crimea gave McClellan every possible facility, but the Russians and French refused him any; *Own Story*, 2.

but all the boldness in executing them was displayed by his subordinates. Short as the campaign was, it showed that he united a hard-headed, practical sagacity about some matters with an astonishing capacity for self-deception in others. He probably really believed, after Morris and Rosecrans had won Corrick's Ford and Rich Mountain respectively, two minor encounters involving minor losses, that he was justified in boasting that he had "annihilated two armies."

McClellan's intensity of purpose was as creditable as his integrity, industry, ability, and constancy to duty. Combined with his singular charm of manner, it diffused an impression of pleased, and even exalted, consecration to his great task, and recalled Wordsworth's portrait of the happy warrior. He could labor with tremendous fixity to reach the objects he had set himself, and at the same time show a warmhearted cheeriness to all associates. He had a sense of mission, a clear understanding of the means to be employed in reaching his goal, and a determination not to be swerved from his direct line. These commendable traits come out clearly in a letter he shortly wrote his wife:

> I shall take my own time to make an army that will be sure of success. . . . I do not expect to fight a battle near Washington; probably none will be fought until I advance, and that I will not do until I am fully ready. My plans depend on circumstances. So soon as I feel my army is well-organized and well-disciplined, and strong enough, I will advance and force the rebels to a battle in a field of my own selection.[8]

Unfortunately, this resolution of temper was lamed by several defects. One was his inveterate perfectionism; all preparations must be complete to the last detail, and all controllable conditions must be just right, before he would make a decisive move. As one Senatorial critic said, he would hesitate to order an advance if he learned that a part of his wagons lacked the extra linchpin required by army rules for each wheel.

Another crippling trait was stated by an observant subordinate in terms of pre-Freudian simplicity—his readiness to seek scapegoats for the inevitable mischances of war: "There are men so peculiarly constituted that when they have once set their hearts on any project, they cannot bear to consider the facts that militate against their carrying it out; they are impatient and intolerant of them; . . . inasmuch as it is impossible for any man to get angry with facts, such men instinctively fix upon certain individuals whom . . . they always accuse . . . of hostility or deception." McClellan, when his plans began to go wrong, wrote his wife: "History will present a sad record of those traitors who are willing to sacrifice the country and its army for personal spite and personal airs." When they had gone further wrong he was writing her: "I am tired of

8 *Own Story;* letter of Oct. 6, 1861.

serving fools." [9] But then his whole attitude toward his superiors was peculiar. He did not regard himself as the servant of the American people, or the subordinate of Lincoln or of Scott. He thought of himself as a man entrusted with a colossal task, under which he staggered; so that any criticism, any interference, even any advice, was an absolutely unforgivable wrong.

Finally, the worst evidence of his self-distrust was his inveterate disposition to exaggerate the magnitude of his difficulties. No matter how large his army, that of the enemy was always greater; no matter how formidable his guns, the opposing fortifications were always stronger. Of these traits we shall find abundant illustrations. The Polish diarist Gurowski, the Thersites of Washington, wrote that his imagination so overrode his sense of fact that he had a faculty for "realizing hallucinations." Charles Russell Lowell, who was on his staff, declared that he was like the Duke of Wellington in that he got everything completely ready, and then unlike the Iron Duke in that, once ready, he did not strike hard. Still another close observer, the war correspondent George W. Smalley, remarked that when the pinch came, McClellan was not a general but a council of war, and it was an axiom that a council of war never fights.[10]

McClellan's intensity of purpose, frequent arrogance in hours of prosperity, tendency to propound a devil-theory for failure, resentment of interference, and egotistic vein, are characteristics not understood in isolation. They are bound together and measurably explained by his conviction that he was under the finger of God. The war produced a number of generals, including Lee, Stonewall Jackson, Rosecrans, and O. O. Howard, of as profound religious fervor as McClellan, but he alone had a Cromwellian sense of selection for God's purposes. Dr. Bellows showed keen insight when he spoke of the general's natural faith in divine protection. This faith supplied a foundation for his loftiness of outlook, personal purity, integrity, and sincerity, qualities which kept for him to the end of his life the esteem of the country. It also gave him, once he had been made the foremost general, a delusion that God had chosen him to be the shield of the Republic; him alone. His Messiah complex was half piety and half disdainful pride.

"I feel sure that God will give me the strength and wisdom to preserve this great nation," he wrote his wife August 9, 1861, adding: "I feel that God has placed a great work in my hands." A little later he writes her of the tremendous responsibility God has laid upon him. "I was called to it; my previous life seems to have been unwittingly directed to this great end; and I know that God can accomplish the greatest results with the weakest instruments—therein

9 James B. Fry, "McClellan and his Mission," *Century*, vol. 48 (Oct., 1894), 931–946; McClellan, *Own Story*, 310, 453.
10 Gurowski, *Diary*, I, 99; Bliss Perry, *Life of T. W. Higginson*, 169; Smalley, *Anglo-American Memories*, 123, 124.

lies my hope." In November, busy drilling his army, he repeats: "I still trust that God will support me and bear me out. He could not have placed me here for nothing."

Those other exalted military organizers, the Emperor Constantine and the Caliph Omar, could not have been more certain of the *instinctu divinitatis*. It was as the instrument of God that he felt he had a right to be loftily contemptuous of older associates, so that the daughter of General James M. Wadsworth, long eminent in New York affairs, indignantly resented his haughtiness to her father. It was this sense of divine selection which enabled him to write his wife so scornfully of Lincoln as a "browsing President," of the Cabinet as "geese," and of the Administration as one which in general made him "perfectly sick." It enabled him to write (August 14) that "General Scott is the most dangerous antagonist I have." As a divine appointee, he had a right to expect his every demand to be met without demur.

Men of such intense religious justification commonly possess a martyr complex, and when hard trials came McClellan was quick to adopt the martyr pose: "I feel that the fate of the nation depends on me, and I feel that I have not a single friend at the seat of government." In all his trials he nevertheless remained confident of his destiny: "I believe in my heart and conscience . . . that all I have to do is to try to keep the path of honor and truth, and that God will bring me safely through." This piety, kept within limits, should have been an added source of strength; but when he carried it to the extreme point of regarding himself as God's lieutenant rather than servant, it became a grave defect. Unlike Cromwell, unlike Stonewall Jackson, who did their best and let Providence do the rest, he alternated between a sense of infallibility when God-inspired, and total fallibility when the inspiration failed. As William H. Russell was quick to perceive, moments of cocky self-certainty were followed by periods of hesitation, timidity, and irresolution.[11]

All in all, splendid gifts were mated with terrible handicaps. And the worst of the handicaps was revealed in the before-quoted letter to his wife in which he spoke of forcing the Confederates to a battle on a field of his own selection. "A long time must elapse before I can do this," he wrote (it was already October 6), "and I expect all the newspapers to abuse me for delay, but I will not mind that." A natural patrician, with little knowledge of or feeling for the plain people, he did not understand that this was a people's war, and that the people's will had constantly to be consulted to ensure popular support.

11 *Own Story*, 168, 175, 176, 316, 317 (see also the biographical introduction by W. C. Prime); Russell, *Diary North and South*, Chs. 55–57. "I like the man," wrote Russell Oct. 10, 1861, "but I do not think he is equal to his occasion or his place." The fact of McClellan's sense of mission under God that astute soldier James B. Fry (*op. cit.*) specially emphasizes.

[II]

All summer and fall new levies of infantry poured into Washington. McClellan dealt with them systematically. As each regiment arrived it was carefully equipped, drilled, and disciplined as part of a provisional brigade, this work being assigned first to Fitz-John Porter, then to Ambrose E. Burnside, and later still to Silas Casey. Artillery and cavalry units were assigned to other officers for equipment and training. As the troops were made ready, they were transferred to permanent brigades on the south side of the Potomac, consisting of four regiments apiece. Then as the drill and field maneuvers progressed, the brigades were formed into divisions—three brigades, meaning twelve regiments, to each division. McClellan had in view a larger unit still, familiar to military men since Napoleon's time, the corps, but he postponed its creation until experience had given the division commanders familiarity in handling large bodies of troops, and until he could determine by actual trial the best generals. Two divisions would theoretically contain 24,000 men, an adequate number for an army corps, and McClellan knew that not many officers are capable of commanding so large a body.[12]

It was part of McClellan's plan that he should command a large force of artillery. Inheriting from McDowell a pitiable 9 batteries, totaling 30 guns, he raised the total to 92 batteries of 520 guns; and he gave each division 4 field batteries, one of them taken from the regular army. McClellan also decided to create a reserve force of 100 guns, and a siege-train of 500. By the time his army was ready to move the amount of ordnance and ordnance stores, far superior to that possessed by the South, sufficed to satisfy even him.[13]

Cavalry presented both a special problem, arising from the fact that army officers had always regarded three years' training as a minimum; it also presented a special opportunity in that it could have been the best intelligence arm of the service as well as a a unique striking force.[14] McClellan put Brigadier-General George W. Stoneman in charge, telling him to whip the volunteers into shape within six months. Stoneman, a West Pointer from upper New York who had been captain in command of Fort Brown, Texas, and had

12 McClellan's *Report*, 53, 57. The corps by McClellan's plan was to have 3 infantry brigades of 4 regiments each, 4 batteries of artillery, and 1 regiment of cavalry, giving it a nominal strength of 12,000 infantry, 1000 cavalry, and 24 guns; an effective strength of 10,000 infantry, 700 cavalry, and 24 guns. *Own Story*, 114. The Confederate army formed no corps in the Army of Northern Virginia until it had received eighteen months of service.

13 Swinton, *Army of the Potomac*, 65. A shrewd Confederate officer, D. H. Hill, later wrote that the Federal artillery was always the most effective arm of the service; *Battles and Leaders*, II, 355.

14 W. W. Averell, in *Battles and Leaders*, II, 429.

escaped with part of his men when Twiggs joined the Confederacy, had gained McClellan's confidence in the West Virginia campaign. He was destined to write his name large in the history of the war. With great rapidity, all obstacles considered, he organized and trained a division of fourteen regiments, with two independent squadrons. To take raw recruits, often unused to arms or horses, and turn them into a disciplined, effective cavalry force was a task of complex difficulty; while they had also to be schooled in meeting problems of the Virginia terrain, with its forest, thickets, rivers, swamps, and hills, its deep mud after rains, and its burning midsummer sun.

Generally speaking, it was impossible to use cavalry as full regiments in Virginia; squadrons were the most efficient unit. When Stoneman got his division into shape it was distributed among the army, with a small body at headquarters, and a special reserve force under Philip St. George Cooke, a former colonel of dragoons who had commanded the Mormon Battalion in Kearny's historic march to California. Stoneman had been quartermaster of the battalion. Cooke, who had later fought the Sioux and Apaches, and had devised an improved system of cavalry tactics, was a stiff disciplinarian. He had the poignant task of fighting a Southern army which contained both his son John and son-in-law J. E. B. Stuart. Beyond hard drill this year Stoneman and Cooke did not go. McClellan by fall might have used the cavalry constantly in reconnaissance raids, but he showed no interest in risking them to gain information.[15]

"Squads right!" "Right oblique, march!" "Hep, hep, hep!" The immemorial bark of sergeants, the rattle of arms, the swirl of dust from red-clay fields trampled to powder, the clamor of fife and drum, encircled Washington north, west, and south. On some clear afternoons the breeze, bringing the fitful strains of massed bands, reported a grand parade in the distance. Visitors glimpsed McClellan galloping hard from post to post, a very Kléber in his hard-bitten, keen-eyed aspect, his staff following breathless and jaded behind. Seldom indeed now did a dirty, drunken soldier stain the Washington streets, for military police snapped such ragamuffins under stringent arrest. Colonel Andrew Porter, whom McClellan had appointed provost-marshal-general, used squads of regulars to close disorderly saloons, clear streets and hotel lobbies of loiterers, arrest every man absent without written leave, and put deserters in fear of their lives. He prohibited civilians from visiting camps or crossing the Potomac without permits. McClellan credited Porter with making Washington one of the quietest cities in the Union. Troop morale rose as men felt that they had both a master and friend at the head of the army.[16]

15 *Battles and Leaders*, II, 429 ff. Cooke was raised from the rank of colonel to that of brigadier-general in the regular army, Nov. 12, 1861.
16 O. R. I, ii, 769; *McClellan's Report*, 55; *Own Story*, 69; Shannon, I, 183; Ropes, I, 163.

The most difficult problems of discipline were presented by several mutinous regiments. Although they had considerable reason for discontent, McClellan properly made an example of them by prompt and severe action. He sent sixty-three men of the Second Maine to the Dry Tortugas for the remainder of the war. Their grievances were probably not unlike those of the Fourth Connecticut at Frederick, Maryland (outside McClellan's purview), who rebelled because of bad officers, bad fare, and such total lack of uniforms that none had coats, few had matching hats, and many appeared even on dress parade in underclothing. Fomenters of revolt in the Connecticut regiment were imprisoned. When the New York Seventy-ninth Highlanders rebelled, McClellan dealt summarily with them. He sent out a force of infantry, cavalry, and artillery to quell them. "The gentlemen at once laid down their arms," he wrote his wife, "and I have the ringleaders in irons. They will be tried and probably shot tomorrow." [17]

Such sternness was indispensable, even though the Highlanders had been badly treated. They had fought bravely at Bull Run, where their colonel, Secretary Cameron's brother, lost his life. After the battle they had been refused permission to return briefly to New York to recruit their ranks, although Secretary Cameron, the commander of the New York militia, and the engineering department of the army had all supported their petition. Later they had been outraged by news that they would be placed in the division of Dan Sickles, whose disreputable record decent men despised. Finally, while preparing to hold elections for a new colonel and other officers, they had suddenly been put under the command of a stranger, Colonel I. I. Stevens of the regular army; whereupon the major, senior captain, and four lieutenants summarily resigned. To cap their discontent, McClellan told them he would not inquire into their "frivolous and unfounded" complaints, and that their behavior laid them open to a charge of "the basest cowardice."

Nobody was shot. Ringleaders were sent briefly to the Dry Tortugas, and the regimental colors still more briefly taken away. Stevens won the devotion of all the men, who served with distinction. The happy subsequent history of the regiment indicated that mismanagement, at a higher level than that of its own officers, had been responsible for the trouble. Nevertheless, McClellan's peremptory course taught the whole army a salutary lesson.[18] He deserves the greatest credit for his insistence on discipline and order.

17 *Own Story*, 86, 99, 100; the Comte de Paris, I, 270, attributes the trouble in the 79th largely to grievances about pay and terms of enlistment. W. H. Russell says "the President was greatly alarmed" by the mutiny.
18 William Todd, *The 79th Highlanders, N. Y. Vols.* (1866), is a superior regimental history; see pp. 56–88.

[III]

The principal impediment McClellan met in bringing his army into efficient discipline arose from the poor quality of many officers, high and low. At a later date it was fashionable to say that no civilian should have been given an important command.[19] This was folly. The regular army simply did not have enough officers to go around. Of its small list, many lacked zeal, some shrank from responsibility, sticking to petty regular army posts when they might have had high volunteer rank, and many were needed in staff rather than field commands. It was out of the question to officer 500,000 men from the army register of 1860, and had it been possible, it would have been unwise.

Anglo-American history gave weighty arguments for using civilians in high posts. Cromwell and Hampden had left Parliament to fight. In colonial days Pepperell of the New England militia had captured Louisbourg from French professional soldiers. During the Revolution, Washington, Greene, and Knox, all with little or no military experience, had bested veteran British soldiers. In the War of 1812, Andrew Jackson, Jacob Brown, and Winfield Scott had all been appointed from civil life, and the two former were militia generals. During and after the French Revolution officers sprang from every walk of life to become generals and marshals.

Moreover, in so vast a people's war as this now beginning, with the armies on both sides representing almost a *levée en masse,* much was to be said for using popular leaders. The idea was to give talent a chance to rise to the top, as it did. Nobody could say in after years that John A. Logan, Jacob D. Cox, Carl Schurz, Benjamin Harrison, Lew Wallace, Joshua Chamberlain and James A. Garfield were not capable generals. On the Confederate side Nathaniel Bedford Forrest showed real distinction. After all, West Point did not differ materially from other good colleges except in a greater study of mathematics, engineering, and drill; the drill there and at army posts never went beyond company and regimental tactics; and Grant, Sherman, and others learned much more outside the army than in.

Yet the process of letting talent rise and incompetence fall took time, and was both painful and debilitating while it lasted. Too often the State authorities evinced an imbecile carelessness in putting the lives of their young men in the hands of stupid, ignorant, and irresponsible leaders. Much depended on the State system, the State adjutant-general, and the fiber of the governor. Ohio had allowed its regiments to choose their higher officers with some appalling results, for competition among aspirants produced neglect of discipline,

19 Ropes takes this view, and naturally some West Point officers always held it.

cheap electioneering, and occasional bribery. A few lucky regiments like the
Twenty-third Ohio, with Rosecrans for colonel and Rutherford B. Hayes for
lieutenant-colonel, obtained admirable officers. But repeatedly some local
politician, an aspiring lawyer or slick talker, took the lead and held it until
resignation or removal furnished relief. It was soon noted that cities and large
towns monopolized the Ohio commissions at the expense of rural areas.[20] In
other States the governors, acting hurriedly under heavy pressures, chose men
sometimes well, sometimes ill.

Morgan in New York shrewdly called on local leaders for advice, and appointed committees to investigate candidates and counsel him. In the three
counties of Chenango, Cortland, and Madison, for example, a committee of
forty-five unanimously designated Elisha B. Smith, who admirably led the local
regiment until he was mortally wounded at Port Hudson in 1863. Andrew in
Massachusetts showed equal sagacity, scouring the State for men of West Point
education, and next them giving preference to seasoned militia officers. He
refused, despite pertinacious demands, to grant a commission to sly Caleb
Cushing. Under still fiercer assaults, he stubbornly declined to make a colonel
of a Democratic politician who had a large following among the Boston Irish.
"I would not commission him," thundered Andrew, "if he was as good a soldier as Julius Caesar, and you should bring an angel from heaven to endorse
him."

But even Andrew blundered in making a colonel out of a militia strutter
who promptly led his men through Boston under the summer sun in a long-
famous "overcoat march." This appointment, he confessed to Sumner, was
inexcusable; but he made others nearly as bad—one hapless regiment getting a
superannuated head who was both dishonest and cowardly, and a lieutenant-
colonel who was an excitable Italian adventurer. The best governors could not
avoid error.[21]

Cameron in a circular letter tried to inculcate greater care. After wisely
urging the governors to commission nobody of doubtful health, morals, or
patriotism, he unwisely suggested that they fix age limits for officers: nobody
over twenty-two to be a lieutenant, nobody over thirty a captain, nobody

20   This was true of other States; see Wm. Croffut and John Morris, *Mil. and Civil History of Connecticut*, 75. Urban leadership was accelerated on a wide front by the war. We
may repeat that officers were everything to morale. The Second Michigan, for example,
did admirably until its colonel was made a brigadier-general, and its lieutenant-colonel took
a post in the regular army. The new lieutenant-colonel and the major being poor heads,
it went to pieces. "The regiment," wrote a Michigan veteran, Wm. W. Duffield, to Governor Austin Blair, "is very much disorganized, and it would be a work of great labor to
bring it up." Aug. 23, 1861; Austin Blair Papers, Burton Hist. Coll.

21   Pearson, *Andrew*, I, 233–235. The colonel who marched his men on a hot day through
the Hub wearing their overcoats, and soon repeated the performance in hotter Washington,
declared that their shoddy uniforms had to be covered up.

over thirty-five a major, and nobody over forty-five a colonel, except when special circumstances dictated a qualification of the rule. Governor Andrew contemptuously declared that he would appoint a good man anywhere short of Methuselah's age. As a matter of fact, an excellent officer might be as old as Wadsworth, who was approaching sixty when slain, or as youthful as Nelson A. Miles, who formed a company but was deemed too immature by his superiors to command men in battle. Beginning with a minor staff position at twenty-two, Miles was major-general four years later. George A. Custer, a graduate of West Point in 1861, earned his spurs as lieutenant at twenty-one and was a general before the war closed. Arthur MacArthur, carrying the flag of his Wisconsin volunteers up Missionary Ridge at eighteen, commanded a regiment before he was twenty. And Thomas W. Hyde of Maine, making a report in Virginia to Major-General Sumner, startled that officer by his juvenile look. "You a major!" exclaimed Sumner, then in his mid-sixties. "My God, sir! You will command the armies of the United States at my age." [22]

Gradually the quality of the officers was bettered, though the work of providing an efficient body of regimental commanders was to take a long time. As one factor, Scott's objections to assigning regular army officers to volunteer units, supported by Cameron, were broken down. As another, the soldiers themselves forced many unfit men to quit. As a third, the examining boards authorized by Congress wielded an effective broom. [23]

Scott gave way slowly. He stood out against a plea by Governor Dennison that he provide five regular army officers, if possible West Pointers, to head five Ohio regiments. Olden of New Jersey met better fortune, however, when he sent an agent to Lincoln with a letter arguing that as he could not find men competent to lead his new regiments, the general government ought to provide at least the colonels. The President asked Scott to see what could be done, and in due course New Jersey got two regular officers as heads of her two newest regiments. [24]

Apparently Cameron did not bestir himself in such matters. Governor Andrew tried in vain to obtain an answer to his plea that Captain T. J. C.

22 DAB; Hyde, Following the Greek Cross, 45, 46.
23 Scott believed the integrity of the little regular army must be protected against all hazards and got Cameron to agree. Under the pleas of Governor Andrew, both Massachusetts Senators—and Henry Wilson and Charles Sumner were powerful men—tried earnestly but in vain to let the Bay State select a few regular army officers for colonels. Adjutant-General Lorenzo Thomas, a narrow bureaucrat, said that more than a hundred such applications had been made, that if they yielded in one instance they must do so in all, and that this would surely damage the army, already hurt by the resignation of so many Southerners. "Your only hope is to obtain if you can the services of some experienced officers now out of the Army. . . ." wrote Wilson sadly to Andrew. June 27, 1861; Andrew Papers, MHS.
24 O. R. III, i, 380, 387; 451, 452. Olden's letter was dated Aug. 24, 1861.

Amory of the regular army should take charge of the Seventeenth Massachu-setts. Finally, late in August, he appealed to McClellan. The general thereupon gave Cameron some common-sense advice. "I do not think it possible to employ our Army officers to more advantage than in commanding divisions, brigades and regiments of new troops," he wrote, "particularly when it is remembered that we have almost none of the old troops at our disposal." Amory was ap-pointed.

Similarly, Frémont in the West made a test case of a regular-army lieutenant who had been sent to St. Louis by Governor Morton of Indiana in command of a regiment, but had been told by the War Department that he could not keep that position. Wishing to retain him and other regular officers, Frémont appealed to Montgomery Blair. The postmaster-general prevailed upon Cam-eron to agree that as many as a hundred regular-army officers of the grade of captain or lieutenant might be allotted to the volunteers, their places to be partially filled by commissioning the two upper classes at West Point as lieu-tenants, and Lincoln endorsed this plan. It went a long way toward making effective the stipulation in the new army law that the commanding general might detail any regular army officer to field service with volunteer regiments. From this time forward an increasing number of veterans of the Western posts began to appear in colonelcies of the new army.[25] The total, however, could not be large among the five hundred and more regiments.

The troops themselves had to take a hand in weeding out misfits and pro-moting able subordinates, and a half-thousand regimental histories prove that they were merciless in exerting pressure. An efficient officer had to have much more than some fair knowledge of tactics, strategy, and camp management; he had above all to be apt in commanding men. This aptitude could neither be acquired by study nor imparted by older officers—it was mainly inborn. One military chronicler speaks of "that rare faculty of enforcing rigid discipline without severity, and of exerting the most absolute command without harshness or arrogance." In unit after unit, the volunteers by giving evidence to examin-ing boards, by letters to Congressmen, or by sharp indications of disapproval brought a bad major or captain down; and good sergeants and lieutenants moved up. Some troop choices were bad, but more were sound.

Thus Edward S. Bragg of Wisconsin wrote his wife from Arlington, October 26, 1861: "Our regiment has taken a purge this week. We have *forced ten resignations* from officers, and put better men in their place." He added: "The men who resigned, did not have our confidence, and we placed the dose to their lips, and made them swallow it." If an officer could not handle his men expertly on the drill ground, their contempt became patent. If he

25 *Ibid.*, 427, 444; F. B. Heitman, ed., *Hist. Register and Dictionary of U. S. Army.*

treated subordinates arbitrarily, flinched in battle, idled, or drank to excess, the contempt became intolerance.[26]

When Cameron appointed the examining boards authorized by Congress, incompetent officers fled like rabbits escaping a meadow before a pack of hounds. In one division two colonels and twenty-five other officers, summoned to appear, incontinently resigned. By the end of the first week in November, 1861, nearly 150 had thus severed their connections. To get rid of such men for good, the War Department lost no time in decreeing that resigned officers would not again receive commissions.[27] Probably more colonels would have gone but for the fact that many were so important politically that they felt well protected. McClellan speeded the work not only of examining boards but of courts-martial, which were specially useful because they were immune from the political pressures which the boards often felt. Having a deep West Point contempt for "scrub" officers, McClellan handled them without gloves. His discharge of one junior commander brought him into conflict with Lincoln himself. Altogether, within eight months after the establishment of the boards, 310 officers were dismissed or resigned to avoid dismissal.[28]

The indirect effect of the board examinations in deterring governors from rash appointments and in stimulating officers to hard study and vigilant effort was doubtless even greater than the direct results. McClellan notes how many of his junior officers taught themselves while teaching their men. They read Hardee, Mahan, Napier, Kinglake, Jomini, and other texts, keeping a few jumps ahead of their subordinates. The Comte de Paris also describes the laborious effort of unschooled officers to educate themselves. Often after a hard day of drill the colonel would first give his juniors a careful lecture on strategy, tactics, and camp management, and then, long after most men were asleep, he, his lieutenant-colonel, and his major would burn their desk lamps far into the night. L. A. Grant of the Fifth Vermont was typical of scores of officers who, entering with no military training whatever, by hard application to details, books, and operations, made themselves into generals. The striking fact is not that failures appeared, but that the citizen army produced so many admirable leaders, brave, conscientious, and resourceful.[29]

Public opinion after Bull Run also had a marked effect on the efficiency of

26 On forced resignations, see Burt, *Memoirs*, 56; Augustus Buell, *"The Cannoneer:" Recollections of Service in the Army of the Potomac*, 24; *History of the Fifty-Fifth Illinois*, 170, 465; Bragg Papers, Wis. State Hist. Soc. Charges against an officer were often tried before a regimental court of other officers; see Henry Lee Papers, MHS, for instances.

27 O. R. III, i, 411; General Order No. 57, Aug. 15, 1861.

28 Shannon, I, 186, 187; Eckenrode and Conrad, *McClellan*, 28; Swinton, *Army of the Potomac*.

29 *Own Story*, 97; Comte de Paris, I, 272, 273; G. G. Benedict, *Vermont in the Civil War*, I, 352, 353.

officers. New York newspapers on August 1 published a telling memorandum by some of the most influential men of the city. It complained of the government's failure to supervise the selection of officers closely; of the wretched intrusion of political, local, and personal considerations into the appointments by various governors; of the bad consequences of company elections of lower officers, and officer elections of colonels; of the lax discipline throughout the volunteer organization, generals hesitating to jerk up weak colonels and colonels to castigate inept captains; and of the reluctance of the government to remove incompetent generals. In dealing with officer efficiency, the people were plainly in advance of Washington. Indeed, they would have supported Lincoln and Cameron in much more vigorous measures than the Administration took. Public sentiment was strongly behind all McClellan's energetic steps in organizing and disciplining the army.[30]

[IV]

In still other ways the steadily increasing army about Washington was made ready for combat. McClellan gave careful attention to provisions, clothing, and health. In this he had willing assistance from that conscientious administrator, Quartermaster-General Montgomery C. Meigs, whose zeal and skill were invaluable. The Secretary of the Sanitary Commission very justly wrote the editors of the National Intelligencer August 12 commending "the prompt and generous action of the enlightened head of the Quartermaster's Department, to whose energetic and comprehensive views of duty the nation has yet to be informed in what innumerable ways it is indebted."

Down to Bull Run the diet of the Union troops had been ill balanced, ill prepared, and ill served. After the first confusions of the spring, abundant supplies of bread, pork, and beef were available in most camps, but army regulations permitted no green vegetables, and except by gift or foraging the soldiers got none. Even when food of proper variety was at hand, bad cooking often ruined it. The army that marched to Manassas was on the verge of severe losses by scurvy and dysentery. But after McClellan took charge, the subsistence department under Colonel H. F. Clarke and the quartermaster's department under Van Vliet acted with energy. They brought in ample stores, established depots, and trained distributing officers. Both had to attend in person to innumerable details, and the reports they soon submitted were not only a story of heavy labors well performed, but a shrewd guide for other officers bearing similar responsibilities. Not once during his command of the army,

30 S. S. Cox, Three Decades, 159–162.

McClellan later declared, did troops go without rations from any fault of the commissary officers.[31]

Though the sanitary and medical system of all American forces remained weak, Surgeon Charles S. Tripler, who in August became medical director of the Army of the Potomac, was able, with the aid of the Sanitary Commission, to effect many improvements. One of his first acts was to move the men camping on Arlington flats, a third of whom were sick with typhoid, malaria, or dysentery. The eagle-eyed Frederick Law Olmsted, famous for his volumes of Southern travel, was secretary of the Commission. Making an inspection just before Bull Run, he had found the captains specially indifferent to foul latrines, garbage-littered camp streets, crowded tents shut tight against "night air," and unbathed men. They tolerated such filthy violations of the most elementary health rules that he called the whole system pestilential.[32] Now they, and colonels and generals above them, were made to understand that discipline included minute attention to cleanliness, fresh air, good water, and recreation.

In September, Olmsted reported that sanitary regulations were being enforced with ten times the old rigor, that even the regiments most demoralized two months earlier were now hardy and cheerful, and that the best-disciplined units were the most contented units. Improvement continued steadily. During the fall and winter (September–February), the number of sick fell to 6.18 per cent, more than half the cases being slight illnesses under treatment in quarters. Meanwhile the Sanitary Commission had launched a determined drive to reform the medical department of the army and oust its feeble head, the aged Surgeon-General C. A. Finley.

Measles, which many regiments brought with them when they left home, was prevalent throughout the camps. Tripler knew of no way to prevent its ravages. Other causes of illness, which Tripler was powerless to remedy, were shoddy blankets, poor tents, and inadequate clothing. On November 8 the surgeon of the Eighth Illinois Cavalry reported that 200 of his men had received no overcoats from the government, and that many of them were reduced to their drawers. The historian of the First Massachusetts Infantry recorded much sickness in their Washington camp because the men's clothing did not protect them from variations of temperature; "when darkness came, instead of sleep, there was a perpetual shiver." Medical men knew how to prevent smallpox, and Tripler recorded with pride that though it was prevalent in many regions

31 See the Olmsted-Harris *Report* on Washington camps, 14 ff.; Sanitary Commission, *Document No. 28*; McClellan, *Report*, 69.

32 Adams, *Doctors in Blue*, 18, correctly attributes much of the bad sanitation to the "incorrigible individualism" of American recruits. Men whose position in society would have demanded cleanliness and decorum washed neither their persons nor their clothes in camp.

from which the army drew its men, vaccination and other precautions kept it from gaining a foothold in the army. They did not know how to prevent typhoid, and in October and November, with an army averaging 130,000 men, there were 7,932 cases of fever of all sorts, about 1,000 of them with a typhoid listing.[33]

The sicklists of regiments from different parts of the country varied greatly. For example, in November, with a mean ratio of 6.5% sick in the whole army, 12 Massachusetts regiments had an average of 50 sick each; 5 Vermont regiments, an average of 144 each; 35 Pennsylvania regiments, an average of 61 each. In January, 1862, the Twelfth Massachusetts, 1005 strong, had only 4 sick; the Thirteenth Massachusetts, 1008 strong, 11 sick; the Fifteenth Massachusetts, 809 strong, had 68; the Fifth Vermont, 1000 strong, had 271 sick; and the Fourth Vermont, 1047 strong, 244. Mortality rates for enlisted men ran twice as high as for officers.

The diseases from which the men suffered most were fevers, measles, various catarrhal complaints, and chronic diarrhea and dysentery. The two last maladies had always been the greatest plagues of armies. In November the Army of the Potomac reported only 280 cases of chronic diarrhea and 69 of chronic dysentery—the best record of any army in the world, Tripler believed. Of the 1331 cases of measles that month, nearly all were of a mild form, and the ailment soon ran its course.

Each regiment had its surgeons who had to be carefully instructed, often in the very rudiments of camp requirements, and kept in hand. Tripler assigned the responsibility for this to the brigade surgeons, competent medical men who had in large part seen the battlefield of Bull Run. Each was required to inspect brigade camps, maintain adequate medical supplies, send Tripler a weekly health report from regimental surgeons, and furnish casualty lists after battle. The improvised base hospitals first used about Washington were a disgrace to the country. Occupying old houses, shops, barns, and schools, with poor plumbing or none and poor ventilation, they literally murdered many a soldier. Their attendants, nurses, and general staff were as green, slipshod, and ignorant as if they had stepped from the pages of Tobias Smollett. When the Sanitary Commission insisted that well-designed new hospitals must be built and competently equipped, Tripler gladly endorsed the demand.[34]

33 Though an English doctor had announced in 1854 the theory that intestinal discharges, carried by flies or other agencies, cause typhoid, and the theory had been proved valid, most Americans still attributed it to "miasmas," fatigue, poor food, and whatnot. Troops refused to believe that it was a filth disease. Adams, *Doctors in Blue*, 203.
34 Stillé, *Hist. of the Sanitary Commission*, 95; McClellan, *Report*, 65–68. The general hospitals in Maryland and about Washington by September had 2700 beds; William Q. Maxwell, *Lincoln's Fifth Wheel*, 53.

Two able officers of the Sanitary Commission, after due investigation, brought forward a plan for building new base hospitals on the pavilion system, each ward to be a self-sufficient structure for forty or fifty patients. The first proposals were modest, providing merely for fifteen thousand sick and wounded. Tripler, Quartermaster-General Meigs, Van Vliet, and others worked out the details. In October Cameron approved them, and asked the Commission to help select five sites. Thus was inaugurated a great hospital system which became one of the noblest triumphs of the war—even though the five buildings were temporarily reduced to two, partly because Tripler did not have enough medical officers for more, partly because McClellan feared graft in hasty construction.[35]

McClellan had laid a sound foundation for future activity. The army was far better organized, officered, equipped, and trained than when he had taken charge, and its morale was infinitely improved. A new sense of confidence spread in early autumn from Washington throughout the North. Men waited eagerly for the young general to deliver an overwhelming blow; for the kind of battle that ends a war—a Ramillies, an Austerlitz.

[V]

As Northerners plucked up confidence in their armies, a piece of happy news from the navy burst upon the nation. On September 2 the press blazed with headlines that sent everybody looking for maps. "Brilliant Naval Victory," ran the captions. "Hatteras Inlet Forts Captured: 730 Prisoners, 35 Cannon Taken." Gideon Welles's department had for the first time seized national attention.

This surprise blow was delivered at a strategic spot. A long thin shield of outlying sea-banks, a prolonged wall flung eastward in bluntly triangular form, protects the Southern coast from Cape Henry, opposite Newport News, Va., down to Cape Lookout, opposite Beaufort, N. C. This sea-wall is composed of pebbly beaches, dunes that shift except where pinned down by wiregrass, and some clay stretches bearing loblolly pine, live oak, and holly. At the apex of the triangle lies Cape Hatteras, the boss of the shield fronting the stormy Atlantic. Here the treacherous Diamond Shoals extend twenty-five miles out to sea, a graveyard strewn with the skeletons of ships. Outside the sea-wall the roaring Atlantic is hag-ridden with fog, winter sleet, autumn hurricane, and year-long tempests; eagles and ospreys soar above the flashing waves. Inside are the calm waters of Albemarle and Pamlico Sounds, where

---

35 Maxwell, 54, 55. Regimental hospitals, usually made of three hospital tents, offered temporary accommodation for small numbers of men.

sailboats glide safely, and ducks, geese, and gulls feed in peace. Hatteras Inlet, ten miles below the cape, opens into these inland seas. Noted in peace-time for its tarpon, dolphin, marlin, and swordfish, it was now the exit from a hornet's nest. Raiders sped out it to harass Union merchantmen; blockade-runners moved in and out. Fort Hatteras and its flank defense, Fort Clark, protected the inlet.

The Union expedition seized these forts in a foray so sudden and easy that it seemed an adventurous lark. General Ben Butler and Commodore Silas Stringham commanded the amphibious force. Their flotilla of some fifteen craft left Hampton Roads August 25, and at sundown next day anchored at the rendezvous. Butler landed a small force of troops at the inlet; Stringham turned the Dahlgren guns of his larger ships—the *Minnesota, Wabash, Susquehanna*— on the defenses, easily outranging their smooth-bores. As shells burst inside Fort Hatteras, its commander saw that the place would soon be a shambles. He surrendered to save needless bloodshed, and the Union commanders decided to hold and garrison the position. On August 30 Ben Butler sent a jubilant official report to his superior: [36]

The importance of this point cannot be overrated. When the channel is buoyed out any vessel can carry 15 feet of water over it with ease. Once inside there is a safe anchorage in all weathers. From thence the whole coast of Virginia and North Carolina from Norfolk to Cape Lookout is within our reach by light-draft vessels which cannot possibly live at sea during the winter months. . . . In my judgment it is a station second in importance only to Fortress Monroe on this coast. As a depot for coaling and supplies for the blockading squadron it is invaluable.

No immediate steps, however, were taken to utilize the advantages which the Union had so swiftly gained. The stroke galvanized the Confederates into hurried action to strengthen their coastal defenses. While they did this, the North, it would seem, might have found it easy to land troops on Roanoke Island, forty miles north of Cape Hatteras, a gateway to all southeastern Virginia. But in fact nothing was done in this direction for three months. Why? One reason lay in diversionary action by McClellan. Just after the capture of Fort Hatteras, he obtained permission from the War Department to organize an amphibious force of ten regiments with a fleet of light vessels, of which Ambrose E. Burnside was appointed head. This force, under McClellan's direct command as part of the Army of the Potomac, was to operate in Chesapeake and Virginia waters as might best assist his main array. Before 1861 ended, Burnside had assembled 20,000 men and a hundred small craft— but McClellan made no use of this potentially quick-striking body.

36 To Gen. John E. Wool; Private and Official Corr. of Butler, I, 229-235.

COAST AND SOUNDS
OF
NORTH CAROLINA.
Scale of Miles

Ben Butler and Commodore Silas Stringham, Driving Through Hatteras Inlet, Seemed to Confederates to Menace Richmond's Southeastern Connections.

If the list of naval achievements was still short, it was clear that the government had capable administrators in the vigilant, hot-tempered Gideon Welles and his chief assistant, the cheerful, robust, self-confident Gustavus Vasa Fox, whose long naval experience gave him sureness of touch.[37] They had to deal with a tremendous complex of problems. When the war began only twenty-four steam-driven vessels were in active service; they were scattered all over the globe; only the newest ships were equipped with powerful guns; although France and Britain had experimented with armored vessels, and such warships had proved their effectiveness in the attack on the Russian works at Kinburn in the Crimea in 1855, the United States had no ironclads; and the supply of trained seamen was inadequate for a sudden expansion of the fleet. But though Welles became a target for acrid criticism, the two men grappled doughtily with their difficulties.

They augmented the naval force at hand by four obvious measures. That is, they recalled all the ships on foreign stations but three; they refitted all the usable vessels laid up in docks or harbors; they began constructing new warships in the navy yards; and they purchased or chartered good vessels wherever they could be found. They gradually put a construction program of fast steamers and ironclads under way. They resisted all efforts to institute State navies, and insisted on the strict equality of the naval establishment with the military establishment. It soon became plain that naval fighting would take place not on the high seas, but in coastal and river waters. It also became evident that the principal contribution the navy could make toward victory would lie in a steady constriction of the blockade. In the end this blockade, colossal and unremitting, was to be one of the greatest naval undertakings of all history.

An impossible task it at first seemed. The Confederate coast line came to 3000 or 3500 miles; it was pierced by innumerable bays, inlets, and rivers; and a considerable part of it, like that bordering the Virginia-Carolina sounds, was really a double line of coast. When Lincoln proclaimed the blockade (April 19, 27, 1861) few ships were available to enforce it. But Welles and Fox persevered. By July in 1861 they had sent 21 purchased or chartered steamers to join the blockade service; and these, with regular naval vessels, made forty-two steamships for the cordon. The list by the closing days of the year rose to about 150 ships. And though Confederates derided the blockade, it was already showing some results; it cut off much of the expected European aid in rearming and refitting the Southern forces after Bull Run.[38]

---

37 Fox, chief clerk of the Navy Department, May 9, Assistant Secretary, Aug. 1, 1861.
38 Owsley, *King Cotton Diplomacy*, 250–253; J. R. Soley, *The Blockade and the Cruisers*, 11 ff.

When the Confederate envoy Slidell held his first interview with high French officials they asked why it was that, if so many vessels had broken the blockade, very little cotton had reached neutral ports. The Foreign Minister was especially inquisitive. "I told him," writes Slidell, "that they were generally of small burden and that spirits of turpentine offered greater profits than an equal volume of cotton. That, although a very large proportion of the vessels that attempted to run the blockade, either to or from our ports, had succeeded in passing, the risk of capture was sufficiently great to deter those who had not a very adventurous spirit from attempting it." [39] A few excerpts from the diary kept by Jacob F. Schirmer in Charleston show how the pinch began to be felt: [40]

May 31 (1861).—News. The war steamers have again appeared for a blockade, and today they stopped a British schooner going out and ordered her back, the British consul has required an explanation.

June 1.—Schooner *Mary Clinton:* news today that she has been captured by a U. S. man of war and sent to New York, she sailed from here on the 10th from New Orleans with 814 casks of rice 285 of which was shipped by H. Corbin & Co.

June 23.—The men of war are still on the blockade, no arrivals of vessels, no more privateers have gone out from here, it is feared that Capt. Welsman's ship *Amelia* has been captured.

July 31.—Our privateers appear to be doing something on the wide ocean and in several cases are successful. Our blockade is still carried on and every article of consumption particularly in the way of groceries are getting very high.

September 9.—Our privateeers appear to have made a close of their business as all of the ports are closed against us.

September 17.—Arrival. The secession gun was fired this morning as a salute to the news of the arrival of a large English steamship owned by John Fraser & Co. into Savannah from Liverpool with a large cargo for our city.

September 25.—The blockade is still an eyesore. Every arrangements were made to send the *Nashville* to Europe, but there is no doubt the news have reached the blockade and they have been reinforced, and the experiment is partly abandoned.

October 16.—Ship *Thomas Watson* from Liverpool for this port went ashore on Folly Island. The blockaders raced her, the crew left the ship in boats and reached the shore, the ship was eventually burnt by the Lincoln rascals.

November 30.—Business perfectly prostrated everything enormously high salt selling at 15 and 20 cents a quart hardly any shoes to be had dry goods of every kind running out.

39 Undated MS entitled "Notes of Interview with Messrs. Thouvenel, Persigny, Baroche, and Fould" in George Eustis Papers, LC.
40 Joseph F. Schirmer Diary, Charleston Hist. Soc. The punctuation has been mended for clarity.

The blockade would have been stronger had it not been necessary to detach war ships at times to pursue Confederate cruisers. Thus when Captain Raphael Semmes with the armed steamer *Sumter* escaped from New Orleans to the high seas late in June, 1861, half a dozen blockading vessels were sent off in a vain effort to seize her. No form of service was more disagreeably monotonous and confined than that on a blockading squadron; its boredoms seemed endless. But no service was more important than this strangling hold on the economy of the South.

The General Who Would Not Dare

AN EXPERT German officer who acted as observer with General Kuropatkin in the Russo-Japanese War was inspired by his irresolution to write that no worse commander can be found than "the leader who does not dare." [1] By late fall of 1861 many Washington observers feared that the North had such a commander. McClellan had properly insisted that thorough preparation must precede his stroke; but how did he define thoroughness?

The first great requisite was to make sure of Washington's defenses. Mc-Dowell had begun to build fortifications, and McClellan with General J. G. Barnard as chief engineer rapidly pressed the work until about fifty posts, mounting three hundred guns, surrounded the capital. The initial redoubts and forts were thrown up to protect particular points. Then, as the engineers found time, additional works were built here and there. The main forts, placed about a half-mile apart, had parapets eleven or twelve feet thick, surrounded by an abattis, but without a glacis; the guns were fired through embrasures, or from barbettes. No continuous entrenchments connected the posts.

South of the Potomac the first line of forts reached from Georgetown to Alexandria in an arc about fourteen miles long and ten miles in radius. Here, before offensive operations opened, the line included eighteen strong posts, extending from the Virginia end of the chain bridge opposite Georgetown (Fort Mary) past Arlington Heights, past the Virginia end of the Long Bridge, and on to Forts Ellsworth and Lyon in front of Alexandria. A similar chain of forts also extended around Washington on the north side of the Potomac, at distances of four to eight miles from the city. Farther south in Virginia the government commenced a second line by building forts at Munson's and Upton's Hills, but when the Confederates retreated from Manassas it decided not to extend this outer arc. British officers who inspected the fortifications were impressed by their strength and by the fact that it would require a large

---

1 Colonel Gaedke quoted in N. Y. *Nation*, vol. 80 (March 16, 1905), 205.

number of troops to man them efficiently. It was plain that unless kept well garrisoned, they might be quickly penetrated and overrun.[2]

With these fortifications at his back, McClellan intended to make his army complete in all respects, perfecting its arrangements with a thoroughness that von Moltke later taught the world to call Prussian. Everywhere improvisation must give way to plan. Each item of equipment—arms, munitions, tents, blankets, clothing, food, medicines, ambulances, entrenching tools, pontoon bridges, depots of supplies, transport—was given meticulous attention. Washington marveled at the endless trains of wagons, mountainous stores, and ever finer *tenue* of the soldiers. It was McClellan's ambition to put into the field the best-organized, best-trained, best-armed, best-fed, and best-uniformed army the hemisphere—perhaps the world—had ever seen.

By fall he was well on the way to his goal. With two glaring exceptions, the surgical and hospital arrangements, and the information system, his foresight covered every prime requirement. Part of the drill he instituted was highly specialized. The engineers, for example, were taught to make trustworthy reconnaissances of the roads in front, to fix the best lines for entrenchments, to choose the most advantageous positions for battle, and to build defensive works and siege lines in the most efficient fashion. The topographical corps, starting without reliable maps of any part of Virginia, became so expert that when heavy fighting took place before Richmond, they knew as much about some of the terrain—though not about the way in which weather affected it—as the Confederates.[3] The nation was to pay heavily, however, for lack of good intelligence agencies to collect data on enemy numbers and movements, for ignorance of streams and floods, and for lack of facilities to deal with an avalanche of battle casualties.

The army reviews, held primarily to inspire confidence among the men, became more and more imposing. They impressed Americans, who traveled even from New York to see them, more than experienced European observers. Régis de Trobriand, for example, son of one of Napoleon's generals and a cosmopolite, thought that the 3000 cavalry who were reviewed September 24 were indifferently mounted, and amateurish in the formation columns and other evolutions; W. H. Russell, looking at several parades, judged the men superior to the three-month militia, but still far from being soldiers. The Washington correspondent of the New York *Times*, describing an artillery-

2 See the confidential report of Captains T. Mahon and R. Grant, and Lieutenant T. C. Price, Aug. 1, 1862, to the British Commander in Chief, Canada; War Office Files, London. These officers visited the United States May 12 to July 7, 1862, spending much time with McClellan. A map of the fortifications is in *Battles and Leaders*, I, 172.

3 General J. G. Barnard not only took able charge of the Washington fortifications, but looked after the training of volunteer engineer forces. Brigadier-General A. A. Humphreys, succeeding J. W. Macomb, was chief of topographical engineers.

cavalry review October 8 on the plain east of the Capitol, praised the troops but criticized the "dull, heavy" way McClellan managed them: "It is a stupid performance generally, and today's was an aggravation of all previous defects." Most observers, however, were delighted, and some journalists, the New York *Herald* heading the McClellan claque, were ecstatic. Bayard Taylor gives us a spirited picture of the general and troops at a late September review:

> There were McDowell, Porter, Keyes, Blenker, Smith, and Marcy, all manly, gallant faces and figures of true military bearing: Cols. De Trobriand and Salm-Salm, with their dashing, chivalresque air; the Prince de Joinville, twisted and stooping, lounging on his horse; the Orleans princes with their mild, amiable faces and aspect of languid interest—in all, a most remarkable group of figures. A horse's length in advance sat the smallest man of the party, broadshouldered, strong-chested, strong-necked, and strong-jawed, one hand upon his hip, while the other, by an occasional rapid motion, flung some communication to the passing squadrons of cavalry. The visor of his cap was well pulled down over his eyes, yet not a man in the lines escaped his observation. His glance seemed to take in at once the whole spectacle, yet without losing any of its smallest details. . . . Something in his figure, his attitude, and the square, tenacious set of his jaws reminded me strikingly of Field Marshal Radetzsky. I scanned the lines of his face. . . . All was cool, prompt, determined, and self-reliant.[4]

On November 20, McClellan staged his grandest exhibition. On a broad plain eight miles from Washington in the direction of Fairfax Court House, he gathered the entire Army of the Potomac. The long columns and solid squares, a hundred thousand men marching and countermarching under waving banners as bands played, made the brightest military pageant ever seen in America. Lincoln, the Cabinet, the diplomatic corps, and thousands of spectators watched. McClellan, escorted by a staff glittering with gold lace, a bodyguard, and two regiments of regular cavalry, radiated confidence. Countless recruits that autumn day, anticipating early victory, had not the slightest premonition of the terrible years of alternate defeat and victory that were to turn the glittering volunteer force into a tougher body of veterans than Hannibal's at Cannae or Frederick's at Leuthen. Yet had they been able to look ahead, few would have quailed, and not many would have repined. Word had run through the army that the review heralded an early advance, and if they were ready to give blows, they were also ready to receive them.[5]

4 Russell, *My Diary North and South;* De Trobriand, *Four Years with the Army of the Potomac,* 89–92; N. Y. *Herald,* Oct. 9; Taylor's letter Sept. 24, 1861, in N. Y. *Weekly Tribune,* Oct. 5, 1862. W. H. Beach, *The First New York (Lincoln) Cavalry,* 50, 51, says the reviews "excited the greatest enthusiasm" among troops.

5 Theodore B. Gates, *The War of the Rebellion,* 165; N. Y. *Herald, Times,* Nov. 21, 22.

[I]

While McClellan was thus imparting vigor and firmness to the army, he was making two blunders, one in his treatment of Scott, and one in his mishandling of Congressional and public opinion.

No real evidence supports McClellan's subsequent complaint that Scott regarded him jealously. It is true that the old general would have preferred the appointment of Henry W. Halleck, disapproved of McClellan's large staff, and thought an army organization by brigades sufficient. But these were the legitimate views of an old-fashioned commander, whose jealousy was for his opinions and dignity only, and whose conservative nature opposed innovation. It is also true that he doubted McClellan's scares about rebel attack. By birth and training a Southerner, he was usually more courteous to men of his own section than to Northerners. But if sensitive and irascible, he was always large-hearted; he felt a high regard for McClellan's abilities, and gave him an honest welcome to his high post.[6]

Had McClellan remembered this fall that he was technically subordinate to Scott, that with all his fussy pomposity the old general had performed unforgettable services, and that courtesy evokes courtesy, friction might have been avoided. He needed but to keep the deferential spirit of his message to Scott during the West Virginia campaign: "All that I know of war I have learned from you. . . . It is my ambition to merit your praise and never to merit your censure." He had arrived in the capital convinced that he would soon supplant Scott. Had he waited patiently, the old general's infirmities would soon have removed him—but, too impatient to wait, he first began lecturing his superior, then openly ignored him, and finally affronted him.

Spoiled by years of quick success, McClellan was made more cockily self-assertive by the adulation Washington gave him. "I find myself in a new and strange position," he wrote his wife: "President, Cabinet, General Scott, and all deferring to me. By some strange operation of magic I have become the power of the land." Not *a* power, but *the* power! Visiting the Senate to press his staff bill, he was "quite overwhelmed by the congratulations I received and the respect with which I was treated." While beseeching God for wisdom, he evinced a self-confidence more than superb. "I . . . am confident that I can lead these armies to victory once more," he wrote the day after reaching Washington. A week later he was more boastful: "I shall carry this thing *en grand* and crush the rebels in one campaign."[7]

6 Elliott, *Scott*, 733. For the West Virginia campaign, Scott even wanted McClellan given a gold medal; *McClellan's Own Story*, 82. E. B. Keyes, *Fifty Years Observation*, 407, calls Scott haughty to Yankees.

7 *McClellan's Own Story*, Ch. 5, with similar statements. Students of history must

As scores of important men spoke to him as the leader who could save the country, suggesting the Presidency or even a dictatorship, his complacency mounted to arrogance. When Scott offered his own choice for inspector-general of the army, McClellan petulantly wrote that the old general was trying "to work a traverse." A few days later, on August 8, he pushed their differences to an open breach. Mistakenly convinced that Beauregard's forces at Manassas could and would try to overwhelm the capital, he sent Scott a description of the danger and a domineering lecture on what to do about it. McClellan in fact thought that Beauregard might attack that very night, though Beauregard was completely immobilized by insufficient subsistence and want of transport.[8] Scott resentfully called McClellan in and rebuked his impertinence. From this "row" the young general strode away angrily. Scott "is always in the way," he wrote his wife; "he understands nothing, appreciates nothing." At once seeking an interview with Seward, who offered sympathy and support, McClellan followed this by visits to other Cabinet officers. Lincoln, whom he held in low esteem, he ignored.[9]

Repeating that Scott was the great obstacle, McClellan wrote his wife on August 9 (only a fortnight, be it remembered, after he reached Washington): "Tomorrow the question will probably be decided by giving me absolute control independently of him." But if he expected his Cabinet friends to produce so abrupt a dismissal of Scott, he counted without the President of the United States.

Lincoln, dismayed by this sudden quarrel, intervened. He induced McClellan to withdraw his pert letter and write Scott a conciliatory note; he induced Scott to withdraw in part a very hurt letter of August 9 to Secretary Cameron complaining bitterly of McClellan's insubordination and proffering his resignation. Had the quarrel broken into the open with publication of the two letters, it would have done Northern morale grievous damage. Scott, withdrawing his offer to resign, refused, however, to abandon his charges of insubordination and in fact added to them. The young commander, he declared, had made arrangements with some members of the Cabinet (he meant Seward, Chase, and Blair) "by whom all the greater war questions are to be settled, without report to or consultation with me, the nominal General-in-

---

always be grateful that McClellan so frankly exposed his own weaknesses in this posthumous book.

8 Beauregard, with Johnston's approval, early in August moved some brigades to the Fairfax Court House area, some advance guards even reaching the heights south of Washington. But Johnston disapproved of his idea of harassing the Union forces in order to provoke them into an attack on ground chosen by the Confederates. Roman, *Beauregard*, I, 131–134. It was doubtless these movements which frightened McClellan.

9 *McClellan's Own Story*, 84 ff.

Chief of the Army." McClellan, he added, had failed to keep him informed of troop arrivals and movements, and had frequently talked with Cabinet members on matters pertaining to Scott himself. This was true. Because McClellan had received his appointment direct from Cameron, without Scott's official endorsement, he felt that he could by-pass the usual army channels of correspondence.[10]

For weeks the bickering continued. When in mid-September the irate Scott issued a general order restricting army correspondence with the President or Secretary of War to proper channels,[11] McClellan ignored it, continuing to write directly to Cameron. He also ignored a direct order from Scott calling for returns of troops with a specification of their stations. At a later date an anonymous friend explained that he did this because he had discovered that Scott's son-in-law, Colonel Henry Lee Scott of North Carolina, serving as the general's aide, had conveyed information to the enemy; but of this grave allegation no proof was ever presented.[12] The old commander, after waiting eighteen days for a response to his order for troop-returns, sent Cameron a pathetic protest. McClellan had furnished returns to the President and some cabinet officers, he wrote, but withheld them from his military superior; he deserved court-martialling.

It is not difficult to comprehend why Scott placed so high a valuation on the abilities of Halleck, which had more than a superficial glitter. While this fifty-one-year-old officer, with degrees from Union College and West Point, had never enjoyed an opportunity to show what he could do in field command, he had distinguished himself as a military theorist, an attorney, and a business administrator. Scott knew that he had talked with two of Napoleon's marshals, had studied military arrangements in France, and had written authoritatively on defense and the art of war. He knew that Halleck, quitting the army because years of effort had brought only the starvation salary of a captain of engineers, had risen so high at the California bar that he might have become judge of the State supreme court. He knew also that Halleck had dexterously seized his

10   Scott's letters of Aug. 9, 12, are in O. R. I, xi, pt. 3, pp. 4–6.
11   O. R. III, i, 382.
12   The text of Scott's letter is in Townsend, *Anecdotes*. The accusation against Henry L. Scott, signed "Smith" and published in the N. Y. *Tribune* of March 12, 1862, declares that the young general learned of the colonel's misconduct. "General McClellan went to the President about the extraordinary denouement, and Col. Scott and Adjt.-General Thomas, who was also suspected of treachery, were summoned to the White House to be confronted on the charge. Colonel Scott confessed his guilt! What was done? Why, Colonel Scott, instead of being shot for his treason, was allowed to be placed on the retired list for life, and to receive the pay and emoluments of a lieutenant-colonel of cavalry! He immediately went to Europe, where he is doing all he can for secession!" An anonymous charge has no weight. C. W. Elliott, *Winfield Scott*, 716, asserts the patriotic constancy of the son-in-law. McClellan, *Own Story*, does not mention him.

business opportunities, becoming head of the New Almaden quicksilver mine, and of a railroad from San Francisco to San José. When the war began he was appointed major-general of the California militia, a position from which Scott lifted him to the same rank in the regular army (August 19, 1861). Of course the old general knew nothing about his personal traits. He did not know that Halleck was essentially a manager and not a leader, a bureaucrat and not a general, whose nerve in any crisis had the strength of a frayed cobweb.[13] He devoutly hoped that Halleck would succeed him, leaving McClellan the Eastern field command.

The controversy was finally ended by Scott's continued decline in health. As his dropsy, vertigo, and paralysis increased, he became unable to attend to business for more than two hours without sleep, and was hardly able to totter from his home.[14] To the approving Cabinet on October 18 Lincoln read a delicately-phrased letter notifying Scott that although he had thus far opposed any request for retirement, he would no longer object; adding that he would sometimes apply to the general for advice, and would deal generously with his official family. It is clear that some Cabinet member told McClellan of this, for next day the young general wrote his wife that although Scott was proposing to retire in favor of Halleck, the Administration had decided to accept his resignation without that condition. McClellan had been talking about forcing the issue, and was jubilant. He, of course, as the seemingly indispensable field general, had held all the trump cards.[15]

The final scene had poignant qualities. The cabinet at an early morning meeting on November 1st agreed to a formal request from Scott to be placed on the retired list. In the afternoon it accompanied Lincoln to Scott's lodgings, where, as the general lay on his couch, the President read the formal order that was required. Helped to his feet, Scott responded, and all shook hands with emotion. That night Lincoln called on McClellan to notify him of his promotion to the post of General-in-Chief. When the President expressed the hope that the vast increase of responsibility would not be embarrassing, McClellan buoyantly assured him that it would not.

A private car was provided by the Philadelphia, Wilmington, & Baltimore for Scott, who wished to go to Europe to consult medical specialists. Next morning at four, in pitch darkness amid a drenching downpour, a distinguished group headed by Cameron and Chase came to the station to see Scott off. Among them was McClellan, to whom Scott gave polite messages for his wife and baby. In a set piece of verbal pyrotechnics, McClellan showered

13 See the estimate of Halleck in J. D. Cox, *Military Reminiscences*, I, 248–262.
14 W. H. Russell had found Scott visibly weakening before Bull Run.
15 *Own Story*, 170; see the N. Y. *Times* October 24, N. Y. *Herald* Oct. 30, 1861, as reflecting the general sentiment for McClellan.

his departing commander with eulogy, which the simple-hearted old soldier received with genuine gratitude. At the same time McClellan characteristically revealed his insincerity by writing his wife: "The [general] order *was* a little rhetorical—but I wrote it *at* him—for a particular market! It seems to have accomplished the object." [16]

One wonders what were the emotions of the old hero of Lundy's Lane and Cerro Gordo as his train rolled north, and whether his classical lore gave him any sense that McClellan might yet pay the penalty of *hubris*. The new leader's impatient tactlessness not only blotted his personal record, but carried more immediate and positive disadvantages. By angering his superior, he caused Scott to diffuse the impression in important circles that Halleck—who had never seen a real battle, who had been in business since 1854, and whose reputation rested on a book, *Elements of Military Art and Science*, published at the outbreak of the Mexican War—was a martial leader of great power. The result was that Lincoln on August 19 appointed Halleck major-general, and expected important work from him. Moreover, by colloguing with Chase, Blair, and certain Congressional leaders, McClellan gave them the idea that he was determined on prompt, forcible, and decisive fighting, from which Scott's fumbling interferences withheld him. He thus aroused anticipations the disappointment of which was to cost him dear.

[II]

"How weary I am of all this business! Care after care, blunder after blunder, trick upon trick," wrote McClellan to his wife October 25. *He* was always the victim of others' acts. After long inaction, his forces did try to strike a blow—and the result was the new disaster of Ball's Bluff, October 21, 1861, only some forty miles from Washington. It illustrated both looseness of command and tactical stupidity. Brigadier-General Charles P. Stone, a West Pointer and Mexican War veteran, had been ordered to make a "slight demonstration." He undertook neither a reconnaissance nor an advance in force, both of which would have been safe, but a risky median venture. The gallant E. D. Baker, moving with somewhat excessive impetuosity, managed to become beleaguered on the Potomac bluff that Sunday afternoon with the right wing of Stone's forces.[17]

16 Nicolay and Hay, IV, 465, 466; O. R. III, i, 613, 614; Myers, *McClellan*, 226. A. K. McClure wrote in 1892 that the inside story of Scott's retirement had never been written, and it was best that it should not be. Gideon Welles gives a vivid account of a truly terrible scene between Scott and McClellan in Lincoln's presence about Oct. 1; *Diary*, I, 240-242.

17 For Ball's Bluff, see *Battles and Leaders*, II, 123-134; Committee on Conduct of the War, 1863, Pt. II, 252-510; Swinton, *Army of the Potomac*, 75-78; J. D. Patch, *The Battle of Ball's Bluff* (1958). McClellan was moving two units, one under McCall and one under Stone, and they coordinated their activities badly. A comrade who knew Baker intimately

Ball's Bluff, with its sickening scene of Union troops falling back under relentless fire in the dusk, half-scrambling, half-tumbling down the steep clay hillside to the water, shot, bayonetted, and clubbed as they searched vainly for the few boats, fell on Northern hearts like a knell of woe. Those who saw Lincoln emerge from the War Department after learning that the beloved "Ned" Baker, one of his staunchest friends, his happy, openhearted Springfield neighbor, his firm Senate ally, was dead, never forgot the moment. The President, his face streaming with tears, groped his way through the door, stricken with griefs both private and public. Stone paid a fearful penalty as scapegoat; while criticism also fell heavily upon McClellan for the vagueness of his orders, which some thought a factor in the defeat.

The army steadily gathered strength. By late November the Union volunteer forces as a whole, east and west, all along the great front from Norfolk to Leavenworth, were surpassing the authorized level of 500,000. On the 27th of that month the War Department, which had so recently been prodding the governors to lift their enlistment levels, began sending out word that all was well. You should make no plans for more regiments, it telegraphed Morgan of New York. "When those that have been authorized are filled we will be fully supplied." Cameron in a report of December 1 to Lincoln placed the total volunteer and regular strength at 660,971; and by General Order No. 135 on December 3 he made the slowing of recruitment official throughout the North. The great feat undertaken in July seemed achieved. This new national army of half a million, moreover, was no product of thoughtless enthusiasm, of heady emotion, but a force of remarkable toughness and determination. Every volunteer of common sense now knew that he was committed to a grueling, exhausting, nerve-racking conflict of uncertain duration, in which he must run a terrible gauntlet of bullets, disease, military folly, poor food, ignorant surgeons, and traitorous equipment. But to countless young men, gladly baring their breasts to the storm of war, the perils were a challenge of which patriotic devotion made light.[18]

Actually, nobody in the War Department knew the precise number of men enlisted, and it was presently found that Cameron had seriously overestimated the total. The stoppage of enlistments was a mistake for which the country would pay dearly. But the forces in hand seemed at the moment all that could be easily raised or effectively managed.

---

wrote: "As gentle and pure and unselfish and generous and eloquent and valiant a man as ever cheerfully gave his life for a noble cause." Elijah R. Kennedy, The Contest for California in 1861, pp. viii, 274–275.

18 O. R. III, i, 553–616, covers Cameron's efforts to stimulate recruiting, and later to slow it down. At the beginning of October he wanted New York to bring its force up to 200,000, and later to 125,000. His report of Dec. 1 is in O. R. III, i, 699.

Of the formidable national army, McClellan held by far the greatest single part. On October 15, his rolls listed 152,051 men. Of these, the men absent, sick, and under arrest totalled 18,850, while about 12,000 more were awaiting arms and equipment. This left 121,201 present for duty; but as about 20,000 were on "extra duty" only a little more than 100,000 were ready for use in active campaigning. Even so, this was a formidable force. Moreover, the totals rose during December, so that by Christmas Day the whole number of officers and men in the Army of the Potomac was not far from 220,000. This was within hailing distance of the figure of 273,000 which McClellan had stipulated as desirable in his midsummer memorandum to Lincoln.[19]

Even in early fall—a fall of warm, dry, pleasant weather prolonged till Christmas—the Northern public began to expect McClellan to use his army, and radical politicians, journalists, and businessmen, growing restive, spoke out bluntly. Montgomery Blair became suspicious of the general. He wrote his father October 1 that the cabinet were perplexed by enemy movements, that he and his friends suspected the Confederates had little force in Virginia but made the utmost show of what they had, and that "Lincoln himself begins to think he smells a rat." Zack Chandler, his irritation rising until he concluded that McClellan was utterly incompetent, descended on Washington late in October to try either to spur the general into action, or to induce Lincoln to replace him. "Trumbull, Wade, and myself have been busy night and day since my arrival," he wrote his wife October 27, "but whether our labor has been in vain or not, time alone must disclose. . . . If Wade and I fail in our mission, the end is at hand." And in mid-December a friend of Wade's wrote him from Indianapolis: " 'Young Napoleon' is going down as fast as he went up." [20]

McClellan, however, still working like a man possessed to bring his army to a higher pitch of efficiency, now regretted his earlier intimations that he might end the war in the autumn by a single blow. Though it would seem that by the shrewd use of spies, Virginia Unionists, and Negroes he could have collected trustworthy information, he possessed no accurate intelligence service. Instead, letting himself be deceived by the reports of his friend Allan Pinkerton, an energetic Scot who had established one of the nation's first private detective agencies in Chicago eleven years earlier, and whose services the general had transplanted from business to war, he grossly exaggerated the strength of Johnston's army at Manassas. The alarmist exaggerations of Pinkerton in handling the so-called Baltimore plot against Lincoln the

19 See Ropes, I, 258, 259, with references.
20 Blair Oct. 1, 1861, Blair-Lee Papers; Chandler Oct. 27, Chandler Papers, LC; A. Denny, Indianapolis, Dec. 16 1861, to Wade, Wade Papers, LC.

previous February showed that the reports of his operatives required much closer analysis than they received. In public and private affairs alike they tended to earn their pay by exaggerated statements of peril.[21] General James M. Wadsworth, whose force lay at Centreville, had a much better intelligence system, for he interviewed Confederate fugitives, and cultivated Negro spies. All fall and early winter he begged McClellan to strike and crush the rebels before him. They numbered only about 50,000, he correctly declared, and could be swept back like chaff. General Daniel Sickles, stationed after October on the lower Potomac, also obtained "valuable and reliable" information on the enemy from Negroes, whom he found faithful and sometimes remarkably intelligent as scouts; but McClellan distrusted Negroes and refused to meddle with slaves.

McClellan now believed, too, that he would have to leave at least 30,000 men to guard Washington, with another 30,000 on the upper and lower Potomac and at Baltimore. He believed that troops who have not been given fully three months of vigorous camp drill could not be trusted to behave with discipline in offensive operations, and knew that a large part of his army was too new to possess any such preparation. Altogether, he was positive that he must wait!

In actual fact, Johnston's army even by the end of the year amounted only to 57,337 men, of whom some 10,200 were kept in the Valley, and 6250 in the Aquia district. Thus only about 41,000 were posted at Manassas. His army was subject to the same deductions of men sick, absent, confined, and on extra-duty as McClellan's.[22] It was far more poorly equipped. We find D. H. Hill writing the Confederate War Department on Christmas Day that poor shells and an entire lack of ammunition for his best gun, a captured piece, made the artillery of his little force at Leesburg "very deficient." The Confederate troops captured at Fort Hatteras late in August had been armed with old pattern muskets, many of them roughly altered from flintlock to percussion, and had used home-made caps and ammunition of poor quality.[23]

Down to the end of December, hard ground and fair skies made military movements quite practicable. With real wonderment, Johnston later wrote that although McClellan had a much superior force near at hand, he never

21 See on Pinkerton the matter in McClellan's *Report;* R. W. Rowan, *The Pinkertons;* and Allan Pinkerton, *The Spy of the Rebellion.* For Wadsworth see Pearson, *Wadsworth,* 90–103; for Sickles, *Committee on the Conduct of the War,* 1863, Pt. 3, pp. 632–643.

22 On October 23, Confederate General Order No. 15 established the Department of Northern Virginia in three districts, the Valley (Jackson), Potomac (Beauregard), and Acquia (Holmes), with Joseph E. Johnston as head of the Department. He remained with the army based on Manassas.

23 D. H. Hill, Leesburg, Dec. 25, 1861, to Adjutant-Gen. Thomas Jordan, extra-illustrated edition *Battles and Leaders,* HL; Hatteras correspondence N. Y. *Tribune* dated Aug. 31, 1861.

interrupted the Confederate military exercises; and as the Southern cavalry was bolder than the Northern, the ground between the two armies was much more open to the Confederates. Johnston was always uneasy over his comparative weakness.[24] Had McClellan advanced with energetic celerity from Arlington against Manassas, or had he made a thrust, as Lincoln proposed, from the mouth of the Occoquan against Johnston's communications, he might have forced the main Confederate army to retreat behind the Rappahannock. In doing so, the Southerners would probably have lost guns and stores which they could ill spare, and would have had to abandon the batteries they had erected on the lower Potomac—positions from which the navy had been anxious to dislodge them. These batteries were in various ways a thorn in the Union flesh. They blockaded an important river channel, raised fears of an incursion into Maryland, threw an additional strain upon the railways reaching Washington, and flaunted Confederate energy in the face of Washington.

It would have been impossible for McClellan to advance farther than the Rappahannock. But even this limited success would have quieted the rising criticism of his inaction, and put heart into the Northern people. The clearing of the Potomac could have been followed, too, by an autumn expedition to capture Norfolk, and thus to put an end to the Confederate refitting of the *Merrimac*. But still McClellan did nothing but drill. Even the New York *Herald*, his special champion, demanded that the Potomac—"the grand highway for stores and reinforcements for the Federal army in front of Washington"—be opened, but the demand was coldly ignored.[25]

The degree to which McClellan was culpable for excessive hesitancy must not be exaggerated. A grave impediment to movement was the shortage of

24 Johnston, *Narrative*, 84 ff.; Ropes, I, 260 ff.
25 N. Y. *Herald*, October 23, 1861. The Navy Department, as Gustavus V. Fox later testified, had proposed to the War Department in June that joint measures be taken to seize the key position of Matthias Point and so assure the navigation of the Potomac. Nothing was done. In August the Navy Department renewed its proposals, but again nothing was done. In October Welles and Fox once more urged the matter, for the Port Royal expedition was soon to start, and the navy wished to send the greater part of the Potomac flotilla with it. If anything was to be done to secure the free navigation of the Potomac, it must be before the flotilla left. The navy assured Lincoln and McClellan that its gunboats would take and destroy the rebel batteries then beginning to appear on the river. This effected, a sufficient number of troops should be landed at Matthias Point to fortify and hold it.
McClellan at first promised to cooperate with 4,000 men, and the navy provided the transports, and assembled its Potomac flotilla at Matthias Point. But twice after agreeing on a date McClellan disappointed the navy. The first time his excuse was that his engineers believed so large a body of men could not be landed—so he did not send them. The navy promised *it* would get them landed. The second time he gave Fox to understand that he feared the landing might bring on a general battle. Fox Papers, N. Y. Hist. Soc.; Committee on the Conduct of the War, 1863, Pt. I, pp. 5–9.

good officers. Many regimental and some division heads were feeble reeds, and most of the men he was considering as corps commanders had never handled a thousand troops before the war. Another impediment was the rawness of numbers of the volunteers, who as W. H. Russell flatly put it, were not yet soldiers. Finally, the question of arms was paramount. Many muskets and part of the ammunition were more dangerous to the holder than to the enemy, while down to December the quantities of both were insufficient. McClellan might well decline any large-scale movement, especially as winter mud and snow could arrive any day. Nevertheless, he should have marched to Manassas, should have cleared the Potomac, and should have forced the enemy out of Norfolk. John G. Barnard, chief of engineers, was as emphatic on this as General James M. Wadsworth. General John E. Wool at Fort Monroe was equally realistic.[26]

As the opening of Congress approached in December the grumbling deepened. Senators Chandler, Wade, and Trumbull, whom John Hay already termed the heads of a Jacobin Club, had been badgering Lincoln to insist on a battle. They felt betrayed, for when they had assailed Scott as feeble, they had promised their friends that McClellan would move promptly. National morale, they told Lincoln, required a show of energy; delay would be as bad as defeat. Greeley was thundering in the *Tribune* that McClellan's inaction had allowed the rebels to close the Potomac east of Washington, and disrupt the Baltimore & Ohio west of the city. Already these Republicans had a suspicion that McClellan was letting politics color his military policy. They perhaps heard reports of such letters as that which he wrote his Democratic friend S. L. M. Barlow on November 8—a missive of the first importance in the light it throws on his thinking. After expatiating on Confederate strength and Union weakness, and declaring that he would "pay no attention to popular clamor," he went on:

I expect to fight a terrible battle. I know full well the capacity of the generals opposed to me, for by a singular chance they were once my most intimate friends.—tho' we can never meet except as mortal foes hereafter. I appreciate too the courage and discipline of the rebel troops. . . . When I am ready I shall move without regard to season or weather—I can overcome *these* difficulties. . . . But of one thing you may rest assured—when the blow *is* struck it will be heavy, rapid, and decisive.

26 Barnard wrote in his report at the close of the Peninsular campaign: "In the winter of 1861 and 1862, Norfolk could and should have been taken. The navy demanded it, the country demanded it, and the means were ample." Wool wrote Stanton February 27, 1862, that Fort Monroe was the proper base from which to assail Richmond. "The rebel army at Manassas ought not to escape capture. It does not amount to more than 30,000 men—at most 35,000 at both Manassas and Centreville." Copy in Hay Papers, Illinois State Hist. Library.

Help me to dodge the nigger—we want nothing to do with him. *I am fighting to preserve the integrity of the Union and the power of the Govt—on no other issue.* To gain that end we cannot afford to mix up the negro question—it must be incidental and subsidiary. The President is perfectly honest and is really sound on the nigger question. I will answer for it now that things go right with him.

As far as you can, keep the papers and the politicians from running over me—that speech that some rascal made the other day that I did *not dare* to advance, and had said so, was a lie. I have always said, when it was necessary to say anything, that I was not yet strong enough, but did the public service require it, I would *dare* to advance with 10,000 men and throw my life in the balance.[27]

Already Zack Chandler and Ben Wade were urging the enlistment of Negroes as soldiers; already they and others were hoping to make the extirpation of slavery a primary result of the war. The press was beginning to debate these demands. Bryant, Greeley, and Medill were urging emancipation; on the other side, the Philadelphia *Evening Journal*, a moderate Democratic sheet, was indicting the Abolitionists as men whose views would lengthen and embitter the conflict. The real struggle in the South, it declared, would be between aristocracy and democracy, not between slavery and freedom. "As affairs have now turned, the disenthralment of the poor white people of the slaveholding States has thrown entirely into the shade the worn-out question of Negro emancipation. . . . It is now becoming apparent that the population of Haiti by the colored people of the country will prove the ultimate and practical solution of the question." [28]

To the Chandlers and Wades such talk was unreal. They meant by hard blows military and political to revolutionize the South. Their violence of language was outrageous and inexcusable.[29] Much saner men, however, were convinced that the high financial costs, the danger of foreign intervention, and the importance of removing the sting of recent defeats, made bold aggressive action imperative. "Let us end the war!" cried the New York *Tribune* on December 18, declaring that winter was the best fighting season in the South. "The offensive," later wrote General Fry, "was demanded from all quarters, and in all ways." [30]

27 Barlow Papers.
28 October 21, 1861.
29 Chandler's letters this fall approached hysteria. "If we fail in getting a battle here now all is lost," he wrote his wife October 27, "and up to this time a fight is scarcely contemplated. Washington is safe. . . . therefore let the country go to the devil. If the South had one-tenth our resources Jeff Davis would today be in Philadelphia." In another letter he remarked that it might be better if the rebels really took Washington, President, Cabinet, and all, for then the true men would make proper use of the nation's powers. Chandler Papers, LC.
30 *Century Magazine*, vol. 48 (Oct., 1894), 931–946.

It was not only McClellan's caution, his perfectionism, and his readiness to exaggerate enemy strength while underrating his own, that was responsible for his immobility, for an even more important factor was involved. Already he was displaying a myopic indifference to those great forces of politics and public opinion which no democratic commander can neglect save at his peril. In a letter the day before he replaced Scott he lashed out at "the impatience of the people, the venality and bad faith of the politicians, the gross neglect that has occurred in obtaining arms, clothing, etc." But in a people's war, the people and their political delegates must be regarded. As they must not make excessively severe demands on military leadership, so military leaders must not make excessively severe demands on them.

In a public speech soon after reaching Washington, McClellan had promised a war short, sharp, and decisive. During his early rides south of the Potomac, he used to point toward the flank of Manassas and say to General McDowell: "We shall strike them there." [31] It was his duty to take account of the morale of the country as well as of the army. By Thanksgiving and still more by Christmas, the nation which had put such implicit faith in him felt it had a right to ask some justification for their faith. For the people were not content, any more than their British cousins in the Crimean conflict had been, to leave all decisions blindly to their military captains; as the historian of the Crimea had written, they "thronged in, and made their voice heard, and became partakers of the councils of state."

But while the East waited, in the Western theater a yet more remarkable series of events had been taking place; events both dramatic and momentous.

31 Swinton, *Army of the Potomac*, 69; McClellan's *Own Story*, 166–177.

16

Frémont and the Impossible Task

THE NORTH by the summer of 1861, as we have seen, had done more than enter upon a grim war effort. It and indeed the whole country had entered upon a revolution. Never before had the American people dreamed of such a mighty effort of organization as that required by the mustering of a volunteer army of half a million, and the commissioning of a tremendous fleet. No government, after such an effort, could ever sink back to the old level of small enterprises pettily pursued. Behind the drilling troops and scurrying ships new industries were taking form, new factories were belching smoke, banks, stores, and warehouses were being enlarged to seize new opportunities, and the wheels of transport were turning with new speed. Novel sources of credit, novel government contracts, and novel concepts of large-scale effort were transforming business and society.

Had some miracle of compromise ended the war in the summer of 1861, the country would have emerged with but minor changes in non-political fields. Bull Run had made it certain that a considerable socio-economic revolution would occur. If the mighty military effort planned for 1862 succeeded, it would be merely considerable. But if it failed, and the conflict continued, the country would face a major revolution, altering many of the organic functions of society. How deep such a revolution might reach, and what social agonies it might involve, first became evident to observers of events in the Western theatre, and especially in Missouri.

The Western situation differed completely from the Eastern in a half-dozen respects. Fighting raged in States—Missouri, Kentucky, Tennessee—whose people were implacably divided; in areas, therefore, where searing hatreds soon generated a vicious guerrilla warfare. In this region long Union lines had to be held: the Missouri River from Kansas City to its mouth, the Mississippi from Quincy to Cairo, the railroad from St. Louis to Rolla, and the Ohio River. The theatre was distant from Washington, the major arsenals, and the centers of greatest population and wealth. Here was the area where commanders first had to come to real grips with slavery. Here, military jealousies showed their worst early forms, and here politics most seriously complicated the military effort. A rougher, harsher temper, derived partly from frontier individualism, pervaded the struggle.

The West required a commander who possessed great political skill as well as military ability. In Missouri he would have to rally loyal elements while repressing the disloyal men intermingled with them; in Kentucky he would have to evince a scrupulous respect for those who supported State neutrality. He would have to deal with difficult political leaders—one in particular. Frank P. Blair, who had thus far led the Union movement in Missouri with more drive than discretion, cherished high political ambitions. Valuing greatly his seat in Congress and chairmanship of the military affairs committee, he did not yet aim at a military command, for which he had no experience whatever. He expected, however, to be the main power in Missouri; and as the first freesoil man elected to Congress from a slave State, co-leader with Edward Bates of the Republican Party there in 1860, and the most brilliant orator of the area, he already possessed national renown and influence. The commander would have to defer to him, or risk the consequences—and he had a most imperious temper. The commander would also have to get along with governors of complex psychology, like Yates of Illinois and Kirkland of Iowa, keeping their confidence, meeting their wants, and enlisting their aid. Nathaniel Lyon had made so many enemies both in Washington and Missouri that he was impossible.

McClellan despised politicians, but the Western commander could afford no such attitude.

[I]

For this post of double danger Lincoln, pressed by the Blair family, selected a man of few military and no political qualifications—John C. Frémont. That Frémont had never commanded more than the few hundred men of his California Battalion, and they briefly and controversially, might not be a crippling disability; very few American officers had led a larger body. That as Senator from California and first Republican Presidential candidate he had shown no political flair was not important; he had been a novice. What did matter was that Lincoln should ignore Frémont's erratic career.

Frémont had indubitably proved himself an explorer of high distinction. Brilliantly intelligent, energetic, daring, and able to inspire expeditions with his own enthusiasm, he had united scientific skill with the ability to endure prolonged hardship. A pathmarker, not pathfinder, he had traversed, mapped, and described great areas of the West in a way that did the nation important service. His knowledge of mathematics, zoology, botany, astronomy, and geology outran that of other famous Western explorers; he wrote with a color and narrative interest that his best rivals hardly approached. The man who had climbed the Wind River Range, discovered Lake Tahoe, scaled the Sierras in midwinter, given the Golden Gate its name, and penned a book which guided the Mormons into Salt Lake Valley, deserved his first fame. The role he had played in the conquest and early government of California, while often indiscreet and at times calculating, contained some heroic pages; and his Presidential candidacy emphasized his rigid freesoil principles.[1]

Close scrutiny of his career, however, disclosed an impetuosity that had repeatedly brought him to the verge of disaster, a want of judgment that disturbed his friends, and a willingness to invade dubious ground for personal advantage. Although cultured, sensitive, and quietly attractive, he had made an equivocal impression. Because he grasped at prizes, such as the civil governorship of California, which he had not honestly earned, he appeared a little the charlatan; because he tempted fortune in so many fields, sometimes failing tragically, as in the fifth expedition, and sometimes succeeding magnificently, as when he emerged from his famous court-martial to find the California senatorship and rich Mariposa estate in his hands, he seemed a little the adventurer. Though he did useful work in helping open the West, all his other labors had an illusory value. While some intimates of great discernment and honesty, like Jessie Benton, Horace Greeley, and Kit Carson, felt a lifelong devotion to him, other people thought that his character was *au fond* questionable. In 1860 he was still a hero to millions of Americans, the recent titular leader of the Republican Party, and a figure of international renown. The Lincoln Administration had to employ him; but why in a post of such multifarious difficulties?

Frémont would have preferred the ministership to France, where his knowledge of the country, fluency in its tongue, and social brilliancy, with the charm of his wife Jessie, would have made him far more successful than the political hack whom Lincoln appointed. The Blairs, after failing to get Lyon the chief command, could have found a West Point man for Missouri. But Frémont and Jessie were old favorites whom they expected to control in Frank's interest and therefore pushed forward. Eager to serve, and convinced that his Western marches qualified him for command, he accepted. When war began he had been in Europe on business, and had shown creditable energy by contracting for $75,000 worth of ordnance and shells and 10,000

---

1 See the author's volumes on Frémont, and especially the third edition of the biography, with the new material on the Civil War in the terminal chapter.

rifles at his personal charge if necessary. He reached Boston June 27 and reported forthwith to Lincoln.

Within less than a week after he landed, on July 3, the government created the Western Department, including not only Illinois and all the States and Territories between the Mississippi and Rockies, but Kentucky as soon as it was safe.[2] It should have taken this action at an earlier date. The fact was that Washington showed a censurable myopia concerning the West, and persisted in it. Once Frémont was appointed he might well have hurried West more promptly. He had his reasons for tarrying—he could learn more about the huge department, covering a third of the nation, in Washington than in St. Louis; when he was about to leave on July 16th or 17th he was told that Scott had further instructions for him; he talked with Governor Yates in Washington, learning that 7000 Illinois infantry were totally unarmed, the cavalry without mounts, and the artillery with few guns; he labored to assemble a staff, and obtain firearms and stores for his destitute forces. But Lincoln became disturbed by the delay. In the end he went West with vague orders and inadequate resources.

The President, Scott, and he agreed that the grand objective, once Missouri was cleared, would be a movement down the Mississippi to Memphis. Lincoln, after consulting with him in the kindliest way, escorted him down the White House steps, saying: "I have given you carte blanche; you must use your own judgment and do the best you can." Thus blithely did the overburdened government entrust the heaviest responsibilities to an untried man, and speak of seizing a river which it was to take two years of heavy fighting to clear! [3]

When Frémont reached Missouri on July 25 he found the Western Department boiling with confusion, shortages, dissension, and perils. The State had far more white manpower of military age than Virginia, and as much as Kentucky and Arkansas combined. It was more fiercely divided among

---

2 From July 3 to Nov. 9, 1861, the Western Department comprised Illinois, Missouri, Iowa, Kansas, Minnesota, Arkansas, Nebraska Territory, Colorado Territory, Dakota Territory and for a time a portion of Kentucky. Indiana and Ohio were in the Department of Ohio; Wisconsin temporarily in no department. Frederick Phisterer, *Statistical Record*, 24–49.

3 Frémont, MS Memoirs, Bancroft Library. Frémont told the Committee on the Conduct of the War that his instructions were vaguely broad, embracing "full discretionary powers of the amplest kind," and that "when I was ready to descend the river I was to let the President know." Montgomery and Frank Blair, though suspect witnesses, doubtless testified correctly to the Committee on Lincoln's uneasiness over Frémont's delay; *Report*, 1863, Pt. 3, pp. 154–186. Rutherford B. Hayes's impressions of Frémont, who reviewed Ohio troops at Camp Chase on his way west, suggest why a high appointment for the explorer was a political necessity. "All his words and acts inspire enthusiasm and confidence," wrote Hayes after a chat, adding: "He is loyal, brave, and persevering beyond compare"; *Diary and Letters*, II, 43.

Southern-born, Northern-born, and foreign-born than any other in the country. Largely ignored by the War Department, it was slipping into a dangerous set of complications.

We have seen that full war had begun in Missouri before mid-June, when General Nathaniel Lyon had arrogantly told Sterling Price that before he made a single concession to the rebels, he would see every man, woman, and child in the State buried. Lyon immediately sent Colonel Franz Sigel to occupy southwestern Missouri, while he himself marched to Jefferson City, the capital, on June 15, and two days later took Boonville in an almost bloodless skirmish. But the Confederates showed equal energy. Governor Claiborne Jackson, resolute and resourceful, issued a call for fifty thousand volunteers to resist the Union "invasion." At Carthage on July 5 his gathering volunteers repulsed Sigel and forced him to retreat. Price, who had been a brigadier-general in the Mexican War, was ready to take the field with the State troops, reinforced by several thousand Confederate soldiers from Arkansas, Louisiana, and Texas under Ben McCulloch, a hard-riding, quick-shooting Texas ranger who had also served in Mexico. Encouraged by the smart victory at Carthage and the news of Bull Run, the Confederate and State forces by the time of Frémont's arrival raised their main army to 10,000 or 11,000 men.

Meanwhile irregular warfare covered half the State. The precipitate actions of Frank Blair and Lyon exposed the loyal population to guerrilla bands and marauders. Some 300 home guard men, driven from Knox and Lewis Counties into Hudson City at the beginning of July, reported that a force of 2700 rebels, chiefly mounted, were seizing food, arms, livestock, and clothing. In other areas Union men were being expelled from their homes. Small, undisciplined, badly-led bands of secessionists, animated by implacable hatred of the North, roved the countrysides. When Union forces appeared, they would separate; little groups would shoot stray soldiers, burn bridges, or waylay loyal farmers; then they would reunite. Particularly in the proslavery counties belting the Missouri River all the way across the State, the most ferocious feeling reigned. Neighbor armed against neighbor in an atmosphere of spreading terror.

The tension laid an iron grip on St. Louis, a Southern city which had recently become a metropolis of freedom for the State. Of its 160,000 people, more than one in four had been born in Germany, more than 30,000 in Ireland, and more than 21,000 in the free States; most of the forces of industry, commerce, and finance were inimical to slavery. Nevertheless, the old aristocratic families, Southern-born men of social position, and some wealthy business leaders, were Confederate in sentiment. Either openly or secretly secessionist, they gave their tone to clubs, restaurants, and drawing-rooms, lent business support to their kind, and influenced their employees. Since the breakup of Camp Jackson and the clashes between German recruits and the people, the malignity of some Southern sympathizers broke all bounds. Women were more rancorous than the men, and even ministers of the gospel spread hatred. After the victory at Carthage one secessionist jubilantly told a free-soil leader: "There is a bullet moulded for every Yankee sympathizer in St. Louis." [4]

Over the Berthold mansion in late July, conspicuous in the heart of the city, flew a Confederate flag, beneath whose folds recruits openly enlisted for the Confederate cause. The streets were bare of Union banners; city authorities were afraid to intervene against rebel activities; danger that the roughest of the unemployed Irish, aided by Southerners, would mount an insurrection, impressed all observers. The German and Yankee volunteers, a determined but undisciplined body of men, would have met such a rising implacably. "Arouse their enthusiasm," Gustave Koerner had written Lyman Trumbull, "and they are uncontrollable." [5] As Lyon had kindled their fervor, so later would Frémont. But bloody civil commotions in St. Louis, the principal Union base for the whole region, were at all costs to be avoided.

[II]

To this angrily divided city and State, humming like a hornet's nest, Frémont was ferried across the Mississippi at nine A.M. on July 25, to convoke a staff meeting at noon. It gave him alarming intelligence. The enemy had their troubles: their State and Confederate troops were separate and often discordant forces, they were ill-armed, and they suffered from Richmond's neglect as the Unionists suffered from Washington's. But Price and McCulloch could concentrate their growing forces in a way that kept the Union commands, necessarily scattered, on the defensive. Lyon was at Springfield with about 7800 men, including Sigel's defeated troops; Brigadier-General John Pope commanded most of the troops north of the Missouri River; and Brigadier-General Benjamin M. Prentiss, a Mexican War veteran, had a weak contingent at Cairo. All three badly wanted reinforcements and supplies. On Frémont's desk lay a telegram from Prentiss, for example, reciting that he had only eight regiments, six of them three-months' men whose term was then

---

4 The MS Autobiography of Charles D. Drake, later Senator from Missouri, is indispensable (Mo. Hist. Soc.). W. L. Broaddus, Hudson City, July 5, describes the situation there; Broaddus Papers, Duke Univ. See also Snead, *The Fight for Missouri*, 99 ff. (anti-Blair); W. G. Eliot in Nevins, *Frémont*, 542 ff.; R. J. Rombauer, *The Union Cause in St. Louis, 1861, passim*; Galusha Anderson, *The Story of a Border City*.

5 Koerner, May 31, Trumbull Papers, LC.

expiring, and desperately needed more to hold his vital point. Lyon's force, rapidly diminishing, also threatened to disappear if the three-months' men left; he was naturally anxious to fight before they quit. Many were without shoes. Food, wagons, medicines, uniforms, but above all arms were wanting. "Our troops have not been paid," Frémont wrote Lincoln July 30, "and some regiments are in a state of mutiny, and the men whose term of service is expired generally refuse to enlist."

Had Washington created its Western Department as soon as hostilities opened, by June 20; had it brought Frémont home earlier, or put someone else in St. Louis betimes; had it paid closer attention to the West, the lowering storm might have been met. Yates, Morton, and other governors had been quite as strenuous as their Eastern compeers in getting men enlisted and brought into State camps; but up to the belated hour of Frémont's arrival too little had been done to assemble, arm, and drill them.

It may seem anomalous that the Confederates in Missouri were able to concentrate more efficiently than the Union forces. The explanation lies partly in the geographical situation of Missouri as an exposed salient, partly in the fierce secessionist passions that Blair and Lyon had aroused, and partly in confused Northern leadership. From southern Kansas, Arkansas, Tennessee, and Kentucky, all contiguous, the Confederates could bring what troops they had—which were few—to aid the Missouri volunteers. Meanwhile, the Union command had, as we have noted, to hold the Missouri River and its hostile belt, the Mississippi to Cairo, the Ohio to Louisville, and three railways, one running to Sedalia three-fourths of the way across the State, one southwest to Rolla, almost halfway across, and a third south to Ironton, also halfway across. It had to hold three vital centers, Jefferson City, St. Louis, and Cairo. All this meant overextended lines. And between Frank Blair's departure for Congress about July 1 and Frémont's arrival three weeks later, Lyon had done nothing to pull the situation together, for he was preoccupied with his own little army. Washington looked on aloof.[6]

Rather, Washington looked the other way! Frémont, rebuffed July 29 when he asked the Treasury office in St. Louis to allot his paymaster some funds, sent urgent telegrams to Montgomery Blair. Reaching Washington just after Bull Run, they fell on deaf ears. "I . . . find it impossible now to get any attention to Missouri or western matters from the authorities here," wired Blair. Jessie Frémont begged permission to hurry to the capital and tell Lincoln of the defenseless condition of the West, but her husband refused. Coming through Ohio, they had met Western troops on their way to the Potomac.

6 *Battles and Leaders*, I, 278 ff.; Nicolay and Hay, IV, Ch. 23; Smith, *Blair Family*, II, 59 ff.; O. R. I, iii, 617 ff.; Nevins, *Frémont*, Ch. 29; Drake, MS Autobiography.

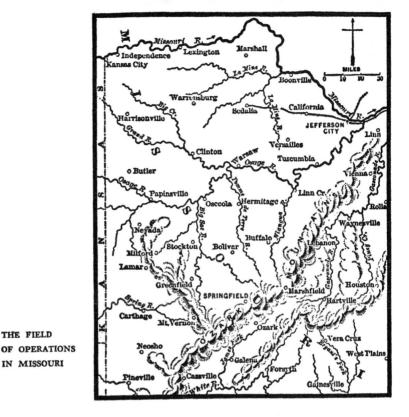

THE FIELD
OF OPERATIONS
IN MISSOURI

In St. Louis she found troops only on paper, an arsenal without arms or ammunition, the enemy thick and unremitting as mosquitoes. If only she could get to the President!—"a Western man and not grown in red tape." But her letters to Washington accomplished nothing. She wrote Montgomery Blair four days after reaching St. Louis that her husband was overwhelmed:

He is doing the best he can without money without arms without moral aid. This city needs a force to repress it. All the arms and well equipped men of Ohio and Indiana we met moving *to the East*. Mr. Frémont says send anything in the shape of arms—but arms we must have. Send money, and both arms and money by the most rapid conveyance.

Frémont sounded the same desperate note in a letter to Blair July 31:

I begin to move today but am distressed by singular inadequacy and scarcity of equipment and great want of arms. At this moment I learn from the Adjutant that two regiments are refusing to move—refusing pay unless they get the whole. My boats have fires up and my movements are checked by this most inopportune lack of money. . . . One regiment had to be compelled to go to Ironton today by arresting officers—it had been in a state of mutiny all day.[7]

7 Jessie Frémont, July 28, Frémont July 31, to Montgomery Blair, Blair Papers, LC.

Frémont had not only to make bricks without straw, but to throw these bricks into hastily improvised walls. Into his first ten days he crowded a series of urgent measures. He policed St. Louis thoroughly, stopping Confederate enlistments at the Berthold mansion, clearing the saloons of soldiers, giving Union residents security, and enforcing rigid drill. Booksellers reported a rising demand for Hardee's *Tactics* and like books. He reorganized the home guard in St. Louis, enlisting men for the war in infantry, cavalry, and artillery divisions. He seized possession of the railroads to Rolla and Ironton, and sent small detachments to protect them. He garrisoned Ironton with a force under Colonel B. Gratz Brown, secured Cape Girardeau, and ordered Pope to organize local committees of safety north of the Missouri to stop guerrilla activities. He *took* from the paralyzed Treasury office in St. Louis $100,000 needed to pay troops. "I have infused energy and activity into the department," he wrote Lincoln, praising the spirit of his forces.[8]

At the outset he had to make a momentous decision. Imminent danger threatened both Lyon at Springfield in southwestern Missouri, and Prentiss at Cairo; he could not adequately reinforce both; and he chose to help Prentiss. Beyond question Cairo was the more important position. Real danger existed that the rebels would sweep all lower Missouri, seize Cairo by a sudden stroke, carry Kentucky into the Confederacy, and rally their sympathizers in southern Illinois and Indiana. If they succeeded in this, they might virtually win the war. Major-General Leonidas Polk, commanding the Confederates at Memphis, had prepared early in July to invade Missouri for a broad-fronted campaign. While McCulloch proceeded against Lyon at Springfield, columns under General Gideon Pillow and W. J. Hardee were to march up the Mississippi, cut off Lyon's retreat, take St. Louis if possible, and on their return to enter Illinois and capture Cairo. This was too grandiose a plan to be practicable. Nevertheless, at the very time Frémont arrived in St. Louis, Polk moved 6000 troops up to New Madrid, Missouri, full of enthusiasm and eager to attack. On July 29, the frightened Prentiss informed Frémont that more than 12,000 Confederates lay within fifty miles of his puny force. On August 1 he telegraphed that Pillow had 11,000 men at New Madrid and was about to be reinforced by 9000 more.

Even if these figures were cut in half, or in three, Cairo was in peril. Lyon was also telegraphing that he wanted "soldiers-soldiers-soldiers." But Lyon could retreat, and Prentiss with his little force could not.

Sending word to Lyon that he had best fall back to his railhead at Rolla, Frémont correctly decided to hurry reinforcements to the vital confluence of the Ohio and Mississippi. Amid the other labors of this first week, he char-

8 O. R. I, iii, 416 ff.; Frémont wrote Lincoln July 30.

tered eight steamboats, loaded them with soldiers, artillery, and stores, and set off down the river. He had hardly slept. Five P.M. on August 2 found his 4000 men landing amid wild cheers at the Cairo wharves. They had come in the nick of time, for Prentiss's force was fast disintegrating. Poorly fed, badly clothed, and only partially supplied with tents, it was suffering from the malarial fever and dysentery that ran rife in its swampy position. Now they could be paid, properly armed (for Frémont was able to bring west some of the equipment he had bought in Europe) and reënlisted. From that hour Cairo was never again in danger.[9]

But Lyon had been left unaided. Frémont was able to order two regiments from Rolla and Boonville, with James Montgomery's small force in Leavenworth, to join him, but their arrival would take time. The consequence was that little over a fortnight after Frémont took up his duties, Lyon came to disaster—and Lyon was a favorite of Frank Blair.

That this disaster was wholly needless there can be little question. Though the Confederate army which marched on Lyon numbered only 13,000 ill-trained, poorly armed men, it was far stronger than his own force of about 5000. It included a large mounted force which fetched it fresh horses and provisions without interference. Lyon's duty, as Ben McCulloch approached Springfield, was to retreat and save his army. His second in command, John M. Schofield, argued this with almost insubordinate vehemence. As he pointed out, while a victory was possible, it was not probable; defeat would sacrifice many lives and much valuable material; and the road back to Rolla was open and safe as late as the night of August 9th. Once Lyon joined the Union troops at Rolla, he could soon build up a strength sufficient to drive McCulloch out of the State. "This, I doubt not," wrote Schofield years later, "must be the judgment of history." Frémont for his part expected Lyon to fall back to meet his reinforcements. On August 6 he sent him instructions that if he were not strong enough to maintain his position, he should retreat until met by fresh detachments; and to a messenger from Lyon he said bluntly, "If he fights, it will be upon his own responsibility."

But Lyon was proud, pugnacious, and headstrong. He exaggerated both the perils of the retreat, and the disaster to loyal citizens if he abandoned them to Confederate wrath; and, stung by being passed over for the chief command,

9 O. R. I, iii, 416–437, cover the main Missouri events; *Comm. on the Conduct of the War*, 1863, pp. 3, 35 ff.; Frémont, MS Memoirs, Bancroft Library; Nevins, *Frémont;* Blair Papers, LC. News of Confederate movements toward Cairo reached the North through the New Albany (Indiana) *Ledger,* which had correspondents in Tennessee, Arkansas, and Southern Missouri. It reported in late July that 12,000 troops had crossed the Mississippi to New Madrid, where they would be joined by others from the three States named, with artillery, to make a swift attack on Cairo. The *National Intelligencer* of August 6 congratulated Frémont on opportunely rescuing Cairo.

he indulged an unworthy jealousy of his superior—his failure to get reinforcements seemed to him, says Schofield, "due to a plan to sacrifice him to another." Of course Frémont might have sent him a peremptory order. But the newly-arrived general deferred to Lyon's West Point education, knowledge of the local situation, and superior information on the enemy's capacities. On the 10th Lyon attacked at Wilson's Creek.

It was a characteristically confused, disorganized battle, the encounter of two badly armed mobs. McCulloch and Price had barely completed the distribution of their men into companies and regiments. Their troops were in great part armed only with the hunting rifles and shotguns they had brought from home. "We have an average of only twenty-five rounds of ammunition to the man," later wrote McCulloch, "and no more to be had short of Fort Smith and Baton Rouge." Not one Confederate in four had anything better than a cotton bag for his ammunition, so that a good shower would almost have disarmed the troops. They had to live on the country. Lyon, deciding to move upon the Confederates in their positions at dawn, lost the advantage of his long-range rifled muskets, and of the fact that later in the day thousands of Confederates would have been absent from the camp foraging. He used a bad battle plan devised by Sigel. Even so, the Union troops seemed winning until a Confederate battery opened on Sigel with heavy effect. Long lines of men battled at close range amid clouds of billowing smoke. In the mêlée a Confederate ball pierced Lyon's breast, and a few minutes later the surviving Union officers, after a hasty council, ordered a retreat.[10] Colonel John M. Palmer delivered his verdict in a letter to his wife: "The truth is that the battle of Wilson's Creek was a folly which the gallant death of Gen. Lyon does not atone for." [11]

The immediate result was an intensification of guerrilla warfare in central and northern Missouri, and an augmentation of Confederate strength. Frémont at once telegraphed Yates, Morton, and Dennison, with the adjutant-general of Iowa, to send him all their disposable forces. He pushed forward plans to fortify St. Louis so that smaller forces might hold it. From New York he ordered arms by fast freight "without further bargaining." He planned that while the remnants of Lyon's army rested and recruited at Rolla, he would occupy all the principal Missouri River towns by the new volunteer army, fortify Ironton, and garrison Warsaw on the Osage River. As soon as he could collect a strong army, he meant to march on Springfield again, and drive the Confederates out of southwestern Missouri into Arkansas. Lincoln,

10 Scofield, *Forty-Six Years*, 40 ff.; Frémont, MS Memoirs; McCulloch, Report dated Dec. 22, 1861, *Mo. Hist. Review*, Vol. XXVI, 354 ff.; Snead, 253.
11 Palmer August 15, 17, 1861, to his wife, describes the battle, Palmer Papers III. State Hist. Lib.

the War Department, and Montgomery Blair, shocked by Lyon's defeat, promised to do everything possible in his behalf.[12]

[III]

It is clear that Frémont found rough work in his first twenty days in Missouri—and his road got rougher and stonier at every step. His initial hardships grew out of the fact that Blair and Lyon had pushed Missouri into full war prematurely, that Washington had made practically no preparations in the West, that the War Department continued to think primarily of the East, and that in Lyon he had a rash subordinate. Thus far the story was simple, but now it grew fearfully, weirdly, calamitously complicated. To comprehend it we must understand the greenness of the troops, the lack of supplies, the difficulties of the contract problem, the bad officer morale, and the political aims of the Blairs. All these difficulties were heightened by his own blunders and miscalculations.

When appointed, Frémont was allowed only three aides from the army line, but the law of August 5 permitted him as major-general to nominate as large a staff as he needed. Lacking McClellan's advantages in choosing old regular-army friends, he gradually assembled a competent group of men, largely of foreign experience.[13] His chief of staff was Brigadier-General A. Asboth, a veteran of Kossuth's revolt, whom John A. Dix pronounced "a very able man as an engineer," and a good planner, "very intelligent on general subjects." He was hardworking and systematic. Asboth chose as personal aid Colonel Anselm Albert, an officer of fourteen years' experience in the Austrian army, of sound executive ability. The duties of adjutant were entrusted to Chauncey McKeever, and those of quartermaster-general to Major Justus McKinstry. The chief topographical engineer was Colonel John T. Fiala, capable in his field. The military secretary was a young chaplain, John H. Eaton, who would later make a creditable record in care of the freedmen and in education. A Cincinnati attorney of note, R. M. Corwine, joined Frémont as judge-advocate, to pass on the many arrests in Missouri, high and low, for disloyalty; and Lincoln himself later assured Stanton that he had done valuable service.

Competent as it was, the staff had in its foreign coloration one pronounced defect: It could give Frémont, himself unfamiliar with many sides of Ameri-

12 Comm. on Conduct of the War, *Report*, 1863, Pt. 3, pp. 110–114. One regiment Frémont wanted was stopped at Louisville as needed there, and another sent to Virginia; *Ibid.*, 117.
13 General Orders No. 15 announced to the staff, St. Louis, September 20; copy in McClernand Papers, Ill. State Library.

can life, little practical counsel in a situation full of political problems. Nor were the civilian aides who nominated themselves to his staff much more helpful. One was Owen Lovejoy, an abolitionist clergyman who had been a Republican member of Congress from northern Illinois since 1857; able, idealistic, and full of learning, humor, and eloquence, but fanatical on slavery. Another was Gustave Koerner, who had fled from the Frankfurt revolt of 1833 to become one of the founders of the "Latin settlement" (he held a Heidelberg doctorate) at Belleville, Illinois, and who after a term on the State supreme court had been elected lieutenant-governor. Still another was William Dorsheimer of Buffalo, a bright young German-American lawyer. Most important of all was Jessie, indefatigably busy, full of ideas, and as impetuous as her husband. This group had an earnest, radical, and impractical stamp.

The new commander toiled day and night, shutting himself all too rigidly away from time-wasting callers. While McClellan spent whole days in the saddle, Frémont stuck closely to his desk, for he had no War Department at hand to assist him, and no such experienced officer as Montgomery C. Meigs to lift part of his burden. For five weeks, according to one of his best aides, he never went farther from the door of his combined residence and headquarters than the sidewalk.[14]

Volunteer regiments swept into St. Louis by train, by steamboat, and afoot, as they swept into Washington. Their greenness was incredible. "The new levies," lamented Frémont, "are literally the rawest ever got together." Officers reported them "entirely unacquainted with the rudiments of military exercises." How could he drill the mob? When he asked permission to scour the nation for veteran officers, Cameron gave it. Not only did he collect a considerable number of drillmasters, but he created a special infantry unit, the Benton Cadets, which he expected to make a school for infantry officers just as his so-called Frémont bodyguard was a school for cavalry officers. Asboth was highly efficient in seeing that the new regiments drilled hard, steadily, and with growing precision. One of Frémont's plans was to form in each regiment a company of sharpshooters which would include the best marksmen, and a company of pioneers to include the most skilled mechanics.

Yet as the flood of volunteers rolled in from all parts of the Northwest, the difficulties grew. Confusion, wrote John Pope from St. Louis August 22, "is worse confounded every moment by the arrival without previous notice of regiments from every Western State in a condition of ignorance and

14 Comm. on the Conduct of the War, *ut supra*, 20 ff. See the *National Intelligencer*, August 20, 1861, for some of Frémont's organizational plans.

greenness altogether appalling. They are sent out to camp on the outskirts of the city without knowledge of their duties and with no one to instruct them in even the most ordinary details of service." [15] Other regiments went to interior railheads. These termini, Pope continued, "have become the seat of a struggling, disorganized mass of men who are swarming among and over each other like ants, and who are organized with the title of a 'military force.' What will be the result when it is attempted to move these disorderly bands forward for action will be hard to say." The Northwestern States had less of a militia tradition than the East, and no such venerable regiments as New York and New England had cherished. Its sons were rougher and more individualistic. Frémont, like McClellan, was determined not to move until his men were partly trained and fairly armed.

Shortages, shortages, shortages! When B. Gratz Brown was first sent to Rolla he had found no provisions, no water, no tents, no cartridge boxes—nothing. He telegraphed that supplies were "absolutely necessary." Lyon's troops had reached Springfield unpaid, ill-fed, in dilapidated clothing, and in part shoeless. S. A. Hurlbut, the drunken brigadier ordered to hold the Hannibal & St. Joe Railroad, had telegraphed July 17 that one of his regiments was wholly unarmed, and he could get weapons neither in St. Louis nor Springfield. And these shortages stubbornly persisted. Frémont had expected to draw arms from the St. Louis arsenal, but found that it afforded no more than 1300 pieces, good and bad.

Of his initial Western strength of perhaps 25,000 men before the three months' militia departed, as we have seen, 7000 Illinoisans had no weapons at all. When Frémont's messages to Montgomery Blair and Major P. V. Hagner gained him nothing, he made an emergency purchase of 25,000 Austrian muskets, 13,000 new and 12,000 old, for whose quality Asboth vouched. While in New York he had ordered 23,000 guns, but Hagner explained that after Bull Run the Administration directed all arms diverted to the Potomac, and the 23,000 went thither! The Hungarian muskets at least gave the incoming volunteers something with which to drill. For a time Frémont in desperation sought weapons wherever he could find them. Naturally, when an Eastern arms dealer telegraphed August 5 that he had 5000 Hall's rifled carbines—new cast-steel breechloaders—Frémont replied that he would take them all at the $22 rate demanded, and wished them shipped by express. This order, later vindicated by a government inquiry, was filled by mid-September, and gave real aid to the West.[16]

15 To Lyman Trumbull; Illinois State Hist. Library.
16 See *Comm. on the Conduct of the War*, III, 78–88, for a full record of the shortages. Hagner, a conscientious officer, had been given charge of War Department purchases from

Nevertheless, Western troops had to continue using whatever arms, if any, they possessed. Three officers who examined John A. McClernand's brigade at Cairo shortly reported that the queer mélange of weapons included Prussian muskets, English Tower muskets, French Minié rifles, three patterns of American muskets, and English muskets by Lacy & Company; of which all the Prussian and English muskets, and part of the American arms, were so defective that the men had no confidence whatever in them. McClernand told Frémont that little over half his force was armed at all, and they with dangerous and insufficient weapons, lacking a supply of available ammunition. One colonel said he would regard himself as a murderer if he took his defenseless men into battle. As late as October 6, McClernand, who had sent a purchaser of his own to Washington for supplies, was frantically writing this agent that he *must* get his requisition filled:

Master its contents and urge upon the Quartermaster-General the necessity of prompt and favorable action. Urge that justice, if not gratitude to Illinois, who has led the way in making pecuniary advances, requires such action. Urge that the faith of the Federal Government requires it. Urge that the public service requires it. If my brigade had been equipped with the expedition contemplated by the letter of the Secretary of War to Governor Yates, I would have routed or captured Jeff Thompson's force at Belmont last week. I would have done it with my own brigade. If necessary, show the accompanying communication to President Lincoln, who I am convinced will favor the most speedy outfit of my brigade.
Persevere! Persevere! Persevere! [17]

Horses, wagons, ambulances, and medical supplies were in equally short supply. Frémont made the error of suggesting that his former attorney Frederick Billings, of the California law firm once headed by Halleck, be empowered to buy horses in Canada. The War Department, holding that they could be obtained more cheaply in the Middle West, peremptorily stopped Billings, and this caused delay. Many of the medical wants went unfilled. At the beginning of July the head of the Sanitary Commission, after making a round of camps in Missouri, Illinois, and Ohio, reported: "We saw no ambulances in any Western camp, and no stretchers." Lyon went into the bloody action at Wilson's Creek with just two ambulances in service, so that it took nearly a week to transport some 700 wounded, suffering in the August heat, to hospitals. Even in November the troops gathering in great masses at Cairo

---

private sources in New York. For light on purchases in general and War Department confusion as well as a justification of Frémont's course see Gordon Wasson, *The Hall Carbine Affair, passim;* the pamphlet, "Vindication of Quartermaster-General McKinstry"; and the inquiry report in House Exec. Doc. No. 94, 37th Cong., 2d Sess.

17 Report of John A. Logan, *et al.,* Camp Cairo, Sept. 30, 1861; McClernand to Frémont, Sept. 17, 30, and to Colonel P. B. Fouke, Oct. 6, McClernand Papers.

possessed only two ambulances, and had done nothing to drill ambulance details for the battlefield. St. Louis organized its own Western Sanitary Commission under W. G. Eliot, and it rather than the Federal Government furnished the western troops their first real facilities for the sick and wounded.[18]

[IV]

The officer problem, as grave in the West as the East, was aggravated by two facts: Western officers, remote from Washington, less closely watched by newspaper correspondents, and working in a freer, bolder atmosphere than Eastern men, showed more carelessness and more aggressiveness; while Frémont's lack of West Point training, and memories of his oldtime troubles in the regular army—his quarrel with S. W. Kearny, court-martial, and popular vindication—fostered a strong antagonism among West Point graduates.

The new volunteer regiments about St. Louis and Cairo had as many wretched colonels, majors, and lieutenants as those about Washington. One reason why many ninety-day men refused to reënlist, West as well as East, was that they could not endure their regimental heads and demanded a complete new reshuffle. Gustave Koerner told Senator Trumbull that more than half the six regiments at Cairo would continue in the army, but never under their old colonels. He predicted that the thirteen new regiments which Yates was offering would be "officered in the usual way by incompetents." [19] More serious, however, was the exceptional degree of insubordination among the higher officers in the West.

John Pope, for example, talked and wrote in the most reckless fashion. An August letter to an Ohio friend foully abused Secretary Cameron: "Everybody in this wide land knows him to be corrupt and dishonest, a public plunderer and an unprincipled politician . . . a man notoriously plundering the Govt betraying his trust and neglecting every vital interest under his charge, cannot be gotten rid of except by public clamor." We have noted his favorite idea that Illinois troops should be formed into an Illinois army under an Illinois general; and he encouraged his men to display their resentment because Illinois units were mingled with Iowa, Missouri, Indiana, Ohio, and Michigan units, heaped confusedly together. In the same letter, pouring out venom upon Lincoln, he actually threatened a mutiny of troops:

18 Adams, *Doctors in Blue;* Nevins, *Frémont,* 491. Frederick Billings, a Vermonter and a graduate of the State university, had been attorney-general of California, and an influential Union leader there. He was destined in time to be the principal builder of the Northern Pacific, and a notable philanthropist; Billings, Montana, is named for him.

19 Koerner, Belleville, Ill., July 29, 1861, to Trumbull; Trumbull Papers, 10. Koerner's chief complaint was that some officers treated German-American recruits "like dogs."

They find themselves neglected, abandoned, and humiliated by the President they have themselves put into the White House, and they have resolved to endure it no longer. A deputation reached Washington yesterday [August 21] representing the State authorities and the military which will force upon Mr. Lincoln either an open rupture or a redress of their wrongs. They warn him that neither Banks nor Hunter will be suffered to take command of Illinois troops, and that if it is attempted the whole of the Illinois forces will march back into the State and have no more to do with the war.

We are certainly cursed with rulers in this country and especially at such a time. This Administration will do in a different manner what Jeff Davis is doing directly. I mean that by neglect, corruption, and outrage, the States of the West will be driven to group together and act without reference to the authority of the General Government. You would be surprised to find how prevalent this idea is today. . . .[20]

These vaporings ill befitted an officer whose father, once territorial secretary of Illinois, had been a friend of Lincoln; and the same irresponsible temper characterized his relations with Frémont. Vain, boastful, ambitious, Pope resented the fact that Lincoln had not made him brigadier-general in the regular army. "The injustice of overslaughing me in this way," he wrote Senator Trumbull, "needs no comment." [21] Brigadier-General Hurlbut was arrested early in September, along with an Iowa colonel, for drunkenness. "I hope it

20 Pope to V. B. Horton, Aug. 22, 1861; Civil War MSS, N. Y. Hist. Soc.
21 Pope to Trumbull June 16, 1861; Trumbull Papers LC. Pope's later epistle to Trumbull, July 6, 1861, deserves quotation at length. He wrote: "Illinois, if properly cared for, occupies today a most peculiar and commanding position in this country. On the one side Missouri has as much as she can do to take care of herself, while Iowa, Minnesota, and Wisconsin have had their troops drawn off for service eastward. On the other hand, Ohio and Indiana have been depleted of their volunteers for service in Western Virginia. Illinois so far stands nearly intact with a powerful force of nearly 20,000 men in the field.

"If this force can be kept together and properly officered and commanded, upon Illinois will devolve largely the reconquest of the Valley of the Mississippi. Where she moves, with such a force, she will of necessity stand first—and hers will be the voice which controls the warlike operations in this valley.

"If we can be kept together we shall constitute two-thirds of any army sent south from this region and our position and influence will cominate in any settlement of affairs west of the Alleghenys. To secure this vital object to our State I have been working from the beginning for some *head* to our troops, even if it be a wooden one—some commander who shall be a citizen and native of this State, and who shall move to the execution of any great military operation, with the concentrated forces of Illinois.

"For this reason I have also objected, whenever I could exercise any influence, to the separation of any isolated regiments from our troops. I deem this object vital to our military efficiency and reputation, and I appeal to you to interfere against this system which is now demoralizing us—frittering away our strength—subjecting our volunteers to the most obscure and odious service—and absolutely destroying the identity of the State. We want a military commander of our own troops, who shall have full authority in this State.

". . . Give us a Major-General and one of our own people to whom the welfare and reputation of our State are dear, and who can enable us to move with the whole military force of Illinois. I feel deeply on the subject and perhaps write too strongly." Trumbull Papers, LC.

will not be long until some of the rest of our drunken officers will have to walk the plank," a private wrote home. Still another brigadier, S. D. Sturgis, was infected by the prevalent West Point animosity toward Frémont as a major-general appointed for political reasons. His temper approached insubordination, so that he was as ready as Pope to impede Frémont's plans; and as the new commander of Lyon's army he occupied a position of critical importance.

Several volunteer officers destined to play striking roles were making their Western debuts. Franz Sigel, after organizing a Missouri regiment, became a brigadier-general in May. A sincere devotee of liberty, this romantic hero of the Baden revolt, still in his late thirties, had led 4000 troops and gained an international name before landing in America to become a humble teacher. The Germans of St. Louis greatly exaggerated his military proficiency. Another striking figure was John M. Palmer. Once a Jacksonian Democrat, he had broken with Douglas in 1854 on the Kansas-Nebraska bill, taken a prominent part in organizing the Republican Party, and supported Lincoln in the Chicago Convention. He was among the first to leap to arms. If the Middle West had a man of Hampden's principle, it was he. He shrewdly remarked of Frémont that he had lived much on the plains without becoming broad, but he was entirely loyal to the major-general.[22]

More important was the before-mentioned John A. McClernand, whose career had touched Lincoln's at many points. A Kentuckian by birth; a fighter in the Black Hawk War; in Congress 1843–51, covering Lincoln's years in the House; a Jacksonian who had turned against Douglas in 1854 as violently as Palmer did; an ardent war Democrat, anxious to mobilize men and money in overwhelming strength—here was an intrepid man who offered much that Lincoln could use. And right ready the President was to employ his services. Leaving Congress, McClernand had raised a brigade in central and southern Illinois. Inasmuch as he and the State authorities were anxious that it should not be sent off until prepared to take the field as an entirety, he lingered in Springfield and Jacksonville till the end of August. Then, as Frémont wished him to go into camp at Cairo for the moral effect his brigade would produce, he got his 2500 men thither at the beginning of September.

In short, McClernand really had a separate command, with its own commissary and quartermaster service and its own objectives. He wished a separate department established with headquarters in Cairo under his charge, coequal in authority with Frémont at St. Louis. Before long he and John A. Logan were

22 Palmer, *Personal Recollections* (1901), *passim*. His letters to his wife in Palmer Papers, Ill. State Lib., reveal fine traits. He read all Scott once a year!

pressing this idea on the semi-acquiescent Lincoln. Frémont could expect no aid from this independent brigadier, a man with a beak of a nose and a headlong, testy, irascible manner.[23]

[V]

While the Western theater was still ill organized, badly equipped, and poorly officered, Frank Blair immediately after the adjournment of the House on August 6 complicated matters by returning to Missouri. Just forty this year, and midway in his second term in Congress, he was anything but radical on the slavery question, for he was one of the chief advocates of gradual emancipation by colonization abroad, but flamingly violent in his demands for a rapid prosecution of the war. He proposed that the government accept all volunteers, take over railroads and telegraphs, and build a ship canal from Lake Michigan to the Illinois River to serve both military and commercial purposes. Seeing everything in black and white, he used language that never lacked heat or pungency. He reached St. Louis expecting to resume the reins of power he had held in June, and from that moment difficulties increased.

A clash between Blair and Frémont—between the attorney-politician who with Nathaniel Lyon had practically ruled St. Louis that spring, and the general who was now winning the warm loyalty of the German population—was almost inevitable. Blair's self-confidence brooked no opposition to his demands. He had broken General Harney, and was ready to break another commander. By his impetuous strokes, forcing premature warfare in Missouri, he had created many of the emergencies against which Frémont contended; and blinded by his affection for Lyon, he blamed Frémont for the recent disaster which was Lyon's own fault. Like Wade and Chandler in their attacks on McClellan, he could not understand military delay.

Seventy-year-old Francis P. Blair of Jacksonian fame and Montgomery Blair, both able to gain Lincoln's ear at a moment's notice, were certain to take Frank's side in any dispute. They hoped to see Frank, who in Lincoln's words was their joy and pride, reach the Presidency; and for that reason they wished him to hold Missouri as a political enclave which he could use as Andrew Jackson had used Tennessee. Montgomery termed his brother the greatest man in the country. Seeing Frémont's energetic acts win over the German population as the potential nucleus of a powerful State party, the Blairs took alarm, while they resented Frémont's apparent disregard of Frank's political henchmen in the letting of war contracts.

Frank Blair asked Major Justus McKinstry, Frémont's quartermaster-

23 See the full letters in McClernand Papers, Ill. State Hist. Lib., Aug.–Dec. 1861.

general, to "give Jim Neal a chance" at supplying horses—Neal being later termed a swindler by a Congressional committee. He urged a firm of wagon-makers on the quartermaster-general, unjustly attacking a rival firm as secessionists. He even sent a would-be contractor to McKinstry with the dictatorial command: "See that he is attended to." He was specially aggrieved when his friend ex-mayor John How, a leather dealer who had allied himself with Walter S. Burnee of Chicago in offering the Western Department clothing, shoes, and other equipment for forty thousand men, was turned away by McKinstry on the ground the order was too large and should be thrown open to competition. Blair naturally distrusted the men who got contracts from McKinstry, some of whom he later described as "obscene birds of prey." [24]

When Frank expressed his irritation to his father, the old Jacksonian decided to take the situation in hand. He wrote Frémont bluntly suggesting "a co-partnership in the West." He and his sons would do everything possible to aid the commander, he said, if Frémont would "exert your utmost influence to carry my points." To begin with, "I want to have Frank made a militia major-general for the State of Missouri." Frémont should induce the new provisional governor, Hamilton R. Gamble, to arrange the appointment for Frémont. The elder Blair had lived in an atmosphere of intrigue and bargain so long that he saw no impropriety in this proposal. Frémont on August 18 duly asked Gamble, as a special favor, to make Frank a brigadier-general at once. When Gamble replied that the State Constitution required the election of brigadiers by subordinate officers, Frémont accepted his statement, but he tried to cushion the blow to the Blairs by explaining that the colonelcy which Frank held, a place which he had gained by election of the regiment, would amount to a brigadiership. This was unsatisfactory to Frank and to his father. [25]

By late August the dispute was serious. Among its origins was of course a fundamental incompatibility of temper, for Frank was shrewd, practical, aggressive, and domineering, while Frémont was erratic, impulsive, and visionary. Both men were proud and hot-tempered. Frank, pluming himself on his repu-

24 For treatment of contracts, see McKinstry's "Vindication"; Frémont's defense in Committee on the Conduct of the War, *Report*, 1863, Pt. 3, 44 ff.; Nevins, *Frémont*, Chs. 29, 30; 37th Cong., 2d Sess., House Report No. 2 on "Government Contracts"; House Exec. Doc. No. 94 on "War Claims in St. Louis." The St. Louis correspondent of the N. Y. *Tribune* wrote in that paper of July 30, 1868: "It was freely asserted, and is believed to this day by thousands, that if the How-Gurnee contract had not failed, then Blair and Frémont would have remained friends." McKinstry wrote How in scathing terms on August 25: "The acceptance of your proposition would involve the expenditure of at least three-fourths of a million dollars—an enormous amount of money to be expended for a public object without throwing open the door to public competition." N. Y. *Herald*, September 23, 1861.
25 The letter of F. P. Blair is in the Frémont Papers, Bancroft Library, Univ. of California; see Nevins, *Frémont*, 310. See also Gamble Papers, Mo. State Hist. Soc., for Frémont-Gamble letters, August–September.

tation as savior of the Union in Missouri, believed that he had a right to control the State; Frémont, as departmental chief, was determined not to let his own authority be weakened.

Frank honestly convinced himself that Frémont lacked the high military talents his position required. Regarding St. Louis as overwhelmingly loyal, he objected to the measures which Frémont and McKinstry took to police it under martial law. Favoring the offensive against the defensive, he condemned Frémont's employment of large bodies of laborers to fortify the city. Later, he declared that Frémont's acts were "the offspring of timidity," an attempt to parry "imaginary dangers." Frémont, on the other hand, knew that his force of effective troops was much smaller than it appeared, and that he might have to denude the city of most of them to meet some urgent demand from the East or the West. He prosecuted his defensive works, including ten forts, until the War Department ordered them stopped in the middle of October. A year later he had the satisfaction of seeing the government order them put in complete readiness for service against attack.[26]

Conferences between the two officers led to no understanding. The tone of Frank's letters to his father and brother changed, as Lincoln recalled later, from doubt to condemnation. Late in August he and Colonel John T. Schofield, a West Pointer recently Lyon's chief of staff, went to Frémont's headquarters. The general, at a map-strewn table, devoted more than an hour to his plan for leading a well-equipped army through southwestern Missouri into Arkansas, and thence descending the Arkansas River to the Mississippi. On their departure, Blair inquired, "Well, what do you think of him?"; and Schofield replied in terms too strong to print. Said Blair, "I have been suspecting that for some time." It is difficult to follow Schofield's condemnation of Frémont's strategic plan. Before many months passed a Union army was to march through southwestern Missouri, defeat the Confederates at Pea Ridge, traverse Arkansas without material opposition, and emerge at Helena on the Mississippi. But it is not difficult to comprehend Blair's ready acceptance and perhaps partial inspiration of Schofield's opinion.[27]

The quarrel rapidly widened into a complete breach. Two political factions, destined to affect deeply the progress of the war, were crystallizing among Missouri Unionists: a conservative, moderate party, the Claybanks, who believed in gradual action against slavery; and a radical, uncompromising body, the Charcoals, ready for vigorous and implacable attacks on it. The Claybanks looked to Blair, Attorney-General Bates, and Provisional-Governor Gamble for leadership, while the Charcoals looked to Frémont and to Benton's

26 See Frémont's St. Louis speech in N. Y. *Weekly Tribune*, November 1, 1862.
27 Schofield, *Forty-six Years*, 48 ff.

old-time political lieutenant B. Gratz Brown. Thus began an alignment which would shortly divide Missouri into two implacable camps, open a battle running into Reconstruction years, and seriously affect national history.

The North as August ended could find even less comfort in the Western than in the Eastern military situation. The army on the Mississippi, as a result of many circumstances, but especially of Washington's neglect, was much less well prepared than that on the Potomac; the quarrel between Frémont and Frank Blair was much more ominous than that between McClellan and Scott; the first offensive would have to move from angrily divided Missouri into angrily divided Kentucky. Then just as the Blair-Frémont quarrel was breaking into the open, the Western commander took a step which electrified the country.

New Star, New Issue

LOW ON the horizon, late this summer, a small dim star began slowly to arise. It was the star of an Ohioan of Puritan ancestry, thirty-nine years of age, who had followed a variety of humble occupations and till lately had been regarded as a rather seedy failure, at times addicted to drink. Indeed, the use of liquor to alleviate homesickness and despondency had caused his resignation of a captaincy in the regular army nearly ten years earlier. He was Ulysses Simpson Grant, of West Point 1839–43, the Mexican War 1845–48, a Missouri farm 1854, and a Galena leather store 1860–61.

The adjutant-general of Illinois when the crisis came was so totally devoid of military experience and organizing capacity that the rush of troops to Springfield threw his office into chaos. The confusion became intolerable. One day Governor Yates exploded with chagrin. "In this bedlam," he said, "we *must* find somebody who can organize regiments." When a friend suggested Captain Sam Grant, who had just arrived in Springfield with the Jo Daviess Guards from Galena, Yates made him mustering officer at $4.20 a day to handle the incoming three-months men. Instantly a change overtook the adjutant-general's office. "In a corner," writes a State functionary, "at a small writing table, might have been seen a man of moderate stature, of exceeding gravity; modest, shy; speaking only when addressed; working busily all day long, making out muster rolls, writing orders, filing papers, bringing order out of confusion, with so little friction and noise that it required a second look to be sure he was doing anything at all." [1]

Grant's clerical duties ended May 22. He vainly wrote to Lorenzo Thomas, an old acquaintance who had become adjutant-general in Washington when Joseph E. Johnston left, and vainly visited McClellan's headquarters in Cincinnati. On the way back from this futile visit he stopped in Lafayette, Indiana, for dinner with several officers. One of them remarked that if he were about

---

[1] MS Reminiscences of Mason Brayman, Chicago Hist. Soc.; see also Lloyd Lewis, *Captain Sam Grant;* Cole, *The Era of the Civil War;* James Grant Wilson, *Life of Grant,* 20 ff.

to give battle to a Southern force, and heard that the Negroes were in insurrection, he would join the Confederates in putting down the slaves. Grant's ire flared. "Colonel W——," he said, "I don't wish to hurt your feelings, but I *must* say that any officer who can make such a declaration is not far from being a traitor!" Their friends had trouble averting an encounter. Then suddenly the grateful Yates offered Grant a regiment—and on June 15 he accepted.

Though soldiers called him "the quiet man," within a few days he had reduced a semi-mutinous camp to order. He marched his command from Springfield much of the way to Quincy on the Mississippi. Before Frémont arrived he reported to Pope, who stationed him at the town of Mexico, about fifty miles north of the Missouri River.[2]

It was on a hot day at Mexico that Grant received an unexpected telegram notifying him that he had been appointed brigadier-general. He knew that this was the work of his Galena Congressman, Elihu B. Washburne, although since Washburne was a Republican and Grant a man of no particular party allegiance they had only a nodding acquaintance. He rose, related his chaplain, pulled his black felt hat nearer his eyes, gave a few extra strokes to his whiskers, and walked off as unconcernedly as if he had been called to supper. One of Frémont's early acts was to order him to Ironton, which he reached August 8. As he totally lacked artillery and cavalry, and did not have enough force to drive away the guerrillas in the area, Frémont suggested that he fortify the town. But Grant objected that he had no engineer officer, while anyway, "drill and discipline are more necessary to the men than fortifications." A collision over rank and authority shortly developed between Grant and General Prentiss, in which Grant was clearly right. Frémont resolved the quarrel by giving him command (August 28) of southeastern Missouri and southern Illinois, with headquarters at Cairo, while sending the irate Prentiss to northern Missouri, which the guerrilla fighting made an uncomfortable place.[3] On September 3 Grant was able to write Washburne a grateful letter from Cairo, announcing that he had decided on John A. Rawlins, a Galena attorney who had helped raise the Forty-fifth Illinois, as chief of staff, and adding:

2 Brayman, MS Reminiscences, tells the traitor story. A clear indication of Grant's quality as an officer is given in his letter to his father from Mexico, Mo., August 3: "My services with the regiment I am now with have been highly satisfactory to me. I took it in a very disorganized, demoralized, and insubordinate condition and have worked it up to a reputation equal to the best, and, I believe, with the good will of all the officers and all the men. Hearing that I was likely to be promoted, the officers, with great unanimity, have requested to be attached to my Command." John H. Gundlach Collection, sold January 5, 6, 1927, Amer. Art Assn.

3 This violent quarrel of Prentiss and Grant, which almost came to fisticuffs, is vigorously described by General B. H. Grierson in his MS autobiography, "The Lights and Shadows of Life," Ill. State Hist. Lib.

I have been kept actively moving from one command to another, more so perhaps than any other officer. So long as I am of service to the cause of our country I do not object, however. . . .

Gen. Frémont has seen fit to entrust me with an important command here, my command embracing all the troops in South East Missouri and at this place. . . .

I can assure you my whole heart is in the cause which we are fighting for and I pledge myself that if equal to the task before me you shall never have cause to regret the part you have taken (in my behalf).

When Grant discovered great abuses in the quartermaster's department at Cairo, he exerted himself so resolutely to correct them that he made enemies both open and secret. One of the bitterest, he thought, was Leonard Swett, Lincoln's old intimate. Swett was hostile, Grant informed Washburne, because of "the course I pursued whilst at Cairo towards certain contractors and speculators who wished to make fortunes off of the soldiers and Government and in which he took much interest whether a partner or not." [4]

Beyond doubt, Grant was the type of officer willing to run risks. Frémont, some of whose associates wished him to send John Pope to Cairo, named Grant instead because he saw in him a man of iron will, dogged determination, great activity, and "promptness in obeying orders without question." Of his power of decision he soon gave a memorable illustration. All summer Kentucky was still "neutral." Neither the national government nor Frémont was anxious to make any movement against the State. It was the Confederacy which first violated its neutrality, General Leonidas Polk on September 3 sending General Gideon J. Pillow to seize Columbus, Kentucky, which was regarded as the key to the Mississippi. Late on the 5th, Grant, without permission, made the appropriate counter-move, capturing Paducah without firing a shot. Intestinal war at once began in the State, the legislature declaring for the Union while Confederate sympathizers summoned a secessionist convention. Had he been permitted, Grant would have tried to take Columbus, for by the end of September he had nearly 20,000 men. [5]

In the preference he showed for Grant, Frémont confirmed Pope's enmity, and made Prentiss violently hostile. But for once his judgment had guided him aright, and he did the country great service by his choice. More even than Washburne or Yates, he saw the qualities of the "quiet man." In his Missouri area of operations, with Hurlbut, Pope, Prentiss, and S. O. Sturgis, the West

4 See Grant to Washburne Sept. 3, 1861, and later letters in 1862, Grant-Washburne Papers, Ill. State Hist. Lib.

5 See Frémont, MS Memoirs, Bancroft Library, for comment on Grant. The first slight technical violation of Kentucky's "neutrality" was John M. Palmer's seizure of a steamer; but Pillow moved in force.

Pointer who had taken over Lyon's force, all holding important commands.[6] he was far more unfortunate in his subordinates than McClellan; and unlike Mc-Clellan, he had to fight at once, for the situation would not wait. He had invading armies and guerrilla bands in his midst.

[I]

Unlike McClellan, moreover, Frémont had to face complex political problems. Against military difficulties he might have made headway, but in the political field he was crippled by his comparative inexperience (for this former Senator and Presidential candidate had done no sustained political work), impetuosity, and excessive readiness to listen to radical advisers. His ripening quarrel with Blair demanded a discretion which he did not possess.

Just as this quarrel, as we have said, was about to become public property, Frémont took his rashest step. Frank Blair wrote Montgomery September 1 that affairs were growing worse in north Missouri; that an army of 10,000 rebels might soon be collecting there; that he had warned Frémont and got no satisfaction; and that the discipline of troops in St. Louis was bad. "He talks of the vigor he is going to use," wrote Blair, "but I can see none of it, and I fear it will turn out to be some rash and inconsiderate move—adopted in haste to make head against a formidable force which could not have been accumulated except through gross and inexcusable negligence." It was Blair's and Lyon's springtime violence which had done most to galvanize this force into action. "My decided opinion," he went on, "is that he should be relieved of his command and a man of ability put in his place." [7]

At that moment Frémont *had* determined on an ill-considered move. He felt driven to desperation by the guerrilla warfare—a warfare by which, wrote James O. Broadhead, "the Union sentiment was being crushed out and the Union men overwhelmed by the tide of rebellion, rapine, and plunder which has literally swept over the State." One loyal man in a loyal district wrote: "All we can hope to do is to escape with our lives." [8]

Frémont's rash step was the first resounding Northern attack upon slavery. The two radical advisers at his elbow, Representative Owen Lovejoy and Jessie,

6 The N. Y. *Tribune* later said editorially that Sturgis was accustomed to declare that the only gentlemen in the country were those of the South. In 1862 he denounced the radical Senator Zack Chandler of Michigan as "liar, scoundrel, and coward." N. Y. *Tribune*, June 30, 1862.

7 Blair-Lee Papers, Princeton University. Blair had been in the State a little over a fortnight when he made these charges.

8 The Carthage, Ill., *Republican*, Aug. 29, 1861, describes the exodus from Missouri into Illinois as astonishing. "Long trains of wagons pass our office almost daily, conveying families who have hastily gathered up a few of their household goods." The Broadhead Papers, Mo. Hist. Soc., contain vivid accounts of the terror by J. O. Broadhead and others.

had been reinforced by John A. Gurley, Representative from the Cincinnati district, a minister, journalist, and politician of strong antislavery views, who had arrived as aide August 6. He was persuasive and earnest. John P. Shanks, an Indiana Congressman of like opinions, had just come or announced his coming. These counselors urged him to fight fire with fire.[9] Slavery nourished the guerrillas; he should strike at slavery.

No doubt Frémont regarded the startling proclamation which he issued under date of August 30 as primarily a military measure. He had placed St. Louis under martial law on August 14; now he extended the regime over the whole State, assuming the administrative powers theretofore exercised by the flabby Gamble. He drew a diagonal line from Leavenworth through Jefferson City, Rolla, and Ironton to Cape Girardeau as separating the areas of Unionist and secessionist control; declared that all civilians caught in arms north of that line should be tried by court-martial and if found guilty, shot; and prescribed the extreme penalty for all persons found guilty of destroying railway tracks, bridges, or telegraph lines. He further announced that the real and personal property of Missourians who actively aided the enemies of the United States was confiscated to public use, and that their slaves would be freed. The geographical distribution of slaveowners in Missouri was peculiar. Of the total of 115,000 slaves listed in the 1860 census, the 31 counties contiguous to the Mississippi and Missouri Rivers north and west of St. Louis held almost 77,000. It was in these counties, and especially in the belt stretching along the Missouri across the State, that guerrilla warfare had its deepest roots. This belt, lying largely along Frémont's line, was subjected to his severe punitive order.[10]

Frémont might well feel desperate. He faced enemies in the field, covert treason within his lines, and insubordination behind his back. The warfare, as the St. Louis *Republican* said, was becoming atrociously savage; both sides killed without quarter, and looted with greedy eagerness. Grant had just written his father from Jefferson City that the country west of that point would be in a starving condition the next winter, for all Unionists were fleeing penniless, leaving farms, crops, and stock to be ravaged by the enemy. Secessionist guerrillas, after firing into many passenger trains, on September 6 weakened a 160-foot bridge over the Little Platte so that at midnight it collapsed under a train loaded with 80 or 90 men, women, and children. Martial law had become a necessity, and to that point Frémont was justified; it was when he went beyond that he invaded a sphere of policy belonging to Lincoln.

9 Shanks's official service as aide began Sept. 20, but he may have arrived in St. Louis earlier. Gurley sat in Congress 1859–63, Shanks 1861–63.

10 Frank Moore, *Rebellion Record*, III, 10, 26, Documents, pp. 33–71, gives the proclamation with some press opinion. Frémont's reasons, as stated in his MS Memoirs, are quoted in Nevins, *Frémont*, 500.

A wiser man would have telegraphed Lincoln in advance concerning the proclamation. Frémont instead followed it with a letter which, however placatory, gave the President no real explanation. He wrote of the enemy (September 3):

He has been fortifying new places, and creeping covertly forward into Kentucky lately, and I have been very anxious to anticipate him, but not quite able yet. Still, I am moving, and we are beginning to roll the war backward. I think the preparation in the South much greater than we had thought, and I believe that you will soon be compelled to exert the whole power of the nation and use every means of aggressive war. Here, I have been compelled to move fast and act with my best judgment as the occasion rose. I trust that the proclamation which I judged it right to issue on the 30th will meet with your approval and support. . . .

Gov. Gamble visits you at Washington. He has been professedly friendly but has shown no real disposition to cooperate. His inefficiency is quite remarkable, and in my judgment he had neither courage nor capacity for his position. . . . You notice that we are driving Pillow back, and you will in a short time see some changes for the better. . . .[11]

Union leaders believed at the time that the Confederacy had 60,000 or 70,000 armed men in Missouri, of whom 40,000 were Missourians.[12] Leonidas Polk had laid plans to hold a great part of the State while attempting to seize control of Kentucky. Nobody knew when Sterling Price and Ben McCulloch would make another attack from the southwest, or Pillow a move from the southeast.

[II]

Even as a military measure, Frémont's proclamation was open to sharp objection. To put Confederate guerrillas to death would simply invite reprisals. To begin the sweeping confiscation of secessionist property would create embittered resistance, not quiet it. And it was far more than a military measure; it was a sharp intrusion into the political field. Already Abolitionists and radical freesoilers of the North were loudly demanding that the war be expanded into a conflict for emancipation as well as Union. Joshua Giddings had published a flaming letter dated June 6 in the New York *Tribune* demanding just such action as Frémont now took; Gerrit Smith, in a letter of July 12 to Owen Lovejoy, had asked why the government took a costly, weary way to suppress

11 Grant's letter on the guerrillas, dated Aug. 27, was in the Gundlach Collection before its sale. Frémont's letter to Lincoln is in the Seward Collection, Rochester University. Lincoln must have referred it to Seward, who kept it.

12 An over-estimate, as subsequent events demonstrated. Military and political conditions are discussed in S. B. Laughlin, "Missouri Politics During the Civil War," *Missouri Historical Review*, v. 23 (April, 1929), 400–26.

the rebellion when a cheap, direct one was at hand. Liberation of slaves had obviously become a necessity, wrote Smith. "Let the President, in his capacity as commander of the army, proclaim such liberation and the war would end in thirty days." Moncure D. Conway was putting through the press a book, *The Great Method of Peace*, which urged emancipation as the key to victory. Charles Sumner was demanding an end to halfway measures. Greeley's *Tribune* declared it was time to stop handling traitors with kid gloves.[13] Frémont's proclamation, followed as it was by his creation of a commission to take evidence and issue deeds of manumission, reverberated on the sounding board these radicals furnished.

If Frémont was rash in issuing this proclamation without prior consultation of the War Department and President, he was to commit a worse folly. Lincoln could never countenance his step, and on September 3rd the President sent him a kindly letter, pointing out his objections. He ordered Frémont to shoot no Confederate without Presidential approbation or consent, for if he did "the Southerners would very certainly shoot our best men in their hands in retaliation"; and he instructed the general to modify his paragraph on the confiscation of property and liberation of slaves so as to conform to the recent Confiscation Act, which sanctioned the seizure of property only when actually used for insurrectionary purposes. It would have hurt Frémont's pride and sense of conviction to yield, and he refused. In a stiff-necked letter he requested Lincoln to *direct* the modification by open order—which Lincoln in a courteous letter of September 11 did.

Frémont was doubtless influenced in this not only by his radical advisers but by the enthusiastic reception of the proclamation in certain quarters. Approval came from a long list of the nation's most important newspapers; not merely radical journals like the Chicago *Tribune*, New York *Evening Post*, and Springfield *Republican*, but moderate papers like the Washington *National Intelligencer* and New York *Times*. In Lincoln's own State it was vigorously applauded. From New England to Kansas most of the clergy, all belligerent haters of slavery, and all citizens who thought Lincoln slow and Seward an evil influence, greeted it jubilantly. Representative George W. Julian of Indiana wrote later that it stirred and united the people of the North during the ten days of life allowed it by the Government far more than any other event of the war. Two Cabinet members approved of it. Secretary Cameron, at home ill, telegraphed his congratulations to Frémont before he found that Lincoln was hostile, and Montgomery Blair thought the emancipation provision justified. In Missouri the effect on loyal and disloyal was all that Frémont had

13 Gerrit Smith Papers, Syracuse University; Clarke, *Julian*, 217-20; N. Y. *Tribune*, Sept. 1, 1861.

hoped—or so at least he believed. "The Union people rejoiced openly," he states in his unpublished memoirs. "To the rebels everywhere it was a blow. It affected not only their principles but their property." [14]

Doubtless Frémont believed that a seemingly voluntary retraction would draw upon his head the censure of all the groups now applauding him, and would send a wave of disappointment and anger—directed against *him*— through much of the North. Though ready to let Lincoln overrule him, he was unwilling to overrule himself. In this he was stubbornly wrongheaded, for it was his duty to obey the Commander-in-Chief without demur, and he could have made it clear that he was yielding to higher authority.

Lincoln, who had to think of the whole country, was fearful of the effect of the proclamation on Kentucky, just now brought to the very crisis of decision as Leonidas Polk invaded her from the South, and Grant followed his example by occupying Paducah. Long poised on the knife edge of neutrality, most Kentuckians were at last coming down on the Northern side. The Frankfort *Kentucky Statesman* termed Frémont's proclamation "infamous"; the Louisville *Courier* thought it "abominable." These journals leaned to secession, but even the loyal Louisville *Journal* thought the general's action deplorable. Joseph Holt wrote Lincoln that while sound Kentuckians accepted the Confiscation Act as a necessary measure, the proclamation transcended and violated it. "You may well judge," he went on, "of the alarm and condemnation with which the Union-loving citizens have read this proclamation." They could not believe that Lincoln would let it be enforced; and anxious that nothing should chill the fervor of loyal citizens at this crucial moment, he asked for Presidential intervention. Condemnatory resolutions were introduced in the legislature. Frémont had some defenders even in Kentucky, but they were few.

Unquestionably, Lincoln was right as to the paramount importance of nurturing loyal sentiment in Kentucky. On the very day that he set aside the objectionable features of the proclamation, the legislature by overwhelming

14 Among the newspapers endorsing the proclamation were Bennett's New York *Herald*, the Chicago *Times*, a violently Democratic organ, and the Chicago *Morning Post*, a Douglasite journal. The measured praise of the *National Intelligencer*, always conservative, was especially notable (Sept. 7). So was the approval given by the St. Louis *Republican*, a Democratic paper highly critical of the Administration and of most of its Missouri measures. The Chase, Wade, Chandler, and Sumner papers contain much enthusiastic comment from a variety of correspondents. Orville H. Browning, Lincoln's old friend of Quincy, Illinois, a highly conservative man, wrote the President on Sept. 30: "His proclamation in my opinion embodies a true and important principle which the government cannot afford to abandon. . . ." Browning Papers, Ill. State Hist. Lib. He added that it rested "upon the well ascertained and universally acknowledged principles of international law," and would greatly weaken the enemy. For Montgomery Blair's approval see Dennett, *Diaries and Letters of John Hay*, 219.

majorities called on Governor Magoffin to demand the immediate withdrawal of the Confederates from the Commonwealth, and when Magoffin vetoed this resolution, the legislature repassed it over his veto.[15] "The mountains are alive with zeal for the Union," declared the Frankfort *Commonwealth*. "Come, then, let us gird up the whole strength of our bodies and souls!" exhorted young John M. Harlan as he began raising a Union regiment. Emancipationist activity would have paralyzed this enthusiasm.

And at this critical moment the Frémont-Blair quarrel burst dramatically into public view. While the press discussed it, Frank had every advantage in laying his side of the dispute before Lincoln. He was effectively abetted by Missourians of the Claybank faction. The impression they made in the White House is reflected by some notes of John G. Nicolay dated September 17:

It is now about in the third week since the Blair family . . . who were mainly instrumental in urging his [Frémont's] appointment upon the Prest., came to him and with many professions of humility and disappointment said they were compelled by the indisputable evidence of experience to confess that in regard to his capabilities for the very important duties to which he had been assigned, he had to their perfect satisfaction proved himself a complete failure, and that they now urged his immediate removal, as strenuously as they had formerly urged his appointment. Their testimony was supported by Governor Gamble of Mo. who came on purpose to Washington to inform the President that he had gone to St. L. to confer with the genl. about the defence of the State, and that after waiting patiently for two days, he was utterly unable to obtain an interview with or admittance to him, and that his necessity had compelled him to come here. A Mr. Broadhead, State Senator of Mo., also travelled all the way here with a similar complaint. Letters were also received from other parties making similar statements, and particularly one from L.I.G., Esq., an eminent lawyer and citizen of St. Louis. The substance of the various statements seemed to be that the Genl. had placed on his staff and surrounded himself with a set of men who had been with him in California and elsewhere and who made it entirely impossible for anyone except his pets to gain access to him etc.[16]

Edward Bates, a Claybank sympathizer, and a rooted conservative on the slavery issue, joined the Blairs in pronouncing Frémont a disaster.

15 For the situation in broad outline see E. M. Coulter, *The Civil War in Kentucky*, 111, 112. The Frankfort *Commonwealth* said editorially: "However objectionable the course of Frémont is in relation to slaves, one fact stands out conspicuously worthy of attention, and it is that rebellion is attended with eminent peril, while loyalty deserves and will receive all the security and protection of life, liberty, and property which the Government can give. Each day—nay, each hour—of the revolution now going on, and which threatens Kentucky, shows the utter recklessness and ruin which must inevitably follow the destruction of our Government. . . ." Sept. 11. The Louisville *Journal*, while regretting Frémont's willingness to give freedom to slaves, compared his proclamation with the far harsher confiscation law of the Confederacy; Sept. 3.

16 Nicolay Papers, LC.

Frémont's view of the quarrel was that Frank's passion had broken all bounds when he found that the general could not be made a tool, that he had laid unjust and unsupported charges before Lincoln through Montgomery Blair, and that the three Blairs were now engaged in a conspiracy to displace him. Gamble had been censured by Frémont for refusing active cooperation in certain measures; Broadhead had been a member of Blair's Committee of Safety. Both the Missouri *Democrat* (Republican) and Missouri *Republican* (Democrat) took Frémont's side, and the German press was strongly with him.[17] But these voices were not heard in Washington.

What could Frémont do to reach the White House? "I began to feel the withdrawal of the confidence and support of the Administration," he wrote later. In his anxiety he allowed Jessie Benton Frémont, gifted, high-strung, and impulsive, to carry a letter to Lincoln. He could have found no worse emissary, for it was in a mood of fierce resentment, steeled by the iron Benton determination, that Mrs. Frémont descended on Washington.

Of the ensuing interview we have two strikingly different accounts, the more authentic her own undated memorandum, and the less trustworthy John Hay's record of a discursive evening talk by Lincoln some two years after the event. Immediately on her arrival in the capital on the evening of September 10 Mrs. Frémont sent a note to the White House explaining that she had come with a letter from the general, and inquiring when she might deliver it. The messenger brought back a card with the reply, "Now, at once, A. Lincoln." She was disconcerted by this, for she had travelled two days and two nights in a hot, dirty day coach and was exhausted. But with Judge Edward Coles of New York accompanying her, she went to the mansion, where she had often played as a little girl in Jackson's day. She was shown into the red room, and after a short wait, Lincoln entered. It was soon plain that the overwrought woman and the anxious, harried President were at cross purposes. Lincoln later said that she taxed him violently with many things, and this is no doubt true. On her way east she had passed a train carrying Montgomery Blair and Montgomery C. Meigs going west to inquire into Missouri affairs; and she doubtless said just what she thought about the Blairs and about the government's neglect of the West. Both she and Coles thought Lincoln's voice hard, his manner repellant, and his anxiety to get rid of her plain. She writes:

It was clear to Judge Coles as to myself that the President's mind was made up against General Frémont—and decidedly against me. . . . Briefly, in answer to his "Well?" I explained that the general wished so much to have his

17 Bates to Chase, Sept. 11, 1861; Chase Papers, Pa. Hist. Soc. Broadhead in a letter of Sept. 17 to the editors of the St. Louis *Democrat* protested against their espousal of Frémont against Blair; Broadhead Papers. On the visit of Meigs see Russell F. Weigley, *Quartermaster General of the Union Army, A Biography of Montgomery C. Meigs.*

attention to the letter sent, that I had brought it to make sure it would reach him. He answered, not to that, but to the subject his own mind was upon, that "*It was a war for a great national idea, the Union, and that General Frémont should not have dragged the negro into it—that he never would if he had consulted with Frank Blair. I sent Frank there to advise him.*" The words italicized are exactly those of the President.

He first mentioned the Blairs, in this astonishing connection.

It was a *parti pris*, and as we walked back Judge Coles, who heard everything, said to me, "This ends Frémont's part in the war. Seward and Montgomery Blair will see to reports against him made by a man authorized to do so, and as everyone knows, with his mind often clouded by drink and always governed by personal motives." [18]

A later statement by Mrs. Frémont [19] discloses that she lectured Lincoln on the difficulty of conquering the South by arms alone, and the importance of appealing to British and world sentiment by a blow against slavery; expressing ideas that Owen Lovejoy and Gurley cherished, but that Frémont never alleged as a reason for his proclamation. The irritated President remarked, "You are quite a female politician." It was at this point that he emphasized Frémont's error in converting a war for the Union into a war against slavery. She also spoke of Frémont's special position as former head of the Republican Party, apparently in terms that heightened Lincoln's irritation.

When old Francis P. Blair saw her next day he was irate. "Look what you have done for Frémont; you have made the President his enemy!" He could not forgive her opposition to Frank. Montgomery would talk with Frémont, he scolded, and bring him to his senses. One account quotes him as saying: "Madam, *I* made your husband what he is, and *I* will unmake him; *I* nominated him for the Presidency in '56, and *I* will defeat him in the future." [20] She sent her husband a cipher message warning him against any advice from Montgomery. Then, having done the general irreparable harm, she returned to St. Louis headquarters.

Frémont, hoping to remain head of the Western Department and soon move forward with his army, took the one step which he believed might appeal to public sentiment. On September 18 he arrested Frank Blair for insubordination, and notified Secretary Cameron that he would submit charges for his trial. Frank had used his family position, he later declared, "to lay private

18 Jessie Benton Frémont MSS, Bancroft Library. She referred to Frank Blair. See Appendix III for details of this interview.

19 In an unpublished biographical section on the explorer written by Mrs. Frémont and her son; Bancroft Library. Her undated memorandum was apparently written just after the interview. Hay's record of Lincoln's talk was made Dec. 9 or 10, 1863, after Lincoln had joined Norman Judd, J. P. Usher, Nicolay, and Hay as they sat "talking politics and blackguarding our friends." Such a record has dubious historical value.

20 So states W. M. Davis of St. Louis in a letter Sept. 17, 1861, to his wife, doubtless quoting Jessie; Davis Papers, Penna. Hist. Soc.

letters with unsustained accusations before the President, disturbing the President's confidence in the Commanding General and seriously impairing the efficiency of this Department." Mrs. Frémont, Montgomery decided, had prompted him—"it was General Jessie's doing." The Postmaster-General telegraphed him asking Frank's release, sensibly adding: "This is no time for strife except with the enemies of the country." When Frémont complied, Frank at first refused to accept a release, for he would have preferred a trial, and he was more implacably hostile than ever.[21]

Western affairs had thus been thrown into a crisis which damaged army morale, and aroused mixed feelings throughout the North. Would Frank Blair break Frémont as he had broken Harney? Or would Frémont redeem himself by a brilliant fall campaign? For the confusion, the resentments, and the embarrassment to military movements it is perhaps less profitable to seek out personal culprits than to analyze general causes. Although Frémont and Frank Blair divide a large culpability, the greater explanation of the sad situation of Missouri affairs lies in the factors already noted—the deep social divisions of the State, half slave and half free; its refractory geography, tying Union defenses to long lines of river and rail; Washington's inexcusable neglect of the trans-Mississippi region; and the readiness of men reared on the frontier to fly to violent measures.

[III]

One development, however, overshadowed all others—the new issue of emancipation. The vigor with which Lincoln rejected the concept of a war fought not only to save the Union but to destroy slavery reflected his concern over a growing public radicalism. He believed in evolution, not revolution; he wished to shorten the conflict, not lengthen it. He knew that to win the war he must keep Democrats and Republicans, conservatives and radicals, reasonably united, and that he must hold the Borderland behind the government. He wished to maintain conditions favorable to a fraternal reunion of North and South after the war. Throughout life Lincoln followed the precepts of the Epistle to the Philippians: "Let your moderation be known to all men " He was pondering his own plan of gradual compensated emancipation in the border area, and Frémont's action threatened to destroy its chances.

But while he rightly insisted that this was a war for a grand national idea, powerful elements now regarded it also as a war for a grand humanitarian ideal.

As a host of liberal citizens had risen to applaud Frémont's proclamation, so

21 Smith, *The Blair Family*, II, 77; Nevins, *Frémont*, 520; see Blair-Lee Papers, Princeton, for the order of release.

a host received Lincoln's modification with anger and disappointment, denouncing it as a fearful blunder. Since Frémont issued his paper, they declared, public credit had improved, recruiting had increased, and patriots had felt greater elation and confidence. The nation could believe, for the first time, that it was fighting for not only a great patriotic object, but a splendid moral goal. Lincoln's action takes away the penalty for rebellion, declared the Chicago *Tribune* of September 16. "How many times," asked James Russell Lowell, "are we to save Kentucky and lose our self-respect?" Judge George Hoadly of Cincinnati reported that indignation in that city had risen to fury, and Moncure D. Conway asserted that if a cheer for Lincoln were proposed to a crowd there, the response would be a groan.[22] A new Philadelphia monthly, the *Continental,* with Charles Godfrey Leland for editor, raised the cry: "Emancipation for the Sake of the White Man." Senator Ben Wade wrote from his northern Ohio home in bitter execration:

What do you think of Old Abe's overruling Frémont's proclamation? So far as I can see, it is universally condemned and execrated in the North, and I have no doubt that by it he has done more injury to the cause of the Union by receding from the ground taken by Frémont than McDowell did by retreating from Bull Run. I shall expect to find in his first annual message a recommendation to Congress to give each rebel who shall serve during the war a hundred and sixty acres of land. Unless the President shall divest himself of such squeamishness, all the mighty exertions of the North to subdue this rebellion will be paralyzed. . . . The President don't object to Genl Frémont's taking the life of the owners of slaves, when found in rebellion, but to confiscate their property and emancipate their slaves he thinks monstrous. . . . Such ethics could come only of one born of "poor white trash" and educated in a slave State.[23]

Beyond question, the war, whatever happened to Frémont, had taken a new turn. His impulsive stroke had crystallized a mass of latent sentiment, and for the first time the idea that the conflict might result in a socio-economic revolution began to grip men's minds.

Meanwhile, Grant was having an interesting time at Cairo headquarters, and showing remarkable decision. He put a popular Illinois colonel, Richard J. Oglesby, in command at Bird Point just across the Mississippi in Missouri.

22 Chase Papers, LC, for Hoadly's letter; Lowell to Sibyl Norton, Sept. 28, 1861 in *Letters,* I, 314; Leland, *Memoirs,* 242–244; Conway to Greeley, Sept. 18, 1861, Greeley Papers, NYPL. Much rejoicing was aroused in radical Northern quarters by news that Frémont had by public advertisement freed two male slaves of Thomas L. Snead, who had taken an active part against the Union. William Pitt Fessenden wrote James S. Pike on Sept. 8 that Frémont's proclamation had had an electrifying effect on the country, and proved him a statesman; he believed that Frémont rather than McClellan might be the coming man. Pike Papers.
23 Wade, Jefferson, Ohio, Sept. 23, 1861, to Zack Chandler; Chandler Papers, LC.

He sent General C. F. Smith, one of the ablest regular army officers, to command at Paducah. A detachment occupied the mouth of the Cumberland hard by. Once he had a narrow escape from capture; while some Confederate prisoners under exchange were in his office for credentials to pass through the lines, somebody mentioned that he was going to Cape Girardeau next day—and though chance prevented his trip, a Union boat in the area was halted by Confederate artillery, and searched by a major confident he had bagged Grant. The general heard that an old acquaintance, the forty-one-year-old brigadier William Tecumseh Sherman, first-year man at West Point in Grant's last year, had arrived in Louisville to assist General Robert Anderson of Sumter fame. He knew that a blue-water naval captain, Andrew H. Foote, had reached St. Louis to take charge of naval operations on the western rivers under Frémont and the War Department. Foote's first task was to hasten the building of gunboats and mortarboats. "Spare no effort to accomplish the object in view with the least possible delay," ordered Frémont.[24]

Plainly, the western theater would soon see action. Whether Frémont realized his plans for clearing Missouri and swinging through Arkansas to the Mississippi, or Grant his plans for moving down that river, large movements impended. They would inevitably have a large influence on wartime policy respecting the slaves.

24 Grant, *Memoirs*, I, 264–268; Lewis, *Sherman*, 181, 182; Hoppin, *Foote*, 158 ff.

18

The Firepower of the North

THE FIRST battle autumn saw fully three-quarters of a million men ranked and accoutered on the American continent. Never in history had such a host been raised so quickly; but east and west on both sides, under McClellan and Johnston, Frémont and Price, troops complained of inadequate and defective arms. The Confederate need was desperate. Governor Isham G. Harris of Tennessee on November 2 earnestly entreated citizens of every county to deliver to his agents "every effective double-barrel shotgun and sporting rifle which they may have." Union troops in the West continued to suffer from crippling shortages, while even in the Washington camps some regiments were kept chafing for weapons. A decent uniformity of pieces and ammunition was beyond the dreams of the most ambitious commander. The world was in the midst of a small-arms revolution, and many problems would have to be solved before men could agree on standard requirements and learn to meet them.[1]

Nothing did more to expose the gangling, adolescent state of American

---

1 The arms revolution now slowly under way had two main parts: Acceptance of rifling (the Enfield standard was three grooves with a spiral twist of one inch in seventy-two to rotate a heavy conical bullet) in place of the old smoothbore; and the gradual acceptance of breechloaders in place of muzzle-loaders. Rifles (that is, guns spirally grooved to give the projectile a rotation which increases the accuracy of its flight) had been invented soon after Columbus discovered America; breechloaders had appeared in the first half of the sixteenth century. During the Revolution Major Patrick Ferguson invented a breechloading rifle used by some British troops. But in 1861 the infantry of practically all nations was still familiar with smoothbore muzzle-loading muskets; direct descendants of the "smoky muskets" of Shakespeare's *All's Well*. Rifles, and muskets converted by rifling, were steadily displacing the inaccurate smoothbores. The United States had adopted a muzzle-loading Springfield rifle for its tiny force of regular infantry in 1855. In various countries limited bodies of troops had been given superior equipment; the French chasseurs, for example, rifles which threw the bullet invented by Captain Minié, an elongated projectile with an iron cup fitting into a hollow cone at the base—this cup, when driven forward by the explosion, expanding the bullet into the grooves. Cavalry, who could not manage ramrods, had to have breechloading carbines or short guns. The Prussians early in the 1840's adopted the needle gun, a breechloader using a cartridge detonated by a spring-driven needle, and slowly improved it. The triumph of this rifle in the war with Austria in 1866 caused all civilized powers to rearm with similar weapons.

society than the effort to arm the swiftly gathered hosts. Both sections confronted an urgent industrial problem without the technological skills, manufacturing resources, and organizational experience required to master it. In no field were both the faults and virtues of large-scale improvisation more strikingly exhibited.

[I]

When Sumter fell the American stock of arms was at the ebb-tide level to be expected in a nation which had never put 50,000 men in the field and never expected to do so. The United States at the beginning of 1861 had in all its forts, arsenals, and armories, North and South, about 600,000 small arms, antique and new, wretched and passable. Of these 35,335 were rifles or rifled muskets, the latest improved arms; 42,000 were older percussion rifles; and about 500,000 were percussion smoothbore muskets.[2] These figures, however, are deceptive, for a great part of the muskets were unserviceable. Not untypical was the Thirtieth Illinois Infantry, which took the field this year armed with 90 "good" Enfield rifles, 183 serviceable American and English muskets, and 357 unserviceable muskets; a total of 357 bad as against 273 good pieces. As this regiment numbered 773 men, 121 possessed no arms at all.[3] Probably half of the 500,000 smoothbore muskets owned by the government were not worth carrying into battle. The other half would be useful, and some Union soldiers carried smoothbores without complaint to the end of the war. They fired an ounce ball at low velocity to a distance of some 600 feet, and could be lethal at nearly that distance; whereas a rifled musket fired a bullet at a velocity of 960 feet a second with a range of 3300 feet. The rifled Springfields and Enfields were usually sighted at 900 feet, and at any distance much above that figure the "drift" of the projectile made accurate sighting impossible.

Just what part of this stock was held in the seceding States it is difficult to say. Lincoln's message to Congress July 4, 1861, stated that a disproportionately large number had been sent to the South, and both Cameron and Scott lent their authority to the charge that Buchanan's Secretary of War, Floyd, had thus denuded Northern repositories. Floyd himself, on returning to Virginia, boasted that he had done so, and absurd assertions on this head crept into the Southern press. The Richmond *Enquirer* declared that by a single order in 1860 Floyd had sent 115,000 improved rifles and muskets from Northern to Southern arsenals; while the Memphis *Appeal* improved on this

2 H. K. Craig to Joseph Holt, Jan. 22, 1861; O. R. III, i, 42.
3 Acting adjutant Dec. 6, 1861, to McClernand; McClernand Papers, Ill. State Library.

by asserting that his transfers, with seizures from Federal posts and purchases abroad, had given the Confederacy more than 700,000 small arms and 200,000 revolvers. The fact is that Floyd had made no exceptional transfers of weapons to the South.[4]

Our best figures on arms allocation indicate that early in 1861 about 336,500 government muskets and rifles were deposited in the free area as against 273,500 in the slave States. Many in the second category, however, were in forts which the Union continued to hold, or in Missouri, Maryland, and the District of Columbia. Another official statement places the number of small arms in Union repositories at the beginning of 1861 at 422,500, a figure which includes deductions for weapons in arsenals already seized or soon to be taken. It did not, however, allow for losses shortly sustained in the capture of Harpers Ferry and the secession of Virginia and Tennessee.[5] Altogether, we are safe in saying that the small arms on hand for Union troops did not exceed 350,000 pieces, of which not more than 250,000 were fit for battle use; while the Confederates could hardly have had more than 200,000 government arms.

Thus the statement of one historian that the United States possessed in its arsenals and posts in April, 1861, enough muskets and rifles for an army of half a million,[6] is simply nonsense. It would, however, have had more than enough for the first armies called up had they been distributed fairly, and cared for efficiently. Unfortunately, systematic allocation was impossible during the first frenzied months, many arms were ruined by misuse, and some were captured at Bull Run, Wilson's Creek, and Ball's Bluff. Viewed broadly, 1861 was a year of distress, search, and complaint among Northern as among Southern officers.

And the armories? When fighting began, the United States had but two, at Harpers Ferry and Springfield, Massachusetts, and the first was immediately lost, with the destruction of all its manufacturing facilities. The nation's fabrication of small arms was therefore confined to one establishment. This armory, planted by Congress on the Connecticut in 1791, had never really emerged from infancy. Consisting of some small buildings on a hilltop, and "water-shops" for heavier operations on a branch of the river, its most imposing structure was the arsenal celebrated by Longfellow, where "from floor to ceiling, like a huge organ" rose the tiers of burnished arms.

4 Meneely, *War Department, 1861*, 41; T. B. Gates, *The War of the Rebellion*, 14; O. R. III, i, 311.

5 O. R. III, i, 321, 322; see the figures also of Craig to Holt, Jan. 21, 1861, O. R. III, *ibid*. The deduction is for weapons seized in arensals in South Carolina, Louisiana, and Alabama, already gone, and in Augusta, Ga., and Fayetteville, N. C., soon to go.

6 Shannon, *Organization and Administration of the Union Army*, I, 110.

When Sumter was taken, only a thousand muskets a month were being made at Springfield. Indeed, in recent years production had fallen to a lower point than that reached in 1815. The government tried to speed up the work, but such bottlenecks developed that even in July only 3000 arms were made. Skilled workmen were hard to find, and the use of machine tools was still rudimentary. Of the 49 parts in the standard Springfield musket many had to be subjected to elaborate processing. The hammer alone, for example, had to be forged, dropped, trimmed, punched, drifted, milled, turned, filed, and finally case-hardened.[7]

Enough guns for only one regiment a month! This April rate meant that both State and Federal authorities had to turn elsewhere in frenzied haste.

[II]

First, let us look at the States.

From the Kennebec to the Sangamon, they sprang forward in a confused mêlée, characterized by inefficiency, duplication, and waste. They and the Washington authorities hurriedly placed contracts with the score of plants capable of producing arms, all concentrated in New England and the Middle Atlantic States, for the West had none. Arms could be made in quantity at Providence, R. I., Worcester, Mass., and Manchester, N. H.; at Hartford, Meriden, Norwich, Norfolk, Windsor Locks, Middletown, and Whitneyville, Conn.; at Watertown, Ilion, and in New York, N. Y.; at Trenton, N. J., at Bridesburg, Pa., and some other places.[8] Contracts were given foreign brokers and manufacturers, but we may first analyze the activities of Federal and State agents in the home markets.

The three principal mistakes made in home arms procurement, broadly considered, were the initial want of system, so that many agencies bid frantically against each other; the excessive orders, for down to July 1, 1862, these agencies contracted for 1,164,000 rifles or rifled muskets of Springfield pattern; and the exorbitant prices paid, averaging fully $20 a gun with appendages.[9] The first error was a product of haste, the second of panic, and the third of a general uncertainty as to costs. In quite a different category stood a more crippling mistake, the failure of the Federal Government to make the most of recent advances in arms design.

7 See description of Springfield armory, *Atlantic Monthly*, Vol. 12 (October, 1863), 436–451, and in Springfield *Republican*, April 22, 1861.

8 Felicia Deyrup, *Arms Makers of the Connecticut Valley*; W. W. Greener, *The Gun and its Development* (6th ed., 1897).

9 Meneely, *War Department, 1861*, 253–254, 262–263; 37th Cong., Sen. Exec. Doc. 72, pp. 15–20 ff.

In the initial scramble for arms on hand, Connecticut and Massachusetts fared especially well, partly because their governors had foreseen the emergency, partly because of their proximity to sources of supply. As early as January, 1861, Buckingham at Hartford had taken personal responsibility for purchasing knapsacks, bayonets, and other equipment for 5000 men. The State owned more than 1000 regular army rifled muskets, and more than 2000 smoothbores good for temporary service, while its factories could quickly turn out supplementary weapons. On Lincoln's first call, Buckingham decided to equip Connecticut forces only with good rifles. State banks furnished money. The first regiment received excellent Sharps rifles, the second Sharps and Enfields, and the third rifled Springfields. Thus a month after Sumter fell the State had sent three well-armed regiments into service. When the first reached Washington May 13, with shining barrels, ample ammunition, tents, and a baggage train, General Scott exclaimed: "Thank God, we have one regiment ready to take the field!" [10]

Before Sumter, William Schouler, the Massachusetts adjutant-general, had begun to press Cameron for arms. The Bay State already had 3000 rifled muskets, and he wished the national government to give it 2000 more. Governor Andrew made still more urgent pleas, demanding arms first from Springfield, and later from the Watertown arsenal. He obtained a supply that gave Massachusetts' early contingents a superior equipment, many of her troops boasting excellent rifles.[11]

In the West, Illinois alone, by dint of luck and enterprise in getting hold of so large a part of the contents of the St. Louis arsenal, was able to equip her early regiments fairly well. We have seen how, late in April, Captain James H. Stokes of Chicago, cooperating with Nathaniel Lyon, seized 21,000 muskets, 500 rifled carbines, 110,000 cartridges, and several cannon, which were promptly moved to Springfield.[12] While Illinois troops were benefited, those of neighboring states suffered. Only 7,000 muskets were left in St. Louis to equip the Union volunteers there. When Governor Dennison of Ohio complained and sent an emissary to Springfield with a requisition which the departmental commander supported by a telegram, Yates with bad grace allowed Ohio 5000 arms. He had good reason to hold on to all the equipment possible, for the State repositories had contained only 362 altered muskets, 105 rifles,

10 Croffut and Morris, *Military and Civil Hist. Conn.*, 67, 83–85.
11 O. R. III, i, 66, 71, 85, 93; Wm. Schouler, *Massachusetts in the Civil War*, I, 219, 220 ff. But some later Bay State regiments were badly armed. At Ball's Bluff the Fifteenth Massachusetts, carrying smoothbores useful only at short range, suffered heavily from Confederates armed with long-range rifles; C. F. Walcott, *Hist. of the 21st Massachusetts*, 14 ff.
12 Report Adjutant-General of Ill., I, 241.

133 musketoons (short, large-bore muskets used by artillery and cavalry), and 297 horse-pistols! Of course his St. Louis spoils did not carry Illinois very far, and the later regiments were as poorly provided as the others of the Northwest. Some got no arms at all until Christmas.[13]

The story of other States may be summed up in the experience of Pennsylvania and her eager, efficient executive Andrew Curtin. At the outbreak of war the authorities found that they had just about 4200 efficient small arms. The totals were much larger, to be sure, coming to 14,700 pieces on paper, but many were antique smoothbores with broken locks or rust-eaten barrels, and some were actually flintlocks that veterans of Valley Forge would have recognized as old friends. As unarmed volunteers fell into line in every town, Curtin sent a wild appeal to Secretary Cameron. Major-General Patterson, just made head of the department embracing Pennsylvania, made similar appeals. They sent demands not only to the War Department but to General Wool in New York.

In response, the War Department ordered Federal arsenals to supply weapons, for as General Scott wrote Patterson, Washington wished no troops sent away unarmed. General Wool also did his best, ordering some 26,000 muskets and more than a million cartridges sent to Pennsylvania. Replying to a special request for 10,000 guns for the 15 reserve regiments which the State was organizing on her own account, Cameron on June 13 announced that the Ordnance Bureau had been told to send them enough smoothbores.[14] Arms did trickle in, but they were never adequate in quantity. The Pennsylvania colonels and General Patterson also protested that many were worthless, and that much of the ammunition was of the wrong caliber. Like other States, Pennsylvania had to make efforts to obtain arms abroad.

The most hot-tempered of all the governors, Oliver P. Morton in Indianapolis, naturally raised the loudest uproar. He had scented approaching danger as soon as the Confederacy was formed. No governor hated slavery more than this explosive man who had walked angrily out of the Indiana Democratic convention the moment it endorsed the Kansas-Nebraska Act, and none stood up more sturdily for his State. "What does this mean? Why this discrimination against Indiana?" he blazed in a telegram to Washington when he thought it slighted. Before Sumter, he had demanded that the War De-

---

13 *Ibid.*, 6 ff. Illinois made vain attempts to buy arms in the East this summer, finding prices too high. When the Fifty-fifth Illinois, recruited during the summer, went to Missouri to fight, it did not draw arms until late December; and they were so wretched that a sergeant wrote Governor Yates that the regiment might better use alder popguns. A Committee of the Regiment, *The Story of the 55th Illinois.*
14 Egle, *Curtin*, 208 ff.; F. H. Taylor, *Philadelphia in the Civil War*, 17 ff.; O. R. III, i, 179–181, 256, 270.

partment store 5,000 small arms and other materials in Indiana in anticipation of trouble. He got approval of the idea, but no shipments. Just after Sumter, while hurrying two agents East and one to Canada to buy arms, he telegraphed Washington that of his 2,400 volunteers in camps, less than half had weapons: "Not a pound of powder or a single ball sent to us, or any sort of equipment." He hastened to Washington, obtained promises, returned home, and then posted to Washington again because the promises were broken. Ten thousand men, he rumbled, were awaiting equipment.[15]

When Cameron explained that a part of the arms ordered to Indiana had been destroyed at Harpers Ferry, Morton refused to be mollified. Nor did Cameron placate him by authorizing Indiana to draw 1500 pieces from the St. Louis arsenal, that arsenal which the Illinoisans had just emptied. Some rifled muskets did arrive from the Pittsburgh arsenal and other points. A peppery debate ensued between Morton and Cameron. Indiana, wrote the Secretary, was unjustified in her bitter scolding, for she had received 3000 new percussion smoothbores, 5000 flintlock muskets altered to percussion, and 1000 Maynard rifled muskets, along with some minor driblets. Altogether, the government had given Indiana 9500 arms for the 5000 men for which it had asked the State. Why, then, the Hoosier ululations? But this was not at all Morton's view. He pointed out that a great part of the arms were abominable, and that he had actually quelled something like a mutiny in the Twelfth Indiana because the men wished to reject unusable old smoothbores. Other troops grumbled that they were given muskets a century old.

The irritated Morton on May 30 appointed Robert Dale Owen the State agent to procure implements of war, and Owen left to join a clamorous group of similar agents in New York. Finally the governor established his own State ammunition manufactory in Indianapolis, which throve so well that in time it sold its surplus to the nation.

So the story went all over the map. New York made appeal after appeal, search after search. Her defeat in getting immediate supplies was writ large in newspaper advertisements on June 1 asking for bids to supply 10,000 Minié rifled muskets and 2000 Minié rifles, with ammunition to equip a force of 12 to 15 regiments of infantry, cavalry and artillery.[16] Iowa, after rebuffs from Cameron and Yates—the latter unwilling to spare any of the St. Louis

---

15 W. D. Foulke, *O. P. Morton*, I, 38, 39, 82, 113-117, 129; O. R. III, i, 64, 65, 89, 93, 116, 122, 149; Anon., *The Soldier of Indiana, passim*. Morton appointed Lewis Wallace the State adjutant-general. He and the quartermaster-general reported many of the Federal arms to be very inferior.

16 Rawley, *E. D. Morgan;* N. Y. *Tribune*, June 1; Burt, Memoirs; Capt. C. E. Minié of Vincennes had gained fame by his elongated bullet, widely used throughout the world. On Robert Dale Owen see the biography by Richard Leopold.

booty—appealed to the governor of Connecticut, to Simeon Draper of the New York Defense Committee, and to arms manufacturers, all without result. The first four Iowa regiments stayed in camp waiting for arms, which finally came as a mixture of antiquated and rubbishy pieces.[17]

To each worried governor, the War Department in the spring and summer of 1861 appeared obtuse and indifferent. Arms were lying at Watertown, Springfield, Pittsburgh: "Why don't they send the arms?" Harassed men in the little War Department took a different view. "It is not possible," James W. Ripley of the Ordnance Bureau wrote the Ohio governor in May, "to meet demands for arms to be distributed among the people without very soon exhausting our entire supplies, and making disproportionate distributions to different parts of the country. There are no Harper's Ferry rifles on hand, and the small supply of rifles should be reserved for the troops of the longer period of service." [18] As national forces grew, the States had to be kept rigorously stinted. As late as the autumn of 1862 Ripley was writing Yates: [19]

I regret very much that it is not within the power of the Ordnance Department to supply to all new troops, such arms as it would afford me pleasure to furnish, if we had or could by any means obtain them; but your Excellency is well aware of the utter impossibility of procuring a sufficient supply of first-class arms to supply to our large armies, and we are therefore compelled to issue the best to be had. In doing this the just rights of the different States are considered. The available arms are arranged in classes and distributed pro rata to the troops called for from each State.

The more energetic States quickly sent arms-buyers abroad. Massachusetts acted with special promptness. On legislative authority given April 20, Andrew appointed F. B. Crowninshield as State agent to procure muskets, rifles, and pistols overseas, and four days later, with a credit of £50,000 and an expert assistant from Springfield, he sailed from New York. His instructions were to buy 25,000 stand of the best quality, as nearly as possible like the guns used in the regular army. Maine and New Hampshire, hearing of his errand, commissioned him to buy for them 3000 and 2000 rifles respectively, and a little later credits came from Connecticut and Ohio. On arriving in London May 6 Crowninshield found that, early as he was, he had to compete with Southern emissaries and buyers from other Northern States, and that speculators were forcing up prices. His assistant, hurrying to Birmingham, where 25,000 first-class Enfield rifles were reported available at £3, found a Southern agent ready to pay £5 apiece for the whole lot, and thought himself lucky to buy

17 Upham, "Arms and Equipment for the Iowa Troops." *Ia. Journal of Hist.*, XVI, 3 ff.
18 Endorsement on letter of Gov. Dennison May 9, 1861; Ordnance Letters, War Dept.
19 Oct. 24, 1862; Ordnance Bureau, Misc. Letterbooks, No. 56, pp. 396, 397.

2000.[20] It was clear to Crowninshield that he should not haggle over prices; and before he sailed back, he obtained 19,380 good Enfield rifles for Massachusetts and shipped part of them, while he also bought 10,000 sets of knapsacks and cartridge boxes, with other equipment.

Leaders in New York meanwhile urged Governor Morgan to buy arms in Europe, and at their suggestion he sent over George L. Schuyler of Schuyler, Hartley & Graham, with authority to obtain about a million dollars' worth of small arms and ordnance. The anxious governor equipped him with a letter to Prime Minister Palmerston which obviously should have gone through the American legation.[21] Howland and Aspinwall also bought arms abroad.

[III]

All this work, however, was swiftly taken over by larger authority; and now we must turn to the national government. We may first summarize its action 1861–62 in two paragraphs.

Clearly, Washington alone could introduce order in place of the confusion and frustration produced by the competing States. As the great new volunteer army came into being, Federal authorities had to accept full responsibility for equipping the men. As fast as possible, they had to take over contract-letting at home and abroad, provide for rigid arms inspection, and accelerate manufacturing at Springfield. Step by step, they gained mastery of the chaotic field, making the Ordnance Bureau one of the nation's most powerful agencies.

Before the end of 1861, War Department contracts had been standardized and a good inspection service created. State purchasing for the national government was permitted only by specific War Department authorization. In many instances the Department refused to compensate States for high-cost purchases in the first months of the conflict, alleging loose methods and disregard of government price specification; in many other instances it reduced the valuation on purchases. Naturally the States were angry, and it was a relief all around when State buying on national account ceased.[22] Federal purchasing

20 Schouler, *Mass. in Civil War*, I, 219, 220; Pearson, *Andrew*, I, 192; Reports of the Master of Ordnance in Mass. Adjutant-General's *Reports*, 1861, 1862. The Master states that Crowninshield bought in all 20,380 rifled Enfield muskets for £73,900.
21 Schuyler bought for New York troops 25,080 rifled Enfields at $16.70 delivered in New York city. He was an able agent, and though his authority to act for the State was suspended in July, on the 29th of that month Cameron authorized him to purchase large consignments for the United States. Rawley, *Morgan;* Burt, *Memoirs;* N. Y. Bureau of Mil. Statistics, *1st Ann. Report* (1863); O. R. III, i, 355. The reports of the New York adjutant-general are singularly unenlightening, and that State lacks a sound history of its war effort. Morgan's 72-page message of January, 1862, contains valuable information.
22 Ripley endorsement on letter of J. N. Ray. March 13, 1862, Ordnance Letters to War Dept.; Cameron to Ripley, War Office Military Bk., No. 47, Jan. 10, 1862; Ripley to Curtin, Oct. 2, 1861, Ordnance Misc. Letterbook No. 55, p. 160.

of arms abroad slackened in the spring of 1862, when everyone hoped for the capture of Richmond, and began again on an improved basis. Government manufacture meanwhile rose until by the spring of 1863 the national armories were producing 30,000 first-class Springfield rifles a month.[23]

But this systematization of arms delivery was not achieved without blunders, delays, and failures of the most disheartening kind. What were they?

War Department confusion at the outset was staggering. Cameron, not allowed before Sumter to prepare for war lest he anger the South, remained ill-prepared because he lacked foresight and energy. When the aging Colonel H. K. Craig had to be dropped as head of the Ordnance Bureau, the Secretary appointed another infirm, incompetent veteran, Lieut.-Colonel James W. Ripley, whom the press soon dubbed Ripley Van Winkle. The bureau staff was so inadequate that extra clerks had to be employed on daily wages.[24] It was a signal misfortune to the North that its supply of arms and munitions was not controlled by a man as able, clearheaded, and progressive as the quarter-master chief, Montgomery C. Meigs.

Ripley was slow, unenterprising, and loath to accept responsibilities. As late as June 3, 1861, possessing no information about the size of the anticipated military force, he asked whether Cameron would approve of provision for 250,000 men in all branches. This was less than half the number envisaged by Congressional leaders, and little over half of what was in Lincoln's mind. Five days later he reported that the government had as yet purchased no muskets, that the Springfield armory was making only 2500 arms a month, and that the service lacked rifled muskets, accoutrements, artillery, and ammunition. But he optimistically declared that supplies on hand would meet all exigencies save the want of rifled muskets, that serviceable smoothbores could be used in their place, and that the Springfield armory and private establishments would maintain the supply and gather a reserve. No need to worry!—no reason even to hurry! Smoothbores would do! [25] A Pennsylvania regiment which compared its Harpers Ferry muskets with Enfield rifles found that the Enfields hit targets at 1000 yards which the muskets missed at 400, and that a mark at 500 yards was riddled by the Enfields while the "buck and ball" of the Harpers Ferry pieces (a ball topped by three buckshot) all fell ignominiously short.

Had the War Department moved with celerity in April–May, 1861, to buy the whole European supply of sound arms and contracted for the whole

23 For a time in the spring of 1862 the Ordnance Bureau refused even the best offers of new contracts like that by Lubback & Co., London, of 100,000 Enfields; Ripley to C. A. Field, April 30, 1862, Ordnance Misc. Letterbook No. 55, p. 160.
24 Meneely, War Department, 1861, 112–113.
25 O. R. III, i, 245, 260.

available output that year, it would not only have acquired an ample store, but would have severely crippled the unindustrialized Confederacy. Such action would have made State buying abroad unnecessary. A few shrewd men urged this. But the whole government, and indeed the American people, underrating the effort ahead and unused to large-scale Federal action, shared the blame. Ripley did not press his early suggestion that a Federal agent be sent abroad to obtain from 50,000 to 100,000 small arms and eight batteries of rifled cannon. He was unduly worried about uniformity of ammunition supply and red-tape standards of quality and cheapness. Cameron also was slow, partly because, like Seward and others, he hoped the war could be quickly ended, and partly because his protectionism made him insist on favoring home industry. Rebuffing Ripley's proposal, as late as July 1 he wrote Lincoln that it was important to encourage domestic manufactures by placing orders in America rather than abroad—especially as war with some European power was a possibility. General Scott and several Cabinet members supported this view.[26]

Two men saw the need of the hour more plainly. One was Henry S. Sanford, minister to Belgium, who tossed on his bed at night worrying about arms. "It distresses me," he wrote Seward a month after Sumter, "to think while we are in want of them, Southern money is to take them away to be used against us." The other was Frémont, who as we have noted had the courage to make provisional contracts. Sanford could merely exhort action; merely urge that because all Europe was arming, because every progressive nation was discarding smoothbores for rifles, because of the machinery shortage, and because supplies were low and prices rising, the United States should move instantly. He begged Seward to send agents to search England and France, to ransack Belgium, and to see if Sweden and Prussia would not sell arms.[27] He himself had no power to act. But Frémont, dropping his European business, did buy. The explorer overcame the Yankee caution of Charles Francis Adams, who reluctantly drew on Treasury funds for $75,000 worth of cannon and shells and $125,000 worth of rifles Frémont had ordered. Frémont, who had been willing to pledge his private means, never forgave Adams for refusing to do the same. A cold, selfish, heartless man, he wrote, who would see the republic sink before he would risk a penny of the Adams fortune!

Adams assured Seward that only his sense of the terrible emergency led him to approve of Frémont's purchases. Lincoln at once ordered the War De-

26 *Ibid.*, 263; Meneely, War Department, 1861, 285.
27 See Report of Committee on Ordnance and Ordnance Stories," July 1, 1862, 37th Cong., 2d. Sess., Senate Exec. Doc. 72; Sanford's warning letter of May 12, 1861, is in O. R. III, i, 277, 278.

partment to honor the drafts, and all the arms were later shipped to the front. But the State Department, agreeing with Cameron, wrote Adams in June that the government would authorize no more foreign contracts. Indeed, except for allowing Sanford to buy 10,000 pieces, Washington temporarily shut down on all purchases abroad, while Cameron and Ripley sat on their hands.[28]

Until Bull Run!—for that thunderclap awakened everybody. It was while its first echoes resounded that Cameron wrote the New York agent, Schuyler, to buy with all speed 100,000 foreign rifled muskets, 10,000 carbines, 20,000 cavalry sabres, and 10,000 revolvers; on July 29 his formal appointment came; and by mid-August, with a $2,000,000-credit at Baring Brothers, he was rummaging the British warehouses. No more home-market coddling!

Unfortunately, Schuyler came too tardily on the scene. He at once found that the Northern States and the Confederacy had almost completely cleared the market of the best rifles, and tied up the best arms factories by their contracts. Prices had risen to double their usual level. Of course antiquated arms, the refuse of decades, in all types, patterns, and calibres, could be had in unlimited quantities, but his instructions and good sense forbade his taking them. When he turned to government arsenals, he found that the British authorities interdicted any sales, but that he might get 45,000 to 48,000 French rifles of an 1853 model. At about the same time he persuaded the Birmingham manufacturers, who were united in a powerful association and had been busily engaged in filling Southern and State contracts, to agree to deliver 35,000 Enfields in New York within six months. Then he was suddenly tripped up by bad luck. He met trouble in getting his money sent from New York to Baring Brothers; the French transaction became public knowledge and Napoleon III forbade it; and Confederate agents snapped up the Birmingham contract at a high price per gun.

In the end, Schuyler did buy a large quantity of arms: 15,000 Enfield rifles in Birmingham at an average price of $18.45 apiece, 4000 French rifles at $17.60, and more than 97,000 good rifles from the government arsenals in Dresden and Vienna at slightly lower prices. These, with 10,000 cavalry carbines and a quantity of revolvers and sabres, cost slightly more than his two millions. His principal purchases were made possible by the friendly attitude of the Austrian Government. Throughout his mission Schuyler, working for only $10 a day and expenses, conducted his affairs with exemplary care, system, and dispatch. He and the expert armorer with him, who meticulously in-

---

28 Nevins, *Frémont*, 3rd ed., 474, 475; O. R. III, i, 293. Frémont bought cannon and shells in England, rifles in France. The Belgian muskets mentioned by Sanford were poor, and Prince Napoleon told D. D. Field they were not worth buying. Cf. T. F. Upson, *With Sherman to the Sea*, 27.

spected all purchases, were repeatedly insulted by men who offered them heavy bribes if they would take inferior equipment.[29]

In his letters home, Schuyler vainly tried to awaken the Ordnance Bureau to the realities of the foreign situation. He emphasized the fact that really excellent arms could not be obtained at any price, even $100 apiece, except from government arsenals, or from private manufacturers already busy with American orders. But Cameron and Ripley, never quite grasping this, contracted with dealers—often mere speculators—for extensive deliveries of foreign arms. They did not comprehend that the government was merely bidding against itself or the States.

The heavy War Department buying of foreign arms through dealers began just after Bull Run with such orders as that to C. K. Garrison, an American, for 10,000 rifled Liége muskets at $27. Ripley agreed in August to accept 4000 foreign rifles from John Pender of Philadelphia at $18.50. The same month J. P. Fitch of New York agreed to deliver 50,000 Enfield rifles at $20, a total later raised to 75,000, while another dealer contracted to bring over 26,000 Enfields at $20. The department bought some Vincennes rifles, a superior arm, at $23.50 delivered in the fall of 1861. This list might be much extended. Such emergency purchases, it will be seen, were at levels materially above those paid by Schuyler in his careful bargaining. He obtained 4000 rifles of Vincennes pattern at almost $6 less than the War Department, and Enfields at $1.55 less, though he gave them a much more rigorous inspection. The alert New Yorker was the keenest businessman abroad.[30]

Altogether, foreign purchases of the Federal Government mounted until by June 30, 1862, they totaled nearly 727,000. Of these Schuyler procured 116,000. Probably if the whole effort had been put in the hands of a purchasing commission directed by Schuyler, he could have obtained much greater firepower at less cost; that is, as many arms, of better quality, at lower rates. At that, the Federal acquisitions were in general better than those of the States. Schuyler kept pointing out how wretched were the weapons shipped to fill State orders, and pleading that State agents be called home and kept there.[31]

Alongside Schuyler labored Minister Sanford, the principal agent in pre-

29 For Schuyler's operations see O. R. III, i, 355, 418, 484–486, 581, 640, etc. See also Schuyler's Report, April 8, 1862, published as a pamphlet. The Chase Papers contain an interesting letter by John J. Cisco, Sept. 24, 1861, on possibilities of buying from Napoleon III; Pa. Hist. Soc.

30 For typical contracts see Ripley to Garrison, July 26, 1861, Ordnance Misc. Letterbook No. 53, p. 280; to Mitchell & Jones, *Ibid.*, 286, 287; to N. V. Barkalow, Letterbook No. 54, p. 42; and see T. A. Scott to Ripley Aug. 5, 1861, War Dept. Military Book No. 45.

31 O. R. III, ii, 855. Asst.-Secretary Peter H. Watson wrote early in 1862 that many arms had been obtained by State agents against the advice of the War Department; to Henry Wilson, Feb. 20, 1862, War Dept. Military Book No. 47.

clusive buying. This bustling, indefatigable, resourceful Connecticut Yankee, not yet forty, with a degree from Heidelberg, found Belgium all too tiny a sphere, and loved to keep an eye on all Western Europe, popping in and out of half the capitals. With insatiable zest, he applied himself to running down Confederate contracts and obstructing or destroying them.

In a single month, with generous credits from the War Department, Sanford obtained 40,000 stand of arms about to go off in a blockade runner, and gobbled up a Confederate contract for 72,000 other arms of low price and quality. He chartered special vessels, in one instance paying a Hamburg company $40,000 for a single voyage, to get his war materials to the United States. After the Trent affair ended, he hurried forward some cargoes which the British had prudently embargoed.[32] All this was in addition to his unwearied prosecution of secret service work and propagandist activities in Europe— activities which, extending to England, gave Charles Francis Adams, jealously sensitive to meddling, acute pain.

As the foreign arms sent across the Atlantic by State agents, reputable dealers, shady speculators, and others were distributed, a roar of indignation and recrimination went up. The best Enfield, Vincennes, and Austrian Government rifles were dependable, but many other pieces were more horrendous to user than to foe. American orders had been a boom to European arsenals anxious to sweep away a clutter of antique and damaged pieces, some of them older than Austerlitz. Newspapers told of regiments taking foreign pieces out to practice, blazing away at the woods, and falling back in disorder with burst barrels and wounded men. Then, too, the conglomeration of arms made replacement of parts difficult, and use of uniform ammunition impossible. A letter which Ripley presently wrote a Pennsylvania officer tells the whole story:

The parts of foreign arms do not interchange. They cannot, therefore, be repaired in the way usual with American arms. It is the practise with some regiments, and should be the case with all regiments armed with foreign arms, to have a mechanic detailed to keep the arms of the regiment in good order. This Dept. will furnish the necesary tools and materials on requisition. If the bayonets do not fit, it is probable that they have been allowed to be mixed up in unpacking the boxes which contained them. In arming the new troops it has been necessary to issue supplies from different points, and in great haste.[33]

[IV]

The War Department's early purchasing of arms from home factories was as blundering and wasteful as the foreign buying. These contracts were chiefly

---

32 Sanford's papers are not yet available. See Meneely, *op. cit.*, 297 ff.; Moran Diary.
33 Ripley to Casey Aug. 25, 1862, Ordnance Misc. Letterbook No. 56, p. 50.

for Springfield pattern rifles, of a quality, if specifications were met, beyond question. Theoretically, they were regulated by laws requiring government advertising for bids, open competition, and systematic inspection. But the emergency was so severe and industrial facilities so weak that at the outset the laws counted for little. The government was no more able to wait than Britain was when Hitler invaded the Low Countries.

Buying had to be done by hurried emergency action outside the law. We have seen how Lincoln had three members of the Union Defense Committee of New York allowed $2,000,000 for immediate war expenditures. As part of this frenzied initial effort Cameron gave his old political supporter Alexander Cummings, now briefly editor of the New York *World*, free rein to make some preposterous purchases. Among other items, Cummings spent $21,000 on straw hats and linen trousers for troops, and bought large quantities of ale, porter, pickles, and tongue. He might have been planning a picnic!

The War Department was at once besieged by contractors and politicians. Its rule was that the Secretary must not directly concern himself with contracts, and Cameron strictly obeyed it. "I had really hoped," he wrote Horace Greeley at the beginning of 1862, "that you had long ago become convinced, from what you have often heard me say, that I have never made any contracts in connection with this Department." But Congressmen were besieged by manufacturers, and wirepulling unquestionably affected contract policy. Even Lincoln was teased into writing a letter for a good Western friend who desired some contracts for building river gunboats.[34] Some of the lesser contract irregularities concerned arms.

As no manufacturer was able to furnish a huge quantity of weapons, and as even the most efficient works often had to erect buildings and install machinery, the contracts had to be scattered in small orders among a variety of suppliers. The Starr Arms Company at Binghamton, New York, got a contract for 80,000 Springfield-pattern muskets, rifled; the Providence Tool Company for 50,000; Eli Whitney of Whitneyville, Connecticut, a son of the inventor, for 40,000; C. B. Hoard of New York for 50,000; and so on. By the spring of 1862 fully a score of orders for small arms had been let. Ripley was scrupulous in insisting that the rifles must conform strictly in design, materials, and workmanship to those made in the Springfield armory, and be subjected to the same inspection. He was rigid about delivery dates. Some manufacturers signed rashly on the dotted line.

Too rashly—for again and again they encountered unforeseen difficulties. Hardworking Eli Whitney, for example, had to build a new factory, and install a new outfit of machinery. He had to prepare four kilns to dry his gun-stocks,

34 Cameron to Greeley, Jan. 15, 1862, Cameron Papers; Lincoln to Commissioner Smith and others, March 28, 1862, *Collected Works*, V, 174.

and order his gun-barrels from another maker. He found it necessary to employ 200 new hands, and might need 325. Even then he was uncertain whether accidents might not prevent his making the first delivery when promised. "I do not think the price, $20, too high, considering the expedition required and the conditions of payment. I do not think the government will obtain more than one quarter of the guns ordered, taking all together, and enforcing stipulations as to time." [35] Whitney's contract, when delays actually occurred, was cut back to 25,000 rifles with a resultant loss.

Similar difficulties were encountered by Lamson, Goodnow & Yale of Windsor, Vermont. They received a government contract in July, 1861, for 25,000 rifled muskets and appendages, which was doubled within three months. At Windsor they had a large plant which had manufactured some 35,000 muskets of the model of 1842, and had furnished a good deal of machinery to the Enfield plant in England. Here they set two hundred men to work making gun machinery and finishing gun parts. They ordered barrels, bayonets, and ramrods from the Bay State works at Northampton, Massachusetts, and a Worcester factory; they forged locks, mountings, and other parts at their own cutlery works in Shelburn Falls; they bought gunstocks. But they, too, met unavoidable delays. After they had invested from $100,000 to $150,000, they plaintively wrote the War Department that they hoped to deliver guns soon, though the contract date had expired; "and now if, for any reason, the government will not receive the fifty thousand, we desire to be informed immediately." They were accepted.[36]

Even so efficient an establishment as Colt's Arms Company, with a factory in Hartford that contained some of the most ingenious machinery in the world, was unable to meet its contract dates. Samuel Colt agreed in July, 1861, to furnish 25,000 rifled muskets of Springfield pattern at $20, the first thousand to be ready in six months. He erected new buildings, installed machinery, and let sub-contracts for barrels, locks, and other parts. Troubles, however, soon thickened about his head—a shortage of skilled labor, the sudden demand of the War Department for special attention to holster pistols, and the tardiness of parts suppliers. The situation was complicated by his long illness, ending in death January 10, 1862. The government recognized that the Colt Company not only had a just claim to some modification, but was too useful to be treated harshly. With a two-million-dollar factory, 1500 employees working day and night shifts, and appliances for making 1000 guns a week, it stood in advance of every other private arms establishment in the land.[37]

35 37th Cong., 2d Sess., Senate Exec. Doc. 72, p. 386; testimony April 11, 1862.
36 Ibid., p. 160.
37 Ibid., 59-61. The destruction of the Colt factory by fire February 10, 1864, was felt as a national blow and caused arms prices to rise. See N. Y. Tribune, Feb. 10, 1864, and picture in London Illustrated News, April 16. It was at once rebuilt.

In general, however, Ripley pursued a severe policy in enforcing contract provisions. The department refused price readjustments, declined to make any allowance to Remington when new Federal taxes imposed a totally unforeseen expense, would not compensate arms importers for fluctuations in international exchange, and brusquely rejected Whitney's anguished appeals for a little more time.[38] Yet these severe policies were coupled, as we have noted, with the two prime errors of ordering too many arms, and paying excessive prices for many of them.

A cost plus system, had Congress been willing to authorize it and the Ordnance Bureau able to police it, would have been better than the allocation of so many hit or miss contracts at hit or miss prices. The before-noted total of 1,164,000 Springfield-type rifled muskets for which the War Department contracted by the summer of 1862 was about twice the amount of home deliveries required; the average price of $20 a gun, with appendages, was about twenty per cent above the proper level. It took time for both government and manufacturers to learn that on bargains for 25,000 rifled muskets or more, $16 would afford a fair profit to efficient makers. Remington & Sons, contracting for a large quantity at that price, gave the Ordnance Bureau its first trustworthy data on costs.[39] The War Department could then regret its numerous $20 contracts, and such orders as that to the Burnside Carbine Company for 7500 carbines at $35 each.[40]

By the summer of 1862 the errors mentioned were cured. The Congressional committee on ordnance reported that it had reduced the domestic orders for Springfields to 473,000, had revised prices, and by other steps had saved the government about $17,000,000. Ripley, in view of the urgent need for arms after the failure of McClellan's advance on Richmond, relaxed the more senseless inspection requirements. The main point, he wrote the Secretary of War, was to secure arms "of the prescribed calibre, of good strong barrels, stocks, and locks, and in all respects serviceable as military weapons." Blemishes could be overlooked.[41]

Disregard of the advertising requirement had not only permitted exorbitant prices, but offered contract jobbers an opportunity to peddle their influence. When the Savage Arms Company failed to get an order, it hired Thomas Dyer, who said he could manage it, and who collected $10,000 for obtaining a pistol contract. Later the same firm employed the adventurer Henry Wikoff, who

38 Ripley's Endorsement Sept. 1, 1863, Ordnance Letters to War Dept., No. 14, pp. 321–323.
39 Report, 37th Cong., 2d Sess., Senate Exec. Doc. 72, pp. 15–18.
40 These were, however, a special weapon weighing 7 pounds, of .54 caliber. Ripley to L. Hartshorne, August 27, 1861; Ordnance Misc. Letterbook No. 53, pp. 307, 308. Senate Exec. Doc. 72, ut sup.
41 Ripley to Stanton August 8, 1862, Ordnance Letters to War Dept. Bk. 13, pp. 464, 465.

actually urged the Savage Company to charge $22.50 for a $19 pistol just because he had filed an application for a contract on which he asked that amount! A specially scandalous offense was proved against Senator James F. Simmons of Rhode Island, a yarn-manufacturer and politician approaching seventy, who introduced a Providence manufacturer to the War Department, helped him get an order for 50,000 rifled muskets, and charged $10,000. As the Congressional committee on ordnance scorchingly put it, he sold his supposed influence; and public opinion forced him to resign in humiliation.[42]

By the end of 1862, but not until that time, the Northern need for proper quantities of weapons as good as the rifled Springfield or Enfield was being met. The helplessness of Frémont's command in Missouri the first war summer, or Sherman's at Louisville that fall, now seemed but a bad dream.[43] Yet it must be remembered that at all times the North had been far better provided with arms and ammunition than the South. When the war began the South, scouring all sources, found that the total number of usable guns for infantry in the Confederacy did not exceed 150,000, and only 20,000 of these were rifles. Several Southern States contracted for Northern arms before Sumter, but shipments were cut off by that event. European purchases brought in but small supplies. General Josiah Gorgas as head of the Ordnance Bureau revealed something like genius in establishing powder mills, arsenals, and arms factories. Weapons were made, altered, repaired, and stored at Richmond, Selma, Macon, Atlanta, Montgomery, Jackson, Little Rock, and other places. The ingenuity and persistence of Southern arms-makers must command the highest admiration. Yet receipts during the first year were negligible, and some Southern boys had to bear shotguns into the battle of Shiloh. Only the tremendous captures of Northern arms during 1862, placed at fully 100,000 pieces, kept the South weaponed.

Southern leaders, in fact, wrung their hands over the situation. When Gorgas on June 29, 1861, reported on all the arms in the Confederacy not in the hands of troops, he found but 15,000 available. The Richmond armory,

42 Report, 37th Cong., 2d Session, Senate Exec. Doc. 72, pp. 515 ff.
43 In fact, from this time surplus stocks began to accumulate. Ripley wrote September 1, 1863, that the government had on hand a very large supply of first-class arms, that monthly receipts from manufacturers constantly increased that stock, and that the Springfield armory alone was now supplying 20,000 arms monthly. Now and then a shortage of special parts appeared, as of gunstocks at the Springfield armory late in 1863, but this was transient. At the beginning of 1864 Assistant-Secretary Watson wrote that in view of the stored surplus and the unfilled contracts, the Springfield Armory could supply every musket needed even if the war continued for years. In the last year of the war the Ordnance Bureau was buying only revolvers and carbines, and it had contracted with the Remington Company, the best private supplier, for quantities of both. Ripley, endorsement on Whitney letter September 1, 1863, Ordnance Letters to War Dept. Book No. 14, pp. 321–323; Watson to Wheelock, Jan. 28, 1864, War Dept. Military Book No. 54b, p. 174; Ramsay to Stanton, Sept. 23, 1864, Ordnance Letters to War Dept., Book No. 15, pp. 180 ff.

beginning late that summer, could supply only a thousand small arms a month; the Fayetteville armory, beginning in March, 1862, could produce only about five hundred. That was the whole domestic picture for the South in the early part of the war! Down to August 16, 1862, the Confederate agent abroad, Caleb Huse, was able to land fewer than 50,000 arms in Southern ports. The Union by comparison held a position of growing wealth; and as the months passed the North also had an advantage in the rising superiority of much of its arms.

The obstacles met by the Confederates in getting arms from abroad were especially frustrating in the first year of the war, for after the foothill difficulties of purchasing came the high cliff of making shipments. Blockade running did not mean much to the arms trade until special steamers of great speed and low visibility were built for the purpose. Huse sent President Davis a gloomy letter from London just after Christmas in 1861, saying that he was miserable in having to look at the immense pile of packages on St. Andrew's Wharf without the power of sending anything: 25,000 rifles, 2,000 barrels of powder, 500,000 cartridges, and 13,000 accoutrements, besides great heaps of miscellaneous supplies. It took time, endless ingenuity, and worry to make inroads on this accumulation. Northern armies met no such frustrations.

The quality of the rifled muskets had steadily improved. Better machine tools counted for a great deal in this advance. Thus the Lamson, Goodnow & Yale Company of Connecticut used the Ball precision lathe machine, previously employed in making sewing-machine needles, the Robbins & Lawrence Company produced an efficient new rifling machine, and Brown & Sharpe of Providence brought on the market a universal milling machine that could be adapted to many purposes other than gun-making. Another important contribution, attributable to the Trenton ironmaster Abram S. Hewitt, was an ample supply of good American gun-metal, of the same quality as the famous Marshall iron imported from England. Hewitt, tremendously aroused by the war peril, did not hesitate to smuggle a spy into the Marshall plant to learn its secret. For this and other services, the Cooper, Hewitt works at Trenton received a glowing War Department citation. Finally, workers in the arms plants everywhere were gaining skill from experience.[44]

With stocks rising, with the Springfield armory getting under such headway that it alone would soon be able to meet national needs, and with prices falling, no more imported arms were needed after 1862. The firepower of the

44 *Mechanics Magazine*, VII, 105 (Feb. 14, 1862), 105. Guy Hubbard, series on "Development of Machine Tools in New England," *American Machinist*, vol. 60 (1924); Nevins, *Abram S. Hewitt*.

North had at all times been greater than that of the South, and the dispropor-
tion inexorably increased. Even when due weight is given the facts that the
South fought mainly on the defensive, initially possessed better marksmen, and
captured great quantities of Northern arms, this disparity was an important
element in deciding the outcome of the war. It might have been made greater.

[V]

The principal indictment against the Ordnance Bureau remains to be stated,
and can be summed up in the current press reproach of "old-fogyism." Critical
newspapers delighted to picture Ripley Van Winkle asleep in the Ordnance
Bureau guarded by two giants, Red Tape and Routine. When disturbed his
face would assume a disgusted frown, he would turn uneasily, and his lips
would mutter: "Keep him out!—inventor!—new idea!—can't come in here!—
Routine! Red Tape!" By the summer of 1862 an ambitious, hard-driving
junior, George T. Balch, was laboring to displace him. But he held power
until September 15, 1863, and continued to offer an unbreachable wall to
progress. In especial, his policy fatally impeded the large-scale adoption of
breechloading rifles.[45]

For the first two years of the war the use of muzzle-loading Springfields
and Enfield rifled muskets as standard patterns was absolutely unavoidable.
Thereafter, however, breechloaders might steadily have been introduced, and
larger and larger bodies of troops might have been equipped with repeating
breechloaders. Their use would have shortened the conflict.

The Springfield and Enfield rifles were effective weapons which used inter-
changeable ammunition, and thus simplified the problem of cartridge supply.
They were made in much the same way, for the Springfield plant had imported
sets of English rolling machines to make gun barrels, with English mechanics,
while the Enfield plant had bought much larger quantities of American machinery. The Springfield caliber was .58, the Enfield .57 plus; as the Springfields tended to foul after twenty-five rounds and become hard to reload,
many soldiers liked then to turn to the slightly smaller Enfield cartridge.
American factories could readily be tooled and manned to make Springfields
in quantity.

Breechloaders, however, posed a far more difficult problem. A number of
usable American models had been devised before 1861, notably the Colt, the
Hall, the Burnside, and the Sharps. Specific offers of the Spencer, Henry, and

---

45 N. Y. *Tribune*, Feb. 21, editorial "Rip Van Winkle in the Army Ordnance Bureau";
Bruce, *Lincoln and the Tools of War*, 260 ff.

Schenck breechloaders were made the War Department in that year. But as patterns varied greatly and the parts were difficult, breechloaders could at first be made only in small quantities and with excruciating delays.[46]

No two breechloaders, in fact, were constructed alike in 1861, so that the replacement of parts would soon have become a Chinese puzzle. Once the armies had been equipped with Springfields, Enfields, Vincennes, and other muzzle-loaders, as they had to be in 1861, it was impossible to arrange for any wholesale replacements before 1863. It can be argued that some buildings of the Springfield Armory might have been set aside to fix standard breechloading designs, to which private manufacturers could have been made to conform. But considering the crushing early demands, paucity of skilled workmen, and undeveloped character of machine tools, the equipment of such a branch would have been a slow task, carried out at the expense of more urgent requirements. When we say that the Colt, Hall, and other existing breechloaders were usable, we do not mean that they did not need great improvement. Army officers objected that they allowed an escape of gas at the junction of barrel sections where they were loaded, that the percussion powder needed for their cartridges was dangerous in jolting wagons, that they were not staunch enough for rough field service, and that troops in the excitement of battle would jam the delicate breech mechanism.[47]

This does not signify, however, that the Ordnance Bureau could not have provided great quantities of good breechloaders in 1863, for by energetic action it could. Not only had the cavalry used breechloading carbines for years, but American seamen and marines had employed them since 1858. The British navy was experimenting with them. Late in 1861 the government placed an order for 10,000 (later 16,000) Gibbs breechloading carbines at $28 each, with appendages.[48]

But this small order, with a delivery schedule of only 500 a month, was not followed up. At the end of 1862 the Ordnance Bureau was still experimenting cautiously with small orders let in a wide variety of quarters. When one contractor asked to have his new type of breechloader tested, Ripley objected on the ground that ten patterns of such arms were already being made, for eight of which tiny government contracts were in course of execution. This multiplicity of designs had caused so much confusion that he could not bear the thought of another.[49] From the ruck two superior arms decisively

46 S. B. Smith, "Military Small Arms," *Papers*, Ohio Commandery Loyal Legion, I, 174 ff. When the British had established their arms factory at Enfield in 1855 they were advised by officers who had carefully inspected American arms factories, and especially Springfield.
47 Ripley endorsement on Schenck's letter, Ordnance Letters to War Dept. Book No. 13, p. 170.
48 Ripley to W. F. Brooks, Dec. 13, 1861; Ordnance Misc. Letterbook No. 54, p. 215.
49 Ripley to Stanton, Jan. 9, 1863, Ordnance Letters to War Dept., Book 14, p. 55, National

emerged· one the Sharps carbine, a familiar single-shot breechloader specially adapted to cavalry, and the other the Spencer repeating rifle, a highly lethal weapon in the hands of infantry. With boldness and vigor, Ripley could have made both of them standard army equipment during the year of Gettysburg and Vicksburg. Had he done so, that might have been the war's last year.

The famous Sharps plant at Hartford was ready for a rapid expansion. Its single-shot breechloader, the most popular such rifle in the war, was especially liked by those who prided themselves on marksmanship. Hiram Berdan, a New York engineer of repute who had Lincoln's encouragement in organizing a famous sharpshooter regiment, did much to advertise it by his warm praise. The Ordnance Bureau placed contracts, especially late in the war, which eventually aggregated more than 100,000 pieces, so that in the last year the Sharps plant, greatly expanded, was employing 500 men day and night. It made more than 30,000 rifles that year. R. S. Lawrence, the master armorer, who under Sharps's direction had full charge of the factory, improved the arm in various ways during the conflict. Perhaps the first highly paid plant manager in the country, he wrote afterward with naïve satisfaction: "With my salary, speculations on machinery, etc., I found myself worth over $100,000." [50]

A good many telescope rifles for sharpshooters like Berdan, it may be interjected, were made by village blacksmiths and gunsmiths in the North. Indeed, telescope rifles had been frequently ordered before the war for the traditional Thanksgiving Day turkey-shoots and other matches. Weighing up to twenty pounds, they were necessarily fired from rests. In New England and the Middle States a village would sometimes not only denude itself of young men, but energetically forge weapons for the best marksmen. One Massachusetts company, going to war in 1861 with telescopic rifles, met first ridicule and then admiration. A member wrote back that the results were

Archives, explains his objection to the multiplicity of designs. Christian Sharps had patented his single-shot breechloading rifle in the 1840's. Christopher Spencer, who had worked in Colt's Hartford factory, patented his seven-shot repeating breechloader early in 1860.

50 *American Machinist*, vol. 60 (Jan. 31, 1924), 172. The Sharps Rifle Manufacturing Company made a variety of patent breechloading and self-priming arms—rifle, carbine, shotgun, and pistol. The superiority of the rifle had been established as early as 1850, when a board of ordnance officers under Major R. L. Baker made a report (Nov. 27), stating that of five makes of rifle and one of carbine presented, the Sharps was much the best. It was loaded with Mr. Sharps' special cartridge, and could be fired several hundred times without cleaning. The Sharps Company, using cast steel, boasted that their arms combined simplicity of design, rapidity of firing, extraordinary range, and perfect accuracy. See advertising circulars, NYPL.

Berdan asked the men he recruited to bring their own rifle with telescopic glass-sight or plain open sights. He wrote one of his enlistment agents, A. B. Stuart, Aug. 22, 1861, "You will see that no man is enlisted who cannot when firing at rest at a distance of 200 yards with a patent sighted rifle put ten consecutive shots in a target the average not to exceed five inches center to center, or with the plain open sight a distance of 300 feet same average." Austin Blair Papers, Burton Hist. Coll.

devastating. "They do good service at a mile, and are certain death at half a mile." At Edwards' Ferry, October 22, 1861, 70 men of this company repelled an advance of 1500 Confederates and drove them from the field with a loss of more than 100 killed, the Yankees suffering not a scratch: "The whistle of every bullet was the death knell of one." Tiffany's in New York offered some very fine and very costly telescopic rifles, among them the imported Whitworth target rifle, which soon sold out at $1250.[51]

Single-shot rifles were all very well, but a good repeating breechloader was something about which soldiers really dreamed. When Rosecrans took over Buell's army in the fall of 1862, he found his cavalry force low, and to compensate for this applied for 5000 Colt's repeating rifles. Raw recruits, he believed, if armed with repeaters that shot five times as fast as Springfields, would be superior to the toughest veterans using the old arms.[52] But while both Colt's and Henry's repeaters had merit, the Spencer carbines and rifles emerged as the cheapest, most durable, and most efficient of such weapons. They could sweep the ground with a deadly hail, and pick out men far beyond Confederate range. All the troops who saw the Spencer repeating rifle became clamorous for it.

That the armies preferred breechloaders, and that officers would have been glad to see at least picked companies in every regiment armed with repeating rifles, there can be no question. Had the soldiers determined Ordnance Bureau policy, they would soon have been adopted. The muzzle-loading smoothbores, which all too closely resembled the Brown Bess of Queen Anne's day, did execution only against masses of men, for they had to be aimed in barn-door fashion. Though troops who had rifled Springfields could pick out distant marks, they found it no fun to stand under fire loading them with ramrod and wad. Ripley's more energetic successor, Brigadier-General George D. Ramsay, grasped the rising demand for quick-firing weapons. He reported to Assistant-Secretary Watson early in 1864 that "repeating arms are the greatest favorite with the army, and could they be supplied in quantities to meet all requisitions, I am sure that no other arm would be used." He wrote again that summer in praise of the Spencer repeater: "It is, to a great extent, the only arm now asked for." [53]

The deadly effect of the repeating rifles used by some Union troops at the

51 American Machinist, vol. 59 (Oct. 18, 1923) 580, 581; "The Use of the Rifle," Atlantic, vol. 9 (March, 1862), 300–306.

52 W. D. Bickham, Rosecrans' Campaign, 25; Bruce, Lincoln and the Tools of War, 114, 115.

53 Endorsement on Applications of Sharps Co. and Burnside Co., Ordnance letters to War Dept. Book No. 14, p. 46; Brigadier-General George D. Ramsay to Stanton, July 14, 1864, Ibid., Book 15, p. 98.

battle of Franklin this year appalled the Confederates who faced them; they were absolutely irresistible in repelling assaults.

After considering all excuses, we must pronounce the Ordnance Bureau under Ripley egregiously slow and cautious in providing both single-shot and repeating breechloaders. In 1861 it had to concentrate on muzzle-loading Springfields, Enfields, and the like. But in 1862 it could have encouraged capable arms manufacturers like the Remington, Colt, Sharps, and Whitney companies—like Merwin & Bray in New York, who made Ballard's very successful breechloading rifles and carbine, and like the New Haven Arms Company, which under Oliver F. Winchester made a variety of arms, including B. Tyler Henry's steadily improved repeater—to press their experiments. They could have agreed upon a standard breechloader design, and soon thereafter have commenced quantity production. By 1864, if not in 1863, it should have been possible to furnish the Northern armies wholesale as good an arm as the famous Prussian needle-gun which played so devastating a part in the Austrian War of 1866. This supply, and even a limited number of repeating rifles, would have transformed the military scene.[54]

What was needed was foresight, energy, and a planned effort to stimulate the great inventive capacity of Americans; what Ripley gave was stubborn caution. It was in spite of his objections that the army in 1863-64 finally contracted for some 41,000 Spencer repeaters—too late. When American makers exhibited arms at the Paris Exhibition of 1867 they gave breechloaders a dominant place, and among them were two magazine guns, the Spencer firing seven shots in twelve seconds, and a rifle made by the Windsor Manufacturing Company (Vermont) firing nine shots in eleven seconds. Of fourteen guns selected for the British breechloading competition in 1867, six were American and two more were made on American principles.[55]

The day of rapid-fire machine guns had not yet arrived. British officers inspecting McClellan's army in the Peninsular campaign found that he had fifty small "repeating guns," each drawn by a horse, but they were unsatisfactory. They were mounted on light wooden carriages. Two dozen cartridges at a time were placed in a hopper, they fell through its bottom into a

54 Cf. N. Y. *Tribune*, Jan. 30, 1864, "Improvements in Fire-Arms"; H. F. Williamson, *Winchester, The Gun That Won the West, passim.*

55 Ripley objected that magazine guns were too heavy, required special cartridges that might explode in transit, and were too costly; see his letter of Dec. 9, 1861, quoted in Williamson, *ut sup.* His attitude remained apparently unchanged until June, 1863, when he put in a trifling order for some 250 Henry repeaters. A British officer who saw seven-shot repeating rifles being made at the Parrott Works at Cold Spring, N. Y., late in 1864, thought them astonishing. He was told that although in action raw troops wasted much ammunition with them, cool marksmen made them very destructive, and a few men armed with them could hold a host at bay on a narrow front. Letter in London *Star*, Dec. 20, 1864, quoted in *Scientific American*, XII, Jan. 21, 1865.

revolving chamber, the gunner turned this chamber by a handle which also worked a percussion hammer, and as fast as he turned, the gun fired. The British observers were told that a hundred shots could be fired a minute; but in some practice at two hundred and fifty yards they observed that most of the ammunition was too small to take the rifling, the gun made few hits, and it soon got out of order. A mechanic, they thought, was needed to keep it in trim, and even then it might prove of little field utility.[56]

Here again, Ripley's disinclination to encourage experiment was unfortunate. Benjamin B. Hotchkiss, who filled war orders for projectiles and other munitions at his New York city factory, and who a decade later designed a five-barrelled weapon which quickly won worldwide adoption, might have been stimulated to devise an efficient rapid-fire piece. McClellan's hopper-and-handle contraption was at best defensive, useful only to hold a narrow bridge; Hotchkiss's gun was suited to offense. Richard J. Gatling, an inventive manufacturer of farm implements in the Middle West, patented a crude rapid-fire gun late in 1862. His first model, with ten revolving barrels, each with its own loading and ejecting mechanism, delivered 200–250 shots a minute. The Ordnance Bureau regarded the weapon with such chilliness that Gatling had to hire his own men to give several battlefield demonstrations during the war. Not until he made important improvements, took out a second patent in May, 1865, and got a Philadelphia arms company to manufacture twelve guns, did the War Department become keenly interested. Had he been given early aid, he might have had the Gatling gun, which the army adopted in 1866, ready for the campaigns of 1864.

[VI]

Ammunition was at first a perplexing problem, since the issuance of a weird variety of arms gave the officers who were responsible for providing it a maddening task. Powder was supplied by a number of firms, but by far the largest shipments came from the E. I. DuPont Company of Wilmington and the Hazard Company at Hazardville, Conn. The brilliant Lammot Du Pont shortly before the war had gone to Europe, inspected foreign powder mills, taken note of improvements resulting from Crimean experience, and returned home to begin a fruitful collaboration with Captain Thomas J. Rodman, ballistics engineer of the Ordnance Bureau. But British observers in 1862 thought the Du Pont method of manufacture inferior to their own.[57]

56 Report of Captains Thomas Mahon and R. Grant and Lieut. T. C. Price, August 1862, to Commander-in-Chief in Canada; Confidential Documents, British War Office.
57 See McClellan's *Report*, pp. 71, 72; William S. Dutton, *Du Pont: One Hundred and Forty Years, passim*; Report of Mahon, Grant, and Price, *ut sup*. Dutton estimates that Du

For muzzle-loaders the standard cartridge was a paper cylinder holding a soft-lead bullet and a charge of powder. Soldiers bit open the cartridge, poured the powder down the barrel, rammed home the ball (with a wad and some extra buckshot in smoothbores), and placed a percussion cap on the nipple to explode the charge. In the fever and noise of battle recruits often failed to notice that a weak hammer had failed to ignite the powder, and rammed down charge after charge until the gun was more dangerous to its holder than to the foe.

Breechloaders of course required a special cartridge. When the war began a number of metallic cartridges for them were available. They included the Burnside, invented by the versatile Ambrose E. Burnside, a percussion-cap cartridge for the Burnside carbine; the Maynard, a reloadable brass percussion cartridge invented by a dentist; and the Smith, with a brass foil or (experimentally) a rubber case. The most popular cartridge for cavalry was the Sharps, originally made of linen with a paper base nitrated for quick ignition, but later of metal. Part of the range, accuracy, and hitting power of the Sharps was attributable to its superior ammunition. The Spencer rifles, which were made in a distinctive bottleneck shape, used a rim-fire cartridge in which the priming charge was placed around the edge rather than in a central core. For all cartridges in all countries, the most troublesome problem was that of checking the escape of gas and fire at the breech, and Britons, Frenchmen, and Americans all toiled to solve it. Wesson of Smith & Wesson, revolver makers, had blazed a hopeful path by giving his rim-fire cartridge a projecting flange around the base.[58]

As the war continued and breechloaders became less rare, the brass or copper rim-fire cartridge became the universal favorite. It was manifestly

---

Pont furnished between 3.5 and 4 million pounds of powder to the Union army and navy, or probably 1 million pounds more than the plant which the Confederacy hurriedly built at Augusta supplied. The Du Pont business, struggling for a solid place, had been put firmly on its feet by the Crimean War, sending Britain and France huge shipments which wiped its books clear of debt. When war came in 1861 the Du Pont mills in Delaware constituted more than a third of the powdermaking capacity of the United States. Lammot Du Pont, the inventor of a new and excellent formula for blasting powder which had swept the markets, was at thirty the nation's leading expert in the chemistry of explosives. The North did not suffer from powder shortages. The South, on the other hand, dependent on its new Augusta mill and a small older establishment at Nashville, was soon paying an average of $3 a pound (more than ten times the normal price) for British powder shipped through the blockade; and seldom during the war was the Confederacy able to supply its infantry with more than 90 rounds a man, though the ordnance manual called for 200 rounds.

58 Leonard Davis, MS Paper on "Cartridges and the Civil War"; Williamson, *Winchester, the Gun That Won the West*. Leonard Davis states that the War Department bought 58,238,924 Spencer cartridges during the war. In spite of a growing uniformity of cartridges, the variety of missiles used remained preposterously wide. On Gettysburg battlefield one collector, J. M. Bush, picked up 125 different kinds of bullets, Union and Confederate, which may now be seen in the Gettysburg Museum.

superior to paper or linen types. As Ramsay wrote in the early summer of
1864, it was waterproof, a great consideration; holding its shape, it was easily
inserted; it required no cap; the charge got the full force of the fulminate in
the circular ring; and the flanged copper case, a perfect gas-check, gave the
powder greater force. Manufacture was then in the hands of three firms, who
charged what the Ordnance Department regarded as an excessive price, $28 a
thousand. As the government would need 42,350,000 cartridges as a year's
supply for the breechloading carbines on hand at the end of 1864, Ramsay
proposed the erection of a special mill at the Frankfort Arsenal. So far as war
needs went, this was a belated demand, for ere the mill could be put in running
order, the war would be in its last stage.[59]

The South did not stand at such a disadvantage in ammunition as in small
arms. Thanks to the energy of sleepless Confederate patriots, even in the
summer of 1861, a stream of material for troops was coming from various
sources: 50,000 to 100,000 rounds of ammunition a day from the Richmond
ordnance laboratory, 20,000 to 30,000 rounds daily from the Augusta arsenal,
15,000 to 20,000 from the Charleston arsenal, and 30,000 to 40,000 from the
Baton Rouge arsenal—with small amounts from other shops. But the quality of
the ammunition fell below the Northern standard, battlefield shortages repeatedly tortured various commanders, and Gorgas and his able lieutenant in
this field, G. W. Rains, worried constantly over the desperate need of the
South for niter and other essentials. It was marvelous that the Confederacy did
as well as it did.[60]

The Civil War was primarily an infantrymen's war, in which artillery
played but a secondary part. Being a war of movement over great distances
and rough terrain, so that the transport even of light fieldpieces like the popular
Napoleon gun often involved great difficulty, it was best suited to mobile
forces. Moreover, the rifled Springfields and Enfields had an effective range
equal to that of field guns using canister, so that infantrymen could usually
silence all but the best sheltered batteries and largest ordnance.

Artillery, like the small firearm, was undergoing a revolution. An English
inventor of genius, William Armstrong, reading how the battle of Inkerman
(November, 1854) was largely decided against the Russians by two eighteen-
pounder guns which almost superhuman effort brought on the field at a late
hour, asked himself whether lighter artillery might not be given equal range.
When he prepared a design for rifled wrought-iron guns, the first in the world,
obtained a contract from the War Office and set about improving his new

59 Ramsay to Stanton, June 25, 1864, Ordnance Letters to War Dept. Book No. 15, pp. 76,
77. Peter Peckham, an Illinois inventor, gained Lincoln's ear for a cartridge never adopted.
60 Frank E. Vandiver, *Ploughshares Into Swords*, 55-117, covers the subject admirably.

ordnance, the artillery revolution was under way. With the precise role played by artillery on American battlefields, however, we shall deal later.

It was a characteristic chapter of the times, this arms story. Initial bewilderment, hurry, confusion, improvisation, streaked with loss and disaster; a hectic meeting of immediate demands; the gradual emergence of a loose system—including termination of foreign orders, coordination of domestic contracts, and increased reliance on the Springfield armory; and finally a successful system. The arms story helps explain McClellan's delays, and Frémont's misfortunes. The steady improvement of arms supply underlay the partial successes of 1862. Only a long array of studies of individual effort, too numerous for general history, could do justice to the enterprise, resourcefulness and determination which dozens of able men, like Whitney, Colt, Winchester, Hewitt, Henry, and DuPont, brought to the service of the country; men far more anxious to save the Union than to promote their individual fortunes. The story of industrial mobilization has color and gallantry, and it touches the very heart of the developmental forces of the nation.

Yet, in the broad view, this chapter also records a very characteristic failure of vision and planning. Only halting, unimaginative use was made of the wide industrial superiority of the North, its fast-awakening energies in business and manufacture. Had the government looked ahead and taken suitable measures, had it by the end of 1863 given the armies a half-million good single-shot breechloaders and a quarter-million repeating rifles, the war might have ended far earlier, with a proportionate diminution of the misery and exhaustion that attended it.[61]

61 Kenneth P. Williams, *Lincoln Finds a General*, II, 782–785, explains the difficulties of introducing breech-loaders; but these difficulties could have been overcome.

19

December Gloom

IT WAS AN anxious autumn upon which the North entered in 1861. The weather in the Middle States and Virginia continued singularly bright, dry, and balmy; day after day throughout November and December the sun shone, mild breezes tossed the many-hued leaves, vehicles raised lines of dust, and men worked outdoors. But a leaden weight lay on the hearts of those who had hoped that the New York bells might ring peace. In the East, McClellan's army quivered and lay still like a basking crocodile. Although public sentiment could not easily forget the October whiplash of Ball's Bluff, McClellan made no response; and in the West, Frémont and Blair seemed more intent on fighting each other than on defeating Price and McCulloch.

Hope for quick action, inspired by McClellan's own words, had risen like a released fountain the moment he replaced Scott. Our young commander, confidentially wrote the Washington correspondent of the Chicago *Tribune*, will put a stop to all Sewardish schemes for paralyzing the war effort. "Look for an advance soon, for it will come, and we shall have some stiff fighting before winter sets in." [1] But still McClellan devoted himself to sedulous drill, admonishing Cameron that the Army of the Potomac should reach 300,000 to ensure decisive success; still the Confederates wondered why he did not move against their puny lines.

Under the delusion of heavy enemy superiority, McClellan believed concentration and caution the only safe policy. Any diversionary movement, any thrust, was too dangerous to be weighed. On August 25 he had written his wife that by the end of the week he would have 75,000 men and feel safer. "Last week he [Beauregard] certainly had double our force." On September 8 he had reported to Cameron that the Confederates meant to take Washington, but would probably move on Baltimore first. That is, they would engage Union pickets on the Potomac and make other demonstrations to draw off McClellan's forces, and then suddenly cross above Washington to

---

1 Henry Smith, Nov. 4, 1861, to the *Tribune* editors; C. H. Ray Papers, Huntington Library.

pour their main army direct on Baltimore. "I see no reason to doubt the possibility of his attempting this with a column of at least 100,000 effective troops." [2]

In other words, the Confederates had the power to launch an attack, but McClellan's army was too weak for one! Actually, the Johnston-Beauregard forces in front of McClellan on October 31 comprised 44,131 men present for duty. These two commanders would have been glad to invade the North with 60,000 seasoned, well-armed, properly wagoned troops, but lacked the men, weapons, and transport. They and General W. H. Smith, at a pivotal field conference attended by President Davis, agreed that the only course was to take a defensive position. Yet weak as they were, the Confederates considered attacking Union forces along the north bank of the Potomac, and rejected the idea because Federal warships controlled the river. McClellan, who enjoyed this control, sabotaged the navy's plan for clearing the south bank.[3]

Allan Pinkerton as McClellan's "chief of the secret service" made army headquarters blench by reporting October 4 that the Confederates in Virginia had the fearful total of 184 regiments, numbering 126,600 men. Of this mythical array, 98,400 under Johnston and Beauregard lay at Fairfax Court House and vicinity, 11,000 under Lee, Floyd, and Wise in western Virginia, 10,400 at Norfolk and Portsmouth, and 6800 under Winder in the Richmond area. The Johnston-Beauregard troops retired to Centerville on October 19, when McClellan's growing army became capable of maneuvering. (Not that McClellan had any intention of maneuvering!) Pinkerton painted another Munchausen picture on November 15 in a memorandum placing Confederate strength (after a deduction of 5 per cent to be conservative) at 116,430. He had founded his first report on information from deserters, contrabands, and his own agents, and the second mainly on the observations of a detective who had visited Manassas, Centreville, and Warrington. This operative declared that the rebels were well armed, well fed, and well furnished with ammunition, but "dam'd badly off for winter clothing." Although McClellan should have realized that deserters would lie, that refugee Negroes could unconsciously exaggerate, and that one operative might be a fool or cheat, he made no real effort at verification.[4]

The pressure for an offensive in these autumn weeks, mistaken insofar as men like Ben Wade and Zack Chandler demanded a major battle, was justified

2 Swinton, *Army of the Potomac*, 72.
3 J. G. Barnard, *The Peninsular Campaign*, 12 ff.; Roman, *Beauregard*, I, 142–145; J. E. Johnston, *Narrative of Military Operations;* Davis Papers (President Davis called the Smith-Johnston-Beauregard council), Duke University; McClellan, *Own Story*, 196–197; Official Report (1864), 110–111.
4 Pinkerton Papers, courtesy of the late Howard Swiggett; J. E. Johnston, *Narrative*, 77.

insofar as it sought bold preparatory action. To clear the south bank of the Potomac and capture Norfolk, we repeat, were objects of prime importance, feasible enough for the hero of West Virginia. Even the mild Senator Foster of Connecticut begged for "energy" along these lines. Union forces held Fort Monroe, Newport News, and Hampton, the Union fleet patrolled Hampton Roads, and the army in this area, well intrenched by contraband labor, was reinforced from time to time. An amphibious assault might have driven the Confederates from Norfolk and compelled the destruction of the *Merrimac*.

For the navy was a fast-growing power, and early in November it once more gave the Union a transient gleam of sunshine. To maintain the blockade, bases not too distant from the Southern ports were required; and the wide, deep Port Royal Sound, lying squarely between Charleston and Savannah, seemed ideal for an establishment. A fleet of seventy ships, carrying—soldiers, sailors, marines—15,000 men, with heavy guns and six months' stores, put into the Atlantic October 29, bands playing, banners flying, and Flag-Officer S. F. Du Pont in the *Wabash* leading the way. Though it encountered a heavy storm, November 4 found it anchored off its goal, "the water as smooth as a pan of milk." Here two forts at Bay Point and Hilton Head, with a trio of weak Confederate gunboats, guarded the entrance to the Sound. The works were scientifically constructed and heavily armed; it was said that the Confederates had hoped to disable their assailants in half an hour. But by fine management of his ships on a semi-circular course and beautifully accurate fire, Du Pont in less than five hours' bombardment forced an evacuation. The *Wabash* alone fired 440 shells. General Thomas W. Sherman's troops took possession of the posts and all the surrounding country.[5]

The Union thus gained a foothold near two of the chief Southern ports, where it could plant a depot for coaling and supplying blockade vessels. The sea islands, lying like peas in the pod of the Sound—Parris, Hilton Head, Port Royal, St. Helena—were perfectly secure. Du Pont reported, "The negroes are wild with joy and revenge," and the Union plainly faced a new problem in administering freedmen. The President was delighted. He was pleased, too, by simultaneous news that General William Nelson, formerly of the navy, had won a fight at Pikesville, Kentucky, taking about a thousand prisoners.

Lincoln had talked frankly with McClellan about the impatience of the radical leaders for action. While public sentiment had to be taken into account, he said, "at the same time, general, you must not fight until you are ready." He had assured McClellan his full support, remarking November 1: "Draw

---

5 For Port Royal, see H. A. Du Pont, *Samuel Francis Du Pont*, ch. VII; Daniel Ammen, *Battles and Leaders*, I, 671–691; Dudley W. Knox, *Hist. of the U. S. Navy*, 202–205. Lincoln's words to McClellan are given in Dennett, *Diary and Letters of John Hay*, Oct. 26, 1861, p. 31.

PART OF THE
Military Department
OF
THE SOUTH
AND OF
SOUTH ATLANTIC COAST

Scale of Miles

on me for all the sense I have, and all the information." Noting the flurry of alarm which Du Pont's expedition sent over the South, he called at McClellan's house the evening of November 11 to say that it seemed a good time to "feel" the Confederate forces. McClellan answered: "I have not been unmindful of that. We will feel them tomorrow." [6] General S. P. Heintzelman indeed made a reconnaissance on the 12th.

When the following day brought news of the capture of Beaufort, South Carolina, it was natural that Lincoln and Seward, attended by John Hay, should pay another evening call on McClellan. The sequel was a disturbing incident. They found the general out at a wedding. Hay records:

6 *Ibid.,* 33.

We went in, and after we had waited about an hour, McC. came in and without paying any particular attention to the porter, who told him the President was waiting to see him, went upstairs, passing the door of the room where the President and Secretary of State were seated. They waited about half an hour, and sent once more a servant to tell the General they were there, and the answer coolly came that the General had gone to bed. . . .

Coming home I spoke to the President about the matter but he seemed not to have noticed it, specially, saying it was better at this time not to be making points of etiquette and personal dignity.[7]

[I]

At this moment the Western drama reached its shabby, destructive climax.

The shortage of arms, equipment, and transportation in Missouri remained lamentable. "It becomes daily plainer that the Mississippi Valley is to be the greatest theatre of the war," wrote the St. Louis correspondent of Greeley's *Tribune* in mid-October; yet "the government fails to comprehend the magnitude of this department, and the extent of its absolute necessities." The Western people, who had poured out their sons generously, felt this bitterly, "and it is engendering a spirit which will prove disastrous if it is not removed." [8] General David Hunter, sent from the East to advise and aid Frémont, was given command of a division which Frémont ordered to move from Jefferson City to Tipton. He reported October 4 that for his forty wagons he had only forty mules; next day that his men had been without rations for twenty-four hours; the day afterward that two regiments had no transportation at all and two only sixteen teams between them, while another lacked side arms, cartridge boxes, gun slings, ammunition, and greatcoats. From Tipton he wrote October 18 that the division would soon be destitute. At Warsaw he found a hospital with 300 sick men who had gone without food for two days.[9] Even making some allowance for exaggeration, since Hunter, a harsh, morose, gloomy man, habitually saw the worst, it is clear that the situation remained painful.

It is unquestionably true that Washington, preoccupied with McClellan's front, still neglected the whole West. William Tecumseh Sherman, commanding in Louisville, raised precisely the same complaints as Frémont and Hunter in Missouri. Early in November he wrote Governor Dennison that the West-

---

7 *Ibid.*, 34, 35. Apparently something nearly as bad happened earlier. W. H. Russell recorded in his diary Oct. 9 that calling on McClellan a few nights earlier, he was told by the orderly: "The General's gone to bed tired, and can see no one. He sent the same message to the President, who came inquiring after him ten minutes ago."

8 Letter dated Oct. 17 in N. Y. *Weekly Tribune*, Oct. 26, 1861.

9 Committee on the Conduct of the War, III, 236–238.

ern State governments, except Ohio and Indiana, were slack, that inexperienced men were put in dangerous places, and that some officers were insubordinate, railing at him and each other. Worst of all was the Federal neglect: [10]

The requisitions made for ordnance and stores have yet been unfulfilled. Some Rifled Guns ordered last August are just received, boxed up and no soldiers to manage them. In like manner wagons came in pieces and time is necessary to set them up. Mules are wild and horses distempered, and worst of all no captains and lieutenants to teach the details—never before was such a body of men thrust headlong into such danger. I will not conceal from you that there is danger. I pointed it out in advance to the Sec'y of War, and wrote to Mr. Chase and the President who paid no attention to any of my warnings and appeals. The people of the country take advantage of our necessities and demand pay in good gold or Kentucky money for everything we want, besides the rails and damage sustained by their fields, and their claims would exhaust any Treasury. Now the Ohio Regiments just arriving come so late that I have no General to command them. These numbers unsupported and uncommanded will accomplish no result.

No one or a half dozen men can attend to all the wants of these new-raised levies, with all their tents and paraphernalia.

Competent observers believed that one main cause of the shortages, confusion, and excessive costs in the Western Department lay in the failure of Washington to provide adequate funds. When the terms of the ninety-day men expired Frémont had kept many of them only by a personal guarantee of their fourth month's pay. He had to buy large quantities of material on credit. Colonel I. C. Woods of his staff estimated that for every dollar lost through the collusion of suppliers, ten dollars were sacrificed for want of ready money. As soon as the department had to buy on credit, control over prices passed from the government into the hands of banks, brokers, moneyed merchants, and speculators, who made themselves intermediaries. In the purchase of mules and horses, waste resulted from want of funds to provide proper corrals, feed, shoeing, and care in St. Louis, and in the purchase of wagons, from want of funds for repairs. Treasury policy was responsible.[11]

"Chase," Montgomery Blair explained to Frémont on August 24, "has more horror of seeing Treasury notes below par than of seeing soldiers killed, and therefore, has held back too soon, I think. I don't believe at all in that style of managing the Treasury. It depends on the war, and it is better to get ready to beat the enemy by selling stocks at fifty percent discount than wait to negotiate and lose a battle." [12]

10 Sherman, Louisville, Nov. 6, 1861, to Dennison; Dennison Papers, Ohio Arch. and Hist. Soc.

11 See Woods' vigorous statement in Committee on the Conduct of the War, 1863, pt. 3, pp. 222, 223.

12 Quoted *Ibid.*, 115, 116.

Violent feeling was aroused in Missouri by a War Department order in mid-October that all claims for supplies sold to the army must be sent to Washington for scrutiny and approval. Both the St. Louis *Republican* and the *Democrat* denounced this action. The government, they declared, had been outrageously slow and parsimonious in doling out funds to the Western army. Since Frémont's arrival his quartermaster's department had received only $1,153,000, not enough to pay for even the army horses. Merchants, manufacturers, and contractors who had furnished supplies and taken vouchers would now have to drop all business, go to Washington, and hang around offices for days. "Our business men," said the *Democrat*, "came forward with great promptness, and have given their time and capital to the proper aiding and equipping of the army." The banks had been equally generous. What was the result? "The Government, after crippling the Department by keeping its officers destitute of funds," now issued this decree, "an outrage on our business community, and an insult to the Commanding General." [13]

The Frémont-Blair quarrel meanwhile had the most unhappy consequences. The two made formal charges against each other. Montgomery Blair took his brother's allegations to the White House, reading them to the President and then handing them to General Scott. He pressed Lincoln for Frémont's removal; "but," he wrote his father October 1, "I think the President does not think it quite fair to squander Frémont until he has another chance." [14]

One of the consequences, an impairment of troop morale, was heightened when the Administration early in October sent out Lorenzo Thomas, the adjutant-general, to review Frémont's activities. His record was that of a mediocre West Pointer who had risen by routine, and was himself under sharp criticism from some governors for delays in furnishing enlistment quotas; an obfuscated and garrulous man, Gideon Welles wrote later.[15] "Frémont ought to be let alone and have full confidence of the government or be removed," Colonel John M. Palmer told Senator Trumbull. "This halfway state is embarrassing. Even private soldiers can sniff trouble in the breeze if it exists." [16] This was the view of a prominent Missourian, J. S. Rollins, who from Columbia inquired of Frank Blair who *was* commander, and where were his

13 St. Louis *Republican*, *Democrat*, Oct. 17.
14 Both sets of charges are unimpressive. Frémont accused Frank Blair of using family position to lay unsustained accusations before the President; Blair accused Frémont of misfeasance in vague general terms. Montgomery Blair's letter to his father is in Blair-Lee Papers, Princeton.
15 C. Cadwalader, N. Y. *Herald* correspondent with Grant, termed Thomas an obstinate, intractable man, long a proslavery Democrat. His unsavory part in the events leading to Andrew Johnson's impeachment belongs to later history.
16 Palmer from Tipton, Mo., Oct. 13, 1861, to Trumbull; Trumbull Papers, LC.

headquarters. "Half of our people are ruined, and the rest will be, and all for the want of a single head." [17]

[II]

Hampered by deficiencies of means and equipment, acutely aware that Montgomery Blair and Bates in the Cabinet were hostile, and certain in advance that Lorenzo Thomas would write an adverse report, Frémont knew that his continued tenure hung by a thread. He later bitterly declared that he had enjoyed barely a month of real command—the month between his arrival in St. Louis and Frank Blair's advent on the scene. He was now blamed for another disaster which, as he protested, was not his fault. Colonel J. A. Mulligan's brigade from Chicago, with enough Illinois and Missouri troops to make a total of 3500 men, had taken an advanced position at Lexington, far up the Missouri River near the Kansas boundary. The indefatigable Price saw his opportunity and advanced. Frémont on September 13–14 ordered Generals Pope, Sturgis, and Jefferson C. Davis at Palmyra, Mexico, and Jefferson City respectively to march to Mulligan's assistance; but not one of them showed the requisite energy and determination. Pope was especially remiss. After promising that by the 18th he would have two infantry regiments, some cavalry, and four guns in Lexington, and that by the 19th he would have 4000 troops there, he completely failed to reach the point. So did the others.[18] Frémont himself on September 15 possessed in St. Louis only 6900 men, including home guards, and had just received imperative orders from Washington to detach 5000 infantry for the East. On September 21 Mulligan's whole force, with seven guns and large stores, was captured.[19]

A bright young New Yorker, George E. Waring, who had managed Greeley's farm at Chappaqua and been drainage engineer for Central Park, and who was soon to become colonel of cavalry in Missouri, gave Frederick Law Olmsted his frank opinion that the regular army generals, including Pope

17 Rollins to Blair, Oct. 18, Blair-Lee Papers.
18 For Frémont's orders to these generals see Frémont Order Book, Bancroft Library; also O. R. I, iii.
19 For Frémont's small numbers, and the Washington demand for 5000 troops, see O. R. I, iii, 493, 494; Schuyler Colfax in Cong. Globe, March 7, 1862, p. 1128. Jefferson C. Davis, who had 9700 troops, including home guards, at Jefferson City on the Missouri, might have sent a relieving force upstream. Frémont, however, chiefly blamed Pope, who was strategically placed; O. R. I, iii, 495. The Washington demand for 5000 men reflected McClellan's flurry of panic lest Beauregard attack. Cameron telegraphed for them "without a moment's delay," and Scott wired, "The President dictates." Frémont spared 2000 troops from St. Louis, 2000 from Kentucky, and 1000 from other sources. This order, Sept. 14, was later countermanded, but not before it had done its harm.

and Hunter, deliberately acted against Frémont, an outsider, through jealousy. Frémont himself was convinced of John Pope's treachery. That leader had a force of 5500 men, ample for Mulligan's relief, which could readily be moved westward by the Hannibal & St. Joe, which he himself had just reported open. He stood inert. Actually, incompetence and timidity offer a better explanation of Pope than treachery, though he certainly showed an insubordinate spirit.

Determined to vindicate himself, Frémont by strenuous efforts concentrated what he thought an adequate army to march through southwestern Missouri against Price and McCulloch. He and his staff reached Jefferson City on September 27. Although the breakdowns among a thousand rotten wagons sent him from the East impeded his march, by October 7 all his troops were on the road to Tipton. Herds of cattle were collected by foraging parties, and grain was fetched in and ground by portable mills, for while he had gathered three million rations in supply depots at Jefferson City and Tipton, he expected to subsist largely on the country, paying loyal citizens for impressed commodities and confiscating produce from the disloyal. The shortage of horses and wagons was partially cured by impressments. He hoped by rapid movement to bring Price and McCulloch to battle. "The army is in the best of spirits, and before we get through I will show you a little California practise," he wrote Jessie—"that is, if we are not interrupted." [20]

This march of some 30,000 men, including 5000 cavalry, with eighty-six guns, was the first formidable aggressive movement yet made by a Northern army. The army furnished evidence that Frémont and his staff had exercised greater organizing power in St. Louis than his critics admitted, and unquestionably its movement was well planned. The commander had divided his force into five divisions headed respectively by Generals Hunter, Pope, Sigel, McKinstry, and Asboth. [21] The proportions of infantry, cavalry, and

20 For Frémont's Missouri campaign see O. R. I, iii, *passim*; his MS Memoirs, Bancroft Library; Jessie B. Frémont, *The Story of the Guard*; Jacob Picard, MS Life of Franz Sigel, kindly lent to author; J. R. Howard, *Remembrance of Things Past*, Ch. 19; and files of the Missouri *Democrat*, leading Republican daily, stanchly on Frémont's side. See also Asa Mahan, *Critical History of the American War*, Ch. 3.

21 Pope revealed his spirit in a letter to his friend V. B. Horton, an Ohio Congressman, Oct. 1 (N. Y. Hist. Soc., Civil War Colls.), and one to General Hunter, Oct. 18 (Frémont MSS, Bancroft Library). The first, written from Boonville, declared that he was at the mercy of Price, with "fifteen or twenty thousand men," if Price advanced. Price, with barely thirteen thousand, was marching the other way. Pope added: "There is a state of dissatisfaction and discouragement among the troops which borders on mutiny." All good accounts agree that the morale of Frémont's troops was exceptionally high. After abusing Frémont roundly, Pope told Horton that since the surrender of Lexington, Price's army had swollen "to 40,000 men." This was more than three times its actual number. In the letter to Hunter, Pope renewed his abuse of Frémont, declared his conviction that half the army would be lost if they went south of the Osage (i.e., south of central Missouri), and asserted that although Frémont had ordered him to bring his whole command to assist

artillery were excellent. The cavalry demonstrated its sound training when a select troop of "prairie scouts" recaptured Lexington with some prisoners and stores, releasing a number of men taken with Mulligan, and when later another force under the Hungarian Charles Zagonyi routed some of the enemy at Springfield. The cardinal source of weakness was the spirit exhibited by Pope and Hunter; a spirit which they would have called distrust of Frémont's capacity, but which Frémont's friends termed one of rank betrayal.

From Tipton, Frémont's march took him south across the Osage, where his engineers laid an 800-foot pontoon bridge in thirty-six hours. His troops advanced rapidly on Springfield, the center of predominantly loyal southwestern Missouri and key to northwestern Arkansas. Here lay an Ozark region antipathetic to slavery. With characteristic exuberance, he spoke of joining Commodore Foote's gunboats on the Mississippi to advance southward. "I think it can be done gloriously, especially if secrecy be kept," he wrote his wife.[22] Late in October he reached Springfield, where by November 1 four of his divisions encamped. From information furnished by his scouts he concluded that a little beyond this town Price and McCulloch would face about and give battle.[23]

He was correct about the decision to fight but mistaken about the position. Price wrote Albert Sidney Johnston on November 7 that although Frémont's army far outnumbered his own, he and McCulloch had agreed to halt and give battle at Pineville, hoping the rugged country would favor them. In fact, they *had* to fight, for Price's Missouri State troops would not move across the boundary, and would shortly disintegrate. But Pineville was not just ahead; it lay deeper in southwest Missouri, seventy-odd miles away.

Frémont was also correct in believing that the chances favored Union victory. "Our combined forces," Price admitted, "cannot cope with them [the Unionists] in numbers." As he informed Jefferson Davis, his Missourians were half-fed, half-clothed, and half-supplied. Ben McCulloch has recorded that they were also undisciplined, officered largely by incompetent politicians, and furnished with an incredible conglomeration of weapons; that five thousand of them, their time up, were anxious to go home; and that cooperation between the Missourians and Arkansans was feeble—"but little cordiality of feeling be-

---

in the movement, he would take only five regiments. Altogether, these utterances fortify Frank Blair's subsequent statement: "Pope is a braggart and liar, with some courage, perhaps, but not much capacity." Welles, *Diary,* I, 104. They should be remembered in their bearing on Pope's subsequent career as head of the Army of the Potomac. As for Hunter, that capable but grimly sour-tempered leader was well aware that the moment Frémont lost the command, he would succeed to it.

22 Jessie B. Frémont, *The Story of the Guard,* 72 ff., 85.
23 See O. R. I, iii, 731, for statements by both Price and McCulloch on their resolve to risk a battle. But Frémont would have had to advance fully four more days to fight it.

tween the two armies." It was with high hopes that Frémont's army, bands pounding, arms glittering, moved out of Springfield. On November 6 Price was near Cassville, fifty miles away. Frémont could get his much-wanted battle only with more time and more marching—and he would be allowed neither.[24]

For while he advanced his critics had been busy. Lorenzo Thomas and Secretary Cameron, visiting Missouri simultaneously, brought back unfavorable impressions. Cameron, talking with Frémont at Tipton on October 14, showed him an order for his removal that Lincoln had authorized him to use at discretion.[25] It is not astonishing that Frémont, as the Secretary wrote, was "very much mortified, pained, and, I thought, humiliated." The explorer made an earnest appeal. He had come to Missouri, he said, at the government's request; he had found his department without troops, preparations, or money; he had organized an efficient army, with which he was in pursuit of the foe; and to recall him at that moment would not only destroy him, but defeat his whole promising campaign. Cameron promised to withhold the order until after he returned to Washington, giving the general time to realize his hope, and Frémont for his part promised to resign if he failed. This was fair enough—but it left Frémont with a concentrating sense of what Damocles suffered.

Lorenzo Thomas made an incredibly hurried Western tour, devoting the single week of October 11–18 to Missouri and Kentucky, heard but one side, and wrote a highly critical report in which the press at once noted inaccuracies. In his loose way this veteran bureaucrat, who had been at West Point with David Hunter, let his supposedly secret statement reach the press.[26]

Raymond of the New York *Times* characterized Thomas' report as the most disastrous blow that the national cause had yet received. Its exposition of the confusion in the Missouri army, the lack of equipment, arms, and transport, and General Hunter's conviction that Frémont was incompetent, all in minute detail, was released "so as to reach Ben McCulloch, Sterling Price, and

24 *Ibid.*, 732 ff.; Ben McCulloch, "Memoirs," *Mo. Hist. Review*, 1932, pp. 354 ff.; Franz Sigel, "The Military Operations in Missouri in the Summer and Autumn of 1861," *Mo. Hist. Review*, 1932 (a view favorable to Frémont); John Hume, *The Abolitionists* (also favorable), 184, 185. At a later date Frémont erroneously claimed that he had been removed in the immediate front of the enemy, about to fight a battle; it was much less than immediate.

25 For Cameron's report see Nicolay & Hay, IV, 430; the N. Y. *Tribune* at once scored it. While Frémont marched, Montgomery Blair was laboring to mobilize opinion against him. "I am hurrying off," he wrote his father Oct. 4, "to see such men as Greeley, Sumner, Andrew, etc. to give them our views and to get them to sustain the Administration. I shall stop in New York and Boston for a day each en route for this purpose—probably shall stay longer in those cities. I saw the President this morning and told him what I intended and he approved. Seward also very cordial." Blair-Lee Papers, Princeton Univ.

26 O. R. I, iii, 540 ff.; N. Y. *Tribune*, Oct. 30, 1861; the two principal dailies, like the German papers, still stood firmly behind Frémont. The *Republican* declared that Lincoln had been deceived by statements wholly *ex parte*, and that the general had exhibited wonderful forbearance during his persecution. The *Democrat* severely condemned Thomas' report, both for its content and for the impropriety of its publication.

A. S. Johnston, and nerve them for the coming fight." Equally injudicious, said the *Times,* was Thomas' account of the situation in Kentucky. "The Southern Confederacy is distinctly told that General Sherman is not sustained by the people of Kentucky; that he has no hope of saving that State to the Union; and that he is preparing only for a hopeless fight before that State is given up." This would indeed be happy news to the rebels! As a matter of fact, Sherman, talking with Cameron and Thomas in a Louisville hotel, had told them in his vehement and excited manner that he would need 200,000 men to drive the Confederates from Kentucky, a statement which led them to conclude that he was insane! [27]

Naturally, Lincoln was deeply impressed by the statements of Cameron and Thomas, concurring with what the Blairs and Bates had told him, and quoting Hunter and other Missouri officers. Brigadier-General S. R. Curtis in St. Louis, for example, gave it as his opinion that Frémont lacked the intelligence, experience, and sagacity necessary to his command. Elihu B. Washburne, visiting St. Louis as head of a Congressional subcommittee on government contracts, was shocked by stories of fraud and extravagance. The Cabinet was divided, for Cameron honestly believed that the government should await the outcome of Frémont's campaign, and the Cabinet meeting on October 22 found Seward and Chase earnestly for delay. The President was then still in painful doubt; but Montgomery Blair and Bates maintained their steady pressure for removal, which Lincoln had to give special weight because of their Missouri connections. On the 24th Lincoln yielded. He wrote an order relieving Frémont, whose command was to be given to Hunter, and sent it to General Curtis for delivery. However, he cautioned Curtis that the order must not be handed to Frémont, if, when the messenger reached him, "he shall then have, in personal command, fought and won a battle, or shall then be in the immediate presence of the enemy in expectation of a battle." [28]

Eight days after Lincoln wrote out the order in Washington it was given to Frémont just beyond Springfield. He believed himself then in the immediate presence of the enemy, for Sigel and Asboth had reported the Confederate

27 Thomas' report went to Cameron Oct. 21. Attorney-General Bates had made sure that the side unfavorable to Frémont should be presented to Thomas with emphasis. He wrote James O. Broadhead on Oct. 9: "Genl. Cameron is gone to St. Louis. Be sure to see him. Talk freely. You need not waste your delicacy nor be baulked by etiquette." Broadhead was Frank Blair's chief lieutenant. A complete text of the report was not made public until given to the Committee on the Conduct of the War (March, 1862), which controverted it. For Sherman's exchanges with Thomas and Cameron see Lloyd Lewis, *Sherman: Fighting Prophet,* 192 ff. Cameron on Nov. 9 appointed Buell to Sherman's place in Kentucky. Proceeding to Missouri, Sherman at once quarreled with Pope and Halleck. His wife took him home amid army reports that he was mad, and at home he frankly told friends: "Sometimes I felt crazy in Kentucky; I couldn't get one word from Washington." Lewis, *Sherman,* 200.
28 *Collected Works,* IV, 562.

advance guard nine miles distant; and he had made all dispositions for an immediate advance and battle. His conviction that Hunter, greedy for command, had hurried the messenger forward, did that high-minded officer injustice. But it was unfortunate that Lincoln had not waited. Sigel believed that if the Union army had pushed onward against McCulloch's position at Cassville, it would have separated him from Price, cut his natural line of retreat, and smashed his force.[29]

The Missouri chapter thus remained a dreary series of blunders and mischances to the end. The Administration was blameworthy for not doing far more to supply arms and money to the West; Frémont was to blame for political if not military ineptness; Frank Blair, who had needlessly accentuated the schism in the State, was blameworthy for his selfish, domineering attempt to exploit the situation; and the Blairs in Washington could be blamed for impetuously taking up the quarrel. It was no real loss that Frémont, like Harney, had been broken. In fact, it was a gain, for the way lay open to abler men. Nor was it any real loss that Frank Blair, whose course decisively lost him the support of the German-Americans, could no longer hope for political control of the State. But the needless deepening of animosities in Missouri, which lay henceforth in a feverish, disordered condition, full of hatreds and violence, was much to be deplored. And had the country peered closely into events, it would have seen displayed in Missouri the frightening fact which Gideon Welles shortly enunciated with reference to the Virginia theater: "Personal jealousies and professional rivalries, the bane and curse of all armies, have entered deeply into ours." [30]

[III]

The immediate results of the Missouri fiasco were bad; the larger and remoter results were worse.

Lincoln, in assigning the command to Hunter, had left him free to determine future operations, but had expressed his own opinion that the best plan would be to give up the pursuit, divide the main army into a corps at Sedalia and another at Rolla (the two rail terminals), and push on the work of drilling and equipping troops. Hunter consulted his subordinates. While Pope was

29 *Ibid.*, 562, 563. Frémont, anxious to fight his battle, fruitlessly tried to obstruct delivery of the order, which was sent into his lines by stratagem. He promptly relinquished the command to Hunter on Nov. 2, and forbade troop demonstrations; O. R. I, iii, 559. Montgomery Blair expressed great satisfaction. "If Rosecrantz [*sic*] could also be dropped," he wrote, "the people would have some idea we are in earnest, care for the Public not for men." Oct. 4; Blair-Lee Papers, Princeton.
30 *Diary*, I, 104.

noncommittal, McKinstry, Asboth, and Sigel were for advancing. Hunter decided to turn back. A pursuit and victory would of course vindicate Frémont's planning.

Sigel later stigmatized this decision as "an outrage without parallel in history," and it did result in terrible human suffering.[31] No sooner did the retreat of Hunter and Pope become known than the Unionists of southwest Missouri were struck with terror and despair. From a radius of more than fifty miles, abandoning their property, they flocked into Springfield and the Union lines. Then, as Sigel's and Asboth's troops reluctantly completed the evacuation of Springfield, the impoverished, woebegone mass of fugitives, including nearly every family in the city who had sympathized with the Union cause, took to the roads with the troops, condemned to the life of refugees and beggars.

After Hunter's superior army fell back, the Confederate forces which had been dispiritedly retreating to a point where they could make their last stand faced about and reoccupied all southwest Missouri. Lincoln had written that the enemy would probably not return to the State from Arkansas, and if they did could easily be repelled.[32] The fact was that they never left Missouri, occupied Springfield and the adjacent country throughout the winter, threatened even Rolla and Jefferson City, and were able to lay waste the country up to the Union encampments. Not until the new year did the Union forces advance again. This time they did not stop halfway, but completed their task—as Sigel believed they might have done under Frémont. Lincoln had been actuated, very reasonably, by a fear that Hunter's communications would become too attenuated, and by his conviction that the Western invasion of the South should be directed down the Mississippi. But after all, Washington was a poor vantage point from which to direct field strategy in Missouri.

Much more important than the Missouri results of Frémont's removal were its national repercussions. The anger in St. Louis spread through wide circles of the East. In New York the *Evening Post* declared that the government's action "smote the community like the loss of a battle." A mass meeting at Cooper Institute on November 27, addressed by Senator Sumner, eulogized Frémont and adopted resolutions defending him and his antislavery measures. Henry Ward Beecher spoke for his large Brooklyn congregation in incensed language. "The North is ripening every day for an abolition war," wrote Ethan Allen Hitchcock from New York on November 15. Whittier penned a poem hailing Frémont's trumpet peal for the emancipation of slaves as a Roland-blast "heard from the van of freedom's hope forlorn." And Thaddeus

31 "Military Operations in Mo. in the Summer and Autumn of 1861," *Mo. Hist. Review*, vol. 26 (July, 1932), 367.
32 O. R. I, iii, 241.

Stevens bade his fellow radicals in Congress rally to the cause: "Who are you that you let the hounds run down your friend Frémont?"

While public indignation was probably strongest in New England, it was stormily evident in many Western centers. The editor of the Cincinnati *Gazette* believed that the region was threatened with a revolution. "Could you have been among the people yesterday, and witnessed the excitement," he wrote Chase just after Frémont's removal; "could you have seen sober citizens pulling from their walls and trampling underfoot the portrait of the President; and could you hear today the expressions of all classes of men, of all political parties, you would, I think, feel as I feel . . . alarmed." The Treasury agent in St. Louis declared that if the President had emptied the government arsenals into the rebel camps, he could not have better strengthened them. The Pittsburgh agent reported that enraged capitalists had stopped their subscriptions for government securities. Another Treasury correspondent, returning from a tour as far west as Iowa, reported: "I never have seen such excitement, such deep indignant feeling everywhere I have travelled."

Frémont had in a double sense made himself a symbol. Neither his effort to free the slaves of those whom Lincoln called "traitorous owners" nor his exhibition of martial energy could be forgotten. While McClellan sat still, he had organized an army of more than 30,000, marched it hundreds of miles, and tried to throw it into battle.[33]

For the Administration the skies were growing dark. Irritation with it ran high as members of Congress gathered in Washington in late November: irritation, anxiety, and discouragement. One disturbing piece of news after another contributed to this.

At Belmont on the Mississippi on November 7, Grant met a check which was accepted quietly only because it might have been much worse. On November 16 the country learned that Captain Charles Wilkes of the warship *San Jacinto* had seized two Confederate envoys to Europe, James M. Mason and John Slidell, aboard the British steamer *Trent*, and although the thoughtless rejoiced, judicious men knew that the stroke portended grave trouble. General

33 Zack Chandler expressed a widespread view when he wrote his wife: "Frémont has accomplished something with eight or ten millions, McL. has accomplished nothing with ten times that amount." Oct. 27, 1861; Chandler Papers, LC. General B. H. Grierson, serving in Missouri at the time, wrote long afterward of Frémont: "I considered him in the midst of his adventures as being, with all his failings, head and shoulders above many of his enemies and traducers. I believed then that he merited, and still think he deserves, a warm place in the hearts of all lovers of freedom, of which he was an earnest, constant, and fearless advocate." MS Autobiography, Ill. State Hist. Lib. Among contemporary defenders of Frémont were William T. Harris, later eminent as an educator, and John F. Hume. Hume believed that if Frémont had commanded a little longer, "he would have achieved a brilliant military success"; that he might have terminated hostilities in Missouri three years earlier than they actually ended. Hume, *The Abolitionists*, 184, 185; Leidecker, *Harris*, 201.

Halleck, who had just replaced Hunter in the chief Western command on November 20, issued an order from St. Louis that no fugitive slaves should thereafter be admitted within Union lines, alleging that Southerner sympathizers used them as spies. This so angered the radicals that when Congress met Lovejoy introduced a resolution of censure, which was defeated by only the close vote of only 78 to 64. The section of opinion for which Ben Wade spoke was bluntly expressing despair of quelling the rebellion under the Administration leaders. "They are blundering, cowardly, and inefficient," Wade confided to Zack Chandler. "I fear the evil is irremediable, having its seat in the very nature of the persons composing the Administration. You could not inspire Old Abe, Seward, Chase, or Bates with courage, decision, and enterprise with a galvanic battery." [34]

Democracy is unhappily prone to demand immediate results, or if unattainable, a dramatic show of action. Many Americans who hoped that they had elected a President of Jacksonian temper began to fear they had gotten a J. Q. Adams, his resolution sicklied o'er with the pale cast of thought. It was impossible as yet to measure the executive stature of Lincoln, for neither by dramatic act nor eloquent word had he illustrated his true qualities. To millions he seemed drifting. That was the precise term a citizen of Freeport, Illinois, writing Elihu Washburne, used: "We of this vicinity feel deeply interested for the welfare of our common country and the way affairs have been drifting our faith in the Administration begins to fail us." So felt C. H. Ray of the Chicago *Tribune*, declaring that although party harmony was important, "when the necessity for making progress is upon us we are ready to quarrel with Lincoln, the Cabinet, McClellan, and anybody else." Neither Lincoln nor McClellan had explained to the country why the troops on the Potomac attempted not even a minor blow. Lincoln did not know why, and in any event had not yet learned to reach the public by effective speech and letter; while McClellan was contemptuous of public opinion. Lost in a fog, the people wondered if they really had a pilot. [35]

Had McClellan dealt a blow to clear the Potomac, successful or unsuccessful, the country would have rejoiced in action. Had Lincoln let Frémont fight the battle which Price awaited at Pineville, win or lose, people would have felt refreshed. Chances of success in both instances were good, but even defeat would have been better than inaction. In war a nation must be ready to meet many defeats; what is important is that it should fight. Thus Americans dumbly, anxiously felt. While radical freesoil and abolitionist sentiment caught

34 Wade to Chandler, Jefferson, Ohio, Oct. 8, 1861; Chandler Papers, LC.
35 Wm. H. Wilson, Freeport, Jan. 11, 1861, to Washburne, Washburne Papers, LC. Ray, Chicago, Dec. 5, 1861, to Washburne Papers, *Ibid.*

up the fallen Frémont banner, it must not be supposed that many people of moderate views did not share the rising distrust. Inside Lincoln's Cabinet both Chase and Bates deemed the President unequal to his duties, Bates writing that he lacked firmness, decision, and grasp. Meanwhile, one of the harshest indictments of Lincoln ever penned came from Frank Blair. The nation in December waited for a sign: either martial action, or an aggressive change of policy.[36]

If the people had pinned high expectations to Lincoln's first annual message, they were disappointed. That long, dull document, dated December 3, holds a place among the more commonplace Presidential papers.[37] It was ill organized, for it unnecessarily summarized materials in the reports of the Cabinet officers. It warily said nothing of the burning question of the moment, the Mason-Slidell affair, nor of the situation in Mexico or Santo Domingo. In dealing with Negroes liberated under the Confiscation Act it took pains not to use the word "slaves," substituting the locution "certain persons." Paying tribute to Scott, Lincoln wrote that the general had repeatedly expressed himself in favor of McClellan as his successor, but did not mention that at the end Scott had earnestly preferred Halleck. The President expressed just satisfaction that Maryland, Kentucky, and Missouri had already furnished 40,000 soldiers to the Union, but he was much too optimistic in pronouncing Missouri comparatively quiet. To the factions of radical and conservative Republicans which were now fast taking shape, by far the most significant passages were his vague proposals for colonizing freedmen abroad, and the statements which followed:

In considering the policy to be adopted for suppressing the insurrection, I have been anxious and careful that the inevitable conflict for this purpose shall not degenerate into a violent and remorseless revolutionary struggle. I have, therefore, in every case, thought it proper to keep the integrity of the Union prominent as the primary object of the contest on our part, leaving all questions which are not of vital military importance to the more deliberate action of the legislature. . . .

We should not be in haste to determine that radical and extreme measures, which may reach the loyal as well as the disloyal, are indispensable.

36 Frank Blair's letter to Montgomery, Oct. 7, 1861, was a characteristic eruption. He wrote that the only way to save the nation was "to kick that pack of old women who compose the Cabinet into the sea"; that he had never dreamed "that such a lot of poltroons and apes could be gathered together from the four quarters of the globe as Old Abe has succeeded in bringing together in his Cabinet"; that the first duty of every patriot "is to stop fighting Jeff Davis and turn in on our own Government and make something out of it"; and that Davis and his whole crew had not done half the harm inflicted "by the cowardice, ignorance, and stupidity of Lincoln's Administration." Smith, Blair Family, II, 83, 85. Bates' acrid comments on Lincoln are in his Diary, 218–220, 223–226, etc.

37 Text in Collected Works, V, 35–53. Only at the close, though failing of eloquence, did Lincoln strike a high note. The nation relied on Providence, he wrote, and "the struggle of today, is not altogether for today—it is for a vast future also."

Before Congress met, Chandler, Wade, and Trumbull, the three Senators who had been badgering Lincoln to insist on a battle, had adumbrated a plan. They would create a Congressional committee which would both carry on a continuous investigation of the war effort and apply frequent pricks of the goad. The session no sooner began than Chandler proposed a Senate committee of three to inquire into Bull Run and Ball's Bluff. Grimes of Iowa substituted a broader resolution for a House-Senate committee of five to explore the causes of the disasters that had attended the public arms, with power to send for person and papers. Further amendments enlarged the committee to three Senators and four Representatives, and stated the mandate in a single comprehensive phrase: "To inquire into the conduct of the present war."

Thus, with nearly unanimous approval, originated the most powerful parliamentary engine of the time, the Committee on the Conduct of the War. This body was not tardy in proceeding to work. Under Wade as chairman, with Zack Chandler, Senator Andrew Johnson, and Representatives Daniel W. Gooch, John Covode, George W. Julian, and Moses F. Odell as members, it began sitting before Christmas. Within a few days this able group ascertained that McClellan's Army of the Potomac had present for duty on December 10 approximately 134,000 equipped infantry, 10,000 equipped cavalry, 10,350 equipped artillery, and 6850 officers.

The establishment of the committee served explicit notice that if the President had war powers, Congress possessed them too, and would jealously assert them. But a majority did not share the Wade-Chandler animosity toward Lincoln. The committee later asserted that it took care to aid and cooperate with the overburdened Chief Executive. Summoning in their first fortnight a series of generals, they made it plain that their inquisitorial gaze would be bent on laggard and incompetent field commanders. This was wise; while interference with President or Cabinet would have been a disaster, the military needed a searching scrutiny.[38]

[IV]

With reason, Lincoln felt much more worry over the Mason-Slidell affair than over the Congressional committee. When the appointment of Captain Charles Wilkes to command an American cruiser with a commission to search for privateers was first announced, a shrewd officer of the Treasury, George

---

38 See introductory matter, 37th Cong., 3rd Sess., *Report of the Joint Committee*, Vol. I (1863). The committee has been treated with undue severity by historians biased in favor of Executive or army. Actually it brought to light much that it was healthful for the public to know, and kept the military arm well reminded of civilian supremacy. In all, it was to issue eight volumes. W. W. Pierson, *American Historical Review*, v. 23 (April, 1918), 550–576, takes a fairer view of it.

Harrington, had urged Seward to get the mandate revoked. "He will give us trouble," said Harrington. "He has a superabundance of self-esteem and a deficiency of judgment. When he commanded his great exploring expedition he court-martialled nearly all his officers; he alone was right, everybody else was wrong." [39] The captain was grandnephew of the fiery John Wilkes famous in the days of Burke, Fox, and Dr. Johnson.

A scene in the Bahama Channel on November 8 verified Harrington's prophecy. Gray sea and gray skies; black smoke from the little warship *San Jacinto* and white smoke from one of her guns trailing across the waves; the jaunty mail-steamer *Trent* lying hove to, her British ensign flapping; a boat filled with armed marines rowing across—this scene heralded trouble. From the *Trent*'s deck the protesting James M. Mason of Virginia and John Slidell of Louisiana, Confederate special commissioners to London and Paris respectively, were haled by Union officers, to be clapped into prison at Fort Warren near Boston.

Fervent Northern jubilation at first greeted this capture of two arch-rebels and this challenge to British insolence. Most newspapers published exultant editorials, Boston tendered Wilkes a banquet, and Secretary Welles rumbled an approval which he was later anxious to forget. The House of Representatives voted Wilkes a gold medal. While the applause still echoed, arrival of the news in Britain on November 28 set off an explosion of resentment. The press blazed with denunciation, influential men expressed indignation over the affront, and talk of possible war at once sprang up. Prime Minister Palmerston blazed to the Cabinet, "You may stand for this but damned if I will!"; and the Ministry, which shared the popular anger, inevitably took steps to meet any eventuality. It ordered a steam squadron made ready, gathered 8000 troops with a supply of munitions for immediate transfer to Canada, and prohibited the export of war materials. That the British Government could easily have used the incident to open hostilities if it wished, there can be no doubt; and Confederates of course ardently hoped it would.

Happily, members of the British Cabinet wished to avoid war with the United States. Palmerston's rapid steps to strengthen Britain's military position were prompted partly by a wish to prepare for the worst, but also partly (as he told Parliament later) by his conviction that the demand for a peaceable restoration of the two prisoners would have to be supported by military strength. Six weeks earlier, he had written the Foreign Minister, Lord John Russell, reaffirming a policy of strict neutrality; British policy must be "to keep quite clear of the conflict between North and South," he declared, interfering only if the American conflagration threatened danger to Europe. Hap-

39 Undated memorandum, Harrington Papers, Mo. Hist. Society.

pily also, the American minister was a man of rare experience, sagacity, and restraint. Charles Francis Adams knew very well that the United States was in the wrong. This son of John Quincy Adams had an inherited animus against Great Britain. He was naturally combative—he had run for the Vice-Presidency on the Freesoil ticket in 1848, and had lately been one of the most active Republican leaders in the House; but he was also naturally cautious, and he possessed shrewd self-control. Realizing the gravity of the crisis, he now waited gloomily and taciturnly. Before news was received of Wilkes's act, Palmerston had spoken at a Lord Mayor's dinner, with Adams present, saying flatly that he was against intervention for the sake of cotton, and treating the American conflict with marked delicacy. Both men could be trusted to show discretion and moderation; and although Palmerston was determined to stand up for British rights, the gouty veteran had too keen a suspicion of Napoleon III—his mind "as full of schemes as a warren is of rabbits"—to care to embroil himself in the New World.

Indeed, Palmerston had foreseen the possibility of just such an incident as this, and had given Adams a hint that it should be avoided. In a friendly private conversation with the American minister on November 15 he had referred to the reckless utterances of Captain John B. Marchand of the U. S. S. *James Adger*, lying at Southampton, who while tipsy had said that he was going to watch for Mason and Slidell and capture them even in sight of the British shore if he could. Palmerston's remark that two additional Southern agents could scarcely make any difference in the course of the British Government once it had made up its mind gave Adams a clear hint (which he failed to take) that it *had* made up its mind adversely to any arguments the Southerners might present.[40]

The Prime Minister had in fact been so disturbed by the possibility of an incident that he had consulted the Crown's law officers on the legality of a possible American seizure of the Confederate envoys. This opinion, dated November 12, 1861, stated that an American warship would have the right to stop and search an English ship, and to take her into port for adjudication of the charge that she carried contraband goods or improper personnel, but would not have any right to remove the diplomatic agents and then allow the ship to proceed. Provision for adjudication was the crux of the matter. When news of the actual happening reached London, the law officers reaffirmed their view of the illegality of Captain Wilkes's step. It was unfortunate for the American position that Wilkes failed to bring the *Trent* into a North-

---

40 *Cambridge History of Br. Foreign Policy*, II, *passim*; E. D. Adams, *Great Britain and the Amer. Civil War*, I, Ch. VII; S. F. Bemis, ed., *Amer. Secretaries of State*, VII, 61–70; *Diplomatic Correspondence*, 1861, pp. 105 ff.

ern port, for if he had done so, the British Government would have been legally disabled from protesting. Palmerston deserved great credit for arming himself with a statement of the law, and for giving Adams an amicable admonition. Seward across the Atlantic had failed to look up any precedents or rulings in advance! [41]

That Wilkes had committed a grave infraction of international law there could be no question. He had a perfect right to search any suspected ship for goods contraband of war, and to take a vessel carrying contraband into port to await the verdict of a prize court. But he had no right to decide the question of a violation of neutrality by personal fiat on the spot, without judicial process. Moreover, it was extremely doubtful whether persons, as distinguished from goods, could ever be deemed contraband. In impressing men from the deck of a neutral ship, Wilkes had committed precisely the kind of act that did so much to provoke the United States to fight the War of 1812. Lord John Russell did not overstate the case when he called it a violent affront to the British flag and a violation of international law. No wonder that the frigid Charles Francis Adams, learning of the exultation of Americans, fell into indescribable sadness, or that the more emotional Henry Adams wrote home that the applauders were "a bloody set of fools." [42]

The situation was rendered more difficult by the fact that British ministers regarded the State Department with a mordant suspicion. They were well aware of Seward's devious ways, remembered some of his recent irresponsible statements, and suspected that just before Sumter he had played with the idea of provoking a conflict with England as a means of gaining Canada. C. F. Adams, Jr., understates the fact when he writes that in 1861 Seward commanded the confidence of no European foreign secretary; Seward in fact had the active distrust of most foreign offices. Dealing with him, the Liberal Cabinet naturally made their note stiff. They avoided an ultimatum, but they did

41   C. F. Adams, Jr., *C. F. Adams*, Ch. XII; J. P. Baxter, "The British Government and Neutral Rights," *Amer. Hist. Review*, v. 34 (October, 1929), 9–29. Palmerston did, however, believe that a division of the American republic would make Britain safer, for he disliked Yankee aggressiveness. He wrote Russell on Jan. 19, 1862, that he liked the scheme of a monarchy in Mexico. "It would also stop the North Americans whether of the Federal or Confederate states in their proposed absorption of Mexico. If the North and South are definitely disunited, and if at the same time Mexico could be turned into a prosperous monarchy, I do not know any arrangement that would be more advantageous for us." Harold Temperley and Lillian M. Fenson, *Foundations of Br. Foreign Policy, 1792–1902*, pp. 219, 220.

42   Russell's statement is quoted in John Bassett Moore, *Principles of Amer. Diplomacy*, 114–118; for the views of the Adamses, see W. C. Ford, ed., *A Cycle of Adams Letters*, I, 70 ff. The *Journal of Benjamin Moran*, II, 904 ff., is useful. Seward had sent Thurlow Weed abroad, and shortly after the Trent affair broke, Weed lunched with Russell at Pembroke Lodge. He found the foreign secretary as chilly as Adams himself always was, but he learned that Queen Victoria was anxious for a friendly settlement.

demand the surrender of the envoys, and an apology. Lord John Russell regarded Wilkes's seizure as a continuation of the old unfriendly American policy, now carried to the point of a direct slap in the face.

However, the language of the ministerial instructions to Lord Lyons was kept within moderate bounds. It was agreed at the Cabinet meeting of November 29 that Russell should draft these instructions, while Palmerston reported all the facts to the Queen. Next day the Cabinet met again, and both shortened and softened Russell's severe language. The revised draft was then sent to Windsor, where Queen Victoria (who had been touched by the cordial American reception of her eldest son the previous year) and Prince Albert were much distressed by the evident danger of war. They realized that the crisis needed emollients, not excitants.

Prince Albert, then in his final illness, could hardly hold a pen. Nevertheless, he wrote for the Queen an earnest memorandum to be laid before Lord Russell—his last political paper. In this document the Queen declared that she would like to have the Government take the position that while it could not allow its flag to be insulted or its mails endangered, it did not believe that the United States intended any insult, or wished to add to the American troubles by a dispute with the British nation; and that London hoped to learn that the American captain had acted without any instructions, or had misunderstood them. Palmerston and Russell immediately made the desired changes. The official biographer of Albert credits him with trying to remove from the dispatch to Lyons everything that could irritate the American people, and to offer them a full opportunity of receding honorably from the position in which Wilkes's indiscretion had placed them.[43]

The fact is that the Palmerston Ministry was so composed as to find a conciliatory policy natural. Such members as Gladstone, Newcastle, and Granville had an ingrained love of peace. The principal ministers, each representing his own group in the Liberal Party, carried on their special work much as they pleased. Palmerston, who had the deciding word in council, was chiefly concerned with keeping the governmental machine running smoothly, avoiding factional rows, and giving the Conservative Opposition few opportunities for attack. He and Russell, who represented different wings of the Liberal Party, curbed each other. Both well remembered the recent Russian war which Britain had entered so insouciantly, and in which victory proved so costly. It is true that the Prime Minister enjoyed living dangerously, or as Cobden put it: "Palmerston likes to drive the wheel close to the edge, and show how

43 Theodore Martin, *Life of His Royal Highness the Prince Consort.* V. A. W. Tilby, *Russell*, 208, 209, credits Gladstone with influencing the Queen and Prince in favor of peace.

dexterously he can avoid falling over the precipice. Meanwhile, he keeps people's attention employed, which suits him politically." Adams, nervous over this precipice-walking, feared that some sudden misstep might send him over the edge, but the old curmudgeon's foot was sure.

Not only was the dispatch to Lyons watered down, but it was accompanied by two private communications from Russell to the British Minister in Washington which lessened the tension. One of them instructed Lyons to see Seward informally before taking him the official paper, prepare him for the demands, and ask him to thresh out the matter with the President and Cabinet before the dispatch was formally read. The other authorized Lyons to give Seward seven days to formulate a reply. If the Secretary rejected the British demands, Lyons was to leave Washington, but from the outset he was to make it plain that he desired to abstain from anything like a menace. No minister could have been happier to pursue a conciliatory line than Lord Lyons. The previous spring, in delivering a Foreign Office dispatch to Seward, he had changed certain expressions to avoid offending the American Government—striking out "measures either by the Northern or Southern Confederacies of North America," for example, and substituting "measures by America." He understood and liked Seward, while he was learning to admire Lincoln.[44]

An unfriendly analyst of the British attitude might describe it as an effort to browbeat the United States by military preparations while privately paving the way for a termination of the quarrel without resort to arms. A truer estimate would credit the British with wishing to uphold their national dignity while giving Americans every opportunity for a graceful retreat. Russell wrote the pacific Gladstone on December 13 that if Washington would liberate the Confederate envoys, he would be glad to make a treaty giving up the British pretensions of 1812 and securing immunity from seizure to unarmed persons aboard neutral vessels. "This would be a triumph for the U. S. in principle, while the particular case would be decided in our favor." Soon afterward he informed Palmerston that if the United States wished to argue the matter, he would allow Washington more time for compliance, adding: "I do not think the country would approve an immediate declaration of war."

The United States, meanwhile, proved very reluctant to back down. The public and official praise of Wilkes was hard to disclaim. Seward, more regardful of public opinion than learned in international law, or skilled in diplomacy, had lost a golden opportunity in not promptly restoring Mason and Slidell on the ground of historic American belief in the illegality of such seizures. Lincoln, however, though at first pleased by the capture, was soon overcome by doubts,—"I fear the traitors will prove to be white elephants," he said—and

44 Lyons, June 17, 1861, to Russell; FO 84/1137.

again impressed on Seward the fact that one war at a time was enough. Charles Sumner, exchanging anxious letters with his friends Richard Cobden and John Bright, told Washington leaders that the government should recede. Edward Everett, former Secretary of State, Thurlow Weed, and numerous business leaders, swung to the same view. The assertion of the French advocate of the Union cause, Count Gasparin, that the Confederate envoys were a hundred times more dangerous in Fort Warren than they would be walking the streets of London and Paris, was echoed by August Belmont, staying in Nice: "Neither the violent and clumsy representations of the demagogue Mason nor all the energy and astuteness of your fierce Slidell could have changed the settled policy of England and France in this controversy."

At the end of November, Seward sent word to Adams that Wilkes had acted without orders, that he hoped the Ministry would consider the question in a friendly temper, and that the United States would show a conciliatory disposition. When Lincoln sent his annual message to Congress at the beginning of December, he wisely ignored the subject. From the moment that Adams on December 19 imparted the contents of Seward's letter to Russell, the situation brightened. Popular feeling on both sides had grown calmer, and the psychological reasons for American sensitivity to British antagonism made also, as Whittier wrote, for a rapid restoration of friendly feeling:

> O Englishmen! in hope and creed,
> In blood and tongue our brothers!
> We too are heirs of Runnymede;
> And Shakespeare's fame and Cromwell's deed
> Are not alone our mother's.

Lincoln thought for a time that the question might be arbitrated, and his Cabinet remained divided. But at a meeting on Christmas day, with Sumner present to read letters from Bright and Cobden, they agreed to admit that Wilkes had committed a wrong, and to restore the two envoys. As Attorney-General Bates put it, all yielded to the logic of the situation. Seward composed a note in his smartest Auburn-attorney vein, castigating British policy past and present even while he apologized for the violation of British rights; and his impudent irrelevances lent comfort to many Yankee jingoes. The peaceful outcome of the dispute gave general gratification on both sides of the water. In America, Everett wrote that a strong feeling of relief pervaded the community; in England, Adams recorded a striking revulsion—"The current which ran against us with such extreme violence six weeks ago now seems to be going with equal fury in our favor."

Dr. Whewell, master of Trinity College, Cambridge, made the right ironic comment: "According to American principles Mason and Slidell ought not to have been seized, but according to English principles their surrender ought not to have been asked." [45] What was perhaps the most perilous moment of the Civil War had been passed. It was already clear that when Mason reached London, he would accomplish—unless some new squall blew up—precious little. W. L. Yancey, Pierre A. Rost, and A. Dudley Mann, whom the Confederate government had sent to Europe as special commissioners just after Sumter, had been received very coldly by the British Foreign Office. In fact, they had hardly been received at all. After a first frigid interview, Lord John Russell had refused to see them again, requesting them to put in writing any communications they wished to make to him. And when they wrote, they got no reply to their letters until early in December the Foreign Minister crushed their hopes with two curt sentences: "Lord Russell presents his compliments to Mr. Yancey, Mr. Rost, and Mr. Mann. He has had the honour of receiving their letters of the 27th and 30th of November, but in the present state of affairs he must decline to enter into any official communication with them." It seemed certain Mason would fare no better.

While the excitement of the *Trent* affair hung over the country, much more stubborn problems were claiming attention. Lincoln's annual message had hardly reached Congress when an irreparable breach between him and the Secretary of War, touching the most sensitive point of national policy, came to light.

45 See MS Diary of Edward Everett, Nov. 1, 1861–Feb. 2, 1862, for comments on the affair. Gasparin wrote in the *Journal des Débats*. The fullest general treatment, T. L. Harris's *The Trent Affair*, is marked by bias. See also the able essay "The Trent Affair, 1861," by Charles Francis Adams, Jr., in *Mass. Hist. Soc. Proceedings*, v. 45 (1911), 35–148. Not only Edward Everett but Sumner at first held the seizure justified, Sumner sending the State Department some citations of favorable precedents; but both changed their minds.

20

"The Bottom Out of the Tub"

THE MOOD of the nation as it came to the end of a year barren of signal victory or real advance was expressed by the long speech of J. A. Gurley of Ohio in the House on the conduct of the war. Men generally felt, he said, that an active policy must be adopted or the conflict would drag on for years and acquire international scope. The army was ready, the troops were eager for action, the country was looking for a commander with the will, enterprise, and skill to gain victories; but where was the leader? More men had been lost by sickness in the past five months than a half-dozen battles would have claimed. The expense had been enormous. An occasional reverse would be better than this inaction, this waste of opportunity, this dreary disappointment.

Gurley had the clerk read an excerpt from the Richmond *Dispatch* which bit deeper than his own acid words. It declared that from the beginning of December the Yankees had possessed on the Potomac the best army on the continent, 200,000 strong, with formidable forces elsewhere. The weather had been favorable; they could have struck at numerous points; their blows could have done the Confederacy serious injury. Instead, they had given the South time to make itself safe at every point where it had been vulnerable. Why? Because, declared the writer, the Yankees enlist not to fight, but only to draw pay. Their factories being closed for want of Southern trade, the men had gone into the army to live, well fed, well clothed, and safe. The war was practically closed.

W. D. Kelley of Pennsylvania was soon making the House echo to a sterner indictment. The public mind and heart were sick, he said, that after all the sacrifices for war, no progress had been made: "Washington is beleaguered and Richmond is not." Even a leader less sensitive to the national mood than Lincoln was would have felt the importance of action to revitalize the War Department, spur McClellan into movement, and place a constructive solution for the problem of slavery among the objects of the war. Within the space of a few weeks the President, awakening to his authority and his capacities, had dealt with all three subjects.

[I]

Lincoln's distrust of Cameron's capacity, irritation with his methods, and hostility to his ideas, had steadily grown. From the first, the two had disliked each other. Lincoln had resented the apparent necessity, under half-promises which his friends had given at the Chicago Convention, of putting Cameron in his Cabinet.[1] He had been warned by various people that Cameron had a corrupt record. As early as May, 1861, one politician judged from separate conversations with both President and Secretary that "much feeling" existed between them. The President heard tales that some of the Pennsylvania contracts of the War Department were dishonest, and told callers that he meant to have them examined. By October, convinced that the Secretary was at least incompetent, he spoke of the man to young Nicolay with unwonted asperity. Cameron, he declared, was "utterly ignorant" of his proper affairs; "selfish and openly discourteous to the President"; "obnoxious to the country"; and "incapable of either organizing details or conceiving and advising general plans." [2]

Incompetent Cameron was; corrupt he was not, save in the sense that he kept a keen eye out for political profit. He made bad appointments, as other executives did. One man was privately denounced by Gideon Welles as infamous; another, placed in an investigative capacity, was assailed by the writer Epes Sargent as unfit save on the theory that one might set a thief to catch a thief. In the unavoidable hurry and confusion of equipping the troops, Cameron often signed bad contracts. But Lincoln himself defended him in the employment of Alexander Cummings to buy military supplies, and William Pitt Fessenden was quite right, as inquiry proved, in saying that much of the clamor against the Secretary was baseless. Rascals who offered regiments and demanded funds when they had no men, contractors disappointed in their hope of plundering the government, and rival politicians with old scores to pay, were prominent among the assailants. Chase defended Cameron's integrity earnestly. Charles A. Dana, who knew him well and was impressed by his personal force, warmth of heart, and literary cultivation, did the same.[3]

His abysmal lack of business capacity and incredible laxity, however, cost the country more than petty dishonesties might have done. Dozens of men

---

1 Ben P. Thomas, *Lincoln*, 234. Cameron equally resented Lincoln's post-election efforts (as he saw it) to wriggle out of a fair political bargain.

2 W. W. Orme, Washington, May 14, 1861, to Leonard Swett, David Davis Papers, Ill. State Hist. Lib.; Helen Nicolay, *Lincoln's Secretary*, 125.

3 Lincoln declared that Cameron's emergency steps in war purchasing "were not moved nor suggested by himself, and that not only the President but all the other heads of departments were at least equally responsible"; *Collected Works*, VII, 193, 194. Fessenden wrote his defense of Cameron Aug. 27, 1861; Fessenden Papers. See Dana's comment to Ida M. Tarbell, Tarbell Papers, Allegheny College.

who did business in the War Department have left us pictures of its bumbling clutter. Cameron refused to protect his time, saw everybody, forgot everything, established no routines, and deputed little to subordinates. "What was the last action I took on your case?" he asked an importunate caller. "You borrowed my pencil, took a note, put my pencil in your pocket, and lost the paper," replied the suitor. In July Trumbull had the Senate call on Cameron for information as to war contracts, but with little result. That same month the House appointed a committee under C. H. Van Wyck of New York to investigate the subject, and most of the evidence it collected of irregularities naturally pertained to the War Department. In August a group of bankers urged Lincoln to get rid of the Secretary. This deputation did not impress the President, who realized that if he yielded to them, they would shift the attack to some other Cabinet member; but even Cameron's best friends grew impatient with his slack, haphazard methods.[4]

Chase, for example, informed John Sherman in the fall that some remedy must be found for the absence of system and economy in war expenditures, and suggested various reforms. When in November he decided that the War Department bills were exorbitant, he refused to accept Cameron's estimates for the next year to lay before Congress. Returning them, he declared in a stinging letter, aimed at the whole executive branch, that both the failures of the armies and the financial difficulties of the nation had been traceable neither to want or an excess of men, but to the lack of systematic administration.[5]

Even more irritating to Lincoln than Cameron's woolly-minded lack of system was his meddling with the sensitive issue of slavery. Although initially Cameron had been under the influence of his conservative friend Seward, early in the war he shifted ground and became more intimate with Chase, who assisted him in military affairs. Already, what Montgomery Blair called a hard underground war had begun between Chase and Seward, and before long, Seward was quite willing to get rid of Cameron as a punishment for his defection. Chase was of course fundamentally hostile to slavery; and two of Cameron's old personal friends, Colonel John Cochrane, a New York Congressman who became colonel of chasseurs, and Samuel Wilkeson, of Greeley's *Tribune*, also used their influence to give the Secretary a growing anti-slavery tendency. The War Department, like the Navy Department, had to deal with innumerable pitiful cases of slaves who escaped into the Union lines, and both Cameron and Welles took the position that they should not be returned to their masters. Cameron sent Ben Butler a letter, written in part by Chase, approving

4 A. G. Riddle, *Recollections of War Times*, is the basis of the pencil anecdote; see also *Cong. Globe*, July 21, 1861; Meneely, *War Department in 1861*.
5 To Cameron Nov. 27, 1861; Schuckers, *Chase*, 279–281.

of that general's "contraband" policy.[6] This was unexceptionable. But the Secretary, who now honestly believed that slavery was the tap-root of rebellion, soon went further.

When General Thomas W. Sherman was preparing for his part in the Du Pont expedition against Port Royal, Cameron had drafted a comprehensive letter of instructions to govern him in the treatment of slaves. Laying down the principle that those who entered the Union lines might be used in government service, it was so worded that the general could have armed them; and it gave assurances that slaves employed by the army would never be sent back to bondage. Cameron had entrusted this letter, just before he left for his Missouri trip on October 9, to Assistant Secretary Thomas A. Scott for issuance. Lincoln saw it, struck out the pledge that slaves would never be returned to their masters, and limited the passage respecting government service by a dozen pregnant words: "This, however, not to mean a general arming of them for military service." As Thomas A. Scott pointed out in reply to an inquiry, this still left the door open, in great emergencies, to the arming of colored men by irregular enrollment; and the New York *Tribune* commented that it went beyond Frémont's proclamation in that it permitted the use of arms, in such emergencies, by slaves who had fled from loyal as well as disloyal masters. But Cameron's effort to commit the army to a radical position on slavery, probably abetted by Chase, had been defeated.[7]

Unquestionably he was sincere in his repeated assertions that to strike at slavery was to strike at the root of insurrection. The theory that he was taking an abolitionist stand in order to gain Radical protection against dismissal is unjust. For one reason, he was aware by October that his fate was determined. "I knew I was doomed when I consented to go to St. Louis," he shortly assured old F. P. Blair, "and was not altogether clear of suspicion that it was intended I should be by one of my associates [Seward], but having determined to shrink from no duty I went cheerfully, only taking care to let the President know my belief, and to get his promise that I should be allowed to go abroad when I left the Department." He knew Lincoln well enough to understand that no Radical intervention could help him. Moreover, this vigorous Jacksonian (now sixty-two, he was destined to live to ninety) had long detested slavery, and believed that blows at it would shorten the war. "I can safely say," he told Blair, "that I have not done an official act that I would not do again, under the same circumstances. But there are many things I would have

6　Welles, *Diary*, I, 127; see also Welles, "Narrative of Events," *Amer. Hist. Review,* XXXI, 486 ff.; Benjamin F. Butler, *Autobiography (Butler's Book),* 259–261.

7　Meneely, 341–343; Nicolay and Hay, V, 123, 124; N. Y. *Tribune,* Nov. 25, 1861.

done, which were omitted only because my associates were not as advanced as I was in hostility to the rebellion." [8]

In mid-November, when the issue was sharply joined between those who would accept restoration of the Union with slavery and those who demanded the Union with emancipation, Cameron took a further step. He visited Springfield, Massachusetts, with Colonel John Cochrane. There he told numerous citizens privately that in outfitting T. W. Sherman's expedition he had included extra guns to be placed in the hands of any men who could use them. At a parade of Cochrane's regiment in Washington a few days later the colonel declared in the Secretary's presence that arming the slaves did not differ from utilizing other captured enemy resources: "We should take the slave by the hand, place a musket in it, and bid him in God's name strike for the liberty of the human race." Cameron, amid cheers by the regiment, stated his hearty approval of every sentiment uttered by Cochrane. This episode provoked a hot discussion in high military and political circles. McClellan, tender toward slavery, and already irritated because Cameron held a strong belief in the immediate striking-power of the volunteer army while the general distrusted the volunteers, became hostile. The conservative Caleb B. Smith lashed out at Cameron in Cabinet meeting, and Lincoln himself was much displeased.[9]

Yet Cameron, applauded by many Radical voices, stuck to his guns. At a reception which John W. Forney gave at his Washington home for George D. Prentice of the Louisville *Journal*, he bluntly reiterated his views. Speaking informally, and belligerently facing Caleb B. Smith, he again declared that he would arm any able-bodied men in the South who offered their services. Smith, who followed him, vehemently condemned any such policy. Reports of this clash appeared in the newspapers, and the New York *Times* advised Cabinet members to push on with the war instead of quarreling in public over controversial issues. Meanwhile, Montgomery Blair, always sensitive to Border State opinion, took sides with Bates and Smith. He found opportunity to twit Cameron upon a newspaper remark that the Secretary had now elbowed Frémont out of the abolitionist boat, and taken the tiller in the stern-sheets.[10]

Something of the temper of the Highland Scot, of the Cameronians who

8 From his home, "Lochiel," Feb. 8, 1862; Blair-Lee Papers, Princeton. A. K. McClure, who differed radically from Cameron in politics, gives a fair estimate of him in *Lincoln and Men of War Times*, 147–168; correctly stating that the most upright and sagacious statesman of the nation could not have administered the War Department in 1861 without flagrant abuses and errors.

9 N. Y. *Herald*, Nov. 14, N. Y. *Tribune*, Nov. 14, 15, 1861; Flower, *Stanton*, 115; *Amer. An. Cyc.*, 1861, p. 645; Bates, *Diary*, Nov. 20, 1861.

10 N. Y. *Times*, Nov. 20, 22, Dec. 2, 1861; Bates, *Diary*, Nov. 20, 27; Smith to Barlow, Nov. 22, 23, Barlow Papers. Prentice at once published a long attack on Cameron.

had battled to the hopeless end at Aird Moss, crying, "Lord, spare the green and take the ripe," had been aroused in Cameron. He defiantly told at least one Cabinet meeting how firmly he believed in arming and organizing Negro soldiers.[11] He also let friends know that his annual report would deal emphatically with the subject. This announcement startled conservative Pennsylvanians, and the editor Forney headed a delegation which late in November bearded Cameron at his house to remonstrate. He read them what he intended to say. "It will never do!" exploded Forney. "I beg of you not to press so certain a firebrand." Wilmot defended the passage. All night the angry debate raged. Then, as early daylight struggled through the curtained windows, Cameron rose, went to the sideboard, filled a glass with whiskey and water, and holding it aloft, declared: "Gentlemen, the paragraph stands."[12]

[II]

Seldom had patriotic Americans passed more anxious days. As December drew in the whole North knew that financial difficulties were thickening and the suspension of specie payments was at hand, that the Mason-Slidell affair held dire potentialities, and that radicals and conservatives would be at each others' throats throughout the session of Congress. No state paper would arouse more interest than the report of the Secretary of War. On November 25th Washington correspondents began announcing that Cameron would advocate the arming of slaves. The Secretary had not only shown his paragraph to intimates, but laid it before the new special counsel for the War Department, Edwin McMasters Stanton, who made changes to strengthen it from a legal standpoint, and gave it full approval. The key sentences ran: [13]

"Those who make war against the Government justly forfeit all rights of property. . . . It is as clearly a right of the government to arm slaves, when it may become necessary, as it is to use gunpowder taken from the enemy. Whether it is expedient to do so is purely a military question. . . . If it shall be found that the men who have been held by the rebels as slaves are capable of bearing arms and performing efficient military service, it is the right, and may become the duty, of the Government to arm and equip them, and employ their service against the rebels, under proper military regulations, discipline, and command."

This was a threat, not a statement of immediate intent, and within a year

11 Hugh O'Reilly, "Arming the Slaves for the Union," pamphlet published 1875; O'Reilly was secretary of the Association for Promoting the Organization of Colored Troops, one of various abolitionist bodies already demanding such action.
12 *Idem.* The MS Reminiscences of X. X. Cobb, NYPL, give a slightly different version.
13 Nicolay and Hay, V, 125, 126; *Cong. Globe*, Dec. 12, 1861. The N. Y. *Tribune's* Washington correspondent sent out word of Cameron's intention Nov. 25.

events were to make the threat good. But the expediency of arming the Negroes was not a purely military question—it was equally a political question; and the nervous condition of the Borderland made such an utterance highly indiscreet.

Why did Lincoln so lose touch with Cameron that the Secretary could pen this paragraph? For one reason, he always drove his Cabinet with slack rein, and often with no rein at all, a matter of frequent complaint by businesslike members. For another, he was engrossed with a multiplicity of urgent affairs, including the *Trent* dispute, Mexico, a memorandum on the military offensive which he sent McClellan about December 1, a plan for compensated emancipation in the Border States, and final touches on his own message. For a third reason, he had asked Cabinet members for an abstract of essential parts of their reports, and Cameron's had apparently given him no uneasiness. Yet all these reasons are unsatisfactory; Lincoln did find time in these days for comparative trifles, and he betrayed a lack of proper vigilance. Perhaps he would not have been so supremely great a man had he been a highly circumspect and efficient administrator. But we cannot excuse his secretaries for not reading the newspapers, listening to Washington talk, and seeing that he was warned betimes.[14]

The sequel was an unfortunate exposure of Administration differences. On Saturday, November 30, Cameron presented his report to Lincoln, who was too busy to read it that day. Next morning the Secretary mailed copies to postmasters in leading cities, to be delivered to newspapers as soon as Lincoln had sent his message to Congress. He also gave confidential copies to Washington correspondents. Sometime on Sunday Lincoln read the report. Astonished and dismayed, he at once called Cameron to the White House. Here two conferences took place in rapid succession, other Cabinet members participating in the second. The President insisted that Cameron suppress the paragraph on arming slaves. As Lincoln was presenting in his message some vague ideas on colonizing freedmen abroad, and was about to attempt to persuade Border State Congressmen to support a plan for compensated emancipation, he could permit no such untimely declaration. Cameron expostulated. His statement contained nothing especially novel, he argued, and it ran parallel with equally explicit and radical, though briefer, statements in Welles's reports.

It appears that Chase outspokenly and Welles at least tacitly supported him.[15] But Bates, Seward, Smith, and Montgomery Blair stood on the other

14 Mrs. Stephen A. Douglas, one of the many visitors, called Nov. 27 for advice on the property of her minor children in the South; *Collected Works*, V, 32.
15 Welles, "Narrative of Events," *Amer. Hist. Rev.*, XXXI, 486 ff.; Flower, *Stanton*, 116; N. Y. *Times, Herald*, Dec. 3–6; N. Y. *Tribune*, Dec. 4, a very full account probably inspired by Cameron or Chase; Nicolay and Hay, V, 126, 127.

side, and of course Lincoln's word was final. Cameron either gave way, or was overruled despite continued protestations; at any rate, he had to submit.[16]

But the mischief had been done. On Monday, December 2, Montgomery Blair telegraphed postmasters to return the packages containing Cameron's report. Congress met at noon buzzing with rumors about the dispute between Lincoln and Cameron, for Cabinet officers on both sides had talked excitedly to friends. The legislative branch had expected to receive the President's message, but this was withheld. The House at once showed its temper by passing a resolution for the emancipation of slaves of rebels within all military jurisdictions; that is, endorsing Frémont's policy. Many predicted an early breakup of the Cabinet and general confusion. On the 3rd Lincoln's message went to Congress unaccompanied by any departmental reports. Though moderate members liked it, radicals greeted it with little bursts of derisive laughter.[17] The press meanwhile took positions on Cameron according to its predilections. Greeley's *Tribune* of course doggedly supported him, while Raymond's *Times* stood doggedly with Lincoln. And to the amazement of millions of citizens who had not heard of the dispute, the newspapers began publishing Cameron's report in two versions!

The inevitable had happened. In some cities postmasters did not receive Montgomery Blair's order for withdrawal, and in others it was not heeded. The Cincinnati *Gazette*, for example, got Cameron's report unaltered. The editors immediately printed it on the front page of the next morning's paper; then, late that night, they got the version as modified under Lincoln's orders, and printed the changes on the inside pages. The New York *Times* and *Herald* on December 4 carried the report as amended, while the *Tribune* that day published it in the Secretary's original form. The *Congressional Globe* of December 12 printed the suppressed portion. Naturally all radicals were enraged. "What a fiasko!" C. H. Ray of the Chicago *Tribune* wrote Elihu Washburne. "Old Abe is now unmasked, and we are sold out." For the moment Cameron was the toast of all men who hoped for hard blows at slavery.[18]

16 Nicolay and Hay, and Flower, say Cameron declined to yield and was overruled; A. K. McClure, in *Lincoln and Men of War Times*, 162, 163, states he "submitted as gracefully as possible," the view taken by Meneely. That he did submit is indicated by the fact that he wrote a substitute passage.

17 Washington corr. in N. Y. *Tribune*, Dec. 5, 1861.

18 Washburne Papers, LC. The Cincinnati *Gazette* published an explanatory editorial Dec. 6, with a long news article from Washington narrating the whole dispute. This article declared that Cameron had refused to budge, but that Lincoln had compelled the change. The revision struck out Cameron's matter on the treatment of Negroes, and substituted a single paragraph. This, after stating that many slaves were in military hands and constituted a military resource which should not be turned over to the Confederacy, went on: "The disposition to be made of the slaves of rebels after the close of the war can be safely left to the wisdom and patriotism of Congress. The representatives of the people will, unquestionably, secure to the loyal slaveholders every right to which they are entitled under the Constitution of the country."

A deputation of Congressional leaders which included Vice-President Hamlin, Owen Lovejoy, John A. Bingham, and other antislavery men descended enthusiastically on the Secretary's house as he entertained W. H. Russell of the London *Times* at dinner, and acclaimed him in fervent speeches. At the next caucus of Republican Representatives others earnestly upheld him. Thaddeus Stevens, long a bitter political antagonist, wholeheartedly endorsed his course. And Stevens had a sensational bit of news. McClellan, he said, had come to Lincoln and threatened to resign if the offensive passages were not struck out. For this assertion he gave no proof.[19]

[III]

Lincoln hesitated to dismiss Cameron summarily because abrupt action would anger the Radical war party. Cameron, for his part, wished to make his now inevitable exit with dignity, taking a foreign post, and hoped to have a voice in selecting his successor. As he knew, he had few friends in Washington. Sumner stood firmly by him in the Senate, and Chase in the Cabinet, but many even of the extreme antislavery group had been alienated by his bad administration and his adroit haste in getting his report before the country. Much of the press comment on his recommendations was scathing; for example, Raymond's *Times* remarked that it was odd to talk of arming the slaves when the War Department had not yet succeeded in properly arming white men.[20] His position was worsened when late in December the House investigative committee under C. H. Van Wyck of New York submitted a report which, published in full by the press, dealt unsparingly with frauds practiced upon the War Department.

A new Secretary had to be chosen, but in a way that would spare Cameron's feelings, respect the growing war party which demanded advanced measures, and persuade the country that a truly constructive step was being taken. He must be acceptable to the editors, governors, Congressmen, and plain citizens who thought aggressiveness the cardinal need. By Christmas Lincoln realized that he and the country were in serious straits. One piece of news after another dampened Northern spirits: General Albin Schoepf's deplorable retreat from the neighborhood of Cumberland Gap, exposing the brave Unionists of east Tennessee; the loss of ground in Missouri, and Halleck's hostility there to Negro refugees; the sudden, one-sided communication of the French foreign minister, E. Thouvenel, taking part with the British in the *Trent* affair; Greeley's declaration that the country could not go on spending its

19 See N. Y. *Tribune*, Dec. 5, and Russell's diary Dec. 4 for the Congressional call; N. Y. *Weekly Tribune*, Dec. 14, 1861, for caucus.
20 Dec. 6, 1861.

colossal sums for another six months; and the unescapable humiliation of surrendering Mason and Slidell.

Union fortunes were in fact at a desperate point. The Treasury was almost empty, high new taxes were a necessity, and on December 28 the principal New York banks decided to stop specie payments. Many were asking with Chase how it was that when the War Department reported 660,000 men under arms, the armies of the Potomac, West Virginia, Kentucky, and Missouri did not contain more than half that many. Congress, President, and a great majority of thoughtful citizens had a fast-ebbing faith in McClellan. The Western army was essentially leaderless. "Our only hope now," General James Wadsworth wrote Sumner, "is in the legislative branch. If you are competent to the crisis you may save the country; but you must do it soon or be too late!" [21] And to cap other misfortunes McClellan fell ill of typhoid. On December 20 he failed to appear at headquarters, next day it was learned he was very sick, and by Christmas staff intimates (but not the President!) knew that his life was in danger.[22]

His illness was disastrous because it paralyzed all military planning. McClellan had never delegated his principal powers, so that Marcy, head of his staff—himself recently ill—dared make no decisions whatever. The general, confined to his bed during some three weeks, saw nobody and kept his condition largely secret from the press. Lincoln lost practically all communication with him. Calling sometimes when McClellan was asleep, the President was denied entrance and given no trustworthy news. As the general later wrote, Lincoln's anxiety induced him to fear that the disease was so acute that it would terminate fatally. Not until January 10, 1862, was McClellan really alert again.

All the while, with a formidable groundswell of opinion demanding action, the leaderless armies stood immobile, giving the country only a few slight successes in Missouri and Kentucky. Perforce, the anguished Lincoln had to step into the breach. In St. Louis Halleck did little beyond oversee Pope, Schofield, and Prentiss in trying to halt marauding and bridge-burning; in Louisville Don Carlos Buell, who had taken command of the Department of the Ohio November 15, was concentrating his troops and eying Nashville as an objective. Hoping some large result could be achieved in the West, Lincoln tele-

---

21 Jan. 10, 1862; Pearson, *Wadsworth*, 102, 103.
22 The Comte de Paris, of McClellan's staff, in *Battles and Leaders*, II, 120, says his life was in danger. McClellan in *My Own Story*, 155, asserts that "although very weak and ill, my strong constitution enabled me to retain a clear intellect" and make decisions. A man very weak and ill of typhoid is not a good judge of his own clarity of intellect, and McClellan had reason to gloss over his disability. The N. Y. *Herald* on Friday, Dec. 27, said he was better, was transacting business, and would be in the saddle again on Monday; he was not in the saddle for at least two weeks more.

graphed Halleck on New Year's eve asking whether he and Buell were acting in concert. He followed this with a message to both generals: "Delay is
ruining us, and it is indispensable for me to have something definite." The
generals responded that they were *not* coöperating with each other, that some
of their regiments were unarmed, and that Halleck opposed any immediate
movement. On a letter from that tactician the President wrote despairingly:
"It is exceedingly discouraging. As everywhere else, nothing can be done."

And Lincoln had reason for depression! He had just presided over a joint
meeting of the Cabinet and the Committee on the Conduct of the War, at
which the radicals—Zach Chandler, Ben Wade, and John Covode—bitterly
denounced McClellan, and clamored for giving McDowell charge of the Army
of the Potomac.[23]

On January 10 Lincoln, in gloom and perplexity, sought out one of the
few administrators who was demonstrating high capacity, Quartermaster-
General Meigs. He seated himself before the blazing office grate. "What shall
I do?" he demanded. "The people are impatient; Chase has no money and he
tells me he can raise no more; the general of the Army has typhoid fever.
The bottom is out of the tub." [24]

Meigs had a ready suggestion: As it was evident that McClellan would be
incapacitated for some weeks, Lincoln should call a conference of the higher
officers to talk over plans. The same night, January 10, what amounted to an
Emergency War Cabinet—Lincoln, Chase, Seward, T. A. Scott, and Generals McDowell and Franklin—met in the first of four sessions. The President
was in such a mood of desperation that he even spoke of taking the field himself. He voiced his anxiety over the exhausted finances, the impatient temper
of Congress, the want of liaison between Halleck and Buell, and above all,
McClellan's illness. He must talk to somebody, he said. "If General McClellan
does not want to use the army, I would like to *borrow* it, provided I could
see how it could be made to do something." While the civilians listened eagerly,
he asked Generals McDowell and Franklin what military plans they would
advise. McDowell proposed that the Army of the Potomac make a frontal
advance in Virginia, moving against Aquia, Centreville, and Manassas; Franklin, who knew something of McClellan's ideas, proposed a lateral movement
on Richmond from the head of the York River.

Next evening, the 11th, the group met again, augmented by Montgomery
Blair. They debated the two plans, Chase arguing for the frontal movement,
and Blair for an attack from the upper York. Lincoln wished that Meigs be

23 *Collected Works*, V, 86, 87; O. R. I, vii, 532–535; Meneely, 359; McClellan, *My Own
Story*, 155 ff.
24 See Meigs's narrative in *American Hist. Review*, XXVI, 292, 293, and MS Diary, Meigs
Papers, LC; Swinton, *Army of the Potomac*, 79–85.

consulted and that officers gather information on the transportation needed to carry troops down the Potomac and up the York. Much perplexed, he made no decision between the two plans, but arranged for a third meeting. To some observers in the group, a struggle for power between McDowell as backed by Chase, and McClellan as supported by Blair and Meigs, seemed emerging; but the President was thinking of the war, not of rival generals.[25] On Sunday afternoon, the 12th, they met again with Meigs present, and after some discussion agreed that as McClellan was better, they would consult with him next day.

Of course McClellan soon learned what was afoot, and to Lincoln's jubilant relief, he was on hand at a fourth White House meeting Monday afternoon. Apparently he was galvanized into action by a warning from the subtle Edwin M. Stanton, who had reasons of his own for wishing to curry favor with the general, and who warned him: "They are counting on your death and are already dividing among themselves your military goods and chattels." If Stanton could ally himself with McClellan, he would stand in a more powerful position.[26] McClellan at once leaped at the conclusion that a plot had been formed to get rid of him and put McDowell in his stead, and that Chase and McDowell were at the bottom of it. He appeared at the White House in a truculent mood. The President opened the meeting by explaining why he had called the Cabinet members and generals together, and then innocently asked McDowell to explain the plan for a direct forward movement. While McClellan glared angrily, McDowell argued that this march could be started in three weeks, whereas a transfer of the army to the peninsula between the York and James Rivers could not be begun, for lack of transports, for a month or six weeks.

Disconcerted by McClellan's haughty stare, McDowell added an excusing sentence about the urgent situation in which the government stood. To this the general replied coldly if not sharply, "You are entitled to have any opinion you please!"—and said no more. He regarded the whole affair—the conferences, the inquiries, the plans—as a treacherous effort to supersede him while ill. He was not advising the President of the United States, but foiling a group of conspirators! [27]

Finally the anxious Lincoln asked, in effect: "What and when can any-

---

25   Meigs, *loc. cit.*; McDowell's memorandum on the meeting, Swinton, 79, 80; McClellan, *Own Story*, 155 ff.; T. H. Williams, *Lincoln and the Radicals*, 84–86.

26   Chase had told Stanton, who told McClellan. But we must not do Stanton the injustice of attributing to him a purely selfish motive. He was already sure of the Secretaryship of War; he and McClellan, as fellow Pennsylvanians, were warm friends. Others, including perhaps Meigs, must have told McClellan as soon as he began to get up, which was Jan. 11th.

27   McClellan had the impression that Lincoln had directed McDowell, Franklin, and Meigs to make a "secret examination" into the state of the army, which he says was un-

thing be done?" The surly general at last spoke up. "The case is so clear a blind man could see it," he snapped. Without explaining, he said he did not know what force he could count on: how many men Burnside would take for a projected attack on Roanoke Island, and Ben Butler for the proposed descent on New Orleans. Finally Secretary Chase, out of patience with him, brought the talk back to the main point by repeating Lincoln's question: "What do you intend doing with your army, and when do you intend doing it?"

A sullen silence ensued. McClellan, who regarded Chase as his principal enemy, ignored him. Finally he unbent enough to offer some remarks about Western operations. An advance in Kentucky was to precede that in Virginia, he remarked, and he had directed General Buell to *take* wagons if he could not hire them. Another pause followed. All were plainly waiting for an answer to Lincoln's and Chase's queries. At last the commander made the evasive statement that he was most unwilling to divulge his plans, always believing that in military matters the fewer people who knew his secrets the better. "I will tell them if I am *ordered* to do so." Lincoln then inquired whether the general had fixed any particular time, which he need not state. "Yes," responded McClellan. "Then," said the President, "I will adjourn this meeting." Already Seward had commented in his amiable way that they had better break up: "I don't see that we are likely to make much out of General McClellan." Chase, previously distrustful, thereafter detested the general.

A wiser leader would at once have gone privately to Lincoln, and given him his full plans and time-schedule, but McClellan remained sullen. During another fortnight he did nothing, keeping Lincoln still in the dark. The worried President thereupon felt himself provoked to a decisive and unhappy step. On January 27, yielding to pleas by the War and Navy departments, but consulting nobody and reading it to the Cabinet for information only, he issued General War Order No. 1. It directed a general movement of land and naval forces against the enemy February 22. The Secretaries of War and the Navy, all officers in national service, and their subordinates, would be held strictly responsible for executing the order. Four days later the President's Special War Order No. 1, addressed to McClellan, bade him use the Army of the Potomac, after safeguarding Washington, in a flanking movement to the southwest of the Confederate position at Manassas—to begin not later than February 22.[28]

---

necessary, for his staff could have informed the President of the "exact condition" of every branch. *My Own Story*, 156. Why the staff never did so is a puzzle. Nothing is more discreditable to McClellan than his willingness to believe that the transparently honest Lincoln, so patient and long-suffering, could be capable of double-dealing.

28 See text in O. R. I, v, 41 ff., and with previously unpublished passages, in Lincoln, *Collected Works*, V, 119 ff. Welles says in his Diary, I, 61, that he and Stanton had pressed for such an order. Both were preparing for the New Orleans expedition. Both wished the

It was obvious that General War Order No. 1 was intended primarily for popular effect. Political rather than military, it was expected to protect the Administration from accusations of inaction rather than to inaugurate a series of battles. Even so, it was unwise. Lincoln would have to learn to handle Congress and public opinion more adroitly. His order seemed impatient, his idea of a "general movement" was amateurish, and his choice of Washington's birthday was undignified. The Special Order to McClellan, however, evinced real sagacity, for it was well devised to make him show his hand. Lincoln waited to see how soon his reply would come and how much of his plans it would reveal.

[IV]

Meanwhile, Cameron's exit had been managed, his successor installed, and an initial effort made to fit a bottom into the tub. We must reëmphasize the fact that the central reason for Cameron's dismissal was not his antislavery position, which counted for little, but his lack of grasp, foresight, administrative energy, and organizing power. However numerous, fierce, and well-founded the charges brought against his successor, Stanton clearly possessed these particular qualities.

Lincoln knew that Cassius M. Clay was anxious to drop his place as minister to Russia and accept an army command. He ascertained through Thurlow Weed that Cameron would be glad to take the post. As the new Secretary, Lincoln thought of naming Joseph Holt, the stanch Kentucky Unionist who had done so much to put courage into the last acts of the Buchanan Administration. But Cameron believed that Stanton, who also had given iron resolution to Buchanan's last months, and who had assiduously curried favor at the War Department, was an abler man. Cameron had urged him on the radicals, introducing him to Zack Chandler at a breakfast party as the best choice, and making the same recommendation to Ben Wade.[29]

"I called on Mr. Lincoln," Cameron later wrote, "and suggested Edwin

---

Confederates driven from the south bank of the Potomac, their batteries demolished, and the river fully opened. Welles writes that "we united in requesting President Lincoln to issue his celebrated order of the 27th of January."

29 Years after, when Cameron was Senator, Charles F. Benjamin saw the ex-Secretary, Cameron told him "that soon after he became Secretary of War he received a call one evening from Stanton, who was cordial and effusive, and fervidly eloquent on the subject of depriving the Confederacy of its slave property and putting it to the use of the Union. Thenceforward, as he told me, Stanton was his confidant and adviser, and when he saw that his days in the Cabinet were numbered he set every agency at work that he could command to make sure of Stanton as his successor, and when he knew he had succeeded he was glad to get out." Charles F. Benjamin, Washington, June 1, 1914, to Horace White; White Papers, Ill. State Hist. Lib.

M. Stanton to him as my successor. He hesitated; but after listening to me for a time, he yielded, and sent me to offer the place of Secretary of War to him, and added: 'Tell him, Cameron, if he accepts, I will send his nomination as Secretary, and yours as minister to Russia, to the Senate together.' " This may be accurate as to Cameron's action, but the story is more complicated. Seward, as Gideon Welles, Montgomery Blair, and others assert, was the prime mover in bringing Stanton forward. He knew the man's strength and was impressed by Assistant-Secretary Peter H. Watson's warm endorsement. It is said that while Lincoln hesitated over Holt, who might have struck some radicals as being too much a Border State man, Winfield Scott, Ben Wade, and Sumner also urged the claims of Stanton. Lincoln of course consulted numerous men.[30] He did not know, and Cameron did not tell him, that Stanton had helped write the antislavery passage in Cameron's report.

The final stroke was not without drama. Lincoln on January 10, by Chase's hand—for Lincoln in his politic way wished Chase to think *he* had a prime part in the matter—sent a note to Cameron. It reached the Secretary late in the evening, and he was staggered to see that it was so worded as to give the public the impression of a curt discharge. At midnight he sought Thomas A. Scott's house in high emotion. Showing Scott and McClure the note, he wept as he said that it meant his personal and political destruction. They assured him of what seems to have been the fact, that Lincoln—then distracted over McClellan's condition—had dashed off the note without perceiving its implications. All agreed that next day they should ask the President to withdraw it, allow Cameron to submit his resignation, and accept it graciously. Speaker after speaker in Congress this month, using the Van Wyck report as ammunition, was assailing the Secretary, and Lincoln must not seem to throw him to the wolves. The result was that the President sent Cameron two letters dated January 11. One was a notification that as Cameron had more than once expressed a wish for another office, he could now gratify him with St. Petersburg; the other was a generous personal communication, declaring his personal esteem and his confidence in the Secretary's ability, patriotism, and fidelity.

Cameron departed with pride in the work he had done to raise and train the great volunteer army. "No man ever served with more disinterested integrity than I did, and I am sure in the end all will say so." In actual fact, the next generation criticized him more harshly than he deserved. The greatest of war ministers, confronted with his staggering tasks, and given the meagre

30 Different views on Stanton's appointment are given in Welles, *Diary*, I, 57-59, 127, 128; Bates, *Diary*; Chase, *Diary*, Jan. 12, 1862; Henry Wilson, "Jeremiah S. Black and Edwin M. Stanton," *Atlantic*, XXVI, 474 ff.; Maunsell B. Field, *Memories*, 267-269; Flower, *Stanton*, 116, 117, and A. G. Riddle, *Benjamin F. Wade*.

resources the government could then muster, would have blundered. In this office he was honest, and he did his best. But he was a misfit, whom Lincoln appointed against his best judgment; clumsy, forgetful, unsystematic, he failed to adapt himself to his responsibilities as Chase and Seward did; and his executive feebleness soon made him a sore clog upon the administration. The War Department, enlarged by Congress in late summer and now shaken down, gave Stanton a far more efficient agency than Cameron had found. Contract letting had been systematized, trustworthy manufacturers had been separated from cheats, and half a thousand regiments had been put in fair order.

The first drivers of the military machine, the men who jerked it into gear, were penalized by circumstance. The nation had to regard them as expendable, and they were all broken.[31]

In choosing Stanton, Lincoln took a man of whose true capacities or character nobody was informed. But he knew well that Stanton had been a Jacksonian Democrat, had held the Attorney-Generalship under Buchanan as a Union Democrat, and had other Union Democrats as his chief friends. He understood his well-earned eminence at the bar. No other aspirant combined so much executive support, Meigs alone disliking the appointment, with so much Congressional approbation. His public reputation overtopped that of Holt. With characteristic magnanimity, Lincoln dismissed any recollection of the slights Stanton had put upon him when they were fellow-counsel in the reaper-patent case in Cincinnati in 1855. He could not know that in recent letters, Stanton had violently abused him and his Administration, and

---

31 Cameron delivered a long defense of his record at a public dinner in Harrisburg just before sailing for Europe (N. Y. *Herald*, May 8, 1862). As a young man, he said, he had often worked twenty hours out of the twenty-four, "but that labor was nothing in comparison with the overpowering toil which I underwent at Washington." He found the Ordnance Department without a head, the man in charge being too old to be competent, and he appointed Colonel Ripley, who was believed capable, "but who soon proved, in the opinion of my associates, to be unequal to the crisis." To safeguard the Department, he directed Thomas A. Scott, his assistant, to see that every contract had a thirty-day cancellation clause to be invoked in case of failure to meet requirements. Cameron revealed that Lincoln had specifically approved one large arms contract. When on Sept. 4 Herman Boker & Co. of New York had offered upwards of more than 100,000 rifled percussion muskets, subject to departmental inspection, at not more than $18 each, Lincoln had endorsed on the letter of offer: "I approve the carrying this through, carefully, cautiously, and expeditiously. Avoid conflicts and interference." The Secretary defended his railroad arrangements to carry Eastern soldiers to Washington in the April crisis when the bridges of the Wilmington & Baltimore were destroyed. Massachusetts capitalists, he asserted, controlled that road, and their resentment when he arranged with the rival Harrisburg, Reading, and New Jersey roads to reduce the New York–Baltimore fare from $6 to $4 inspired the attack by Dawes. Cameron also charged that some of his Congressional assailants, who had passed a vote of censure in the House, had asked him for improper contract favors. "Having my whole time occupied in preparing an army out of raw and undisciplined soldiers, of course I may have run counter to the desires of such gentlemen."

had even advised the violent overthrow of the government, to be replaced by a military dictatorship under McClellan. If he had, he would have ignored the fact. Lincoln was willing to pay any personal price to obtain a powerful organizer of victory.

The transfer of the War Department to Stanton was widely hailed as a great national victory.[32] Its moral effect was tremendous. Senators and Representatives who in the dark winter of 1860–61 had seen how Stanton nerved the weak Buchanan to duty, and had exposed the dark purposes of Floyd and Cobb, particularly rejoiced. They recalled how fiercely he had risen to meet the crisis, what iron resolution, industry, and vigilance he had brought to this task, and how carefully, using Howard of Michigan and Sumner of Massachusetts as intermediaries, he had kept the Republicans informed of every movement tending to endanger the nation. They remembered gratefully how he had decided that his fellow Cabinet-member, Isaac Toucey, ought to be arrested, and had inspired a House resolution on that subject. Henry Wilson, as member of a Republican committee of vigilance, had received almost daily warnings and suggestions from Stanton. Sometimes they had conferred at one in the morning on the secession crisis. The Congressional radicals were also aware that for months now, Stanton had chafed over the seeming inaction of the army, and in intimate talk had berated the Administration for not pursuing a more determined and aggressive policy.[33]

The fact that Stanton was no politician, but simply a leader of the bar noted for his prodigious industry and powerful argument, pleased the public. The press drew the portrait of a man of large brain, complete absorption in any task he undertook, and absolute fearlessness. Greeley's *Tribune* credited him with "the highest qualities of talent, courage, and uncompromising patriotism." He told Winfield Scott that he would give the public but one pledge, to throttle treason, and everybody knew that he brought to his work no commitments, attachments, or predilections that could embarrass it. Joseph Holt wrote a friend that he found everybody rejoicing; "but that rejoicing would be far greater did the people know, as I do, the courage, the loyalty, and the

32 The Washington correspondent of the N.Y. *Times* wrote (issue of Jan. 14) that the capital was stunned by the news, and the Washington correspondent of the *Tribune* called it a bombshell.
33 McClellan, a friend of Stanton, was astonished but delighted, writing S. L. M. Barlow, the Democratic leader in New York City, that the nomination was an unexpected bit of good fortune. Stanton had been on the point of going to New York to become law partner of Barlow. Jan. 18, 1862, Barlow Papers. The rejoicings of the radicals in Congress are described by Henry Wilson, "Edwin M. Stanton," *Atlantic*, Feb. 1870. The Cleveland *Plain Dealer* said: "We know Edwin M. Stanton well. He has more of the Bonaparte in his composition than any other man in America. The army will move on now, even if it goes to the devil."

genius of the new secretary. . . . He is a great man intellectually and morally —a patriot of the true Roman stamp, who will grapple with treason as the lion grapples with his prey." [34]

And the first steps of the Secretary showed that his earnestness had method. He asked the Senate to postpone further consideration of military nominations till he could scrutinize the list. He had a frank talk with the Committee on the Conduct of the War, getting their views and making suggestions for further legislation. He rearranged his office space. He laid down firm rules of business: [35]

> 1. He would receive nobody at his house and transact no business there (Cameron had been overrun at home with callers).
> 2. The Department would attend to letters and other written communications the first thing each morning, this taking precedence of other business.
> 3. Instead of giving six days a week to members of Congress, as Cameron had done, he would give them one day, Saturday.
> 4. He would give all other callers one day, Monday.
> 5. The other days, Tuesday to Friday inclusive, he would give to the war, and only to business pertaining to the armies in the field.

Finally, Stanton announced he would strike from the Army rolls all officers found in Washington except those ordered there by superiors on military business.

[V]

The bottom had indeed seemed nearly out of the tub in this midwinter crisis. But early in the year the North could feel a greater firmness and confidence; the tub was being strengthened.

Not Chase's financial measures, nor Seward's surrender of Mason and Slidell, nor the new War Department administration, did this. The central fact was that Lincoln, on whom all the fortunes of the Union depended, had begun to lead firmly. In his early months he had shown sagacity, moderation, poise —but not a strong captaincy. He had frequently fumbled. He had hesitated to call out the full strength of the North, so that Zack Chandler had some grounds for declaring the Administration timid, vacillating, and inefficient. Not a single public utterance, not one letter, not even a dramatic act, had been stamped with the qualities men later learned to term Lincolnian. But in the last weeks of the year he faced the bluster of Wade and Chandler, the

34 Flower, *Stanton*, quoting E. D. Townsend on Stanton's remark to Scott; Curtis, *Buchanan*, II, 480, for Holt's letter; N. Y. *Tribune*, Feb. 12, 1862, for Greeley's opinion. A full treatment of Stanton's character, resources, and limitations will appear later in this narrative, as will a study of Chase's financial policies.
35 N. Y. *Weekly Tribune*, Jan. 25, 1862.

suaver pressures of Sumner and Trumbull, without yielding an inch. Zack Chandler dared to tell him: "I am in favor of sending for Jeff Davis at once, if your Administration views are carried out!" But the Washington correspondent of the *Times* correctly reported just before Christmas that Lincoln was adamant. "All thought of overruling the policy of President Lincoln in regard to the war is now virtually abandoned. After full consideration of all the reasons that have been presented to induce him to modify his plans to please the radicals, the President has firmly resolved to stand by his original purpose to regard the Union as unbroken, to restore the national laws over the seceded States as rapidly as possible, and to protect the lives and property of all loyal men." He had his own proposals for slavery, his first great constructive plan, which he was now about to present to the Border States, and which fitted his fundamental policy of the restoration of a truly fraternal Union.

This was the firmness of a strong leader, a chieftain who grew with the demands laid upon him. And the appointment of Stanton was the first great decided step, showing real statesmanship, which Lincoln had taken in front of the embattled nation. The President was beginning to feel his strength; to ride in the tempest, and direct the storm.

THE FIRST and worst year of the war, 1861, was over; an unhappy year, that upon a casual review seemed to contain far more of Union failure than achievement. It had been a year of hysterical excitements and skin-deep patriotism, of contract grabbing, office mongering, and political jobbery, of shortages, shoddy, and corruption. In foreign affairs it had been a year of humiliation: of Seward's wayward hankerings for war, of Napoleon III's sly meddling in Mexico and Spain's greedy intervention in Santo Domingo, and of America's chagrined surrender of Mason and Slidell. In the military sphere it had been stained with the blood of Bull Run, Ball's Bluff, and Wilson Creek, with the failure of McDowell, Patterson, and Lyon, with the dramatic collapse of Frémont, and with a widespread loss of faith in McClellan.

It had been a year of improvisation, and of the errors inseparable from haste, amateurishness, and disorganization. The loose, irresponsible management of half the recruiting had been almost incredibly faulty; the selection of untested incompetents to hold the lives of hundreds in their hands and spend enormous sums had often been shocking. Some new functions of the national government had never gained efficiency. The paymaster service in the army, for example, continually broke down. It was shameful that soldiers who risked their lives for a paltry thirteen dollars a month should not receive that sum; disgraceful that their families should often suffer for want of part of it. Yet it was a fact, and army morale felt its effects. Some weakness in the national character seemed involved in the early deficiencies of camp sanitation, the ill-checked indulgence of officers and men in drink, the easy habit of going absent without leave, and the general antipathy to discipline.

Yet on careful view the Northern achievement seemed more impressive. When in history had a people of twenty-five millions, so unused to martial pursuits and completely devoted to tasks of peace, compressed so mighty a war effort into nine months? To enlist nearly 700,000 men, soldiers, sailors, and marines; to clothe, arm, and train them, however roughly; to collect powerful naval squadrons out of nothing, and institute a new era of armored steam warships—this was a prodigious feat. As 1861 ended, Northern hosts were poised on the Potomac, Ohio, and Mississippi to march southward. Already they had made West Virginia, Kentucky, and Missouri seemingly secure, if but half pacified, for the Union. The navy had seized two footholds on the South Atlantic coast, had begun a blockade whose effectiveness was evidenced by the price of Southern products on the world market, and was preparing to strike at New Orleans. The *Monitor* was building. For the whole effort money and materials had been found in sufficiency, if not in abundance.

The war had shown that the North was still under-developed industrially; but it had demonstrated that the Union had a wide advantage over the South —little Massachusetts alone manufactured sixty per cent more goods in 1860 than the entire Confederacy, and New York more than twice as much. The North was actually overbuilt in railroads, and events already proved that this would be the first great railway war of history, the Northern lines carrying armies and material to every invasion point. Economically and militarily, they knit the North into a compact whole. Already perceptive men saw that the four trunk lines which bridged the Allegheny barrier guaranteed a closer union of East and Northwest, and a steady growth of population and power while the battle raged.

Like a tocsin awakening a lethargic giant, the war had brought into play unsuspected powers of mobilization and administration. Against the ineptness of Cameron could be set the proved resourcefulness of the shrewd, untiring Connecticut Yankee, Gideon Welles, in making the most of scattered ships and neglected yards. If Chase at the Treasury as yet offered only promise, that was because the formidable difficulties would have baffled a Hamilton. A chaotic, ramshackle structure of State banks; a body of investors too small, too unused to Federal securities, and too cautious to give the government proper aid; House and Senate committees which even under strong men like Thaddeus Stevens and William Pitt Fessenden were clumsy in framing large-scale financial legislation; a steady march of inflation—these difficulties were compounded by the general belief in a short war. But Chase had grasp, earnestness, and courage. Among the men of lesser prominence who proved the nation's latent organizational capacities stood Montgomery C. Meigs as head of the all-important quartermaster services, Gustavus V. Fox as the efficient second leader at the Navy Department, and, now emerging, Thomas A. Scott as Stanton's invaluable aid. Of each, observers could say what one Congressman wrote of Scott: "What a relief to deal with him, with his electric brain and cool, quiet manner."

Amid the confusion, blundering, and selfishness patriots could also find cheer in the unanticipated resourcefulness of the State governments. Generally regarded as weak, shackling mechanisms corroded by politics, they had shown both zeal and power. Three war governors in especial, Andrew of Massachusetts, Curtin of Pennsylvania, and Oliver P. Morton of Indiana, had earned honorable places in the nation's history. When the War Department telegraphed its first call for troops Andrew made instant reply: "Dispatch received. By what route shall we send?" He proved his acumen by a following letter stuffed with shrewd suggestions. This trio of governors had a special capacity for enlisting business and financial talent, and for arousing popular determination. Curtin in his insistence on a body of trained reserve regiments saw further ahead than Washington. Morton helped kindle a fervor which brought out 150,000 volunteers in Indiana, making the draft practically a superfluity. Other governors—Yates, Kirkwood, Morgan, Buckingham—did well, but these three proved the resilient strength of a union of States.

All over the map, too, voluntary effort had exhibited a vision and strength which shamed inertia and self-seeking. It was already clear that women could write a lustrous page in public affairs. Partly from the foresight of one feminine organization—the Women's Central Association of Relief in New York—was born a body which finely typified the possibilities of expert private endeavor: the United States Sanitary Commission. Its two principal founders, Dr. Henry W. Bellows, a Unitarian minister, and Dr. Elisha Harris, a prominent New York physician, rallied a devoted group of men: A. D. Bache, Wolcott Gibbs, Cornelius R. Agnew, George Templeton Strong, and others. They made felicitous choice of an executive secretary in Frederick Law Olmsted. This body had a rough road just ahead. But nothing quite like it, in its combination of specialized skill, sturdy common sense, and consecrated devotion to a great aim, had previously been known in American annals; and its success was to show that a new era of national organization was opening.

As mid-January brought news of the victory of George H. Thomas, with 4000 effective troops, over an equal force of Confederates at Mill Spring, Kentucky, Northerners hoped for a turning of the tide. Most people ardently wished that McClellan, Buell, and Grant would make the war short; some hoped it would be prolonged sufficiently to ensure the downfall of slavery. Actually the year of improvised war was giving way to a year in which the war would become revolution; for the nation had been deeply aroused, and it would not stop.

Bibliography and Appendices

BIBLIOGRAPHY

Abel, Theodore, "The Element of Decision in The Pattern of War," in *American Sociology Review*, vol. 6 (December, 1941), 853–859; Adams, Charles F. Jr., *Charles Francis Adams*, by his son (Boston, 1900), "The Trent Affair, November, 1861," in Mass. Hist. Soc. *Proceedings*, vol. 45 (1911), 35–148; Adams, C. F. Jr., and Henry, *A Cycle of Adams Letters 1861–65*, ed. by Worthington C. Ford (2 vols., Boston, 1920); Adams, E. D., *Great Britain and the American Civil War* (2 vols., New York, 1925); Adams, George W., *Doctors in Blue: the Medical History of the Union Army in the Civil War* (New York, 1952); Alexander, De Alva S., *A Political History of the State of New York, 1774–1882* (3 vols., New York, 1906–09); Ambler, Charles H., *History of West Virginia* (New York, 1933); Anderson, Galusha, *The Story of a Border City during the Civil War* (Boston, 1908); Angell, James B., *The Reminiscences of James Burrill Angell* (New York, 1912); Angle, Paul M., ed., *The Lincoln Reader* (New Brunswick, N. J., 1947)

Bailey, Thomas A., *A Diplomatic History of the American People* (New York, 1940 and later eds.); Bancroft, Frederic, *The Life of W. H. Seward* (2 vols., New York, 1900); Barnard, John Gross, *C. S. A. and the Battle of Bull Run: a letter to an English Friend* (New York, 1862), *The Peninsular Campaign and Its Antecedents*. . . . (New York, 1864); Bates, Edward, *The Diary of Edward Bates, 1859–66*, ed. by Howard K. Beale (Washington, D. C., 1933); Baxter, James P., "The British Government and Neutral Rights 1861–65," *American Historical Review*, vol. 34 (October, 1928), 9–29; Beach, W. H., *The First N. Y. (Lincoln) Cavalry from April 19, 1861 to July 7, 1865* (New York, 1902); Belmont, August, *A Few Letters and Speeches of the Late Civil War* (New York, 1870); Bemis, Samuel F., ed., *American Secretaries of State and Their Diplomacy* (10 vols., New York, 1927–29), *A Diplomatic History of the United States* (New York and London, 1936 and later eds.); Benedict, G. G., *Vermont in the Civil War* (2 vols., Burlington, 1886–88); Benton, Thomas Hart, *Thirty Years' View: a History*. . . . (2 vols., New York, 1854–56); Bickham, W. D., *Rosecrans' Campaign with the Fourteenth Army Corps* (Cincinnati, 1863); Bicknell, George W., *History of the Fifth Maine Volunteers* (Portland, 1871); Bill, Alfred Hoyt, *The Beleaguered City, Richmond 1861–65* (New York, 1946); Bishop, James L., *History of American Manufactures from 1608 to 1860* (3 vols., Philadelphia, 1861–68); Black, Robert C. III, *The Railroads of the Confederacy* (Chapel Hill, 1952); Blaine, James G., *Twenty Years of Congress: From Lincoln to Garfield* (2 vols., Norwich, 1884–86); Botts, John Minor, *The Great Rebellion: Its Secret History, Rise, Progress and Disastrous Failure* (New York, 1866); Boykin, Samuel, *A Memorial Volume of the Hon. Howell Cobb* (Philadelphia, 1870); Boynton, E. C., *History of West Point and its Military Importance*. . . . (New York, 1864); Bradford, Gamaliel, *Confederate Portraits* (Boston, 1912), *Union Portraits* (Boston, 1914); Bragg, Jefferson Davis, *Louisiana in the Confederacy* (Baton Rouge, 1941); Brooks, Noah, *Washington in Lincoln's Time* (New York, 1895); Brown, G. W., *Baltimore and the Nineteenth of April, 1861: a Study of the War* (Baltimore, 1887); Browning, Orville H., *The Diary of Orville H. Browning*, ed. by T. C. Pease and J. G. Randall (2 vols., Springfield, Ill., 1925–31); Bruce, Robert V., *Lincoln and the Tools of War* (Indianapolis, 1957); Buckingham, Samuel Giles, *The Life of William A. Buckingham, the War Governor of Connecticut.* . . . (Springfield, Mass., 1894); Buell, Augustus C., *"The Cannoneer": Recollections of Service in the Army of the Potomac.* . . . (Washington, D. C., 1890); Burlingame, Roger, *March of the Iron Men: a Social History of Union through Invention* (New York, 1938); Burt, Silas W., *My Memoirs of Military History of . . . New York During the War for the Union* (Albany, 1902); Butler, Benjamin, *Autobiography and Personal Reminiscences of Major General Benjamin F. Butler; Butler's Book* (Boston, 1892); Butler, William Allen, *A Retrospect of Forty Years 1825–65* (New York, 1911)

Callahan, James Morton, *History of West Virginia, Old and New* (2 vols., Chicago, 1923); *Cambridge History of British Foreign Policy 1783–1919*, ed. by Sir A. W. Ward (3 vols., Cambridge, 1922–33); Carman, Harry J., and Luthin, Reinhard H., *Lincoln and the Patronage* (New York, 1943); Carr, Lucien, *Missouri: a Bone of Contention* (Boston, 1888); Catton, Bruce, *This Hallowed Ground* (Garden City, N. Y., 1936); Charnwood, Lord, *Abraham Lincoln* (London, 1916); Chase, F. H., *Lemuel Shaw: Chief Justice of the Supreme Judicial Court of Massachusetts 1830–60* (Boston, 1918); Chase, Salmon P., *Inside Lincoln's Cabinet: The Civil War Diaries*, ed. by David Donald (New York, 1954), *Diary* (Annual Report Amer. Hist. Assoc., vol. II, Washington, D. C., 1902); Chesnut, Mrs. Mary Boykin, *A Diary from Dixie*, ed. by I. D. Martin and M. L. Avary (New York, 1905), new edition ed. by Ben Ames Williams (Boston, 1949); Churchill, Winston, *The Crisis* (New York, 1901); Clark, George L., *History of Connecticut; Its People and Institutions* (New York, 1914); Clarke, Mrs. Grace Giddings, *George W. Julian* (Indianapolis, 1923); Cleland, R. G., *A History of Phelps-Dodge, 1834–1950* (New York, 1952); Cole, Arthur Charles, *The Era of the Civil War 1848–70* (Springfield, Mass., 1919); Coleman, Mrs. Ann Butler, *The Life of John J. Crittenden with selections from his correspondence.* . . . (2 vols., Philadelphia, 1871); Commager, Henry Steele, ed., *The Blue and the Gray* (2 vols., Indianapolis, 1951); Commons, John Rogers, et al., *History of Labor in the United States* (4 vols., New York, 1918–35); Conger, A. L., *The Rise of U. S. Grant* (New York, 1931); Connor, Henry G., *John Archibald Campbell* (Boston, 1920); Cooper, James Fenimore, *The Correspondence of James Fenimore Cooper*, ed. by his grandson (2 vols., New Haven, 1922); Corbin, Diana F. M., *A Life of Matthew Fontaine Maury* (London, 1888); Corliss, C. J., *Main Line of Mid-America: the Story of the Illinois Central* (New York, 1950); Coulter, Ellis M., *The Civil War and Readjustment in Kentucky* (Chapel Hill, 1933), *The Confederate States of America 1861–65* (Baton Rouge, 1950); Cowley, Charles, *A History of Lowell* (Boston, 1868); Cox, Jacob D., *Military Reminiscences of the Civil War* (2 vols., New York, 1900); Cox, Samuel S., *Union—Disunion—Reunion, Three Decades of Federal Legislation 1855–85* (Providence, 1885); Crawford, Col. Samuel W., *The Genesis of the Civil War; the Story of Sumter, 1860–61* (New York, 1887); Croffut, William and Morris, John, *The Military and Civil History of Connecticut During the War of 1861–65* (New York, 1868); Cubberley, E. P., *Public Education in the United States.* . . . (Boston, 1934), *State and County School Administration.* . . . (New York, 1915); Cudworth, W. H., *History of the First Regiment of Massachusetts Infantry 1861–64* (Boston, 1866); Curtis, George Ticknor, *The Life of James Buchanan* (2 vols., New York, 1883)

Dahlgren, M. V., ed., *Memoirs of John A. Dahlgren* (Philadelphia, 1872); Daniel, Fred S., *The Richmond Examiner During the War* (New York, 1868); Davis, Jefferson, *Jefferson Davis, Constitutionalist: His Letters, Papers and Speeches*, ed. by Dunbar Rowland (10 vols., Jackson, 1923), *The Rise and Fall of the Confederate Government* (2 vols., New York, 1881), "Lord Wolseley's Mistakes," *North American Review*, vol. 149 (October, 1889), 472–482; Dawes, Henry L., "Two Vice Presidents, John C. Breckinridge and Hannibal Hamlin," *Century Magazine*, vol. 50 (o.s.) (July, 1895), 463–467; De Leon, T. C., *Four Years in Rebel Capitals: an Inside View of Life in the Southern Confederacy* (Mobile, 1890); Detroit Post and Tribune, *Life of Zachariah Chandler* (Detroit, 1879); Deyrup, Felicia, *Arms Makers of the Connecticut Valley* (Northampton, 1948); Dix, Morgan,

Memoirs of John Adams Dix (2 vols., New York, 1883); Donald, David, *Lincoln's Herndon* (New York, 1948), *Lincoln Reconsidered: Essays on the Civil War Era* (New York, 1956); Douglas, Stephen, "Reminiscences of Stephen Douglas," *Atlantic Monthly*, vol. 8 (August, 1861), 205–213; Dowdey, Clifford, *The Land They Fought For: the Story of the South as the Confederacy: 1832–65* (New York, 1955); Dupuy, R. E., *Where They Have Trod: the West Point Tradition in American Life* (New York, 1940); Dutton, William S., *Du Pont: One Hundred and Forty Years* (New York, 1942); Dwight, Theodore F., *Campaigns in Virginia, 1861–62* (Military Hist. Soc. of Mass., Boston, 1895)

Early, Jubal, *Autobiography, Sketch and Narrative of the War Between the States* (Philadelphia, 1912); Eaton, Clement, *A History of the Southern Confederacy* (New York, 1954); Eckenrode, Hamilton and Conrad, Bryan, *George B. McClellan, the Man who Saved the Union* (Chapel Hill, 1941); Eckert, Thomas T., *Recollections of the U. S. Military Telegraph Corps during the Civil War* (New York, 1907); Eggleston, George C., *A Rebel's Recollections* (New York, 1875); Egle, William H., *Life and Times of Andrew Gregg Curtin* (Philadelphia, 1896); Elliott, C. W., *Winfield Scott, the Soldier and the Man* (New York, 1937); Evans, Clement A., *Confederate Military History: a Library of Confederate States History* (12 vols., Atlanta, 1899)

Fairchild, C. B., *History of 27th Regiment New York Volunteers 1861–63* (Binghamton, 1888); Fertig, James W., *The Secession and Reconstruction of Tennessee* (Chicago, 1898); Fessenden, Francis, *Life and Public Services of William Pitt Fessenden* (2 vols., Boston, 1907); Field, Maunsell B., *Memories of Many Men and Some Women. . . .* (New York, 1874); Fish, Carl Russell, *The American Civil War, An Interpretation*, ed. by William Ernest Smith (New York, 1937); Fiske, John, *The Mississippi Valley in the Civil War* (Boston, 1900); Flower, Frank A., *Edward McMasters Stanton, the Autocrat of Rebellion, Emancipation and Reconstruction* (Akron, 1905); Forbes, John Murray, *Letters and Recollections*, ed. by Sarah Forbes Hughes (2 vols., Boston, 1899); Forney, John W., *Anecdotes of Public Men* (2 vols., New York, 1873–81); Foulke, William D., *Life of Oliver P. Morton, including his important speeches* (2 vols., Indianapolis, 1899); Fox, Gustavus V., *Confidential Correspondence of G. V. Fox 1861–65* (2 vols., New York, 1918–19); Freeman, Douglas S., *R. E. Lee, a Biography* (4 vols., New York, 1934–35); Frémont, Jessie B., *The Story of the Guard: A Chronicle of the War* (Boston, 1863); Fry, James B., "McClellan and his 'Mission,' a Study," *Century Magazine*, vol. 48 (October, 1894), 931–946; Fulton, John, *Memoirs of Frederick A. P. Barnard* (New York, 1896)

Gates, Theodore B., *The War of the Rebellion, with a Full and Critical History of the First Battle of Bull Run. . . .* (New York, 1884); Gordon, John B., *Reminiscences of the Civil War* (New York, 1904); Gosnell, H. Allen, *Guns on the Western Waters: The Story of River Gunboats in the Civil War* (Baton Rouge, 1949); Grant, Ulysses S., *Personal Memoirs of U. S. Grant* (2 vols., New York, 1885–86); Gray, Wood, *The Hidden Civil War: the Story of the Copperheads* (New York, 1942); Grinnell, Josiah B., *Men and Events of Forty Years. . . .* (Boston, 1891); Gurowski, Adam, *Diary 1861–62* (3 vols., Boston, 1862–66)

Hale, Edward Everett, *Memories of a Hundred Years* (2 vols., New York, 1904); Hamilton, Joseph De Roulhac, ed., *The Correspondence of Jonathan Worth* (2 vols., Raleigh, N. C., 1909); Hamlin, C. E., *Life and Times of Hannibal Hamlin 1809–1891* (Cambridge, Mass., 1899); Harlow, Alvin Fay, *Old Waybills: The Romance of the Express Companies* (New York, 1934); Harrington, Fred H., *Fighting Politician: Major-General N. P. Banks* (Philadelphia, 1948); Harris, Thomas Le Grand, *The Trent Affair. . . .* (Indianapolis, 1896); Harwell, Richard B., *The Union Reader* (New York, 1958); Hassler, Warren W., Jr., *General George B. McClellan, Shield of the Union* (Baton Rouge, 1957); Hawthorne, Nathaniel, "Chiefly About War Matters," *Atlantic Monthly*, vol. 10 (July, 1862), 43–61; Hay, John, *Lincoln and the Civil War, in the Diaries and Letters of John Hay*, ed. by Tyler Dennett (New York, 1939), "Life in the White House in the Time of Lincoln," *Century*

Magazine, vol. 41 (November, 1890), 33–37; Hayes, Rutherford B., *Diary and Letters*, ed. by Charles Richard Williams (5 vols., Columbus, O., 1922–26); Hazard, Blanche E., *Organization of the Boot and Shoe Industry in Massachusetts* (Cambridge, Mass., 1921); Heitman, F. B., ed., *Historical Register and Dictionary of the U. S. Army from 1789 to 1903* (Washington, D. C., 1903); Hendrick, Burton J., *Statesmen of the Lost Cause* (Boston, 1939), *Lincoln's War Cabinet* (Boston, 1946); Hesseltine, William B., *A History of the South 1607–1936* (New York, 1936), *Lincoln and the War Governors* (New York, 1948); Hill, Louise Byles, *Joseph E. Brown and the Confederacy* (Chapel Hill, 1939); Hitchcock, Ethan Allen, *Fifty Years in Camp and Field, A Diary of Major-General E. A. Hitchcock*, ed. by William Croffut (New York, 1909); Hoar, George Frisbie, *Autobiography of Seventy Years* (2 vols., New York, 1903); Hooper, Oscar C., *The Crisis and the Man* (Columbus, O., 1929); Hoppin, James M., *Life of Andrew Hull Foote, Rear Admiral* (New York, 1874); Horn, Stanley F., ed., *The Robert E. Lee Reader* (Indianapolis, 1949); Howard, John R., *Remembrance of Times Past* (New York, 1925); Howe, George F., *Chester A. Arthur, A Quarter Century of Machine Politics* (New York, 1934); Howe, Mark A. De Wolfe, *The Life and Letters of George Bancroft* (2 vols., New York, 1908); Hume, John, *The Abolitionists, Together with Personal Memories of the Struggle for Human Rights 1830–64* (New York, 1905); Hungerford, Edward, *The Story of the Baltimore and Ohio Railroad 1827–1927* (New York, 1928); Hurlburt, William H., *General McClellan and the Conduct of the War* (New York, 1864); Hyde, Thomas, *Following the Greek Cross; or Memories of the Sixth Army Corps* (New York, 1895)

Ingersoll, L. D., *History of the War Department of the U. S.* (Philadelphia, 1879)

Johnson, Rossiter, *A Short History of the War of Secession 1861–65* (New York, 1910); Johnson, R. V. and Buell, C. C., *Battles and Leaders of the Civil War* (4 vols., New York, 1887); Johnston, Joseph E., *Narrative of Military Operations Directed during the late War between the States* (New York, 1874); Johnston, R. M., and Browne, W. H., *Alexander H. Stephens* (Philadelphia, 1878); Jones, John B., *A Rebel War Clerk's Diary at the Confederate States Capitol* (2 vols., Philadelphia, 1866); Jones, John W., *Life and Letters of Robert Edward Lee, Soldier and Man* (New York, 1906)

Kennedy, Elijah R., *The Contest for California in 1861. . . .* (Boston, 1912); Keyes, Erasmus D., *Fifty Years' Observation of Men and Events, Civil and Military* (New York, 1884); Kinglake, Alexander W., *Invasion of the Crimea, Its Origin and Progress* (8 vols., New York and London, 1863–87); Kirkland, Edward Chase, *Men Cities and Transportation, a Study in New England History 1820–1900* (2 vols., Cambridge, 1948); Koren, John, *The History of Statistics; Their Development and Progress in Many Countries* (New York, 1918); Körner, Gustave, *Memoirs 1809–1896* (2 vols., Cedar Rapids, Ia., 1909)

Lamon, Ward Hill, *Recollections of Abraham Lincoln 1847–65* (Washington, D. C., 1911); Laugel, Auguste, *The United States During the War: 1861–65* (New York, 1866); Laughlin, Sceva B., "Missouri Politics during the Civil War," *Missouri Historical Review*, vol. 23 (April, 1929), 400–426; Leech, Margaret, *Reveille in Washington, 1860–65* (New York, 1941); Leidecker, Kurt F., *Yankee Teacher, the Life of William Torrey Harris* (New York, 1946); Leland, Charles G., *Memoirs* (New York, 1893); Lewis, Charles Lee, *Admiral Franklin Buchanan, Fearless Man of Action* (Baltimore, 1929); Lewis, Lloyd, *Sherman, Fighting Prophet* (New York, 1932), *Captain Sam Grant* (Boston, 1950); Lewis, Virgil A., *How West Virginia Was Made. . . .* (Charleston, 1909); Lincoln, A., *Collected Works of Abraham Lincoln*, ed. by Roy Basler (8 vols., New Brunswick, 1953); Livermore, Thomas L., *Days and Events, 1860–1866* (Boston, 1920); Lossing, Benson, J., *A History of the Civil War 1861–65* (3 vols., Hartford, Conn., 1868); Lowell, James Russell, *Letters of James Russell Lowell*, ed. by Charles Eliot Norton (2 vols., New York, 1894)

McClellan, George B., *McClellan's Own Story: the War for the Union. . . .* (New York, 1887), *Report of the Organization and Campaigns of the Army of the Potomac* (New York, 1864), McClure, A. K., *Abraham Lincoln and Men of War Times. . . .* (Philadelphia, 1892), *Col. A. K. McClure's Recollections of Half a Century* (Salem, 1902); McElroy, John, *The Struggle for Missouri* (Washington, D. C., 1909); McGregor, James C., *The Disruption of Virginia* (New York, 1922); McPherson, Edward, *Political History of the United States . . . During the Great Rebellion* (Washington, D. C., 1864)

Macrae, D., *The Americans at Home. . . .* (Edinburgh, 1870); Magruder, Allan B., "A Piece of Secret History—President Lincoln and the Virginia Convention of 1861," *Atlantic Monthly*, vol. 35 (April, 1875), 438–445; Mahan, Asa, *A Critical History of the Late American War* (New York, 1877); Martin, E. W., *The Standard of Living in 1860* (Chicago, 1942); Martin, Theodore, *Life of His Royal Highness, the Prince Consort* (London, 1875–80); Maurice, Sir Frederick, "A System for the Conduct of the War," *Atlantic Monthly*, vol. 137 (June, 1926), 772 ff.; Maxwell, William Q., *Lincoln's Fifth Wheel: the Political History of the U. S. Sanitary Commission* (New York, 1956); Meigs, Montgomery, "General M. C. Meigs on the Conduct of the Civil War," *American Historical Review*, vol. 26 (January, 1921), 285–303; Meneely, Alexander H., *The War Department, 1861, a Study in Mobilization and Administration* (New York, 1928); Merrill, Samuel, *The 70th Indiana Volunteer Infantry in the War of the Rebellion* (Indianapolis, 1900); Mill, John Stuart, *Dissertations and Discussions: Political, Philosophical, Historical* (5 vols., Boston, 1864); Milton, George F., *The Eve of Conflict* (New York, 1934); Mitchell, Silas Weir, *In War Time* (Boston, 1886); Moore, Frank, ed., *The Rebellion Record* (12 vols., New York, 1861–63); Moran, Benjamin, *Journal of Benjamin Moran 1857-65*, ed. by Sarah A. Wallace et al. (2 vols., Chicago, 1948–49); Munford, Beverley, *Virginia's Attitude Toward Slavery and Secession* (New York, 1909); Myers, William Starr, *A Study in Personality: George B. McClellan* (New York, 1934)

Nevins, Allan, *Ordeal of the Union* (2 vols., New York, 1947), *The Emergence of Lincoln* (2 vols., New York, 1950), *Abram S. Hewitt: and some account of Peter Cooper* (New York, 1935), *Frémont: Pathmarker of the West* (New York, new ed., 1955); Newell, J. K., "Ours," *Annals of Tenth Regiment Massachusetts Volunteers. . . .* (Springfield, 1875); Newman, Ralph, with E. B. Long and Otto Eisenschiml, *The Civil War* (Vol. I, *The American Iliad*, Vol. II, *The Picture Chronicle*, New York, 1956); Newton, Thomas W. L., *Lord Lyons: a Record of British Diplomacy* (2 vols., London, 1913); Nicolay, Helen, *Lincoln's Secretary: a Biography of John G. Nicolay* (New York, 1949), "Characteristic Anecdotes of Lincoln," *Century Magazine*, vol. 84 (August, 1912), 697–703; Nicolay, John G., and Hay, John, *Abraham Lincoln: a History* (10 vols., New York, 1890); Norton, Charles E., *Letters of Charles Eliot Norton* (2 vols., Boston, 1913); Norton, Clarence C., *The Democratic Party in Ante-Bellum North Carolina 1835-61* (Chapel Hill, 1930); Norwood, William F., *Medical Education in the United States Before the Civil War* (London, 1944)

O'Reilly, Hugh, "Arming the Slaves for the Union," pamphlet, 1875; Owsley, Frank L., *King Cotton Diplomacy; Foreign Relations of the Confederate States of America* (Chicago, 1931)

Packard, F. R., *History of Medicine in the United States* (2 vols., New York, 1931); Palmer, John M., *Personal Recollections* (Cincinnati, 1901); Paris, Comte de (L. P. A. d'Orleans), *History of the Civil War* (4 vols., Philadelphia, 1875–88); Parks, Joseph H., *General Edmund Kirby Smith, C. S. A.* (Baton Rouge, 1954); Parton, James, *General Butler in New Orleans. . . .* (New York, 1864); Patterson, Robert, *A Narrative of the Campaign in the Valley of the Shenandoah in 1861* (Philadelphia, 1865); Patton, James W., *Unionism and Reconstruction in Tennessee 1860-69* (Chapel Hill, 1934); Pearson, Henry G., *The Life of John A. Andrew, Governor of Massachusetts* (2 vols., New York, 1904), *General James S. Wadsworth* (New York, 1913); Peckham, James, *General Nathaniel Lyon and Missouri in 1861: A Monograph of the Great Rebellion* (New York, 1866); Perry, A. F., "A Chapter in Interstate Diplomacy," *Loyal Legion Papers, Ohio Commandery*, vol. 3, 333–363; Perry, Bliss, *Life and Letters of Henry Lee Higginson* (Boston,

1921); Peto, Sir S. Morton, *Resources and Prospects of America*. . . . (London and New
York, 1866); Phillips, Ulrich B., *The Life of Robert Toombs* (New York, 1913); Phisterer,
Frederick, *New York in the War of the Rebellion, 1861-65* (5 vols., Albany, 1912), *Statistical Record of the Armies of the United States* (New York, 1883); Piatt, Donn, *Memories
of the Men Who Saved the Union* (New York, 1887); Pierce, Edward L., *Memoir and
Letters of Charles Sumner* (4 vols., Boston, 1877-94); Pierson, William W., "The Com-
mittee on the Conduct of the Civil War," *American Historical Review*, vol. 23 (April,
1918), 550-576; Pinkerton, Allan, *The Spy of the Rebellion; Being A True History of the
Spy System of the U. S. Army during the late Rebellion* (New York, 1883); Poor, Henry V.,
History of the Railroads and Canals of the U.S. (New York, 1860); Potter, David M.,
Lincoln and his Party in the Secession Crisis (New Haven, 1942); Pratt, Edwin A.,
The Rise of Rail Power in War and Conquest, 1833-1914 (London, 1915); Pratt, Fletcher,
Civil War on Western Waters (New York, 1956)

Quint, Alonzo, *The Record of the Second Massachusetts Infantry 1861-65* (Boston,
1867)

Radcliffe, G. L., *Governor Thomas H. Hicks of Maryland and the Civil War* (Balti-
more, 1901); Ramsdell, C. W., "Lincoln and Fort Sumter," *Journal of Southern History*,
vol. 3 (August, 1937), 259-288; Randall, James G., *The Civil War and Reconstruction*
(New York, 1937), *Lincoln the President* (4 vols., New York, 1945); Rawley, James A.,
Edwin D. Morgan, 1811-1883: Merchant in Politics (New York, 1955); Reagan, John H.,
Memoirs: With Special Reference to Secession and Civil War (New York, 1906); Reavis,
Logan U., *The Life and Military Services of General William Selby Harney* (St. Louis,
1878); Reid, Whitelaw, *Ohio in the War: Her Statesmen, Her Generals and Soldiers* (2 vols.,
Cincinnati, 1868); Rhodes, James F., *History of the United States from the Compromise
of 1850*. . . . (9 vols., New York and London, 1893-1929); Rice, Allen Thorndike, *Remi-
niscences of Abraham Lincoln by Distinguished Men of his Time* (New York, 1909);
Riddle, A. G., *Recollections of War Times: Reminiscences of Men and Events in Wash-
ington, 1860-65* (New York, 1895); Robinson, W. M., *The Confederate Privateers* (New
Haven, 1928); Roman, Alfred, *Military Operations of General Beauregard in the War
Between the States 1861-65* (2 vols., New York, 1884); Rombauer, R. J., *The Union Cause
in St. Louis in 1861*. . . . (St. Louis, 1909); Ropes, John Codman and Livermore, W. R.,
The Story of the Civil War . . . 1861-1865 (4 vols., New York, 1893-1913); Rosewater,
Victor, *History of Cooperative Newsgathering in the U. S.* (New York, 1930); Rowan,
Richard W., *The Pinkertons: A Detectvie Dynasty* (Boston, 1931); Russell, William H.,
My Diary North and South (2 vols., London and New York, 1863); Rutherford, Mary L.,
The Influence of the American Bar Association on Public Opinion and Legislation (Phila-
delphia, 1937)

Sandburg, Carl, *Abraham Lincoln* (6 vols., New York, 1926-39); Schaff, Morris, *The
Spirit of Old West Point, 1858-1862* (New York, 1907); Schofield, John M., *Forty-Six
Years in the Army* (New York, 1897); Schotter, H. W., *The Growth and Development
of the Pennsylvania Railroad Company . . . 1846-1926* (Philadelphia, 1927); Schouler,
William, *A History of Massachusetts in the Civil War* (2 vols., Boston, 1868-71); Schuckers,
Jacob W., *Life and Public Services of Salmon Portland Chase*. . . . (New York, 1874);
Schurz, Carl, *The Reminiscences of Carl Schurz 1852-63* (2 vols., New York, 1907-08);
Schwab, John C., *The Confederate States of America 1861-1865*. . . . (New York, 1901);
Seward, Frederick W., *Seward at Washington as Senator and Secretary of State 1846-61*
(2 vols., New York, 1891), *Reminiscences 1830-1915* (New York, 1916); Seward, William H.,
Works, ed. by George E. Baker (5 vols., New York, 1883-84); Shafer, Henry B., *The
American Medical Profession: 1783-1850* (New York, 1936); Shanks, Henry T., *The
Secession Movement in Virginia, 1847-1861* (Richmond, 1934); Shannon, Fred A., *The Or-
ganization and Administration of the Union Army 1861-65* (2 vols., Cleveland, 1928);
Sheldon, George W., "Old Shipping Merchants of New York," *Harpers' Magazine*, vol.

84 (February, 1892), 457–471; Sherman, William Tecumseh, *Memoirs, Written by Himself* (2 vols., New York, 1890); Sigel, Franz, "Military Operations in Missouri in . . . 1861," *Missouri Historical Review*, vol. 26 (July, 1932), 354–366; Smalley, George W., *Anglo-American Memories* (New York, 1911); Smith, Edward C., *The Borderland in the Civil War* (New York, 1927); Smith, William E., *The Francis Preston Blair Family in Politics* (2 vols., New York, 1933); Snead, T. L., *The Fight for Missouri. . . .* (New York, 1886); Soley, J. R., *The Blockade and the Cruisers*, Vol. I of *The Navy in the Civil War* (New York, 1883); Stampp, Kenneth, *And the War Came* (Baton Rouge, 1950); Stevens, W. B., *Centennial History of Missouri . . . One Hundred Years in the Union, 1820–1920* (2 vols., St. Louis, 1921); Stoddard, William O., *Inside the White House in War Times* (New York, 1890); Stovall, Pleasants, *Robert Toombs, statesman, speaker, soldier, sage; his career in Congress and on the hustings—his work in the courts—his record with the army—his life at home* (New York, 1892); Strode, Hudson, *Jefferson Davis, American Patriot 1808–1861* (New York, 1955); Strong, George T., *Diary*, ed. by Allan Nevins and Milton H. Thomas (4 vols., New York, 1952); Summers, Festus P., *The Baltimore and Ohio in the Civil War* (New York, 1939); Swinton, William, *Campaigns of the Army of the Potomac. . . .* (New York, 1882); Switzler, W. F., *Switzler's Illustrated History of Missouri from 1541 to 1877* (St. Louis, 1879)

Tasher, Lucy L., "The *Missouri Democrat* and the Civil War," *Missouri Historical Review*, vol. 31 (July, 1937), 402–419; Taylor, Frank H., *Philadelphia in the Civil War, 1861–65* (Philadelphia, 1913); Temperley, Harold, and Fenson, Lillian, *Foundations of British Foreign Policy from Pitt (1792) to Salisbury (1902). . . .* (Cambridge, 1938); Thomas, Benjamin P., *Abraham Lincoln: a Biography* (New York, 1952); Thomas, David Y., *Arkansas in War and Reconstruction 1861–74* (Little Rock, 1926); Thomas, Joseph W., "Campaigns of McClellan and Rosecrans in West Virginia," *West Virginia Magazine of History*, vol. 5 (July, 1944), 245–308; Thompson, Robert L., *Wiring a Continent, the History of the Telegraph Industry in the United States 1832–66* (Princeton, 1947); Tilley, John Shipley, *Lincoln Takes Command* (Chapel Hill, 1941); Townsend, E. D., *Anecdotes of the Civil War in the U. S.* (New York, 1884); Trobriand, R. de, *Army Life in Dakota; selections from the Journal of Philippe Regis . . . de Trobriand* (Chicago, 1941); Trollope, Anthony, *North America* (2 vols., London, 1862)

Upham, Cyril B., "Arms and Equipment for the Iowa Troops in the Civil War," *Iowa Journal of History*, vol. 16 (January, 1918), 3–52; Upson, Theodore F., *With Sherman to the Sea. . . .* (Baton Rouge, 1943); Upton, Emory, *Military Policy of the United States* (Washington, 1917)

Van Deusen, Glyndon G., *Thurlow Weed: Wizard of the Lobby* (Boston, 1947), *Horace Greeley, Nineteenth Century Crusader* (Philadelphia, 1953); Van Oss, S. F., *American Railroads as Investments* (New York, 1893); Vandiver, Frank, *Ploughshares into Swords: Josiah Gorgas and Confederate Ordnance* (Austin, 1952); Villard, Henry, *Memoirs 1835–1900* (2 vols., Boston, 1904); Violette, Eugene and Forest, Wolverton, *A History of Missouri* (St. Louis, 1955)

Walcott, C. F., *History of the Twenty-First Regiment Massachusetts Volunteers. . . .* (Boston, 1882); Wallace, Lew, *An Autobiography* (2 vols., New York, 1906); Warren, Charles, *A History of the American Bar* (Boston, 1911); Wasson, Robert Gordon, *The Hall Carbine Affair. . . .* (New York, 1948); Watson, William, *Life in the Confederate Army. . . .* (New York, 1888); Wayland, Francis, *Thoughts on the Present Collegiate System in the U. S.* (Boston, 1842); Webb, Elizabeth, "Cotton Manufacturing and State Regulation in North Carolina 1861–65," *North Carolina Historical Review*, vol. 9 (April, 1932), 117–137; Weber, Thomas, *The Northern Railroads in the Civil War, 1861–1865* (New York, 1952); Weed, Thurlow, *Autobiography of Thurlow Weed*, and Weed, Harriet A., *Life of Thurlow Weed* (2 vols., Boston, 1884); Weeden, William B., *War Government, Federal and State, 1861–1865* (Boston, 1906); Welles, Gideon, *The Diary of*

Gideon Welles, Secretary of the Navy under Lincoln and Johnson, ed. by John T. Morse (3 vols., Boston, 1911), "Narrative of Events," *American Historical Review*, vol. 31 (April, 1926), 486-494, *Lincoln and Seward: Remarks upon the Memorial Address of Charles F. Adams on the late Wm. H. Seward.* . . . (New York, 1874); West, Richard S., *Gideon Welles: Lincoln's Navy Department* (Indianapolis, 1943); White, Andrew D., *Autobiography* (2 vols., New York, 1922); White, Horace, *The Life of Lyman Trumbull* (Boston, 1913); White, Leonard D., *The Jacksonians: A Study in Administrative History, 1829-1861* (New York, 1954); Wiley, Bell I., *The Life of Johnny Reb, The Common Soldier of the Confederacy* (New York, 1943), *The Life of Billy Yank, The Common Soldier of the Union* (Indianapolis, 1951); Wilkinson, Spenser, *War and Policy: Essays* (New York, 1900); Willey, W. P., *An Inside View of the Formation of West Virginia* (Wheeling, 1901); Williams, Kenneth, *Lincoln Finds a General: A Military Study of the Civil War* (4 vols., New York, 1949-56); Williams, T. Harry, *P. G. T. Beauregard: Napoleon in Gray* (Baton Rouge, 1954), *Lincoln and His Generals* (New York, 1952), *Lincoln and the Radicals* (Madison, 1941); Williamson, Harold F., *Winchester, the Gun that Won the West* (Washington, D. C., 1952); Wilson, Henry, "Jeremiah S. Black and Edwin M. Stanton," *Atlantic Monthly*, vol. 26 (February, 1870), 463-475; Wilson, James Grant, *The Life and Campaigns of Ulysses Simpson Grant.* . . . (New York, 1868); Wilson, James H., *Under the Old Flag: Recollections of Military Operations.* . . . (2 vols., New York, 1912); Wilson, W. B., *A Few Acts and Actors in the Tragedy of the Civil War in the U. S.* (Philadelphia, 1892); Winthrop, Theodore, "Washington as a Camp," *Atlantic Monthly*, vol. 8 (July, 1861), 105-118; Wise, John S., *The End of an Era* (Boston, 1902); Woodward, Ashbel, *The Life of General Nathaniel Lyon* (Hartford, 1862); Wright, Marcus J., *General Scott* (New York, 1897)

A full list and description of manuscript sources will be published in the next volume of this work. It should be noted here that HL refers to Huntington Library, MHS to Massachusetts Historical Society, and NYPL to New York Public Library.

APPENDIX I

Northern and Southern Resources, 1860

I. WHITE POPULATION NORTH AND SOUTH

It is roughly correct to say that the Northern States had a white population of twenty millions, while the Southern white population was about five and a half millions. An accurate picture, however, requires a somewhat fuller statement.

The white population of New England by the census of 1860 was 3,110,000; that of New York, Pennsylvania, New Jersey, Maryland, and Delaware was 8,745,000; that of Ohio, Indiana, Illinois, Iowa, and Kansas was 6,126,000; and that of Michigan, Wisconsin, Minnesota, and Nebraska was 1,708,000. The total white population in this area, where strength could most effectively be mobilized and deployed by the Federal Government, was 19,689,500. In the Far Western area—California, Oregon, Washington, Dakota, New Mexico, Utah, Nevada, and Colorado—the white population was 587,500. This gave the North a total white population of approximately 20,275,000.

The border States of Missouri, Kentucky, and Tennessee, whose strength was divided between North and South, had a white population of 2,810,000. Of this the population of Tennessee, a member of the Confederacy, was 827,000.

The census of 1860 gave the white population of the ten Confederate States excluding Tennessee as 4,622,000. If the white population of Tennessee is added, the whole number of whites in the eleven Confederate States falls barely short of 5,500,000.

Looking at whites alone, the population odds against the Confederacy were thus almost four to one. The South, however, had an immense asset in its Negro population.

II. COLORED POPULATION NORTH AND SOUTH

Speaking in rough terms, the North had fewer than a half million colored people available for the war effort, while the South had not far from three and three-quarters millions. Again a fuller array of statistics is required for an accurate picture of the situation.

The colored population of New England, New York, Pennsylvania, and New Jersey by the census of 1860 was 153,983. That of the eight Middle Western States from Ohio and Michigan to Kansas, together with Nebraska Territory, came to 65,642. The total for these seventeen Northern States and one Territory was 221,625. If we add the Negro population of Delaware, Maryland, and the District of Columbia, the aggregate is almost 430,000. The Far Western States and Territories would add fewer than 5,000, nearly all of whom lived in California.

The colored population of the ten Confederate States excluding Tennessee, which was invaded and partly occupied in 1862, came to 3,371,000. If we add the 289,000 colored people of Tennessee, the eleven Confederate States had in all 3,654,000 Negroes and mulattoes.

III. POPULATION TOTALS

Missouri and Kentucky were so divided between North and South that an accurate brief comparison of strength is furthered by their omission. Leaving them out, the North had a combined white and colored population of approximately 20,700,000—just over that total. The eleven States of the Confederacy had a combined white and colored population of approximately 9,105,000. The North therefore had an advantage of more than two to one, even reckoning the colored population on a parity with the white. The Union, moreover, had the assistance of unrestricted immigration from Europe.

IV. POPULATION OF MILITARY AGE

The census of 1860 lists white males in two age categories, one 15 to 20, and the other 20 to 30, but does not break them down by years. The total white male population 15 to 30 in the seventeen Northern States of New England, the Middle Atlantic area, and the Middle West, with Nebraska, the main reservoir of manpower, was 2,582,678. But the whole number of white males 15 to 30 in the Confederate States came only to 791,000. This omits from computation on either side Missouri, which had 166,000 white males of 15 to 30 years, and Kentucky, which had 134,000. The whole number of white males in this age group available to the North was certainly a good deal more than three times the number in the South.

V. MANUFACTURES IN 1860

The census credited New York with 22,624 establishments holding a capital, in round numbers, of $172,896,000. It gave Pennsylvania 22,363 establishments, with a capital of $190,056,000. Ohio had 11,123 establishments of $57,295,000 capital, while Massachusetts was listed as possessing 8,176, with a capital of $132,792,000. In round numbers the North had 110,000 manufacturing establishments, with 1,300,000 industrial workers.

The South fell far behind. Virginia had 5,385 manufacturing establishments with a capital of $30,840,500; Alabama had 1,459, with a capital of less than $9,100,000; Louisiana had 1,744 with a capital of only $7,151,000; and Mississippi had 976, with a capital of but $4,384,500. The total number of manufacturing establishments in the Confederacy was about 18,000, with 110,000 industrial workers.

The value of the product of manufacturing in the four Southern States named in 1860 did not reach $85,000,000. But that of New York was placed at $379,000,000, and that of Massachusetts at $255,500,000.

VI. IRON MANUFACTURES

In 1860 the United States had 286 iron furnaces scattered through 18 States. Pennsylvania led with 125. Tennessee was the largest Southern producer of pig iron, with 17 furnaces, and Virginia came next with 16.

The number of forges and rolling mills in the country, producing bar, sheet, and railroad iron, was 256, in twenty States. Pennsylvania was by far the largest manufacturer, with 87 forges or rolling mills, employing more than half the whole capital investment of the country in this line. The value of its product amounted to between $15,000,000 and $16,000,000 a year. New York was the second largest producer. Virginia had 20 establishments with a product valued at $1,667,000, and Tennessee was proud of 35, with a product, however, of only a little over a half-million dollars.

Of 470 locomotives built in the United States in the year ending June 1, 1860, Virginia made 19, and no other Southern State any. In the manufacture of agricultural implements in 1860, the aggregate Southern production was worth a little over $1,000,000. But during the previous decade the Western States had raised their production from $1,900,000 to $8,700,000.

Firearms in 1860 were manufactured in 239 establishments, New England being far in the lead. Of the whole product, worth $2,342,700, the Southern States made less than $73,000 worth. One county in Connecticut—Hartford—valued its product at well over a million dollars.

VII. DRAFT ANIMALS

The dependence upon horses and mules in transporting troops and supplies makes statistics upon them important. The Middle and Western States in 1860 had more than 4,000,000 horses. The Southern States had less than one and three-quarters millions, of which more than one-sixth were in remote Texas, and nearly one-sixth in vulnerable Tennessee. But in the number of asses and mules the South had a distinct advantage. Its total for the eleven States of the Confederacy was 822,047; the total of the Middle and Western States was only a little over 310,000, while New England had practically none.

The eleven Confederate States had approximately 2,566,000 horses, asses, and mules combined, while the Northern States, excluding the Far West, had almost 4,600,000. The South had about one horse to every five inhabitants; the Middle Western States, about two horses to every seven inhabitants.

VIII. RAILROADS

Of the total railroad mileage in the United States in 1861, which by Poor's *Manual* was 31,256, the South contained 9,283, or less than 30 per cent. Federal inroads soon reduced this to something over 6,000 miles (J. C. Schwab, *Confederate States*, 273).

APPENDIX II

Documents on Mrs. Frémont's Interview With Lincoln

The Frémont Papers in the Bancroft Library of the University of California contain a copy, undated, of a letter which Montgomery Blair sent the general in St. Louis soon after his arrival, when Blair was still supporting him. This is the letter in which he criticized Secretary Chase for his parsimony, writing: "Chase has more horror of seeing Treasury notes below par than of seeing soldiers killed." (Nevins, *Fremont*, third edition, 509). He also criticized Lincoln in a passage worth quoting in full:

"I showed the President, Billings' letter, and read him yours about Adams. He says that you were right in saying that Adams was devoted to his money-bags.

"Schuyler had already gone to Europe about arms when I wrote and telegraphed you, and your letter in reply was handed to Mr. Seward, to be forwarded to him. . . . The main difficulty is, however, with Lincoln himself. He is of the Whig school, and that brings him naturally not only to incline to the feeble policy of Whigs, but to give his confidence to such advisers. It costs me a great deal of labor to get anything done, because of this inclination of mind on the part of the President or leading members of the Cabinet, including Chase, who never voted a Democratic ticket in his life. But you have the people at your back, and I am doing all I can to cut red tape and get things done. I will be more civil and patient than heretofore, and see if that won't work."

The MS continuation of Frémont's published volume of *Memoirs* (1887) which Mrs. Frémont and her son Frank wrote, partially from his dictation, contains a full account of the circumstances in which he prepared his proclamation of military emancipation. This is given almost in full in Nevins, *Frémont,* 500. It emphasizes the fact that, with an insufficient number of troops, ill-armed and unpaid, to repress guerrilla warfare, he felt that sharp measures were necessary to deal with the great numbers of secessionist sympathizers who would flock almost overnight to the Confederate camps, assist in some sudden stroke, and then return to their farms and villages. "He determined to force the rebel sympathizers, who did not join the rebel armies as soldiers, to remain at home, and to make them feel that there was a penalty for rebellion, and for aiding those who were in rebellion." When Judge Edward Davis warned him that "Mr. Seward will never allow this," for he wished to wear down the South not by blows but by steady pressure, Frémont persisted. "The time has come for decisive action; this is a war measure, and as such I make it." (Op. cit., 503.) Then as relations between Frémont and Frank Blair worsened, and he felt that Lincoln did not understand his position, he agreed to Mrs. Frémont's taking a letter to the White House. She was not only the wife of the departmental commander; she was daughter of a great American Senator.

Jessie Benton Frémont left St. Louis the evening of September 8 with the letter, dated that day. It dealt exclusively with strategic movements. The most significant passage concerned advances which Frémont wrote that he contemplated ordering in Kentucky and if possible Tennessee. On August 28 he had placed Grant in command in southeast Missouri, and had declared his intention of occupying Columbus, Ky. On September 2d Union forces had occupied Belmont just across the river from this place; and immediately thereafter Polk's Confederates had seized Columbus, while Grant had occupied Paducah. Frémont's letter to Lincoln looked to the future, not the past, and to the taking of strong Kentucky positions. He wrote:

"I have reinforced, yesterday, Paducah with two regiments, and will continue to strengthen the position with men and artillery. As soon as General [C. F.] Smith, who commands there, is reinforced sufficiently to enable him to spread his forces, he will have to take and hold Mayfield and Lovelaceville, to be in the rear and flank of Columbus, and to occupy Smithland, controlling in this way the mouths of both the Tennessee and Cumberland Rivers. At the same time, Colonel Rousseau should bring his force, increased, if possible, by two Ohio regiments, in boats to Henderson, and, taking the Henderson & Nashville Railroad, occupy Hopkinsville, while General Nelson should go with a force of 5,000 by railroad to Louisville and from there to Bowling Green."

Already Frémont had sent a spy, Captain Charles D'Arnaud, recommended to him by Colonel Lovell Rousseau and Judge Corwine of Cincinnati, to map the principal highways, bridges, and forts of Kentucky and western Tennessee, a mission from which D'Arnaud returned with maps showing the construction work the Confederates were doing on Forts Henry and Donelson. In this, and in his emphasis on securing the mouths of the Cumberland and Tennessee, Frémont showed foresight.

He wrote Lincoln that the movements he outlined were readily feasible, for the population in the area was predominantly loyal. If all went well, subsequent movements could be made against Columbus, Hickman, and eventually Nashville. He wished to have the bounds of the Western Department enlarged to cover Indiana, and, contemplating their partial occupation, Kentucky and Tennessee.

But while this letter carried by Mrs. Frémont treated military matters alone, Frémont had sent a separate letter by mail dated September 8 to Lincoln explaining his proclamation at some length, and asking Lincoln to send him an open order for its modification. It may have arrived on the afternoon of the 10th. When Lincoln answered it on the 11th he wrote that it was "just received." If it did arrive just before Mrs. Frémont descended upon the White House, that fact might account for the curtness of the reception he gave her, his failure to ask her to sit down, and his evident desire to cut the visit short. He did not wish to argue with her about the stubborn position of the general. If he had read the New York *Herald's* Washington correspondence published the previous day (September 9) it would not have soothed his feelings. For it asserted that the Cabinet had been taken aback by the proclamation; that for twenty-four hours they discussed it fully; and that then "it was finally unanimously determined that the proclamation was just the right thing made at precisely the right time, in exactly the right manner, and by the right man." The *Herald* was criticizing the Administration savagely for its dilatoriness in reinforcing the Western army.

But if Lincoln was abrupt in receiving Mrs. Frémont, a partial explanation might be found in physical fatigue. He had spent the greater part of the day with the troops. Early in the morning he had gone with Cameron and McClellan to attend a tedious ceremony at a camp beyond Georgetown where Governor and Mrs. Curtin presented Pennsylvania flags to the regiments of the reserve corps of that State, and had reviewed the ten thousand troops. Then he, Cameron, McClellan, the Curtins, and others had crossed the Chain Bridge to Virginia, where he saw McClellan restore the colors to the Seventy-ninth New York, heard Cameron make a speech, reviewed more troops, and inspected some of the new fortifications. He did not regain the White House until dusk.

It is certain that in this interview Mrs. Frémont exceeded her commission. Frémont, as he insisted in his letter to Lincoln and later said in his MS memoirs, had been inspired by military motives alone in writing his proclamation. But Mrs. Frémont, after referring to the opposition of the Blair family, began to talk about the political value of the proclamation, speaking of the difficulty of conquering by arms alone, and of the importance of appealing to public sentiment in Britain and France by a stroke against slavery. This justified Lincoln's remark: "You are quite a female politician." Some of the ideas that were in her head are disclosed by an undated letter which she wrote later, apparently just before Frémont's removal, to Dorothea Dix, an old friend. It is not certain she sent it, for the letter is in the Frémont papers, but it is revealing. It reads:

"I can but think that if the President had had an interview with Mr. Frémont there never would have grown up this state of injury to the public service—two honest men can quickly understand each other but the same good brain and bad heart that made the President so unjust and deaf to me has influenced not only the President but the newspapers of the kind that daren't offend Govt patronage. The truth has to come out victorious finally. Mr. Frémont can well afford to wait, but this lost time can never be regained for the country. Soon the river will be filling with ice and land work will be harder than the Valley Forge records. While it is yet day the work should be done.

"All we knew in the early summer, of the intrigue with France is becoming more and more sorrowfully apparent. If the South can bring themselves to play that last card—and you know as I do that Mr. Slidell is a gambler every way—politically as well as with money—then recognition by both England and France is very near. The worst would be that with all their enormities they would have the moral triumph too. You know from long experience abroad that America was neither loved nor hated, but very much feared and very much resented.

"Their chance has come to push us back and they will not lose it. The double bait of free trade and gradual emancipation (*very gradual* it will be) but enough to make a pretext for England, will not be repulsed by them, and Slidell has the backing of the Rothschilds. Their feelings have been sufficiently shewn by the *Times*. This is our last chance—it is a very hard pull—but a strong pull, above all a *pull altogether*, will bring us through. My dear chief is doing his duty . . . . but it is a shame and a crime to hamper and as far as they can disable him."

APPENDIX III

The Newspaper Press and the Impact of War

The country in 1860 had slightly more than 3,000 newspapers, and a decade of stormy political agitation had raised their influence to an unprecedented height. Their editors displayed a considerable amount of independence and courage. In August, 1861, the New York *Herald* was at pains to collect the names of "secession papers" in the North, and "Union papers" in the South, with some information on what had happened to them.

The phrase "secession paper" did not necessarily mean a newspaper giving outright and disloyal support in the North to the Confederacy, though a few of them ventured beyond that line. It meant rather a newspaper which, like the *Daily News* in New York or the *Times* in Chicago, had wished to see the erring sisters depart in peace; objected vehemently to any enlargement of war objectives beyond the restoration of the Union; and criticized Administration measures in terms so harshly as to lower the morale of their readers. The New York *Tribune* at this very time was denouncing the *Courrier des Etats Unis*, which stood for peaceable separation, as traitorous, and calling for its suppression. Most of the journals here listed did not go so far as this French-language paper. It will be noted that surviving "Union papers" in the South were all actually in the border States, and with few exceptions, like the Knoxville *Whig*, were safe under the protection of the Union flag.

SECESSION-PAPERS YET IN EXISTENCE IN THE NORTH.

NEW YORK.

Argus, Albany.
News, New York.
Journal of Commerce, N. Y.
Day Book, New York.
Freeman's Journal,N. York.
Prattsville News,Prattsv'le.
Budget, Troy.
Observer, Utica.
Watchman, Greenport, L. I.
Courier, Syracuse.
Advertiser, Lockport.
Union, Troy.
Herald, Sandy Hill

Register, Paterson.
Journal, Newark.
Republican Farmer.
Journal, Belvidere.

Republican, Saratoga.
Democrat, Ithica.
Gazette, Hudson.
Union, Watertown.
Gazette, Geneva.
American Union,Ellicotville.
Herald, Yonkers.
Franklin Gazette.
Democrat, Niagara.
Democrat, Schenectady.
Gazette, Malone.
Sentinel, Mayville.

NEW JERSEY.

Democrat, Hunterdon.
Herald, Newton.
Gazette, Plainfield.

PENNSYLVANIA.

Valley Spirit, Chambersb'g.
Patriot, Harrisburg.
Catholic Herald, Phila.
Examiner, Washington.
Star, Easton.
Democrat, Allentown.
Christian Observer, Phila.

Democrat, Coshocton.
Republican, Pittsburg.
Union, Wilkesbarre.
Herald, Honesdale.
Republikaner (German),
Allentown.

CONNECTICUT.

Times, Hartford.
Mercury, Middletown.
Advertiser, Bridgeport.

Register, New Haven.
Sentinel, Middletown.

IOWA.

Bugle, Council Bluffs.
Herald, Dubuque.

State Journal, Iowa City.
Citizen.

NEW HAMPSHIRE.

Patriot, Concord.

Gazette.

WISCONSIN.

Democrat, Kenosha.

See Bote (Ger.), Milwaukee.

MAINE.

Argus, Portland.

Watchman.

OHIO.

Enquirer, Cincinnati.
Crisis, Columbus.

Democrat, Galion.
Empire, Dayton.

MINNESOTA.

State, Winona.

RHODE ISLAND.

Post, Providence.

ILLINOIS.

Union, Cass county.
Democrat, Alton.

Times, Bloomington.
Signal, Joliet.

INDIANA.

Gazette, Evansville.
Journal, Terre Haute.

Sentinel, Indianapolis.

VERMONT.

Spirit of the Age, Woodstock.

CALIFORNIA.

Express, Marysville.

KANSAS.

Bulletin, Atchison.

———

SECESSION PAPERS IN THE LOYAL SOUTHERN SECTIONS.

Sun, Baltimore.
Exchange, Baltimore.
South, Baltimore.
Courier, Louisville.
Argus, Weston, Mo.

Yeoman, Frankfort, Ky.
Statesman, Lexington, Ky.
Gazette, Wilmington, Del.
Mail, Hagerstown, Md.
News, Cynthiana, Ky.

UNION PAPERS IN THE SOUTH.

American, Baltimore.
Commonwealth, Frankf't, Ky.
Clipper, Baltimore.
Citizen, Centreville, Md.
Democrat, St. Louis.
Democrat, Louisville.
Examiner, Frederick, Md.
Eagle, Maysville, Ky.
Herald, Wellsburg, Va.
Herald, Hagerstown, Md.
Intelligencer, Wheeling, Va.
Journal, Louisville, Ky.
Journal, St. Joseph, Mo.
Journal, Wilmington, Del.
News, Milford, Del.
NationalUnion, Wino'ter, Ky.
Observer, Lexington, Ky.
Patriot, Baltimore.
Press, Wheeling, Va.
Republican, St. Joseph, Mo.
Star, Morgantown, Va.
Union, Frederick, Md.
Whig, Knoxville, Tenn.

EFFECT OF THE WAR ON SECESSION JOURNALS.

NORTHERN SECESSION PAPERS DESTROYED BY MOBS.

Jeffersonian, Westchester, Pa.
Sentinel, Easton, Pa.
Farmer, Bridgeport, Conn.
Democrat, Canton, Ohio.
Standard, Concord, N. H.
Democrat, Bangor, Me.
Clinton Journal, Kansas.

NORTHERN SECESSION PAPERS SUPPRESSED BY CIVIL AUTHORITY.

Catholic Herald, Phil'a.   Christian Observer, Phil'a.

NORTHERN SECESSION PAPERS DIED.

Herald, Leavenworth.   American, Trenton.

NORTHERN SECESSION PAPERS DENIED TRANSPORTA-TION IN THE MAILS.

Journal of Commerce, New York.
News, New York.
Day Book, New York.
Freeman's Journal, New York.

SECESSION PAPERS CHANGED TO UNION.

Eagle, Brooklyn, N. Y.   *Democrat, Haverhill, Mass.
Republican, St. Louis.
*Editor tarred and feathered and rode on a rail.

SOUTHERN SECESSION PAPERS DIED.

News, Charleston, S. C.
Tribune, Mobile.
Register, Mobile.
News, Mobile.
Courier, New Orleans.
Union, Wheeling, Va.
Herald, Paducah, Ky.
Herald, Norfolk.
Crescent, Columbus, Ky.
Courier, Hickman, Ky.
Telegraph, Rutherford, Tenn.
Courier, Gallatin, Tenn.
Confederation, Montgomery, Ala.

SOUTHERN SECESSION PAPERS SUSPENDED BY MILITARY AUTHORITY.

State Journal, St. Louis.
Observer, Booneville, Mo.
Bulletin, St. Louis.
Missourian, St. Louis.
Sentinel, Alexandria, Va.
Democrat, Savannah, Mo.
Gazette, Alexandria, Va.
Register, Macon, Mo.
Paper in Weston, Va.

SOUTHERN SECESSION JOURNAL CLEANED OUT BY A MOB.

Alleghanian, Cumberland, Md.

RECAPITULATION.

Northern secession papers	73
Union papers South	23
Secession papers in loyal Southern sections	10
Northern secession papers mobbed	7
Northern secession papers stopped by civil authority	2
Northern secession papers died	2
Northern secession papers denied mail facilities	4
Northern secession papers changed to Union	3
Southern secession papers died	13
Southern secession papers suppressed by military authority	9
Southern secession papers mobbed	1

FROM N. Y. *Herald*, AUGUST 29, 1861

Index